ISLAM AND TIBET – INTERACTIONS ALONG THE MUSK ROUTES

The first encounters between the Islamic world and Tibet took place in the course of the expansion of the Abbasid Empire in the eighth century. Military and political contacts went along with an increasing interest in the other side. Cultural exchanges and the transmission of knowledge were facilitated by a trading network, with musk constituting one of the main trading goods from the Himalayas, largely through India. From the thirteenth century onwards the spread of the Mongol Empire from the Western borders of Europe through Central Asia to China facilitated further exchanges. The significance of these interactions has been long ignored in scholarship.

This volume represents a major contribution to the subject, bringing together new studies by an interdisciplinary group of international scholars. They explore for the first time the multi-layered contacts between the Islamic world, Central Asia and the Himalayas from the eighth century until the present day in a variety of fields, including geography, cartography, art history, medicine, history of science and education, literature, hagiography, archaeology, and anthropology.

Islam and Tibet – Interactions along the Musk Routes

Edited by

ANNA AKASOY
CHARLES BURNETT
RONIT YOELI-TLALIM

Routledge
Taylor & Francis Group
LONDON AND NEW YORK

First published 2011 by Ashgate Publishing

Published 2016 by Routledge
2 Park Square, Milton Park, Abingdon, Oxfordshire OX14 4RN
711 Third Avenue, New York, NY 10017, USA

First issued in paperback 2016

Routledge is an imprint of the Taylor & Francis Group, an informa business

British Library Cataloguing in Publication Data
Islam and Tibet – interactions along the musk routes.
1. Islam – China – Tibet – History. 2. Culture diffusion – China – Tibet – History. 3. Culture diffusion – Islamic countries – History. 4. Tibet (China) – Civilization – Mongolian influences. 5. Tibet (China) – Relations – Islamic countries. 6. Islamic countries – Relations – China – Tibet.
I. Akasoy, Anna. II. Burnett, Charles (Charles S. F.) III. Yoeli-Tlalim, Ronit.
303.4'8251501767–dc22

Library of Congress Cataloging-in-Publication Data
Islam and Tibet – interactions along the musk routes / [edited by] Anna Akasoy, Charles Burnett, and Ronit Yoeli-Tlalim.
p. cm.
Includes bibliographical references and index.
ISBN 978-0-7546-6956-2 (hardcover : alk. paper)
1. Islamic countries—Relations—China—Tibet. 2. Tibet (China)—Relations—Islamic countries. 3. Islamic countries—Civilization. 4. Tibet (China)—Civilization—Islamic influences. 5. Islam—China—Tibet—History. I. Akasoy, Anna. II. Burnett, Charles (Charles S. F.) III. Yoeli-Tlalim, Ronit.

DS35.74.C6I84 2010
303.48'217670515—dc22

2010008294

ISBN 13: 978-1-138-24704-8 (pbk)
ISBN 13: 978-0-7546-6956-2 (hbk)

Contents

List of Figures and Maps

FIGURES

MAPS

List of Plates

Preface

Most of these papers originated in a conference entitled *Islam and Tibet: Cultural Interactions*, which was held at the Warburg Institute, University of London, on 16-18 November, 2006 as part of a project supported by the Arts and Humanities Research Council (AHRC) (APN19294 and website http://warburg.sas.ac.uk/islamtibet/indexit.htm). In addition to the contributors to this volume, Yossef Rapoport talked about the evidence for trade route through Tibet in a map in the eleventh-century *Book of Curiosities* (see p. 7 below). Benno van Dalen of Frankfurt University presented his findings on the astronomical handbook of al-Sanjufīnī ('Islamic Astronomy in Northeastern Tibet (14th century)': see pp. 11-12 below). John Newman, of the New College of Florida, discussed the Kālacakra Tantra as a source for Tibetan knowledge of Islam, and Deborah Klimburg-Salter of the University of Vienna gave an illustrated evening lecture in the elegant Islamic setting of Leighton House, investigating the most likely kind of Buddhist statue that was allegedly sent by the King of Tibet to the caliph al-Maʾmūn in the early ninth century. The conference was enriched by the expert chairing of the sessions by Alexander Berzin, Peter Jackson, Charles Ramble, Emilie Savage-Smith and Edward Henning, and by the concluding discussion led by Geoffrey Samuel. In addition to the AHRC, the conference received generous funding from the Shelley and Donald Rubin Foundation, the British Academy and the Wellcome Trust. Further support towards the publication of this book was made by the Shelley and Donald Rubin Foundation. We are very grateful to Bruce Payne, the Executive Director of the Foundation, for his constant encouragement of research in Islam and Tibet. We would also like to thank the following libraries for having granted us permission to reproduce images: the Nasser D. Khalili Collection of Islamic Art, the Archaeological Survey of India, the British Library, the Forschungs-und Landesbibliothek Gotha and the Bodleian Library (Oxford). The lion's share of the editorial work has been done by Anna Akasoy, but all three editors have contributed their expertise in their respective fields, and Charles Burnett has prepared the index. We would like to thank Tsering Wangyal Shawa for designing the maps. We are very grateful to the Warburg Institute for providing congenial surroundings and much practical support for the pursuit of the Islam and Tibet project in general, and for hosting this conference in particular.

The transliteration of non-European languages has been standardized in this volume except where authors have preferred a different system. Diana Altner's article, referring to present-day issues, uses the simplified Chinese character system (we are grateful to Tim Barrett for checking the Chinese characters). Unless otherwise indicated, years are those of the Common Era.

The only abbreviations for publications referred to in this volume are *EI*^{2} (*Encyclopaedia of Islam*, second edition [Leiden, 2006], online edition) and *EIr* (Ehsan Yar-Shater [ed.], *Encyclopaedia Iranica* [14 vols to date, London, 1982-2008]; available at www.iranica.com).

Languages are abbreviated as follows:

Ar. – Arabic
Arm. - Armenian
Ch. – Chinese
Mo. - Mongolian
Pe. – Persian
Sa. – Salar
Skt. – Sanskrit
Syr. – Syriac
Tib. - Tibetan
Tu - Turkish
Uy. – Uyghur

The Editors

Chapter 1

Islam and Tibet: Cultural Interactions – An Introduction

Ronit Yoeli-Tlalim

In the mid-eighth century three major empires abutted each other: the Abbasid Empire, founded in 750, which established its new capital at Baghdad in 762 and embraced the culture of Persia; the Tibetan Empire, which reached its height in the early ninth century; and Tang China (618-907) in the east, with its capital of Chang-an (Xi'an), spilling out into the Tarim Basin (East Turkistan, now Xinjiang). Cutting across these political regions were two powerful religious movements: Buddhism, which from its origins in northern India, challenged and eventually displaced local religions in China and Tibet, and Islam, which spread from the West over the Indian subcontinent and South East Asia, reaching China and the Tibetan borderlands. These political and religious movements of the eighth century were to shape the development of Central Asian civilizations for many centuries to come, and can still be discerned in the societies of the region today. It is to the ways in which the Islamic empire, in particular, impinged on Tibet (and *vice versa*), and to the role of Muslims in Tibetan society that this book is devoted.

By 'Tibet' is meant more than the geographical area of the Tibetan Plateau, or any current political construct such as the 'Tibetan Autonomous Region' (TAR). Regions that participated in Tibetan culture, such as Ladakh and Baltistan, are also included. Above all, Tibet is viewed as it was conceived throughout its changing history by its Islamic neighbours. And similarly, the lands of Islam are considered as viewed in Tibetan literature. Thus this book begins with an essay by Anna Akasoy on Tibet in Islamic geography and cartography: what names did the Arabic authorities have for Tibet, and what land did they mean when they referred to 'Tubbat' (which is taken to be the Arabic equivalent to Tibet)? How did they obtain their information? And did their knowledge of the area change over time? The primary aim of the article is to trace the tradition of the concept of Tibet in Arabic literature, rather than to exploit that literature for reliable information about Tibet in historical times. Thus the Arabic tales refer to conversions to Islam in Tibet; they claim that those who visit the country are so overwhelmed with such joy that they cannot refrain from laughing and that the country abounds with gold and musk.

In Tibetan there are a number of terms that refer to the Islamic empire and its people, of which the most important are *stag gzig*, *par sig*, *khrom/phrom* and

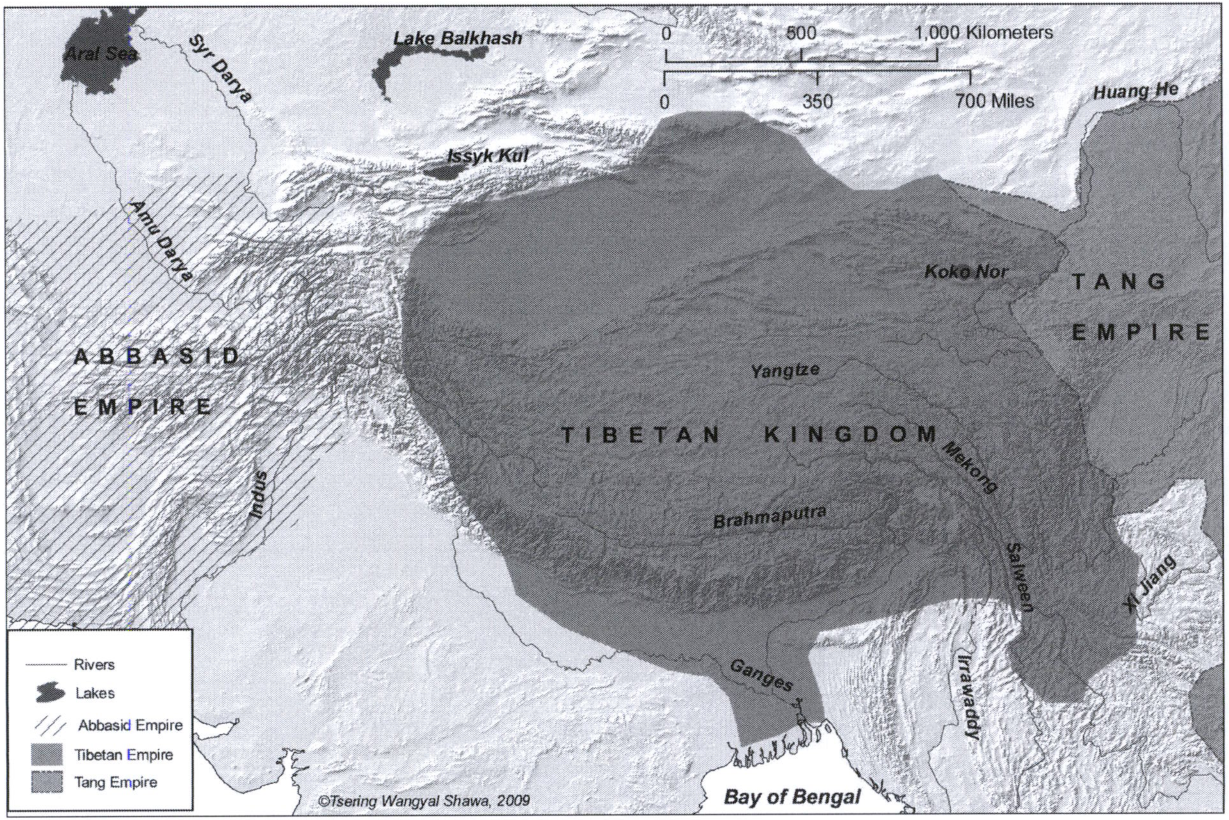

1.1 Tibetan Empire, 8th century (estimation)

kha che. *Stag gzig* in its various spellings (*stag gzigs, ta zig, ta zhig, ta chig*) as well as *par sig* (*par sil, pa ra si ka*) refer in many cases, but not always, to Muslims or to Arabs in general. The earliest mentions of these names are to be found in the Tibetan Dunhuang material.[1] In Pelliot Tib. 1283, dated to the second half of the eighth century or the first half of the ninth,[2] we find a reference to the *par sil* tribe[3] along with a mention of the *ta zhig*.[4] A reference to the land of *ta zig* is documented in a Tibetan medical text from Dunhuang which describes methods of moxibustion, and mentions the land of *ta zig* as a source for paper.[5] The early renderings of the name *par sig* support a direct linguistic link, as suggested by Uray, between Tibetan and Early Middle Persian or possibly Sogdian.[6]

The name *ta zig* is related to 'Tajik', now the name of Tibet's closest Persian-speaking neighbours. Another Tibetan term that refers to lands in the West derives from 'Rome' (or 'Rum', Byzantium): Khrom (or: Phrom). As Dan Martin explains in his contribution here, it is hard to know where the exact delineation between Tazig and Khrom stands from the Tibetan point of view, and probably

---

1 The Mogao caves at Dunhuang, western China, were discovered at the beginning of the twentieth century. In addition to the multitude of artistic treasures found there, the discovery of Cave 17, nicknamed 'the library', has had a revolutionary effect on Asian studies. The manuscripts have been dispersed among libraries in Paris, London, St Petersburg, Tokyo, Beijing and elsewhere. For electronic versions of some of these texts, and a bibliography see: otdo.aa.tufs.ac.jp and the website of the International Dunhuang Project: idp.bl.uk.

2 See Louis Ligeti, 'À propos du "Rapport sur les rois demeurant dans le nord"', in *Études Tibétaines dédiées à la mémoire de Marcelle Lalou* (Paris, 1971), pp. 166-89, at p. 172.

3 Pelliot Tib. 1283, l. 10. See Jacques Bacot, 'Reconnaissance en Haute Asie Septentrionale', *Journal Asiatique*, 244 (1956): pp. 137-53, at pp. 141 and 145. Imaeda et al., however, have transliterated the name as *par mil*, see Yoshiro Imaeda, Tsuguhito Takeuchi et al., *Tibetan Documents from Dunhuang* (Tokyo, 2007), p. 179, l. 542.

4 Pelliot Tib. 1283, l. 85. Clauson, basing himself on old Turkic inscriptions, infers that the reference to the *ta zhig* in Pelliot 1283 refers to Arabs (and not to Persians). See Gérard Clauson, 'À propos du manuscript Pelliot Tibétain 1283', *Journal Asiatique*, 245 (1957): pp. 11-24.

5 Saying: 'If there is bleeding from the nose use paper from *ta zig*': Pelliot Tib. 127, l. 174. Luo Bingfen et al. (eds), *Tun hong nas thon pa'i bod kyi gso rig yig cha gces bsdus* (Pe cin, 2002), p. 222.

6 Géza Uray, 'Tibet's Connections with Nestorianism and Manicheism', in Ernst Steinkellner and Helmut Tauscher (eds), *Contributions on Tibetan Language, History and Culture*, vol. 1 (Vienna, 1983), pp. 399-429, at p. 409. Uray discusses another early (eighth century) mention of the name *par sig*. In the *Vimalaprabhā*, the commentary on the *Kālacakra tantra*, the Tibetan version of the name appears to be based, as one would expect, on the Sanskrit (*pārasika*) – *pā ra si ka* in Bu-ston, see Bu-ston Rin-chen-grub, *The Collected Works of Bu-ston*, ed. Lokesh Chandra (New Delhi, 1965), vol. 1, fol. 391, l. 5. It might be the case that when the transcription is *par sig* (or *par sil*) the name is derived from Sogdian or Early Middle Persian, and when it is *pa ra si ka* it is derived from the Sanskrit.

all we can state with any degree of certainty is that in Tibetan they refer to areas in close proximity to each other.

A significant contact with Muslims was through neighbouring Kashmir. So many Muslims had arrived in Tibet through plying their trade via Kashmir that Muslim settlers in Tibet were called by a name deriving from the name 'Kashmir': *kha che*. Whether this term already meant 'Muslim' in general, rather than 'Kashmiri' in a mention of *kha che* silk in a Dunhuang manuscript from the ninth century is not clear.[7]

Kashmir had already been an important cultural junction in the seventh and eighth centuries when Buddhist scriptures and scientific works were transmitted from there both to Tibet and to the emerging Islamic culture. This is the subject of the article by Kevin van Bladel. Barmak, the father of the Barmakid family, was an educated Buddhist official from Tokharistan (Bactria), an area where Buddhism and its related Sanskrit sciences flourished at the time the Arabs arrived. The family then became very important in the Abbasid court in Baghdad and the Barmak's grandson, Yaḥyā, became the tutor and then the powerful minister of the caliph, Hārūn al-Rashīd (reg. 786-809). Van Bladel demonstrates how, as a result of Yaḥyā's Buddhist roots and his family ties with Tokharistan and Kashmir, Yaḥyā facilitated a substantial translation enterprise from Sanskrit to Arabic in the Caliph's court. A major outcome of this enterprise was the monumental translation of the Indian medical classics into Arabic: the *Suśruta*, the *Aṣṭaṅgahṛdaya saṃhitā* of Vāgbhaṭa and the *Siddhasāra* of Ravigupta. These same texts were also translated into Tibetan a short while later and thereafter became core texts in the Tibetan medical tradition. Although the full impact of the Indian tradition on Arabic medicine is yet to be studied, van Bladel provides sufficient evidence to show its importance, particularly in the area of pharmacopoeia. The cultural links facilitated by the Barmak family are inherently rooted in the special conditions developed in Central Asia in the century after the Arabs arrived and when Buddhism was still widely practised.

Another outcome of the coexistence of Buddhists and Muslims in Central Asia is discussed by Christopher Beckwith, who suggests that the adoption of the scholastic method in the Islamic world was a result of the conversion of the Central Asian Buddhist *vihāras* (monastic colleges) into Islamic *madrasas*. According to Beckwith, the conversion incorporated not only the structure, but also the people - and with them their method of learning too. The earliest known examples of the scholastic method appear to be, Beckwith suggests, in commentarial texts of the *Sarvāstivādin* school of Buddhism, which flourished in Central Asia. The first Muslim writer known to have used the scholastic method is Ibn Sīnā, who was born and educated in Central Asia. The sudden appearance

[7] In IOL Tib J 756 l. 33. The term is: *kha che dar*, which could be rendered either as Kashmiri or Muslim silk. See Bingfen et al. (eds), *Tun hong nas*, p. 133. A similar expression is found in the *Li yul lung bstan pa*, where it appears as: *kha cher dar*. See Ronald E. Emmerick, *Tibetan Texts Concerning Khotan* (London, 1967), p. 33.

of the scholastic method in Western Europe followed the translation of one of the most important of Ibn Sīnā's works from Arabic into Latin, and coincided with the transmission of the *madrasa* to Europe as the college.

Whereas texts can often demonstrate precise details of transmission between cultures, as in the cases presented by van Bladel and Beckwith, visual evidence of transmission is not always so clear-cut. Souren Melikian-Chirvani, however, draws attention to some tantalizing hints at this evidence in regard to links between Tibet and Iran. The evidence suggests that at a very early age – at least as early as the mid sixth century BCE – the artefacts of horsemanship, of hunting and warfare of a type known from western Iran, became familiar to the populations of present-day Tibet. Other, later evidence, suggests a clearer link: Melikian-Chirvani discusses three types of silver wine banquet vessels made in the Iranian world which reached Tibet around the seventh–eighth century CE. He also explores the provenance of Persian silk amongst Tibetans: pictorial and material evidence indicate that Persian brocaded silks were used as royal garments in Tibet as early as the seventh century. This includes a fragment of Sasanian silk with a Pahlavi inscription establishing its royal ownership which was recovered from a Tibetan tomb. He also notes the enduring memory of these textiles in the traces they left in western Tibetan mural paintings in Ladakh (Alchi) and Spiti (Tabo). Could it be that the reference found in the Dunhuang manuscript to *kha che* silk refers to what Melikian-Chirvani is describing from visual evidence? This question is yet to be investigated.

A study conducted by Christopher Beckwith in the late 1970s[8] brought to light the significance of the influence of medical knowledge originating in areas lying to the west of Tibet on Tibetan medicine. Beckwith mentioned references to medical influence deriving from Tazig and Khrom. These links, as mentioned in one of the earliest histories of Tibetan medicine, are further discussed in this volume by Dan Martin.

The sources discussed by Beckwith, as well as other sources which have come to light in the three decades since he published his article, mention a certain *Ga le nos*, as one of the four sages who introduced medicine into Tibet. This 'Galenos' obviously does not refer to Galen himself, but rather to the transmission of elements of Galenic medicine, which could have arrived in Tibet via Arabic, Persian or Syriac intermediaries.

Interestingly enough, in the earliest extant Tibetan medical history discussed by Martin, this 'Galenos' is not mentioned. In this medical history by Che rje, composed in the thirteenth century, there is a reference to another figure who is associated with medicine originating from the West: Tsan pa shi la ha, or as Martin suggests reading his name: Tsan Bashilaha. He suggests 'Tsan' refers to his origin from the shores of the Black Sea, and reading 'Bashilaha' as 'Basileos'. More research will be needed to ascertain more about this figure, and the

---

[8] Christopher I. Beckwith, 'The Introduction of Greek Medicine into Tibet in the Seventh and Eighth Centuries', *Journal of the American Oriental Society*, 99 (1979): pp. 297-313.

knowledge he may have brought with him. Martin also embarks on a revealing account of the medical content of the book ascribed to this Tsan Bashilaha: the *Bi ci'i pu ti kha ser*, which has recently been published. A method for detecting invisible skull fractures discussed in this text resembles methods described in Greek and Arabic medicine.

How one might explain the later appearance of the name 'Galenos' in Tibetan medical histories remains an open question for the time being. In any case, by the seventeenth century details concerning this 'Galenos' are abundant in the Tibetan historical narratives. One of the most detailed accounts of the contacts between Tibetan and Western (Persian) medical sciences is in the medical history by De'u dmar bstan 'dzin phun tshogs (b. 1672).[9] De'u dmar tells us not only about Ga le nos and Biji Tsan pa shi la ha, the representatives of what seems to be an Arabo-Persian tradition, but also about an entire 'Biji' lineage, spanning from Persia to Tibet, or rather from the Persian court and into the Tibetan court. One of the predecessors of the Biji lineage was a certain Ga le thos, who, according to De'u dmar, served as the personal physician to the king of the *stag gzig*.[10] According to De'u dmar, Biji Ga le thos's son was the Ga le nos who was invited to Tibet during the reign of Srong btsan sgam po (617–49). We are told that he cured Srong btsan sgam po's illness and hence was requested to become chief doctor. The younger brother of Ga le nos had two sons – the older was Biji Tsan pa shi la ha, who was invited to Tibet by the Tibetan prince Ljang tsha lha dbon, son of Mes ag tshom (d. 755). Furthermore, De'u dmar tells us, Tshan pa shi la ha: '... arrived in the Tibetan kingdom after having been dispatched by the king of Khrom together with 300 [other] masters and students [of medicine] and hence the medical teachings spread'.[11]

What is particularly interesting about De'u dmar's account is that it portrays the links with *stag gzig* doctors as spanning through a continuous period of time. Not only the famous 'Galenos', but an entire lineage is associated with *stag gzigs* and *khrom*. The significant input from the *stag gzig* doctors described by De'u dmar leaves us with the question: what was the nature of the medical knowledge that arrived from the Arab-Persian world into the Tibetan medical system? This is a vast question. But some indications can be gained from the analysis of the urine section from the early Tibetan medical text, the *Zla ba'i rgyal po*,[12] in which doctrines and practices from Western medicine appear among the more evident

[9] For a discussion of this source, see Frances Garrett, 'Critical Methodologies in Tibetan Medical Histories', *Journal of Asian Studies*, 66 (2007): pp. 363-87.

[10] De'u dmar bstan 'dzin phun tshogs. 'Gso ba rig pa'i chos byung rnam thar rgya mtsho'i rba rlabs drang srong dgyes pa' 'dzum phreng', in *Gso rig gces btus rin chen phreng ba bzhugs so* (Zi ling, 1993), pp. 632-764, at p. 704.

[11] De'u dmar bstan 'dzin phun tshogs. 'Gso ba rig pa'i chos byung', p. 705.

[12] Ronit Yoeli-Tlalim, 'On Urine Analysis and Tibetan Medicine's Connections with the West', in Sienna Craig et al. (eds), *Studies of Medical Pluralism in Tibetan History and Society* (Halle, 2011), pp. 195-211.

influences deriving from the Indian and the Chinese spheres. The *Zla ba'i rgyal po* is an early example of a synthesis of medical ideas deriving from different cultures. How and when did the Western input come to Tibet is still a question to be resolved, but the material acquired so far suggests that further research into theses questions will be highly worthwhile.

Following the initial relations between Tibet and its Muslim neighbours during the time of the Tibetan Empire, contacts continued predominantly via trade. There is evidence that a trade route from Arabia to Persia, via northern India and into Tibet was in operation already in the eighth century and continued to be active until modern times. Another trade route is described by Binyamin of Tudela, the Spanish Jewish traveller who appears to have travelled to Baghdad in the second half of the twelfth century. He writes that Jewish traders with Tibet proceeded from Baghdad to Persia, to Shiraz, Ghazna and Samarkand. From there, he says: 'it is four days to Tibet, which is the land where musk[13] is found in its forests'.[14]

A medieval map in the Arabic *Book of Curiosities*, written in Egypt in the eleventh century discussed in the Islam and Tibet conference by Yossef Rapoport, follows what seems to be a trade route which begins in India, goes to Tibet and from there to China.[15] This not only highlights the place of Tibet along the Muslim trade routes, but also is interesting in locating Tibet on the route to China. Indeed Tibet can also be seen as an intermediary between China and the Islamic world in a cultural sense, a point which is reflected in Paul Buell's contribution.

Tibet was an important point on the Eurasian trade routes and a source for a number of exotic goods. The most famous among these was musk, used both in medicine and in perfumery. This is the focus of Anya King's contribution. We know that musk from Tibet was traded and used in the Near East and the Mediterranean from as early as the third century CE. Musk appears as a highly desired substance in a great variety of Arabic genres (geography, zoology,

13 The word used here is: מור (mor). On the identification of mor with musk in Hebrew sources see Shapirah, 'Al khomrei ha'bosem meha'khai bamkorot ha'ivriim' ('On Animal Perfume Substances in the Hebrew Sources'), *Harofé Haivri: The Hebrew Medical Journal*, 2 (1959): pp. 95-103.

14 *Benjamin of Tudela*, fol. 82, in *The Itinerary of Benjamin of Tudela*, ed. and trans. Marcus Nathan Adler (London, 1907).

15 Emilie Savage-Smith and Yossef Rapoport (eds), *The Book of Curiosities: A Critical Edition*. Online publication (www.bodley.ox.ac.uk/bookofcuriosities) (last accessed: March 2007). The map in question is in Book 2, chap. 18. See also Yossef Rapoport and Emilie Savage-Smith, 'Medieval Islamic View of the Cosmos: The Newly Discovered Book of Curiosities', *The Cartographic Journal*, 41 (2004): pp. 253-9 and Yossef Rapoport, 'The *Book of Curiosities*: A Medieval Islamic View of the East', in Andreas Kaplony and Phillip Forêt (eds), *The Journey of Maps and Images on the Silk Road* (Leiden, 2008), pp. 155-71.

medicine, religion) as well as in accounts of merchants and travellers. In most of these it is the musk from Tibet that is deemed the best.

Musk, in addition to being a highly desired perfume, is a substance which is found both in Tibetan and Arabic medical literature. Based on a comparative study between the Arabic and the Tibetan uses of musk in medical contexts, we have come to the conclusion that, alongside trade, there were also exchanges of ideas.[16] Hence the overall name we have suggested for the cultural exchanges discussed here: the Musk Route.[17]

The case of musk is an example of the ways in which 'super-drugs', as well as other luxury goods, were marketed through their exotic appeal. The construction of desirability and its associated lucrativeness are intertwined with trade and power. A similar point is raised by van Bladel with respect to Central Asia, where the patronage of wealthy rulers funding Buddhist travellers, is intertwined with the existence of Buddhist texts where precious commodities were promoted.

An echo of trade contacts is also attested in the nature of many of the loan-words from Arabic and Persian which are found in Tibetan.[18] These include, for example, the words in Tibetan for saffron (Tib. *kur kum*; *gur kum* or *gur gum*) from the Persian and Arabic *kurkum*; or the word for gold brocade: *zar babs* (from Pe. *zar baft*, discussed here by Melikian-Chirvani), or the word *nal*, the Tibetan word for ruby, from the Persian *lāl*, a much sought-after commodity in the Arab world which arrived from Central Asia.

A pivotal period of cultural exchanges between Tibet and the Islamic world occurred during the Mongol period, which is discussed here by Peter Zieme, Paul Buell and Arezou Azad. During the thirteenth and early fourteenth centuries, the Ilkhan Mongol rulers in Iran maintained close relations with Tibetan Buddhism. With the help of Arabic, Persian, Tibetan, Syriac and Armenian sources we can trace the extensive Tibetan presence in the Ilkhanid court in Tabriz, where most of the rulers were Buddhist and their spiritual advisers were lamas (*bakhshi*).[19]

Rashīd al-Dīn (1247-1318), a court physician, who became an extraordinarily powerful (and rich) minister of the Ilkhans, realized the exceptional cosmopolitan milieu that the Mongol rule had created.[20] As he tells us:

---

16 Anna Akasoy and Ronit Yoeli-Tlalim, 'Along the Musk Routes: Transmissions between Tibet and the Islamic World', *Asian Medicine: Tradition and Modernity*, 3 (2007): pp. 217-40.

17 I would like to thank Philip Denwood for first discussing this idea with me.

18 Berthold Laufer, 'Loan Words in Tibetan', *T'oung Pao*, 17 (1916): pp. 404-552. For the sections on loan words from Persian and Arabic see pp. 474-85.

19 For a discussion on the *bakhshis* in the Ilkhanid court see Rashīd al-Dīn, *Histoire des Mongols de la Perse*, trans. Étienne Quatremère (Amsterdam, 1968), pp. 184-99, n. 51. See also Leonard van der Kuijp, '"Bayši" and Bayši-s in Tibetan Historical, Biographical and Lexicographical Texts', *Central Asiatic Journal*, 39 (1995): pp. 275-302.

20 See Anna Akasoy, Charles Burnett and Ronit Yoeli-Tlalim (eds), *Rashīd al-Dīn: Agent and Mediator of Cultural Exchanges in Ilkhanid Iran* (London, forthcoming).

> Now that the world from one end to the other is under one or the other branch of the Chingiz Khanids, philosophers, astronomers, scholars and historians of all sects and religions connected with China [Khita], ancient India, Kashmir, Tibet, Uyghur, as well as other people like the Turks, Arabs and Franks are before our eyes in large numbers and every one of them has books containing the history, chronology and religious thought of those countries ...[21]

In addition to the more well-known association of Qubilai Khan with Tibetan Buddhism through the Sa skya Paṇḍita, we now also have evidence of the influence of Tibetan Buddhism in the Ilkhanid as well as the Chagatai Khanates.[22] The first Ilkhan, Hülegü (Tib. Hu la hu or: Hu la; reg. 1256-65), was, like his brother Qubilai in China, a follower of Buddhism. As has been discussed by Sperling, Hülegu became a patron of the Tibetan Buddhist Phag mo gru sect and repeatedly sent gifts to their abbot, rGyal ba Rin po che Grags pa brtson 'grus.[23] The *Red Annals* (*Deb ther dmar po*), a Tibetan historical chronicle of the fourteenth century, tells us that the last presents reached Phag mo gru two years after the death of Hülegü (i.e. in 1267).[24] We also know that Hülegü, while already ruling in Iran, had a representative in Tibet, who is named in several Tibetan sources as Go go chu (Kokochu), and that through this representative, Hülegü maintained his jurisdiction over a number of areas in Tibet. There are also references to this representative's son taking part in the political life of the Phag mo gru several years later.[25] The Phag mo gru in central Tibet (in Ü, based at sNe'u gdong) had considerable religious and political power at the time, and it appears that the financial and military support from Hülegü was key in the power struggle between the Phag mo gru on the one hand, and on the other the Sa skya rulers, who were supported by the Mongol court of the Great Khans.

An interesting testimony of the link between Geikhatu (reg. 1291-95), the fifth Ilkhan, and Tibetan Buddhism, is found on a coin minted in his time, which includes his Tibeto-Mongol religious name: Rinchen Dorje (rin chen rdo rje,

---

21 Rashīd al-Dīn, *Jāmiʿ al-tawārīkh*, translation in Thomas Allsen, *Culture and Conquest in Mongol Eurasia* (Cambridge, 2001), p. 83.

22 See Samuel Grupper, 'The Buddhist Sanctuary-Vihāra of Labnasagut and the Il-Qan Hülegü: An Overview of Il-Qanid Buddhism and Related Matters', *Archivum Eurasiae Medii Aevi*, 13 (2004): pp. 5-77.

23 These relations are attested to in a number of Tibetan sources. See, for example, Kun dga' rdo rje (1309-65), *Deb ther dmar po* (Peking, 1981), pp. 122-4. The *Blue Annals* say in reference to rGyal ba rin po che: 'Having heard about the fame of his accomplishments, king Hu-la from sTod presented on three occasions great offering to him.' 'Go lo tsā ba gzhon nu dpal, *The Blue Annals*, trans. George Roerich (Delhi, 1996), p. 580. For a detailed study see Elliot Sperling, 'Hülegü and Tibet', *Acta Orientalia Academiae Scientiarum Hungaricae*, 44 (1990): pp. 145-57.

24 *Deb ther dmar po*, p. 122. Discussed by Sperling, 'Hülegu and Tibet', p. 151.

25 Sperling, 'Hülegü and Tibet', p. 153.

meaning 'precious diamond') in its Mongolian form in Arabic transliteration , in addition to the Muslim profession of faith.[26]

Ghāzān (reg. 1295-1304), the seventh Ilkhan, grew up as a Buddhist. Rashīd al-Dīn tells us that Ghāzān's grandfather, Abāqā, surrounded him with Buddhist lamas, and hence he maintained a great affection for their religion. According to Rashīd al-Dīn, Ghāzān spoke Tibetan. He also patronized and constantly consorted with lamas who came from Tibet and Kashmir, and who were very influential among the Mongol upper classes up to his generation.[27]

A revealing text in this respect is Rashīd al-Dīn's *Life of the Buddha*, based on the input of the Kashmiri pandit, Kamalaśrī, and which is a part of Rashīd al-Dīn's *History of India*.[28] As I have discussed elsewhere, the text reflects some interesting connections with Tibet and Tibetan Buddhism. The *Life of the Buddha* section contains, for example, one of the earliest (if not *the* earliest) piece of external evidence for the assembling of the Kanjur (bka' 'gyur).[29] Considering that Rashīd al-Dīn's *Life of the Buddha* was composed around 1310, being more or less contemporary with the assembling the first Kanjur in Narthang, this mention is very interesting.

The Ilkhanate court was influenced not only by Tibetan Buddhism, but also by Kashmiri, Uyghur and Chinese Buddhism.[30] The significant input of Tibetan Buddhism in Kashmiri Buddhism of the time,[31] as well as in Uyghur Buddhism, helps to explain the mirroring of a Tibetan type of Buddhism in Rashīd al-Dīn's *Life of the Buddha*. The important role of Tibetan Buddhism amongst the Uyghurs

---

[26] De Saulcy, 'Lettres sur quelques points de la numismatique orientales', *Journal Asiatique*, 13 (1842): pp. 113-49, at pp. 129-32; Stanley Lane Poole, *Catalogue of Oriental Coins in the British Museum* (10 vols, London, 1875-90), vol. 6, p. 32.

[27] Arsenio P. Martinez, 'Third Portion of the History of Ġāzān Xān in Rašīdu 'd-Dīn's *Ta'rīx-e Mobārak-e Ġāzānī*', *Archivum Eurasiae Medii Aevi*, 8 (1994): pp. 99-206, at p. 111, n. 13. The relevant sections in Rashīd al-Dīn's *Tārīkh-e Mobārak-e Ghāzānī* quoted by Martinez are: pp. 165ff., 171ff. and 188.

[28] See Karl Jahn, *Rashīd al-Dīn's History of India* (The Hague, 1965); Gregory Schopen, 'Hīnayāna Texts in a 14th Century Persian Chronicle', *Central Asiatic Journal*, 26 (1982): pp. 225-35.

[29] See the facsimiles in *Die Indiengeschichte des Rašīd ad-Dīn*, trans. Karl Jahn (Vienna, 1980), ms. Istanbul, Topkapı Sarayı. Hazine 1654, fol. 348r, l. 28 (Persian version) and ms. Khalili collection (formerly Royal Asiatic Society A 27), fol. 2077v, l. 1 (Arabic version). The text says that after the death of Śākyamuni, a stranger 'collected the words and useful sayings of Śākyamuni in a book, the entirety of which he called Kashurdy (A: قشوردي P: قسوردي)'. 'Kashurdy' is presumably a transcription of 'Kanjur'. See Ronit Yoeli-Tlalim, 'Rashīd al-Dīn's *Life of the Buddha* – Some Buddhist Perspectives', in Akasoy et al. (eds), *Rashīd al-Dīn*.

[30] See Grupper, 'The Buddhist Sanctuary'. See also: Klaus Röhrborn, 'Die Islamische Weltgeschichte des Rašīduddīn als Quelle für den zentralasiatischen Buddhismus?', *Journal of Turkish Studies*, 13 (1989): pp. 129-33.

[31] See Jean Nadou, *Les Bouddhistes Kaśmiriens au moyen age* (Paris, 1968).

is discussed here by Peter Zieme. Influence of Tibetan Buddhism on Uyghur culture during the Yuan (Mongol) period is attested to both in the numerous Buddhist texts that were translated from Tibetan into Uyghur during this time, and also in the influence which can be detected in Buddhist art in the Kurutka caves near Turfan. This influence went hand in hand with increasing Muslim presence. The tension between Buddhism and Islam in the Turfan area at the time, is attested to by an Uyghur Buddhist poem, that exhibits a hostile attitude to Islam.

Indeed, also in Iran the Buddhist days were not to last. Upon his ascension to the throne, Ghāzān converted to Islam. He then:

> Commanded that all idols be smashed and all temples and other places of worship disallowed by law in the lands of Islam be destroyed. Most of the idol-worshipping *bakhshis* were converted to Islam, but since God had not slated them for success, the faith they held was not correct: outwardly they appeared to be Muslims, but from their foreheads showed traces of infidelity and error.

The text goes on to say that, after a while the Padishah of Islam [ie: Ghāzān] comprehended their hypocrisy and said, 'Let any of you who so desires, go to India, Kashmir, Tibet or his native country.'[32]

The Persian term for a Buddhist place of worship is *butkhāna*. The aim of the research expedition on which Arezou Azad reports here, was to assess whether the references to *butkhānas* by Persian historians of the Ilkhanid period can be identified with any of the three rock-cut sites in the regions of Marāgha and Sulṭāniyya. During the Mongol period, Marāgha was the focus of scholarly exchanges between Iranian and Chinese astronomers, following the creation of an observatory commissioned by Hülegü and supervised by the famous scholar Nāṣir al-Dīn Ṭūsī (d. 1274). Having examined these sites, Azad reaches the conclusion that, despite the literary evidence, in the absence of any specifically Buddhist epigraphy, iconography or artefacts, it is difficult to confirm that any of these caves indeed served as Ilkhanid Buddhist worship sites. They rather seem to be a monumental mélange of Mithraic, Buddhist, Islamic and Christian episodes.

The exchanges between Iranian and Chinese astronomers and the possible role of Tibetans in the process was the topic of Benno van Dalen's paper at the Islam and Tibet conference (not included here).[33] In addition to the observatory at Marāgha, there was also an Islamic Astronomical Bureau with an observatory

---

[32] *Rashiduddin Fazlullah's Jami'u't-tawarikh: Compendium of Chronicles. A History of the Mongols*, trans. Wheeler M. Thackston (3 vols, Cambridge, 1999), vol. 3, p. 676.

[33] See Benno van Dalen, 'Islamic and Chinese Astronomy under the Mongols: A Little-Known Case of Transmission', in Yvonne Dold-Samplonius, Joseph W. Dauben, Menso Folkerts and Benno van Dalen (eds), *From China to Paris: 2000 Years Transmission of Mathematical Ideas* (Stuttgart, 2002), pp. 327-56.

founded by Qubilai Khan in his new capital near present-day Beijing in 1271, which was headed by Zhamaluding (presumably the Muslim Jamāl al-Dīn al-Bukhārī), and had a large number of Muslim astronomers. The main surviving source for the achievements of the Bureau is a Chinese translation of an Islamic astronomical handbook with tables, called the *Huihuilifa*, which was composed in the early Ming dynasty (1383) and was later reworked in Nanjing in 1477, as well as in Seoul in 1442. In recent years a Persian manuscript in St Petersburg and an Arabic one from the Bibliothèque Nationale de France in Paris have been found to be related to the *Huihuilifa*. The Paris manuscript is an astronomical handbook by the otherwise unknown astronomer al-Sanjufīnī, who worked for the Mongol viceroy in northeastern Tibet in the 1360s and who based himself heavily on the material which is also included in the *Huihuilifa*. Van Dalen discussed the various characteristics of this work and showed through which route the knowledge it contains may have reached Tibet.

As in the court of the Great Khans, a major attraction for the Ilkhans was Buddhist medicine, and particularly substances, which supposedly had life-prolonging effects. Indeed, the parallels found between Tibetan and Arabic or Persian alchemy, as signalled by Michael Walter's studies on the Tibetan Jābir, provide scope for further illuminating research in this direction.[34]

Tibetan medicine provides an interesting case of a cultural intermediary, as discussed here by Paul Buell. Looking at the role of Tibetans as key conduits of knowledge between 'East' and 'West', particularly between China and the Islamic world, Buell shows how the Tibetans played a decisive role in interpreting medicine at the Mongol court, since their own medicine involved some of the same syntheses as the cosmopolitan 'Muslim' medicine of Mongol China. As a medical system which synthesizes Greco-Arab, Indian and Chinese systems, Buell argues that Tibetan medicine stood in a favoured position, bridging the Chinese and Islamic systems during the Yuan dynasty. Tracing Tibetan influences in the Chinese *Huihui yaofang* ('Muslims Medicinal Recipes') and in the imperial dietary manual of Mongol China, the *Yinshan zhengya* ('Proper and Essential Things for the Emperor's Food and Drink'), Buell argues that the role of Tibetan medicine as a cultural intermediary was central.

Following the demise of the Mongol empire, another area of cultural interactions emerged in Ladakh and Baltistan, also known as: 'Middle Tibet' and 'Little Tibet' respectively. Inhabited by ethnic Tibetans, who speak Tibetan dialects, north-western India has witnessed various forms of co-existence between its two main religions: Tibetan Buddhism and Islam. An essential form of interchanges is seen in the reciprocal exchange of princess-brides, as told here by Georgios Halkias. Halkias discusses the practice of royal inter-marital

---

34 Michael Walter, 'Jâbir, the Buddhist Yogi I', *Journal of Indian Philosophy*, 20 (1992): pp. 425-38; 'Jâbir, the Buddhist Yogi II: 'Winds' and Immortality', *Journal of Indian Philosophy*, 24 (1996): pp. 145-64; 'Jabir, the Buddhist Yogi, Part III: Considerations on an International Yoga of Transformation', *Lungta*, 16 (2003): pp. 21-36.

alliances across the Buddhist–Muslim divide in the Himalayas, primarily as depicted in local folk-songs and written histories. Bridal exchanges among peasants and aristocrats in Ladakh and Baltistan preserve accounts of an age-old Muslim–Buddhist symbiosis, celebrating the influence enjoyed by the Muslim queens in the Ladakhi court and by the descendants of such marriages. The marriages widened the basis of power of the royal families in question. Both parties were expected to respect each other's faith and neither party had to undergo religious conversion. The convention of Islam and Buddhism coexisting in a family was common in Ladakh until recent times.

As Akasoy mentions, the conversion theme also appears in the earliest Muslim sources. Already Yaʿqūbī (ninth century), for example, claims that under al-Maʾmūn the King of Tibet converted to Islam and then sent a golden image of the Buddha as a token of his conversion.[35] A fascinating visual account of this episode was presented by Deborah Klimburg-Salter in the Islam and Tibet conference, but unfortunately it is not included in this collection.

Looking at conversion narratives in a broader sense, we find that it is often alliances – whether military or for love and marriage – that serve the background for these conversion narratives. The conversion stories are often found to use mythical devises to reverse agonizing realities. The powerful 'other' becomes subdued in one form or other. The case of the Buddhist *Kālacakra tantra* and its Shambhala myth provide such a case of a conversion narrative. The *Kālacakra,* composed in India in the eleventh century and subsequently translated into Tibetan, contains an eschatological account describing the reign of the 25th ruler (*rigs ldan*) of Shambhala at the time when the entire earth will be conquered by Muslims (referred to as 'barbarians', Tib: *kla klo*). The *Kālacakra* recounts that at that time the Shambhala army will enter into battle with the *kla klo*s and defeat them. Following that, the 25th ruler of Shambhala will reign over the entire earth, propagating the teachings of the Buddha in general, and the *Kālacakra* specifically. This eschatological account has been widely disseminated both in Tibet and Mongolia and used to various political ends.

Although it is often stated that the *Kālacakra* was composed in north India as a reaction to the growing dangers of Islam, it also reflects co-existence with Islam and, indeed, an assimilation of several Islamic ideas.[36] Echoes of the *Kālacakra*'s

---

[35] Christopher I. Beckwith, *The Tibetan Empire in Central Asia: A History of the Struggle for Great Power among Tibetans, Turks, Arabs, and Chinese during the Early Middle Ages* (Princeton, 1987), pp. 160-62.

[36] For some of these see Giacomella Orofino, 'Apropos of Some Foreign Elements in the Kālacakratantra', in Helmut Krasser et al. (eds), *Tibetan Studies: Proceedings of the 7th Seminar of the International Association for Tibetan Studies, Graz 1995*, vol. 2 (Vienna, 1997), pp. 717-24 and Alexander Berzin, 'Holy Wars in Buddhism and Islam: The Myth of Shambhala'; 'The Kalachakra Presentation of the Prophets of the Non-Indic Invaders'; 'Religious Conversion in Shambhala', all in *The Berzin Archives*, available online: www.berzinarchives.com.

references to Islam are found in later Tibetan literature. One such case is found in the writings of the sixteenth-century author Tāranātha. In his account of how Islam began, Tāranātha recounts that Muhammad was in fact a Buddhist disciple who had lost his faith in the Dharma, violated his vows and was subsequently expelled from the *sangha*. Later he:

> Concealed himself under the name Ma-ma-thar, changed his robes, composed the *mleccha* scripture preaching violence and kept it concealed in the place of Bi-śli-mi-lil, the great demon ...

The story then continues (in quite a peculiar way!) and then Tāranātha tells us:

> [fol. 42b] Along with a thousand attendants, he became the sage of the *mleccha*s under the name Bai-kham-pa [Pai kham pa]. He went to the region in the vicinity of Makha city.[37]

Here we encounter another sphere of loan-words: the religious. In addition to the words which have come from the *Kālacakra* (via the Sanskrit), such as the mention of Mecca and the 'mantra' Bismillāh, here we encounter another interesting word – the word Tāranātha uses for the name of the sage of the Muslims, Pai kham pa. The Tibetan here is derived from the Persian word for 'prophet', *paygambar* (P: پيغمبر).[38] We may also note that the name used here for Muhammad is different from that which is known in the Sanskrit *Kālacakra* literature – Madhumatī (and its Tibetan equivalent, sbrang rtsi'i blo gros).[39] This sphere of loan-word usage seems to reflect direct contacts with Muslims, which at this time existed not only in neighbouring countries, such as Mughal India, but also in Tibet itself.

Religious conversion becomes a key issue in later narratives, although it is often not clear whether they are historical or mythical. Important accounts of religious conversion can be found among the Tibetan Kashmiri Muslim community, who trace their arrival to Tibet to the time of the Fifth Dalai Lama (1617-82). An oral tradition which has previously been recounted by Marc Gaborieau, tells the story in which Khayr al-Dīn secretly converted the

---

37 *Tāranātha's History of Buddhism in India*, trans. Lama Chimpa and Alaka Chattopadhyaya (Delhi, 1997): pp. 117-18. This account has been mentioned by Cabezón. See: José Ignacio Cabezón, 'Islam in the Tibetan Cultural Sphere', in Abdul Wahid Radhu, *Islam in Tibet: Tibetan Caravans*, Louisville, KY, 1997, pp. 13-34, note 45 at pp. 30-1.

38 See Laufer, 'Loan Words in Tibetan', p. 481.

39 I have not come across this form of Muhammad's name in other Tibetan sources. The more common form, as it appears in the *Kālacakra* literature is Ma-dhu-ma-ti. For appearances of this form see John Newman, 'Islam in the Kālacakra Tantra', *Journal of the International Association of Buddhist Studies*, 21 (1998): pp. 311-71, at p. 333.

Fifth Dalai Lama to Islam, after defeating him in a competition of magic.[40] In Gaborieau's contribution here, the presence of Muslims in Tibet before the time of the Fifth Dalai Lama's reign is testified by Portuguese missionaries in Tibet in the early seventeenth century.

With clearly documented Muslim presence in and around Tibet from this period onwards, the evidence of Buddhist–Muslims relations is attested to in various forms. Some of these are discussed here by Papas, Zarcone and Elverskog. Papas and Zarcone deal with the genre of conversion narratives, stemming from areas where Buddhism and Islam were in actual close contact. These narratives of conversion tread, as Papas puts it, 'a delicate path between history and legend along collective memory and representation'. He relates these conversion narratives to a broader tradition among the Muslims of the Himalayas and Central Asia – the tradition of secret conversion to Islam of prominent Buddhist figures.

Some of the ways in which historical accounts of religious encounters have been perceived and shaped throughout the last millennium by particular agendas, specific to time and place, is evidenced in Elverskog's essay here. Throughout the periods Elverskog describes, two points emerge as the main reasons for Islam and Buddhism's representation of the other as 'evil': one is particular political agendas, and the other ignorance. The narration of religious interactions along lines of 'clash of civilizations' is found both in Buddhist sources from the eighth century onwards[41] and in much Western scholarship.

Throughout this collection there are various discussions of the role of intermediary cultures. This includes, certainly, the Islamic culture as whole, spreading from Samarkand to Cordova, but also, more specifically, the Persian language (Gaborieau, Bray), the role of Kashmir and Kashmiris (Bray, Melikian-Chirvani and van Bladel) and the role of Uyghur culture (Zieme).

Gaborieau discusses the role of Muslims and of the Persian language as an intermediary between Tibet and the West. Focusing on the use of Persian language for Portuguese missionaries, he discusses its importance in shaping Western understanding of Buddhism. John Bray discusses the mediation role of the Persian language, particularly as used by Kashmiris, for the dissemination of knowledge about Tibet. Although focusing on one case from the nineteenth century, many of the points of cultural intermediaries raised in his essay are also relevant for earlier times: the way in which commerce and diplomacy are intertwined in various forms of mediation; and the way Kashmiris, with their international network, and bilingual skills in Tibetan and Persian, served as important cultural intermediaries.

In present-day Tibet, there are three different Muslim groups: Muslims whose origins are in Kashmir, Ladakh and India, Muslims whose ancestors came

---

40 Marc Gaborieau, *Récit d'un Voyageur Musulman au Tibet* (Paris, 1973).

41 See Leonard van der Kuijp, 'The Earliest Indian Reference to Muslims in a Buddhist Philosophical Text of *circa* 700', *Journal of Indian Philosophy*, 34 (2006): pp. 169-202.

from China, and Tibetan converts to Islam. These groups, and how they relate to the modern Chinese general category of *hui* is the focus of Diana Altner's contribution. Another contemporary aspect is presented here by Jan Magnusson, who discusses the intertwining of the political and cultural agendas of the contemporary Baltistan Movement. Demonstrating how tradition is mobilized as a strategy in the reassertion of a cultural, political and regional identity, he discusses how the Baltistan movement, whose membership is made up mostly by Muslims, has mobilized historical narratives of Greater Ladakh, emphasizing the link with 'Old Tibet'. He analyses their struggle to reintroduce Tibetan script and the production and promotion of the very popular pop *ghazal*s within this context. These contemporary issues have their resonance in the historical parts of the book. The juxtaposition of the historical and the contemporary in this collection may help us to further understand the multiple facets of the interactions discussed in these essays.

Chapter 2

Tibet in Islamic Geography and Cartography: A Survey of Arabic and Persian Sources

Anna Akasoy

ABBASID BAGHDAD AND ISLAMIC GEOGRAPHY

From the earliest days of Islam, interactions between diverse religious, ethnic and cultural groups contributed to the dynamics of its history. The Muslims, initially almost exclusively Arabs, had to deal with various groups of non-Muslims who came under their control during the first expansion, and as they settled in the provinces formerly belonging to the Byzantine and Sasanian empires and Islam became more attractive for the locals, the Arab character of the religion was substituted by a more universal approach and new ideas were absorbed. By the time of the Abbasid revolution in 750, the Islamic empire stretched from the Iberian Peninsula to Central Asia where the Arab Muslim armies defeated those of Tang China at the river Talas in 751.

Arabic and, later, Persian literature reflects the contacts with these diverse peoples.[1] If we want to study the attitudes of medieval Muslims to other cultures, we may find ourselves in a more or a less fortunate situation. Abundant material is available concerning contacts with the Abrahamic cousins of Islam, Christianity and Judaism, both of which had an enormous impact on the early development of Islam. In both cases, the need for the Muslims to distinguish themselves was greatest, too. Another case of relatively early and intense contact is that of the intellectual heritage of ancient Greece. The translation of texts on philosophy and science gives a unique impression of how Muslims (or the Christian translators) understood elements of a different culture which was no longer practised. A similar phenomenon, albeit on a much smaller scale, can be identified in the imports of Indian intellectual culture to the Islamic world. In this case, however, we are in the fortunate position of having at our disposal an account of a true expert, the scholar al-Bīrūnī who completed his famous book on India in 1030. Al-Bīrūnī had been trained in the Greek sciences and obtained knowledge of Sanskrit and Indian philosophy when he accompanied Maḥmūd of Ghazni on his campaigns into north-west India. Even though the exceptional

---

[1] For Islamic attitudes to other religions and cultures in general see the volumes edited by Jacques Waardenburg (*Muslim Perceptions of Other Religions* [New York, 1999]) and Robert Hoyland (*Muslims and Others in Early Islamic Society* [Aldershot, 2004]).

character of the author and his work renders these hardly representative of Muslim attitudes, at least they provide starting points for investigation.

In other cases, we have neither a broad textual basis nor such exceptional documents. If we want to study Islamic attitudes to peoples in sub-Saharan Africa before the bloom of Islamic culture in West Africa, for example, we have to rely on snippets collected from a variety of texts.[2] We are faced with a similar dearth of information in the case of Tibet. There are several circumstances which explain this situation. Geography is one of them: both sub-Saharan Africa and the Himalayas are difficult terrains and relatively far away from the main lands of the Islamic world. Cultural reasons may have been even more important: thriving cosmopolitan cities with a vibrant literary tradition were probably more interesting. Presumably, there were not many literati in the main lands of the Arab world who spoke the necessary languages or who found the local beliefs doctrinally challenging. For the medieval Arabs, Tibet clearly did not constitute a prestige culture. The relatively slow spread of Islam into the Himalayas in particular might have been another contributing factor.

In cases where according to our present knowledge no medieval Muslim author has devoted a substantial study to a certain culture, we cannot avoid the cumbersome task of collecting short references and anecdotes from all sorts of Arabic and Persian texts. There is one genre, however, which usually turns out to provide promising starting points, and this is geographical literature.[3]

The rise of geographical literature needs to be understood against the backdrop of the events referred to above: that is, the creation and expansion of an Islamic empire. When the Abbasid family took over the caliphate and moved the capital from Syria to Iraq, thereby reflecting the interests of the growing number of Persian Muslims, they presented their self-image in a very visible form. The second caliph, al-Manṣūr, secured his place in history in 762 as the founder of Baghdad, *madīnat al-salām*, 'the city of peace', as he called it. The creation of this future metropolis alone could serve as an exemplary case of cultural exchanges within Asia. The date of the foundation was set by three men: Māshā'allāh, a Jew, and Nawbakht, a Zoroastrian convert to Islam, were well-versed in astronomy, and they were joined by Khālid ibn Barmak about whom more will be noted later.[4] The round outlook of the heart of the city itself

---

2 See Anna Akasoy, 'Paganism and Islam. Medieval Arabic Literature on Religions in West Africa', in John Marenbon and Carlos Steel (eds), Proceedings of the Conference *Paganism in the Middle Ages and the Renaissance*, Cambridge University, 19-20 September 2006 (forthcoming).

3 See the authoritative work by André Miquel, *La géographie humaine du monde musulman jusqu'au milieu de 11e siècle* (3 vols, Paris, ^{2}1973-75) and Fuat Sezgin, *Geschichte des arabischen Schrifttums*, vols 10-12 (Frankfurt, 2000).

4 Charles Wendell, 'Baghdâd: *Imago Mundi*, and Other Foundation-Lore', *International Journal of Middle East Studies*, 2 (1971): pp. 99-128.

may have been influenced by Central Asian models.[5] The city reflected the image the Abbasid caliphs wanted to convey of themselves. Al-Manṣūr's mosque and palace were at the centre of the round city and the caliph was at the heart of the known world.

Intellectual life in Baghdad was shaped not only by the image its cultural patrons intended to promote, but perhaps even more by the more cosmopolitan and egalitarian character of Abbasid society. The capital offered opportunities to a great variety of people. The best-known example is probably the family of the just mentioned Khālid ibn Barmak, the Barmakids, who were formerly guardians of a Buddhist temple in what is modern-day Afghanistan and rose to a position of immense power at the court of Hārūn al-Rashīd.[6] When people from diverse and distant places came to Baghdad, they brought along their linguistic, literary, religious, political and intellectual traditions as well as their material culture. Medical and pharmacological treatises testify to the presence of goods, or at least the knowledge of them, from all over Asia.[7] The reputation of exotic drugs to allow swift recovery and even eternal life is an ancient legacy,[8] but in Arabic medical literature we find substances from the East which do not appear in Greek sources. Musk, the main import good from Tibet, is one of them.[9]

Like the theoretical framework of Islamic medicine which was largely derived from Greek sources, Arabic geographical literature too was inspired by the ancient tradition. However, from its early days onwards and like medicine, it included new elements which bear witness to the wider geographical scope. It is also in these early geographical texts that we find the earliest descriptions of Tibet in Islamic sources.[10]

---

[5] Wendell, 'Baghdâd: *Imago Mundi*'; Christopher Beckwith, 'The Plan of the City of Peace: Central Asian Iranian Factors in Early ʿAbbāsid Design', *Acta Orientalia Academiae Scientiarum Hungaricae*, 38 (1984): pp. 143-64. But see Kevin van Bladel in this volume for doubts.

[6] See also the contribution by Kevin van Bladel in this volume.

[7] An exemplary study of this subject is R.A. Donkin, *Dragon's Brain Perfume: An Historical Geography of Camphor* (Boston, 1999).

[8] Laurence M.V. Totelin, 'Mithridates' Antidote – A Pharmaceutical Ghost', *Early Science and Medicine*, 9 (2004): pp. 1-19.

[9] Anna Akasoy and Ronit Yoeli-Tlalim, 'Along the Musk Routes: Exchanges between Tibet and the Islamic World', *Asian Medicine: Tradition and Modernity*, 3/2 (2007): pp. 217-40; and the contribution by Anya King in this volume.

[10] Most of the texts referred to in this article are written in Arabic, a smaller number in Persian. The expression 'Islamic geography' is not only warranted by the fact that the authors were exclusively Muslims, but by the worldview which had a region shaped by Islamic culture at its heart. The term does not suggest a genuinely or primarily religious nature for this genre.

TIBET IN ISLAMIC GEOGRAPHY – METHODOLOGICAL PROBLEMS

Geographical literature needs to be understood here in a broad sense. Generally speaking, there are two branches, human and mathematical geography. The former includes descriptions of the culture and the history of different regions as well as legends and anecdotes, whereas the latter owes its existence to the tradition of Ptolemy and determines latitudes and longitudes. But I will also look into texts which are usually described as 'encyclopaedias' of various kinds or works of *adab*. The borders between these genres are often blurred, and we shall see how this might affect our assessment of the different accounts of Tibet. In addition to purely textual sources I will examine cartographic evidence at the end of this article.

Some of the testimonies to early contacts between Tibetans and Arabs in *adab* have been fruitfully exploited by historians of Tibet, who naturally adopted a Tibeto-centric perspective and tried to identify the corresponding people, places and historical events in the Tibetan past. There can be little doubt concerning the heuristic value of matching entities in texts and in the 'real world'. The aim of the present contribution, however, is a different one: that is, to read these references to Tibet within a body of texts that has its own logic determined by its character as literature, its sources, its authors, their patrons and audiences and their respective environments.[11] While I discuss the methodological implications elsewhere in greater detail, using the popular topos of the happiness of the Tibetans as an example,[12] this article offers a survey of Arabic and Persian primary sources, pointing out lines of development as well as elaborating on specific contexts.

There are several questions I would like to raise throughout this article:

- The Arabic name for Tibet is Tubbat. Yet, as we shall see, it is far from certain what Tubbat refers to exactly in Islamic sources and whether this is the only way in which Muslim authors referred to Tibet.[13]
- Where did Muslim authors obtain their information from and did they have any particular reasons for including a certain kind of information?

---

11 For similar approaches to non-fictional medieval Arabic literature as literature see Stefan Leder (ed.), *Story-Telling in the Framework of Non-Fictional Arabic Literature* (Wiesbaden, 1998); Philip F. Kennedy (ed.), *On Fiction and Adab in Medieval Arabic Literature* (Wiesbaden, 2005); Julia Bray (ed.), *Writing and Representation in Medieval Islam* (London, 2006). In the last volume see especially Robert Hoyland, 'History, Fiction and Authorship in the First Centuries of Islam' (pp. 16-46).

12 Anna Akasoy, 'Dying of Laughter in Lhasa: Tibet in Islamic Geographical Literature' (forthcoming).

13 Luciano Petech, 'Il Tibet nella geografia musulmana', *Atti della Accademia Nazionale dei Lincei, Classe di Scienze morali, storiche e filologiche*, 2 (1947): pp. 55-70, at p. 55. According to Petech, it is not necessarily the case that Tubbat means Tibet (see below, pp. 38-9).

- How does the description of Tibet in Islamic literature change throughout the centuries? Should we assume with Luciano Petech that all relevant information on Tibet had been gathered during the first military campaigns of the Arabs without later authors taking notice of changes within the Himalayan region, or should we rather assume that Muslim authors remained up-to-date with their information on Tibet?

HUMAN GEOGRAPHY AND THE EARLY TRADITION

Among the earliest sources of Arabic geographical literature are two narrative genres, *akhbār* and *ʿajāʾib* (stories about marvellous events and things). A famous example is the *Akhbār al-Ṣīn wa'l-Hind*.[14] These 'Stories about China and India' were collected by a merchant with the name Sulaymān in the middle of the ninth century, edited in the tenth century by a certain Abū Zayd al-Sīrāfī and used by many authors of important geographical treatises.[15] Sulaymān's home was probably South Arabia. He went several times to China and composed the earliest report of such a journey. His text includes many ethnological details and anecdotes. In modern academic literature it is sometimes stated that the text was compiled without literary ambition, but rather as a guidebook for sailors and merchants, a distinction which might be rather artificial.[16]

One passage in Sulaymān's book leads us into the immediate neighbourhood of Tibet.[17] The author mentions the people of Mūja who are white and dress like the Chinese. They possess musk of excellent quality, inhabit a land of white mountains higher than any others and are at war with the surrounding kingdoms. The kings of Mādbud are neighbours of the Mūja. They are greater in number than the Mūja and resemble the Chinese more than they do. They are also in close contact with the Chinese and exchange gifts on an annual

[14] Gerald Tibbetts, 'The Beginnings of a Cartographic Tradition', in J.B. Harley and David Woodward (eds), *Cartography in the Traditional Islamic and South Asian Societies* (Chicago, 1992), pp. 90-107, here p. 90.

[15] Sauvaget lists Ibn Khurradādhbih, Ibn al-Faqīh, Ibn Rusta, al-Masʿūdī, al-Bīrūnī, al-Marwazī, al-Idrīsī, al-Qazwīnī and Ibn al-Wardī. See *Aḫbār aṣ-ṣīn wa'l-hind, Relation de la Chine et de l'Inde*, ed. and trans. Jean Sauvaget (Paris, 1948), pp. xxiii-xxviii.

[16] For similar problems cf. James Montgomery, 'Serendipity, Resistance, and Multivalency: Ibn Khurradādhbih and his *Kitāb al-Masālik wa-l-mamālik*', in Kennedy (ed.), *On Fiction and Adab*, pp. 177-232.

[17] For the following account see *Aḫbār aṣ-ṣīn wa'l-hind*, pp. 14-15 (nn. 31-2). The passage about the Mūja has been translated into English in *Arabic Classical Accounts of India and China*, trans. S. Maqbul Ahmad (Shimla, 1989), p. 45. For a German translation of the passages under consideration here see Ingeborg Pahlke, 'Die Chinareise des Sulaimān at-Tāǧir', *Zeitschrift für Geschichte der arabisch-islamischen Wissenschaften*, 5 (1989): pp. 190-224, at pp. 209 and 224.

basis, but they are not their subjects. Between their land and China there are only mountains and steep paths. In the final paragraph of his text, Sulaymān describes the people of Tibet. They live close to the Toghuzghuz, a Turkic people. The Tibetans are also Turks, and their leader is the Khāqān of Tibet.[18]

Who exactly are these people? And what is Sulaymān's source of information? Even if the Mūja are described as different from the Tibetans,[19] the description of their land - musk of excellent quality, high snow-covered mountains - fits exactly that of Tibet in later Islamic literature, where the high quality musk is one of the most recurrent features. In the section on musk in his *Akhbār*, Sulaymān also praises the quality of the Tibetan kind and does not mention the Mūja. The kings of Mādbud are probably the kings of lower Tibet, *smad bod* in Tibetan. In other Islamic sources we find the expression *Tusmat* which probably represents Tibetan *stod smad*, upper and lower Tibet: upper Tibet being the centre and the west, lower Tibet the eastern region around Lake Kokonor.[20] The already mentioned eleventh-century author al-Bīrūnī speaks in his *al-Qānūn al-Masʿūdī* of inner and lower Tibet (*Tubbat dākhil* and *adnā*), listing inner Tibet as part of the third and fourth climates[21] (for which see below) and explaining that the Indian method of calculating the year is used in lower Tibet.[22] There is a parallel in the Arabic geography of China which distinguishes between inner China (*Ṣīn*) and outer China (*Māṣīn*).[23]

Some of the information displayed by Sulaymān seems to be what can be expected from a merchant: musk was a highly prized trading good, as were the white hawks Sulaymān mentions in his last sentence on Tibet. The information on ethnicity, habits and political structure might have provided a merchant with a basic orientation.

Political organization equally remained one of the most important themes in Islamic descriptions of Tibet, which often repeat the claims that the Tibetans are Turks and that their leader is a Khāqān, the common term for a Turkish ruler. Sometimes they are described as merely similar to the Turks. Maqdisī, an author of the tenth century, declared the Tibetans a category between Turks and Indians. The style of their clothes is Chinese, but they have the flat noses of the Turks and the brown skin of the Indians. Unlike other authors, Maqdisī adds

---

18 *Aḫbār aṣ-ṣīn wa'l-hind*, p. 27 (n. 73).

19 For their identity cf. the translation of the passage and the notes in *Aḫbār aṣ-ṣīn wa'l-hind*, pp. 54-5.

20 Luciano Petech, 'Nota su *Mābd* e *Twsmt*', *Rivista degli Studi Orientali*, 24 (1949): pp. 142-4.

21 Al-Bīrūnī, *Kitāb al-qānūn al-Masʿūdī fī al-hay'a wa'l-nujūm* (3 vols, Haydarabad, 1954-56), vol. 2, pp. 563 and 573. See also *Biruni's Picture of the World*, ed. A. Zeki Validi Togan (Delhi, 1937), p. 45.

22 Al-Bīrūnī, *Kitāb al-qānūn al-Masʿūdī*, vol. 1, p. 92.

23 Michal Biran, *The Empire of the Qara Khitai in Eurasian History* (Cambridge, 2005), pp. 98-101.

that they have a literary tradition and sciences of numbers and stars (*al-kitāba wa'l-ḥisāb wa'l-nujūm*).[24] Often they are described as close neighbours. The remark by Ibn al-Faqīh who wrote in 903 that Tibet forms part of the border of the land of the Turks seems to suggest that the Tibetans themselves are not Turks.[25] Similar remarks are included in geographical lexica such as Yāqūt's (574 or 575/1179-626/1229) *Muʿjam al-buldān*[26] (although he introduces Tibet as part of the Turkish region – *balad bi-arḍ al-Turk* – it lies to the East of the lands of the Turks – *bilād al-Turk*) and its abbreviation, Ṣafī al-Dīn's (d. 739/1338) geographical lexicon *Marāṣid al-iṭṭilāʿ*[27] and several other sources dependent on it. Al-Bakrī, on the other hand, an author of the eleventh century (d. 487/1094) in al-Andalus, to whom I shall return later, presents the historical background of the Tibetan affiliation with the Turks as follows:

> The largest part of the empire (of the Turks) belongs to China and Khorasan ... They had a king, the Khāqān of the Khāqāns, who united their lands. When he died their kingdom dispersed (?). A fraction (*farīq*) in Tibet received their name, and they were the ones who submitted to a Khāqān. When their political order dissolved, they were called by a similar name.[28]

Yāqūt presents a similar story and adds that the Tibetans were highly respected among the Turks, because their king used to be one of them and it was believed among their learned men that he would return.[29] This is not the only version of the origins of the Tibetans early Arabic literature has to offer. Masʿūdī for example, an author of the tenth century, quotes a verse by Diʿbil ibn ʿAlī al-Khuzāʿī (148/765-246/860) which might be the earliest mentioning of Tibet in Arabic sources. In his verse Diʿbil refers to the Yemenis and says:

---

[24] Muṭahhar ibn Ṭāhir al-Maqdisī, *Kitāb al-badʾ wa'l-tārīkh*, ed. and trans. Clément Huart (6 vols, Paris, 1899-1919), vol. 4, p. 63.

[25] Ibn al-Faqīh, *Mukhtaṣar Kitāb al-buldān*, ed. M.J. de Goeje (Leiden, 1885), p. 329. For a French translation see *Abrégé du livre des pays*, trans. Henri Massé (Damascus, 1973), p. 388. Not much is known about his biography other than that he was born in Hamadan, see the article by Henri Massé on Ibn al-Faqīh in *EI*^{2}. While Massé mentions that he was indebted to Jāḥiẓ and Jayhānī, Petech sees him as part of the tradition dependent on the material collected under al-Maʾmūn (Petech, 'Il Tibet nella geografia musulmana', p. 61).

[26] Yāqūt, *Jacut's Geographisches Wörterbuch*, ed. Ferdinand Wüstenfeld (6 vols, Leipzig, 1866-73), vol. 1, pp. 817-20.

[27] Ṣafī al-Dīn ʿAbd al-Muʾmin ʿAbd al-Ḥaqq al-Baghdādī, *Marāṣid al-iṭṭilāʿ* (3 vols, Cairo, 1954-55), vol. 1, p. 251.

[28] Al-Bakrī, *Al-Masālik wa'l-mamālik*, ed. Adrian van Leeuwen and André Ferré (2 vols, Tunis, 1992), vol. 1, p. 261, n. 389.

[29] Yāqūt, *Geographisches Wörterbuch*, vol. 1, p. 818.

> They composed writings on the gate of Merw and were scribes (?) at the gate of China
> They called Samarkand 'Shammar' and placed the Tibetans there[30]

Diʿbil is another good example if we want to find out where these early reports about Tibet and the Tibetans came from.[31] Born in the Middle East, he had to leave his native Kufa after being involved in highway robbery. From 789 until 792 he served as a governor in Siminjan and Tokharistan in present-day north-eastern Afghanistan. His association of the Tibetans (*Tubbatiyyūn*) with the ancient kings of Yemen (*Tabābiʿa*) might be a simple etymological explanation, but forms part of a set of widespread legends about the Himyarites in Samarkand promoted by those who advocated the South Arabian legacy.[32] Yāqūt too quotes Diʿbil's verse and explains that as time passed, the Tibetans forgot their Arab ways and resembled more and more the Turks, calling, among other things, their king *khāqān* instead of *tubbaʿ*.[33]

In fact, the legend of the Yemeni origin of the Tibetans is one of the most popular elements in the descriptions of Tibet in Arabic literature. Abū Saʿīd ʿAbd al-Ḥayy al-Gardīzī, who wrote his *Zayn al-akhbār* in Persian in around 1050, offers in his chapter on Tibet one of the most extensive accounts of the Yemeni roots of the Tibetans, in which a great variety of Tibetan and Islamic elements are intertwined in the unusual story of Thābit.[34] Having heard from his mother of the natural riches of Tibet, Thābit, a governor for the Tubbaʿ, travels there, but the devil (*Iblīs*) has him kidnapped. Thābit agrees on a pact with Iblīs and returns to the earth where he becomes the king of Tibet. In the story, Thābit's long hair and attire are reminiscent of Tibetan style. The devil eats a louse and declares

---

30 Quoted by Masʿūdī, *Murūj al-dhahab*, ed. Charles Pellat (3 vols, Beirut, 1965-70), vol. 1, pp. 187-8 (§389).

وهم كتبوا الكتاب بباب مرو　　وباب الصين كانوا الكاتبينا
وهم سموا السهام بسمرقند　　وهم غرسوا هناك التبتينا

31 On Diʿbil cf. the article in *EI*² on him. Al-Bakrī quotes a verse according to which Diʿbil died in Zawīla (southern Libya). See Nehemia Levtzion and J.F.P. Hopkins, *Corpus of Early Arabic Sources for West African History* (Princeton, ²2000), p. 63.

32 Tilman Nagel, *Alexander der Große in der frühislamischen Volksliteratur* (Walldorf-Hessen, 1978), p. 21. See also the article by Alexandre Papas in this volume.

33 Yāqūt, *Geographisches Wörterbuch*, vol. 1, pp. 818-19.

34 Abū Saʿīd ʿAbd al-Ḥayy Gardīzī, *Zayn al-akhbār*, ed. ʿAbd al-Ḥayy Ḥabībī (Tehran, 1347/1948; repr. 1969), pp. 263-5. Hansgerd Göckenjan and István Zimonyi, *Orientalische Berichte über die Völker Osteuropas und Zentralasiens im Mittelalter: Die Ğayhani-Tradition (Ibn Rusta, Gardīzī, Hudūd al-ʿĀlam, al-Bakrī und al-Marwazī)* (Wiesbaden, 2001), pp. 128-34, where parallels in the Tibetan tradition are pointed out; A. Martinez, 'Gardīzī's Two Chapters on the Turks', *Archivum eurasiae medii aevi*, 2 (1982): pp. 109-217, pp. 128-31 for an English translation of the passage on Tibet.

that it grants a long and safe life – a legend which has parallels in the Tibetan tradition. In Gardīzī's text we can see that a Khāqān does not necessarily have to be of Turkish origin. When the Yemeni Thābit becomes a king in Tibet, Gardīzī refers to him as Khāqān. Al-Bakrī too mentions later in his text the Himyarite origin of the Tibetans.[35]

Other authors, however, such as Iṣṭakhrī who wrote in 951, were more sceptical. He concludes his brief note about the South Arabian roots of the Tibetans with the words 'and God knows it best'.[36] The same remark appears in the geographical work *Ṣūrat al-arḍ* by Ibn Ḥawqal who wrote in 977 and relied heavily on Iṣṭakhrī.[37] The North African Ibn Khaldūn in the *Introduction* (*Muqaddima*) to his *History*, written in 1377, even dismissed such connections between the Yemenis and Tibet as utter nonsense:

> It would ... ordinarily have been impossible for the Tubbaʿs to traverse the land of the Persians on their way to raid the countries of the Turks and Tibet, because of the nations that are interposed on the way to the Turks, because of the need for food and fodder, as well as the great distance ... All information to this effect is silly and fictitious.[38]

As I argue elsewhere,[39] this Yemeni legend may very well have developed as a counter-narrative to the Alexander legend – the great king is also credited with the foundation of cities in Central Asia. In an etymology which might be just as simple as the above-mentioned, it is claimed that Alexander left behind (*taraka*) the Turks (*turk* or *atrāk*) in Central Asia.[40] Others, however, claimed that the Turks were left behind by the Tubbaʿ and the Himyarites.[41] For those with less pronounced sympathies for South Arabia, the Yemeni legend might have been an attempt to incorporate the Tibetans into the legacy of the Arab Muslims. The legend may also simply reflect an employment of Yemeni soldiers in the early Arab conquests in the East, but this issue requires further investigation.

---

35 Al-Bakrī, *Al-Masālik wa'l-mamālik*, vol. 1, p. 269 (n. 410).

36 Iṣṭakhrī, *Viae regnorum*, ed. Michael Jan de Goeje (Leiden, 1870), p. 10.

37 Ibn Ḥawqal, *Configuration de la terre*, trans. Johannes Hendrik Kramers and Gaston Wiet (2 vols, Paris, 1964), p. 15. The text includes a number of references to Tibet's location and to trading goods.

38 Ibn Khaldūn, *The Muqaddimah: An Introduction to History*, trans. Franz Rosenthal, Edited and abridged by N.J. Dawood (Princeton, 1989), p. 16.

39 Anna Akasoy, 'Alexander in the Himalayas: Competing Imperial Legacies in Medieval Islamic History and Literature', *Journal of the Warburg and Courtauld Institutes*, 72 (2009): pp. 1-20.

40 Nagel, *Alexander der Große*, p. 21.

41 Thus al-Qurṭūbī (d. 1273) in an eschatological text, *Tadhkira fī aḥwāl al-mawtā* (Cairo, n.d.), p. 682.

Sulaymān and Diʿbil, the former a man of trade, the latter involved in administration, exemplify the way in which this early material of Islamic geography was assembled. Both of them might have encountered ‘real’ Tibetans, either in the ports of China or in Central Asia. They could have relied on oral tradition from other merchants, soldiers, administrators, travellers or local people, or they could have been ‘armchair geographers’ and simply used earlier written sources. The fact that they personally visited these places did not prevent them from using accounts by other writers in their own descriptions. In both cases the information has to a certain extent a ‘real’ basis, but it is almost impossible to find out if Sulaymān and Diʿbil tried to verify it. Both are among the earliest testimonies of the key Tibetan themes in Islamic literature, the Turkic or Yemeni origin and the musk.

Travellers continued playing an important role in the development of geographical literature and often provide sources for fresh Muslim impressions of Tibet which do not rely on previous texts. A good example is Abū Dulaf who wrote two treatises about his journeys, which took place in the middle of the tenth century.[42] The first treatise, which is preserved with a number of later additions, describes his journey from Bukhara to Sandābil which has been identified as Kan-čou. Among several Turkish tribes in the area Abū Dulaf mentions the Tubbat and gives an account of their way of life which is unrelated to any previous descriptions of Tibet in Arabic literature, at least as far as we know them.[43] In the second *Risāla*, the traveller mentions the campaigns of the Tubbaʿ to China who had a castle built between Tus and Nishapur in which he placed his treasures and family. When he returned, he took some of his belongings, but left others behind in a secret place. As Vladimir Minorsky has pointed out, ‘as a native of Yanbuʿ, Abū Dulaf is only too willing to connect local antiquities with south-Arabian lore’.[44] The same can be said about others who spread the legend of the Tibetans’ Yemeni legacy. Abū Dulaf’s account was used by later authors of geographical literature. The passage on the Tubbat, for example, appears in the work of Amīn Rāzī written in *c.*1593. Another source, fortunately preserved in a manuscript in the Bodleian Library, is a cosmography entitled *The Book of Curiosities of the Sciences and Marvels for the Eye* by an anonymous author, possibly someone involved in trade, and written in Egypt between 1020 and 1050. One of the maps which accompany the text shows the route from Daybul to the ‘Gate of China’, one of the stations being Tibet.[45]

---

[42] See the article on him by Vladimir Minorsky in *EI*².

[43] About the text see Josef Marquart, *Osteuropäische und ostasiatische Streifzüge: Ethnologische und historisch-topographische Studien zur Geschichte des 9. und 10. Jahrhunderts (ca. 840-940)* (Leipzig, 1903; repr. Darmstadt, 1961), pp. 74-93.

[44] Abū Dulaf, *Travels in Iran (circa A.D. 950)*, ed. and trans. Vladimir Minorsky (Cairo, 1955), p. 59 and pp. 106-7 for Minorsky’s commentary.

[45] Accessible via http://cosmos.bodley.ox.ac.uk/hms/home.php (last accessed 21 August 2008). See Jeremy Johns and Emilie Savage Smith, ‘The Book of Curiosities: a Newly

AL-MAʾMŪN

More important for the creation of systematic entries on Tibet in Islamic geographical literature than this kind of sporadic information are the data collected under the Abbasid Caliph al-Maʾmūn (reg. 196/812-218/833). Relations between the caliphs and the Tibetans started as early as the second decade of the eighth century. Yaʿqūbī in his *History*, written around 891, reports for the reign of the Umayyad ʿUmar II (99/717-101/720) of an embassy despatched from Tibet to the governor of Khorasan, Jarrāḥ ibn ʿAbdallāh, to ask for missionaries to teach Islam in Tibet.[46] Yaʿqūbī also mentions the king of Tibet as one of the rulers who submitted to the Abbasid Caliph al-Mahdī (158/775-169/785). Under al-Maʾmūn, Yaʿqūbī claims, the king of Tibet converted to Islam and sent as a token of his conversion a golden idol set on a throne to Khorasān.[47] Again, although Yaʿqūbī's *History* reveals something about the historical relationship, we should carefully evaluate the text within its own literary context.

Yet, our scepticism should not go too far. As Christopher Beckwith has shown, Chinese sources confirm some of these details and mention political alliances between the Arabs and the Tibetans in the years in question. But what about the Tibetan interest in Islam? The local population of the newly conquered territories should have been confronted with the choice between conversion and expulsion or death, as demanded by Islamic law, but it seems little likely that there were any substantial conversions among the Tibetans. Other authors such as the Andalusian geographer Ibn Saʿīd (610/1213-685/1286) claim that Islam entered Tibet as a consequence of the Islamization of the Turks who were unbelievers in the era of the Barmakid al-Faḍl ibn Yaḥyā and entered later the service of the Seljuks.[48] As in other cases, the submission to the Islamic faith might not have meant more than a submission to an Islamic army,[49] as is also

---

Discovered Series of Islamic Maps', *Imago Mundi*, 55 (2003): pp. 7-24; Evelyn Edson and Emilie Savage-Smith, *Medieval Views of the Cosmos* (Oxford, 2004); Yossef Rapoport and Emilie Savage-Smith, 'Medieval Islamic View of the Cosmos: The Newly Discovered Book of Curiosities', *The Cartographic Journal*, 41 (2004): pp. 253-9.

46 Yaʿqūbī, *Ibn-Wādhih qui dicitur al-Jaʿqubī historiae*, ed. Martijn Theodoor Houtsma (2 vols, Leiden, 1883; repr. 1969), vol. 2, p. 362, and *Kitāb al-boldān*, ed. Michael Jan de Goeje (Leiden, 1892), p. 301. Christopher I. Beckwith, *The Tibetan Empire in Central Asia: A History of the Struggle for Great Power among Tibetans, Turks, Arabs, and Chinese during the Early Middle Ages* (Princeton, 1987), p. 87. Douglas M. Dunlop, 'Arab Relations with Tibet in the Eighth and Early Ninth Centuries A.D.', *Islâm Tetkikleri Enstitüsü Dergisi*, 5 (1973): pp. 301-18, at pp. 307ff.

47 Yaʿqūbī, *Historiae*, vol. 2, p. 550. The idol is also mentioned by Ibn al-Faqīh in his *Mukhtaṣar Kitāb al-buldān*, p. 21; *Abrégé*, p. 26. See Beckwith, *The Tibetan Empire in Central Asia*, pp. 160-62.

48 Ibn Saʿīd, *Kitāb al-jughrāfiyā*, ed. Ismāʿīl al-ʿArabī (Beirut, 1970), p. 175.

49 Yohanan Friedmann, 'A Contribution to the Early History of Islam in India', in Myriam Rosen-Ayalon (ed.), *Studies in Memory of Gaston Wiet* (Jerusalem, 1977), pp. 309-33,

pointed out by Jan Magnusson in his contribution to this volume. Alexandre Papas and Thierry Zarcone analyse conversion narratives which point to much later periods. Further information regarding al-Maʾmūn's contacts with the Tibetans can be gleaned from Ṭabarī (224-5/839-310/923). His account shows a confused terminology and he seems to refer to the ruler of the Tibetans as being king of Tibet as well as king of the Turks.[50] As we have seen, such a confusion is far from uncommon among medieval Muslim writers.

In the history of Islamic geography al-Maʾmūn is credited with a decisive impact. In connection with the military campaigns al-Maʾmūn ordered the collection of information about the history, geography and culture of the newly conquered peoples. One of the best-known testimonies to this geographical enterprise is the famous world map, which was probably produced for political purposes, to show that al-Maʾmūn ruled over all that mattered. The map is not preserved, and its form remains an enigma. Many Islamic geographical treatises are believed to depend on this information.

A key figure in this early formation of Arabic geography as a science was al-Khwārizmī (*c.*184/800-*c.*232/847). His table with geographical data has been described as the 'progenitor of the Maʾmūnic group'.[51] In this table, Tibet appears among the places of the fifth climate with the longitude 130° and the latitude 38°.[52] This position and similar ones are also given by several other Muslim writers.[53] I will return to the problem of the position of Tibet further below.

When it comes to the numerous anecdotes and legends, the ethnographic and cultural information in Arabic and Persian geographical literature, it is more difficult to determine where it came from and whether it was connected with al-Maʾmūn. Let us consider the following example: in his *Book on Animals* the well-known contemporary of Diʿbil, Jāḥiẓ (160/776-255/868), says:

---

at p. 322.

50 We should probably refrain from following Beckwith's suggestion to emend Ṭabarī's expression (*The Tibetan Empire in Central Asia*, p. 159), which would be an artificial harmonizing of a terminology which is inconsistent in the original. For Ṭabarī's methodology cf. the article on him in *EI*².

51 Edward S. Kennedy and Mary Helen Kennedy, *Geographical Coordinates of Localities from Islamic Sources* (Frankfurt, 1987), p. xxiii.

52 Al-Khwārizmī, *Das Kitāb ṣūrat al-arḍ des Abū Gaʿfar Muhammad ibn Mūsā al-Huwārizmī*, ed. Hans von Mžik (Leipzig, 1926), p. 28 (n. 405). Hubert Daunicht, *Der Osten nach der Erdkarte al-Ḫuwārizmīs* (4 vols, Bonn, 1968-70), vol. IV/1, pp. 95-6.

53 Al-Battānī (d. 317/929) who relies on al-Khwārizmī and was influential himself (*Opus astronomicum*, ed. Carlo A. Nallino [3 vols, Milan, 1899-1907], vol. 3, p. 239 for the Arabic text, vol. 2, p. 44 for the Latin text). The otherwise unknown Zayn al-Dīn al-Dimyāṭī in his *Kitāb al-tahdhīb fī maʿrifat al-qibla wa-naṣb al-maḥārīb* gives 140° and 38° (Ms. Oxford, Bodleian Library, Marsh 552, fols 103r-114r). For an extensive list see Kennedy and Kennedy, *Geographical Coordinates*, pp. 360-61 for Tibet.

> The merchants of Tibet, from among those who have entered China and Jâvaka, who have explored those islands and investigated these countries, maintain that whoever stayed in the heart (*qaṣaba*) of Tibet is overwhelmed with joy; he does not know the reason for it, and does not stop smiling, laughing without astonishment, until he departs from it.[54]

Jāḥiẓ is the first author to mention this widely diffused anecdote in Arabic literature. Petech assumed that it stemmed from the material collected under al-Maʾmūn,[55] but his view has been challenged by Christopher Beckwith who claimed that Jāḥiẓ's description of Tibet could have hardly referred to the real place, since merchants on their way to China and Jâvaka took the sea route which does not lead into Tibet.[56] I think this is a misreading of the Arabic text. Jāḥiẓ does not present a proper travel route, but rather a loose association in the sense of 'those who travel to the Far East'. The passage appears among several others on pleasant smells in different regions, and for the entertaining effect evoked by the curiosity of the phenomenon, the accuracy of the place names is of little significance. What neither Petech nor Beckwith have discussed in any more detail is in which ways Jāḥiẓ could or should have been connected to al-Maʾmūn's geographical project. Even though the Caliph admired his work, there is no reason why Jāḥiẓ should have borrowed this particular information from the geographers involved in the enterprise and not from traders themselves.

In another passage in his *Book on Animals* also related to Tibet, the author mentions such a source. In his chapter on mice, Jāḥiẓ describes an animal called the 'musk-mouse' or 'musk-rat'. The existence of this animal is at least in part due to a terminological confusion. The Arabic word for musk pod is *fārat al-misk* which could easily be read as *faʾrat al-misk*, 'musk mouse'. The existence of such an animal is supported by accounts of small animals which leave a pleasant smell behind. In the passage in question, Jāḥiẓ explains that he enquired from a fellow Muʿtazilite who was a perfumer what this 'musk mouse' was. The perfumer replied that it was not a mouse, but rather a small gazelle which was the source of musk.[57]

With Jāḥiẓ' *Book on Animals* we have already left the genre of geographical literature which, however, is a necessary step if we want to consider this corpus

---

54 Jāḥiẓ, *Al-Ḥayawān*, ed. ʿAbd al-Salām Muḥammad Hārūn (7 vols, Cairo, 1938-45), vol. 7, p. 230. Beckwith's translation is slightly misleading. See Christopher I. Beckwith, 'The Location and Population of Tibet According to Early Islamic Sources', *Acta Orientalia Academiae Scientiarum Hungaricae*, 43/2–3 (1989): pp. 163-70, at p. 164.

55 Petech, 'Il Tibet nella geografia musulmana', p. 58. Among the earlier authors, it also appears in Ibn al-Faqīh, *Mukhtaṣar Kitāb al-buldān*, p. 255; *Abrégé*, p. 308.

56 Beckwith, 'The Location and Population of Tibet', p. 164.

57 Al-Jāḥiẓ, *Al-Ḥayawān*, vol. 5, p. 304. See also Herbert Eisenstein, *Einführung in die arabische Zoographie* (Berlin, 1990), pp. 214 and 221 for animals which produce perfumes. See also Akasoy and Yoeli-Tlalim, 'Along the Musk Routes'.

of texts within its literary context: that is, *adab* in a broader sense. In a variety of encyclopaedic works, Tibet appears often in connection with musk and the animal that produces it, but sometimes also as the home of another curious creature, the Ṣannāja. This animal which resembles a dragon is, according to Zakariyyāʾ ibn Muḥammad al-Qazwīnī (d. 682/1283), the largest beast on the earth and lives in Tibet. Other animals which see it die.[58] In illustrations of the Qazwīnī's *ʿAjāʾib al-makhlūqāt*, the flaming wings of the Ṣannāja betray Chinese influences. The existence of such an animal in Tibet confirms the impression of its liminal status, at the edges of the civilized world.

In texts about precious goods, Tibet is praised mainly for its musk, but also for its gold and armour.[59] Finally, another context in which Tibet is sometimes mentioned, are apocalyptic Sibylline traditions in which various peoples and places are destroyed by others.[60] All these diverse bits of information combined to a more detailed picture of Tibet in the minds of medieval readers and listeners.

Another genre of geographical literature which developed from the data collected under al-Maʾmūn is treatises which are often entitled *Kitāb al-masālik wa'l-mamālik* ('Book of Highways and Kingdoms'), which largely rely on non-literary sources such as lists of pilgrimage and post stages and information about the distance between these stages. The earliest example of this type which survives is Ibn Khurradādhbih's geographical book, written about 846. Ibn Khurradādhbih (205/820 or 211/825-c.272/885 or 300/911) was a postal official and had a professional interest in geography.[61] Later, he became the *nadīm*, boon-companion of the Caliph al-Muʿtamid (reg. 256/870-279/892), and

---

58 Bilha Moor and Efim A. Rezvan, 'Al-Qazwīnī's *ʿAjāʾib al-Makhlūqāt wa Gharāʾib al-Mawjūdāt*: Manuscript D370', *Manuscripta Orientalia*, 8/4 (2002): pp. 38-68, at p. 50 and Fig. 8. Another example of the Ṣannāja can be found in the Aleppo room in the Museum for Islamic Art (Berlin). See Karin Rührdanz, 'Fabeltiere des Aleppo-Zimmers vor dem Hintergrund der Illustrationen naturhistorischer Kompendien', in Julia Gonnella and Jens Kröger (eds), *Angels, Peonies, and Fabulous Creatures: The Aleppo Room in Berlin* (Münster, 2008), pp. 47-53, at pp. 47-8. Also Gerda-Henkel-Stiftung, Jahresbericht 2007, p. 71. I would like to thank Bilha Moor for having alerted me to this inhabitant of Tibet.

59 See, for example, Aḥmad ibn al-Rashīd ibn al-Zubayr, *Book of Gifts and Rarities/Kitāb al-hidāya wa'ltuḥaf*, trans. Ghada al Hijjawi al-Qaddumi (Cambridge, 1996), p. 62.

60 David Cook, *Studies in Muslim Apocalyptic* (Princeton, 2002), p. 265 ('the Sind [will be destroyed] by the Hind [Indians], the Hind by the Tibetans, and the Tibetans by the Chinese'). See also David Cook, 'Muslim Apocalyptic and Jihād', *Jerusalem Studies in Arabic and Islam*, 20 (1996): pp. 66-102, at p. 100 ('The army attacking China will bring back its kings in chains, along with the kings of al-ʿAqāba [perhaps Tibet], receive a great reward and find that Jesus has arrived in Syria.'). Lists of various peoples destroying each other are included in geographical sources such as Ibn al-Faqīh's *Mukhtaṣar Kitāb al-buldān*, p. 258; *Abrégé*, p. 312.

61 Montgomery, 'Serendipity, Resistance, and Multivalency', pp. 185ff. For the postal system see Adam J. Silverstein, *Postal Systems in the Pre-Modern Islamic World* (Cambridge, 2007).

as such he probably possessed certain skills and the necessary knowledge for entertaining at court.

In his *Kitāb al-masālik* there are several passages on Tibet, some of which contain information already mentioned in earlier sources, but Ibn Khurradādhbih added further material. In one of the passages on Tibet he describes how Alexander the Great after having defeated and killed the king of India, sends his army into Tibet and China. The kings of the East have heard of Alexander's victory over Darius, 'king over Persia and India', and know of his justice and good manners. The report goes on with the following speech of the Tibetan king ('Ṭarkhān'):

> 'O king (Alexander), I have heard so much about how just and loyal you are and that you defeat those who oppose you that I understood that you act by God's will. I would like to put my hand in yours, and I wish neither to oppose nor to fight you in any matter. For he who combats you and fights you fights the divine command, and he who fights the divine command will be defeated. I belong to you with my people and my kingdom. Do with it as you like.' Alexander replied to him politely and said: 'The right of him who recognises the truth/right of God is an obligation for us. I wish that what you see of our justice and loyalty will satisfy you.' ... He (the Tibetan king) gave him presents, but he (Alexander) rejected them. He continued offering them, until he accepted them. Then he (the Tibetan king) brought him 4,000 donkey loads of gold and an equal amount of musk. He (Alexander) gave a tenth of the musk to Rushank, the daughter of Darius, the king of Persia, his (Alexander's) wife. He distributed the rest among his comrades and made the gold part of his treasure. The king of Tibet asked him to lead his army to China.[62]

A less elaborate version of this story appears in Ṭabarī's slightly later *History*.[63] As far as I can see, this story of Alexander in Tibet appears only in Islamic versions of the Alexander romance and from the ninth century onwards. It is, of course, very similar to the above-mentioned accounts of Alexander as the founder of Central Asian cities, yet here he assumes the role of the great conqueror.

62 Ibn Khurradādhbih, *Kitāb al-masālik wa'l-mamālik*, ed. Michael Jan de Goeje (Leiden, 1889), p. 263.

63 Ṭabarī, *The History of al-Ṭabarī* (40 vols, Albany, 1985-2007), vol. 4, p. 94. See also p. 80 in the same volume for the Yemeni king al-Rāʾid, and note the mention of Thābit who appears prominently in the account of the eleventh-century Persian writer Gardīzī. See Göckenjan and Zimonyi, *Orientalische Berichte*, p. 128, with a different etymological explanation for the name Tibet which appears in many other texts too. According to this explanation, *Tubbat* is derived from *thabata*, i.e. to stay somewhere. Yāqūt adds that the *thāʾ* was exchanged for a *tāʾ* as non-Arabs did not pronounce the original letter (*Geographisches Wörterbuch*, vol. 1, p. 818).

In the brief passage in Masʿūdī's encyclopaedia, both roles are combined.[64] Not unlike the Yemenis in Tibet, this might have been an attempt to accommodate the geography of the Greek original to the more extensive Islamic empire as happened in Spain and East Africa. These new versions seem to have followed the principle that if Alexander went to the extreme ends of the world, he must have visited the extreme West as well. Again, one can imagine that such stories were designed to be presented at court where Alexander was known as an exemplary ruler.

In another passage Ibn Khurradādhbih relates the anecdote about the happiness in Tibet which we have already encountered in Jāḥiẓ' work.[65] As the anecdote was copied over centuries and in different regions of the Islamic world, more details were added. Al-Bakrī, the already mentioned author of the eleventh century, quotes this story, adds that families in Tibet do not mourn if someone dies, and offers an explanation for the happiness of the Tibetans: 'In this country,' he says, 'the humour [or: nature, *ṭabīʿa*] of the blood dominates over the living creature ...'.[66] We can find the same words in *Tuḥfat al-albāb*, another collection of curious information written by Abū Ḥāmid al-Gharnāṭī who, like al-Bakrī, was born in al-Andalus and wrote a century later, in the early 1160s.[67] Unlike his earlier compatriot, however, Abū Ḥāmid from Granada travelled through Eastern Europe, Khwārazm and Iraq. Yet, the fact that he uses almost the same words to render this phenomenon confirms that we should not read his account simply as a direct reflection of what he witnessed and heard during his journey, but also as part of an already existing substantial corpus of literature. In other versions this element assumes increasingly fantastical and complex features. The Persian author Qazvīnī (d. 740/1339) recounts the story with an almost alchemical tendency:

> It is said that in the country of Tibet there is a stone of fine colour, and transparent; now every foreigner who looks at this stone falls to laughter against his will, and laughs so much that he dies. On the natives of this land, however, this stone has no effect.[68]

---

64 Masʿūdī, *Murūj al-dhahab*, vol. 2, p. 9 (§673). For Masʿūdī depending on Ibn Khurradādhbih cf. Montgomery, 'Serendipity, Resistance, and Multivalency', pp. 188-9.

65 Ibn Khurradādhbih, *Kitāb al-masālik wa'l-mamālik*, p. 170.

66 Al-Bakrī, *Al-Masālik wa'l-mamālik*, vol. 1, p. 269 (n. 410).

67 Abū Ḥāmid al-Gharnāṭī, *Tuḥfat al-albāb/El regalo de los espíritos*, trans. Ana Ramos (Madrid, 1990), p. 107. For his background and biography see the article on Abū Ḥāmid al-Gharnāṭī in *EI*². For a further elaboration of the theme see Yāqūt, *Geographisches Wörterbuch*, vol. 1, p. 818, and for a similar account in Ottoman geography see the passage edited and translated in Raphael Israeli, 'An Arabic Manuscript on China and Tibet', *Arabica*, 39 (1992): pp. 207-15, at pp. 214-25.

68 Qazvīnī, *The Geographical Part of the Nuzhat al-Qulūb*, ed. and trans. Guy Le Strange (London, 1915-19), p. 279.

Another variation of the laughing story is quoted by the twelfth-century geographer Idrīsī (work completed in 548/1154) who mentions a 'castle of laughter' in his section on Tibet:

> This castle has no door, and whoever approaches it, feels joy and delight like somebody does who drinks wine. It is said that who attaches himself to the castle and climbs it, does not stop laughing. He throws himself into the castle and is never seen again. I believe that this story is not true. It is made up, but is a precise and well known account.[69]

These stories of the dangerous happiness in Tibet might have become mixed up here with another anecdote with is frequently quoted in Islamic sources, for example by Qazvīnī:

> In the Khotan province there is a mountain, which is called Kūh Samm (Poison Hill), and it is for this reason. There is here a valley through which the usual high road from China to Tibet passes, and in that valley the high road is clearly marked out, and many images have been set up here on either side. Should anyone who passes by that high road wander away from the straight line, his breath is caught by the vapours arising from the ground here round about, and he perishes therefrom.[70]

To some degree these stories have a true background: travelling through the Himalayas must have been a straining experience for foreigners. But one could also think of the perils reported in Arabic texts for other distant lands, such as the cannibalism in Africa. We should consider the possibility that the local population or traders were involved in the creation of these myths.[71] Furthermore, some of the elements of these accounts probably derived from an

---

[69] Roberto Rubinacci, 'Il Tibet nella Geografia d'Idrīsī', in *Gururājamañjarikā: Studi in onore di Guiseppe Tucci* (2 vols, Naples, 1974), vol. 1, pp. 195-220, §17.

[70] Qazvīnī, *The Geographical Part of the Nuzhat al-Qulūb*, p. 280. The same story is already quoted by his compatriot Zakariyyā᾽ ibn Muḥammad al-Qazwīnī (d. 682/1283) in his *ʿAjā᾽ib al-makhlūqāt*. See al-Qazwīnī, *Zakarija ben Muhammed ben Mahmud el-Cazwini's Kosmographie*, ed. Ferdinand Wüstenfeld (2 vols, Göttingen, 1948-49), vol. 1, p. 164. In both texts, Jayhānī is mentioned as the source (see below). The bridge over the poisonous mountain is also mentioned by Gardīzī, *Zayn al-akhbār*, p. 264. Yāqūt, *Geographisches Wörterbuch*, vol. 1, p. 820, says that while some people die, others get a 'heavy tongue'.

[71] For a parallel see James Montgomery, 'Spectral Armies, Snakes, and a Giant from Gog and Magog: Ibn Faḍlān as Eyewitness among the Volga Bulghārs', *The Medieval History Journal*, 9/1 (2006): pp. 63-87, at p. 71.

even older literary tradition, the story of the City of Brass which is popular in world literature and appears also in the Arabian Nights.[72]

However, the issue of the joy and laughter requires a more complex reading. Let us first consider another example: in the twelfth century the great poet Niẓāmī interwove these different threads into a whole new account of Alexander's visit to Tibet in his *Iskandarnāma*:

> When his diadem reached to the height of Tibat,
> All his army began to laugh.
> He asked: —'For what is this laughter
> 'In a place where it is proper to weep for ourselves?'
> They declared:—'This soil, saffron-like,
> 'Makes man laughterful without cause.'
> At that Paradise-like city the king was amazed:
> 'Involuntarily, how produces it laughter?'
> ...
> He beheld all the plain full of musk (dropped from the musky deer).
> When he saw the musk-possessing deer of the plain,
> He ordered that none should hunt the deer (so that the musk should not be lost).
> In every place where the army used to hold the road-pass,
> He used to take up musk in ass-loads.[73]

This paradisiacal description of Tibet coincides with the image of Tibet in the West since the nineteenth century which still prevails. Were the Arabs the first 'prisoners of Shangrila,' to borrow an expression of Donald Lopez in his critique of the Western idealisation of Tibet?[74] It does seem as if what the Muslim authors display here is a similarly 'Orientalist' image of the 'noble savage'. Yet, the notion of joy and laughter has a negative, even deadly side, which is evident in the stories about the stone and the castle. What these accounts reminded me of is the episode of the lotus-eaters in the Odyssey. In their *Dialectic of Enlightenment*, Adorno and Horkheimer took this episode as an example for the mimetic state of men, a stage before the development of civilization. The lotus-eaters live in a blissfully innocent state, unaffected by the treacherous emancipation of civilization. Yet, if we return to this early stage of human history, of pre-history,

---

72 For the City of Brass see, among many other publications, Andras Hamori, 'An Allegory from the Arabian Nights: The City of Brass', *Bulletin of the School of Oriental and African Studies*, 34 (1971): pp. 9-19. I intend to explore the sources of the story of the deadly laughter and its development more fully in 'Dying of Laughter in Lhasa'.

73 *The Sikandar nāma, e bara: or, Book of Alexander the Great*, trans. H. Wilberforce Clarke (London, 1881), pp. 585-6. For a German translation see *Das Alexanderbuch/Iskandarname*, trans. Johann Christoph Bürgel (Zurich, 1991), p. 261.

74 Donald S. Lopez, *Prisoners of Shangri-La: Tibetan Buddhism and the West* (Chicago, 1998).

we have to remove the seemingly emancipated concerns from our minds, and man as a civilized being has to die. It is this ambiguous notion that the later Islamic sources present.[75]

THE JAYHĀNĪ TRADITION

Another milestone in the history of Islamic geography is the Jayhānī tradition, a complex corpus of versions written by a family.[76] The originals are not preserved, but several well-known authors rely on them. The two authors from Qazwīn, for example, mention Jayhānī as the source for their story about the Poison Hill. Among the writers dependent on this tradition is also the eleventh-century Andalusian al-Bakrī. His *Kitāb al-masālik wa'l-mamālik* contains information which does not appear in the earlier sources which rely on the al-Ma'mūn tradition. Al-Bakrī states for example that the source of the Oxus – or: Amū Darya (Jayḥūn in Arabic) – is in Tibet. This curious bit of information appears in many Arabic geographical treatises[77] and is key to any attempt to find out where on a map Muslim writers located Tibet. The Amū Darya is the result of several headwaters which come together in the western border region of Tajikistan and Afghanistan, which was Islamic territory since the mid-eighth century. Arabic sources seem to have been quite confused about the number and location of the headwaters of the Amū Darya, and this leads to a very substantial general problem.

A dilemma we are facing very often with these descriptions is that they are equations with too many unknowns. As is also evident in mathematical geography, it is by no means certain that Tubbat always refers to a region and not a city, and in either case there are great differences among Muslim writers when they determine the location. Since the course of the Amū Darya was also surrounded by uncertainties, these confusions add up and any attempt to establish what exactly medieval Muslim authors referred to remains extremely

---

75 A nineteenth-century Arabic testimony to legends which circulate in the West is discussed in my forthcoming article 'Alexander in the Himalayas'.

76 James Montgomery, 'Ibn Rusta's Lack of "Eloquence", the Rūs, and Samanid Cosmography', *Edebiyât*, 12 (2001): pp. 73-93, at pp. 84-5. In general see Göckenjan and Zimonyi, *Orientalische Berichte*.

77 Al-Bakrī, *Al-Masālik wa'l-mamālik*, vol. 1, p. 231, n. 341. Also mentioned by Dimashqī (d. 727/1327), *Manuel de la cosmographie du moyen âge, traduit de l'arabe "Nokhbet ed-dahr fi 'Adjaib-il-birr wal-bahr" de Shems ed-Dîn Abou-'Abdallah Mohammed de Damas*, trans. August Ferdinand Mehren (Copenhagen, 1874; repr. Amsterdam, 1964), p. 114 for the Amū Darya (see also, among other passages, p. 123 for the origin of the Brahmaputra in Tibet, p. 129 for musk and p. 376 for the Yemeni connection); Ibn Rusta who wrote between 903 and 913 also mentions Tibet as the source of the Amū Darya which may suggest that this information is not related to Jayhānī after all, see *Kitāb al-a'lāq al-nafīsa*, ed. Michael Jan de Goeje (Leiden, 1892), p. 91 and Ibn Rusteh, *Les atours précieux*, trans. Gaston Wiet (Cairo, 1955), p. 104.

hazardous. Another problem is whether the mentioning of regions such as China or India and possibly Tibet implies states with borders or rather cultural regions.[78]

As we have already seen from several cases such as Gardīzī, who wrote on the Yemeni legend, Islamic geography clearly developed after these major authoritative traditions were established. I would like to mention briefly two further examples.

Marwazī, who wrote in the 1120s what is essentially a zoological book (*Kitāb ṭabāʾiʿ al-ḥayawān*), used the Jayhānī tradition, but his text reflects a better ethnological knowledge of Tibet than earlier sources. He states – like other authors – that Tibetans, Chinese and Turks resemble each other, but emphasizes that the Tibetans are independent and have their own language.[79] More remarkable is a long passage on several Tibetan tribes, in which Marwazī mentions the following detail:

> There is a tribe of Tibetans called Arā, who live in a land and place called in Tibetan Akhāy.l, which possesses thick woods, meadows and pastures. They are of the king's people. When the Tibet-khāqān dies childless and there is no one else in the khāqān's family, a man from among them is elected and made khāqān.[80]

He also included important geographical information such as the 'Gate of the two Tibets' (Bāb al-Tubbatayn):

> As regards the place called Bāb al-Tubbatayn, it is a gate between the mountain Shīwa and the river Kh.rnāb, fixed on a weak wall built of thorns and earth, and the Tibetans have there a military post where toll is levied from anyone travelling that way, to the amount of one part out of forty.[81]

Another, earlier example is the anonymous *Ḥudūd al-ʿālam* composed in Persian in 372/982, which relies also on the Jayhānī tradition, but includes a very precise description of Tibet that appears in no other Islamic source.[82] The author of the *Ḥudūd al-ʿālam* begins with a general introduction in which he describes Tibet as a central point for trade between India and the Islamic world.

---

78 Biran, *The Empire of the Qara Khitai*, pp. 97-101.

79 Marwazī, *Sharaf al-Zamān Ṭāhir Marvazī on China, the Turks and India*, ed. and trans. Vladimir Minorsky (London, 1942), p. 28.

80 Marwazī, *On China, the Turks and India*, p. 28.

81 Marwazī, *On China, the Turks and India*, p. 28.

82 For the following references see *Ḥudūd al-ʿālam: The Regions of the World. A Persian Geography*, trans. Vladimir Minorsky (London, 1937), pp. 92-4. A facsimile has been published by Vasilii Vladimirovich Bartol'd (Leningrad, 1930), fols 16a-b.

It is a land of few commodities, but there are gold mines, musk and animals like black foxes, grey squirrels, sable-martens and ermine. 'Its king,' the anonymous author states, 'is called Tubbat-Khāqān and he has great numbers of troops and arms.' These general remarks are followed by a description of individual places in Tibet, which is rather unusual. Most astonishing is the short description of Lhasa: 'A small town with numerous idol temples and one Muslim mosque. In it live a few Muslims.'

The interesting question is how to interpret the additional information provided by and after the Jayhānī tradition. A key difficulty we encounter here is that even though by and large we are able to determine which texts were influenced by the Jayhānī tradition, this is hardly possible for every bit of information. Moreover, the texts are related to each other in an extremely complex way which barely allows reconstructing a 'linear' way of transmission. In other words: the fact that a certain piece of information or anecdote on Tibet appears for the first time in a text associated with the Jayhānī tradition does not mean that it was unknown to Muslim authors before that time. It might very well have entered the literary tradition in the eighth century or under al-Maʾmūn. It is also difficult to divide the information into categories which are characteristic of a certain phase in Arabic and Persian geographical literature, given that the passages on Tibet are usually very short and that there are several parallel and partly overlapping developments. Nevertheless it is my impression that once the Jayhānī tradition started dominating Arabic geographical literature we tend to find information which is more precise than in those sources which rely 'merely' on al-Maʾmūn, and this seems to be a continuous development. However, this does not necessarily imply that the information is more accurate in the sense that it gives a 'better', more realistic picture of Tibet, even though it is probably easier to identify corresponding 'real' entities. Luciano Petech might have very well been right when he suggested that from early on Arabic literature preserved an image of Tibet which reflected at least in terms of geography a certain historical phase.[83] Michal Biran makes a similar observation concerning the image of China in Arabic literature which was based on the acquaintance with Tang China (618-906) and maintained an anachronistic character.[84] Yet, Petech's claim that information on Tibet in Arabic literature was basically gathered under al-Maʾmūn and remained unchanged ever since, requires reconsideration as we shall see in more detail below.

MATHEMATICAL GEOGRAPHY

During the age of translations in early Abbasid Baghdad, Persian and Greek literature exercised a great influence on Arabic geography. The Arabs adopted

83 Petech, 'Il Tibet nella geografia musulmana'.

84 Biran, *The Empire of the Qara Khitai*, p. 97.

both the Persian system of seven *keshvār*, six regions around a central (Iranian) region, and the Greek idea of seven climates, but they did not simply identify *keshvārs* with climates. Tibet was placed together with China in the seventh *keshvār* (see Plate 2.1), but in various divisions of the world we can find it as part of the third, fourth and fifth climates.

Alongside these general concepts the Muslims adopted what is referred to as mathematical geography, a tradition based on Ptolemy. They re-measured the longitudes and latitudes of place-names given by Ptolemy, but their corrections often seem quite arbitrary and are not necessarily closer to the real position of a place.[85] In Islamic geography a whole tradition of tables with place-names developed in which either only the climates with latitudes as climate boundaries were given or latitudes and longitudes. Al-Khwārizmī mentions a city in the fifth climate with the name T-b-t. Petech stressed that the position indicated for this place (long. 130° lat. 38°) corresponded approximately with the position of Khotan, a centre of military administration when the Tibetan Empire was at its height.[86] He claimed that 'Tubbat' in Islamic literature referred on the one hand to a region in Turkestan and on the other hand to a very specific place: that is, Khotan. One of Petech's main arguments was that the exact place indicated in Arabic geographical literature was so precise it could only refer to a city.[87] Beckwith challenged this argument and argued that tables with latitudes and longitudes in Arabic geographical literature include also regions.[88] Indeed, in al-Khwārizmī's *Kitāb ṣūrat al-arḍ*, Tibet is listed alongside cities as well as regions under the general heading *mudun* (pl. of *madīna* which is usually translated as 'city').[89] Moreover, the position given for 'Tubbat' in Islamic sources varies from text to text, as can be seen from the table compiled by Edward and Mary Helen Kennedy.[90] In addition to that, some authors (such as Maqdisī) make a clear distinction between Khotan and Tibet.[91] Likewise, the Andalusian geographer Ibn Saʿīd distinguished between Tibet as a region and a Tibetan city (*madīna tubbatiyya*).[92] Beckwith drew the conclusion that Arabs authors were very well aware of the position of Tibet and its neighbouring countries.[93] Yet, one should

85 For the use of the Greek tradition see Tibbetts, 'The Beginnings of a Cartographic Tradition', pp. 96-107.

86 Petech, 'Il Tibet nella geografia musulmana'.

87 Petech, 'Il Tibet nella geografia musulmana', p. 60.

88 Beckwith, 'The Location and Population of Tibet', p. 165.

89 Al-Khwārizmī, *Kitāb ṣūrat al-arḍ*, p. 28, n. 405, for Tibet.

90 Kennedy and Kennedy, *Geographical Coordinates*, pp. 360-61.

91 Beckwith, 'The Location and Population of Tibet', p. 166. Maqdisī, *Kitāb al-badʾ waʾl-tārīkh*, vol. 4, p. 63, and al-Bīrūnī in his *Taḥqīq mā liʾl-Hind: Alberuni's India: An Account of the Religion, Philosophy, Literature, Geography, Chronology, Astronomy, Customs, Law and Astrology of India about A.D. 1030*, ed. Edward C. Sachau (2 vols, London, 1888), vol. 1, p. 165.

92 Ibn Saʿīd, *Kitāb al-jughrāfiyā*, p. 176.

93 Beckwith, 'The Location and Population of Tibet', p. 165.

stress with Petech that there are some confusions in Islamic geographical literature which suggest that at least some authors were not aware of the position of Tibet or that what they referred to as 'Tubbat' was different from what other authors understood it was.

The Andalusian writer and poet Ibn ʿAbd Rabbih (246/860-328/940) in his encyclopaedic *The Unique Necklace* (*al-ʿIqd al-farīd*), for example, describes 'Tubbat' as belonging to the land of the Turks and as a place full of musk, but introduces the brief remark with the words 'among the last cities of Khorasan is a city (*madīna*) which is called Tubbat'.[94] Likewise, Ibn al-Faqīh who wrote at about the same time speaks of a 'city of Tubbat' (*madīnat Tubbat*) built by the Himyarite ruler Tubbaʿ al-Aqran.[95] Finally, Idrīsī included in the world map he made for the Sicilian ruler Roger II (1095-1154) Tibet in the form of a city.[96]

CARTOGRAPHY

A kind of material which has not been considered for the question of Tibet in Islamic geography is of a visual nature: that is, cartography. Tibet appears in a number of different types of maps. There are, for example, maps which show the different climates or the *keshvārs* (Plate 2.1).[97] In another type of map, the *qibla* map, we occasionally find the name Tibet (Plate 2.2).

The most interesting case is a different type of map, something we may usually have in mind when we think of a map – rather than the highly schematic maps which divide the world into different zones. The cases I will discuss now are either world maps or sections taken from them.

The most important tradition here is that of the school of al-Balkhī (236/850-322/934). Al-Balkhī's geographical work itself is not preserved, but it seems to have been a short commentary on a set of maps. A later author, the already mentioned Iṣṭakhrī, wrote a commentary on these maps in the middle of the tenth century. Some 25 years later this version was updated by Ibn Ḥawqal, also introduced above, a traveller and trader and possibly also a missionary for the Fatimids. According to Tibbetts, he became carried away with his

---

94 Ibn ʿAbd Rabbih, *Al-ʿIqd al-farīd*, ed. Mufīd Muḥammad Qumayḥa (9 vols, Beirut, ³1987), vol. 7, p. 281.

95 Ibn al-Faqīh, *Mukhtaṣar Kitāb al-buldān*, p. 336; *Abrégé*, pp. 386-7.

96 The map is reproduced in Konrad Miller, *Mappae Arabicae: Arabische Welt- und Länderkarten des 9.-13.Jahrhunderts* (6 vols, Stuttgart, 1926-31), 1. Band, 2. Heft, part III (IX/III) shows Central and South Asia.

97 In a drawing of the seven climates with inserted place names with the title *Kitāb hay'at ashkāl al-arḍ wa-miqdāruhā fī al-ṭūl wa'l-ʿard al-maʿrūf bi-jughrāfiyah* (an abridgement of Ibn Ḥawqal's map), dedicated to Sayf al-Dawla (d. 356/967), a Hamdanid Sultan, Tibet appears together with Kashmir in the third and fourth climate. Harley and Woodward (eds), *Cartography in the Traditional Islamic and South Asian Societies*, p. 78, Fig 3.6.

own improvements and inserted into Iṣṭakhrī's commentary miscellaneous information relating to his own travels.[98] As far as the position of Tibet is concerned, the maps which belong to the Balkhī tradition contain a very curious feature: Tibet appears here, between Hind (India) and Ṣīn (China) as a land with access to the sea. Some of these maps, especially in the later Ibn al-Wardī (d. 861/1457) tradition, even indicate a *baḥr al-Tubbat*, a 'sea of Tibet' (Plate 2.3). There is a curious parallel in the Marco Polo manuscripts which mention corals of Tibet which – together with the information stemming from Arabic sources – must have given the impression that Tibet was a coastal region or at least included one.[99]

How are we to interpret this? There are two options: one of them is to suspect that Tibet follows here the pattern of the better known regions, India and China. The other option is to assume along the lines of Luciano Petech that Islamic cartography 'froze' the image of the Tibetan Empire at its height when it stretched as far as the Gulf of Bengal. The only parallel in the textual tradition I have identified so far is Iṣṭakhrī who mentions the 'shores of Tibet' (*sawāḥil Tubbat*) as part of the borders of the Persian Sea (*baḥr Fars*).[100] Al-Bakrī, on the other hand, describes Tibet and Kabul as examples of lands far away from the sea.[101] Another possible explanation for the 'sea of Tibet' is that it was confused with a 'lake of Tibet' (*buḥayrat Tubbat*) which is mentioned by Ibn Saʿīd and which Daunicht identifies with the Tengri-nōr or Namtso (gnam mtsho).[102]

As we have seen for the geographical texts, Petech's claim, although it accounts for some features in descriptions of Tibet, needs to be modified, and the same applies to cartography. In the twelfth century a new tradition developed in Islamic cartography – that of al-Idrīsī, who added new information on Tibet in his text as seen above, but also in his maps the position of Tibet is different from that in the Balkhī tradition: it is clearly hidden behind the mountains and offers a more up-to-date account (Plate 2.4).

Why did this change come to pass? Did Idrīsī have more accurate data at his disposal? Was it because the Arabs had known for a long time that the balance of power had shifted in the Himalayas and Idrīsī was simply the first who expressed this in a map? Or was it because of the formal, stylistic changes he introduced

98 Gerald Tibbetts, 'The Balkhī School of Geographers', in Harley and Woodward (eds), *Cartography in the Traditional Islamic and South Asian Societies*, pp. 108-36, at p. 110.

99 Braham Norwick, 'Why Tibet Disappeared from "Scientific" 16th-17th Century European Maps', in Shōren Ihara and Zuihō Yamaguchi (eds), *Tibetan Studies: Proceedings of the 5th Seminar of the International Association for Tibetan Studies, Narita 1989* (Narita-shi, Chiba-Ken, 1992), vol. 2, pp. 633-44, at p. 635.

100 Iṣṭakhrī, *Viae regnorum*, p. 29. Ibn Ḥawqal, who depends on Iṣṭakhrī, has the same passage: *Configuration de la terre*, p. 41.

101 Al-Bakrī, *Al-Masālik wa'l-mamālik*, vol. 1, p. 208, n. 299.

102 Ibn Saʿīd, *Kitāb al-jughrāfiyā*, p. 176. Daunicht, *Der Osten nach der Erdkarte al-Ḫuwārizmīs*, p. 96.

in his map compared with the Balkhī tradition? At this stage we can note that a change took place, but we might never be in the position of explaining it. Suffice it to say that alongside the cartographic tradition which had Tibet bordering the sea another parallel tradition conveyed a substantially different picture.

CONCLUSION

It is difficult to end this article with general conclusions, given that what I would like to emphasize here is that it is too early for such conclusions. Historians of Tibet such as Luciano Petech or Christopher Beckwith have presented very pronounced views regarding the identity of Tibet and the Tibetans in Islamic geography, but further research needs to be conducted in this area in order to reach more certain conclusions.

We have only started to explore the descriptions of Tibet in Arabic and Persian geographical literature on a superficial level. One of the next steps that is needed has been pointed out by James Montgomery who stresses that 'we must pay scrupulous attention to the context of these texts. This attention may involve questions of patronage, or considerations of genre and type, or investigations of audience and intended readership, or an assessment of the religious environment in which they were composed'.[103] Descriptions of Tibet in Arabic geographical literature are, as we have seen, usually very brief. It is often impossible to determine at which stage a particular piece of information has entered the complex geographical tradition and whether any particular purpose may have triggered its inclusion. We should probably abandon rigorous divisions such as the one between oral tradition and the fanciful elaboration of written sources, or that between fiction and accurate 'realistic' descriptions. One of the questions we can address at this stage is in which way the particular context of a particular author might have determined his access to information about Tibet or his interest in this region. Factors to be taken into consideration include trade, science, administration and the existing literary corpus. Two further steps which need to be taken for a more comprehensive analysis of our material are those I have attempted here in the form of a first outline: (1) to read geographical texts as literature, and (2) to take the cartographic tradition into account. What I have tried to offer here are a few more detailed glances into a material that is very rich, but also very demanding. A comprehensive analysis of Tibet in Islamic geography and cartography is a time-consuming task, but we have reason to believe that it is also a very rewarding one.[104]

103 Montgomery, 'Serendipity, Resistance, and Multivalency', p. 185.

104 Ahmed Zaki Velidi Togan, *Ibn Fadlan's Reisebericht* (Nendeln, 1966), p. xii, n. 2.

Chapter 3
The Bactrian Background of the Barmakids

Kevin van Bladel[1]

In the course of the eighth century, Arabic was established as the new language of prestige and interregional communication from North Africa to the edges of India. A long period of translations began, in which the parts of older literatures useful to the new elite were converted into Arabic (*c*.750-1000). The contents of these translations, the social contexts that called for them, and their varied receptions are well documented and have received increasingly refined and convincing treatments in modern scholarship.[2] For more than two hundred years, wealthy intellectuals in the new capital of Baghdad paid translators large amounts of money to make much older texts available to them in Arabic.[3] Justly the most famous of these translations are the ones from Greek, which, taken all together, included hundreds of works by dozens of ancient authors, and came to constitute one of the foundations of early Arabic thought. All this is well known to historians. But, in the first decades of this period of translations, a relatively small number of works were translated from Sanskrit into Arabic, including texts on astronomy, medicine and political maxims. These have received very little attention among modern scholars, and the social circumstances of these translations from Sanskrit remain unclear. The utility of such works may be self-evident, but that does not suffice to explain their westward transmission. Why would anyone in Baghdad, Muslim or not, have sought translations from the literary language of a distant country like India, and not, say, from Chinese or

---

[1] The following abbreviations are used in the notes. BD1 = Nicholas Sims-Williams, *Bactrian Documents from Northern Afghanistan I: Legal and Economic Documents.* (Oxford, 2000). BD2 = Nicholas Sims-Williams, *Bactrian Documents from Northern Afghanistan II: Letters and Buddhist Texts* (London, 2007). *Fihrist* = Al-Nadīm, *Kitāb al-fihrist*, ed. Gustav Flügel (2 vols, Leipzig, 1871-72), vol. 1. My thanks are due to Anna Akasoy, Christopher Beckwith, Michael Cook, Patricia Crone, Christopher Minkowski, Everett Rowson and Jonathan Skaff for valuable comments on different drafts of this article. The remaining errors are all my own.

[2] Noteworthy accounts include Gerhard Endress, 'Die wissenschaftliche Literatur', in *Grundriss der arabischen Philologie* (3 vols, Wiesbaden, 1987-92), vol. 2, pp. 400-506 and vol. 3, pp. 3-152; Dimitri Gutas, *Greek Thought, Arabic Culture: The Graeco-Arabic Translation Movement in Baghdad and Early 'Abbāsid Society (2nd-4th/8th-10th C.)* (London, 1998); Cristina D'Ancona (ed.), *Storia della filosofia nell'Islam medievale*, vol. 1 (Turin, 2005).

[3] Gutas, *Greek Thought, Arabic Culture*, pp. 121-50.

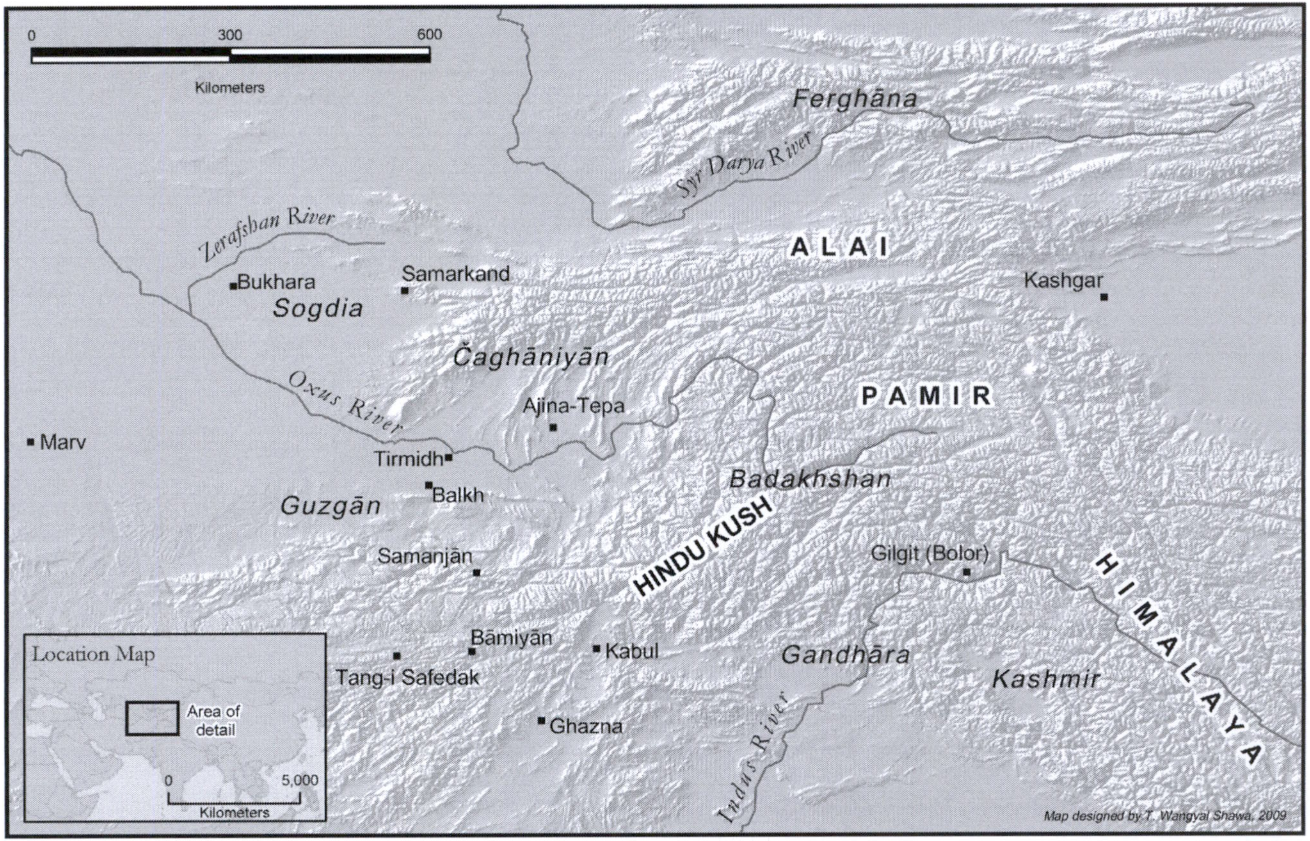

3.1 Tokharistan and its region

Latin? Who would have had the interest and the means to sponsor such projects? Where would they have found the necessary manuscripts? If an interest in Sanskrit texts existed in Baghdad, in the late eighth century, why then did that interest soon disappear completely?

This study shows that one particular family was responsible for a substantial number of these early Arabic translations of Sanskrit works, indeed almost all of them, and moreover that their background in Tokharistan, a country whose culture and history are increasingly coming to light through new discoveries, explains their interest in Sanskrit learning. The Barmakid family is fairly well known to historians. They include some of the most powerful secretaries and governors under the Abbasid dynasty during its first half-century (750-803). Though several modern studies have dealt with their careers in detail, it is worthwhile to begin with a brief summary of their best-known achievements.[4] Khālid, the son of Barmak, was part of the Abbasid revolution. From the beginning of Abbasid power in 750, he played a major role in administering the Arab empire as the head of different secretarial bureaus and governing provinces. His son Yaḥyā was tutor to the future caliph Hārūn al-Rashīd and then, after al-Rashīd's accession in 786, he became his vizier, having near total administrative control for the next 17 years. Yaḥyā's sons were similarly important during this period, governing provinces, leading armies, and tutoring young caliphs-to-be. Reports stress that the Abbasid family and the Barmakid family were personally very close even early on.[5]

What has received less attention is the cultural background of the Barmakids. Historians know that the father of this family, the Barmak, was an educated Buddhist official of some sort from Tokharistan: that is, Bactria. Beyond this odd

---

4 Lucien Bouvat, 'Les Barmécides d'après les historiens arabes et persans', *Revue du Monde Musulman*, 20 (1912): pp. 1-131 and Dominique Sourdel, *Le vizirat 'Abbāside de 749 à 936 (132 à 324 l'Hégire)* (2 vols, Damascus, 1959-60), vol. 1, pp. 127-81 are the standard accounts. Clifford Edmund Bosworth, 'Abū Ḥafṣ 'Umar al-Kirmānī and the Rise of the Barmakids', *Bulletin of the School for Oriental and African Studies*, 57 (1994): pp. 268-82, presents substantial, fundamental new information not available in these works. Tayeb El-Hibri, *Reinterpreting Islamic Historiography: Hārūn al-Rashīd and the Narrative of the 'Abbāsid Caliphate* (Cambridge, 1999), pp. 31-58, contextualizes the tales of the Barmakids in the historical romances and narratives (as such) told about them as members of the caliphal court. Also useful are the articles on the Barmakids in the *EIr* and *EI*[2].

5 Bosworth, 'Abū Ḥafṣ 'Umar al-Kirmānī', pp. 271-2, discusses reports that the women of the Barmakid and Abbasid families suckled each others' children even before Abū 'l-ʿAbbās became caliph in 750. Such an arrangement would have created a bond considered equivalent to kinship (article 'Raḍāʿ' in *EI*[2]). Nevertheless, as pointed out by Nabia Abbott (cited by Bosworth, 'Abū Ḥafṣ 'Umar al-Kirmānī', pp. 271-2, n. 26), the closeness of this relationship may have been exaggerated in later accounts to justify further al-Rashīd's action against the Barmakids, which was supposedly a punishment when the Barmakid Jaʿfar had amorous relations with the caliph's sister. See also the passages translated by Bosworth, 'Abū Ḥafṣ 'Umar al-Kirmānī', p. 276.

fact, often mentioned, it is not a subject much pursued. This is partly because historians of the early Arab empire have tended to treat Iran under the Arabs as a single cultural unit, so that the Barmakid past was more or less a Persian one. In fact, Iran was a land of many countries with distinctive populations having different cultures.[6] The more one knows about Tokharistan in the seventh and eighth centuries, the more obvious it becomes that educated individuals from that region in particular would be interested in Sanskrit books. A clearer picture of life in Tokharistan at the time the Arabs colonized it emerges through a combination of evidence from sources in Chinese, Arabic, Sanskrit and, importantly, Bactrian, the recently rediscovered and deciphered language of Tokharistan now attested in numerous short texts. To this must be added the findings of archaeologists and art historians who have investigated the region and discovered remains not yet well publicized.[7] What appears from the evidence collected below is that Tokharistan was the one and only area colonized heavily by the Arabs where Buddhism flourished at the time the Arabs arrived, and the only area that was firmly incorporated into the empire where Sanskrit studies were pursued up until the conquest.[8] It will become evident that it was no coincidence that the Barmak's grandson, who became the vizier of this huge empire, took a personal interest in Sanskrit works and Indian religions. When the Barmak's descendants were suddenly and forcibly removed from power by the caliph al-Rashīd in 803, and the Barmakids' influence disappeared, no further translations from Sanskrit into Arabic are known to have been made until al-Bīrūnī, two centuries later in India itself, under very different circumstances.[9] To explain the background of the Barmakids, one must begin with Bactria itself.

BACTRIA-TOKHARISTAN AT THE TIME OF THE ARAB CONQUESTS

Today the territory of Tokharistan, roughly the ancient Bactria known from Greek sources, is divided between the modern states of Afghanistan, Uzbekistan and Tajikistan, but in the seventh and eighth centuries, it was recognized by Chinese travellers as a culturally and linguistically distinct unity, though

---

[6] Here and throughout I am not referring to the modern state of Iran or its modern concept, but to the regions in which Iranian languages were spoken.

[7] In particular the publications of Boris A. Litvinsky and Tamara Zeimal', mostly published in Russian, deserve a wider audience.

[8] Here I am overlooking Sind, which seems to have lacked continuous direct social contact with the Abbasid court and about which under early Arab rule there is little information.

[9] This point in the argument admittedly rests on a lack of evidence. Nevertheless, any translations from Sanskrit into Arabic made in the period between the Barmakids and al-Bīrūnī have either not come to light so far or their dates have not been recognized.

politically fragmented.[10] According to the most general usage of the name, Tokharistan is the wide valley around the upper Oxus River surrounded on three sides by mountain ranges, before the Oxus flows out into the open plains. The Oxus River descends into this valley from the towering Pamir mountains. It winds down around the mountain highlands of Badakhshan before passing on its way westward. To the north are the Alai and Buttamān mountains, which send several tributary rivers into the Oxus; beyond these mountains are Sogdia and Ferghāna and long desert roads to China. To the south is the Hindu Kush range, which separates Iran from Kābul, Gandhāra, and India beyond. Some geographers consider also the northern Hindu Kush to be a part of Tokharistan, so that the region includes both the mountain highlands in the south up to Bāmiyān and the valley plains around the Oxus. This makes some sense in defining the region, since, as evidence shows, the Bactrian language was used as far south as Bāmiyān and even farther.[11] In an official document from the governorship of Abū 'l-ʿAbbās ʿAbdallāh ibn Ṭāhir (reg. 828-45), registering the payments of the *kharāj* tax due from each town of his domain, there is a list of the districts (*kuwar*) of Tokharistan. These include lands as far north as Ṣaghāniyān and as far south as the edges of Kābul, one of the 'frontiers of Tokharistan (*min thughūr Ṭukhāristān*)'. Among the other places listed as part of Tokharistan are Tirmidh, Juzjān, Bāmiyān, and Rūb and Samanjān, names that will appear again in the present study.[12] However, some Arabic geographers used the name Tokharistan more narrowly to refer just to the southern side of the Oxus valley.[13]

The major city of Tokharistan was Balkh,[14] since ancient times one of the great urban centres of northeasternmost Iran, built where a river (the Balkh-āb)

---

10 Xuánzàng in the early seventh century said that Tokharistan was divided into 27 states dependent on the Türks (Samuel Beal, *Si-Yu-Ki: Buddhist Records of the Western World* [2 vols, London, 1884], vol. 1, pp. 36-68). He includes the valleys north of the Oxus, such as Čaghāniyān, and all of the Hindu Kush region as far as Kapiśa, in the Bactrian language area.

11 Beal, *Si-Yu-Ki*, vol. 1, pp. 36-54.

12 Ibn Khurradādhbih (fl. late ninth century) copied this document into his book of itineraries (*Kitāb al-masālik wa'l-mamālik*, ed. Michael Jan de Goeje [Leiden, 1889], pp. 36-7). His position as Director of Posts and Intelligence (*ṣāḥib al-barīd wa'l-khabar*; see 'Ibn Khurradādhbih', in *EI*[2]) in Jibāl and then in Baghdad, and as a companion to the caliph al-Muʿtamid, must have given him access to such documents. See the article by Akasoy in this volume.

13 Barthold and Bosworth, 'Ṭukhāristān', in *EI*[2]. Vasili Barthold, *Turkestan down to the Mongol Invasion* (London, [3]1968), pp. 64-8. Ibn Khurradādhbih (*Kitāb al-masālik wa'l-mamālik*, p. 34) distinguishes Upper Tokharistan, *Ṭukhāristān al-ʿUlyā*, as a special region, apparently the area up the valley to the east from Balkh (including Khulm, a place called Bahār, and other towns).

14 Al-Yaʿqūbī (d. *c*.900), *Kitāb al-buldān*, ed. Michael Jan de Goeje (Leiden, 1892), p. 287: 'Balkh is the greatest city of Khorasan. The King Ṭarkhān, King of Khorasan, used to reside there.'

descends from the Hindu Kush.[15] It was one of the most important stopping points for travellers overland between Iran and India, since it was situated near some of the easier ways southward over the mountains. As the author of the tenth-century Persian work *Ḥudūd al-ʿālam* put it, Balkh is a 'resort of merchants', 'it is the emporium of Hindūstān'.[16] The route between India and Balkh was used also by the travellers between India and China who made the long journey around, rather than over, the difficult Himalaya, Pamir and Karakorum mountains.[17] Other ways led eastward from Balkh up into the Himalayas, through Badakhshan and the kingdom of Balūr (Bolor, modern Gilgit), ultimately to Tibet. In short, Balkh was situated upon important crossroads and conduits of trade in many directions, and control of Balkh facilitated control of these trade routes.

When the Arabs conquered the region in the late seventh and early eighth centuries, they had passed beyond the lands of the Sasanian Empire that they had previously overthrown through nearly twenty years of war (633-51). Tokharistan had been outside Sasanid Shahs' control for the preceding three centuries, during which several dynasties of Hunnic and Turkic origin in succession had ruled the local population. Most recently the lords of Tokharistan were subordinates of the Western Türk Khaganate of Inner Asia. It took the Arab armies several generations of regular campaigning to subdue Tokharistan and the neighbouring lands.

Through all these pre-Islamic dynasties, one important sign of cultural continuity is now clear. Thanks to recent discoveries, the language of Tokharistan is now much better known, attested from the second century until the ninth century, both before and after the beginning of Arab domination, in texts on coins, inscriptions and on more than one hundred and fifty legal and commercial documents, mostly on leather. This Bactrian language, a member of the Iranian language family, is similar in different respects to the other Iranian languages known from the same period, such as Parthian, Sogdian and Middle Persian.[18]

---

15 'Balk̲āb' in *EIr*. Its waters do not actually reach the Oxus, since they are carried off as irrigation into the arid plain around the city. *Ḥudūd al-ʿĀlam: 'The Regions of the World', a Persian Geography 372 A.H.-982 A.D.*, trans. Vladimir Minorsky (Cambridge, ²1970), p. 73 (written 982-83), says of the Balkh river, 'All of its waters are used up for cultivation.' Satellite imagery today shows a fan of green spreading out around Balkh until it dissipates into dry lands.

16 *Ḥudūd al-ʿālam*, p. 108.

17 There were other routes in use between India and China directly over the Himalayas, on which see Jason Neelis, 'The *Vieille Route* Reconsidered: Alternative Paths for Early Transmission of Buddhism beyond the Borderlands of South Asia', *Bulletin of the Asia Institute*, 16 (2002): pp. 143-64.

18 Even before the majority of the new documents came to light, this much was clear: Sims-Williams 'Bactrian Language', in *EIr*. One should avoid confusion between Bactrian and the languages today called 'Tocharian', which are entirely different and constitute another branch of the Indo-European language family. The Tocharian languages are attested in texts mostly from the northern Takalamakan region, not in Tokharistan, but

It was written, however, in a local adaptation and development of the Greek script, a legacy of the Graeco-Bactrian kingdom that had persisted after Alexander's conquest centuries earlier. Most of the surviving Bactrian texts found so far were probably preserved in the mountainous highlands of the northern Hindu Kush. The great majority of these texts have come to light only in the last two decades, and they have been deciphered by Nicholas Sims-Williams and his colleagues. Historians have only begun to benefit from these newly available texts in creating a narrative account of the history of the region.[19] It is apparent that this language was once the vehicle of a literature now lost.

Tokharistan was a region with a distinctive language, script and culture, different from those of Persia and India. It had distinctive gods and artistic styles of its own, and, owing to its position at a major crossroads in the network of routes between India, Iran and China, it enjoyed material and cultural exchanges in every direction.[20] The masters of Balkh could profit from the major conduits of a lucrative trade in luxury goods that had moved along these roads for centuries. Some Bactrian goods were definitely involved in this long-distance trade, as shown by the example of a silver vessel found in Gansu, China, bearing a short Bactrian inscription.[21]

Before the Arab conquest, Tokharistan was in the westernmost part of a far-flung domain in which Buddhism was cultivated and practised with great energy and expense, and, through Buddhism, its population shared in social, artistic and intellectual traditions common to the regions to its south and east. A brief explanation of the role of Buddhism in this great area will help to explain how the

a number of loan words indicate contact between speakers of Bactrian and Tocharian. See Sims-Williams, 'Ancient Afghanistan and its Invaders: Linguistic Evidence from the Bactrian Documents and Inscriptions', in id. (ed.), *Indo-Iranian Languages and Peoples* (Oxford, 2002), pp. 225-42, at pp. 229-30, and Georges-Jean Pinault, 'Tocharian and Indo-Iranian: Relations between Two Linguistic Areas', in Sims-Williams (ed.), *Indo-Iranian Languages and Peoples*, pp. 243-84.

19 Nicholas Sims-Williams, *New Light on Ancient Afghanistan: The Decipherment of Bactrian* (London, 1997) and 'Ancient Afghanistan and its Invaders'. Frantz Grenet, 'Regional Interaction in Central Asia and Northwest India in the Kidarite and Hephthalite Periods', in Sims-Williams (ed.), *Indo-Iranian Languages and Peoples*, pp. 203-24, at pp. 220-21, provides a timeline of the region up to the eighth century.

20 On the material culture of the region, see B.A. Litvinsky, 'An Outline History of Buddhism in Central Asia', in Bobodzhan Gafurovich Gafurov et al. (eds), *Kushan Studies in U.S.S.R.* (Calcutta, 1970), pp. 53-132; Benjamin Rowland, *The Art of Central Asia* (New York, 1974), pp. 45-119; B.A. Litvinsky and T.I. Zeimal', *The Buddhist Monastery of Ajina Tepa, Tajikistan: History and Art of Buddhism in Central Asia* (Rome, 2004); Grenet, 'Regional Interaction in Central Asia and Northwest India', and the bibliographies in these works.

21 Nicholas Sims-Williams, 'A Bactrian Inscription on a Silver Vessel from China', *Bulletin of the Asia Institute*, 9 (1995): p. 225.

society and rulers of Tokharistan were linked with their eastern neighbours.[22] As numerous texts in many languages tell, and material remains show, for centuries before the arrival of the Arabs in the area, many Buddhist missionaries travelled long distances between India, Afghanistan, Tibet, the kingdoms of the Tarim Basin such as Khotan, and China in the pursuit of learning and the propagation of Buddhism. The first signs of their activity in the Bactrian area dates to the period of the Kushan Empire (*c.* first to third centuries), which through its rule united Bactria and northern India into one domain.[23] The activity of these travelling monks, in this area and beyond, had in itself helped to create an international market for the luxury goods traded over this network of far-flung routes. Buddhist travellers received the patronage of wealthy rulers and some Buddhist texts promoted a canonical list of precious commodities, including such objects as banners of silk from China, jewels from India, and silver and gold, all required for the endowment of Buddhist monuments. In turn, the patrons accumulated merit, and, of course, prestige in the eyes of others, through their generosity and donations, providing for monks, founding monasteries, and enriching reliquary monuments or *stūpas*. These *stūpas* became centres of pilgrimage, stimulating further travel and the movement and collection of precious commodities and relics. Many of the dynasties east of Iran shared in their common lavish support of Buddhist scholarship and practice, for which the rulers received acclamations, and which in some cases even facilitated flattering claims that the kings were bodhisattvas. According to this doctrine, Buddhist kings ruled, in effect, by right, because they owed their rank to the merits of previous lives. Buddhist literature written in Sanskrit supported this notion, and these Sanskrit texts were actively sought in translation all over Asia. Since many social groups stood to gain, especially the powerful, the interregional movement and exchange flourished.[24]

From India to China, an extensive common Buddhist vocabulary and iconography came into use, derived ultimately from northern India, through the work of missionaries over several centuries, but nevertheless naturalized and developed differently in each region. The Buddhist populations of these regions shared an ideal of a social order distinguishing monastics from lay people,

---

22 This is not intended to be a general history of Tokharistan, but only to document and describe the presence of Buddhists there. Xinru Liu, *Ancient India and Ancient China: Trade and Religious Exchanges AD 1-600* (Delhi, 1988) provides an economically-oriented historical introduction, on which part of the following is based. For a recent overview of Buddhism, and the evidence for its presence, throughout Inner Asia see Xavier Tremblay, 'The Spread of Buddhism in Serindia – Buddhism among Iranians, Tocharians, and Turks before the 13th century', in Ann Heirman and Stephen Peter Bumbacher (eds), *The Spread of Buddhism* (Leiden, 2007), pp. 75-129.

23 Tremblay, 'The Spread of Buddhism in Serindia', pp. 82-8.

24 On the trade in precious commodities and its links to Buddhist ideology, see Liu, *Ancient India and Ancient China*, pp. 53-123.

protected by a *dharmarāja* or king in the *dharma*,[25] and an economy of gifts given for merit (and prestige).[26] These dynasties also allied themselves with one another through the exchange of brides, enhancing their cultural bonds with personal connections. For evidence of Buddhism in Tokharistan itself, one must turn to Chinese sources, the Bactrian texts, and to the finds of archaeologists. Taken together, the evidence shows practices flourishing in the ancestral home of the Barmakids like those just described in neighbouring regions.

Xuánzàng 玄奘 was a Buddhist monk who travelled from 629 to 645 from China to India. There he learned Sanskrit, collected numerous Buddhist texts, brought them back to China, and became a famous translator. His description of countries outside of the control of the Tang dynasty is one of the most important sources for the historical geography of Asia available for this period. In 630, while far away the Byzantine emperor Heraclius was reclaiming Jerusalem from the Sasanians, Xuánzàng observed Tokharistan and had quite a bit to say about the region and about the city of Balkh. All around the valley of Tokharistan Xuánzàng found Buddhist monks, monasteries and *stūpas*, especially at Balkh, where he estimated one hundred monasteries and 3,000 monks. He describes the **Nava-saṅghārāma* 納縛僧伽藍,[27] or 'New Monastery', as a place lavishly decorated with precious materials. Near the monastery was a **stūpa* 窣堵波, also lavishly adorned. He also says that here alone north of the Hindu Kush, at this monastery in Balkh, did scholars continue to make *lùn* 論 (equivalent to Sanskrit *śāstra*): that is, commentaries on *sūtras* or philosophical texts. Xuánzàng was a learned scholar and translator who used such terms fairly precisely.[28] Buddhist scholarship thus appears to have flourished at Balkh in the early seventh century.

A century later, around 726, another Buddhist monk from Silla (what is today Korea), named Huìchāo 慧超, travelled in the region. Huìchāo wrote in Chinese a description of India and Central Asia, including Tokharistan, discovered in 1908 in a unique ninth-century manuscript at Dunhuang, called *Huìchāo wǎng wǔ tiānzhúguó zhuàn* 慧超往五天竺國傳, 'Account of Huìchāo's Journey to the Five Lands of India'.[29] This neglected historical source gives a view of Iran from the

[25] The ideal of this dharmic king is described, on the basis of Pali texts, by Uma Chakravarti, *The Social Dimensions of Early Buddhism* (Delhi, 1987), pp. 150-76.

[26] Of course, market economies also flourished throughout these regions. The point here is to describe the role of Buddhists in interregional exchange, because it is important for the following argument. For more on various kinds of exchange between India and China in this period, see Tansen Sen, *Buddhism, Diplomacy, and Trade: The Realignment of Sino-Indian Relations, 600-1400* (Honolulu, 2003), pp. 1-102.

[27] Modern Mandarin *nàfò sēngjiālán*.

[28] Beal, *Si-Yu-Ki*, vol. 1, pp. 43-8.

[29] Walter Fuchs, 'Huei-ch'ao's 慧超 Pilgerreise durch Nordwest-Indien und Zentral-Asien um 726', *Sitzungsberichte der Preussischen Akademie der Wissenschaften, phil.-hist. Klasse*, 22 (1938): pp. 426-69, and *The Hye-Ch'o Diary*, ed. and trans. Han-Sung Yang, Yün-Hua Jan, Shotaro Iida and Lawrence W. Preston (Seoul, 1984).

east after the Arabs had conquered Iran and Khorasan, but before the Abbasid revolution. While the importance of this work has been recognized by specialists on the Silk Road, to my knowledge no Arabist has ever used it as a source on the activities of the Arabs or the history of this region.

After coming to India from China by sea, Huìchāo made his way through much of India, and then travelled over the Hindu Kush into Tokharistan before returning to China overland through the Tarim basin. In the time since Xuánzàng's visit, Arab armies had conquered all of the Persian Empire and had been making war on Tokharistan already for a long time. Recently, in 725, the Arab garrison had been moved into Balkh proper, as Arabic sources tell. The latest edition offers the following text.[30]

> 又從此犯引國。北行廿日。至吐火羅國。王住城名為縛底那。見今大是兵馬。在彼鎮押。其王被[31]逼。走向東一月程。在蒲持山住。見屬大是所管。言音與諸國別。共罽賓國少有相似。多分不同。衣著皮毬氎布等。上至國王。下及黎庶。皆以皮毬。為上服。土地足駝騾羊馬氎布蒲桃。食唯愛餅。土地寒冷。冬天霜雪也。國王首領及百姓等。甚敬三寶。足寺足僧。行小乘法。食肉及葱韮等[32]。不事外道。男人並剪鬚髮。女人在髮。土地足山。

> From this land of Bāmiyān I travelled northwards twenty days, and I arrived in Tokharistan (*Tŭhuŏluó-guó* 吐火羅國). The home city of the king is called Balkh. At this time the troops of the Arabs are there and they occupy it. Its king was forced to flee one month's journey to the east and lives in Badakhshan. Now it (Balkh) belongs to the Arabs' domain.
>
> The language (here) is different from that of the other lands; though somewhat similar to that of Kāpiśa, for the most part it is different. For clothing there is fur and cotton; up to the king and down to the lowly people, they all wear fur as outerwear. In the land there are plenty of camels, mules, sheep, horses, cotton, and grapes.[33] For food, people like just dry cakes. The land is very cold, and in winter there is frost and snow.
>
> The king, the nobles, and the people revere the Three Jewels [i.e. practise Buddhism]. There are many monasteries and monks; they practise the Lesser

---

30 *The Hye-Ch'o Diary*, ed. and trans. Yang et al., pp. 100-103. Their readings, based on a fresh examination of the manuscript, differ in several details from those of Fuchs, 'Huei-ch'ao's 慧超 Pilgerreise', p. 466. I have followed Fuchs only in a few details. Thanks to Sunhee Yoon for help with several Chinese characters. As for the translation, I have benefited from both Fuchs, 'Huei-ch'ao's 慧超 Pilgerreise', p. 449, and *The Hye-Ch'o Diary*, p. 52.

31 Here I follow *The Hye-Ch'o Diary*, p. 100, l. 13 in deleting the dittography in the manuscript: 其王被其王被逼.

32 Following the readings of Yang et al., *The Hye-Ch'o Diary*, p. 103, l. 4.

33 Vineyards (ρoζγo) are mentioned in a number of the Bactrian documents dating from the fourth to the eighth century. See BD2, p. 260.

> Vehicle (*Hīnayāna*) teachings and eat meat, onion and leeks. No one practises heretical teachings. The menfolk cut their beard and head hair. The womenfolk, by contrast, let their hair grow. The land has many mountains.

It is apparent from Huìchāo's description that, in his view, the true ruler of Balkh was still alive, in exile. From his description alone, one might think it quite possible that the king of Balkh could be restored to his domain in the course of time, and that the Arabs would be evicted. The Arabs are clearly still newcomers, foreign occupiers. It is also worth emphasizing that he described all the inhabitants of the region as Buddhists even while the Arabs rule the region.

While Buddhism was evidently widespread in Tokharistan, other sources indicate that different religions were in fact practised by Bactrians.[34] The famous Nestorian Christian stele, bearing a bilingual Chinese–Syriac inscription, erected in 781 at Cháng'ān 長安, capital of the Tang empire, was made by churchmen including 'Mār Yazdbôzîd, priest and Chorepiscopus of Kûmdân,[35] capital of the Kingdom [i.e. of the Tang Empire], son of the late Miles, priest of Balkh, capital of Ṭəḥwārastān'[36] *mry yzdbwzyd qšyšʾ w-kwrʾpysqwpʾ d-Kwmdʾn mdynt mlkwtʾ br-nyḥ npšʾ Mylys qšyšʾ d-mn Blḥ mdyntʾ d-Ṭḥwrstn*. As it says, his father was a priest in Balkh, indicating the presence of a Christian community in Tokharistan in the mid-eighth century, one connected somehow with Christians in China.[37] Furthermore, a fragment of Bactrian text written in the Manichaean script, found at Turfan, indicates that at least some Bactrian-speakers living abroad were Manichaean.[38] Nevertheless, however many of the local population were Christian or Manichaean, one has the distinct impression from Huìchāo that

34 As Litvinsky, 'An Outline History of Buddhism in Central Asia', p. 119, already said of Huìchāo's high estimation of the adherence to Buddhism in Tokharistan, 'We think he was a little guilty of exaggeration.'

35 Kumdan is Cháng'ān.

36 Henning recognized this text, like the Chinese rendering of the name cited above, as attesting to an older pronunciation of the name Tokharistan (Walter Henning, 'Argi and the "Tocharians"', *Bulletin of the School of Oriental Studies*, 9 [1938]: pp. 545-71, at pp. 545-6). This is now confirmed in the Bactrian documents, where the name appears circa the fifth century as τοχοαραστανο (BD2, p. 270).

37 The name Yazdbôzîd, meaning 'Saved by God', is evidently Middle Persian (thanks to Nicholas Sims-Williams for explaining to me why it is probably not a Bactrian name). *Yezid* is attested for God in the 'Bactrian bismillah' at the beginning of the Bactrian document Y (BD1, p. 145) of the mid-eighth century: πιδο ναμο ιεζιδασο. (The name is ιεζιδ-, Yezid, with the attached clitic -ασο referring to what follows.) One may suppose that Christians in Balkh had already used this Persian name for God already before Muslims arrived.

38 Nicholas Sims-Williams, 'The Bactrian Fragment in Manichaean Script (M1224)', in Desmond Durkin-Meisterernst, Christiane Reck and Dieter Weber (eds), *Literarische Stoffe und ihre Gestaltung in mitteliranischer Zeit* (Wiesbaden, 2009), pp. 245-68. This Manichaean text, coincidentally or not, 'has a strong Buddhist colouring' (Sims-Williams at p. 255).

most of people in Tokharistan revered or respected the Buddha, including, importantly, the rulers. They did not follow 'heretical' doctrines, as he put it. At least it was a country with 'many monasteries and monks', and this corresponds with the earlier description of Xuánzàng and the finds of archaeologists (on which more below).

It is important to note that Huìchāo was describing Tokharistan on the basis of direct experience. He says that when he was in Tokharistan, he encountered a Chinese envoy (*hànshǐ* 漢使) to foreign peoples. On the occasion of their meeting he composed some verses of poetry expressing his homesickness, which he cites. He then adds some other verses that he composed on a freezing cold, snowy day in Tokharistan, addressing the difficulty of crossing the mountains separating him from his homeland.[39] These anecdotes confirm that his report on the country is an eyewitness account, apparently in the winter. He is the only contemporary author to describe the local culture of the region at the time of the Arab conquest.

Besides these Chinese texts, there are Bactrian texts giving evidence about the local population. One of the most important of these is a recently published inscription in Bactrian made on a now-ruined Buddhist *stūpa* 25 kilometres to the west of Bāmiyān.[40] It gives its own date for the foundation of the *stūpa*, equivalent to the year 714,[41] not long before Huìchāo's visit to the region. The author of the text was the lord of Gazan (i.e. Ghazna) (γαζανο χοδδηοο). He says he established this *stūpa* (στοπο) when there was a Türk ruler and an Arab ruler (καλδο δορκο χαρο δο ταζιγο χαρο σταδο). This is apparently a reference to the situation described also by Huìchāo, when the Arabs held western Tokharistan and Balkh, but the Türk ruler, king of Balkh, persisted in the mountains to the east.[42] It is striking that this Bactrian speaker, the lord of Ghazna, founded a new *stūpa* in the midst of the Arab incursions and wars in the region. He dedicates the merit of the foundation to the success of his family and gives homage to the Buddhas (ναμω βοδδανο). The text uses a number of Buddhist Sanskrit terms in somewhat naturalized Bactrian forms.

---

39 *The Hye-Ch'o Diary*, pp. 55-6.

40 Jonathan Lee and Nicholas Sims-Williams, 'The Antiquities and Inscription of Tang-i Safedak', *Silk Road Art and Archaeology*, 9 (2003): pp. 159-84.

41 This date, like the other dates given in this article for the Bactrian texts, assumes the Bactrian era of 2 October 223 recently proposed by F. de Blois, 'Du nouveau sur la chronologie bactrienne post-hellénistique: l'ère de 223-224 ap. J.-C.', in *Comptes rendus des séances – Académie des Inscriptions et Belles-Lettres*, juin 2006, pp. 991-7; this is the Sasanian era, imported to Tokharistan during the earlier period of Sasanian domination of the region. Previously the era was tentatively identified as beginning in 233 (Sims-Williams, *New Light on Ancient Afghanistan*, p. 9).

42 Qutayba ibn Muslim successfully fought and killed a major local ruler, Nēzak Ṭarkhān, in 709-10. Lee and Sims-Williams, 'The Antiquities and Inscription of Tang-i Safedak', pp. 167-8, offers several other possible, similar interpretations.

Some of the Bactrian documents on leather that have come to light also inadvertently indicate the presence of Buddhist monks in the Hindu Kush mountains as late as the mid-eighth century. One partially preserved Bactrian letter, of uncertain date, is addressed to a monk bearing the Sanskrit name Rahulabhadra and the title of an eminent scholar, *ācāryārya* (ρυολοβαδρο ασαριαριιο).[43] Two dated documents contain an apparently traditional formula used in the sale of land, stating that the land may be used by the new owner for any purpose, including for a temple or a Buddhist monastery: that is, a *vihāra* (βαυαρο /βahār/).[44] One document was written in 729 in a place called Rizm, the other in 747 in Gandar,[45] both by men serving the lord of Rob (Bactrian ρωβο, Arabic *Rawb*), a region in the mountains south and east of Balkh. In both, the payment in the transaction was in 'Arab silver dirhams'. The exact chronology of the Arabs' control over the valleys of the Hindu Kush requires further investigation, but it is noteworthy that the contracts were made 'in the presence of the god Wakhsh' (πισο βαγο οαχþο), perhaps meaning they were made at a temple or shrine of this god. These documents show that a local god continued to have at least symbolic authority in the area for some years after the Arab conquest of the region. One of these documents states explicitly that the land was being sold by its owner in order to make money to pay the Arab poll-tax (Bactrian ταζιιαγγο γαζιτο, or Arabic *jizya*) levied on non-Muslims. Here the *jizya* is paid by a man acknowledging a local god.

Two short, specifically Buddhist, texts in Bactrian have come out of Afghanistan. One of the recently deciphered Bactrian fragments contains a formulaic colophon to a Buddhist work, including a dedication of the merit from copying the text.[46] This traditional Buddhist expression, common to colophons of Buddhist texts, must be the last leaf in a once larger manuscript. It is impossible to think that this is the only Buddhist manuscript ever written in Bactrian; it must be the trace of a larger body of texts now lost. Another Buddhist text in Bactrian survives on what appears to be a small cloth pennant. It invokes the bodhisattvas and is decorated with drawings.[47] All of these Bactrian texts have been deciphered and interpreted by Nicholas Sims-Williams.

Some other legal documents in Bactrian (dated 659-722) originating in Guzgān, to the west of Balkh, do not give any direct indication of Buddhism.

---

43 BD2, ji1. After the obeisant greeting, the matter of the message is unfortunately not legible.

44 BD1, V24, W21. The spelling βιυαρο, closer to the original Indic loan-word, also occurs in a Bactrian Buddhist amulet full of Bactrianized Sanskrit terms (BD2, za190, line 19).

45 In the Arabic documents Ghandar; thus not to be interpreted as Gandhāra (BD2, p. 206).

46 BD2, za and zb; see also the small fragment zc. Previously published in Nicholas Sims-Williams, 'A Bactrian Buddhist Manuscript', in Jens Braarvig (ed.), *Buddhist Manuscripts Volume I. Manuscripts in the Schøyen Collection I* (Oslo, 2000), pp. 275-7.

47 BD2, za.

The god Wakhsh, on the other hand, enjoys great prestige there: βαγο οαχþο βαγανο þαυο, 'the god Wakhsh, king of the gods'.[48] Wakhsh is a witness to legal transactions in Guzgān as in the Bactrian documents from the Hindu Kush. Yet among all the Iranian names in the Guzgān documents, the appearance of 'Rāhul, leader of the people of Lizag', points indirectly to Buddhism: Rāhula was the Buddha's son, his name being therefore not uncommon among Buddhists.[49]

Not only Bactrian but pieces of Sanskrit texts have been discovered in Tokharistan, attesting that this language, too, was studied in the region up until the Arab conquest. For the most part, Sanskrit texts were brought out of India into other regions only in association with the propagation of Buddhism. Both the find-spots of these fragmentary texts, where known, and their contents, where legible, confirm this in the case of Tokharistan and the neighbouring regions. Pieces of Sanskrit manuscripts in Brāhmī script dating as late as the eighth century have been found both in the Hindu Kush, at Bāmiyān[50] and nearby Shahr-i Zohak,[51] and also in the valley of the Oxus, north of the river, at Ajina-Tepa and Zang-Tepa.[52] These finds, though highly fragmentary, show that Buddhist Sanskrit scholarship was pursued in the area until the advent of the Arabs and perhaps even afterwards. The Sanskrit manuscripts at Shahr-i Zohak, a ruined castle 15 kilometres east of Bāmiyān, included medical texts.[53] A number of other Buddhist Sanskrit texts, dated on palaeographic grounds to the first to sixth centuries, have emerged from Afghanistan with no clear indication of their find-spots, but the Brāhmī scripts used are very close to those employed at Bāmiyān and Gilgit.[54] Much earlier Buddhist texts, written on birch bark scrolls in Gāndhārī, in the Kharoṣṭhī script, have also come to light in Afghanistan; despite their great importance for the history of Buddhism, these are not directly relevant to the present study because these date from the first centuries of the Common Era.[55]

---

48 Nicholas Sims-Williams, 'Bactrian Legal Documents from 7th- and 8th-Century Guzgan', *Bulletin of the Asia Institute*, 15 (2001): pp. 9-29, pp. 14-15 (O3').

49 Sims-Williams, 'Bactrian Legal Documents from 7th- and 8th-Century Guzgan', pp. 20-21 (Uu 4-5).

50 Sylvain Lévi, 'Note sur des manuscrits sanscrits provenant de Bamiyan (Afghanistan) et de Gilgit (Cachemire)', *Journal Asiatique*, 220 (1932): pp. 1-45, at pp. 1-13.

51 Bernard Pauly, 'Fragments sanskrits d'Afghanistan (fouilles de la D.A.F.A.)', *Journal Asiatique*, 255 (1967): pp. 273-83.

52 Litvinsky, 'An Outline History of Buddhism in Central Asia', p. 111. One page in Buddhist Sanskrit at Zang-tepa apparently contains part of a *vinaya* text: that is, it deals with the monastic code.

53 Pauly, 'Fragments sanskrits d'Afghanistan'.

54 Braarvig (ed.), *Buddhist Manuscripts Volume I* (see especially the appendix by Lore Sander on the dating of the scripts, pp. 285-300).

55 Richard Salomon, *Ancient Buddhist Scrolls from Gandhāra: The British Library Kharoṣṭhī Fragments* (Seattle, 1999); id., 'The Senior Manuscripts: Another Collection of

North of the Oxus, in the side of Tokharistan that was formerly part of the Soviet Union, Russian archaeologists have made additional important discoveries of Buddhist sites that have not received sufficient attention.[56] At Ajina-Tepa, east of Tirmidh, ruins of a Buddhist *vihāra* were unearthed containing the remains of wall paintings and sculpture dated from the fifth to the eighth centuries. Among the remains was a giant statue of the Buddha reclining just before his *parinirvāṇa*. Though mostly badly damaged, these material finds give an idea of what must once have been a lively culture of images blending ancient Iranian and Buddhist visual arts into new, local forms.[57] Another Buddhist *vihāra* was discovered north of the Oxus by the same archaeologists at Kala-i Kafirnigan, on the Qubādhiyān River, dated by the coins found there to the early seventh to mid-eighth century.[58]

In short, both fragmentary texts and material remains attest to the living presence of Buddhism, and learning both in Sanskrit and probably also in the local, Bactrian language, in Tokharistan in the eighth century, before, during, and, for a time, after the settlement of Arabs in the region. By contrast with this evidence attesting to Buddhist scholarship and practice in the area, Arabic sources do not relate any information about Buddhism as such in this region; they speak only vaguely of polytheism and idolatry if they mention the local inhabitants at all. This in itself shows that they recognized that they were dealing not with Christians, Manichaeans or Jews. Huìchāo's account around 726 gives a Buddhist point of view, stating simply that in this time both the Persians and the Arabs 'serve heaven, and do not know the *buddhadharma*' 事天不識佛法.[59]

In retrospect, the eventual ascendancy of Islam in Tokharistan and writing in Arabic may seem to have been inevitable, but to people of the region during the mid-eighth century, when resistance to the Arabs was ongoing, it was probably not so clear that the Arabs were there to stay. It seems, indeed, on the basis of the sources just reviewed, that Buddhism and local polytheism coexisted with Arab Muslim rule for a period of decades. For now, it is hard to

---

Gandhāran Buddhist Scrolls', *Journal of the American Oriental Society*, 123 (2003): pp. 73-92. Richard Salomon, 'New Manuscript Sources for the Study of Gandhāran Buddhism', in Pia Brancaccio and Kurt Behrendt (eds), *Gandhāran Buddhism* (Vancouver, 2006), pp. 135-47 summarizes the significance of the newly discovered early Gāndhārī texts.

56 For an overview of the sources and earlier archaeology demonstrating the presence of Buddhist institutions in this area, see Litvinsky, 'An Outline History of Buddhism in Central Asia', pp. 110-20.

57 B.A. Litvinsky and T.I. Zeimal', *Adžina-Tepa: Arkhitektura, Živopis', Skul'ptura* (Moscow, 1971) and *The Buddhist Monastery of Ajina Tepa*, with numerous photographic plates, especially in the former. The coin finds at Ajina-Tepa date *c.*650-750 (*The Buddhist Monastery of Ajina Tepa*, pp. 19-20).

58 B.A. Litvinsky, 'Kalai-Kafirnigan. Problems in the Religion and Art of Early Medieval Tokharistan', *East and West*, 31 (1988): pp. 35-66.

59 *The Hye-Ch'o Diary*, p. 53, text 7a10 and 7b2-3.

know about the daily relations between the Arab colonizers and the people of Tokharistan. However, the latest dated Bactrian documents, together with 32 Arabic documents on leather from Tokharistan that have also recently come to light, dated 755-77, afford glimpses of the assimilation and accommodation of the population to their new rulers. These Arabic documents of Bactria have been edited and studied by Geoffrey Khan.[60] They are apparently from the same archive containing many of the Bactrian documents and refer to members of the same family. Some 23 of these Arabic documents are tax receipts dated 764-74. The tax officials commonly have Arabic names with Iranian patronymics, such as al-Ḥasan ibn Warazān.[61] These are evidently local converts to Islam or the children of converts who gave their sons Arabic names.[62] The sons likely learned Arabic through social intercourse with their Arab Muslim neighbours and, no doubt, from the study of the Qur᾽ān in buildings converted to mosques. Subsequently they became local governors, officials and secretaries.[63]

The Bactrian name Mir son of Bek (*Mīr ibn Bēk*) appears a number of times in the Arabic documents, the same name also appearing in three of the latest Bactrian documents (μιρο βηκο πορο), which are dated to about 747-72.[64] This in itself shows a society with two languages in different official uses for different legal concerns.[65] Mir was a landowner who had disputes with his brothers; they shared lands and three of them were married polyandrously to one wife, polyandry being an ancient local practice long attested, and noticed most recently by Huìchāo.[66] The Arabic and Bactrian documents mention some of the same places, such as Madr and Rizm.

---

60 Geoffrey Khan, *Arabic Documents from Early Islamic Khurasan* (London, 2007), and 'Newly Discovered Arabic Documents from Early Abbasid Khurasan', in Petra Sijpesteijn et al. (eds), *From al-Andalus to Khurasan* (Leiden, 2007), pp. 201-15.

61 *Waraz-*, οαραζ-, is an element in several attested Bactrian names. See BD2, p. 241b.

62 The latter type would reflect Richard Bulliet's theory (*Conversion to Islam in the Medieval Period: An Essay in Quantitative History* [Cambridge, 1979], pp. 18-19) that the last non-Arabic name in a Muslim's genealogy indicates the ancestor who converted.

63 Similarly also Khan, *Arabic Documents from Early Islamic Khurasan*, p. 19: 'It would appear that members of Iranian administrative families were incorporated into the Abbasid administration.'

64 Khan, *Arabic Documents from Early Islamic Khurasan*, pp. 20-22, assembles the data on this family and constructs a family tree of its known members.

65 Khan, *Arabic Documents from Early Islamic Khurasan*, pp. 64-5, compares the distribution of functions of the Arabic and the Bactrian documents.

66 Huìchāo: 'In the country of Tokhāristān and those of Kāpiśa, Bāmiyān, and Zābulistān, two, three, five, or even ten brothers are jointly married to one wife. They are not allowed to marry separately as they are afraid that separate marriages would ruin their livelihood' (*The Hye-Ch'o Diary*, p. 54). The translators' 'livelihood' renders *jiājì* 家計, perhaps better understood as 'household economics' or 'family economy'. It seems that the point is rather about inheritance laws and ownership rather than livelihood per se. This is precisely what the disputing brothers in Bactrian Document X, including this Mir,

The latest dated Bactrian document, from 771-2, tells us more about this Mir son of Bek.[67] Mir's brother Bab has apparently now separated from their fraternally shared estate, and Mir has requested the governor, who bears a Türkic name, that he be freed from any liabilities or debts for which his brother was responsible. This document, unlike the previous ones, contains no references to local religion; rather it begins with an expression in Persian: 'in the name of God' (πιδο ναμο ιεζιδ).[68] This clearly indicates that the formulae, if not the religion, of the ruling Muslims had been adopted. One can only wonder if Bab's departure reflects a new family pattern brought by the norms of the Arab settlers and Islam, but it is impossible to say very much on the basis of one document alone.

Al-Jahshiyārī (d. 942) tells in his history of viziers and secretaries how Arabic became the official language of government accounts in the province of Khorasan in 741-42. The capital, including the offices of administration, had very recently been shifted eastward to Balkh for a few years (736-38) by Asad ibn ʿAbdallāh. Naṣr ibn Sayyār, Asad's replacement, apparently had just moved it back to Marw in 739.[69] Al-Jahshiyārī writes:[70]

> Most of the secretaries of Khorasan at that time were Magians (*majūs*). The accounts were kept in Persian (*bi'l-Fārsiyya*). So Yūsuf ibn ʿUmar [al-Thaqafī], who was then governor of ʿIrāq, in the year 124 sent a letter to Naṣr ibn Sayyār [governor of Khorasan], ... ordering him not to resort to any of the polytheists

have to say, *c*.760 (ed. and trans. BD1, pp. 136-7): 'Now it has been thus agreed by us, that it is not necessary for us to quarrel and it is not necessary (for us) to destroy (our) house; so now .. a mutual agreement has been made by us, and our ditches and .., and our houses and persons and homes and estates, much and little, good and bad, mountain and river-valley, slave-girls and slaves, (shall) belong (to us) equally, and we shall live just as it is the custom (for) brother to live with brother. And we shall possess the woman whose name (is) Zeran as a three-(some) ..' By 'house' here the Bactrian text refers not only to property but to the family itself. A Bactrian polyandrous marriage contract survives from as early as 333 CE (Document A, BD1, pp. 32-5).

67 BD1, document Y.

68 BD1, pp. 144-5.

69 Al-Ṭabarī, *Tārīkh al-rusul wa'l-mulūk*, ed. Michael Jan de Goeje (15 vols, Leiden, 1879-1901), series 2, part 3, p. 1591, under year 118: *wa'ttakhadha Asadun madīnata Balkha dāran fī sanati 118 wa-naqala ilayhā al-dawāwīna wa'ttakhadha al-maṣāniʿa thumma ghazā Ṭukhāristāna thumma arḍa Jabghūya*. From this point on, Asad's narrative is centred on Balkh. When Naṣr next took over the government of Khorasan, the first campaign was from Balkh, but he then returned (*qafala*) to Marw, which again became the base of Arab operations in Khorasan, and, presumably, of the administration, too (Ṭabarī, *Tārīkh al-rusul wa'l-mulūk*, series 2, part 3, p. 1688). Cf. Hamilton Alexander Rosskeen Gibb, *The Arab Conquests in Central Asia* (London, 1923; repr. New York, 1970), pp. 80-81, and Khalid Yahya Blankinship, *The End of the Jihād State* (Albany, 1994), p. 183.

70 Al-Jahshiyārī, *Das Kitāb al-Wuzarā' wa-l-Kuttāb des Abū 'Abdallāh Muḥammad ibn 'Abdūs al-Ǧahšiyārī*, ed. Hans Mžik (Leipzig, 1926), pp. 64-5.

> (*ilā aḥad min ahl al-shirk*) in his government and his books. The first one to translate the writing from Persian into Arabic was Isḥāq ibn Ṭulayq the Scribe.

This description is quite likely for Marw, a city of the former Sasanian Empire. One expects that literate Magians would be keeping the records there in Persian. However, for the recently dominated territory of Tokharistan, I have found no substantial trace of Magians in this period in the available materials, and the Bactrian language was in current use for the purposes of record-keeping.[71] The capital and its administration had just been moved to and from Balkh. Could the passage then refer not only to Magians but also to Buddhists and Bactrian polytheists who wrote in Bactrian, not Persian? In that case, it would not be the only time that later authors in Arabic would conflate the people of Tokharistan and the Persians, or mistake Buddhism for Magianism. For example, a contemporary of the Barmakids disparaged the Buddhist *vihāra* at Balkh as a fire-temple.[72] In any case, the Arabic sources usually do not distinguish clearly the people of the former Persian Empire from those of Tokharistan, even though they had previously lived under separate governments for centuries.

ABŪ ḤAFṢ AL-KIRMĀNĪ'S *AKHBĀR AL-BARĀMIKA*

It is in this background of the Arab occupation of Tokharistan, and contact between the colonists and the locals, that the Barmakid family became involved

71 Nicholas Sims-Williams, 'Some Reflections on Zoroastrianism in Sogdiana and Bactria', in David Christian and Craig Benjamin (eds), *Realms of the Silk Roads: Ancient and Modern* (Turnhout, 2000), pp. 1-12, presents evidence for 'Zoroastrian' words and gods in Bactria. Strictly speaking, these are Bactrian words with cognates in Avestan and gods shared in common with Sasanian Zoroastrianism, not evidence for a Bactrian Zoroastrianism, as such, particularly in the confessional sense encountered in western Iran under the later Sasanids. Tremblay, 'The Spread of Buddhism in Serindia', p. 88, appears to think that the scribes of the Bactrian documents were in fact Mazdaeans, albeit 'apathetic as to the choice between Mazdeism and Buddhism' in their terminology. I think, however, that the legal terms of their documents are formulaic and do not reflect the scribes' religious preference. Nor do I think it is entirely clear whether references to gods such as Wakhsh are 'Mazdaean' in any meaningful sense. The character of eastern Iranian Mazdaism, clearly different in some respects from the Sasanian type, requires further research.

72 In a poem by Abū 'l-Hawl al-Ḥimyarī (fl. from al-Mahdī to al-Amīn: Fuat Sezgin, *Geschichte des arabischen Schrifttums* [vols 1-9, Leiden, 1967-1984; vols 10-, Frankfurt, 2000-], vol. 2 p. 599), mocking al-Faḍl ibn Yaḥyā al-Barmakī as having suspiciously un-Islamic roots, the Nawbahār is described as 'a house of polytheism and unbelief in which a fire is worshipped' *wa-baytu shirkin wa-kufrin bihī tu'aẓẓamu nārū* (cited by Yāqūt, *Buldān*, see *Jacut's geographisches Wörterbuch*, ed. Ferdinand Wüstenfeld [6 vols, Leipzig, 1866-73], vol. 4, p. 820).

in the politics of the caliphate. There are several excellent modern surveys of the history of the Barmakids, based on numerous reports gleaned from the extant medieval sources. However, a large amount of the information available on the Barmakids derives in fact from just one source, an Arabic author who lived *c.*800, Abū Ḥafṣ ʿUmar ibn al-Azraq al-Kirmānī. Al-Kirmānī wrote a history of the Barmakids, called *Akhbār al-Barāmika wa-faḍāʾiluhum* (*The History and Virtues of the Barmakids*).[73] Because some of al-Kirmānī's history is related on the authority of the Barmakid Muḥammad ibn Yaḥyā ibn Khālid, the great-grandson of the Barmak, it must reflect to some extent an account from the Barmakid family itself. It includes remarkable, personal details not found elsewhere, but its narrative is motivated by the purpose to glorify the Barmakids.[74] Unfortunately, the work is not extant in its entirety. Only separate passages from it survive, cited by Ibn al-Faqīh (wrote *c.*903), al-Ṭabarī (d. 923), Yāqūt (d. 1229), Ibn al-ʿAdīm (d. 1262) and others.[75] The Persian historian Yazdī used it as the basis of a short historical romance about the Barmakids, *Tārīkh-i Āl-i Barmak*, written in 1360.[76]

One long excerpt surviving from al-Kirmānī's work deals with the origins of their family in the person of the Barmak himself; it has been known since the publication of Ibn al-Faqīh's geography in 1885. Three main versions of this text have been published, all of which are to some extent defective. De Goeje's edition of Ibn al-Faqīh was the first, and it has served as the basis for most scholars dealing with the Barmak. However, a manuscript in Mashhad containing the text of Ibn al-Faqīh was published in facsimile in 1987;[77] this was not available to de Goeje, but here the relevant passage has a substantially better text, including whole sentences left out by the manuscripts used in de Goeje's edition. Importantly, the Mashhad manuscript includes the citation of al-Kirmānī as its source for this passage, whereas that citation is lost in de Goeje's edition.[78]

---

[73] Bosworth, 'Abū Ḥafṣ ʿUmar al-Kirmānī', p. 268.

[74] Ibid., pp. 269-70.

[75] Bosworth, ibid., presents all of this information with analyses of several passages.

[76] Yazdī, *Chrestomathie persane a l'usage des élèves de l'école spéciale des langues orientales vivantes*, ed. Charles Schefer (2 vols, Paris, 1883-85), vol. 2, pp. 2-104 (Persian side).

[77] Ibn al-Faqīh, *Mukhtaṣar Kitāb al-buldān*, facsimile of ms. 5229 Riḍawīya Library, Mashhad in *Collection of Geographical Works by Ibn al-Faqīh, Ibn Faḍlān, Abū Dulaf al-Khazrajī*, Series C Facsimile Editions 43, ed. Fuat Sezgin (Frankfurt, 1987).

[78] Bosworth did not recognize that al-Kirmānī was also the source of Ibn al-Faqīh on the Barmakids, because the citation by name was not indicated in de Goeje's edition. It is, however, explicitly stated in the Mashhad ms. of Ibn al-Faqīh (presented below) and in Yāqūt's quotation of the passage. The missing citation led Bosworth ('Abū Ḥafṣ ʿUmar al-Kirmānī', p. 271) to think that Ibn al-Faqīh's account was from a different source and supposed a chronology in conflict with the other reports also derived from al-Kirmānī. In fact, however, he guessed the solution rightly himself, suggesting that there are *two* individuals named Barmak under discussion, one the father of the last Barmak, that is,

Nevertheless the Mashhad text is not without its own problems. Finally, Yāqūt's geographical encyclopaedia *Muʿjam al-buldān* contains the same text, and while it shows the editorial hand of its learned author, it gives a third witness often corresponding more closely with the Mashhad manuscript than with de Goeje's edition.[79] Here I present the text following the Mashhad manuscript, using Yāqūt and de Goeje's edition in the following translation only in the few places marked. I have standardized the language and eliminated some grammatical mistakes in the Mashhad text without note, only indicating a few more important and necessary alterations to the wording of the passage. Section numbers have been added to the translation to facilitate the discussion to follow.[80]

1. وببلخ النوبهار وهو من بناء البرامكة قال عمر بن الأزرق الكرماني

2. كانت البرامكة أهل شرف على وجه الدهر ببلخ قبل ملوك الطوائف وكان دينهم عبادة الأوثان فوصفت لهم مكة وحال الكعبة بها وما كانت قريش ومن والاها من العرب تدين به فاتخذوا بيت النوبهار مضاهاة لبيت الله الحرام ونصبوا حوله الأصنام وزينوه بالديباج والحرير وعلقوا عليه الجواهر النفيسة

3. وتفسير النوبهار البهار الجديد وكانت سنتهم إذا بنوا بناء حسناً أو عقدوا طاقاً شريفاً أن يكلّلوه بالريحان ويتوّجوا بذلك أول ريحان يطلع في ذلك الوقت فلما بنوا ذلك البيت جعلوا عليه أول ما ظهر من الريحان وكان البهار فسمي نوبهار

4. وكانت العجم تعظمه وتحج إليه وتهدي له وتلبسه أنواع الثياب وتنصب على أعلى قبته الأعلام وكانوا يسمون قبته الأستب[81] وكانت مائة ذراع في مثلها وارتفاعها فوق مائة ذراع بأروقة مستديرة حولها وكان حول البيت ثلاثمائة وستون مقصورة يسكنها خدامه وقوامه وسدنته وكان على كل أهل مقصورة من تلك المقاصير خدمة يوم لا يعود إلى الخدمة حولاً ويقال إن الريح كانت ربما حملت الحريرة من العلم الذي فوق القبة فتلقيه بالترمذ وبينهما اثنا عشر فرسخاً وكانوا يسمون السادن الأكبر برمكاً لأنّهم شبهوا البيت بمكة وقالوا سادنه ابر مكة فكان كل من ولي منهم السدانة يسمى برمكاً وكانت ملوك الهند والصين وكابل شاه وغيرهم من الملوك تدين بذلك الدين وتحج إلى هذا البيت وكانت سنتهم إذا هم وافوه أن يسجدوا للصنم الأكبر ويقبلوا يد[82] برمك وكانوا قد جعلوا للبرمك ما حول النوبهار من الأرضين سبعة فراسخ في مثلها وسائر أهل ذلك الرستاق عبيد له يحكم فيهم ما يريد و كانوا قد صيروا للبيت وقوفا

the grandfather of Khālid ibn Barmak. This is indeed the case, as clarified below in the notes to the text.

79 Ibn al-Faqīh, *Mukhtaṣar Kitāb al-buldān*, ed. Michael Jan de Goeje (Leiden, 1885), pp. 322-4. Yāqūt, *Geographisches Wörterbuch*, vol. 4, pp. 817-19.

80 Previous translations appear in English (Assadullah Souren Melikian-Chirvani, 'The Buddhist Ritual in the Literature of Early Islamic Iran', in Bridget Allchin [ed.], *South Asian Archaeology 1981* [Cambridge, 1984], pp. 272-9, at p. 275, based on Ibn al-Faqīh and Yāqūt, and leaving out the part on the Barmak's life) and French (*Abrégé du Livre des pays*, trans. Henri Massé [Damascus, 1973], pp. 383-5, based on de Goeje's edition; and Assadullah Souren Melikian-Chirvani, 'L'évocation littéraire du bouddhisme dans l'Iran musulman', in *Le Monde Iranien et l'Islam: Sociétés et Cultures*, vol. 2 [Geneva, 1974], pp. 1-72, at pp. 12-14 and 21-2).

81 Mashhad ms., p. 321, l. 18 الاسبت.

82 *Yad* supplied in Yāqūt, *Geographisches Wörterbuch*, vol. 4, p. 818, l. 15.

كثيرة وضياعاً عظيمة سوى ما يحمل إليه من الهدايا التي تتجاوز كل حد[83] وسائر اموال ذلك مصروفة الى البرمك الذي يكون عليه

5. فلم يزل يليه برمك بعد برمك إلى أن افتتحت خراسان أيام عثمان بن عفان رضي الله عنه وقد صارت السدانة إلى برمك أبي برمك أبي خالد[84] فسار إلى عثمان مع دهاقين كانوا ضمنوا مالاً من[85] البلد ثم إنه رغب في الإسلام فأسلم وسمي عبد الله ورجع إلى ولده وأهله وبلده فأنكروا إسلامه وجعلوا بعض ولده برمكاً فكتب إليه نيزك طرخان وهو أحد الملوك يعظم ما أتاه من الإسلام ويدعوه إلى الرجوع في دين آبائه فأجابه برمك إني إنما دخلت في هذا الدين اختياراً له وعلماً بفضله عن غير رهبة ولا خوف[86] لم أكن لأرجع إلى دين بادي العوار مهتك الأستار فغضب نيزك وزحف إلى برمك في جمع كثيف فكتب إليه برمك قد عرفت حبي للسلامة وإني قد استنجدت[87] الملوك عليك فأنجدوني فاصرف عني أعنة خيلك وإلا حملتني على لقائك فانصرف عنه

6. ثم استغره وبيته فقتله وعشرة بنين له فلم يبق له خلف سوى برمك أبي خالد فإنّه أمّه هربت به وكان صغيراً إلى بلاد القشمير فنشأ هناك وتعلم النجوم والطب وأنواعاً من الحكمة وهو على دين آبائه ثم إن أهل بلده أصابهم طاعون ووباء فتشاءموا بمفارقة دينهم ودخولهم في الإسلام فكتبوا إلى برمك فقدم عليهم فأجلسوه في مكان أبيه وتولى النوبهار فسمي برمكاً

7. فتزوج برمك بنت الصغانيان فولدت له الحسن وبه كان يكنى وخالداً وعمراً وأم خالد وسليمان بن برمك من امرأة غيرها من أهل بخارا واهدى صاحب بخارا الى برمك جارية فولدت له كاك بن برمك وأم القسم

8. وللبرامكة أخبار كثيرة يطول أمرها وإنما ذكرنا هذا الخبر بسبب بناء النوبهار

1. [Following a list of the cities founded by Dhū 'l-Qarnayn, i.e. Alexander the Macedonian, including Balkh:] In Balkh is the Nawbahār, built by the Barmakids. ʿUmar ibn al-Azraq al-Kirmānī said:
2. The Barmakids were a noble people for a long time in Balkh before the petty kings.[88] Their religion was idol worship. Then Mecca was described to them, and the circumstances of the Kaaba therein, and the religious practice of the Quraysh and the Arabs who supported them. Therefore they made the house of the Nawbahār in imitation of the sacred house of God, and erected idols around it, adorned it with silk brocade (*al-dībāj*) and silk cloth (*al-ḥarīr*), and attached precious gems to it.

---

83 *Ḥadd* following Yāqūt, *Geographisches Wörterbuch*, vol. 4, p. 818, l. 18, rather than Mashhad ms., fol. 322, l. 10 *wāḥid*.

84 Mashhad ms., p. 322, l. 12 الى برمك أبي خالد. Clearly de Goeje's emendation of his codices (Ibn al-Faqīh, *Mukhtaṣar Kitāb al-buldān*, p. 323, l. 13) from 'Barmak ibn Barmak Abī Khālid' to 'Barmak Abī Barmak Abī Khālid' is correct, as this alone makes what follows sensible. I follow his emendation here.

85 *Min* with *ḍaminū* emending Mashhad ms., p. 322, l. 12 *fī* and Yāqūt, *Geographisches Wörterbuch*, vol. 4, p. 818, l. 21 *ʿan*.

86 The text here is uncertain between *rahba* and *la-arjiʿu*, having different readings in de Goeje's edition (Ibn al-Faqīh, *Mukhtaṣar Kitāb al-buldān*, p. 323, ll. 17-18), the Mashhad ms., p. 322, l. 16 (where the words are written unclearly), and Yāqūt (*Geographisches Wörterbuch*, vol. 4, p. 719, l. 2).

87 Mashhad ms., p. 322, l. 18 استنجرت.

88 This identifies their family origin as supposedly pre-Sasanian. The 'petty kings', *mulūk al-ṭawāʾif*, refer to the many kings who are supposed to have ruled after the destruction of Alexander.

3. The meaning of Nawbahār is 'the New' (Bahār). Their custom, whenever they built a fine building and constructed a noble vault, was to festoon it with fragrant herbs (*al-rayḥān*) and to crown it with[89] the first herbs to arise in that moment. Therefore, when they built that house, they put the first fragrant herb to spring up in that time: it was the *bahār* [oxeye], so it was named *Nawbahār*.[90]
4. The Iranians (*al-ʿAjam*) used to glorify it and make pilgrimage to it, send gifts to it, drape it in different kinds of cloth, and fix flags on top of its dome, the name of which among them was *al-Ustup* [Bactrian στοπο, from Sanskrit *stūpa*]. The dome was one hundred cubits in its diameter, its height over one hundred cubits, with circular arcades around it.[91] Around the house there were three hundred and sixty compartments in which dwelt its servants, attendants, and custodians. For each resident in those cells there was the service of a day; they did not serve again for a year. It is said that the wind would sometimes carry the silk from the flags on top of the dome and cast it to Tirmidh; the distance between the two [from there to Tirmidh] was twenty-two *farsakhs*. They used to call its chief custodian 'Barmak', because they likened the house to Mecca, and they said its custodian is 'in charge of Mecca' (*abar Makka*).[92] Whoever among them took the office of custodianship used to be called Barmak.[93] The kings of India, China, the Kābūl Shāh and other kings used to practice that religion (*dhālika al-dīn*) and make pilgrimage to that house. Their custom, whenever they arrived at it, was to bow down to the biggest idol and kiss Barmak's hand. They had granted the Barmak seven *farsakhs* in

[89] Everett Rowson informs me of another variant given in the edition of Yāqūt at his disposal: *wa-tawakhkhaw li-dhālika* 'and they had recourse for that to'. This may be preferable to the reading *wa-yutawwijū bi-dhālika* in the texts I have at hand.

[90] Melikian-Chirvani's suggestion ('The Buddhist Ritual in the Literature of Early Islamic Iran', p. 275), based on Yāqūt's text, was that the word was vowelled Nawbuhār, supposedly reflecting a Sogdian pronunciation. This must be abandoned now that the Bactrian word βαυαρο has come to light.

[91] One hundred Abbasid cubits in the time of al-Maʾmūn is 48.25 meters, or about 158.3 feet (cf. 'Dhirāʿ' in *EI*²). Xuánzàng's description says it is two hundred *chǐ* 尺 in height. One *chǐ* in the Tang period was 30.3 cm (Endymion Wilkinson, *Chinese History: A Manual, Revised and Enlarged* [Cambridge, 2000], p. 238), so he estimates it is as 60.6 meters, or 198.8 feet, in height.

[92] Middle Persian *abar* is preserved only in the Mashhad ms.; it became meaningless to other copyists who changed the phrase to *bāb Makka* 'the gate of Mecca' (as in de Goeje's edition of Ibn al-Faqīh, p. 323, l. 6), and Ibn Makka (as in Yāqūt, *Geographisches Wörterbuch*, vol. 4, p. 818, l. 12). Clearly the latter two phrases are not as apt as folk etymologies as *abar Makka* since neither captures the sound of 'Barmak' so well.

[93] In this translation, the presence or absence of the definite article before Barmak follows the Arabic text throughout this passage.

diameter[94] of the lands around the Nawbahār [de Goeje's ed.: and a farm district called Zuwān in Tokharistan, eight *farsakhs* by four *farsakhs*].[95] All the inhabitants of that district (*rustāq*)[96] were slaves of his upon whom he adjudicated however he wished. The house had many endowments of property (*wuqūf*) and great estates, beyond the extraordinary gifts that exceeded all limits, and all its wealth (*amwāl*) was for the expenses of the Barmak in charge of it.

5. Barmak after Barmak continued to administer it until Khorasan was invaded in the days of ʿUthmān ibn ʿAffān [caliph 644-56], may God be pleased with him. The office of custodian had gone to Barmak, father of Barmak who was Khālid's father.[97] Barmak went to ʿUthmān together with *dihqāns*[98] who were guarantors of money for the country.[99] Then he was attracted by Islam, so he submitted [i.e. converted to Islam] and was named ʿAbdallāh. He returned to his children, his household, and his country, but they disapproved of his Islam. They put one of his children in his place as Barmak.[100] Nēzak Ṭarkhān,[101] one of the kings, wrote to Barmak, appalled by his conversion to Islam and appealing to him to return to the religion of his fathers. Then Barmak wrote to him, 'It is only by choice, and knowing its superiority, without fear or dread, that I have entered this religion. I am not about to return to an obviously flawed

---

94 Perhaps rather 'seven square *farsakhs*'.

95 Ibn al-Faqīh, *Mukhtaṣar Kitāb al-buldān*, ed. de Goeje, p. 323, l. 10, gives this phrase where the Mashhad ms. does not.

96 Middle Persian *rōzdāg* (perhaps also a similar word in Bactrian), referring to a farm district. See 'Rustāḳ' in *EI*².

97 Here the Mashhad ms. (p. 322, l. 12) shows a haplography, *ilā Barmak Abī Khālid*, where de Goeje's edition (p. 323, l. 13) has a correct emendation *ilā Barmak Abī Barmak Abī Khālid* (the codices at de Goeje's disposal had *ilā Barmak ibn Barmak Abī Khālid*, with the easy confusion of *ibn* and *abī*).

98 *Dihqāns* were the traditional aristocratic land-owning class in Iran. Both Yāqūt and de Goeje's edition have instead the similarly spelled *rahāʾin*, 'hostages'.

99 De Goeje, p. 323, ll. 13-14 has a different sentence here: 'Barmak went to ʿUthmān among hostages given as security (*fī rahāʾin*) and went down to Medina'. I cannot tell whether the sense of the verb *ḍaminū* is that these were aristocrats liable for the produce of their land as taxes or whether, as hostages, they were guarantors of a treaty in favour of the Arabs. See 'Ḍamān' in *EI*².

100 Here the Mashhad ms. has an illegible word made clear by Yāqūt, *Geographisches Wörterbuch*, vol. 4, p. 818, l. 22. De Goeje's edition, p. 323, ll. 14-15: 'He returned to his children and the Barmak-hood (*al-barmakatu*) went to one of his children'.

101 Nēzak Ṭarkhān is a name apparently held by several rulers of Tokharistan (as suggested by Grenet, 'Regional Interaction in Central Asia and Northwest India', pp. 214-18). See also 'Ṭarkhān' and 'Nīzak, Ṭarkhān' in *EI*². The title ταρχανο occurs in three Bactrian documents, dated about 629-671, and in the Bactrian letter jg.1 (BD2 pp. 134-5 and p. 269a), though not with the name Nēzak.

religion, the shame of which has been laid bare'. Nēzak became angry and advanced toward Barmak with a strong troop. The Barmak wrote to him, 'You already know my love of peace. I have asked the kings for help against you, and they have responded, so turn the reins of your horses back from me, lest you compel me to meet you'. So he turned back from him.

6. Then he [Nēzak Ṭarkhān] came to him by surprise with a night attack, and killed him and ten of his sons. He had no successor remaining except the Barmak, that is, the father of Khālid, for his mother fled with him, he being still a child, to the land of Qashmīr. He grew up there and studied astrology, medicine, and the branches of philosophy (*anwāʿan min al-ḥikma*), while remaining in the religion of his ancestors. A plague and pestilence befell the people of his country and they took it as a bad omen due to abandoning their religion and entering Islam, so they wrote to Barmak and he came to them. They seated him in his father's place and he took over control of the Nawbahār, and he was called Barmak.
7. He married a daughter of the king of Čaghāniyān. She bore for him al-Ḥasan, for whom he was given the *kunya* Abū 'l-Ḥasan, and Khālid, ʿUmar, and Umm Khālid. Sulaymān ibn Barmak was from another woman from the people of Bukhara. The lord of Bukhara had given a slave girl to Barmak as a bride. She bore for him Kāl ibn Barmak[102] and Umm al-Qāsim.
8. There are many historical reports about the Barmakids, but it was because of the building of the Nawbahār that we wanted only [to give] this report in particular.

Sections 1 and 8 of this translation are Ibn al-Faqīh's introduction and conclusion. Sections 2-7 are part of the al-Kirmānī's report written down *c.*800, either just before or just after the fall of the Barmakids. Modern scholars have not addressed the ideological significance of this report, but instead have mined it for information about Bactrian Buddhism or dismissed it as purely legendary. It is indeed a very important source about Buddhism in Tokharistan,[103] but it was preserved only because it conveys special messages about the status of the Barmakids. The purpose of sections 2-4 of the report is to show that, before Islam, the Barmakid family enjoyed a prestige among the Iranians and indeed among all eastern nations like that of Quraysh among the Arabs. This is totally explicit. All the kings of the entire east bowed down to them and respected them. The implicit message is that they are the Iranian twins of the Hāshimite

---

102 Mashhad ms., p. 323, l. 7: Kāk ibn Barmak. Kāl or Kāk is evidently a Bactrian name. Cf. perhaps Bactrian letter cq (BD2), designated as from καλ, an abbreviation of the full name καλοοιαρδαγο appearing in the letter's opening address.

103 Melikian-Chirvani, 'The Buddhist Ritual in the Literature of Early Islamic Iran', pp. 275-6. David Alan Scott, 'The Iranian Face of Buddhism', *East and West*, 40 (1990): pp. 43-77, at pp. 64-5.

Abbasid caliphs, whose viziers they became, and that these Barmakids by right of inheritance should continue to receive high honours. It is emphasized that they were extraordinarily wealthy even before their conversion to Islam, and that everyone bore rich gifts to them. The Nawbahār at Balkh is equivalent to the Kaaba at Mecca; this is no small assertion about the status of Balkh. The claim this passage makes about the Barmakids' enduring inheritance is typical of Arabic literature around the time of the Barmakids, when massive genealogical works were compiled to prove whose family had precedence.[104] It justifies the success of the Barmakids under the Abbasids by emphasizing their glorious and wealthy past. They enjoy their status by right of inheritance.

Despite the tendentious character of the report, there can be no doubt that much of the information it contains is authentic, since the descriptions of Buddhist practices and the institution of the Nawbahār exactly match what is known from neighbouring regions. The religion of the Barmakids was recognized as a distinct religion (*dīn*) followed also by kings of India, China, and Kābul. The monastery and the *stūpa* received lavish gifts and donations from their supporters. *Stūpas* are objects of pilgrimage, and so was the Nawbahār. The *stūpa* was richly decorated and silk flags, banners, or pennants, flying from the top of the dome of the *stūpa*. There was a large statue before which people prostrated themselves. Servants of the shrine lived in cells around the *stūpa*, in a type of Buddhist architecture perhaps like that known from neighbouring regions.[105] Contemporary Buddhist monasteries in China and India possessed inalienable land properties, called in China *fēng* 封, or appanage, and so did the Nawbahār, called by the Arabic term for religious endowments of this type, *waqf*.[106] Huìchāo says, for example, that in Kashmir, 'Whenever a monastery is built, a village and its inhabitants are immediately donated as an offering to the Three Jewels. Building a monastery without making any donation of a village and its folk is not done.'[107] In China, the workers on these properties were practically owned by the monasteries. Moreover, monasteries in China sometimes did possess true slaves for menial tasks and cleaning.[108] Huìchāo says again of Kashmir, 'Since there are no slaves [in India], it is necessary to donate villages and their inhabitants'.[109] Whatever their exact legal status near Balkh, the Nawbahār possessed land

104 'Nasab' in *EI*².

105 Until archaeological investigation around Balkh discovers the exact site, it is possible to see examples of *stūpas* surrounded by cells in reference works such as Pierre Pichard and François Lagirarde (eds), *The Buddhist Monastery: A Cross-Cultural Survey* (Paris, 2003), pp. 32-3.

106 The monastic codes (*vinayas*) specified that land properties were held by the monastic establishment in perpetuity (Jacques Gernet, *Buddhism in Chinese Society* [New York, 1995], pp. 67-8).

107 *The Hye-Ch'o Diary*, p. 47.

108 Gernet, *Buddhism in Chinese Society*, pp. 94-141.

109 *The Hye-Ch'o Diary*, p. 47.

endowments populated by what are described as slaves (*ʿabīd*) by al-Kirmānī's source. All these practices are typical of monasteries and *stūpas* in neighbouring countries in the same period.[110]

Specific terminology shows that al-Kirmānī's source knew real Bactrian words, though evidently not the Bactrian language. The name of the Nawbahār has long been recognized as meaning 'New (Buddhist) Monastery'. The Bactrian documents show us in fact that the name Nawbahār is a Bactrian word, naturalizing what would be in Sanskrit *navavihāra*.[111] The spurious folk etymology, connecting the monastery's name with fragrant herbs, shows that the true meaning was lost within a short time of the Arab conquest.[112] The dome at the Nawbahār is called *al-Ustup*, obviously a rendering of the Bactrian loan-word στοπο, from Indic for a reliquary monument, or *stūpa*.[113] As seen above, the title of the custodian, Barmak, is interpreted in the text by a tendentious folk etymology to prove that the Nawbahār was a pious and well-intended imitation of Mecca. More than sixty years ago, however, Harold Bailey recognized the name Barmak as a Bactrian word derived from Sanskrit *pramukha*, meaning 'chief' or

---

110 See also Melikian-Chirvani, 'Buddhism ii. In Islamic Times', in *EIr.*

111 Bactrian βαυαρο '*vihāra*' is mentioned in BD1, Document V, line 24 and Document W, 21, 19. The adjective for 'new' in Bactrian is written νωγο by itself, but in compounds, νω- is attested, as in βιδδιιο-νω-σαρδο 'Second (month of the) new year' Document T, line 1. νωγοσαρδο '(first month of the) new year' is transcribed into Arabic script as *nwsrd*, apparently indicating that the final -γο had ceased to be pronounced (Nicholas Sims-Williams and François de Blois, 'The Bactrian Calendar', *Bulletin of the Asia Institute*, 10 [1996]: pp. 149-65, at pp. 158-9, 161).

As late as the eleventh century, the Khwārizmian polymath al-Bīrūnī could report the word *bahār* in a discussion of the sect we know as Buddhists, whom he knew by the eastern Iranian name *shamanān*, saying 'their monuments, the *bahār*s of their idols (*bahārāt aṣnāmihim*) and their *farkhār*s are visible on the borders of Khurāsān adjacent to India' (*Chronologie orientalischer Völker von Albêrûnî*, ed. Eduard Sachau [Leipzig, 1878], p. 206). This obviously refers to Bactria and its mountains. *Farkhār* was the Sogdian (and Khwarezmian?) word for a Buddhist *vihāra* (*βrγʾr*, *frγʾr*; see Émile Benveniste, *Études sogdiennes* [Wiesbaden, 1979], pp. 22-3, and Badr-ol Zaman Gharib, *Sogdian Dictionary* [Tehran, 1995], pp. 108b and 154a). Al-Bīrūnī knew something of Buddhist cosmology and belief in reincarnation as well, as he relates. For him, however, Buddhism was only one survival of the primordial, Ṣābiʾan religion of idol-worship, another manifestation of which was Hellenic paganism.

112 Melikian-Chirvani ('L'évocation littéraire du bouddhisme', p. 15) cites M. Filliozat, saying that the practice of using fragrant herbs in this way is authentic.

113 It is interesting to note that the originally long vowel of *stūpa* has become short. Perhaps this reflects either a feature of the Bactrian language or the ambiguity of vowel length in the Bactrian script, or (less likely) that the vowel was shortened in Arabic as a normal result of a *sukūn* on the final letter.

'leader'.[114] The title is also attested in Khotanese documents and it appears in the Tibetan *Li yul lung bstan pa* as *bar-mag*.[115] Nevertheless, the practical significance of the title and the nature of the office to which it referred are still unknown and should form the subject of a future study.

Al-Kirmānī then relates another tale, in section 5 and the beginning of section 6, doubtless also fictional, designed to give the Barmakids another kind of glory: priority in Islam. The father of the Barmak – that is, the second to last man to bear the title Barmak – allegedly converted to Islam after visiting the early caliph ʿUthmān in Medina. It is impossible to believe that a Buddhist official from Tokharistan would have travelled to Arabia to convert to Islam when the Arabs had only begun to raid Khorasan. Upon the Barmak's return to Tokharistan, the new convert was allegedly threatened by the local Türk ruler, who advanced with an army, for abandoning his religion. This second-to-last Barmak defied him, saying he had powerful friends to protect him, and at first this Türk was held at bay by the threat. The story superficially resembles the tale related by Xuánzàng about the Türk, son of the Yabghu Khan, who recently wanted to attack the New Vihāra there to plunder its riches, but was deterred by the *deva* Vaiśravaṇa, protector of the monastery.[116] It is conceivable, though unlikely and impossible to verify, that the tale related to al-Kirmānī about the threat against the Barmak reflects a distorted narrative of this early seventh-century event.

In any case, when the second-to-last Barmak and most of his family were killed by Nēzak's treachery, his wife fled, bearing his sole surviving son to Kashmir. It is with this child that we encounter a historical figure, the father of Khālid. He was raised and educated in Kashmir in his ancestral 'idol-worshipping' religion, and he would eventually return to become the Barmak who fathered the viziers of the Abbasids. There is no reason for his immediate descendants to have fabricated a story about studies in Kashmir (it cannot have enhanced the prestige of the Barmakids in any special way) and there is every reason to expect them to know about their immediate ancestor's upbringing. Indeed, while even the hereditary character of the office of Barmak is subject to doubt without further information about what a *pramukha*'s status entailed, we can be sure that the father of Khālid was the last Barmak, and that he had studied in Kashmir.

---

114 Harold Walter Bailey, 'Iranica', *Bulletin of the School of Oriental and African Studies*, 11/1 (1943): pp. 1-5, at p. 2.

115 Tibetan *par-mog*, *bar-mag*, Khotanese *prramuha-*, Ronald Emmerick, *Tibetan Texts Concerning Khotan* (London, 1967), p. 137; Harold Walter Bailey, 'Hvatanica IV', *Bulletin of the School of Oriental and African Studies*, 10/4 (1942): pp. 886-924, at p. 921. For resolution of initial cluster *pra-* in Bactrian cf. the Indic loanword in Bactrian πραμανο / παρομανο /parmān/ 'authoritative' ultimately from Sanskrit *pramāṇa* (BD2, pp. 251-2). For Barmak, one would expect Bactrian *πραμοκο, *παρμοκο or *παρομοκο.

116 Beal, *Si-Yu-Ki*, vol. 1, pp. 44-5. Vihāras normally had protective *devas*, as seen in the examples from Khotan in the *Li Yul Lung bstan pa*, passim.

The subjects that the Barmak studied there are cited as *nujūm*, *ṭibb* and *anwāʿ min al-ḥikma*: astrology, medicine and different branches of philosophy.

It is relevant, therefore, to review what is known about Kashmiri scholarship of the seventh and eighth centuries, to determine why it would make a desirable destination for the last Barmak and his mother, or what in particular he might have studied there. Historians of Buddhism have long known that Kashmir was an important centre of Buddhist scholarship from very early times. It remained so in the late seventh and early eighth century. Texts on logic, *abhidharma*, commentaries on canonical texts, and medical works were composed in Sanskrit in Kashmir in this period.[117] It is impossible to know exactly what years the Barmak spent there, except that it was before he came to the court of Hishām (reg. 724-43) and probably also before the birth of Khālid in 709.

The twelfth-century Sanskrit history of Kashmir, Kalhaṇa's *Rājataraṅgiṇī*, based on earlier, lost sources, describes the ascent of the powerful Kārkoṭa dynasty there in this period, and, among other things, their foundation of a large number of Buddhist monasteries and *stūpas*. The eighth-century Kārkoṭan king Lalitāditya-Muktāpīḍa receives a lot of attention in this history, because under his leadership Kashmir is supposed to have conquered surrounding regions and to have repelled foreign invaders, no doubt enriching the country greatly. Among their foreign foes was *Mummuni*, tentatively interpreted by Lévi and Chavannes as a garbled rendition of *al-muʾminīn* (Arabic for 'the commander of the believers', i.e. the Caliph).[118] The *Rājataraṅgiṇī* also relates that under Lalitāditya-Muktāpīḍa, a sage from Tokharistan (*Tuḥkhāradeśa*) named Caṅkuṇa, 'brother of the alchemist (*rasasiddha*) Kaṅkaṇavarṣa', was brought to the Kashmiri court, where he became court minister and allegedly produced a great deal of gold by magical means. Both he and his wife, as well as his son-in-law, the physician Īśānacandra, founded *vihāras* in Kashmir.[119]

Unfortunately, the chronology of these Kashmiri kings is not entirely clear. Aurel Stein calculated that Muktāpīḍa's reign lasted 699-735 based on his reading

---

117 Jean Naudou, *Buddhists of Kaśmīr* (Delhi, 1980), esp. pp. 61-77. Charles Willemen, Bart Dessein and Collett Cox, *Sarvāstivāda Buddhist Scholasticism* (Leiden, 1998), pp. 138-254. Ronald Emmerick, 'Ravigupta's Place in Indian Medical Tradition', *Indologica Taurensia*, 3-4 (1975-76): pp. 209-21, esp. pp. 219-21. See also, in general, Hartmut Scharfe, *Education in Ancient India* (Leiden, 2002).

118 Sylvain Lévi and Édouard Chavannes, 'L'itinéraire d'*Ou-k'ong* (751-790)', *Journal Asiatique*, 6 (9e série) (1895): pp. 341-84, p. 354, on Kalhaṇa, *Rājataraṅginī*, ed. and trans. Marc Aurel Stein (3 vols, Delhi, 1892-1900; repr. 1979 and 1987), IV.167 (where see Stein's note to his translation of the text). Hermann Goetz, 'The Conquest of Northern and Western India by Lalitāditya-Muktāpīḍa of Kashmīr', *Journal of the Bombay Branch Royal Asiatic Society*, 28/1 (1952): pp. 43ff.; repr. in id., *Studies in the History and Art of Kashmir and the Indian Himalaya* (Wiesbaden, 1969), pp. 8-22 presents a case arguing that the conquests of Lalitāditya-Muktāpīḍa reached very far abroad, but the argument is full of speculation.

119 Kalhaṇa, *Rājataraṅginī*, vol. 1, pp. 143-7 (IV.211-12, 215-16 and 246-64).

of Kalhaṇa. However, as he soon acknowledged, this conflicts with the dates of envoys to China from the different Kashmiri kings as given in the Chinese court chronicle *Tángshū* 唐書; these Chinese reports would require Muktāpīḍa's 37-year reign to begin no earlier than 724, if Kalhaṇa's terms of reigns are to be accepted.[120] In any case, it is certainly excessive to suppose that this Caṅkuṇa from Tokharistan, or his son-in-law, was the Barmak himself (the chronology does not seem to permit it), or even a Barmakid, but it does show that scholars and aristocrats from Tokharistan did visit Kashmir. Then again, if the Barmak was related to rulers of Tokharistan, a family connection cannot be ruled out.

The Chinese traveller Wùkōng 悟空 went to Kashmir in 759 and stayed for four years, taking ordination as a Buddhist monk and learning Sanskrit (*fànyǔ* 梵語).[121] His book on his travels notes the presence of three hundred monasteries there, at one of which – probably one founded by the king Muktāpīḍa himself[122] – Wùkōng studied the Mūlasarvāstivāda *vinaya*. Just over a century before, Xuánzàng reported the existence of one hundred monasteries in Kashmir.[123] Even if the figures are imprecise, and the number of monasteries did not exactly triple in this time, one has a strong impression that Buddhism flourished greatly there and found lavish support between 650 and 750.[124] Huìchāo says as much around 726: 'The kings, the chiefs, and the common people greatly revere the Three Jewels' in Kashmir.[125] Among the prominent monasteries that Wùkōng lists are a *vihāra* founded by Caṅkuṇa 將軍, a striking verification of the Sanskrit report of Kalhaṇa much later, and two other *vihāra*s, one founded by the Yě-lǐ *Tegin[126] 也里特勤, 'son of the king of the Türks', and another founded by the *Qatun (*kědūn* 可敦), queen of the Türks.[127] This implies political and family connections between the court of Kashmir and that of the Türks, including aristocratic visitors from Tokharistan, further confirming the impression one takes from Kalhaṇa of relations between the rulers of the two regions in the early eighth century. All of this adds verisimilitude to al-Kirmānī's report that the Barmak came from Balkh to study in Kashmir. It was a thriving centre of

---

120 Naudou, *Buddhists of Kaśmīr*, p. 266. Marc Aurel Stein, 'Notes on Ou-k'ong's Account of Kaçmīr', *Sitzungsberichte der Kaiserlichen Adademie der Wissenschaften in Wien, phil.-hist. Cl.*, 135 (Vienna, 1896): pp. 1-32, at p. 2, n. 2. Cf. Édouard Chavannes, *Documents sur les Tou-Kiue (Turcs) occidentaux* (St.-Petersburg, 1903), pp. 166-7.

121 Lévi and Chavannes, 'L'itinéraire d'*Ou-k'ong* (751-790)', pp. 354-6.

122 Stein, 'Notes on Ou-k'ong's Account of Kaçmīr', pp. 5-7.

123 Beal, *Si-Yu-Ki*, vol. 1, p. 148.

124 Stein, 'Notes on Ou-k'ong's Account of Kaçmīr', p. 21, has already made this observation.

125 *The Hye-Ch'o Diary*, p. 46.

126 Chavannes, *Documents sur les Tou-Kiue (Turcs) occidentaux*, p. 367b. See also Stein, 'Notes on Ou-k'ong's Account of Kaçmīr', pp. 19-21.

127 Lévi and Chavannes, 'L'itinéraire d'*Ou-k'ong* (751-790)', pp. 354-5.

Buddhist scholarship where members of the ruling elite of Tokharistan invested considerable resources and enjoyed personal connections.

Melikian-Chirvani suggests that the collapse of the Buddhist kingdoms of eastern Iran provoked a wave of immigration from there to Kashmir.[128] Since so many sources of Tibetan Buddhism were in Kashmir during this very period, future research should look for signs that Bactrian Buddhism was part of what the Tibetans received.

To return to al-Kirmānī's account: Eventually the Barmak was summoned back to Balkh to take the role and title of Barmak at the Nawbahār. There he had a family, the description of which closes al-Kirmānī's report as cited by Ibn al-Faqīh (Part 7 of the translation above). The continuity of the narrative afterwards is broken because the other known citations of al-Kirmānī are somewhat disconnected.[129] We are told that the Barmak was brought later with a number of other Khorasani hostages to the Umayyad caliph Hishām ibn ʿAbd al-Malik in al-Ruṣāfa in Syria, where he converted to Islam. Hishām's reign (724-43) is indeed the period in which Balkh was brought totally under control by the Arabs, in that the city itself was occupied by the Arab garrison.

By this time, the Barmak already had children by a princess (*bint malik*) of Čaghāniyān, a valley in the north of Tokharistan that was part of the Bactrian language area, as implied by Xuánzàng.[130] One of these children was Khālid, born in 709 according to Ibn ʿAsākir.[131] As a youth (*ṣabīy*) Khālid accompanied his father the Barmak to the court of Hishām, but he had already spent his early years in Tokharistan.[132] There can be little doubt that, before arriving in Syria, Khālid's first language was Bactrian, the language of both his parents, and that his first religion was that of the Nawbahār, Buddhism. Thereafter, al-Kirmānī relates, Khālid grew up in the Umayyad court as a very close friend of the Arab prince Maslama ibn Hishām ibn ʿAbd al-Malik.[133] Khālid developed fluency in Arabic, the subject of a later report, in which he nevertheless identifies himself as 'Iranian' (*min al-ʿAjam*).[134] Supposedly his father, the Barmak, held that the caliphate belonged to the heirs of the prophet, and this encouraged Khālid to work for the Abbasid *daʿwa* in Jurjān already in 742-743, after his family had returned to Khorasan.[135]

---

128 Melikian-Chirvani, 'L'évocation littéraire du bouddhisme', p. 22.

129 Bosworth, 'Abū Ḥafṣ 'Umar al-Kirmānī', has collected, translated, and masterfully commented on many of these reports and what follows here is based on his work.

130 Beal, *Si-Yu-Ki*, pp. 36-9. Xuánzàng found five Buddhist monasteries in Čaghāniyān.

131 Bosworth, 'Abū Ḥafṣ 'Umar al-Kirmānī', p. 271.

132 Ibn al-ʿAdīm, *Bughyat al-ṭalab fī tārīkh Ḥalab*, ed. Suhayl Zakkār (12 vols, Damascus, 1988-89), vol. 7, p. 3019.

133 Bosworth, 'Abū Ḥafṣ 'Umar al-Kirmānī', p. 274. Ibn al-ʿAdīm, *Bughyat al-ṭalab*, vol. 7, p. 3019.

134 Not 'Persian', as rendered by Bosworth, 'Abū Ḥafṣ 'Umar al-Kirmānī', p. 275. Ibn al-ʿAdīm, *Bughyat al-ṭalab*, vol. 7, p. 3021.

135 Bosworth, 'Abū Ḥafṣ 'Umar al-Kirmānī', pp. 272 and 274-5.

The Barmak's medical education was useful in Hishām's court. He is said to have treated Maslama for infertility (and this is, according to al-Kirmānī, on the authority of Maslama's own son, the product of the prescription).[136] The last we ever hear of the Barmak himself is that in 725-26 Asad ibn ʿAbdallāh, governor of Khorasan, put him in charge of rebuilding the city of Balkh, when the Arab army camp moved into the city.[137] Presumably the Barmak was eventually able to retire to Balkh, but one cannot say for certain what became of him.

In fewer than twenty years after his arrival at the court of Hishām, the Barmak's son Khālid had become politically active back in Khorasan. He became the chief secretary for the Abbasid revolution and then for the new Abbasid administration. For these roles he must have been literate, skilled in arithmetic and knowledgeable in the administration of lands. From the first Abbasid successes, Khālid ibn Barmak is said to have been in charge of the *dīwān*s of the army and the *kharāj*.[138] According to al-Kirmānī, it was Khālid who first organized the records of the *dīwān* of the army in bound books (*dafātir*) rather than 'loose documents rolled up in scrolls' (*ṣuḥuf mudraja*).[139] As new Arabic documents from Tokharistan become available, it may be possible to discern administrative innovations of Khālid ibn Barmak.

Several anecdotes surviving from al-Kirmānī emphasize the extraordinarily close living arrangements that arose between the Barmakid family and the Abbasid family. Already the mutual suckling relationship of the Abbasid and Barmakid women has been noted, an ancient Arab practice.[140] We also have such remarkable statements attributed to the first Abbasid caliph Abū 'l-ʿAbbās as this one:[141]

قال ابن الأزرق وقال له أبو العباس يوماً وخرج على الناس يوماً وأحب أن يعرفهم مكانه منه يا خالد ما أحد أخص بأمير المؤمنين منك أنت معي وأهلك مع أهلي وولدك مع ولدي

> Ibn al-Azraq [al-Kirmānī] said: Abū 'l-ʿAbbās said to him [i.e. to Khālid ibn Barmak] one day, when he went out before the people (of his court) one day

---

136 Bosworth, 'Abū Ḥafṣ 'Umar al-Kirmānī', p. 274. Ibn al-ʿAdīm, *Bughyat al-ṭalab*, vol. 7, p. 3019.

137 Ṭabarī, *Tārīkh al-rusul wa'l-mulūk*, series 2, part 3, p. 1490, under year 107 (i.e. 725-26).

138 Ṭabarī, *Tārīkh al-rusul wa'l-mulūk*, years 132-35 (749-53, end of each year's entry) lists Khālid as in charge of the *dīwān al-kharāj*, showing that he held this role very early. See Bosworth, 'Abū Ḥafṣ 'Umar al-Kirmānī', pp. 275-6, Ibn al-ʿAdīm, *Bughyat al-ṭalab*, vol. 7, p. 3022.

139 Translation of the phrase by Bosworth, 'Abū Ḥafṣ 'Umar al-Kirmānī', pp. 275-6. Ibn al-ʿAdīm, *Bughyat al-ṭalab*, vol. 7, p. 3022. Ibn al-Azraq remarks that the *dīwān* of the army remained organized as *dafātir* until his own time.

140 See note 5 above.

141 Ibn al-ʿAdīm, *Bughyat al-ṭalab*, vol. 7, p. 3022. Bosworth, 'Abū Ḥafṣ 'Umar al-Kirmānī', p. 276.

> and wanted to let them know his relationship to him, 'O Khālid, no one is more intimate with the Commander of the Believers than you. You are together with me, your household is together with my household, and your children are together with my children.'

Such close relations between the families eventually led to the promotion of Khālid's son Yaḥyā, the Barmak's grandson. Yaḥyā was tutor of the caliph al-Mahdī's son Hārūn and, late in the eighth century, after his student became the caliph al-Rashīd, Yaḥyā became the principal administrator of the entire empire. Yaḥyā probably grew up largely away from Tokharistan in a mostly Muslim, Arabic-speaking, imperial court. One can only wonder if he ever learned to speak Bactrian, as his father and, no doubt, many of his less privileged and less successful relatives in Tokharistan continued to do.

YAḤYĀ AL-BARMAKĪ'S INTEREST IN INDIA AND SANSKRIT SCIENCES

Sources tell that the great vizier Yaḥyā al-Barmakī was a patron of scholars and poets, and he himself dabbled in the sciences.[142] He took an interest in discussions of religion, and, along with his family and some of his associates, he was suspected of secretly-held heretical views, or *zandaqa*.[143] The contemporary philologist al-Aṣmaʿī (d. 828) composed mocking verses about the Barmakids on the occasion of their fall from power: 'When polytheism (*al-shirk*) is mentioned in a learned session, the Barmakids' faces light up / and if a verse (of the Qurʾān) is recited among them, they bring stories about Mazdak.'[144] (Mazdak was a famous pre-Islamic Iranian heretic.)[145]

---

142 His own works are lost, including 'The Book of Experiences', *Kitāb al-tajārib* (Franz Rosenthal, 'From Arabic Books and Manuscripts', *Journal of the American Oriental Society*, 83/4 [1963]: pp. 452-7, at p. 455) and a book on perfume (*Fihrist*, p. 317). Al-Nadīm lists Yaḥyā al-Barmakī as one of many authors on alchemy (*Fihrist*, p. 353). He wrote a little poetry (*Fihrist*, p. 166).

143 *Fihrist*, p. 338: 'It is said that every one of the Barmakids, except Muḥammad ibn Khālid ibn Barmak, was a *zindīq*'. On the history of the term *zandaqa* see 'Zindīḳ' in *EI*². Muḥammad ibn Layth al-Khaṭīb, secretary of Yaḥyā al-Barmakī, was suspected of *zandaqa* (*Fihrist*, p. 120; he also wrote a book for Yaḥyā of *adab* and *ḥikam*, *Fihrist*, p. 315), as was Abān al-Lāḥiqī, their favourite poet ('Abān b. ʿAbd al-Ḥamīd al-Lāḥiḳī', in *EI*²). On the other hand, he supported Hishām ibn al-Ḥakam, a contentious Shiite fond of writing refutations, including a refutation of the *zanādiqa* (*Fihrist*, pp. 175-6).

144 Al-Jahshiyārī, *Kitāb al-Wuzarāʾ*, p. 252. El-Hibri (*Reinterpreting Islamic Historiography*, p. 45, n. 73) suggests that the accusation of heresy would invalidate Jaʿfar's marriage to ʿAbbāsa, and that the story of their marriage could have arisen 'as a corollary of the *zandaqa* charges'.

145 The 'Mazdakite' movement is supposed to have lasted beyond the ninth century in eastern Iran. Among other things, it is supposed to have entailed 'sharing women',

Yaḥyā al-Barmakī had a conspicuous concern for Indian religions and Indian medicine. Al-Nadīm wrote:[146]

الذي عني بامر الهند في دولة العرب يحيى بن خالد وجماعة البرامكة ويوشك ان يكون هذه الحكاية صحيحة اذا اضفناها الى ما نعرف من اخبار البرامكة واهتمامها بامر الهند واحضارها علماء طبها وحكمائها

> The one who was concerned with the subject of India under the Arab dynasty was Yaḥyā ibn Khālid ibn Barmak, as well as the Barmakids in general. This story is probably true, when we relate to it what we know from the history of the Barmakids,[147] their interest in the subject of India, and the fact that they summoned Indian medical scientists and Indian philosophers.

Al-Nadīm then records a few excerpts of a report on Indian religion written for Yaḥyā al-Barmakī, which he knew in a manuscript copy written by the philosopher al-Kindī. According to al-Kindī's sources, Yaḥyā had sent a mission to India for two purposes: to collect Indian medicinal plants and to learn about the religions there. The surviving portion of the report mentions the way to India from Balkh and discusses the giant Buddha statues at Bāmiyān (located in the Bactrian language area), among other things.[148]

Vladimir Minorsky argued that many of the later reports on India circulating in early Arabic and Persian literature derive in one way or another from this lost book written originally for Yaḥyā al-Barmakī. These include the accounts on India, or portions of them, by Ibn Khurradādhbih, al-Maqdisī, al-Marwazī, Gardīzī, al-Shahrastānī and others. If this is correct, the book written for Yaḥyā may well have been the most important source on Indian religions available west of India before al-Bīrūnī.[149] Minorsky's theory has found some confirmation in a

---

perhaps on the pattern of Bactrian polyandry. Abān al-Lāḥiqī, poet of the Barmakids, is supposed to have composed a poem of the story of Mazdak. See 'Mazdak' and 'Abān b. 'Abd al-Ḥamīd al-Lāḥiḳī' in *EI*[2].

146 The passage just translated is based on al-Nadīm, *Kitāb al-fihrist*, ed. Riḍā Tajaddud (Tehran, 1971), p. 409, which has a more complete and grammatical sentence than *Fihrist*, p. 345.

147 It is possible that the phrase *akhbār al-Barāmika* here refers to the title of al-Kirmānī's book.

148 *Fihrist*, p. 345 and the following pages. The passage just translated is based on *Fihrist*, ed. Tajaddud, p. 409.

149 Vladimir Minorsky, *Sharaf al-Zamān Ṭāhir Marvazī on China, the Turks and India* (London, 1942), pp. 6-11 and 125-42; id., 'Gardīzī on India', *Bulletin of the School of Oriental and African Studies*, 12 (1947-48): pp. 625-40, at p. 626. On many of the same texts, see also Daniel Gimaret, 'Bouddha et les bouddhistes dans la tradition musulmane', *Journal Asiatique*, 258 (1969): pp. 273-316.

study by Bruce Lawrence, but the reconstruction of the report written for Yaḥyā al-Barmakī requires further research.[150]

The Barmakids had a hospital in Baghdad (*bīmāristān al-Barāmika*),[151] at which Yaḥyā indeed employed Indian physicians who translated Sanskrit medical works into Arabic. Two translators who worked there are named: Ibn Dahn[152] and Manka, both bearing apparently truncated Indian names.[153] Among the Sanskrit medical books they translated were the *Suśruta*, the *Aṣṭāṅgahṛdaya-saṃhitā* of Vāgbhaṭa and the *Siddhasāra* of Ravigupta.[154] According to the modern editor of the *Siddhasāra*, Ronald Emmerick, the latter text was probably composed in Kashmir by Ravigupta in about 650 CE.[155] Vāgbhaṭa, author of the *Aṣṭāṅgahṛdaya*, was also apparently a Kashmiri of the mid-seventh century.[156] That would mean that these two medical works, both translated by Ibn Dahn for Yaḥyā al-Barmakī, were current, fairly new texts in Kashmir when the Barmak studied medicine there. It seems more than fortuitous that the Barmak's grandson in Baghdad sent for Indian translators and had these two particular Kashmiris' works translated. Translations of some of these same works from Sanskrit into Tibetan were carried out in the late eighth to the eleventh centuries; two of them

150 Bruce Lawrence, *Shahrastānī on the Indian Religions* (The Hague, 1976).

151 *Fihrist*, p. 245.

152 The name usually Romanized as Ibn Dahn probably represents an Indian name beginning with *dh-*. Ibn Dahn is called master of the hospital (*Ṣāḥib al-bīmāristān*) (*Fihrist*, p. 303).

153 *Fihrist*, p. 245, ed. Tajaddud, p. 303. The latter passage lists twelve works translated from 'the Indian language' (*al-Hindī*, meaning Sanskrit) into Arabic. Three translators are named, and two, Manka and Ibn Dahn, are explicitly stated to have worked in the hospital of the Barmakids as their translators; three of the twelve medical works are explicitly attributed to them. As for the other nine works, whose Sanskrit names are sometimes distorted beyond recognition, one may suppose that the same translators were responsible for them. The third translator, ʿAbdallāh ibn ʿAlī, is said to have put a work into Persian (*al-Fārisī*) first, and then into Arabic. It is now perhaps questionable, however, whether 'Persian' always refers to Middle Persian, and not to Bactrian. The same doubt perhaps applies to other works reputed to be early translations from *al-Fārisī*. An anecdote preserved by Ibn Qutayba, *Kitāb ʿuyūn al-akhbār* (4 vols, Cairo, 1925-30), vol. 1, pp. 24-5, tells how Manka al-Hindī served Yaḥyā ibn Khālid as a physician and consoled the latter in prison; Manka is characterized as practicing astrology as a part of his medicine.

154 *Fihrist*, p. 303, Manfred Ullmann, *Die Medizin im Islam* (Leiden, 1970), pp. 104-6.

155 Emmerick, 'Ravigupta's Place in Indian Medical Tradition'.

156 Claus Vogel, *Vāgbhaṭa's Aṣṭāṅgahṛdayasaṃhitā: The First Five Chapters of its Tibetan Version* (Wiesbaden, 1965), p. 13: 'Judging by the fact that he (Vāgbhaṭa) expressly defines Āndhra and Draviḍa as the names of two southern peoples or kingdoms and repeatedly mentions Kashmirian terms for particular plants, he is likely to have been a Northerner and a native of Kashmir.' Vogel (p. 18) also suggests that the work gives evidence of 'Buddhistic tendencies'.

subsequently became part of the Tibetan Buddhist canon.[157] One may suspect that the coincidence between the works translated into Arabic and Tibetan is due to widespread use of them in the training of physicians in northern India, and specifically in Kashmir, from the seventh century onward.

In Arabic, these works of Sanskrit origin could not compete with the huge number of translations of Galen that were to follow in the next several decades. Physicians in Syria and Mesopotamia were already using Galenic medicine and were probably unwilling to accept a foreign system that differed in its very principles from that of their accustomed practice.[158] Consequently, only a few of the Sanskrit translations, as well as a number of citations from them in Arabic medical compendia, survive. One of the few Arabic authors to give them special attention was a court physician of the caliphs, ʿAlī ibn Rabban al-Ṭabarī (fl. *c.*830-50). He included in an appendix to his compendium, *Firdaws al-ḥikma*, a summary of Indian medicine based on these translations. In this he cited the work of Caraka, the *Suśruta*, the *Nidāna* of Mādhava and the *Aṣṭāṅgahṛdaya* of Vāgbhaṭa, fully aware that the Indian system conflicted in several respects with that of 'the Roman philosophers' (*falāsifat al-Rūm*), but noting the interest of Indian medicine nevertheless.[159]

Traces of the Sanskrit medical translations ordered by Yaḥyā al-Barmakī survive in other works. A few decades later, the famous physician al-Rāzī became master of a hospital at Baghdad – perhaps the same hospital attributed earlier to the Barmakids. His great medical compendium, *al-Ḥāwī*, is based largely on the then-predominant Galenic medicine as well as his own research, but it also includes a number of excerpts from the Arabic translations of Sanskrit works, including fragments of the *Siddhasāra* and the *Aṣṭāṅgahṛdaya*.[160] Much later, in early thirteenth-century Andalusia, Ibn al-Bayṭār copied some of the same citations from the *Ḥāwī* into his encyclopaedia of simple drugs. In these two works we find fragments of the early Arabic translations of Sanskrit works.[161]

---

157 Ronald Emmerick, 'Sources of the Rgyud-bźi', in Wolfgang Voigt (ed.), *XIX. Deutscher Orientalistentag, Vorträge* (Wiesbaden, 1977), pp. 1135-42; id. (ed.), *The Siddhasāra of Ravigupta. Volume 1: The Sanskrit Text* (Wiesbaden, 1980), p. 2; for the Tibetan text, see id. (ed.), *The Siddhasāra of Ravigupta. Volume 2: The Tibetan Version with Facing English Translation* (Wiesbaden, 1982) (reference to two Sanskrit texts in Tibetan translation on p. VII). For the *Siddhasāra* in the Tibetan Tanjur, see Derge vol. 53, 4441#4434, pp. 166-93, (fols. 191b-286b); Narthang vol. 219, pp. 275-472 (fols. 138a-236b); Peking vol. 148, pp. 59-100 (fols. 142a-248b).

158 As remarked much later by al-Bīrūnī in his pharmacopoeia: Hakim Mohammed Said (ed. and trans.), *Al-Biruni's Book on Pharmacy and Materia Medica* (2 vols, Karachi, 1973), vol. 1, p. 7.

159 ʿAlī ibn Rabban al-Ṭabarī, *Firdausu'l-Ḥikmat*, ed. Muḥammad Zubayr Ṣiddīqī (Berlin, 1928), p. 557. Max Meyerhof, ''Alī aṭ-Ṭabarī's "Paradise of Wisdom", one of the Oldest Arabic Compendiums of Medicine', *Isis*, 16 (1931): pp. 6-54, at p. 43.

160 Ullmann, *Die Medizin im Islam*, p. 105.

161 Ullmann, *Die Medizin im Islam*, p. 105. Ronald Emmerick, 'Ravigupta's Siddhasāra in Arabic', in Hans R. Roemer and Albrecht Noth (eds), *Studien zur Geschichte und Kultur des*

Where a Sanskrit work dealt with a special topic, its translation might hold enough interest to survive entire and independently. Such is the case with the book on poisons and their antidotes (*Kitāb al-sumūm*) attributed to Shānāq al-Hindī: that is, the legendary Indian sage Cāṇakya. The introduction of the book explains its origin:[162]

فسّره من اللسان الهندي الى اللسان الفارسي منكه الهندي وكان المتولي لنقله بالخط الفارسي رجل يعرف بأبي حاتم البلخي فسّره ليحيى بن خالد بن برمك ثمّ نقل للمأمون على يدي العباس بن سعيد الجوهري مولاه وكان هو المتولّي لقراءته على المأمون قال العباس بن سعيد الجوهري قال شاناق عظيم الهند في أول كتابه بعد أن حمد الله وأثنى عليه وحلف بعظيم البدّ...

> Manka al-Hindī interpreted it from the Indian language into the Persian language (*al-Fārisī*). A man known as Abū Ḥātim of Balkh was the one charged with translating it (*li-naqlihī*) into the Persian script. He interpreted it for Yaḥyā ibn Khālid ibn Barmak. Then it was translated (*nuqila*) for al-Maʾmūn by al-ʿAbbās ibn Saʿīd al-Jawharī, his client. He was the one charged with reading it out loud to al-Maʾmūn.
>
> Al-ʿAbbās ibn Saʿīd said: Shānāq, the great Indian, said at the beginning of his book, after he praised and commended God and swore by the great Buddha[163]... (The first chapter follows.)

This introductory notice contains important information.[164] First, Manka translated the text from Sanskrit into 'Persian', and a man from Balkh wrote it in the 'Persian' script. (Presumably this was not merely transliteration of a Sanskrit text into a Persian script, but actual translation.) The interpretation was made for Yaḥyā al-Barmakī.[165] Knowing what we know now about the languages around Balkh in the 780s, it seems likely that this Persian language is really Bactrian (keeping in mind that Bactrian is a modern designation and

---

vorderen Orients (Leiden, 1981), pp. 28-31, pointed to the existence of the Arabic version of the *Siddhasāra* and identified the title in Arabic.

162 Bettina Strauss, 'Das Giftbuch des Śānāq. Eine literaturgeschichtliche Untersuchung', *Quellen und Studien zur Geschichte der Naturwissenschaften (Berlin)*, 4/2 (1934): pp. 1-64 + 66 pages of Arabic text, pp. 3-4.

163 Lit. 'the great one of the Buddhas (collective)', parallel to Cāṇakya 'the great Indian', lit. 'the great one of the Indians'.

164 Ullmann's scepticism over this passage is unjustified (*Die Medizin im Islam*, pp. 324-5). As he himself admits, the work truly contains passages demonstrably translated from Sanskrit. No other translators or patrons of such translations are evident in the historical record. Yaḥyā al-Barmakī and al-ʿAbbās ibn Saʿīd al-Jawharī are not 'hermetic' figures.

165 It is, strictly speaking, unclear whether the subject of the second instance of the verb *fassara* is Manka or al-Balkhī. Grammatically, al-Balkhī is more likely, but perhaps the verb is repeated twice with the same subject intended, i.e. Manka.

that we do not yet know the contemporary designation for this local language).[166] The Indian translator would perhaps be more likely to know an Iranian language from the borders of India, such as Bactrian; the man from Balkh would certainly be expected to know Bactrian, not Persian, in the eighth century; Yaḥyā al-Barmakī may well have known Bactrian himself, as his father surely did.[167] If Manka translated it into 'Persian' and explained it to Yaḥyā, presumably only the second translation mentioned, in the time of al-Maʾmūn, was the translation into Arabic.[168] The passage appears for now to describe a translation from Sanskrit into Bactrian, and then Bactrian into Arabic.

Also crucial is the reference to the Buddha.[169] Buddhist Sanskrit works frequently begin with homage to the Buddha, to a particular bodhisattva, or to some or all the buddhas and bodhisattvas together.[170] Here it says the author 'swore by the greatest Buddha' at the beginning of the work. The Sanskrit writings ascribed to the legendary sage Cāṇakya, however, are not especially Buddhist, and do not normally begin with homage to the Buddha, but rather, if anything, to Indian gods. Therefore reference to the Buddha here implies

---

166 It may well have been called just 'Iranian'. Much earlier, in Kaniṣka's Bactrian inscription at Rabatak (Baghlan province, Afghanistan) of the second century CE, the Bactrian language is designated as Aryan (Iranian): αριαο (See Nicholas Sims-Williams and Joe Cribb, 'A New Bactrian Inscription of Kanishka the Great', *Silk Road Art and Archaeology*, 4 [1996]: pp. 75-142, pp. 78, 83 and 90; again in Nicholas Sims-Williams, 'Further Notes on the Bactrian Inscription of Rabatak, with an Appendix on the Names of Kujula Kadphises and Vima Taktu in Chinese', in id. [ed.], *Proceedings of the Third European Conference of Iranian Studies, held in Cambridge, 11th to 15th September 1995, Part 1: Old and Middle Iranian Studies* [Wiesbaden, 1998], pp. 79-92, at p. 81). Similarly Darius I, in the sixth century BCE, had called Old Persian *Ariyā* 'Aryan, Iranian' (DB 4.89). This term might apply to any Iranian language of the period, doubtless causing confusion among Arabic authors, who knew the Iranian peoples uniformly as *ʿAjam*. Such terms persisted: writing in Arabic in the mid-tenth century, the Iranian chronographer Ḥamza al-Iṣfahānī calls the Iranians in general *Aryān* 'Aryans' (using a NW Iranian, not Persian, form of the word), glossing the term in Arabic as *Furs*, 'Persians' (*Tārīkh sinī mulūk al-arḍ wa'l-anbiyā'*, ed. I.M.E. Gottwaldt [Leipzig, 1844], pp. 3-4, preface to the work). Another possibility is that the language of Tokharistan was called 'Tokhari', a term not attested in the texts so far, and to be avoided as likely to cause confusion today with the 'Tocharian' (see note 18 above).

167 If Yaḥyā did know Bactrian, as the passage might suggest, then who knows what sort of texts he had at his disposal?

168 The expression *nuqila li'l-Maʾmūn ʿalā yaday al-ʿAbbās ibn Saʿīd al-Jawharī* could conceivably refer also to the recension of the text made for al-Maʾmūn, who requested that at least one passage be removed, as the text says explicitly. This could also be the stage in which pieces of information lifted from Greek texts were added to the translation from Sanskrit (see Strauss, 'Das Giftbuch des Śānāq', pp. 23-4 and 26-30).

169 This does not refer merely to an 'idol', as Strauss ('Das Giftbuch des Śānāq', pp. 25 and 31) suggested.

170 *oṃ namo buddhāya* and the like; cf. the Bactrian half-calque from Sanskrit ναμωο σαρβοβοδδανο, 'homage to all the Buddhas' (BD2, document za1).

that the text, as it stands in Arabic, was transmitted by Buddhists, or at least by a Buddhist at some stage, who added a standard Buddhist formula to the beginning. Perhaps this was done by Manka himself, the translator summoned from India by the Barmakid vizier.

These Indian physicians knew more of Sanskrit tradition than just medicine. The little known early Arabic theologian Maʿmar Abū 'l-Ashʿath[171] testifies to this in a passage preserved by al-Jāḥiẓ (d. 868/9),[172] describing his personal encounter with an otherwise unknown Indian physician in the service of Yaḥyā al-Barmakī:

> In the days in which Yaḥyā ibn Khālid imported the physicians of India – like Manka, Bʾzykr, Qlbrql, Sindbādh, so-and-so and so-and-so – I said to Bahla the Indian, 'What is eloquence (*al-balāgha*) in the view of the Indians?' Bahla said, 'There is with us a leaf[173] written on that subject, but I cannot translate it for you proficiently, nor have I taken up this art, so that I might with self-confidence undertake (to explain) its special features and summarize its subtler meanings.'

His modesty notwithstanding, Bahla provided two paragraphs' worth of material summarizing a Sanskrit text on fine style and its requisites. This was copied by Maʿmar Abū 'l-Ashʿath and, from him, by al-Jāḥiẓ. The entire passage, the authenticity of which there is no reason to doubt, is a remarkable testimony to several important facts about the Indian scholars in the employ of Yaḥyā al-Barmakī. We see from Maʿmar's statement that there were other Indians in the group, besides Ibn Dahn and Manka, whose names have not been well preserved. Anyone in the company of the Barmakids might have access to these Indian scholars. The passage demonstrates that these physicians, while specializing in medicine, apparently had some knowledge of other branches of Sanskrit learning, including exposure to Sanskrit literary theory, to which indeed any learner of Sanskrit, then purely a language of formality and erudition, can be expected to have been exposed. The physicians apparently had brought some Sanskrit works on subjects other than medicine along with them to western Asia, but these were for the most part not translated into Arabic. The brief epitome of the Sanskrit text on 'eloquence', as copied by Maʿmar Abū 'l-Ashʿath, achieved a peculiar longevity far from its original context since it was adopted by the widely-read al-Jāḥiẓ; in later centuries, both Ibn Qutayba and Abū Hilāl

171 On this figure and his name see Josef van Ess, *Theologie und Gesellschaft im 2. und 3. Jahrhundert Hidschra* (6 vols, Berlin, 1991-7), vol. 2, pp. 37-8.

172 Al-Jāḥiẓ, *Kitāb al-bayān wa'l-tabyīn*, ed. ʿAbd al-Salām Muḥammad Hārūn (4 vols, Cairo, 1960), vol. 1, pp. 92-3.

173 It is unclear whether the word *ṣaḥīfa* here refers to a work literally of one sheet or not.

al-ʿAskarī copied it in their well-known literary works, the latter even providing it with a commentary.[174]

Yaḥyā al-Barmakī's interest in India manifested itself in other ways beyond ordering direct translations. The private poet of the Barmakids, Abān al-Lāḥiqī (d. *c.*815), of eastern Iranian origin, is said to have turned several early works of pre-Islamic origin into Arabic verse for his patrons. These include the Iranian version of the life of the Buddha, *Kitāb Bilawhar wa-Būdhāsaf*, and the stories of Sindbad and Mazdak. Abān also reportedly wrote a book of *Wise Sayings of the Indians* (*Kitāb fī ḥikam al-Hind*).[175] An anecdote preserved by al-Jahshiyārī – cited from the *History of the Poets* by Muḥammad ibn Dāwūd ibn al-Jarrāḥ (d. 908)[176] – says that Yaḥyā al-Barmakī wanted to memorize the famous Indian book of political instruction, *Kalīla wa-Dimna*, in the Arabic version (translated from the Middle Persian version of the Sanskrit original). Abān turned it into verse to facilitate the effort and made it a gift to Yaḥyā's son, Jaʿfar. In return he was awarded 100,000 silver *dirhams*.[177]

It is true that Yaḥyā al-Barmakī was not the only person in western Asia interested in Indian books. A few works of Indian origin were already known in Arabic before his time. These, however, came into Arabic mostly by way of Middle Persian intermediaries, as with the case of *Kalīla wa-Dimna* just mentioned. Importantly, astrologers present already in the court of al-Manṣūr (reg. 754-75), no doubt familiar to Yaḥyā from his youth, were using some astronomical materials of Indian origin, and a few Indian astrologers may have been among them.[178] There are approximately forty books of Indian origin listed in the *Fihrist* of al-Nadīm, most of which are totally unknown today.[179] It is difficult to say whether these are forgeries, or translations from Sanskrit by way of a Middle Iranian language, or direct translations from Sanskrit. In any case, Yaḥyā al-Barmakī remains the only important patron of translations directly from Sanskrit in this period, and Yaḥyā's order is explicitly given as a

---

174 Ibn Qutayba, *Kitāb ʿuyūn al-akhbār*, vol. 2, p. 173; Abū Hilāl al-ʿAskarī, *Kitāb al-ṣināʿatayn*, ed. ʿAlī Muḥammad al-Bajāwī and Muḥammad Abū 'l-Faḍl Ibrāhīm (Cairo, 1971), pp. 25-9.

175 *Fihrist*, p. 119. The edition says *ḥilm*, 'prudence', but Everett Rowson suggests to me the emendation to *ḥikam*, which is surely correct.

176 Sezgin, *Geschichte des arabischen Schrifttums*, vol. 1, pp. 374-5.

177 Al-Jahshiyārī, *Kitāb al-Wuzarāʾ*, p. 259. In Sanskrit literature, too, books, including scientific texts, are ordinarily written in verse to facilitate memorization.

178 David Pingree, 'Astronomy and Astrology in India and Iran', *Isis*, 54 (1963): pp. 229-46, at pp. 242-3; id., *From Astral Omens to Astrology: From Babylon to Bīkānēr* (Rome, 1997), pp. 51-62 (on Kanka al-Hindī); David King and Julio Samsó, 'Astronomical Handbooks and Tables from the Islamic World (750-1900): An Interim Report', *Suhayl*, 2 (2001): pp. 9-105, pp. 31-3.

179 *Fihrist*, pp. 270-71, 303, 305 and 312.

reason for several of these translations. There are, however, a few exceptions to be discussed presently, two minor and one important.

One minor exception has just been encountered: Maʿmar Abū ʾl-Ashʿath requested and received a snippet in a summary translation on Sanskrit 'eloquence'. The other minor exception involves the translator Manka al-Hindī. Manka served Yaḥyā al-Barmakī, for whom he translated the *Book of Poisons* discussed above, among other works, and worked in the hospital of the Barmakids.[180] But we are also told that Manka 'used to translate the names of Indian medicaments in the company (*jumla*) of Isḥāq ibn Sulaymān ibn ʿAlī al-Hāshimī',[181] a figure at the court who was briefly appointed governor of Egypt by al-Rashīd in 793-4.[182] The circumstances under which Manka translated these Indian drug-names for him are unclear, but there can be little doubt that it was Yaḥyā al-Barmakī who initially brought Manka to the court. Whether Manka's association with Isḥāq ibn Sulaymān was a formal one or not, we cannot know, but it could have occurred after the fall of the Barmakids in 803, when Manka must have lost Yaḥyā al-Barmakī's patronage. In any case, the character of the anecdote implies that Manka did not translate whole works for Isḥāq ibn Sulaymān, but merely provided expertise in Indian materia medica.

The more important exception is in the case of a Sanskrit astronomical translation. The transmission of astronomical science from Sanskrit into Arabic is more complicated than the transmission of Indian medical texts, and it does not so clearly involve the Barmakids. In Sasanian Iran, scholars were apparently already making use of Indian astronomical parameters and astrological methods in Middle Persian translation.[183] As just mentioned, astrologers in al-Manṣūr's employ, such as Māshāʾallāh, were still using this information in a tradition going back to Sasanian times.[184] The Barmakids obviously had no role in this earlier transmission of elements of Indian astronomy into Iran.

David Pingree has argued that an astronomical handbook was translated from Sanskrit into Arabic in Sind, in India, as early as 'shortly after 735',[185] and

---

180 See note 153.

181 *Fihrist*, pp. 345 and 303.

182 Muḥammad ibn Yūsuf al-Kindī, *The Governors and Judges of Egypt*, ed. Rhuvon Guest (Leiden, 1912), p. 136.

183 Pingree, 'Astronomy and Astrology in India and Iran', pp. 242-3; id., 'The Persian "Observation" of the Solar Apogee in ca. A.D. 450', *Journal of Near Eastern Studies*, 24 (1965): pp. 334-6; id., 'The Greek Influence on Early Islamic Mathematical Astronomy', *Journal of the American Oriental Society*, 93 (1972): pp. 32-43, at pp. 36-7.

184 David Pingree, 'Māshāʾallāh: Some Sasanian and Syriac Sources', in George Hourani (ed.), *Essays on Islamic Philosophy and Science* (New York, 1975), pp. 5-14.

185 David Pingree, ''Ilm al-Hayʾa' in *EI*^{2}, at 1136a. This date is based only on one short excerpt given by al-Bīrūnī (*Alberuni's India*, trans. Eduard Sachau [2 vols, London, 1910], vol. 2, pp. 48-9), who says it is from a 'corrupt translation' (*naql fāsid*) of the *Zīj al-Arkand*. In this passage there is mention of an epoch of 'the dominion of Sind' (*mulk al-Sind*), cited

that no fewer than four separate astronomical handbooks were eventually translated from Sanskrit into Arabic: *al-Arkand*, *al-Harqan*, the *Sindhind* and the Arjabhar.[186] The last of these is supposed to have been translated about 800. More research on this topic is required to verify these theses, which rest on scanty and complicated evidence. For now, the only certain and presently indisputable report of an astronomical translation from Sanskrit into Arabic (before al-Bīrūnī) was the influential handbook known in Arabic as *Sindhind*, translated already in the time of al-Manṣūr (reg. 754-75). Later sources say that an Indian man, or delegation, came to the court of al-Manṣūr bearing an astronomical work, and 'al-Manṣūr ordered that it be translated into the Arabic language'.[187] One of the caliph's astrologers, al-Fazārī, was in charge of editing the Arabic version.[188] The resulting book, called in Arabic *Zīj al-Sindhind al-kabīr*, became a model for astronomical handbooks for the important first generation of astronomers writing in Arabic.[189] As just related, the reports make this translation work to be the order of the caliph himself. Since the caliph was employing astrologers already working in an Indian–Iranian tradition of astrology, the interest in Indian astronomy must have been pre-existing and requires no further explanation. It is just a guess to suppose that Barmakid advice also played a role here. The only suggestion of a connection is a report of al-Marzubānī (d. 994), according to which Yaḥyā al-Barmakī considered al-Fazārī, who reworked the Sanskrit translation, as one of the four scientists unmatched in his special field of study (in this case, astronomy).[190] This does not argue for much. But creating an astronomical handbook out of materials translated from Sanskrit was al-Fazārī's main achievement, on which Yaḥyā's appreciation must have been based. This fits with his involvement in Indian sciences already evident. The *Sindhind* system remained influential until what Pingree has called the 'Ptolemaicisation'

---

as Ṣafar 117 *hijrī*, i.e. March 735. Pingree thinks that this proves that the *Arabic translation* was written in Sind. Of course, it does not prove that, but only that the work became known in Arabic sometime after that date.

186 Pingree, "Ilm al-Hay'a' in *EI*², under 'The translations from Sanskrit', summarizes his views on the subject.

187 Different but related reports on this event appear in several sources. Ibn al-Ādamī quoted by Ṣā'id al-Andalusī, *Ṭabaqāt al-umam*, ed. Ḥusayn Mu'nis (Cairo, 1998), pp. 68-9, and Ibn al-Qifṭī, *Tārīkh al-ḥukamā'*, ed. Julius Lippert (Leipzig, 1903), pp. 270-71 (following Ṣā'id verbatim) say that the *Sindhind* was brought by a man (*rajul*) from India. Al-Bīrūnī, *Alberuni's India*, vol. 2, p. 15, and al-Hāshimī, *The Book of the Reasons behind Astronomical Tables (Kitāb fi 'ilal al-zījāt)*, facsimile and trans. Fuad I. Haddad, Edward S. Kennedy and David Pingree (Delmar, 1981), f. 95v, line 3 (see also commentary on pp. 216-17), say that it was brought by delegation (*wafd*) from Sind.

188 David Pingree, 'The Fragments of the Works of al-Fazārī', *Journal of Near Eastern Studies*, 29 (1970): pp. 103-23 presents the extant information on al-Fazārī and his work.

189 David Pingree, 'Sindhind' in *EI*².

190 Reported by Yāqūt, *Irshād al-arīb ilā ma'rifat al-adīb, or Dictionary of Learned Men*, ed. David Samuel Margoliouth (7 vols, Leiden, 1907-27), vol. 6, p. 268, ll. 9-12.

of Arabic astronomy by al-Khwārizmī, under al-Maʾmūn (reg. 813-33).[191] It was during this caliph's reign that the philhellenic taste in Arabic, and the number of works translated from Greek, grew enough to displace the demand for Indian and Iranian books.[192] Previously, in the court in the time of the Barmakids, Indian and Iranian astronomy and astrology (both having more distant Greek roots) predominated.

The best way to explain Yaḥyā's unusual and broad interest in India and in Sanskrit works – again, practically unique in Baghdad over a long period – is to suppose that he knew something of these things from his grandfather, the Barmak himself, or from his father Khālid, and perhaps in general from his family connections in Tokharistan. If al-Kirmānī could report about the Barmak's education in Kashmir, and his life in Tokharistan where, until recently, Buddhism flourished and the study of Sanskrit had been cultivated, then Yaḥyā al-Barmakī must have known about it, too. It makes sense in this context that he alone, as far as is known, actively supported research on India, and sent a mission to India to collect medicinal plants and information about Indian religions. In particular, the interest in Indian medicine is striking, since this is the one area in which we have an anecdote about the Barmak's own activities under Hishām. It seems that Yaḥyā al-Barmakī was interested in Sanskrit science and medicine because of his personal connection with those subjects through his grandfather Barmak, who studied those very subjects in Kashmir, and perhaps some of the very same texts later translated into Arabic at Yaḥyā's order.

Scholarship on the formation of Arabic literature views history from the perspective of a learned person in Baghdad. Baghdad is the centre and Arabic is the recipient. However, in this case, one could equally take Kashmir as the point of reference for a narrative about the diffusion of Sanskrit learning. In the seventh and eighth centuries, Sanskrit works were actively sought in translation in many languages of Asia, including Chinese, Tibetan, Khotanese, 'Tocharian' and so on, and probably also in Bactrian, almost always as part of the propagation of Buddhism. Arabic is, in this view, just one more of these recipient languages in the Sanskrit diffusion. Though specifically Buddhist works were not translated into Arabic under the patronage of the Barmakids (as far as surviving evidence shows), one may reasonably suppose that Yaḥyā's special interest in Sanskrit learning, almost unique among the Muslims of western Asia, was nevertheless due to the high prestige attributed to it by his immediate Buddhist ancestors in Tokharistan. The originally Sanskrit materials surviving in early Arabic medical compendia are traces left by a Bactrian élite in transition from Indian-oriented Buddhist learning to a more westward-looking, increasingly Hellenistic, Arabic science supported by Muslims. This transition was effected by the Arab conquest

---

191 Pingree, 'Sindhind' in *EI*². Also King and Samsó, 'Astronomical Handbooks and Tables', pp. 31-5.

192 Gutas, *Greek Thought, Arabic Culture*, pp. 75-104, provides the most convincing analysis yet of the social context for this newly vigorous philhellenic attitude.

and colonization of Tokharistan. The early reception of Sanskrit works in Arabic, however short-lived it may have been, reflects the status of Sanskrit as a language of learning in that country.

It is interesting to note that the first person reported to demand an Arabic translation of Ptolemy's *Almagest* was also Yaḥyā the Barmakid.[193] This early translation was probably from Middle Persian or Syriac, and not from Greek, although sure evidence is lacking.[194] As Dimitri Gutas has shown, Greek philosophy, with its utility for the theological debates incipient in the new capital, was just entering into circulation in Arabic translation in Yaḥyā's time.[195] There are hints suggesting that Yaḥyā al-Barmakī was involved with these new Hellenistic currents as well. For example, his associate, the theologian Hishām ibn al-Ḥakam, wrote a refutation of Aristotle, probably against the eighth book of his *Physics*.[196] A translation of the *logica vetus* of Aristotle, together with Porphyry's *Introduction*, was made, perhaps from Middle Persian, for Yaḥyā al-Barmakī.[197] It is unclear to what extent his sponsorship of translations of Greek philosophical works went. Nevertheless, Yaḥyā al-Barmakī does appear highly educated and among the first patrons of translation at this early stage in the Abbasid period. How much, then, did Yaḥyā's interest in scholarship of all kinds, including the Greek, owe to his grandfather? To what extent was the pre-existing interest in Indian learning, and the patronage of translations from Sanskrit by Asian kings, a factor in creating precedents and models for the later, more extensive, translations from *Greek* into Arabic? It is impossible to answer these tantalizing questions.

An adequate chronology of works translated into Arabic is still wanted. Nevertheless, one may suppose for now that Sanskrit learning, in Arabic translation, together with works translated from Middle Persian, was for a brief time, around the 790s, more important at the court of the caliphs than were translations from Greek. This was due to Yaḥyā ibn Khālid the Barmakid. In this period, the only subjects for which the Greek tradition appears to have been uniquely valued were dialectic, and its attendant logic, as used by

---

193 *Fihrist*, pp. 267-8. That Yaḥyā al-Barmakī took an interest also in astrology has already been shown. It is also indicated by the note that the astrologer al-Khayyāṭ dedicated a book to him (*Fihrist*, p. 276).

194 Nallino argued that it was a translation from Syriac. See al-Battānī, *Al-Battânî sive Albatenii Opus astronomicum*, ed. Carlo A. Nallino (3 vols, Milan, 1899-1907), vol. 2, pp. viii, 192, 211. Paul Kunitzsch (*Der Almagest: Die Syntaxis Mathematica des Claudius Ptolemäus in arabisch-lateinischer Überlieferung* [Wiesbaden, 1974], pp. 115-25) makes a strong case for its being a translation from Middle Persian.

195 Gutas, *Greek Thought, Arabic Culture*, pp. 61-74.

196 *Fihrist*, p. 175, Gutas, *Greek Thought, Arabic Culture*, p. 73.

197 Paul Kraus, 'Zu Ibn al-Muqaffa', *Rivista degli Studi Orientali*, 14 (1933): pp. 1-20, pp. 10-11. If the translator really was the son of the famed Ibn al-Muqaffaʿ, then it would be hard to imagine that the translation was from Greek.

Christian theologians, and the Greek tradition of pure physical theory (as opposed to the applications in astrology and medicine).[198] Besides these special subjects, translations from Sanskrit, supported at that time by the head of the administration, may well have seemed for a while to represent the future type of scholarship in both astrology and medicine, not to mention in the applied political philosophy represented in 'wisdom literature'.[199] With the new capital in Mesopotamia, the passing of the Barmakids, and the rise of Christian secretaries and physicians of Aramaean background, the ninth century became instead the heyday for translations of Syriac and Greek works on all subjects. Sanskrit learning almost disappeared in Arabic with the passing of an élite family which included the sole individuals with both the interest and the means, and also, importantly, the familiarity, to pursue it.

CONCLUSION

It is perhaps not wise to have emphasized the Barmakids' interest in Sanskrit texts to the exclusion of others who may have played a part. In fact, so little is known about the chronology of the earliest Arabic works that discoveries are likely to emerge requiring the picture painted here to be modified somewhat. However, evidence stating directly that it was because of his grandfather that Yaḥyā al-Barmakī esteemed Indian learning highly is unlikely ever to come to light. One should not expect a specific report on the matter, since Yaḥyā was just as much a normal part of his time and society as the Barmak was of his. It did not require any remark. Nevertheless, the Bactrian background of the Barmakids and the status of Sanskrit in the culture of Tokharistan are firmly established. The correspondence between that culture and the special interests of Yaḥyā al-Barmakī remains quite striking.

198 There do not appear to have been any translations of Indian logic into Arabic. Greek dialectic was surely more appropriate for Muslim use in debates with Christians, Jews and other Muslims, since the terms of their theology were shaped in combination with Greek logical tradition. Two of the Syriac letters of the Catholicos Patriarch of the Church of the East Timothy I, written between 782/3 and 799, one under al-Mahdī and one under al-Rashīd, illustrate this nicely for the Barmakid period. Timothy had been ordered by the caliph to obtain an Arabic translation of Aristotle's *Topics*, and then he eagerly sought commentaries on the subject. The Catholicos Timothy's concern is with the more or less totally Hellenistic science of late antique Christian Syria and Mesopotamia, steeped in the study of Aristotle and his Christian successors. His society had little to do with Indian sciences. On the current interests in Greek learning in this period, see also Gutas, *Greek Thought, Arabic Culture*, pp. 61-74.

199 The Indian and Iranian traditions of political wisdom persisted much later in Arabic, sometimes even in a fabricated Greek garb (Kevin van Bladel, 'The Iranian Characteristics and Forged Greek Attributions in the Arabic *Sirr al-asrār* (*Secret of Secrets*)', *Mélanges de l'Université Saint-Joseph*, 57 [2004]: pp. 151-72).

The place of Tokharistan in the early Abbasid period clearly requires further investigation, and the future prospect of more discoveries in the Bactrian language offers the most hope for this. It is normal for historians to refer to the 'Persianizing' culture of the Abbasid caliphs that arose in Khorasan. The resurgence of the manners, fashions and concerns of Persian élites are commonplaces in modern descriptions of the Abbasid court. But one must remember that 'Iran' is a land of many countries. There were other Iranian components of the Abbasid culture beyond the Sasanian, Persian legacy, such as that of Tokharistan, which was not Persian, but Bactrian (though the word was never used in Arabic).

Along similar lines, others have proposed a number of hypotheses suggesting contacts of different kinds between Muslims and Buddhists in eastern Iran. Taken individually they do not seem very strong, and they have never been treated together. Christopher Beckwith argues that the round city of Baghdad was a 'Central Asian' design of Khālid ibn Barmak.[200] Richard Bulliet points to the anti-Abbasid rebellions in the east motivated by an ideology, according to him Buddhist in origin, that their leaders were reincarnations of Abū Muslim.[201] Barthold and Litvinsky argue that the architectural model of first *madrasas*, which, they say, originated in Tokharistan, was actually the Buddhist *vihāra*.[202] Stories about two early Sufis from the region, Ibn Adham (born in Balkh, d. *c*.777)[203] and his disciple Shaqīq al-Balkhī,[204] strongly suggest some form of contact with Buddhists or at least Buddhist models in their hagiography, although this has been disputed.[205] Shlomo Pines argues that contact between Buddhist philosophers and Muslim dialectical theologians influenced the latter, but the results he obtained are highly uncertain and speculative.[206] The best

---

200 Christopher Beckwith, 'The Plan of the City of Peace. Central Asian Iranian Factors in Early 'Abbāsid Design', *Acta Orientalia Academiae Scientiarum Hungaricae*, 38 (1984): pp. 143-64, holding (p. 150) that Khālid ibn Barmak was himself a 'Buddhist priest' with 'much experience in architecture'. Ṭabarī, *Tārīkh al-rusul wa'l-mulūk*, series 3, part 1, p. 320, gives a report that Khālid ibn Barmak laid out the city and advised al-Manṣūr about it (*khaṭṭa madīnata Abī Ja'far lahū wa-ashāra bihā 'alayhi*). Contrary to Beckwith's view (p. 150), the round city at the Sasanian capital of Ctesiphon, just downstream from Baghdad, seems likely to have been a model; see Giorgio Gullini, 'Problems of an Excavation in Northern Babylonia', *Mesopotamia: Rivista di Archeologia*, 1 (1966): pp. 7-38 + plate, at pp. 15, 22, and the accompanying map plate.

201 Richard Bulliet, 'Naw Bahār and the Survival of Iranian Buddhism', *Iran: Journal of the British Institute of Persian Studies*, 4 (1976): pp. 140-45, at p. 145.

202 Most recently Litvinsky and Zeimal', *The Buddhist Monastery of Ajina Tepa*, p. 189. See also the contribution by Beckwith in this volume.

203 'Ibrāhīm b. Adham' in *EI*²; Litvinsky and Zeimal', *The Buddhist Monastery of Ajina Tepa*, p. 188. See also the contributions by Zarcone and Papas in this volume.

204 Van Ess, *Theologie und Gesellschaft im 2. und 3. Jahrhundert Hidschra*, vol. 2, p. 545.

205 'Ibrāhīm b. Adham' in *EI*² for references.

206 Shlomo Pines, 'A Study of the Impact of Indian, Mainly Buddhist, Thought on Some Aspects of Kalām Doctrines', *Jerusalem Studies in Arabic and Islam*, 17 (1994): pp. 182-203.

candidate for such contact is in Jahm ibn Ṣafwān of Bactrian Tirmidh (d. 746), who is expressly said to have had debates with the Buddhists (*Sumaniyya*, the traditional Arabic reading for what should be *Shamaniyya*) that forced him to develop his line of reasoning.[207] Other possible theological contacts have been cited in modern scholarship.[208] On firmer ground, Melikian-Chirvani has shown clearly that the material remains of Buddhism, and particularly the Buddha image, became common motifs in Persian song.[209] Those pursuing such theories have done so with varying degrees of success. In focusing on the Barmakids here, it was possible to indicate specific historical agents involved in the contact between two foreign societies, and to show simultaneously that 'influence' is too simplistic a way to explain the transformation of the culture of Tokharistan into one in which Islam prevailed as normative and authoritative. We are dealing not with two ideologies (Buddhism and Islam) bouncing off one another like stones, sending both in different directions, but rather with human populations in daily contact, one dominating the other, both changing their beliefs and practices as a response to that contact over several generations, and with those in power most successfully demanding conformity to their ways.[210]

---

207 While the epistemological views attributed to the Buddhists in these discussions are reported at several removes, and are probably distorted beyond recognition, it remains that the only early theologian supposed to have such contact was in Khorasan in the early eighth century.

208 Gimaret, 'Bouddha et les bouddhistes', pp. 292-3.

209 Melikian-Chirvani, 'L'évocation littéraire du bouddhisme' and 'The Buddhist Ritual in the Literature of Early Islamic Iran'.

210 I would like to draw attention to Étienne de La Vassière's important study of the history of Tokharistan's Iranian neighbour to the north, Sogdia (*Sogdian Traders: A History* [Leiden, 2005]). Going into much greater detail than I could here for the much more limited present subject, this book provides evidence for the social and economic changes taking place in Sogdia during the same period. The history of the two regions will need to be integrated in future studies on early Islamic Khorasan in general. Parallels in the social histories of the two regions should be expected.

Chapter 4
Iran to Tibet

Assadullah Souren Melikian-Chirvani

The notion that there might be a connection between the Iranian world and Tibet may seem odd at first glance. Actually, these two areas were not so far apart. While they were separated by formidable mountain barriers, they were almost next door neighbours.

If this geographical reality is easily forgotten, this is in part due to the changing political and ethnographic map of the area loosely referred to as Central Asia. Of the present day republics of Turkmenistan, Uzbekistan and Tajikistan, only Tajikistan now rates as part of the Iranian world and has Persian (in its 'Tajik' guise) as its official language. All three, however, were part of the first Iranian Empire unified by the Achaemenid dynasty, and in more recent times they played a major part in the first blossoming of Iranian culture in its Islamic garb under the Samanid dynasty from the late ninth century on.[1]

It is therefore no great surprise that the Iran–Tibet connection stretches as far back as the early first millennium BCE and continued right down to the seventeenth century. When the Portuguese missionary António de Andrade entered Tibet from northern India, he communicated with Tibetans in Persian, the international language of all communities in seventeenth-century India.[2]

Visual evidence alone is at hand to substantiate the connection during a proto-historic period that may have begun before 1000 BCE, followed by a second period corresponding to Sasanian rule in Western Iran (224-651 CE), when written sources tell us a little more, and a third period corresponding with the first six centuries of the Islamic period.

Unfortunately, it is in the nature of visual evidence to lend itself to various interpretations when it comes to putting forward a chronology or identifying the means and ways of transmission of forms and patterns.

In the case of Tibet, it is at present virtually impossible in most cases to determine whether the Iranian influence revealed by the visual evidence of artefacts and paintings came in through direct contacts, or was relayed by cultures thriving in territories adjacent to Tibet–Kashmir to the south, the various (and changing) Turkic-speaking groups to the north which were at

1 Pierre Briant, *Histoire de l'Empire Perse* (Paris, 1996), pp. 44-5. On chronology problems, see p. 50. On the Samanids, see the excellent essay by Richard Frye, *Bukhara* (Oklahoma, 1965).

2 Hugues Didier, *Les Portuguais au Tibet*, revised edition (Paris, 2002), p. 9.

times incorporated with the Tibetan Empire, or China where north-east Iranians (the Sogdians) and Turkic communities introduced some of their traditions. The observations submitted here are primarily intended to draw attention to the considerable period during which Iranian influence, direct or indirect, made itself felt on Tibetan art and culture.

I. WESTERN IRAN TO TIBET: A PROTO-HISTORIC JOURNEY

Despite the lack of precisely datable material, there seems to be little doubt that the earliest contacts took place before the Achaemenid dynasty rose to power in the mid-sixth century BCE.

1. THE PROTO-HISTORIC TIBETAN ARTEFACTS

Attention was drawn long ago in very general terms to the similarities that exist between small bronze objects found in Tibet and other bronzes dug up in the Western Iranian province of Lorestan.

Bernard Goldman briefly touched, among other things, on the specific case of a bird pendant that formed part of a 'mixed collection of small bronzes gathered in Tibet by Giuseppe Tucci', first published in 1935 by the Italian dean of Tibetan art history.[3]

Goldman, observing that 'it is only necessary to point out [for comparison] a few Luristan bronzes to show the possibility of a non-Tibetan ancestry', concluded that the Lorestan bronzes must be earlier than their Tibetan offshoots.[4] Tucci himself tackled the subject in the vaguest possible fashion in his overview of Tibetan art published in 1973. Noting that 'Goldman drew comparisons with Iran', Tucci stated, somewhat hypothetically, that 'such connections [in French: *correspondances*] are also likely, for contacts with Iranian cultures (more particularly concerning Western Tibet) no doubt go back to very early times, and artistic and decorative motifs may well have travelled from Iran to Tibet via migrations and commercial exchanges'.[5]

While the objects selected by Tucci in his book on Tibet obviously belong to different traditions, two of them do reveal a close connection with the art of Lorestan and two more point to a connection with other West Iranian artefacts around the late second or early first millennium BCE.

---

3 Bernard Goldman, 'Some Aspects of the Animal Deity: Luristan, Tibet and Italy', *Ars Orientalis*, 4 (1961): pp. 16-35.

4 Goldman, 'Some Aspects', respectively p. 175 B and p. 176 A.

5 Giuseppe Tucci, *Tibet* (Geneva, 1973), p. 16.

A pendant in the form of a pair of addorsed birds closely resembles some Lorestan pieces (Plate 4.1).[6] Goldman did not cite the most obvious parallel, a type of seal in which two birds back to back rise from a short stump (Plate 4.2).[7]

Pendants in which the foreparts of two birds back to back are merged into a single bird are common in Lorestan,[8] and the pairing of animals was widespread in the entire Western Iranian region.[9] The stylistic handling of the twin birds from Tibet with their globular eyes and their crests, and the Expressionist mood of the object, clearly point to a Lorestan connection. However, the bronze discovered by Tucci is not a Lorestan artefact. The deep sinuous grooves across the body are enough to indicate a different provenance.

A second Tibetan bronze lending itself to a rapprochement with Lorestan is a harness ring with two stylized feline heads attached to a loop.[10] These bear an unmistakable kinship to some Lorestan feline heads such as the animal topping a bronze haft holding a crescent moon axe blade published by André Godard.[11] The stylized feline heads on the Tibetan ring also call for comparison with those seen on artefacts conventionally associated with the site of Ziviye on the edge of southern Azarbayjan.[12]

A connection with the art of the Caspian province of Gīlān is suggested by another harness ring from Tibet about which Tucci says almost nothing (Plate 4.4).[13] The twin loops are each topped by an animal motif made up from the foreparts of two stylized quadrupeds, possibly mountain goats, which are joined back to back. Both in structure and figural design, the object has a typically West Iranian look.

Another piece from the Tucci collection points in the same direction. The single ring with four pierced lugs projecting outside and two stylized bird figures

6 Tucci, *Tibet*, pl. 19-21 (three views); mentioned p. 35 regarding its symbolism.

7 Nicolas Engel et al., *Bronzes du Luristan* (Paris, 2008), p. 131, n. 109 and 110 where these are given a broad dating 1300-650 BCE. Three more examples in Yolande Maleki, 'Une fouille en Luristan', *Iranica Antiqua*, 6/1 (1964): pp. 1-35. See pl. VII, 1.

8 Maleki, 'Une fouille', p. 129, n. 101. Further examples from Lorestan in P.R.S. Moorey, *Ancient Persian Bronzes in the Adam Collection* (London, 1974), p. 93, n. 57 and 58. Eric de Waele, *Bronzes du Luristan et d'Amlash: Ancienne collection Godard* (Louvain-la-Neuve, 1982), p. 171, fig. 141, n. 261, 262 etc.

9 Ezzatollah Negahban, *Marlik: The Complete Excavation Report*, vol. 2 Illustrations (Philadelphia, 1996), pl. 34, n. 77, pl. 44, n. 131.

10 Tucci, *Tibet*, pl. 2.

11 André Godard, *Les Bronzes du Luristan* (Paris, 1931), pl. XXII, fig. 67.

12 André Godard, *Le trésor de Ziwiye (Kurdistan)* (Haarlem, 1950), p. 41, fig. 31. De Waele, *Bronzes du Luristan et d'Amlash*, p. 30, n. 23. The book uncritically accepts attributions to sites based on dealers' reports. Oscar Muscarella put to rest the Ziviye myth in: '"Ziwiye" and Ziwiye: the Forgery of a Provenance', *Journal of Field Archaeology*, 4 (1977): pp. 197-219.

13 Tucci, *Tibet*, pl. 7, left-hand piece.

projecting in the intervening space might go unnoticed if seen amidst sundry items from Iran (Plate 4.3).[14]

In addition to the harness rings from Tibet that present similarities to horse equipment devices from Iran which are not later than the early first millennium BCE, a second group of artefacts belonging to the art of warfare and hunting independently suggests early contacts with the Iranian world. Tucci, illustrating some arrowheads in his book, loosely refers to them as 'arrows [*sic*] with a central ridge' and states that they are 'too common as a type to allow even approximate dating'.[15]

The three specimens illustrated by him represent variants of a specific type of arrow head of which one is matched by a model excavated at Bard-e Bāl in Lorestan.[16] This includes the tang, apparently of lozenge section. It would be indispensable to handle the objects, only known to this writer from black-and-white plates, to take the discussion further.

While it would be imprudent to draw sweeping conclusions on the basis of five samples, the parallels to which these lend themselves are too precise to be ignored and justify submitting the following working hypothesis. At some point, the artefacts of horsemanship (the harness rings) and of hunting and warfare (the arrow heads) of a type known from Western Iran in the late second or early first millennium BCE, became known to the populations of present-day Tibet. The objects, which are not of Iranian make, may tentatively be assumed to have been wrought in Tibetan lands, offering an early case of influence from the Iranian world over the Himalayan area.

Was this the result of direct transmission, or did intermediary groups play a part? Or was there a dual process involving direct and indirect transmission?

Historical geography from later times suggests that direct transmission is likely to have taken place. Early Iranian treatises in Arabic and Persian refer to Tibet as adjacent to Iranian Central Asia, called in Islamic times *Mā warā' al-nahr* (Ar.) *Māverā an-Nahr* (Ar./Pe.), 'the lands beyond the river'.

This is the case with the Iranian geographer Eṣṭakhrī who wrote in Arabic and died in 323/920.[17] Later, an anonymous geographical treatise written in Persian in 372/982, *The Frontiers of the World from East to West* [*Ḥodūd al-ʿĀlam men*

14 Tucci, *Tibet*, pl. 7, right-hand piece.

15 Tucci, *Tibet*, p. 38.

16 Compare Tucci, *Tibet*, pl. 33 far right and Lucien Vanden Berghe, 'Recherches archéologiques dans le Pusht-i Kuh, Luristan', *Bastan Chenassi va Honar-e Iran*, 6 (1971): pp. 14-43. See p. 29, pl. 31, fourth arrow head from left.

17 Abū Isḥāq Ibrāhīm ibn Muḥammad al-Fārīsī al-Iṣṭakhrī *al-maʿrūf bi'l-Karkhī* ['known as al-Karkhī'], *Kitāb al-masālik wa'l-mamālik* [*The Book of Itineraries and Kingdoms*], ed. Michael Jan de Goeje (Leiden, [3]1967), p. 297; Abū Esḥāq Ebrāhīm Eṣṭakhrī, *Masālek va Mamālek*, ed. Iraj Afshār (Tehran, 1340/1961), p. 233. Arabic text: *bayna Wakhān wa-Tubbat qarīb*; Persian version: *Ḥadd-e Vakhān be ḥodūd-e Tobbat peyvaste-ast*, 'the border of Wakhan is adjacent to the marches of Tibet'.

al-Mashreq ela'l-Maghreb], notes that Tibet is bordered to the west by 'part of the marches of Māverā an-Nahr'.[18]

The anonymous geographer, who is extremely concise, takes the trouble to inform the reader that 'all goods from India come to Tibet, and from Tibet come to the cities of the Muslims'.[19] His statement implies that direct commercial traffic with India was problematic at the time he (or an earlier informer on whose work he drew) was writing, and that Tibet was the area through which it transited towards the Iranian world.

All this suggests a continuous flow of commercial traffic between Tibet and historical Iranian lands, particularly the great cities of Samarqand and Bokhara.

The nature of the goods imported from Tibet into Iran is well known concerning the Islamic period. The anonymous author of 982 says that Tibet 'produces musk in abundance, black fox furs, squirrel furs, sable, ermine, and rhinoceros horn'.[20] How extensive this trade was may be inferred from the innumerable references to 'the musk of Tibet' and, more broadly to its exquisite perfumes, that occur in Persian poetry from the earliest times.

Abū Ṭayyeb Mosʿabī, at one time the Vizir of the Samanid *Amīr* (ruler) Naṣr b. Aḥmad, writes in a couplet bemoaning the guiles of the universe, seemingly seductive but intrinsically ferocious:

چو عود قماری وچون مشك تبت   چو عنبر سرشت يمان وحجازی

You are like the aloe wood of Cambodia and like the musk of Tibet
Like the ambergris nature of Yemen and Ḥijāz[21]

Out of the thousands of verses mentioning the musk of Tibet, a couplet from a panegyric written in the early fifth/eleventh century by Farrokhī Sistānī, a court poet of Sultan Maḥmūd the Ghaznevid, shows best how musk was totally identified with Tibet in the earliest Persian tradition:

---

18 Anon., *Ḥodūd al-ʿĀlam men al-Mashreq ela'l-Maghreb*, ed. Manūchehr Sotūde (Tehran, ^{2}1362/1983), p. 73. Under the heading 'Discourse on the Tibet area and its cities', the author says: 'To the east there are parts of Chīnestān (China); to the south, Hendūstān (India); the west is partly bordered by Māverā an-Nahr and partly by the Khallukh (=Qarluq Turks) country; and the north is partly bordered by the Khallukh country and partly by the Toghuzghuz (= a confederation of Turkish clans).'

19 *Ḥodūd al-ʿĀlam*, p. 73.

20 *Ḥodūd al-ʿĀlam*, p. 73.

21 Cited by Maḥmūd Modabberī, *Sharḥ-e Aḥvāl va Ashʿār Shāʿerān-e Bī-dīvān az qarnhā-ye 3,4,5 hejri-e qamarī* [*Biographies of Poets without a Dīvān from the Third, Forth, and Fifth Centuries of the Lunar Hijra and their Verses*] (Tehran, 1370/1991), p. 56. On the poet, ibid., p. 55. I correct both for the sake of the metre and meaning *ʿanbar-sereshte-ye* to *ʿanbar-seresht*.

تا ز کشمیر صنم خیزد واز تبت مشگ همچو کز مصر قصب خیزد واز طائف ادیم

As long as Kashmīr produces idols and Tibet musk
Just as Egypt produces muslin and Ṭā'if scented leather[22]

Kashmir is one of the lands frequently associated with beautiful Buddhist idols in early Iranian literature[23] and Tibet here is presented as the land of musk par excellence.

Rare allusions to the presence of Iranians in Tibet crop up in Persian literature. In the tenth century, Manṭeqī Rāzī, says in a partially preserved ode:

بسان مرد ایرانی به تبت به باغ اندر گلی بشکفت خندان

Like an Iranian man in Tibet
A rose blossomed, smiling in the garden[24]

The comparison echoes the myth repeated in the anonymous geographical treatise of 982 according to which all men start smiling as they step into Tibet.[25] That myth must have originated in Iranian travellers' oral accounts of the smiling images of Buddhist iconography and of the contented expressions of Tibetan bonzes.

Further evidence of the presence of Iranians in the heart of Tibet is indirectly provided in his usual terse manner by the author of *The Frontiers of the World*. A town with the spelling L-H-Ā-S-Ā, faithfully transcribing the name Lhasa in the Arabic-Persian alphabet, is thus briefly described:

> Lhāsā is a small town. In it there are Buddhist temples [*botkhāne-hā*, 'Buddha Houses'] and one mosque for the Muslims. There are Muslims in it [Lhāsā], few in numbers.[26]

It must be left to Tibetologists to check whether this information is corroborated by Tibetan sources, establishing some form of Muslim presence in tenth-century

---

22 *Dīvān-e Ḥakīm-e Farrokhī-e Sīstānī*, ed. Moḥammad Dabīrsiyāqī (Tehran, ²1349/1970), p. 245, l. 4872.

23 Assadullah Souren Melikian-Chirvani, 'L'évocation littéraire du Bouddhisme dans l'Iran musulman', *Le Monde Iranien et l'Islam*, 2 (1974): pp. 1-72. See pp. 44-5. I have since come across many more mentions of 'the Buddhas of Kashmir'.

24 Modabberī, *Sharḥ-e Aḥvāl*, p. 203. On the poet, who died between 367/19 August 977 – 8 August 978 and 380/31 March 990 – 19 March 991, see p. 199.

25 *Ḥodūd al-ʿĀlam*, p. 73.

26 *Ḥodūd al-ʿĀlam*, p. 74. 'Kārsang' mentioned ibid., p. 76 seems to fit Lhasa better, judging from the 'many' Buddhist temples that it contains. The anonymous writer may have had had in mind two different cities and reversed their respective names.

Tibet. In the absence of contradictory evidence, the mention of a mosque and of established Muslims may be accepted as an indication of a small Iranian presence in Tibet – at that point, Islam had barely touched the Indian subcontinent or the various Turkic groups north of Tibet. The Iranian presence was obviously linked to commerce, the musk trade particularly.

When *Khʷāje* Naṣīr (Naṣīr al-Dīn al-Ṭūsī) wrote in the middle of the thirteenth century his treatise on precious stones, metals and perfumes titled *Tansūq-Nāme-ye Īlkhānī*, Tibetan musk was still highly rated, coming second for quality after Khotani musk.[27] In earlier times, Tibetan musk was the preferred variety. This is implied by a brief mention in the treatise on gems and metals written in Arabic in the early fifth/eleventh century by the Iranian polymath from Central Asia Abū Rayḥān Muḥammad al-Bīrūnī.[28] Quoting 'the Accounts of the Ancient Iranians' [*Akhbār al-Furs*], *Khʷāje* Abū Reyḥān describes presents made to the Sasanian emperor [Khosrow I] who reigned from 531 to 579.[29] After citing those of 'the master of Ceylon' and 'the King of India', the polymath names 'the Khāqān', without any further characterization. The Khāqān's presents consisted of 'one hundred cuirasses with gilt and silvered abstract decoration and four thousand *manns* of Tibetan musk'. The Turkish title 'Khāqān' evidently refers to the ruler of the Turkish confederation ruling Iranian Central Asia, Istämi Khāqān whose daughter Khosrow married according to the ninth-century historian Balādhurī.[30]

The musk trade alone would be enough to account for the establishment of a small Iranian merchant community in Tibet, from Samarqand in particular. Masʿūdī writing around 930 reports that he 'met in Khorasan several people who had travelled from Soghd to Tibet and China via the Sal Ammoniac Mountains'.[31]

The Tibetans for their part imported luxury goods from Iran.

---

27 Moḥammad b. Moḥammad b. Ḥasan *Khʷāje* Naṣīr ad-Dīn Ṭūsī, *Tansūq-Nāme-ye Īlkhānī*, ed. Modarres Rażavi (Tehran, 1348/1969), p. 249.

28 Abū Rayḥān Muḥammad b. Aḥmad al-Bīrūnī, *[Kitāb] al-Jamāhir fi'l-Jawāhir*, ed. Yūsof al-Hādī (Tehran, 1374/1995), p. 145.

29 On *mann* as a weight unit, see Walter Hinz, *Islamische Masse und Gewichte* (Leiden, 1970), p. 17. The closest to a Sasanian period *mann* might be that of highly conservative Tabarestān, nearly 2 kgs. Arthur Christensen, *L'Iran sous les Sassanides*, revised edition (Copenhagen, 1944), pp. 361 and 441.

30 Christensen, *L'Iran*, p. 380, n. 2, citing Schaeder *Iranica*, p. 41, remarks that Khosrow's taking the daughter of Istämi Khaqan is an historical fact.

31 Etienne de la Vaissière, *Histoire des marchands sogdiens* (Paris, 2002) cites the passage p. 318 in the translation given by Marcel Pellat, vol. 1, p. 142, but makes a slight mistake in equating the name Sughd/Soghd used in the fourth/tenth century with Sogdiana. It then referred to a much smaller territory: Iṣṭakhrī, *Kitāb al-masālik wa'l-mamālik*, p. 295 where he sees it as part of the Bokhara district, 'the rest of Soghd being attached to Samarqand'. In p. 316, Eṣṭakhrī, placing Sughd to the East of the Bokhara district, notes that its 'metropolis' [*qaṣaba*] is Samarqand and enumerates its cities: Karmīniyya, Rabinjan, al-Kushāniya, Istikhān, Samarqand. These, he says, are 'the heart of Sughd'.

According to James Russel Hamilton's translation of a tenth-century chronicle mentioning the appointment of [Ts'ao] Yuan-Tchong and his son [Ts'ao] Yuan-Kong to imperial military commandments in the prefecture of Kua under the reign of Che-Tsong (954-60), these officials offered to the court a tribute of 'sal ammoniac, antelope horns, Iranian ('Persian' [Posseu]) brocades and Ngan-si cotton cloth'. The newly appointed officers were Tibetans from Kwachu in Gansu.[32]

Offering Iranian brocades to the Chinese court was a long-established tradition. The *Annals of the Liang* mention 'Persian Brocades' sent in 520 CE as a tribute to Emperor Wu from the Hwa land: that is, the land of the Hephtalites,[33] which, at that period, according to Ṭabarī writing in the fourth/tenth century, included the Balkh area (later rating as the easternmost corner of Khorasan), Tokhārestān along the northern shores of the Oxus and Gharchestān.[34]

Similarly, the route between Tibet and the north-east Iranian areas is staked out by documents preceding the advent of Islam. A large number of Sogdian inscriptions were cut on rocks near Tankse in Ladakh, the westernmost area of historical Tibet. One is of considerable interest concerning Sogdian–Tibetan relations. According to Etienne de la Vaissière, the only elements that do not raise problems of decipherment or interpretation say: 'during the year 210 [...] the Samarqandian [...] Nōsh-farn [...] messenger to the Tibetan Khaqan'.[35] La Vaissière believes that the era given is that of Yazdegerd III, which would date the inscription to 841-42 CE. What it tells us, the French scholar concludes, is that a mission from Samarqand headed by a Sogdian was on its way to Tibet.

Western Tibet, the area closest to those travelling from the south-east Iranian world, was best known to Iranians. In the *Frontiers of the World*, the first Tibetan region mentioned by the author is indeed Zhang-zhung.[36]

32 James Russell Hamilton, *Les Ouïghours à l'époque des cinq dynasties d'après les documents Chinois* (Paris, 1955, repr. 1988), p. 57. Berthold Laufer, *Sino-Iranica* (Chicago, 1919), p. 488, n. 9 already cited the text translated by Hamilton as an example of 'Persian' brocades sent from Kwachu in Gansu to the Chinese court. Hamilton notes in *Les Ouïghours*, p. 26, n. 9, that the Tibetans took control of Kwachu ('Koua-tcheou') in 776.

33 Laufer, *Sino-Iranica*, p. 488 and n. 5, and Edouard Chavannes, *Documents sur les Tou-kiue occidentaux* (Paris, 1904), p. 222.

34 Chavannes, *Documents*, pp. 223-4, with n. 1 citing Zotenberg's translation of the Persian version of Ṭabarī's *Annals*, vol. 2, p. 131.

35 La Vaissière, *Histoire des marchands sogdiens*, p. 310. The author briefly discusses the possibility that the date might be given according to the Muslim era which would be equivalent to 825-6, but does not retain it: see p. 311.

36 *Ḥodūd al-ʿĀlam*, p. 73. The name appears without the diacritical dots, reading 'r' instead of 'zh' in the printed edition as in the manuscript, see facsimile 16A of the Kabul edition with the Persian translation of Vladimir Barthold's preface and the commentary of Vladimir Minorsky by Mīr Ḥosayn Shāh in *Ḥodūd al-ʿĀlam* (Kabul, 1342/1963). Minorsky, *Ḥudūd al-ʿĀlam*, ed. Clifford Edmund Bosworth, revised edition (London, 1970), p. 257 did

For the moment, no earlier written documentation is available to map out the route from East Iranian lands to Tibet, but commercial routes tend to be remarkably constant through history. It is not stretching the imagination too far to posit that the Iran–Tibet route was the same in earlier times. Nor is it wildly adventurous to presume that the earlier contacts paved the way, so to speak, for the significant impact that Iranian culture had on Tibet from the seventh–eighth centuries on, resulting in the adoption of a royal ceremonial, the wine banquet, and of the Sasanian regalia ranging from the royal silk brocades called in Pahlavi and Persian *parniyān* and *parand*, to the attributes of the universal royalty traditionally claimed by Iranian rulers.

II. THE INSTRUMENTS OF THE IRANIAN WINE BANQUET IN TIBET

Art proves that silver vessels made in the Iranian world reached Tibet not later than some time around the seventh–eighth centuries CE. These were of a type used at Iranian courts in the ritualized wine libations which I have described in several monographs.[37] Three types of Iranian wine banquet vessels can be shown to have reached Tibet: wine bowls, wine horns terminated with animal heads, and animal-headed ewers.[38]

1. OF WINE BOWLS AND WINE CUPS

The wine bowls are represented by one silver piece of immense importance that appeared in 1985 at a London auction as the property of Professor David Snellgrove (Plate 4.5).[39] The bowl was ascribed to 'Central Asia, probably Bactria'

---

not consider the possibility that diacritical dots were omitted, a common occurrence in early manuscripts, and transliterated the name as 'Rang-Rong'.

[37] On the early Iranian royal wine banquet (*bazm*) see A.S. Melikian-Chirvani, 'The Iranian *Bazm* in Early Persian Sources', in *Res Orientales: Banquets d'Orient* (Bures-sur-Yvette, 1992), pp. 95-119, one fig.; on the distant sacrificial origins of the wine libations and their cosmic symbolism, see A.S. Melikian-Chirvani, 'The Wine Bull and the Magian Master', in *Studia Iranica*, Cahier 11 *Current Patterns in Iranian Religions* (Bures-sur-Yvette, 1992), pp. 101-34, 3 figs.

[38] On the identification of the ancient Pahlavi and Persian names and symbolism of wine horns see A.S. Melikian-Chirvani, 'The Iranian Wine Horn from Pre-Achaemenid Antiquity to the Safavid Age', *Bulletin of the Asia Institute*, N.S., 10 (1996): pp. 85-139 and 28 figs. On animal-headed ewers, their ancient names and symbolism, see A.S. Melikian-Chirvani, 'Les taureaux à vin et les cornes à boire de l'Iran islamique', in Paul Bernard and Frantz Grenet (eds), *Histoire et cultes de l'Asie Centrale Préislamique* (Paris, 1991), pp. 101-38, 17 figs and 2 colour plates.

[39] Sotheby's *Antiquities* (London, 9 October 1985), lot 64, four unnumbered pages. Denwood's 'Greek Bowl from Tibet', in *Iran* (London, 1973), pp. 121-7, does not take into account the Hellenistic aspects of Iranian art.

meaning the land known as Bakhtrish in Achaemenid Persian (sixth century BCE), and Balkh in Persian. No qualification is necessary.

The figural scenes executed in repoussé, with individual sections crimped in according to the Iranian technique used on Sasanian silver wares, clearly point in that direction. Executed in a style derived from the enduring legacy of Hellenism which spread with regional variants across the entire Iranian world,[40] these scenes are stylistically comparable to others on pieces that have come to light in the East Iranian domain.

The latter include a shallow footed dish now in the British Museum which was preserved in the Treasury of the Amīrs [=Rulers] of Badakhshān until 1829 and another silver dish acquired in Rawalpindi.[41] On both, characters are clad in light drapes that do not conceal the naked forms of the body. The handling of the low relief on the shallow bowl from Tibet is closely comparable to the dish acquired in Rawalpindi. A similar remark applies to the trees with twisted trunks and stumps of pruned branches which also carry unreal blossoms at the top. On the underside of the footed dish from Tibet, six fishes are swimming. The stylization of the water finds an exact parallel on an eight-lobed elongated vessel of the type called *rekāb* in early Persian sources.[42] This vessel, now in the Louvre, was tentatively ascribed to Eastern Iran by Françoise Demange.[43]

Interpreting the scene featuring the standing characters engaged in wine drinking on the bowl formerly owned by David Snellgrove is problematic. As on other Iranian silver bowls that likewise draw on the Hellenistic legacy, the Greek motifs or themes were probably recast in Iranian terms as happened throughout the history of Iran whenever literary themes were borrowed from foreign sources. Given the loss of all Iranian secular literature preceding the advent of Islam, there is scant hope of ever putting forward an interpretation founded on textual evidence.

By contrast, the motif of the swimming fish on the underside of the base clearly renders the motif of the river/sea (in Persian *dariyā* or, using the Arabic loan word, *baḥr*), hinting at 'the sea of wine' that each wine cup or wine bowl

---

40 On the Hellenistic garb of Iranian art and culture, see A.S. Melikian-Chirvani, 'Rustam and Herakles, a Family Resemblance', *Bulletin of the Asia Institute*, N.S., 12 (1998): pp. 171-99, 8 figs.

41 Ormonde Maddock Dalton, *The Treasure of the Oxus* (London, [3]1964). Respectively n. 196, pp. 49-50 and pl. XXVII, n. 208, pp. 62-4, pl. XXXVIII. On the dish n. 208, see latterly *Les Perses Sassanides* [*sic*] *Fastes d'un empire oublié 224-642* (Paris, 2006), p. 98, n. 36.

42 A.S. Melikian-Chirvani, '*Rekāb*: The Polylobed Wine Boat from Sasanian to Saljuq Times', *Res Orientales*, vol. 8 *Au Carrefour des religions: Mélanges offerts à Philippe Gignoux* (Bures-sur-Yvette, 1995), pp. 187-204, 9 plates.

43 Françoise Demange, 'Nouvelles acquisitions', in *Revue du Louvre* (Paris, 2004), p. 87, figs 5 and 6. – *Les Perses Sassanides*, p. 104, n. 42, see colour plate p. 104, central lobe.

metaphorically contains.[44] That this is indeed a wine bowl is further confirmed by the depiction of glass decanters held by two characters.

The significance of this wine bowl concerning the Iranian world–Tibet connection lies in its provenance. According to Sotheby's catalogue, it was acquired in Nepal in 1961 'from a member of an aristocratic Tibetan family which had been resident in Lhasa for many generations. The bowl was regarded as a family heirloom; its previous provenance was not known.'[45] The silver piece would appear to have been kept above ground through time, inasmuch as visual inspection not verified by laboratory examination can be trusted. This raises the tantalizing possibility that an East Iranian piece of silver not later than the seventh century, and possibly earlier, might have been passed on from hand to hand in Tibet during the last 1300 years or thereabouts. In any case, its verified presence in Tibet in more recent times establishes the import of East Iranian silver vessels for the royal wine banquet.

Evidence that Tibetan artists became familiar with north-east Iranian precious metal wares is independently supplied by the discovery of a remarkable gold wine cup with a ring handle that came to light in Paris in September 2008 (Plate 4.6).[46]

The shallow bowl, about 9.5 cm across, reproduces an age-old type known in Iranian art since Pre-Achaemenid times. It rests on a low beaded foot of a type commonly found in Sogdian silver datable to the eighth century CE.[47] The ring-handle topped by a five-lobed thumb-rest likewise derives from Sogdian silver models of that period.[48] A Tibetan inscription carefully incised on the underside has been read by the eminent historian of Tibetan art, Amy Heller, as *'o rgyad 'phan lod.*

Whatever interpretation is ultimately retained, the inscription tells us that the cup was in Tibetan hands in early times, probably around the eighth century

44 On 'the sea of wine' in Persian poetry when referring to the wine in the drinker's bowl, see for example, Melikian-Chirvani, 'The Wine Bull and the Magian Master', pp. 116-17. This is an ancient Middle Eastern theme, like others relating to wine in Iranian literature. It passed into ancient Greek literature: See François Lissarrague, *Un flot d'images: Une esthéthique du banquet Grec* (Paris, 1996), chapter headed 'La mer vineuse', pp. 104-18.

45 Sotheby's, *Antiquities* (see n. 39 above), same entry lot 64 (not paginated) last paragraph.

46 Unpublished. Displayed on the stand of the renowned dealer in Chinese art Christian Deydier at the Biennale des Antiquaires, Grand Palais, 2008.

47 Vladislav Petrovich Darkevich, *Khudozhestvennij Metall Vostolk VIII-XIIIw.* [*Artistic Metal Wares of the East*] (Moscow, 1976), n. 29, pp. 21-2, pl. 8, figs 1-4. For an accessible illustration of Darkevich n. 29 with outdated regional attribution and date, see Arthur U. Pope (ed.), *A Survey of Persian Art* (Ashiya, 1981), vol. 7, pl. 222 or, better, Boris Ilich Marshak, *Sogdiisko Serebro* [*Sogdian Silver*] (Moscow, 1971): see respectively pl. T 28 (line drawing) and T 42; see also the six-lobed cup with ring handle in T 46.

48 Compare Marshak, *Sogdiisko Serebro*, handle plate in T 46.

CE. There is no way of determining whether the inscription was written in Tibet, in the areas of present-day east Turkistan (now Xinjiang) where Sogdians mixed with a growing Turkic Uyghur population, or even further east in Dunhuang, originally a Sogdian outpost (Durwanga, hence the Sinicized pronunciation 'Dunhuang'), or in China where numerous Sogdian communities settled.[49] The material, gold, in conjunction with the high quality of the object, makes it legitimate to speculate that it had a princely or royal destination.

There is reason to believe that, in addition to silver and gold plate, another class of Iranian royal table ware became known to Tibetan artists: precious metal vessels studded with gemstones. These formed part of the broader category of precious metal artefacts studded with gemstones, from wares for the royal table to the hilts of edged weapons. Called *moraṣṣaʿāt*, an Arabic loan-word which replaced various early Persian words such as *bar-āmūde*, these were kept in the royal treasury.[50]

Indirect evidence concerning the transmission from Iran to Tibet of table wares in gold studded with gemstones is yielded by one of the murals discovered by Thomas Pritzker 'in the valley of Pu Khar, in the Western Kingdom of Guge'. On the east wall, Ganapati is seen holding an object that has not attracted attention[51] (Plate 4.7). The profile of the squat bowl rising from a narrow circular base with slightly curving sides flaring at a very low angle before briefly curving back over the inside at the top bears an unmistakable resemblance to much earlier Iranian models (Plate 4.8).

A horizontal row of lotus buds pointed downwards reproduces a motif encountered on scores of Iranian vessels. Judging from the yellow colour of the reproduction, the painter had in mind a gold bowl studded with alternately red and green gems. In the Iranian tradition these would have been rubies, or possibly red spinels, and emeralds.[52] The gems are cut in the shape of a pointed lotus bud. Found on gold, silver and bronze vessels form the earliest times, the motif is

---

49 Etienne de la Vaissière and Etienne Trombert, 'Des Chinois et des Hu. Migration et intégration des Iraniens orientaux durant le haut Moyen-Age', *Annales. Histoire, Sciences Sociales*, 5-6 (2004), pp. 931-69, and La Vaissière, *Histoire des marchands sogdiens*, particularly pp. 49-53 and pp. 217ff. One of the so-called 'Ancient Letters' found near Dunhuang was contained in a sealed linen envelope inscribed in Sogdian: 'to be sent to Samarqand'. See *Histoire des marchands sogdiens*, pl. I, n. III, facing p. 212.

50 A.S. Melikian-Chirvani, 'The Jewelled Objects of Hindustan', *Jewellery Studies*, 10 (2004): pp. 9-32, 22 figs. See p. 9 on Iranian *moraṣṣaʿāt*.

51 Thomas Pritzker, 'The Wall Paintings of Nyag Lhakhang Kharpo', *Orientations* (March 2008): pp. 102-12. See p. 103, fig. 1a.

52 A.S. Melikian-Chirvani, 'The Red Stones of Light in Iranian Culture I. Spinels', *Bulletin of the Asia Institute*, N.S., 15 (2001): pp. 77-110, 2 figs. Red and green stones are associated in poetry, e.g. pp. 94-5.

called *peykānī* ('arrow-head like') in early Persian treatises on gemmology – in early Persian poetry 'arrow heads' are often compared with buds.[53]

Was the original model that gave rise to the image in the mural an Iranian pre-Islamic import or, as seems more likely, a Tibetan artefact? If so, did it precede the execution of the murals in the Pu Khar valley by centuries? These questions cannot be answered for now. All that is clearly established is the reproduction of an early Iranian model in an eleventh-century painting in Tibet.

2. AN IRANIAN TYPE WINE SERVICE

It is against this background of apparent imports of precious metal royal vessels from the Iranian world and closely related Tibetan artefacts that the case of a set of three parcel gilt silver vessels – a beaker, a wine horn and a decanter – acquired in 1988 by the Cleveland Museum of Art, must be reconsidered (Plates 4.9-11).[54] All three pieces were obviously made in the same centre, perhaps the same workshop, within a short lapse of time, and may be assumed to have been acquired by their original owner to form part of a wine service. The stylistic consistency of the repoussé motifs noted by previous commentators is evident as a glance.

On all three pieces, the figural motifs are enclosed within twin framing rope-like bands carrying highly stylized blossoms or leaves which curl back. Whether lions, birds, or dragons, they are handled in a highly expressive style which may be described as Baroque, but they do not appear to be the work of a single artist. To cite but one example, the lion standing on its rear legs depicted on the beaker is quite different from the lion leaping on the wine horn.[55]

While the rearing lion and the eagle with spread wings ultimately go back to the Iranian repertoire, the reptile with a horned head calls to mind Chinese dragons.

The shapes again betray a dual origin. The wine horn is a typically Iranian model, with its wide opening at the top and its small tubular outlet projecting from the mouth which allowed the wine to flow in a straight jet.[56]

---

53 The 'arrow-head' cut (*peykānī*) is described in 'Red Stones of Light', pp. 94-5.

54 Stan[islaw] Czuma, 'Tibetan Silver Vessels', *The Bulletin of the Cleveland Museum of Art*, 80/4 (1993): pp. 131-5 with mention of the earlier publication by the same writer. Stanislaw Czuma, 'Some Tibetan and Tibet-Related Acquisitions of the Cleveland Museum of Art', *Oriental Art*, 38/4 (1992-93): pp. 231-42, see p. 231. Martha Carter, 'Three Silver Vessels from Tibet's Earliest Historical Era: A Preliminary Study', in *Cleveland Studies in the History of Art* (The Cleveland Museum of Art, 1999), pp. 22-47, see pp. 22-37.

55 Compare Czuma, 'Tibetan Silver Vessels', p. 131, fig. 1 and p. 133, fig. 3 respectively.

56 On the way in which the wine horn was held in the eighth century, see Melikian-Chirvani, 'The Iranian Wine Horn', p. 113, fig. 15.

The beaker with its cylindrical body and flat base reproduces a model that has a long history in Iran, and the ring handle with its polylobed thumb-rest harks back to Sogdian models of the seventh or eighth century.[57]

The vase-like container, only 22.9 cm high, has been understood to be a vase by previous commentators. However, it is rather small for a vase, whereas its size is right for a decanter in the Iranian tradition, and such a function is consistent with that of the beaker and the wine horn. All three pieces are evidently part of a wine service in the Iranian fashion.

The Tibetan make of the pieces has so far been taken for granted. One reason is the presence of an early Tibetan inscription on the underside of the beaker and another reason may have been the provenance which would have been known to the commercial source.

A third argument may now be invoked, the broad epigraphic kinship of the inscriptions on the underside of the beaker and on the newly discovered gold wine cup.[58] In addition, both vessels have ring handles with comparable lobed thumb-rests. The Tibetan manufacture of the two objects is therefore highly likely, although it is more difficult to assure with any degree of certainty that the actual place of execution was Tibet rather than, perhaps, adjacent territories to the east or north, where Tibetan communities lived and where Tibetan rule held sway at certain periods.[59]

The importance of the Cleveland Museum set goes beyond establishing the existence of a Tibetan workshop creating silver vessels in an original style derived from Sogdian, that is, north-east Iranian models. It points to the adoption of the Iranian royal wine banquet.

The inscription on the base of the beaker has been translated as 'personal possession of the high-born princess', a reading questioned by Hugh Richardson who observed that the inscription may name a place rather than a person.[60]

---

57 On cylindrical vessels from Jīroft datable to the third millennium BCE see anon., *Farhang-e Ḥāshiye-ye Halīl-Rūd va Jīroft* [*Culture Around Halīl-Rūd and Jīroft*] (Tehran, 1384/2005). See p. 44, figs. 13 and 14, p. 45. Metal buckets of cylindrical shape are represented at Takht-e Jamshīd ('Persepolis') in the sixth century BCE : Roman Ghirshman, *Perse: Proto-iraniens. Mèdes. Achéménides* (Paris, 1963), p. 206, pl. 205, far right. Compare Czuma, 'Tibetan Silver Vessels', p. 132, fig. 2.

58 Tibetologists will be the ultimate judges of the degree of kinship.

59 Helmut Hoffman, 'Early and Medieval Tibet', in Denis Sinor (ed.), *The Cambridge History of Early Inner Asia* (Cambridge, 1990), pp. 385, 390. Amy Heller, 'Recent Findings on Textiles from the Tibetan Empire', in *Riggisberger Berichte* (Zurich, 2006), pl. 175, notes: 'in about 666, Tibet occupied first Khotan, then Kucha and the northern oases, which it held until 692'.

60 Czuma, 'Tibetan Silver Vessels', p. 131. Carter, 'Three Silver Vessels', p. 23 and p. 41, n. 2, acknowledging the original reading by Heather Stoddard (Karmay) as *phan:shin g:gong:skyes:sug:byad(or byang)*, and n. 3 noting Hugh Richardson's comments. See further p. 41, n. 3. Richardson's remarks on the earliest use of the Tibetan terms suggest that the wine service might date from the eighth century CE rather than the late seventh century.

It is however clear that the set had a royal destination. I have described the special character of the Iranian royal wine banquet which goes back to the deepest past of Iran when wine libations were substituted to blood libations, probably at the advent of Zoroastrianism. Loaded with a cosmic symbolism, the wine libations took place in an atmosphere of great solemnity.[61]

The utensils used included the wine horn, called *pālogh* in Pahlavi. Also used in early Persian, the term soon gave way to the more common *shākh*, 'horn', used alone or in conjunction with nouns referring to wine, as in '*shākh-e bāde*', literally 'wine horn'.[62]

From Pre-Achaemenid times down to the seventh century at least, the extremities of the wine horns were fashioned in the shape of animals which had once been sacrificial victims: bulls, deer, gazelles, goats and others.[63]

The wine horn, like the entire wine banquet ceremonial, knew no religious boundaries. Wine horns have come to light in a Buddhist context in the eastern Iranian world, at Bagram north of Kabul for example, and wine horns were still used at Islamic courts across the Iranian world as late as the thirteenth century.[64]

3. ON A TIBETAN ANIMAL-HEADED EWER

Evidence that the Iranian wine banquet was adopted in Tibet is provided by another type of vessel, of which a specimen is preserved in the Jokhang in Lhasa (Plate 4.12).[65] The parcel-gilt silver ewer, worked in a style of its own that does not lend itself to specific comparison with anything else, has a neck topped by a camel's head. The wine would be poured into the ewer through an opening in the head and come out of the circular outlet lodged in the mouth. This structural

---

[61] On the early Iranian royal banquet, see n. 37 above. Its symbolism is dealt with in several monographs by this writer dealing with wine vessels. On wine boats: 'From the Royal Boat to the Beggar's Bowl', in *Islamic Art* (New York, 1990-91), vol. 5, pp. 3-106 with 106 figs. On bird-shaped wine-ewers: 'The Wine Birds of Iran from Pre-Achaemenid to Islamic Times', *Bulletin of the Asia Institute*, N.S., 9 (1995): pp. 41-97, 27 figs. On wine horns (so-called 'rhyta'): 'The Iranian Wine Horn'. On wine-legs (ewers shaped as feet/legs): 'The Iranian Wine Leg from Prehistory to Mongol Times', *Bulletin of the Asia Institute*, N.S., 11 (1997): pp. 65-91. On the distant origins and esoteric connotations of the Wine Bull (ewer shaped as a bull, or as a vase topped by a bull's head): 'The Wine Bull and the Magian Master': see n. 38 above.

[62] Melikian-Chirvani, 'The Iranian Wine Horn'.

[63] See n. 61.

[64] Joseph Hackin, *Recherches archéologiques à Begram* (2 vols, *Texte* and *Planches*, Paris, 1939). See *Planches*, pl. IX, fig. 20, n. 176 and *Texte*, p. 33 where the object is mistakenly described as a 'support d'oeuf d'autruche en forme de rhyton'. On the use of wine horns at thirteenth-century courts, see Melikian-Chirvani 'The Iranian Wine Horn', p. 95.

[65] Heller, *Early Himalayan Art*, p. 23 where the vessel is called a 'jug'.

model is Iranian (Plate 4.13),[66] even if the *sui generis* style of decoration owes nothing to Iran.

Dating such an object in the absence of stylistically comparable pieces is hazardous. Commentators have put forward the eighth century. However, the highly mannered rendition of a dancing character raising his lute above his shoulder with one hand while holding a plectrum in the other and the formal motifs almost Baroque in spirit, make it conceivable that the decanter might be later by a century or two.

What is clear is the connection of the animal-headed ewer to the Iranian concept of the royal wine banquet. The dancing character plays an Iranian-type instrument as Iranian tradition required at wine banquets[67] and wears a crown consisting of a ring with a frontal clasp, in which two eagle wings are stuck. This is the Sasanian crown model.

I am in no position to suggest whether the character represents a ruler dancing or an allegorical figure. The Iranian wine banquet ceremonial was probably recast in the cultural terms of what Tibet was then. But however the dancing character may be construed, it will have had some form of royal connotation, literal or metaphorical, given his crown with eagle wings of Sasanian derivation.

Indeed, the adoption of the Iranian royal wine banquet ceremonial reflects a broader trend that led early Tibet to borrow Iranian royal custom and paraphernalia.

III. THE IRANIAN REGALIA IN THE EARLY ART OF TIBET

This has not been realised so far, in part because the nature of the important brocaded silk decorated with tangent roundels called *parniyān* and *parand* in Persian literature was identified relatively recently by this writer in a publication dealing chiefly with Iran and Central Asia.[68] It was the most important of all textiles that travelled along the so-called 'Silk Road'.

1. PARNIYĀN/PARAND BROCADED SILKS IN TIBET

In the Persian lexicon of the mid-eleventh century attributed to Asadī Ṭūsī, *parniyān* is said to be 'silk from Eastern Turkistan that has patterns and roundels'

---

[66] Melikian-Chirvani, 'Les taureaux à vin et les cornes à boire de l'Iran islamique', see pl. XLIX, figs 12, 13; pl. figs 14, 15; figs 16, 17.

[67] Melikian-Chirvani, 'The Iranian *Bazm*', pp. 97 and 98 (quoting the tenth-century *Shāh-Nāme*). Thousands of verses associate the banquet and music playing.

[68] A.S. Melikian-Chirvani, '*Parand* and *Parniyan* Identified: The Royal Silks of Iran from Sasanian to Islamic Times', *Bulletin of the Asia Institute*, N.S., 5 (1991): pp. 175-9, one fig.

[*ḥarīr-e Chīnī bāshad ke naqsh-hā va charkh-hā dārad*].[69] *Parand* is characterized as a monochrome [*sāde*] version of the silk while *parniyān* is 'polychrome' (*haftrang*, literally 'of seven [primary] colours'), a distinction maintained in later dictionaries.[70] The distinction, which may go back to Pahlavi literature, is echoed in the opening couplet of an ode written in the early eleventh century by Farrokhī:

چون پرند نیلگون بر روی پوشد مرغزار
پرنیان هفت رنگ اندر سر آرد کوهسار

As the wilderness pulls the deep blue *parand* over its face
The mountain crest brings over its head the polychrome *parniyān*[71]

The border framing the *parniyān/parand* roundels is a stylized rendition of the sky and its stars. The circle or ring is an age-old symbol of the sky in Iranian thinking and the beads stand for stars perceived in the Middle East as small circular spots,[72] as witness many Persian verses. The eleventh-century poet Lāmeʿī Gorgānī writes:

از روی چرخ چنبری رخشان سهیل ومشتری
چون بر پرند ششتری پاشیده دینار ودرم

On the face of the arched sky, Canopus and Jupiter scintillate
Like dinars and dirhams strewn on Shoshtarī *parand*[73]

69 Asadī Ṭūsī, *Loghat-e Fors*, ed. Moḥammad Dabīrsiyāqī (Tehran, 1337/1968), p. 144. Missing in the more recent edition given by Fatḥollāh Mojtabāʾī and ʿAlī-Ashraf Ṣādeqī, Abū Manṣūr Aḥmad b. ʿAlī Asadī Ṭūsī, *Loghat-e Fors* (Tehran, 1365/1986).

70 Moḥammad b. Hendūshāh Nakhchevānī, *Ṣeḥāḥ ol-Fors*, ed. ʿAbd ol-ʿAlī Ṭaʿatī (Tehran, 1341/1962), p. 75.

71 On the Pahlavi use of the words, see W.B. Henning, 'Two Central Asian Words', *Transactions of the Philological Society* (1945): pp. 150-62, notably p. 153. Henning quotes Farrokhī's couplet (ibid., p. 156) and retains *bīdgūn* ('of weeping willow colour') because the word is more rarified. *Nīlgūn* is preferable because it fits into the repertoire of Iranian images. *Dīvān-e Ḥakīm-e Farrokhī-e Sīstānī*, p. 175, verse 3711.

72 Abū Naṣr ʿAlī b. Aḥmad Asadī Ṭūsī, *Garshāsp-Nāme*, ed. Ḥabīb Yaghmāʾī (Tehran, 1317/1938) writes in the mid-eleventh century:

When the sun plucked out of the turquoise glazed
Vault all the crystal beads

73 *Dīvān-e Lāmeʿī Gorgānī*, ed. Moḥammad Dabīrsiyāqī (Tehran, 2535sh/1976), p. 97. Nakhchevānī, *Seḥāḥ ol-Fors*, p. 75.

The mention of dinars, which are gold coins, and dirhams, which are silver coins, is not random. The seventh-eighth century *parand* beads are golden or white when standing out on a deep blue ground, the colour of the sky at night in the Iranian mental repertoire.[74]

Evidence that Iranian-type *parniyān* illustrated in Plate 4.14 was used for royal garments in Tibet as early as the seventh century is supplied by Chinese painting.

In an important study of Tibetan costume from the seventh to the eleventh century, Heather (Stoddard) Karmay was the first to draw attention to 'the earliest representation of a Tibetan we have at present'.[75] This refers to Blon-po mgar, the minister of Srong-btsan sgam-po portrayed in a Chinese scroll attributed to Yan Liben (627-73). The scroll depicts Blon-po mgar rejecting the hand of a granddaughter of the Chinese Emperor Taizong. The minister wears a cloak cut from the silk with roundels enclosing the effigy of a duck.

Heather Karmay pointed out that 'this type of brocade' was 'very widespread in Asia by the time of the Tang' dynasty. It should simply be added that the model spread from Iran as far East as Japan via the north-east Iranian areas populated by Sogdians, and as far west as Arab Spain by the tenth century.[76]

Miss Karmay, who had the merit of drawing attention to the fabric worn by the minister and of pointing out its Iranian connotation, mentioned 'the symmetrical pearl bordered "Sasanian" roundels', noting the Sasanian connection in inverted commas.[77]

These are justified in so far as a textile from Turfan illustrated by her as a material example of silk with beaded roundels may have been woven in that city where a massive Sogdian presence is established by various Chinese manuscripts of the sixth century CE and thus would qualify as an example of the East Turkistan *parniyān* silks cited by Asadī Ṭūsī. But textiles with roundels enclosing figural motifs are already represented on the early seventh-century bas relief at Ṭāq-e Bostān where the Sasanian emperor Khosrow II wears trousers cut from such a fabric and so are, more precisely, textiles with the effigies of birds framed by circular bands of beads broken up by square devices.[78]

---

74 As shown, for example, by Farrokhī's couplet quoted above.

75 Heather Karmay, 'Tibetan Costume, Seventh to Eleventh Centuries', in Ariane Macdonald and Yoshiro Imaeda (eds), *Essais sur l'art du Tibet* (Paris, 1977), pp. 65-81, at pp. 65-7. Discussed by Amy Heller, 'Two Inscribed Fabrics and their Historical Context: Some Observations on Esthetics and Silk Trade in Tibet, 7th to 9th Century', in *Riggisberger Berichte*, 6 *Entlang der Seidenstrasse* (Riggisberg, 1998), pp. 95-118. See pp. 108-9 where the robe is more clearly reproduced (fig. 47, p. 109) after Valrae Reynolds, 'Luxury Textiles in Tibet', in Jill Tilden (ed.), *Asian Art* (London, 1995), pp. 86-97, 190-91.

76 See Melikian-Chirvani, *The Royal Silks of Iran* (in preparation).

77 Karmay, 'Tibetan Costume', p. 67.

78 Shinji Fukai and Kiyoharu Horiuchi, *Taq-i-Bustan* (2 vols, Tokyo, 1969-72), pls XLIV, XLV, XLVI for a detail of the emperor's trousers with roundels in a repeat pattern but

Material proof of the import of Sasanian silk into lands inhabited by Tibetans is available. At Dulan in Qinghai, a fragment of a Sasanian silk with a Pahlavi inscription establishing its royal ownership was recovered from a Tibetan tomb.[79]

Sogdians, that north-east Iranian group of indefatigable traders, played the lead role in the transmission to Tibet of Sasanian *parniyān* and *parand* as well as of their own versions. Whether these were woven in their original homeland, perhaps in Samarqand, or in their easternmost cities in what is now East Turkistan, makes no difference to the cultural significance of the use of Iranian-type royal silk in Tibet.

How enduring the memory of *parniyān/parand* was can be measured from the traces it left in Western Tibetan mural painting in Ladakh at Alchi and in the Spiti region (now part of Himachal Pradesh in India) at Tabo.[80] There, on the north wall of the 'entrance *stūpa*' in the village of Mangyu, the Amitayus Buddha is clad in a mantle cut from a Tibetan fabric with a pattern of tangent roundels each enclosing figures of animals passant (see Plate 4.15).[81] Robert Linrothe noting that the paintings are contemporary with those in the Sumtsek temples, dates them to 'the early twelfth to the early thirteenth century'.

It is impossible to determine whether the north-east Iranian *parniyān/parand* silks to which the textile depicted in the Mangyu 'entrance *stūpa*' goes back is a comparatively early model of the seventh or eighth century, or whether later examples of Islamic period *parniyān/parand* overlaid that memory. The precise if limited evidence of a strain of East Iranian influence reaching Tibet in the early Guge Kingdom established by the twelfth-century murals at Dungkar warns us of possible overlayers of different strands of influence from various periods. In any case, the adoption of *parand* mantles for Buddha figures echoes royal Iranian usage.

By the time Ferdowsi was writing the *Book of Kings* (*Shāh-Nāme*) completed shortly before 1000 CE, the symbolism of royal glory attached to the *parniyān/parand* silks was still very much alive. Praising Sultan Maḥmūd the Ghaznevid, Ferdowsi writes:

بنام جهاندار محمود شاه   ابو القاسم آن فرّ دیهیم وماه
خداوند ایران وتوران وهند   ز فرّش جهان شد چو رومی پرند

not yet tangent. For the variant with beaded frames on the tunics of the royal hunter's retinue standing on flat-bottomed boats, ibid., vol. 1, pl. LVII b.

79 Zhao Feng, 'Weaving Methods for Western Style *Samit* from the Silk Road in Western China', in *Riggisberger Berichte*, 9 *Central Asian Textiles and their Contexts in the Early Middle Ages* (Riggisberg, 2006), pp. 189-210. See p. 199 reproduced fig. 142. Zhao writes (English text, possibly mistranslated) that 'the Persian language was not used in Persian territory after the mid-8th century', presumably meaning Pahlavi. That is also incorrect.

80 Robert N. Linrothe, 'The Murals at Mangyu: A Distillation of Mature Esoteric Buddhist Iconography', *Orientations* (November 1994), repr. in *Art of Tibet: Selected Articles from Orientations 1981-1997* (Hong Kong, 1998), pp. 194-205. On dating see p. 194.

81 Linrothe, 'The Murals at Mangyu', p. 203, fig. 17.

In the name of the world ruler Maḥmūd *Shāh*
Abo'l-Qāsem, that glory [*farr*] of the crown and the throne
The Lord of Iran, Turan and India
The world by his glory became like a Rūmī *parand*[82]

The adjective Rūmī refers to Anatolia, called Rūm in Iran before and after Islam because the Byzantines claimed to be *Romaioi*, 'Romans'. (Other manuscripts, however, have *Chīnī parand*, 'East Turkistan *parand*'.) Ferdowsi says that the world is made to look like a *parand* loom by the king's glory, in Persian *farr*, because the halo of glory surrounding the king's head is shaped like a ring similar to the large circular borders framing the *parand* roundels. Both signify the sky, the halo of glory being the sky filled with the golden light of the sun at the apex.

The memory of buddhas wearing *parniyān/parand* garments (in Persian *bot-e parniyān-pūsh*) which rings in early Persian poetry survived as a literary cliché into the fourteenth century. Khʷājū Kermānī thus writes:

پری چهره ساقی مه سیمتن   بت پرنیان پوش پسته دهن

Angel-faced cupbearer, moon with a silver body
Parniyān-clad Buddha with a mouth [small as a] pistachio[83]

It is for its royal significance that the Buddha was clad in *parniyān/parand* attire as the Lord of the Universe, a concept which almost certainly entered Buddhism when it was refashioned to a considerable extent in Iranian lands.[84] That the royal symbolism attached in Iran to *parniyān/parand* was understood in Buddhist Tibet may be inferred from its representation on bronze figures of the bodhisattva Avalokiteshvara and the Amitayus Buddha, the Lord of the Universe.

Amy Heller has drawn attention to the representation of a textile with roundels that 'recall earlier designs of a single figure in a medallion' on the statue of a crowned Buddha from Gilgit dated 715/716 by its dedicatory inscription.[85] This, of course, describes a *parniyān/parand*-type brocade.

---

82 *Shāh-Nāme*, ed. Jalāl Khāleqī-Moṭlaq (9 vols, New York, 1366/1998-1386/2008), vol. 5, p. 439, l. 8 - p. 440, l. 9. On variant, see p. 440, n. 6.

83 Khʷājū Kermānī, *Homāy va Homāyūn*, in *Khamse-ye Khʷājū-ye Kermānī*, ed. Saʿīde Niyāz-Kermānī (Tehran, 1370/1991), p. 437 l. 3780.

84 The extent to which Buddhism took hold in Iranian lands is reflected, among others, in the metaphorical evocations of perfect beauty in Persian literature. See Melikian-Chirvani, 'L'évocation littéraire du Buddhisme'. On the Iranian origins of the Buddhist ritual of the adorning of the Buddha, see A.S. Melikian-Chirvani, 'The Buddhist Ritual in the Early Literature of Islamic Iran', in Bridgit Allchin (ed.), *South Asian Archaeology, 1981* (Cambridge, 1984), pp. 272-9, at pp. 274-6.

85 Heller, 'Recent Findings on Textiles from the Tibetan Empire', p. 181. See fig. 125, p. 182, fig. 126.

The roundels in question follow the model prevalent in the late seventh to eighth century from Iran to Tang China where it was adopted.[86] The beads are arranged in four clusters of four beads each, separated from each other by devices which are not square as on Sasanian silks, but of a more elaborate outline. These designs may be assumed to be of Tibetan invention like the figures that the roundels enclose.

In the same article Amy Heller illustrates another bronze figure of the seated Buddha datable to the eighth century tentatively ascribed to Kashmir, and cites two more examples, one in the Lahore Museum and the other in Beijing which was presented by the Seventh Dalai Lama to the Qianlong Emperor.[87] The cushions in all three cases are covered with beaded tangent roundels, in other words with *parniyān/parand*-type silks.

It was therefore established practice in Kashmir and Tibet to represent the Buddha as the Lord of the Universe seated on a cushion covered in a *parniyān/parand*-type silk. Whether such silks were woven in Tibet, or only imported, cannot be determined. Either way, the use of *parniyān/parand*-type textiles for this type of Buddhist iconography indicates that the royal connotation of the Iranian brocaded silk was understood.

This fits with the Tibetan adoption of another set of highly important royal symbols in Sasanian and early Islamic Iran.

2. THE TIBETAN ADOPTION OF THE IRANIAN CROWN

A globe set on a crescent moon, mostly associated with two stoles fluttering down or sideways, is frequently seen on the head of the Buddha or at the top of the uppermost parasol crowning a *stūpa*. It was so important that the artists making seals took care to represent them, however minute the scale, as is shown by the early clay seal imprints (*tsa-tsa*) which Tucci collected in Tibet.[88] To the best of my belief, no attempt has been made to account for the origin, let alone

---

86 A different view is taken by Wu Min, 'The Exchange of Weaving Technologies between China and Central and Western Asia from the Third to the Eighth Century Based on New Textiles Finds at Xinjiang', in *Riggisberger Berichte*, 9, pp. 211-41. However, our learned colleague provides arguments against her own thesis: among others, the order given by Emperor Wendi to a man called He Chou 'to make silks that imitated Persian silks': see pp. 239-40. His grandfather came from a town in the greater Samarqand area called al-Kushāniyya in Arabic texts. The assumption that frames with clusters of beads/pearls separated by square devices is Chinese ignores the fact that such frames were widespread in Iranian art. Taking the opposite view to Wu Min's, Zhao Feng ('Weaving Methods') assures us on the basis of the weaving techniques, that *samit* textiles cannot have been woven in China proper (see p. 209).

87 Heller, 'Recent Findings on Textiles from the Tibetan Empire', p. 178, n. 6.

88 Tucci, *Tibet*, pls 89, 90, 91, 94, 96, 101 (to the left of the bodhisattva's head), 108 and corresponding captions, pp. 221-3. According to Tucci, all date from the twelfth or thirteenth century.

the meaning of the symbols. In Sasanian art, these regalia were carved on rock bas-reliefs, executed in repoussé on royal silver plate and struck on imperial coinage.[89]

The *raison d'être* of the orb and the crescent moon as part of the Sasanian regalia has yet to be elucidated. A simple explanation might lie in the formula 'Lord of the Sun and the Moon' (*Khodāvand-e khorshīd-o māh*) used 30 times in the *Shāh-Nāme* when celebrating God as the Lord of the World.[90] Whatever their exact meaning, their presence in the imperial headdress establishes their imperial significance. Associated with the Buddha, they would have hailed him as 'the Lord of the Universe', and when crowning a *stūpa*, the regalia would have retained the same significance, the *stūpa* symbolizing the cosmic body of the Buddha.[91]

This set of regalia comes together with the use of yet another Iranian royal symbol: the parasol. This is an age-old Iranian metaphor for the sky. In a panegyric on an unnamed ruler, Shams Ṭabasī thus writes in the early thirteenth century:

هر روزِ شاه شرق بر این چتر آبگون
در ظلّ رایت تو علم بر فراشته

Everyday the Shah of the Orient [= the sun] above that bluish parasol [=the sky]
Raises its ensign in the shadow of your standard [92]

The parasol as an imperial symbol goes back to the Achaemenid empire. At Takht-e Jamshīd ('Persepolis' in Western Orientalist literature), an attendant holds a parasol over the head of Emperor Darius I in the bas-relief carved on one of the doorways.[93] It persisted in Sasanian Iran where it appears on the Ṭāq-e Bostān imperial relief and in the East Iranian lands won over to Buddhism, as at

---

89 Monumental sculpture: Roman Ghirshman, *Parthes et Sassanides* (Paris, 1962), p. 192, pl. 235 (at Taq-e Bostan, the emperor standing on the upper tier) and for details Fukai and Horiuchi, *Taq-i-Bustan*, vol. 2, pls. V, VI, VII. Royal silver: *Parthes et Sassanides*, p. 212, pl. 253; p. 206, pl. 245. Coinage: pp. 250, n. 318; 320.

90 E.g. *Shāh-Nāme*, ed. Khaleqī-Moṭlaq, vol. 1, p. 139, l. 817 (I retain the version given by Jules Mohl I p. 184, l. 846 which has *namāyam* rather than *namānam*):

[That] by the might of the Lord of the Sun and the Moon
I will show him [the full power of] my equipment

91 Adrian Snodgrass, *The Symbolism of the Stupa* (Ithaca, 1985), pp. 360ff.

92 *Dīvān-e Asīr ad-Dīn Akhsīkatī*, ed. Rokn ad-Dīn Homāyūn Farrokh (Tehran, 1337/1958), p. 461.

93 Ghirshman, *Perse*, p. 186, pl. 233.

Siyāhgerd in the Fonduqestān valley where a mural shows a king behind whom an attendant holds up a parasol.[94]

The explicit royal connotation of the parasol still prevailed in Western Tibet by the time Iranian influence came afresh from the eastern areas of Iran, now Islamicized, more specifically from Khorasan under Ghaznevid rule in the course of the eleventh century. This much may be inferred from several murals in the caves at Alchi which specialists date between the middle of the eleventh and the first half of the twelfth century.

A mural in the Dukhang cave depicts what Pratapaditya Pal rightly called 'a royal drinking scene' (Plate 4.16[95]) without specifying its origin.[96] This is an Iranian-style royal banquet. The king is seated cross-legged, in the manner of the Iranian aristocracy. On his left, a wine taster is seated on his heels, in the respectful posture that behoves members of the court in the presence of the king. The taster raises to his lips a footed cup of a shape known from Iranian metalwork of the thirteenth century while the queen holds up another footed cup of a model known from Iranian glass. On his right, the king's consort is seated cross-legged like the king himself and holds a footed bowl which, again, is of an Iranian type.[97] Together, they form a royal couple such as may be seen in Iranian polychrome ceramics with figural scenes from the twelfth and thirteenth centuries.[98]

The king wears Iranian-style attire. The turban is loosely interpreted, but the two widening strips coming down are duly depicted.[99] The long cloak (or *qabā*)

---

[94] Ghirshman, *Parthes et Sassanides*, p. 197 showing part of pl. 237 (the imperial boar hunt). Behind the emperor mounted on his steed, an attendant raises the parasol. See Joseph Hackin, J. Carl and J. Meunié, *Diverses recherches archéologiques en Afghanistan* (Paris, 1959), figs 195 and 199. The two characters were mistakenly described as 'dieu solaire et dieu lunaire'.

[95] In a three word caption, in his list 'Illustrations of Dukhang'. See next footnote.

[96] Pratapaditya Pal, *A Buddhist Paradise: The Murals of Alchi. Western Himalayas* (Hong Kong, 1982), pl. D.23, text pp. 50-51.

[97] Footed bowl with curving sides: A.S. Melikian-Chirvani, *Islamic Metalwork from the Iranian World 8-18th Centuries* (London, 1982), p. 164, pl. 71, text pp. 162-4. For a glass footed cup of closely related type, see Kjeld von Folsach, *Islamic Art: The David Collection* (Copenhagen, 1990), p. 144, n. 222 where it is broadly dated '8th-10th century'. By the same author, *Art from the World of Islam in the David Collection* (Copenhagen, 2001), p. 206, n. 304, where it is dated '9th-10th century'. Footed bowl with inverted truncated conical cups: several glass examples seen by this writer in the art market.

[98] Arthur Upham Pope (ed.), *A Survey of Persian Art* (18 vols, New York, 51981), vol. 9, pl. 651.

[99] E.g. *Survey of Persian Art*, vol. 9, p. 675, pl. 674, showing the inside of the pottery plate now in the Freer Gallery of Art, Washington where two horsemen appear with their turban bands fluttering behind them, and p. 674 showing the outside, where the hero slaying an *ezhdehā* (dragon) also has the two bands coming down from his turban. See also pl. 664, where the bands likewise flutter behind the horsemen's headdresses.

is cut from a *parniyān*-like fabric, with the characteristic rows of tangent beaded roundels which enclose effigies of felines *passant*. The beads form continuous rows instead of being arranged in clusters of four separated by devices, thus pointing to a later type of *parniyān* fashionable by the tenth–eleventh centuries in Islamic Iran.[100] The couple is seated under a royal parasol.

Two couples appearing behind another lobed line are part of the court inner circle – the two men may be princes for they wear a royal headdress. One is identified as royal by the fact that his headdress is identical to the turban worn by the king. The other wears the 'two-horned skull cap', in Persian *kolāh-e do shākh*, mentioned several times in the chronicle of the eleventh-century historian Beyhaqī, and reproduced on eleventh-century bronze vessels from Khorasan.[101] It still occurs in Persian manuscript painting of the early thirteenth century in relationship with an eleventh-century text, the romance of Varqe and Golshāh.[102]

The Tibetan scene and its theme, the Iranian royal wine banquet, therefore, obviously find their iconographic source in the domain of the Ghaznevid rulers.

The question of transmission is more complex and must be considered in the light of what the style tells us. While the composition, the perfectly linear rendition of the characters and even the colour scheme also point to Iranian models, the conventional stylized faces do not.

These bear some kinship to a couple of well-known Persian manuscripts executed in Western India around the mid-fifteenth century, according to the authors who have studied them.[103] However, it is in manuscripts of Hindu or Jain

---

100 See Melikian-Chirvani, *The Royal Silks of Iran* (forthcoming). *Parniyān* silk roundels are depicted at Bamiyan at a date which this writer believes to be as late as the seventh or eighth century. In cave D, a roundel encloses two birds clutching a pearl necklace. The beaded frame encloses four clusters of pearls/beads separated by square clasp-like devices: Joseph Hackin in collaboration with J. Carl, *Nouvelles recherches archéologiques à Bâmyan* (Paris, 1933), p. 9, fig. 1. For an easily accessible plate, Jeanine Auboyer, *The Art of Afghanistan* (Paris, 1968), pl. 75, text p. 53. At Siyāhgerd, in the Fonduqestān valley 117 km to the north-west of Kabul and 120 km to the west of Bamiyan, a painted sculptural group representing a king and his consort was recovered from the remains of a Buddhist 'monastery' (as described by the excavators). The king seated, one leg folded, wears a tunic covered with roundels that were 'framed by a row of pearls' and enclosed birds and possibly human masks judging from the faint traces still visible at the time. See Hackin, Carl and Meunié, *Diverses recherches*, fig. 192 and p. 56.

101 *Khʷāje* Abo'l Fażl Moḥammad b. Ḥoseyn-e Beyhaqī *Dabīr*, *Tārīkh-e Beyhaqī*, ed. Khalīl Khaṭīb-e Rahbar (3 vols, Tehran, 1368/1989), vol. 1, p. 41, l. 24.

102 A.S. Melikian-Chirvani, *Le Roman de Varqe et Golšâh: Essai sur les rapports de l'esthétique littéraire et de l'esthétique plastique dans l'Iran pré-mongol, suivi de la traduction du roman* (Paris, 1970), 246 pp., 65 figs and four colour plates. See p. 217, pl. 4, far left.

103 A dispersed manuscript of the Persian 'Quintet' [*Khamse*] by Amīr Khosrow Dehlavī, discussed by Richard Ettinghausen, *Paintings of the Sultans and Emperors of India* (New Delhi, 1961), pl. 1, dated by Ettinghausen to the second half of the fifteenth century;

texts that the corner of the eye projecting beyond the face of characters seated three-quarters such as the king may be seen.[104]

All told, the handling of the facial types with their brick-red complexion, and the rendition of the eyes, raises the possibility that the Iranian iconographic details could have reached Tibet via Indian intermediaries or, alternatively, that artists of Indian (perhaps Kashmiri?) stock, familiar with East Iranian art and attempting to use its formulae, came to Tibet. The presence in Ghaznevid territory of Indian stone-cutters and even builders, presumably Muslims, some trained in the tradition of Hindu style architecture, is proven by the existence of a small twelfth-century monument of purely Indian style and craftsmanship in central Afghanistan, that is, East Iranian territory, where it is unrelated to the vernacular style.[105] If Indian masons exercised their talents in the East Iranian territories under Ghaznevid rule, so could painters.

The mural paintings in the Sumtsek constructions that also form part of the Alchi monastic complex provide further examples of Iranian royal *iconography* handled in a non-Iranian *style*.

The paintings which cover the left leg of the statue of the bodhisattva Avalokiteshvara are particularly remarkable.[106] One detail shows a typical Iranian royal hunt in Ghaznevid times[107] (Plate 4.17). A turbaned king charges on in full gallop. Behind him, that is, at his side according to pictorial convention, his hawking master (*bāzdār*) looks at the kestrel which he holds by the legs with a bare hand unprotected by a leather gauntlet required to prevent it from being lacerated by the claws of the bird. Perhaps a Tibetan (or Kashmiri artist working in Tibet) intended to follow the Iranian iconographic model of a royal hunter hawking without being aware of the precise detail of the indispensable outfit. Hunting valets of diminutive size (to signify their humble status) wear protective helmets as if they were soldiers. The frontman running alongside the hawking master on horseback holds a long bow with his left hand and arrows in his right hand stretched out behind him.

Both the king and his hawking master wear Iranian-style turbans and their heads are set off by halos of glory with beaded edges which go back to Iranian models of the ninth or tenth centuries, as may be seen by comparison

and a *Shah-Name* studied by B.N. Goswamy, *A Jainesque Sultanate Shahnama and the Context of Pre-Mughal Painting in India* (Zurich, 1988).

104 Goswamy, *Jainesque Sultanate Shahnama*, p. 17, fig. 20 from a fifteenth-century manuscript of the *Kalpasutra*, and p. 21, fig. 30 from a *Kalakacharya katha* manuscript of the fifteenth century.

105 G. Scarcia and Maurizio Taddei, 'The Masgid-i Sangi of Larvand', *East and West*, 23 (1973): pp. 89-108. See p. 94 where the structure, probably a mausoleum, is located at Malekān in the Ghōr mountains bordering Zamīndāvar.

106 Pal, *A Buddhist Paradise*, detail showing both legs pl. S5.

107 Pal, *A Buddhist Paradise*, pl. S8.

with metal dishes.[108] They also wear Iranian-style armlets. The slight cusps to the halos point to an interpretation of the Iranian halo perhaps influenced by greater familiarity with Buddhist mandorlas occasionally cusped. Once more, this makes one wonder whether the model of the hunting scene became known to the Tibetan artist via some non-Iranian (Kashmiri? Nepalese?) intermediary.

A major set of questions to be addressed in the future concerns the purpose of such Iranian iconography on the legs of the bodhisattva Avalokiteshvara. They presumably relate to the life of Prince Siddharta Gautama, the historic character who would become the Buddha and is depicted in the guise of a ruler from Islamic Iran. Murals in the main temple at Tabo (Gtsug lag khang) show that the royal symbolism of the 'parasol of majesty' (*chatr-e homāyūnī* in Persian), perfectly understood, was put to such use in other Tibetan shrines.[109] Attendants hold it over the head of the mother of the Buddha, princess Mahamaya, as well as over the head of the Buddha Shakyamuni. The parasol is closer to those of twelfth-century Iran than to those in Gandharan sculpture borrowed from Sasanian Iran.

The meaning attached to such loans, unlikely to have been a matter of fashion or individual taste in this religious context, is as intriguing as the identity of those who inspired them.

Similar questions arise about other cases of Iranian connections.

Stūpa architecture reveals such contacts, possibly via Kashmir. The 'entrance *stūpa*' at Mangyu village not far from Alchi, looks like a direct imitation of the traditional East-Iranian Islamic mausoleum with a square ground plan topped by a dome.[110] Inside, the ceiling simulates the structure of the cave ceilings at Bamiyan and in the valley of Foladi near by, in the south-east Iranian domain, in present-day Afghanistan.[111] How, and why, this imitation came about is unknown. There is little point in speculating, however, before much-needed in-depth monographic studies of Kashmiri Buddhist architecture, early Tibetan

---

108 Josef Orbeli and Camilla Trever, *Orfèvrerie Sasanide/Sasandiski Metall* (Leningrad, 1935), pls 17 and 18 (French text, p. XLI), both 25.8 cm across. Probably originating from the same workshop, they display stylistic features unlikely to predate the ninth century: note the ewer held by an attendant in pl. 18 and the trilobate cusped motif extending from the rectangular carpet.

109 Peter van Ham and Aglaja Stirn, *The Forgotten Gods of Tibet* (Paris, 1997), p. 74, 2 and p. 77, 4. On Tabo dates, see Thomas Pritzker, 'The Wall Paintings of Tabo', in *Art of Tibet: Selected Articles from Orientations*, pp. 71-3.

110 Linrothe, 'The Murals at Mangyu', p. 194, fig. 2.

111 Compare what Linrothe calls 'the lantern ceiling' of the 'entrance *stūpa*', p. 195, fig. 4 and the ceiling in a cave from the 'F group' at Bamiyan in J. Hackin with J. Carl, *Nouvelles recherches archéologiques à Bâmyan*, pl. XXXIX, fig. 46 or the 'lantern ceiling' in a cave of the present-day town near Bamiyan in Auboyer, *The Art of Afghanistan*, pl. 97a. Additional examples including two that are perfectly identical in design to the 'entrance *stūpa*' will be found in Bruno Dagens, Marc Le Berre and Daniel Schlumberger, *Monuments Préislamiques d'Afghanistan* (Paris, 1964), pl. XXIX, text p. 46.

architecture, and, not least, a careful search through written sources, Tibetan, Kashmiri and Indian, are undertaken. Only then will it be possible to have some clearer idea of the way in which Iranian objects, forms, iconography and concepts travelled to Tibet.

A NOTE OF THANKS AND APOLOGY

I wish to thank colleagues who have helped me: Dr Ariane Macdonald to whom I owe, in addition to a precious volume, the privilege of having been first intrigued by the Tibetan world over four decades ago; Dr Amy Heller, who kindly sent me a bibliography of her impressive work on Tibetan culture; and Étienne de la Vaissière, who was kind enough to present me with his exemplary book on Sogdian merchants. I am grateful to the editors for inviting me to contribute to the theme of this volume from the standpoint of a cultural historian of Iran. I am aware that many of my remarks will seem unsophisticated and occasionally mistaken to Tibetologists, but my hope is that they may stimulate better-qualified researchers to answer the questions raised here. I apologise for having cut down footnotes drastically due to space reasons. Arabic words/names are transliterated according to the international system where they appear in an *Arabic context*. Persian is transliterated as pronounced in standard Western Persian according to the system adopted in my *Islamic Metalwork from Iranian Lands* (London, 1982). Names commonly used (e.g. Khorasan, Bamiyan) have no diacritical signs.

Chapter 5

Greek and Islamic Medicines' Historical Contact with Tibet:

A Reassessment in View of Recently Available but Relatively Early Sources on Tibetan Medical Eclecticism[1]

Dan Martin

Giuseppe Tucci's Tibetan library was, for several decades in the middle of the twentieth century, by far the most significant such collection to be found in all of Europe west of St Petersburg. In 2003 the second tome of a catalogue of his massive collection was published in Rome. While leafing through the catalogue pages, I was startled and then a little excited to notice the title of an early history of Tibetan medicine that I had listed in my bibliography, *Tibetan Histories*, published in 1997, where the title appears as *Shes-bya Spyi'i Khog-dbub Rgyal-mtshan Rtser 'Bar*. Although not entirely unknown to scholarship, we would

[1] I would like to dedicate this article to my dissertation adviser Christopher I. Beckwith, whose 1979 paper entitled 'The Introduction of Greek Medicine into Tibet in the Seventh and Eighth Centuries' (*Journal of the American Oriental Society*, 99/2 [1979]: pp. 297-313) is the classic and by far the most important piece of scholarship on the subject ever written. His paper has stood the test of time and is still to my mind perfect, or very nearly so. It was also far ahead of its time, if we may judge from the fact that for two decades its ideas did not receive very much attention from the sluggish realm of academia: a few brief mentions and little more than that. Its most appreciative reader by far has been a Tibetan doctor and medical historian, Sman-rams-pa Pa-sangs-yon-tan, *Bod-kyi Gso-ba Rig-pa'i Lo-rgyus-kyi Bang-mdzod G.yu-thog Bla-ma Dran-pa'i Pho-nya* (Leh, 1988), who cites it frequently. If there is anything to add to it today it is because the earliest Tibetan-language source on the subject then available to him dates to the mid-sixteenth century. A number of older sources have surfaced in intervening years, and I would mainly like to focus on the evidence they provide. The existence of a few as-yet unpublished early medical works was announced a few years ago in an unpublished conference paper by Yangga Trarong, a doctor and scholar from Tibet, who has worked on the problem of Greek influence on Tibetan medicine in collaboration with a classical philologist (the conference paper, entitled 'Studying Early Tibetan Medical Manuscripts', was delivered at the Tenth Seminar of the International Association for Tibetan Studies in September 2003). So I see real hope of further progress in this area in the near future, far above and beyond what I will have to say here.

have to say that it has hardly ever been mentioned in modern Tibetological literature, and in the last few centuries it seems no one has directly made use of the information it contains. Of course, I immediately dispatched an electronic mail to Elena De Rossi Filibeck, who very kindly helped me to obtain a microfilm of the manuscript, and I went to work on it.[2]

At the end of his medical history of 1704, the Regent Sangs-rgyas-rgya-mtsho discusses the sources he used (including the history in question), as well as the sources that he might have used if only they had been available. He names what he believed was the earliest medical history under the title *Rin-chen Spungs-pa* (*Heap of Precious Substances*). I still have not been able to identify the text the Regent had in mind.[3]

In any case, my point for the moment is just to say that the manuscript preserved in the Tucci collection has as few as two rivals for the honour of being considered the earliest Tibetan work specifically devoted to medical history. It is always a danger to speak of 'firsts' in human history, of course, and I will not push this point further, just to admit that a number of obscure and fairly early medical history titles have been listed in the literature. If we limit ourselves to those that are available and known to us at the moment, we may say that three medical history texts survive from around the year 1200, and the next somehow available, even if not yet published, history dates about 200 years later. But then old medical histories continue to surface, including some that, while known to exist in the past, remained unavailable in recent times. As an example, we might point to Olaf Czaja's recent article about a previously unavailable and still unpublished manuscript of a medical history by Mtsho-smad Mkhan-chen dated to the middle of the sixteenth century.[4]

I have compiled a listing of 16 medical histories that preceded the Regent's history, of which to my knowledge only six are, in one form or another, available today (see Appendix A). I am certain this is not a complete listing.[5] Still, I think it gives a fair idea about the wealth of early historical writings that concern medicine. These earlier works have been largely neglected by Tibetan authors

[2] Elena De Rossi Filibeck, *Catalogue of the Tucci Tibetan Fund in the Library of IsIAO* (Rome, 2003), vol. 2, p. 429, no. 1281. See also Dan Martin and Yael Bentor, *Tibetan Histories: A Bibliography of Tibetan-Language Historical Works* (London, 1997), p. 37, no. 36.

[3] Sde-srid Sangs-rgyas-rgya-mtsho, *Dpal-ldan Gso-ba Rig-pa'i Khog-'bugs Legs-bshad Bai-ḍūrya'i Me-long Drang-srong Dgyes-pa'i Dga'-ston* (Lanzhou, 1982), pp. 562-9. On the composition of this medical history, completed in 1703 or 1704, see especially Kurtis R. Schaeffer, 'Textual Scholarship Medical Tradition, and Mahāyāna Buddhist Ideals in Tibet', *Journal of Indian Philosophy*, 31 (2003): pp. 621-42, at pp. 623-5.

[4] Olaf Czaja, 'A Hitherto Unknown "Medical History" of mTsho-smad mkhan-chen (b. 16th cent.)', *Tibet Journal*, 30/4-31/1 (2005-06): pp. 153-72. This manuscript was kept in the library of the former Maharaja of Sikkim, and was made available in microfilm by the Nepal-German Manuscript Preservation Project (Kathmandu).

[5] There are in fact still more titles listed in the passage of the Regent's history just mentioned.

in recent centuries in favour of the Regent's history, which was and largely continues to be the standard reference for both earlier scholars in Tibet and contemporary Tibetologists.

There are indeed chapters on medical history in broader histories of Tibetan Buddhism. There is also a genre for the history of the traditional sciences that always includes medicine. Still, the usual genre-term for a medical history in Tibet is *khog-dbubs*, a word with several different spellings, which makes it difficult to explain with certainty. I once speculated in print about the meaning of the word, but now I believe the most likely explanation is one supplied by Olaf Czaja. According to him it may be etymologized as meaning 'piercing to the interior cavity', or perhaps 'piercing to the internal parts'. In practice it sometimes seems to indicate a type of commentary that gets to the heart of the original text and reveals its basic structure, its general outlines. The reason it came to be used for the genre of medical histories is still rather mysterious, and can remain so for the time being.[6]

Going back to the Tucci manuscript, I believe it represents one of the first two medical history texts of the *khog-dbubs* genre. Allow me to clarify somewhat the matters of authorship and dating, but without too many detailed arguments, since these have recently been published in a separate paper.[7]

I will just summarize some of my findings. The manuscript actually contains two titles. We will pay most attention to the first and longer text, in 46 numbered folios, since the second is nothing but an outline. The outline does at least tell us that the author had planned to write an extremely detailed and lengthy commentary on Vāgbhaṭa's *Aṣṭāṅgahṛdayasaṃhitā* (*Compendium on the Heart of the Eight Branches* [*of Medicine*]).[8] From the outline we may also see that the first text is merely part of the introduction to the projected commentary. The commentary proper never got beyond commenting on the first lines of the text. As we know – well, it is a bitter fact of life, and please excuse me for reminding you of it – for better or worse, people often enter the grave without completing everything they had wanted to do.

The manuscript is largely written in very clear cursive letters. The ink was probably mostly silver ink, with some shorter parts in gold ink that are not very

---

6 See Czaja, 'Hitherto Unknown', pp. 154-6; Martin and Bentor, *Tibetan Histories*, p. 14. There are indeed a few puzzling instances of titles that employ the term *khob-dbubs* that have to do with neither history nor the sciences.

7 Dan Martin, 'An Early Tibetan History of Indian Medicine', in Mona Schrempf (ed.) *Soundings in Tibetan Medicine: Anthropological and Historical Perspectives* (Leiden, 2007), pp. 307-25.

8 The Tibetan translation has the title *Yan-lag Brgyad-pa'i Snying-po Bsdus-pa*. The *Aṣṭāṅga* was, incidentally, one of the works used by al-Ṭabarī in his summary of Indian medicine composed in about 850 CE. See Max Meyerhof, ''Alî aṭ-Ṭabarî's "Paradise of Wisdom", One of the Oldest Arabic Compendiums of Medicine', *Isis*, 16/1 (1931): pp. 6-54, at p. 43 ('Ashtânqahradî'). The *Aṣṭāṅga* has been subject of a number of studies and editions by Claus Vogel, the late Ronald Emmerick and others.

clear in the black-and-white microfilm at my disposal. The paper was sized with a dark sizing, probably the dark-blue-sized paper known in Tibetan as *mthing shog*.[9] Unfortunately the final page of the first text is the least legible one, and it was not possible to make out the author's name in the colophon. Still, with the evidence of the title and some further evidence in the interior of the text it has been possible to establish beyond any doubt who the author was. His full name is Che-rje Zhang-ston Zhig-po Thugs-rje-khri-'od. We will simply call him Che-rje.

It is frustrating that very little is known about the life of the author, and what we do know mainly comes either from the content of the Tucci manuscript itself, or descends from a brief passage in the just-mentioned medical history by the Regent Sangs-rgyas-rgya-mtsho.[10] The Regent's biographical sketch is not very enlightening, although it does inform us who his teachers and students were, and which texts he composed. Of his six compositions, the first is our medical history, while the second is the outline text. The other four texts I have been unable to locate. Mention, too, is made of two texts, the *Yang-tig* and *Zin-tig*, written by his student Gtsang-ston Dar-ma-mgon-po. Remarkably enough, both of these texts are available in reprint editions published in India. These quite lengthy works by his student are significant in that they preserve Che-rje's practical medical instructions. For this reason and more, they should be studied further.[11]

We may know from still other sources, thanks to Roberto Vitali, that the hereditary lineage of physicians to which Che-rje belonged was closely attached to the court of the Western Tibetan kings and that they even intermarried with the royal family.[12] Some of the most important information about Che-rje comes from reading his own medical history. He relates in detail his own medical lineage, one that descended from none other than the illustrious 'Great Translator' Rin-chen-bzang-po, who translated the *Aṣṭāṅga* into Tibetan in 1015 CE. The information on the date of this translation seems to be unique to Che-rje's history. The translation was done together with the Kashmiri Janārdana with financial support in the form of gold from the Western Tibetan king and others. We may also know from Che-rje's history that he, like his near-contemporary G.yu-thog-pa, may be considered a follower of the Nyingma school, since he

---

9 It would be good to learn more about the history of this particular type of paper, but about all I can say at the moment is that it was certainly being made in the late twelfth century, and was probably used already in late imperial times. *Mthing* means 'azurite', most likely employed in its manufacture in earlier centuries.

10 Sde-srid, *Dpal-ldan Gso-ba Rig-pa'i Khog-'bugs*, pp. 178-9. This passage has often been repeated in more recent medical histories without adding any new information.

11 Gtsang-stod Dar-ma-mgon-po, *Slob-ma'i Don-du Zin-thig and Bu-la Gdams-pa Yang-thig* (2 vols, Leh, 1975); Gtsang-stod Dar-ma-mgon-po, *Slob-ma-la Phan-pa'i Zin-tig: A Collection of Instructions on Tibetan Medicine and Treatment* (2 vols, Gangtok, 1976).

12 Roberto Vitali, 'On Some Disciples of Rinchen Zangpo and Lochung Legpai Sherab, and their Successors, who Brought Teachings Popular in Ngari Korsum to Central Tibet', in Alex McKay (ed.), *Tibet and her Neighbors: A History* (London, 2003), pp. 71-9, at pp. 74-5.

discusses Buddhism within the framework of the Nine Vehicles.[13] I see this as just another instance of something that may be seen more generally in Tibetan medical history, which is that medical lineages have little to do with sectarian boundaries. Well, at least they tend to cross those boundaries with ease.

It is mainly on the basis of Che-rje's medical lineage that I have ventured to place the period of his main activities to decades surrounding the year 1200. I feel rather confident in translating the 60-year cycle date given in the colophon, a Wood Mouse year, into the Common Era date of 1204. Still, the date 1264 cannot be entirely excluded. I have done my best to disprove the earlier in favour of the later date, but with no success so far. He does not seem to mention any figures who lived much beyond the year 1200. So I am satisfied for now that the date 1204 may be accepted as a working hypothesis. A close inspection of the physical manuscript's colophon page may turn up evidence not visible in my microfilm that would yield a more confident statement on the dating problem.

Now we will limit ourselves to a few general comments on the contents of the work. The work as a whole may be considered a 'completed' history of medicine, even though originally conceived as the historical introduction to a much larger commentary. The properly historical part ends on folio 33, while the final 14 folios discuss the title, general outline, and chapters of the *Aṣṭāṅga*. Generally it would be accurate to say that it is a history of Indian medicine with a very strong focus on the biography and writings of Vāgbhaṭa and his immediate circle. This generalization holds true regardless of the presence of brief parts that concern Tibetan or other non-Indian medical traditions. This is just what we might expect in an introduction to a commentary on a work by Vāgbhaṭa.[14]

We can say in general about Che-rje's style that he was a very systematic and logical thinker. He wrote in detail, yet tersely, according to a preconceived outline, moving from topic to topic. The prose does not exactly 'flow'. Sometimes one is not sure whether to say that he is following an outline or that he is simply giving an outline. It is obvious that he must have received some training in formal, philosophical logic. In his day Gsang-phu Ne'u-thog Monastery was the main or most influential source of this kind of training.[15] But I am not even certain if Che-rje was a monk or not (given the importance of his family

---

[13] For a historical exploration of the idea of the Nine Vehicles (Theg-pa Dgu), see David Snellgrove, *Indo-Tibetan Buddhism: Indian Buddhists and their Tibetan Successors* (Bangkok, 2004), pp. 405-7.

[14] Che-rje's account of Vāgbhaṭa would, five centuries later, form the most important source for the chapter on Vāgbhaṭa in the Regent's medical history. What this ought to tell us is that the Regent could locate no finer source on Vāgbhaṭa in the Tibetan literature that came before him.

[15] For the early history of Gsang-phu Ne'u-thog, see especially Shunzo Onoda, *Monastic Debate in Tibet: A Study on the History and Structures of Bsdus-grwa Logic* (Vienna, 1992), pp. 13-14; Leonard W.J. van der Kuijp, 'The Monastery of Gsang-phu Ne'u-thog and its Abbatial Succession from *ca.* 1073 to 1250', *Berliner Indologische Studien*, 3 (1987): pp. 103-27.

lineage, I doubt he could have been a monk for at least most of his life), and it is likely only monks would have studied at Gsang-phu Ne'u-thog. I have no way of knowing what formal education he might have received outside his own family medical lineage. In any case, he often employs standard scholastic methods for the ordering of his arguments, starting with the idea that is going to be refuted, then putting forward the thesis to be defended, and finally clearing up possible objections.[16] In general, he is so enamoured with outlining that one of his chief criticisms directed against certain other near-contemporary Tibetan medical writers is that they did not know how to outline properly.

Everything said here so far was intended to serve as introduction to a closer investigation of one of the less typical passages that deals with the world-history of medicine. Its subject matter is less typical, but its style is very typical indeed: terse statements and sets of lists rigorously structured by an outline. I have given the outline in Appendix B. Here, too, Vāgbhaṭa is at the centre of Che-rje's interests, and his main aim is to situate Vāgbhaṭa and his *Aṣṭāṅga* within certain analytical categories. Let us now look at each of the four parts of the general outline and see how Che-rje situates Vāgbhaṭa in each one of them.

Under the first, The Seven Schools: Vāgbhaṭa is located at the top of the list of the 'Scholars of the Five Sciences', in its turn the fifth in his list of the Seven Schools. This should become clearer from a reading of the Appendices.

Under the second, The Four Cycles: Vāgbhaṭa's medical text is classified under the first: Outer textual items of knowledge.

Under the third, The Four Translations: The Tibetan translation of Vāgbhaṭa's text belongs to the 'highland' (meaning western Tibetan) translations.

Under the fourth, The Two Times of Translation: It was translated in the period of later translations.

Regarding the listing of the Seven Schools in Appendix C, I would like to suggest that in the content and ordering of this sevenfold outline alone there are several interesting messages. The list is all about authorship of texts belonging to various medical systems. The first significant omission in the outline – in any case, the first thing I personally notice – is the absence of any medical scripture from the words of the Buddha.[17] The top of the list is occupied by bodhisattvas, and I would suggest that there is a kind of descending order.

---

16 On this particular pattern for ordering arguments, see Christopher I. Beckwith, 'The Medieval Scholastic Method in Tibet and the West', in Lawrence Epstein and Richard F. Sherburne (eds), *Reflections on Tibetan Culture: Essays in Memory of Turrell V. Wylie* (Lewiston, 1990), pp. 307-13. See also Beckwith in this volume.

17 This omission stands out precisely because one of the continuing debates in Tibetan medical history turns around whether or not the *Rgyud-bzhi* might be considered to be scripture, or in other words, the 'Word' of the Buddha. For more on this debate, which did not seem to be of any interest to Che-rje since he did not even know about any *Rgyud-bzhi* text, see Olaf Czaja, 'Zurkharwa Lodro Gyalpo (1509-1579) on the Controversy

The first four have transcendent or enlightened beings as their authors. Of these, the first two are transcendent beings, both Buddhist and non-Buddhist. The second pair, nos 3 to 4, are enlightened humans, the 'sages' or rishis of non-Buddhists and the Enlightened humans of the Buddhists. The last three items are devoted to the schools associated with texts composed by 'ordinary' humans, humans who are not necessarily enlightened, who may not be Buddhists. No. 5 represents non-Tibetan physicians, although Chinese medicine gets its own category, no. 6. Certain Tibetan medical authors are named under no. 7.

Now when we turn to Appendix D, we can make several generalizations about this listing as well. It, too, is all about particular texts by particular authors that are somehow, along with still other unnamed texts, representative of national or regional schools of medicine. We could think of them as Vāgbhaṭa's peers in the world outside Tibet and China. Geographically speaking, it 'roughly' (even if not exactly) moves from the area of the Indian subcontinent in the first half of the list to areas in the periphery of Tibet in the last half.

In no. 1 we get the two Indic names in Tibetan translation. Nos 2-4 have transcriptions of Indic names. Nos 5 and 10 are apparently Tibetan transcriptions from the languages of the areas indicated, while nos 6–9 are given in Tibetan translation (these names obviously should not be Sanskritized).

One general and, I think, quite necessary thing to say is this: what we have here is a listing of foreign writers on medicine. This is not a listing of foreign physicians who visited Tibet, and it is not meant to be. Che-rje ends this list with the statement that 'The texts, procedures and practical advice of these ten gradually spread in Tibet'. He does not say that the persons themselves came to Tibet. There seems to be neither a time frame nor any sense of chronology. Elsewhere (see Appendix B, third part) he does imply that medical teachings from all the four main countries surrounding Tibet were translated into Tibetan in Imperial Times. More on these points later, since I think they gain clarity when looking into the problematic identities of the individual authors.

Of course it has not yet proven possible to provide positive identities for most of the names listed here. My impression is that they all – somehow – represent real names.

No. 1a is the most clearly identifiable person, of course. Che-rje's history is probably the ultimate source for the Tibetan belief that Mātṛceta, Aśvaghoṣa, Āryadeva and Vāgbhaṭa (among others) are all names for the same person. Modern scholars of Indian literature have long rejected this traditional idea. I believe that to the Tibetan mind all the stories about Brahmin converts to Buddhism tended to blur and blend together. Incidentally, this confusion of identities also made it possible to conceal the fact that some of them, and particularly for our

---

of the Indian Origin of the *rGyud bzhi*', *Tibet Journal*, 30/4-31/1 (2005-06): pp. 131-52, especially p. 133.

purposes Vāgbhaṭa, were not Buddhists. Che-rje gives Vāgbhaṭa a list of 21 (or 22) names, a list that is repeated in the Regent's history.[18]

The next person in the list, Sthiramati, presents some difficulties. Of course our immediate tendency is to identify him as the most famous Sthiramati, a sixth-century disciple of Vasubandhu, who authored several Buddhist commentaries. But there were a number of Indians and Tibetans by this name. What we need to find is a Kashmiri Sthiramati who was known to be active in the medical field. For the moment, I guess, we will have to be satisfied to accept this so-far unavailable information that there was a Kashmiri Sthiramati who wrote a medical text. He could have been the disciple of Vasubandhu, I suppose, but there does not seem to be a way to validate this any further.

Jinamitra is a different story. But with him, too, we surely have an immediate tendency to identify him with the famous Kashmiri Jinamitra who was active as a translator in Tibet in the first decades of the ninth century. His name appears in countless translation colophons in the Tibetan Kanjur. But there were several Indian Buddhist Jinamitras. Fortunately we have helpful information elsewhere in medical historical literature. Just a few years ago, a work which must belong to the eleventh century was published for the first time. It was by an interesting character known as Bha-ro Lag-rdum or Skyes-bu Me-lha. The book is called the *Snyan-brgyud Be-bum Nag-po*. Unfortunately, I have not seen this publication yet, but I do have a long citation from the verse history that forms the first chapter of this work.[19] He was a very learned physician who became the court physician of the king of Orgyan. His father's name was Jinamitra. The reason for his epithet Bha-ro Lag-rdum is this. While treating the queen for an illness, it became known that he had committed the sin of incontinence. He was punished by having his hands cut off and was then banished. Lag-rdum means 'Arm Stump'. He arrived in Tibet during the reign of the Western Tibetan king Rtse-lde, therefore in the last part of the eleventh century, and was mainly active at the capital city of Tho-ling, although he travelled to central Tibet and had very many students there. His medical teachings were primarily those orally transmitted to him by his father Jinamitra.[20]

I think this 'external' source of verification (and there is more to be found in the later medical histories) is quite important. It confirms that the physician Jinamitra - who we should emphasize never came to Tibet - lived in Orgyan. Although there is of course much discussion on this point, I believe that Orgyan

---

[18] Sde-srid, *Dpal-ldan Gso-ba Rig-pa'i Khog-'bugs*, p. 146.

[19] Byams-pa-phrin-las, *Gangs-ljongs Gso-rig Bstan-pa'i Nyin-byed Rim-byon-gyi Rnam-thar Phyogs-bsgrigs* (Beijing, 1990), pp. 114-16. The details for the published version ought to be as follows: *Snyan-brgyud Be-bum Nag-po dang Man-ngag Rin-chen Gter-mdzod* (*Snyan-nas Snyan-du brgyud-pa Man-ngag Be-bum Nag-po*) (Chengdu, 2001). On the title page, two authors are named: Skyes-bu Me-lha and Tshe-rig-'dzin-pa O-rgyan-blo-'phel.

[20] For more on Skyes-bu Me-lha, see Vitali, 'On Some Disciples of Rinchen Zangpo', pp. 75-6.

means the Swat Valley in present-day northern Pakistan. (Tibetologists generally have no doubt about this, although Indologists sometimes do.) Since Bha-ro Lag-rdum spent much time at Tho-ling in western Tibet, it is all the more likely that Che-rje, active shortly thereafter in the same general area, would have known about him and his father. We know from an outline of his work that his diagnostic methods included both pulse and urine analysis. So it is also interesting to see that a physician named Jinamitra is said to have composed a text on urinalysis.[21] I still have not procured any information that would shed light on the title Che-rje gives for Jinamitra's composition: 'One Thousand and Ninety-One Healings'.

No. 3: I have spent a great deal of time puzzling over the impossible Sanskrit name Pra-a-nan-ta, and have been unable to decide how it ought to be fixed. It could intend something like Prajñānanda, Jayānanda, etc. I thought it could also be a corrupted reading for Bram-ze ('Brahmin') Ananta. A translator active in Tibet in the mid-eighth century, he originally came to Tibet as a merchant until his abilities as a translator were required by the Tibetan emperor. He was, after all, a Kashmiri and not from Magadha.[22] Note the different reading Shrī A-nanda in the Regent's history. By far the most famous physician in the history of Magadha was Jīvaka (or Jīvakakumāra, in Tibetan 'Tsho-byed Gzhon-nu), the physician of King Bimbisāra and Gautama Buddha. I will say no more since I have nothing more to say, at least at this moment. One hates to admit defeat.

No. 4, Sumatikīrti, would seem fairly simple to identify with a degree of certainty. He is well known as a pundit who worked on translations, belonging to the 'later spreading' (*phyi-dar*) period, which begins in the last decades of the tenth century. He stayed in the Nepal Valley, and it is not certain if he ever set foot in Tibet, perhaps not. Given the dates of the Tibetan translators with whom he worked, he must have been active in the last part of the eleventh century. It is known that Mar-pa Do-pa Chos-kyi-dbang-phyug (dates not certain, but perhaps 1042-1136) studied with Sumatikīrti, among others, in Nepal. Rngog Lo-tsā-ba Blo-ldan-shes-rab (1059-1109) also is known to have worked with Sumatikīrti. It is rather troubling that this pundit does not seem to be credited with the composition or translation of any medical works. But I do not know of any other

---

21 Byams-pa-phrin-las, *Gangs-ljongs Gso-rig*, p. 117. The source of this information is said to be in the *Subsequent Tantra* (one of the four tantras that make up the *Rgyud-bzhi*, or perhaps rather a commentary on the same), where it is referred to as *Dzi-na-mi-tra'i Chu-dpyad*. I have not yet traced this reference in the text of the *Subsequent Tantra*.

22 On the Brahmin Kashmiri Ananta, personal translator for Śāntarakṣita during his first trip to Tibet in about 763 CE, see Cristina Scherrer-Schaub, 'Enacting Words: A Diplomatic Analysis of the Imperial Decrees (*Bkas bcad*) and their Application in the *Sgra sbyor bam po gñis pa* Tradition', *Journal of the International Association of Buddhist Studies*, 25 (2002): pp. 263-340, at pp. 275, 293. Ananta was already in Tibet working as a translator when Śāntarakṣita arrived. It is quite remarkable that, even though an 'Indian', he is consistently called a translator (*lo-tsā-ba*), and not a pundit.

South Asian with the name Sumatikīrti.[23] I am going to neglect no. 5 for the moment and quickly comment on nos 6–9. No. 6 is rather interesting, since here Dolpo is obviously regarded as a separate kingdom. It was not a part of Nepal (its annexation took place, I believe, only in the late eighteenth century). I have seen other indications of Dolpo's independent status in early Tibetan literature. Of course, Dolpo language was very closely related to Classical Tibetan, and so the name Rdo-rje-'bar-ba can probably be taken as the actual name of the author of the medical works entitled, 'The Shorter and Longer [texts called the] Weapon of Fearlessness'.[24] As for nos 7–9, I really cannot offer any positive arguments for the identity of any of them. Presumably their original names would have been in Uyghur Turkish, Tangut and Khotanese, and what we have here are the Tibetan translations of those names. The Ga-gon in the title of the Uyghur medical text is interesting, since it is sometimes encountered as a place name. It could refer to one or another Khaganate that might have neighboured the Uyghur Kingdom.[25] There are a number of old Uyghur medical manuscripts, but I have not looked into them. Perhaps the most famous episode in early Uyghur medical history is the visit to China of the Turk, apparently an Uyghur Turk, named Nanto as known from the records of the Sung Dynasty.[26]

Before dealing with nos 5 and 10, which constitute the Holy Grail of our quest, I would like to give my present opinions about the locations of Phrom and Tazig in pre-Mongol Tibetan geographical understanding. These ideas come from a study of geographical conceptions of the eleventh–thirteenth centuries as known primarily from Bon histories. To start with Tazig: All early Tibetan geographies are in agreement that Tazig is a large kingdom to the west of Tibet, just as India lies to the south and China lies to the east. And obviously, if we stand in Tibet and look west, the large country beyond Kashmir (which is not in question here) would of necessity be Iran or Persia. Michael Walter has recently criticized those who simply translate Tazig as 'Persia', saying that in the time in question for Bon texts, it must have meant the Abbasid Empire of the early Middle Ages (which at its height included all of Western Central Asia, present-

23 Of course there have been Tibetans with the Tibetan-language equivalent of the name, Blo-bzang-grags-pa, most famously Tsong-kha-pa Blo-bzang-grags-pa (1357-1419), renowned as founder of the Dge-lugs school.

24 Remarkably, the *Weapon of Fearlessness* (*Mi-'jigs-pa'i Mtshon-cha*) is given by Sde-srid, *Dpal-ldan Gso-ba Rig-pa'i Khog-'bugs*, p. 150, as the title of a seven-fascicle text composed by three foreign doctors in the time of Emperor Srong-btsan-sgam-po (first half of the seventh century). Notice also Rechung, *Tibetan Medicine*, p. 15. This book was in seven fascicles (*bam-po*), and not seven chapters as Rechung's translation of the title would have it.

25 This was suggested to me by Christopher I. Beckwith.

26 See, for example, Aydın M. Sayılı, 'Turkish Medicine', *Isis*, 26/2 (1937): pp. 403-14, at p. 406.

day Afghanistan and into the Sindh).[27] I do not wish to spend too much time on this problem, just to say that in my own study of what Bon sources of the period have to say about Olmo Lungring and Tazig, I have found that several different types of geographies: the general country geography, the river geography and the language geography all point to the area of northern Afghanistan, starting at the latitude of Kabul, and perhaps including territory north of the Oxus or Amu Darya; in effect, the area of what is now northern Afghanistan, and perhaps part of Tadzhikistan.[28] Even if Tazig does refer to the entire Abbasid Empire, it could also be that Tibetans were more likely to intend by it the parts closer to themselves.

As for Phrom, we ought to pronounce it as 'From'. Middle Iranic languages (according to Nicholas Sims-Williams) regularly spell the name 'Rome' with an initial 'fr-'. Although standard Lhasa-style language of today may pronounce it T'rom, in Amdo it may still be pronounced From. In early Bon sources, From Gesar is always a place name, never a name of a person. We could simply say that From means 'Rome' and therefore the Eastern Roman Empire or Byzantium (in Greek, called Ρωμανία, *Rōmanía*). However, we know from numismatic evidence (and also from the records of the T'ang Dynasty) that Fromo Kesaro, 'Caesar of Rome', was an epithet used by an eighth-century Turkish ruler in the larger area of Kabul, an area that probably enlarged to include the Swat Valley in northern Pakistan. He received this laudatory epithet because he, like the Byzantines, was successful at holding back the Muslim conquerors.[29] There is much more to discuss here, but one thing is clear, that the areas of Tazig and From seem to fall into the same place in the map. I am satisfied to say, for now, that they were in close proximity. Perhaps, but only perhaps, we could say that *for Tibetans in those times*, Tazig denoted the part of this area that had fallen under Islamic rule while From was used for the area to its east, dominated by Turks, that continued to resist invasion. This could also explain why it is that many later Tibetan geographies locate the land of Gesar in the north, rather than in the west. The lines of resistance to the Islamic conquest, after all, moved in that direction.

Now one of the most interesting of the early Bon sources for the geography of From is a passage from one of the Rma Family histories which I would date to

---

[27] Michael Walter, 'Jabir, the Buddhist Yogi, Part III: Considerations on an International Yoga of Transformation', *Lungta*, 16 (2003 = special issue on *Cosmogony and the Origins*, ed. Roberto Vitali): pp. 21-36, at p. 31.

[28] Dan Martin, "Ol-mo-lung-ring, the Original Holy Place', in Toni Huber (ed.), *Sacred Spaces and Powerful Places in Tibetan Culture: A Collection of Essays* (Dharamsala, 1999), pp. 258-301.

[29] See Helmut Humbach, 'New Coins of Fromo Kêsaro', in Gilbert Pollet (ed.), *India and the Ancient World: History, Trade and Culture before A.D. 650* (Leuven, 1987), pp. 81-5; Helmut Humbach, 'Phrom Gesar and the Bactrian Rome', in Peter Snoy (ed.), *Ethnologie und Geschichte: Festschrift für Karl Jettmar* (Wiesbaden, 1983), pp. 303-9.

the thirteenth century. It is talking about the reign of the legendary Emperor Dri-gum-btsan-po:

> In about that time, in India there was Dharma [Buddhism], it is said; in China, *gtsug-lag* calculation [astro-sciences and divination]; in From, medical treatments; in Tibet and Zhangzhung countries, apart from practising and being civilized by Bon there was nothing else. This medical treatment was practiced at the hand of Bon.[30]

This is at least interesting for closely connecting the area of From with medical treatments, and for insisting that this medicine was in the Bon religion's hands.

I would like to look now at the names of the physicians of Tazig and From. I can be very brief with Ur-pa-ya, also spelled Ur-ba-ya, and just say that I cannot identify him. I have had a few different ideas, which I could find no way to substantiate. Attempts to explain it as an Indic name led to failure, although we might think it closely resembles Sanskrit *urvaya*, an indeclinable meaning 'far off'; a close match, perhaps, but all the same it would seem to be far off the mark. One idea is that it is simply *ʿarabiyya*, Arabic for 'Arabic', 'Arab' or 'Arabian'.[31] I also entertained the idea that it might be somehow Oribasios, a fourth-century successor of Galen at Pergamon and physician to Julian the Apostate, who produced huge and influential compendia of medical lore. Even if one or another of these ideas might be correct, I have found no method of substantiation, no sure way to overcome some of the chronological and linguistic problems that would of necessity be involved. I had thought that the title of his medical work, *The Six Phenomenal Origins*, might be a reference to the basic idea of the Six Necessities (Arabic: *sitta ḍarūriyya*) known to Galenic medicine in general.[32] I have not been

---

[30] See *G.yung-drung Bon-gyi Rgyud-'bum*, as contained in *Sources for a History of Bon* (Dolanji, 1972), pp. 1-46, at pp. 22-3: *dus de tsam na / rgya gar na chos yod skad / rgya nag la gtsug lag rtsis / phrom la sman spyad / bod dang zhang zhung gi yul na bon gyis 'dul zhing spyod pa las / gzhan gang yang med pa lags so // sman spyad 'di bon gyi lag tu spyod pa lags so*. It is interesting that Beckwith, 'Introduction of Greek Medicine', p. 306, could cite a slightly abbreviated version of this quote from Shar-rdza's twentieth-century history, which is very surely based on the earlier Rma history.

[31] Ibn al-ʿArabī (1165-1240), born in Spain, travelled a great deal, but spent the last ten years of his life in Damascus. He is after all too late, or very nearly so, to appear in Che-rje's history. He is not known to have written anything on medicine.

[32] References were supplied in Dan Martin, 'An Early Tibetan History of Indian Medicine'. The relevant footnote on the 'six necessities' is no. 15 on p. 317. On the six 'non-naturals' ('necessities') see, for example, Peter E. Pormann and Emilie Savage-Smith, *Medieval Islamic Medicine* (Edinburgh, 2007), pp. 44-5. We might add that these were known in thirteenth-century England, to Roger Bacon at least, under the name 'Six Causes'. See the words of John Charles, 'Roger Bacon on the Errors of Physicians', *Medical History*, 4/4 (1960), pp. 277-8:

able to further substantiate this either, so again, I can just say that I have found no satisfactory solution to the identity of Ur-ba-ya; only a few guesses that may all prove to be nothing more than that.

For the identity of the physician from From, I believe I can come up with something that is at least more persuasive. First let me say that when Tibetanists are faced with the syllables Tsan-pa-shi-la-ha they are bound to parse them as Tsanpa and Shilaha. This is for two reasons: firstly because we are accustomed to seeing the syllables -pa and -ba as common functional suffixes, and secondly because the syllables Shi-la look so much like the Sanskrit Śīla, 'moral discipline', which occurs in a number of Indic names like Kamalaśīla etc. The 'ha' is simply puzzling.[33] After much thinking on this problem, I believe that the Indo-Tibetanist reading leads nowhere. It may take a little imagination to solve this problem, along with the understanding that we are dealing with a name that is to be interpreted neither in a Tibetanizing nor a Sanskritizing way. Rather we ought to be looking for an explanation with the understanding that it represents a name that would have belonged to either (1) someone from the place known to Arabs as Rūm, or in Middle Iranic language as From, meaning the Byzantine realm, or (2) someone from a place roughly between northern Afghanistan and northern Pakistan in an area ruled by Turks.

I recommend taking the syllable Tsan as the 'surname' (perhaps a clan name, place name or the like) or at least a specifier, and the remainder, Bashilaha, as the given name. The Tsan (there are in fact many different spellings) were a people who inhabited the Tsanik region in the hills above the port city of Trabizon (modern Turkish spelling: Trabzon) on the shores of the Black Sea at the extreme north-east of Asia Minor. They lived in close proximity to (and are sometimes carelessly confused with) the Laz. Both peoples were Christianized in around the sixth century and remained so until the thirteenth. Behind Bashilaha, I read the very common name Basileos. Besides being a popular personal name, it was also used in the Byzantine Empire as a term for its own rulers. I believe that this explanation has a certain cogency and conforms to the principle of parsimony, since it manages to explain three things at once: (1) His place of origin, From, being the Byzantine Empire, (2) the Tsan is explained as a nationality within the

---

> The signs and symptoms of old age (and his [Bacon's] catalogue of these is very extensive) are due to a drying up of the natural juices, with which is unhappily combined, an invasion of excessive extraneous humours, as exemplified by his special morbific bug-bear, the phlegm. Seeking for the real causes of this gradual failure of vital powers, he blames the air we breathe, excesses of food and drink, lack of sleep, restlessness of the body, and agitation of mind.

Bacon was an avid reader of works by Muslim scientists.

33 'The final syllable [ha] of his personal name ... is so far inexplicable. However, the facts that his name is obviously of Sanskrit derivation ...' Beckwith, 'Introduction of Greek Medicine', p. 303.

Byzantine Empire, and (3) Bashilaha is explained as Basileos or Bāsil, a title or name commonly used by both kings and subjects of the Byzantine Empire.

But I have not exactly dazzled myself, even, with the brilliance of my own suggestion. I would still hope for more reasons for finding it justifiable, and of course more ways of substantiating or falsifying it, or if necessary discarding it altogether. One might, and probably ought to, assume that since this doctor disappeared into Tibet where he obtained only local fame, we ought not expect his existence to be recorded in sources external to Tibet. Of course, most of Che-rje's list of doctors never went to Tibet, as I said, but in the case of Tsan Bashilaha, we do have the information from an independent thirteenth-century source, the history by Mkhas-pa Lde'u, that he did enter Tibet and translated medical works in the time of Mes-ag-tshom, in the middle of the eighth century.[34] Most but not all later medical historians agree on this point. In the Lde'u history he uniquely bears the name Be-ci Btsan Pa-ha-la.[35]

The term *be-ci* requires a little discussion. Some later sources (cited by Beckwith) say that the Bi-ci or Bi-ji in his name is a word from 'his own language' for 'doctor'. Indeed, the Middle Iranian word (as Beckwith pointed out) is *pezeshk*, surely related historically speaking to the Sanskrit *bhiṣaj*, and borrowed into Armenian as *bzhishk*.[36] In the early-fifteenth-century history by Brang-ti, he tells how Tsan Bashilaha settled down in Tibet and married, with his descendants carrying with them the name of the Bi-ci lineage.[37]

Now among the several reputedly ancient Tibetan medical works that have reached publication in recent years is one entitled *Bi-ci'i Pu-ti Kha-ser*, 'The Yellow-Covered Volume of the Biji'.[38] It is made from a very badly spelled manuscript.

---

34 Christopher I. Beckwith, *The Tibetan Empire in Central Asia* (Princeton, 1993), p. 227, gives Emperor Mes-ag-tshom (aka Khri-lde-gtsug-brtsan) the reign dates of 712-55 CE.

35 Mkhas-pa Lde'u, *Rgya Bod-kyi Chos-'byung Rgyas-pa* [*Extensive Dharma History of India and Tibet*] (Lhasa, 1987), p. 300: *be ci btsan pa ha las sman dpyad bsgyur*. For details on this historical work, see Martin, *Tibetan Histories*, pp. 43-4, no. 54. Since this is a modern publication based on a cursive manuscript (proven by the colour plate that serves as the frontispiece of the book), we might expect imperfect readings, especially in the case of unfamiliar foreign names.

36 All these words mean 'physician'. See Louis H. Gray, 'Certain Parallel Developments in Pali and New Persian Phonology', *Journal of the American Oriental Society*, 20 (1899): pp. 229-43, at p. 241.

37 Beckwith, 'Introduction of Greek Medicine', p. 303. Leonard W.J. van der Kuijp, 'The Earliest Indian Reference to Muslims in a Buddhist Philosophical Text of Circa 700', *Journal of Indian Philosophy*, 34 (2006): pp. 169-202, at p. 191.

38 Zur-mkhar Blo-gros-rgyal-po, *Sman-pa-rnams-kyis Mi-shes-su Mi-rung-ba'i Shes-bya Spyi'i Khog-dbubs* (Chengdu, 2001), p. 294: *de nas tsan pa shi la ha rang yul du 'byon khar rang gi sras la gdams pa be'u bum nag po'i skor 'jal tshad dang bcas pa dang / tsa ra kas mdzad zer ba'i drang srong snying brgyud mgo byang khog yan lag gi pra khrid skor gsum dang / mgo byang khog yan lag 'du ba thor bu dang bcas pa'i bcos thabs bi ji pu ti kha ser du grags pa rnams phul ba las / phyi ma la rgyal po'i bla yig 'od 'bar du grags*. It is interesting that the title *Bi-ji Pu-ti Kha-ser*

The content is divided into six chapters. I would like to draw attention to the first three chapters: chapter 1 is on wounds of the head; chapter 2 on wounds of the trunk; chapter 3 on wounds of the limbs.[39] These chapters on wounds take up nearly half of the book.[40] Chapter 4 very systematically covers first the types and symptoms of the main diseases associated with the three humours, then types and symptoms of diseases associated with specific bodily organs and, finally, types and symptoms of diseases that seem to affect the body in general. Then the same categories are covered once more, only this time offering methods of treatment. Chapter 5 is a very brief one on miscellaneous diseases. The last chapter, chapter 6, starts out with an explanation of various forms of medicines followed by a number of miscellaneous recommendations for treating specific diseases divided more according to their treatment methods. Unfortunately the colophon is not very informative. It does tell us that the volume was made for the sake of Emperor Khri-srong-lde-btsan, while it does not tell us it is a translation of a foreign medical text. There are a few names of doctors, so far unidentifiable. There are some warnings not to make more than two copies. We can see that the manuscript is not the 'original' since it says that there were many things in Indic (or Chinese?) script in the exemplar that were not copied out. There are also warnings not to steal the text, so evidently the theft of medical books was a problem. All of this tells us what the narratives also suggest, which is that this was for a long time a zealously guarded text kept as a kind of family heirloom for the exclusive use of a dynasty of doctors.

---

is given together with an outline that corresponds to the actual chapter outline of the published text: *Bi-ci'i Pu-ti Kha-ser* (Lhasa, 2005). We have to understand that the 'title' of this work is merely a description of a physical volume, a 'volume' (*pu-ti* is more properly spelled *po-ti*, which anyway corresponds to Indic *poṭhi*) with a yellow cover (*kha ser*), which belonged to the Bi-ci family lineage of physicians. In this passage by Zur-mkhar we also learn something interesting, which is that Tsan Bashilaha returned to his own country, leaving behind at least one son who inherited his books. If it were not for this we might assume that he lived out his remaining days in Tibet. I have not attempted to analyse the narratives about Tsan Bashilaha, mainly because the Brang-ti history would seem to be key to the historical development of some of the narrative elements, and this history is not yet available to me. See now Frances Garrett, 'Critical Methods in Tibetan Medical Histories', *Journal of Asian Studies*, 66/2 (2007): pp. 363-87, where the Brang-ti history is utilized, with a comparative study of its narratives.

[39] See Beckwith, 'Introduction of Greek Medicine', p. 303, where the same succession of head, trunk and limbs appears, but in three different text titles.

[40] These three kinds of wounds are covered by three chapters in the *'Bum-bzhi*, as well as the *Rgyud-bzhi*. Generally speaking, the chapter titles of the two texts very closely correspond. On this point one may consult Tseyang Changngoba, Namgyal Nyima Dagkar, Per Kvaerne, Dondrup Lhagyal, Dan Martin, Donatella Rossi, and Tsering Thar, *A Catalogue of the Bon Kanjur*, volume editor, Dan Martin; project coordinator, Per Kvaerne; series editor, Yasuhiko Nagano, Bon Studies series no. 8 (Osaka, 2003), p. 192.

I searched within the pages for some general theory about diseases, and the only thing I found was the statement that there are a total of 404 diseases, of which only 101 can be cured by physicians (p. 91). The text makes use of the three (not four) humours as the basic causes of disease.[41] The idea that there are 404 diseases is well known in Indian Mahāyāna Buddhist scriptures (the *Vimalakīrti Sūtra*, for example).[42] It is interesting to note in this connection that a Sanskrit text on the 404 diseases was translated into Arabic in Abbasid times.[43] In general, I think that the 404 diseases is a canonical Buddhist idea, and probably not an Ayurvedic one.[44]

---

41 A theory of four humours, the fourth one being 'blood', is known in Tibet, even if rare, and passages demonstrating this have been located in the lengthy *Gzi-brjid* biography of Lord Shenrab, founder of the Bon religion. In Sman-rams-pa Pa-sangs-yon-tan, *Bod-kyi Gso-ba Rig-pa'i Lo-rgyus*, pp. 12, 76, is a citation from the *Gzi-brjid* which confirms Tibetan knowledge of a four-humour system: *ma rig nyon mongs dug lnga de / dug gsum rgyu la nad kyi rgyu bzhi ldang / rlung mkhris bad kan khrag nad 'du ba bzhi*. The source of this quotation, according to the note, is *Gzi-brjid* vol. JA, fol. 28 'na' side of the page, line 1. Although I could not locate this exact quotation in the version of the *Gzi-brjid* at my disposal, I did notice in *Mdo Dri-med Gzi-brjid* (Lhasa, 2000), vol. 7, p. 291, the following: *rgyu dang rkyen las gyur pa yi // rlung 'khris bad kan khrag las sogs // 'du ba rnam bzhi 'khrugs pa dang // nad rigs sum brgya drug cu yang // skad gcig nyid la zhi bar 'gyur*. It is interesting that, besides saying that there are four humours (here called *'du-ba* rather than *nyes-pa*), it says there are 360 diseases instead of the more expected number of 404. We know that the three-humour system was well known in Tibet's Imperial Period, certainly if we may count on the authenticity of the letter of Buddhaguhya: see, for example, Ronald M. Davidson, *Tibetan Renaissance: Tantric Buddhism in the Rebirth of Tibetan Culture* (New York: Columbia University Press, 2005), p. 22. For a critical reconsideration of the appropriateness of 'humour' as a translation of Tibetan *nyes-pa* (or Sanskrit *doṣa*), see Yonten Gyatso, '*Nyes-pa*: A Brief Review of its English Translation', *Tibet Journal*, 30/4-31/1 (2005-06): pp. 109-18. The term *'du-ba* is used to refer to the *nyes-pa* in view of their action. See the definition of the three *'du-ba*, 'aggregators' or '[re]combiners', in the medical dictionary by 'Go-'jo Dbang-'dus, *Bod Gangs-can-pa'i Gso-ba Rig-pa'i Dpal-ldan Rgyud-bzhi Sogs-kyi Brda dang Dka'-gnad 'Ga'-zhig Bkrol-ba Sngon-byon Mkhas-pa'i Gsung-rgyun G.yu-thog Dgongs-rgyan* (Beijing, 1982), p. 265. Among the most interesting discussions of the humours of Tibetan medicine, aside from the one just mentioned, are those of Marianne Winder, 'Tibetan Medicine Compared with Ancient and Mediaeval Western Medicine', *Bulletin of Tibetology*, N.S., 1 (1981): pp. 5-22, at pp. 5-8, and Terry Clifford, *Tibetan Buddhist Medicine and Psychiatry: The Diamond Healing* (York Beach, 1984), pp. 90-95.

42 See Étienne Lamotte, *The Teachings of Vimalakīrti (Vimalakīrti Nirdeśa)*, trans. Sara Boin (Oxford, 1994), p. 36, and references given there. See also Robert A.F. Thurman, *The Holy Teaching of Vimalakīrti: A Mahāyāna Scripture* (University Park, 1976), at pp. 22 and 114.

43 Khaliq Ahmad Nizami, 'Early Arab Contact with South Asia', *Journal of Islamic Studies*, 5/1 (1994): pp. 52-69, at p. 64.

44 The sources cited by Meulenbeld have different disease numbers. The *Suśrutasaṃhita*, for example places the number of illnesses at 1,120. The *Kāśyapasaṃhita* states that illnesses are 'innumerable'. See Jan Meulenbeld, *A History of Indian Medical*

One person conspicuous by his absence from Che-rje's list is the famous Ga-le-nos. It is of course remarkable that Galenos appears at all in Tibetan medical histories, let alone with a proper Greek ending on his name.[45] Some histories of more recent centuries have him entering Tibet, in the flesh, in the first half of the seventh century. Beckwith has argued convincingly that the coming of Galenos, together with the Yellow Emperor of Chinese medicine and the rishi Bharadhvāja of India, is little more than a myth, although a myth that may yet convey the information that these three systems of medicine were influential in Tibet in those early times. Still, by the time of the Regent's history rather elaborate stories could be told about his visit. The Regent says he settled down in Tibet and had three children (I think this part of his biography was taken away from that of Tsan Bashilaha, and there are still other signs that their biographies and accomplishments were in some ways confounded).[46]

Before ending this article, I at least want to mention the list of Nine Foreign Physicians who came to Tibet during the time of Khri-srong-lde-brtsan (see Appendix E). No trace of this list or any of the individual names contained in it may be found in the three earliest medical texts. This list begins to appear only in the fifteenth-century histories.

No. 1, Śāntigarbha, is best known as one of the consecrators of Samye Monastery upon its completion in the late eighth century. In the field of medicine, he is credited with the translation of the main old text on Tibetan medical botany.[47] Only four of his very brief works are preserved in the Tanjur,

---

Literature (Groningen, 1999), vol. IA, p. 332 and vol. IIA, p. 26. I would like to thank Ronit Yoeli-Tlalim for supplying these references.

45 There were mentions of Galenos in earlier English-language Tibetological literature (arranged in roughly chronological order): Rolf Alfred Stein, *Tibetan Civilization* (Stanford, 1972), p. 61 (first published in French in 1962); Yeshey Donden, 'Tibetan Medicine: A Brief History, translated by Gyatsho Tshering', *The Tibet Society Bulletin*, 5 (1972): pp. 7-24, at p. 18, mentions 'Persian' scholars 'Galay Ne, Cehanpa Sila', by which he surely means Galenos and Tsan Bashilaha; Rechung, *Tibetan Medicine*, p. 15, says 'Perhaps a Persian translator of Galen, or a pen-name adopted by a Persian doctor'; Per Kvaerne, in his review of Rechung Rinpoche's book in *Kailash*, 3/1 (1975): pp. 6-73, at p. 71, said, 'It is interesting to note that a Persian (or perhaps a Byzantine Greek) doctor styled Galenos is supposed to have settled in Lhasa during the reign of Sroṅ-bcan sgam-po i.e. during the 7th century.' However, Beckwith, 'The Introduction of Greek Medicine', was the very first to consider critically the narratives as a whole and place them in historical context.

46 Sde-srid, *Dpal-ldan Gso-ba Rig-pa'i Khog-'bugs*, p. 151. Beckwith, 'Introduction of Greek Medicine', p. 301. That there was an exchange of biographical elements was suggested in Czaja, 'A Hitherto Unknown Medical History', p. 165, n. 27.

47 The authorship of this herbal is credited to the feminine bodhisattva Tārā. It survives in at least three published manuscript versions, and no doubt many unpublished ones. For Śāntigarbha's translation of the three-chapter herbal entitled *Sngo'i 'Khrungs-dpe Rin-chen Sgrol-ma (~Sgron-ma?)*, with authorship attributed to Tārā, see Sde-srid, *Dpal-ldan Gso-ba Rig-pa'i Khog-'bugs*, p. 173 (other medical texts he translated are listed on p. 171,

and he is generally one of the least frequently mentioned of the Indian pundits that resided in Imperial Tibet, although his name does occur in a Dunhuang manuscript.[48] None of the others in this list of nine would seem to be known from any other context besides this list and, of course, a biographical work that I will discuss shortly.

I am not at the moment prepared to sort out all the details and come to an airtight conclusion on this matter, but I believe this new list of foreign doctors does not hold the same degree of historical validity as the list in Che-rje's history. Here are three of my reasons for thinking so:

1. The lack of sources of verification outside the context of the medical histories (and the biography to be mentioned presently).
2. None of the names appears in Che-rje's listing.
3. Then there is the unconvincing nature of the Chinese, Tazig and Turkish names. Now it is true that the listing, with somewhat different spellings for the names, appears in the biography of the Elder G.yu-thog-pa. Note also that in this particular listing we do find the addition of Tsan Bashilaha as no. 10. The biography of the Elder G.yu-thog-pa was written, according to its colophon, by a member of the G.yu-thog-pa family. It has not been possible to identify the author, let alone give his dates.[49] All we can say is that this biography was made known in the seventeenth century during the time of the Fifth Dalai Lama. We could say it probably dates from that time. One reason for doubting its authority is because it is very likely that the chief subject of this biography, the Elder G.yu-thog-pa, never existed. Che-rje's history knows of his own near-contemporary G.yu-thog-pa, but

where we may notice a 120-chapter herbal, here called *Sngo-'bum*, pronounced by Tārā). For a classic study of the history of the herbal, see Charles Singer, 'The Herbal in Antiquity and its Transmission to Later Ages', *The Journal of Hellenic Studies*, 47/1 (1927): pp. 1-52. (On p. 48 we read how the herbal of Dioscorides was translated from Greek directly into Arabic – some, Singer not being among them, think it was first translated into Syriac, then into Arabic – in Baghdad in about 854 by Stephanos, son of Basilios..). So far as I know no one has offered even the briefest historical sketch of the Tibetan genre of herbals known as *'khrungs-dpe*. This is a pity.

48 Jacob Dalton, 'The Early Development of the Padmasambhava Legend in Tibet: A Study of IOL Tib J 644 and Pelliot tibétain 307', *Journal of the American Oriental Society*, 124/4 (2004): pp. 759-72, at p. 768.

49 Ven. Rechung Rinpoche Jampal Kunzang, *Tibetan Medicine Illustrated in Original Texts* (Berkeley, 1976). The biography of the Elder G.yu-thog-pa is found on pp. 141-327. The corresponding Tibetan text has been published a number of times. It would appear unlikely that the biography's author, who we know from the colophon had a claim to belong to the G.yu-thog family, ought to be identified with the Lhun-grub-bkra-shis who founded the monumental *stūpa* at Grwa Byams-pa-gling in 1472, since the latter belonged to the Thu-mi family, claiming descent from Thon-mi Sambhoṭa, reputed inventor of Tibetan script in the seventh century.

> nothing about a G.yu-thog-pa in Imperial Times. Even the historical works by G.yu-thog-pa and his disciples never mention an 'Elder G.yu-thog-pa'. What we do find in the histories of the fifteenth and following centuries is a listing of nine young men of the mid-to-late eighth century chosen for their intelligence who were made to study medicine. Since this list includes together with G.yu-thog-pa names such as Che-rje himself, it is abundantly clear that it was formed by taking names of famous Tibetan physicians of the eleventh–thirteenth centuries and placing them as a group back into the eighth century. That this is what happened was already evident to at least two Tibetan historians in the sixteenth and nineteenth centuries.[50] It should be no surprise to anyone that certain Tibetan history writers were often critical of their sources, just as some of us are today.[51]

So, at the risk of sounding like a stone-carved philologist of the often detested kind, I would say that Che-rje's list, given its relative age, needs to be taken most seriously in its account of the foreign medical figures and their works. I have tried to show that the medical figures listed by him also need taking seriously, although I should say again that some of these figures date as late as the late eleventh century. Of course there is something disappointing in all this, especially since the idea that there was a kind of international medical conference in Imperial Tibet would seem to unravel. Surely such international meetings of medical minds were taking place in such places as third- and sixth-century Gund-ī Shāpūr in southwestern Persia,[52] and ninth-century Baghdad,[53] to give some examples.

---

50 Long ago Samten G. Karmay, in his article entitled 'Vairocana and the Rgyud-bzhi', *Tibetan Medicine*, 12 (1989): pp. 19-31, at p. 29, n. 13, expressed his amazement that the Elder G.yu-thog-pa could be awarded a birthdate of 790 CE, since he is a 'fictitious character'.

51 I could point to a partial parallel in the narrative of nine young men chosen for their intelligence to become translators in the mid-to-late eighth century. Here, too, we have a thirteenth-century listing of partly unfamiliar names. In yet later histories these names were displaced by names of translators who were in fact probably active in the early ninth century. Their translations, unlike those done by the translators in the first list, still survive. For a critical study of the list of nine medical students, see Manfred Taube, *Beiträge zur Geschichte der medizinischen Literatur Tibets* (Sankt Augustin, 1981), pp. 15-16, in addition to references already given in my earlier paper.

52 S.H. Taqizadeh, 'Some Chronological Data Relating to the Sasanian Period', *Bulletin of the School of Oriental and African Studies*, 9/1 (1937): pp. 125-39, at p. 136. Samir Johna, 'The Mesopotamian Schools of Edessa and Jundi-Shapur: The Roots of Modern Medical Schools', *The American Surgeon*, 69/7 (2003): pp. 627-30. For a reassessment of what they term as 'the myth of Gondēshāpūr', see Pormann and Savage-Smith, *Medieval Islamic Medicine*, pp. 20-21. I would like to thank the editors for supplying this reference.

53 This means the translations of Greek and other medical works at the *Bayt al-ḥikma* ('House of Wisdom') under Ḥunayn ibn Isḥāq (809-77 CE). See, for example, Samir Johna,

Why not also in Tibet in the seventh or eighth century? Of the eleven medical writers in Che-rje's list, we may only be relatively sure that Tsan Bashilaha actually visited Tibet, since we at least have an independent thirteenth-century source for this, in which we learn for the first time that this visit took place in the middle of the eighth century. I would like to suggest in closing that perhaps the study of historical narratives may not be our most sure way to demonstrate medical influence. A thorough study of some of the earliest medical texts, which are only now beginning to appear, would reveal some significant clues.

Apart from the question of theriac, studied by Beckwith in a brief note,[54] here is just one more example: The *Bi-ci'i Pu-ti Kha-ser*, which I mentioned before as the text preserved by the early Tibetan medical school that descended from Tsan Bashilaha, in its first chapter devoted to head wounds,[55] describes a method for detecting invisible skull fractures. It says that when the bone has been exposed, and you are still unable to see any fracture, you cover the bone with vermillion or black ink and bandage it. When the ink is later wiped off, there will be a coagulation of the red or black indicating that there is a fault.[56]

'Hunayn ibn-Ishaq: A Forgotten Legend', *The American Surgeon*, 68/5 (2002): pp. 497-9. See also Manfred Ullmann, *Islamic Medicine* (Edinburgh, 1978) and Pormann and Savage-Smith, *Medieval Islamic Medicine*.

[54] The Tibetan word *dar-ya-kan*, clearly of foreign origins, occurs in a title that forms part of a lengthy list of the works translated by Tsan Bashilaha. See Christopher I. Beckwith, 'Tibetan Treacle: A Note on Theriac in Tibet', *The Tibet Society Bulletin*, 15 (1980), pp. 49-51. Beckwith's findings were reviewed, in Tibetan, in Sman-rams-pa Pa-sangs-yon-tan, *Bod-kyi Gso-ba Rig-pa'i Lo-rgyus*, p. 296, n. 76. See as well the long entry on *dar-ya-kan* in Pasang Yonten Arya, *Dictionary of Tibetan Materia Medica* (Delhi, 1998), pp. 97-9. *Dar-ya-kan* is still used today as part of the names or epithets of many medicinal simples and preparations. It means either 'elixir' (*bdud-rtsi*) or something that can cure disease with a single application.

[55] Even though the word *rma* in the chapter title literally means 'wound(s)', it does in fact cover head traumas of all kinds, including fractures and contusions. On p. 10 we even see lists of symptoms that resemble those of concussion or of still more serious types of brain injuries. For example, among the diagnostic symptoms of damage to the brain sheath or membrane(s) (*klad rgya nyams-pa*), we can see listed unclear cognition (*shes-pa mi gsal*), constant vomiting (*dus rtag-tu skyug bro*), forgetfulness (*brjed-ngas*), shaking of the feet etc. (*rkang-pa la-sogs-pa 'dar*), and sleep talking (*gnyid log-pa'i dus-su blab-bcol smra*). For a survey article on the history of medical ideas about concussion, see Paul R. McCrory and Samuel F. Berkovic, 'Concussion: The History of Clinical and Pathophysiological Concepts and Misconceptions', *Neurology*, 57 (2001): pp. 2283-9. This article denies that Asian medical systems had any methods for dealing with head traumas: 'Although many medical tracts and writings survive from Chinese, Persian, Indian and Hindu medicine, there are no surviving accounts regarding the management of head injury or concussion' (p. 2284). As we marvel at their confident command of all surviving Asian medical literature, we should point out the brief section of the *Bi-ci* book (on pp. 19-21) on treatments for brain injuries.

[56] On p. 8: *byug pa rdzas gyi (~kyi) sgo nas brtag pa ni / rus pa mngon nas gas chag ma rtogs na / mtshal lam snag [tsha] rus pa g.yog par gdab ste / phyis pas dmar breng (~hreng) ngam gnag*

Now this method for detecting invisible skull fractures was used in Greek Hippocratic medicine (Hippocrates' treatise 'On Injuries of the Head'), although he does not identify the substances used in his 'black ointment'.[57] Al-Zahrāwī, the famous Islamic surgeon of the tenth century, also employed this technique, and he is explicit about using ink.[58] This is quite intriguing, although I have not yet had the opportunity to look very far into the history and implications. For one thing, I really have no idea whether this ink procedure was or was not used in early Ayurvedic or Chinese medicines. An obvious place to look would be Vāgbhaṭa's chapters on wounds.

Meanwhile, at the eleventh seminar of the International Association of Tibetan Studies, held at Winterthur on the Rhine in 2006, Ronit Yoeli-Tlalim showed, with utter clarity, that the categories used in an early Tibetan medical text known as the *So-ma-ra-dza* in its treatment of urinalysis very surely have their source in Graeco-Islamic texts on the subject.[59] I would say that much concentrated research remains to be done along these lines. It may actually encourage these comparative studies if we were to declare a temporary moratorium on the repetition of traditional stories about one or more international medical conferences in seventh- or eighth-century Tibet.[60] That might be true regardless of whether such a conference actually took place, or not. Indeed, the absence of a conference would be no indication of the absence of exchange. If anything, the conference stories were developed as a way of accounting for something that was obvious to the storytellers, which is that international medical exchanges did happen.

(~nag) breng (~hreng) byung na skyon yod pa yin. The passage continues. The parenthetical material represents emendations and insertions by the modern editors of the text.

57 I.G. Panourias et al., 'Hippocrates: A Pioneer in the Treatment of Head Injuries', *Neurosurgery*, 57/1 (2005): pp. 181-9, especially p. 185, column B, 'Latent Cranial Injuries'. See also Guido Majno, *The Healing Hand: Man and Wound in the Ancient World* (Cambridge, 1975), pp. 166-9 (particularly the illustration on p. 169). For another brief discussion see McCrory and Berkovic, 'Concussion', p. 2284.

58 'The hairy fracture is difficult to discover and can be diagnosed by exposing the skull, and smearing it with ink; the linear fracture thus appears stained.' Ezzat Abbouleish, 'Contributions of Islam to Medicine', http://www.islam-usa.com/im3.html (accessed 1 Nov. 2006). Al-Zahrāwī lived in Islamic Spain from 936 to 1013 CE. In European literature he was called by his Latin name Albu[l]casis, and is today a well-known figure in the history of surgery.

59 This paper, entitled Ronit Yoeli-Tlalim, 'On Urine Analysis and Tibetan Medicine's Connections with the West', in Sienna Craig et al. (eds), *Studies of Medical Pluralism in Tibetan History and Society* (Halle, 2011), pp. 195-211.

60 Clifford, *Tibetan Buddhist Medicine and Psychiatry*, p. 53: 'In particular pursuit of medical knowledge, King Srongtsan Gampo held the first international medical conference in Tibet. Doctors came from India, Persia, and China.' This is just one example of numerous such statements one may find in the literature.

APPENDIX A: LIST OF EARLY MEDICAL HISTORIES

Note: 'TH' means Dan Martin and Yael Bentor, *Tibetan Histories* [London, 1997]; this listing does not include chapters on medical history contained within larger works. Those known to be extant are marked with §§§:

circa 1200 (?): G.yu-thog-pa Yon-tan-mgon-po (1127-1203), *Khyung-chen Lding-ba*. Published. TH no. 17. §§§

1204 (possibly 1264): Che-rje's history. Che-rje Zhang-ston Zhig-po Thugs-rje-khri-'od, *Sman-gyi Byung-tshul Khog-dbubs Rgyal-mtshan Rtse-mo 'Bar-ba* [*Blazing Tip of the Victory Banner: The History of Medicine*], a manuscript (still unpublished) in 46 folios preserved in the Giuseppe Tucci collection in Rome. TH no. 36. §§§

1200s (?): Anon., *G.yu-thog Bla-sgrub-kyi Lo-rgyus: Nges-shes 'Dren-byed Dge-ba'i Lcags-kyu* [*A Virtuous Hook for Drawing up Certainty: History of the Guru Services of G.yu-thog-pa*]. TH no. 37. This has been published (thanks to Gavin Kilty for pointing this out to me): *G.yu-thog Snying-thig-las Byin-rlabs Bla-ma Sgrub-pa'i Chos-skor Sdug-bsngal Mun-sel Thugs-rje'i Nyi-'od ces-pa'i Thog-mar Lo-rgyus Dge-ba'i Lcags-kyu*, contained in: *G.yu-thog Snying-thig-gi Yig-cha: The Collected Basic Texts and Ritual Works of the Medical Teachings Orally Passed from G.yu-thog Yon-tan-mgon-po*, 'arranged and largely restructured by Khams-smyon Dharma-seng-ge', Smanrtsis Shesrig Spendzod series no. 106, D.L. Tashigang (Leh, 1981), pp. 5-21. According to the colophon, it was written by a direct follower of G.yu-thog-pa named 'Dznyā-na-dha-ri', which must mean Ye-shes-gzungs. §§§

Early 1400s: Brang-ti Dpal-ldan-'tsho-byed, *Gso-rig Chos-'byung Shes-bya Rab-gsal* [*Making Knowable Objects Clear: A History of Healing Science*]. According to a review by Kurtis R. Schaeffer (*Journal of Asian Studies*, 57/3 [1998]: p. 857), the author must be placed at the beginning of the fifteenth century. He adds that it is extant in a 48-folio cursive manuscript (which remains unpublished). TH no. 35 (with mistaken dating). §§§

circa 1450: Stag-tshang Lo-tsā-ba Shes-rab-rin-chen (b. 1405), *Gso-dpyad Byung-tshul-gyi Lo-rgyus Sman-gyi Spyi-don dang bcas-pa Mkhas-pa'i Yid 'Phrog*. TH no. 105.

Late 1400s: Byang-pa Bkra-shis-dpal-bzang, *Khog-'bugs 'Dzum Dkar Bzhad-pa'i Nyi-ma*. TH no. 128.

— Byang-smad-pa [Byang-sman] Bsod-nams-ye-shes-rgyal-mtshan, *Gso-rig Chos-'byung Pad-tshal Bzhad-pa'i Nyin-byed*. TH no. 129.

— Byar-po Paṇ-chen Rdo-rje-pha-lam, *Khog-'bugs Legs-bshad Gser-gyi Snye-ma*. TH no. 130.

1500s: Ska-ba Shākya-dbang-phyug (= Mtsho-smad Mkhan-chen), *Khog-'bugs Legs-bshad Dngul-dkar Me-long*. Still unpublished, although subject of a study (with resumé and outline) by Olaf Czaja. TH no. 153. §§§

— Blo-bzang-rgya-mtsho ('Rin-chen-sdings Sems-dpa'-chen-po', = 'Tsho-byed Blo-gros-brtan-pa), *Chos-'byung Drang-srong Dgongs-rgyan*. A history, primarily of medicine. TH no. 154.
— Mnga'-ris 'Tsho-byed Chos-skyong-dpal-bzang (b. 1479), *Gso-ba Rig-pa'i Khog-'bugs Bdud-rtsi Chu-rgyun*. A copy exists in Norbu Lingka. Unpublished. TH no. 158.
— Dpa'-bo Gtsug-lag-phreng-ba (1504-66), *Sman-gyi Chos-'byung dang 'Bam Bcos*. TH no. 169.
— Zur-mkhar Blo-gros-rgyal-po (= Legs-bshad-tshol, b. 1509), *Khog-'bugs Gtan-pa Med-pa'i Mchod-sbyin-gyi Sgo 'Phar Yangs-po* (= *Drang-srong Kun-du-dga'-ba'i Zlos-gar*). Now published. TH no. 172. §§§
— Mi-pham-bzang-po, *Khog-'bugs 'Chi-med Phun-tshogs Lnga-ldan*. TH no. 176.
1588: Bde-chen-chos-'khor-gyi Sman-pa Ratna'i-ming-can, *Gso-ba Rig-pa'i Khog-'bugs Legs-bsdus*. TH no. 185.
circa 1700 (?): 'Phan-yul Gro-sa-ba Tshogs-gnyis-rgya-mtsho, *Rgyud-bzhi'i Khog-'bugs Bai-dûrya'i Chu-rgyun*. TH no. 241.
1704: Sde-srid Sangs-rgyas-rgya-mtsho (1653-1705), *Dpal-ldan Gso-ba Rig-pa'i Khog-'bugs Legs-bshad Bai-dûrya'i Me-long Drang-srong Dgyes-pa'i Dga'-ston* (= *Sman-gyi Khog-dbub*). Published. TH no. 259. §§§

APPENDIX B: GENERAL OUTLINE

The general outline used in Che-rje's passage on the 'Universal' History of Medicine paraphrased with details [lists of text titles etc.] omitted:

1st — *The Seven Schools*. ***See Appendix C.
2nd — *The Four Cycles*. These are: [1] Outer textual items of knowledge. [2] Inner advice about the meaning [of the text]. [3] Secret procedural guidance. [4] Super-secret experiential guidance.
3rd — *The Four Translations*. These are [1] highland [western], [2] lowland [eastern], [3] southern and [4] northern. Che-rje adds a brief geography here, about the Five Great Countries: China in the east, India in the south, Stag-[g]zig in the west, and Ge-sar in the north, with Tibet as the fifth Great Country in the centre. He says that India and China, being fonts of the sciences, were the main sources for many translations, that the Buddha's compassion manifested medical treatments in every country, that during the time of the expansion of the Tibetan kings' domains, they were all translated into Tibetan.
4th — *The Two Times of Translation*. These are, of course, the earlier translations (*lnga 'gyur* being a careless spelling for *snga 'gyur*), and the later translations. No translators and no titles of Imperial Period translations are given, unfortunately. Included among the medicine

text translators of the later period are not only Rin-chen-bzang-po, but also Skyes-bu Me-lha, the Red Ācārya, and one named Be-nag Brag-'khar-ba (the latter's translations were from Chinese).

APPENDIX C: THE SEVEN SCHOOLS

(Lugs Bdun; folios 21r-22v):

1. Rgyal-sras Byang-chub-sems-dpa'i Lugs (Bodhisattva School).
2. Lhas Mdzad-pa'i Lugs (School [of Texts] Composed by Devas).
3. Drang-srong-gis Mdzad-pa ([School of Texts] Composed by Sages [*ṛṣi*]). The eight sages who taught the Caraka texts (the *Tsa-ra-ka Sde Brgyad*).
4. 'Phags-pa'i Lugs ('Saint' School). This means primarily Nāgārjuna's medical texts and commentaries on the same, although a few works by Sadāprarudita are also mentioned.
5. Mkhas-ldan Mnga' Rig[s] gi Lugs (School of the 'Scholarly Powerful Families' [?], but they are later referred to as Lnga Rig-pa'i Mkhas-pa, 'Scholars of the Five Sciences'). ***See Appendix D.
6. Ha-shong gi Lugs (School of the [Chinese] Hoshangs). Names mentioned here: Ha-shong Ma-ha-yan and Li-ga-zin-ta.
7. Rigs-ldan Bod-kyi Lugs (School of Worthy Tibet[ans]). Names mentioned here: Yid-'ong-legs-pa'i-rgyan, Zhang Gzi-brjid-'bar, Gyong-sman Phan-ne, and 'myself' [meaning Che-rje].

APPENDIX D: SCHOLARS OF THE FIVE SCIENCES

	Source: Che-rje's history of 1204 (1264?).	For comparison, the Regent's history of 1704, p. 176.
	Mkhas-ldan Mnga' Rig[s]-gi Lugs (School of the 'Scholarly Powerful Families' [?], but they are later referred to as Lnga Rig-pa'i Mkhas-pa, 'Scholars of the Five Sciences').	Prefaced only with the information that the list is that of some persons of earlier generations (*snga-rabs-pa kha-cig ltar-na.*).
[1a] [India]	Slob-dpon Dpa'-bo [Ācārya Śūra, here meaning Vāgbhaṭa] composed four texts (titles listed).	

[1b] Kashmir	Brtan-pa'i-blo-gros [Sthiramati] composed *Dri-ma-med-pa'i* [xxx], etc. Kashmiri (Kha-che) System.	The text[s] by Brtan-pa-blo-gros [Sthiramati] entitled *Dri-med Gzi-brjid* and others. Kashmir System (Kha-che'i Lugs).
[2] Orgyan	Dzi-na-mi-tra [Jinamitra] composed *Gso-ba Stong-dgu-bcu-rtsa-gcig*, etc. Orgyan (U-rgyan) System.	The text[s] by Dzi-na-mi-tra [Jinamitra] entitled Gso Stong-dgu-bcu-rtsa-dgu and others. Orgyan System (U-rgyan-gyi lugs).
[3] Magadha	Pra-a-nan-ta composed *Gnas-'gyur Gsum* ['Three Transformations in the Situation/Location'], etc. Magadha (Dbus-'gyur-'chang) System.	The text[s] by Shrī A-nanda [Śrī Ānanda] entitled *Gnas-'gyur Gsum* and others. Magadha System (Yul-dbus-kyi Lugs).
[4] Nepal	Su-ma-ti-kirti [Sumatikīrti] composed *Bsdus Sbyor Gsum* ['Three Abbreviated Preparations'], etc. Newar (Bal-po) System.	The text[s] compiled by Su-ma-ti-kirti [Sumatikīrti] entitled *Bsdus Sbyor Gsum* and others. Newar System (Bal-po'i Lugs).
[5] Tazig	Ur-pa-ya composed *Chos 'byung Drug*, etc. Arabo-Persian (Stag-gzig) System.	The text[s] by Urba-ya entitled *Chos-'byung Drug* and others. Arabo-Persian System (Ta-zig-gi Lugs).
[6] Dolpo	Rdo-rje-'bar-ba composed *Mi-'jigs-pa'i Mtshon-cha Che Chung*, etc. Dolpo (Dol-po) System.	The text[s] by Rdo-rje-'bar-ba entitled *Mi-'jigs Mtshon-cha* and others. Dolpo System (Dol-po'i Lugs).
[7] Uyghur	Legs-pa'i-rgyan composed *Ga-gon-gyi Rdol-thabs Su[m]-bcu-rtsa-lnga* ['Thirty-five Methods for Spontaneous Emergence of Ga-gon'], etc. Uyghur (Hor) System.	The text[s] by Legs-pa-rgyal-mtshan entitled *Ga-gon-gyi Brdol-thabs Sum-cu-rtsa-lnga* and others. Uyghur System (Hor-gyi Lugs).
[8] Tangut	Brtson-'grus-snying-po composed *Sum Khugs*, etc. Tangut/Xixia (Me-nyag) System.	The text[s] by Brtson-'grus-snying-po entitled *Su Khugs* and others. Tangut System (Mi-nyag-gi Lugs).

[9] Khotan	Rgyal-ba'i-rdo-rje [Jinavajra or {Vi}jayavajra??] composed *Yan[-lag] Bdun-pa*, etc. Khotanese (Li) System.	The text[s] by Rgyal-ba-rdo-rje entitled *Yan-lag Bdun-pa* and others. Khotanese System (Li'i Lugs).
[10] Phrom	Btsan-pa-shing-la-ha composed the *Tshad-pa'i 'Gros 'Ded*, etc. Phrom ('Brom, sic!) System.	The text[s] by Tsan-pa-shi-la-ha entitled *Tshad-pa 'Bros 'Ded* and others. Khrom System (Khrom-gyi Lugs).

APPENDIX E

The nine physicians who came to Tibet at the invitation of Emperor Khri-srong-lde-brtsan according to Zur-mkhar-ba's sixteenth-century medical history (pp. 255-6), evidently based on Brang-ti's early fifteenth-century medical history (extant, but not available to me):

From India (Rgya-gar):
1. Shan-ti-garbha [Śāntigarbha].

From Kashmir (Kha-che):
2. Guhya-badzra [Guhyavajra].

From China (Rgya-nag):
3. Stong-gsum-gang-ba.
4. Bha-la Ha-shang.
5. Ha-ti-pra-ta.

From Tazig (Stag-gzig):
6. Sog-po Ha-la-shan-ti.

From 'the Turks' (Dru-gu):
7. Seng-mdo-'od-chen.

From Dolpo (Dol-po):
8. Khyol-ma-ru-rtse.

From Nepal (Bal-po):
9. Dharmā-shi-la [Dharmaśīla].

The comparable passage in the biography of the Elder G.yu-thog-pa composed by Lhun-grub-bkra-shis is translated into English in Rechung Rinpoche Jampal Kunzang, *Tibetan Medicine Illustrated in Original Texts* (Berkeley, 1976), pp. 202-9.

The same text in the original Tibetan (based on the 1982 edition, pp. 100-101) reads as follows:

[1] *rgya gar shantiṃ garbha'i lugs la lus spyi gso ba'i yan lag bdud rtsi'i chu rgyun.*
[2] *rgya nag ni sman pa stong gsum gang ba'i lugs la byis pa gso ba'i yan lag chung dpyad nyi ma'i 'od zer.*
[3] *ma hā de wa'i lugs la mo nad gso ba'i yan lag zla ba'i dkyil 'khor.*
[4] *dharma buddha'i lugs la gdon nad gso ba'i yan lag rdo rje pha lam.*
[5] *bal po'i sman pa da na shī la'i lugs la rgas pa gso ba'i yan lag gnad kyi mdzub tshugs.*
[6] *kha che'i sman pa khun badzra gyi lugs la dug nad gso ba'i yan lag rus sbal gyi 'gyur 'gros.*
[7] *sog po'i sman pa na la shan dir pa'i lugs la rgas pa gso ba'i yan lag bcud kyi rgya mtsho.*
[8] *dol po'i sman pa khyo ma ru rtse'i lugs la ro rtsa gso ba'i yan lag dga' bde 'phel byed.*
[9] *gru gu'i sman pa seng ge 'od can 'phel byed kyi lugs la btsal ba thig gi yan lag ro bkra 'phrul gyi me long.*
[10] *khrom rgyal mu rtse the khrom gyi sras btsan pa shi la hi'i lugs la khrom gyi dbye ba drug pa la sogs pa yin no.*

Chapter 6
Tibetan Musk and Medieval Arab Perfumery[1]

Anya King

INTRODUCTION

Early medieval Tibet was an integral part of the Eurasian trading networks known today as the Silk Road.[2] Tibet imported goods such as fine silks from China,[3] and aromatics and *materia medica* from India, while it exported metalwork such as shields and armour[4] as well as musk. Musk, produced by the musk deer, was surely the most famous product of Tibet, and probably the most widely used in the early medieval world.

---

[1] Much of the material in this article is presented more fully in my unpublished dissertation, 'The Musk Trade and the Near East in the Early Medieval Period' (Indiana University, 2007). All translations quoted are my own unless explicitly noted otherwise. Since this article was written in 2006, a new study on musk by Anna Akasoy and Ronit Yoeli-Tlalim has appeared: 'Along the Musk Routes. Exchanges between Tibet and the Islamic World', *Asian Medicine: Tradition and Modernity*, 3/2 (2007): pp. 217-40.

[2] Christopher I. Beckwith, 'Tibet and the Early Medieval *Florissance* in Eurasia: A Preliminary Note on the Economic History of the Tibetan Empire', *Central Asiatic Journal*, 21 (1977): pp. 89-104.

[3] See Amy Heller, 'Two Inscribed Fabrics and their Historical Context: Some Observations on Esthetics and Silk Trade in Tibet, 7th to 9th Century', in Karel Otavsky (ed.), *Entlang der Seidenstraße: Frühmittelalterliche Kunst zwischen Persien und China in der Abegg-Stiftung* (Riggisberg, 1998), pp. 95-118, which discusses the history of the silk trade and the relationship of silk textiles found in Tibet to Chinese and Iranian textiles.

[4] Fine Tibetan armour (*kashkhūdah*) saved the life of a Khagan of the Turgesh, see al-Ṭabarī, *Ta'rīkh al-rusul wa'l-mulūk*, ed. Michael Jan de Goeje et al. (15 vols, Leiden, 1879-1901; repr. 1964-65), vol. 2, pp. 1521-2 and Christopher I. Beckwith, *The Tibetan Empire in Central Asia: A History of the Struggle for Great Power among Tibetans, Turks, Arabs and Chinese during the Early Middle Ages* (Princeton, 21993), p. 109, n. 4. Arabic sources frequently mention the bucklers (*turs/tirās*) of Tibet, e.g., Ibn Ḥawqal, *Kitāb ṣūrat al-arḍ*, ed. Michael Jan de Goeje and rev. Johannes Hendrik Kramers (Leiden, 1938; repr. 1967), p. 472, and shields, e.g., Ibn al-Faqīh, *Mukhtaṣar Kitāb al-buldān*, ed. Michael Jan de Goeje (Leiden, 1885; repr. 1967), p. 255, and al-Masʿūdī, *Murūj al-dhahab wa-maʿādin al-jawhar*, ed. Charles Barbier de Meynard and Abel Pavet de Courteille, rev. Charles Pellat (7 vols, Beirut, 1966-79), vol. 4, p. 279 (§ 2657).

In tracing Eurasian trade it is often difficult to account for the different sources of goods. Musk, however, if genuine, was exclusively an import into the Near East as the musk deer which produced it lives only in the highlands of the eastern end of Eurasia.[5] The eponymous musk deer, *Moschus moschiferus*, native to Northern China, Mongolia and Siberia is not the musk deer of the Himalayas, which is *Moschus chrysogaster*.[6] Musk was completely unknown in classical antiquity in the Near East and Mediterranean; it first begins to appear there in late antiquity.[7] The incorporation of musk into medicine, along with some other familiar Asian substances like camphor and ambergris, occurred in early Islamic times.

Musk was easily the most important aromatic substance known to the medieval Arabs. Muḥammad ibn Abī Bakr ibn Qayyim al-Jawziyya (d. 751/1350) said of musk in his book *al-Ṭibb al-nabawī*: 'It is the king of the varieties of aromatics, their noblest and sweetest [*aṭyab*]. It is that about which proverbs are coined, and other things are compared to, while it is not compared to anything else. It is the sand-dunes [*kuthbān*] of the Garden.'[8] The importance of musk was such that all of the works on aromatics commenced with a discussion of musk or musk perfumes, usually followed by ambergris and then aloeswood.[9] Among the different varieties of musk known to the medieval Arabs, Tibetan had a special place and usually was considered the best musk.

The musk deer, of several species of *Moschus*, is a small animal standing about 50-60 cm at the shoulder and weighing from 7 to 17 kg.[10] The mature male produces musk in a vesicle just above the genitals. Hunters would remove the

---

5 Scientific literature on the musk deer is dominated by the important works of Michael J.B. Green. See especially his articles 'The Distribution, Status and Conservation of the Himalayan Musk Deer *Moschus chrysogaster*', *Biological Conservation*, 35 (1986): pp. 347-75 and 'Musk Production from Musk Deer', in Robert J. Hudson et al. (eds), *Wildlife Production Systems: Economic Utilisation of Wild Ungulates* (Cambridge, 1989), pp. 401-9.

6 The taxonomy of the musk deer is reviewed in Colin P. Groves, Wang Yingxiang and Peter Grubb, 'Taxonomy of Musk Deer, Genus *Moschus*, Moschidae, Mammalia', *Acta Theriologica Sinica*, 15/3 (1995): pp. 181-97.

7 The introduction of musk into the Near East and Mediterranean lands is discussed in chapter 3 of my dissertation.

8 Muḥammad ibn Abī Bakr ibn Qayyim al-Jawziyya, *Al-Ṭibb al-nabawī* (Cairo, 1978), p. 437.

9 So Ibn Māsawayh, *Kitāb jawāhir al-ṭīb al-mufrada*, ed. Paul Sbath, 'Traité sur les substances simples aromatiques', *Bulletin de l'Institut d'Égypte*, 19 (1936-37): pp. 5-27, Sahlān ibn Kaysān, *Mukhtaṣar fī 'l-ṭīb*, ed. Paul Sbath, 'Abrégé sur les arômes', *Bulletin de l'Institut d'Égypte*, 26 (1943-44): pp. 183-213, al-Nuwayrī, *Nihāyat al-arab fī funūn al-adab* (33 vols, Cairo, 1923-2002), vol. 12, p. 1, and al-Qalqashandī, *Ṣubḥ al-aʿshā* (14 vols, Cairo, 1913-20; repr. Cairo, 1964), vol. 2, p. 119.

10 In addition to the works of Green cited above, descriptions of the musk deer are found in Ronald M. Nowak (ed.), *Walker's Mammals of the World* (2 vols, Baltimore, 1991), vol. 2, pp. 1364-5; Vladimir Georgievich Heptner et al., *Mammals of the Soviet Union*, vol. 1

entire vesicle filled with about fifteen to thirty grammes of musk.[11] The vesicle containing the musk is called a musk pod; musk still in the pod was the most desirable. Musk removed from the pod is waxy and granular, and this loose musk is called grain musk. In modern times musk deer have begun to be farmed by the Chinese and Indians so that the musk can be extracted without killing the animal; musk deer adapt poorly to captivity and the quantity of musk produced is insufficient for the demand.[12] Modern perfumery almost entirely uses synthetic substitutes for musk, but musk is very much in demand for traditional Asian medicine in East Asia.

The present-day range of the different species of musk deer encompasses much of the forested highlands of eastern and eastern inner Asia, from Siberia in the north down into Burma and Vietnam, and from Korea in the east into the Altai Mountains, and in the Himalayas perhaps as far as Afghanistan. Musk deer do not live in desert or steppe conditions, so the inner part of Central Eurasia which is too arid to support forest vegetation is devoid of them. In earlier times the range of the musk deer may have been greater, but, in general, the medieval sources on the distribution of the musk deer reveal a picture similar to the modern understanding of its range.

ARABIC SOURCES ON THE ORIGINS AND TYPES OF MUSK

The medieval Arabs had a fairly detailed concept of the geographical origins of musk. In pre-Islamic times musk was attributed to India, through which it was transported, as well as to the East Arabian port of Dārīn through which it was traded into Arabia.[13] The appellations of musk in Arabic poetry include terms like *faʾrat hindiyyin* 'Indian mouse' for the musk pod.[14] By the mid-ninth century musk was known to have originated from Tibet and China. The Christian physician Ibn Māsawayh (777-857) wrote of the kinds of musk:

(Washington, 1988), pp. 101-24; and Volker Homes, *On the Scent: Conserving the Musk Deer. The Uses of Musk and Europe's Role in its Trade* (Brussels, 1999).

[11] Information on musk deer hunting can be found in my dissertation, pp. 17-18.

[12] On musk deer farming, see Baoliang Zhang, 'Musk Deer, their Capture, Domestication and Care according to Chinese Experience and Methods', *Unasylva*, 35 (1983): pp. 16-24 and Rob Perry-Jones, 'TRAFFIC Examines Musk Deer Farming in China', www.traffic.org/species-reports/traffic_species_mammals34.pdf (accessed 2 August 2008).

[13] E.g. al-Bīrūnī, *Kitāb al-ṣaydana fī 'l-ṭibb*, ed. ʿAbbās Zaryāb (Tehran, 1991), p. 4. Much discussion of the musk of Dārīn and its appearance in poetry is in King, 'The Musk Trade', pp. 133-6.

[14] Cf. ʿAntara quoted by Abū Ḥanīfa al-Dīnawarī, *Kitāb al-Nabāt: The Book of Plants: Part of the Monograph Section*, ed. Bernhard Lewin (Wiesbaden, 1974), p. 192. The musk pod was originally denoted by the Arabic term *faʾra*, 'mouse', which was later replaced by the Persian loanword *nāfija*, see King, 'The Musk Trade', pp. 40-43.

> The best of them is the Sogdian; it is what arrives in Sogdiana from Tibet, and then it is carried to the horizons overland (lit. 'by the back', *ʿalā al-ẓahr*). Next is the Indian; it is what arrives in India from Tibet, and then to al-Daybul.[15] It is then transported by sea; it is inferior to the first type because of its transport by sea. Next is the Chinese; it is inferior to the Indian because of the length of time it is kept at sea. Perhaps, moreover, they differ because of the difference in grazing land originally because these compete for superiority. The best of it is musk which was produced from grazing on the plant called *al-kandasa*;[16] it is found in either Tibet or Kashmir or in both places. Next is that which is produced from grazing on the spikenard (*sunbul*) which is used by the perfumers, and it is found in Tibet. The inferior is that which is produced from grazing on the plant whose root (*aṣl*) is called bitter (*murr*), and the scent of that plant and its root is the scent of musk except that musk is stronger and more redolent than it.[17]

Thus Ibn Māsawayh regarded the best musk as the Tibetan, and he noted that the musks called Sogdian and Indian were really Tibetan musk transported through either of these lands. The Basran writer al-Jāḥiẓ (d. 255/868 or 869) says in his *Kitāb al-ḥayawān* that the musk animal 'is a small animal (*duwaybba*) which lives in the region of Tibet.'[18] Elsewhere al-Jāḥiẓ mentions that the musk animal resembles a small gazelle (*khishf*).[19]

The geographer Ibn Khurradādhbih (205/820 or 211/825–300/911?) gives some important early information on the musk trade in his book *Kitāb al-masālik wa'l-mamālik*. Unfortunately, this book survives only in an abridged version. Ibn Khurradādhbih mentions musk several times, and specifically discusses it as a product of China. But the abridgement of his work contains no discussion of the products of Tibet. However, he does mention in his discussion of Alexander the Great that the king of Tibet gave Alexander a gift of four thousand donkey loads

[15] The major port of Sind in early medieval times.

[16] Discussed in chapter 6 of my dissertation. This plant is also mentioned by al-Yaʿqūbī, quoted by al-Nuwayrī, *Nihāyat al-arab*, vol. 12, p. 7, who also gives the form *k.d.h.m.s* apparently from al-Tamīmī; De Goeje's glossary merely explains the word as a plant which grows in Tibet. *K.n.d.s* or *q.n.d.s* can mean the white hellebore, and this must be why Levey, who gives no explanation for his translation of this rare word, has translated it as hellebore. Another, more usual meaning for Arabic *kundus*, is the soapwort, Greek *στρούθιον*, *Saponaria officinalis* and *Gypsophila struthium*.

[17] Ibn Māsawayh, *Kitāb jawāhir al-ṭīb al-mufrada*, pp. 9-10. Cf. also the translation by Martin Levey, 'Ibn Māsawaih and his Treatise on Simple Aromatic Substances', *Journal of the History of Medicine*, 16 (1961): pp. 395-410, at p. 399.

[18] Abū ʿUthmān ʿAmr ibn Baḥr al-Jāḥiẓ, *Kitāb al-ḥayawān*, ed. ʿAbd al-Salām Muḥammad Hārūn (8 vols, Cairo, 1966), vol. 5, p. 301.

[19] Al-Jāḥiẓ, *Kitāb al-ḥayawān*, vol. 5, p. 304.

of gold and a similar amount of musk.[20] Alexander gave a tenth of the musk to his wife Roxanne, who was the daughter of Darius, king of Persia, and distributed the rest among his companions, while he placed the gold into his treasury. This story, while ahistorical, shows the popular association of musk with Tibet in the time of Ibn Khurradādhbih. Four thousand donkey loads of musk is an incredible quantity, as befits the Alexander legends, and it is doubtful that even in a time when the musk deer was not so endangered such a large quantity of musk could have been accumulated.

Additional important information on the land which produced musk appeared in the early tenth century. This information stems from the circle of Abū Zayd al-Sīrāfī (active during the first half of the tenth century), who collected information on the eastern trade from his hometown, the trade emporium Sīrāf on the Iranian coast of the Persian Gulf. Sīrāfī included a discussion of musk in his supplementary chapter to the anonymous text known as the *Akhbār al-Ṣīn wa'l-Hind* of 851.[21] Sīrāfī's account of musk is paralleled by the account of musk in the *Murūj al-dhahab* of his acquaintance al-Masʿūdī.[22] Masʿūdī's version is not quoted directly from al-Sīrāfī's text; rather it seems to have been created from either the source used by al-Sīrāfī or from information gathered by him in discussion with al-Sīrāfī; the latter is more probable. This general account was very influential and often quoted by later writers who dealt with musk. Al-Sīrāfī says of the land from which musk comes: 'The land which has the Chinese musk gazelles and Tibet is one land with no distinction between them. The people of China carry off the gazelles which are close to them and the people of Tibet those which are close to them.'[23]

During the middle of the tenth century awareness of a new place which produced musk is attested in Arabic literature. The first attestation of this is in Muḥammad ibn Aḥmad ibn Saʿīd al-Tamīmī's (d. 370/980) book *Jayb al-ʿarūs wa-rayḥān al-nufūs*.[24] This work is apparently lost, but it is quoted extensively by al-Nuwayrī in his encyclopaedia *Nihāyat al-arab*. Al-Tamīmī writes:

> Musk has many types and differing kinds. The best and most excellent of them is the Tibetan which is brought from the place called *dhū s.mt*; between it and Tibet is a journey of two months, then it is brought to Tibet and then it is

[20] Ibn Khurradādhbih, *Kitāb al-masālik wa'l-mamālik*, ed. Michael Jan de Goeje (Leiden, 1889; repr. 1967), p. 263. See Akasoy in this volume.

[21] Ed. ʿAbdallāh al-Ḥabashī, *Riḥlat al-Sīrāfī* (Abu Dhabi, 1999), pp. 75-7. Cf. also Jean Sauvaget, *Akhbār aṣ-Ṣīn wa l-Hind: Relation de la Chine et de l'Inde* (Paris, 1948).

[22] Al-Masʿūdī, *Murūj al-dhahab*, vol. 1, pp. 188-9.

[23] *Riḥlat al-Sīrāfī*, p. 75.

[24] On al-Tamīmī's work, see Manfred Ullmann, *Die Medizin im Islam* (Leiden, 1970), p. 315.

transported to Khurāsān. He said: The origin of musk is in a four-footed animal (*bahīma*) whose form resembles a small gazelle.[25]

The place name *Dhū sm.t* is a transcription of the old Tibetan *mdosmad*, referring to northeast Tibet (modern Amdo), which is given in the *Ḥudūd al-ʿālam* as *Tūsm.t.*[26] The work of the Egyptian Christian physician Sahlān ibn Kaysān (d. 380/990) includes a discussion of the varieties of musk, and he includes the *Ṭūm.s.tī*,[27] which is another independent attempt at reproducing *mdosmad* in Arabic, adding an adjective ending (*ī*). Ibn Kaysān ranks it below the Tibetan in quality, but his work is also unusual in that he advocated Chinese musk as the best.

It is common in the Arabic literature to give lists of the different products of the world arranged according to their respective excellences. Musk is no exception, and several lists of the different types of musk are available. Musk was classified according to its origin, as well as whether it was still in the pod or was loose, in the form of grain musk. Apart from Ibn Māsawayh's account, which favoured Tibetan musk under the names of the peoples who traded it, the Sogdians and the Indians, there are two other notices of musk which discuss the different varieties from the ninth century. One of these is contained in the merchant's handbook called the *Kitāb al-tabaṣṣur bi'l-tijāra* which is traditionally attributed to the polymath al-Jāḥiẓ, although this is by no means certain.[28] In any case, it seems to be a work of the ninth century and there is nothing in it to indicate a later date. This book was written to assist the merchant or would-be merchant to distinguish between different trade goods, and appraise their qualities. The author writes: 'The best musk is the dry, light coloured (*al-fātiḥ*) Tibetan; the inferior (*ardāhu*) is *al-buddī*.'[29] The *buddī* musk refers to musk which the Arabs believed was plastered upon Buddhist statues in India and subsequently removed and sold after its scent had deteriorated.[30]

---

25 Al-Nuwayrī, *Nihāyat al-arab*, vol. 12, p. 2.

26 *Ḥudūd al-ʿālam*, ed. Manuchihr Sutudah (Tehran, 1983), 11:9 on p. 75; Vladimir Minorsky, *The Regions of the World: A Persian Geography 372 A.H. -982 A.D.* (London, ²1970), pp. lxxii and 257; Luciano Petech, 'Nota su *Mābd* e *Twsmt*', *Rivista degli Studi Orientali*, 25 (1950): pp. 142-4; repr. in his *Selected Papers on Asian History* (Rome, 1988), pp. 45-7; Christopher I. Beckwith, 'The Location and Population of Tibet according to Early Islamic Sources', *Acta Orientalia Academiae Scientiarum Hungaricae*, 43 (1989): pp. 168-9.

27 Sahlān ibn Kaysān, *Mukhtaṣar fī 'l-ṭīb*, p. 188. I have prepared a translation and study of this important source.

28 Its translator Charles Pellat doubts it: 'Ǧāhiẓiana, I. Le Kitāb al-Tabaṣṣur bi-l-Tiǧāra attribué à Ǧāḥiẓ', *Arabica*, 1 (1954): pp. 153-65, at p. 153.

29 Al-Jāḥiẓ [attr.], *Kitāb al-tabaṣṣur bi'l-tijāra fī waṣf mā yustaẓraf fī 'l-buldān min al-amtiʿa al-rafīʿa wa'l-aʿlāq al-nafīsa wa'l-jawāhir al-thamīna*, ed. Ḥasan Ḥusnī ʿAbd al-Wahhāb al-Tūnisī (Cairo, 1994), p. 17.

30 Cf. King, 'The Musk Trade', pp. 250-51, 265-6, for further references.

The other early source on the different varieties of musk is the geographer and historian Aḥmad ibn Abī Yaʿqūb ibn Jaʿfar al-Yaʿqūbī (d. 284/897). One of his works which is lost discussed aromatics and is known from quotations by the tenth-century writer Muḥammad ibn Aḥmad ibn Saʿīd al-Tamīmī, whose work was used by both al-Nuwayrī and al-Qalqashandī in their encyclopaedias. While aware of other varieties of musk, al-Yaʿqūbī regarded Tibetan musk as the most important, as evinced by his discussion of the origins of musk:

> Aḥmad ibn Abī Yaʿqūb, *mawlā* of the Banī al-ʿAbbās, said: A group of those well versed in the source of musk mentioned to me that its sources in the land of Tibet and other places are well known. The traders set up there structures resembling a minaret (*manār*) the length of the arm bone. When this animal from whose navel musk originates comes, it rubs its navel on that minaret and the navel falls there. The traders come to it in a time of the year which they know, and they gather what they are permitted to. When they bring it into Tibet [proper], one tenth of its value is taken from them.[31]

This account is interesting because it implies that the land where the musk deer live is not in central Tibet, but rather on the periphery, which is correct, since musk deer do not live in the arid interior of the Tibetan plateau but rather in the mountainous areas to the south and east. Al-Yaʿqūbī further regards Tibet as a trading centre for musk, where musk was collected for trade, presumably from those who hunted for the animals.

Al-Yaʿqūbī's list of the varieties of musk forms the basis of the lists of types in the chapters on musk in al-Nuwayrī's and al-Qalqashandī's encyclopaedias.[32] The two versions give an identical ranking of the varieties of musk except for the last, which al-Nuwayrī has transposed with the next to last.[33] The list runs thus, in descending order of excellence: 1. Tibetan, 2. Sogdian, 3. Chinese, 4. Indian, 5. Qinbār, 6. Tughuzghuzī, 7. Qasārī, 8. Khirkhīzī, 9. ʿIṣmārī, 10. Jabalī.

The account of musk of Abū Zayd al-Sīrāfī, which is paralleled by al-Masʿūdī, contains the most detailed reasoning for the excellence of Tibetan musk. Al-Sīrāfī had noted that the land which produced the musk deer was a single land located between China and Tibet, from which they both acquired their musk. The reasoning for the excellence of the musk of Tibet, which he takes for granted, is, then, not to be sought in a difference of the land which produced it. He says:

> Rather, the superiority of Tibetan musk over Chinese musk is for two reasons. The first is that the musk gazelle which is in the territory of Tibet has grazing lands of fragrant spikenard (*sunbul*) while those which lie near the land of China have grazing land of other herbs. The second reason is that the people

31 Al-Nuwayrī, *Nihāyat al-arab*, vol. 12, p. 4.

32 Al-Qalqashandī, *Ṣubḥ al-aʿshā*, vol. 2, pp. 210-11.

33 See King, 'The Musk Trade', p. 243.

> of Tibet leave the pod in its original condition while the people of China adulterate the pods which come to them; their routes are also over the ocean and moisture[34] clings to them. If the people of China left the musk in the pods and placed them into pots (*barānī*, i.e. pots with lids) and secured them, it would arrive in the land of the Arabs like the Tibetan in its goodness. The best musk of all is that which the gazelle scrapes on the rocks of the mountains; it is a substance which forms in its navel as fresh blood collects in the manner in which blood collects when it appears from boils. When it ripens, he rubs it and it torments him so he flees to the stones until he tears a hole in it, and what is inside it flows out. When it comes out from him, he dries and heals over and the substance returns and collects in him as before.
>
> There are men in Tibet who go out in search of this. They have a knowledge of it and when they find it, they pick it up and collect it and put it inside the pods and carry it to their kings. This is the best musk when it has ripened in its pod upon its animal. Its excellence over other musk is like the excellence of fruit which has ripened on its tree over the other which has been torn from it before its ripening. Other than this is musk which is hunted with set-up nets and arrows. The pod might be cut off from the gazelle before the musk has matured inside it. Although when it is cut from its gazelle it has a bad odour for a time until it has dried over long days, as it dries it changes until it becomes musk.[35]

There are thus three different aspects to the excellence of Tibetan musk according to al-Sīrāfī: the fodder of the animal, the condition in which the musk was procured and the condition in which it was transported. The production of musk by the musk deer was, in the opinion of al-Sīrāfī and most other writers, due to the consumption of fragrant herbs by the animal. This belief is seen as early as Ibn Māsawayh, who was quoted earlier, but in later times it became almost universally believed that the musk deer grazed on spikenard. The various plants which are known by the Arabic name *sunbul* have a distinctly musky quality which was then supposedly transferred to the musk, and this is the reason for this belief.[36] However, not everyone believed in this; for example, Sahlān ibn Kaysān dismissed it 'because there are gazelles which graze on wheat, barley, and grasses, and musk comes from them'.[37]

The second reason for the excellence of the Tibetan musk was that the Tibetans supposedly allowed the musk to mature naturally, which al-Sīrāfī likened to the superiority of tree-ripened fruit to that which was picked prematurely. All of the

---

34 The text has *al-ʾīdhāʾ*, but the parallel in Masʿūdī has *al-andāʾ*. Ferrand has also translated this 'celui-ci s'imprègne d'humidité', see Gabriel Ferrand, *Voyage du marchand arabe Sulayman en Inde et en Chine rédigé en 851* (Paris, 1922), p. 110.

35 *Riḥlat al-Sīrāfī*, pp. 75-7.

36 See King, 'The Musk Trade', pp. 247-8.

37 Sahlān ibn Kaysān, *Mukhtaṣar fī 'l-ṭīb*, p. 190.

writers examined who discuss the transformation of blood into musk emphasize that this process takes a long time. Al-Tamīmī claims that musk, having been separated from the animal, was hung in a privy for forty days.[38] The mention of the privy must be an attempt to account for the slightly urinous element in the scent of the musk. The English chemist Robert Boyle noted that the air of the privy could restore the scent of musk.[39] The forty-day period reflects the common notion of forty days as a period of waiting and preparation.[40] For Sahlān ibn Kaysān the period is defined as a year (*ḥawl*).[41]

Thirdly, the adulteration and mishandling of musk could detract from its quality. It was believed that musk was best stored in its own vesicle, and this can be seen in al-Sīrāfī's statement that loose musk was stuffed into pods. Al-Masʿūdī's version explicitly states that the Chinese removed the musk from the pods and adulterated it; while al-Sīrāfī only states that the Chinese adulterated it, presumably within the pod. Finally, the conditions of the transportation of musk could affect it. The dry overland journey from Tibet through Khorasan was considered more salubrious for musk, which was considered hot and dry, than the moisture which it encountered on the sea voyage from China. This same reasoning for the excellence of Tibetan musk is given by al-Masʿūdī,[42] who is quoted by later writers such as the pharmacologist Ibn al-Bayṭār (d. 646/1248) in his influential *Jāmiʿ li'l-mufradāt*.[43]

Sahlān ibn Kaysān's account of musk is contained in his short work *Mukhtaṣar fī 'l-ṭīb*, in which he gives information on musk, ambergris, aloeswood and camphor, as well as formulas for compound perfumes. As mentioned, Ibn Kaysān's account is unusual in that he preferred Chinese musk to the Tibetan. His reasoning for this was that the Chinese musk pods were larger, with finer skin and thus a higher proportion of musk in the weight of the pod overall. He also says that it is stronger, with a third of a *mithqāl* of it being equal to two *mithqāl*s of Tibetan musk in compounding. He also describes the colour as more yellow than the Tibetan, which contained grains which were yellow and black, although he also noted that there was no difference between the colours in quality. Evidently the musk available to Sahlān ibn Kaysān, who lived in Egypt and apparently prepared perfumes for the Fatimids, led him to these conclusions. In the nineteenth century Chinese 'Tonkin' musk was often preferred to the Tibetan as well, and it was thought to be less adulterated.

---

38 Al-Nuwayrī, *Nihāyat al-arab*, vol. 12, p. 3.

39 Robert Boyle, 'The Usefulness of Natural Philosophy II. Sect. 2', in *The Works of Robert Boyle*, vol. 6, ed. Michael Hunter and Edward B. Davis (London, 1999), pp. 523-4.

40 Annemarie Schimmel, *The Mystery of Numbers* (Oxford, 1993), pp. 247-8.

41 Sahlān ibn Kaysān, *Mukhtaṣar fī 'l-ṭīb*, p. 190.

42 Masʿūdī, *Murūj al-dhahab*, vol. 1, pp. 188-9.

43 Ibn al-Bayṭār, *Al-Jāmiʿ li-mufradāt al-adwiya wa'l-aghdhiya* (4 vols, Būlāq, n.d.), vol. 4, pp. 155-6.

Be that as it may, in the conclusion of the *Laṭāʾif al-maʿārif* of al-Thaʿālibī, which catalogues the most precious things at the beginning of the eleventh century, the finest aromatics are given as 'the musk of Tibet, the aloeswood of India, the ambergris of al-Shiḥr, the camphor of Fanṣūr, the citron of Tabaristan, the orange of Basra, the narcissus of Jurjān, the lotus of Shīrwān, the rose of Jūr', etc.[44]

It was thus well understood in the early medieval Near East that musk originated from the lands of Eastern Asia, and also that the Tibetan was usually considered the best variety.

MUSK IN PERFUMERY

Musk was used, first and foremost, for its scent. Genuine musk has an almost overpowering animal scent far removed from the compounds today described as 'musk' which are synthetic. During the twentieth century, with the introduction of synthetic musks and the increasing cost of natural musk, the substance gradually disappeared from European perfumery. The effects of musk on a perfume are difficult to quantify, but a tiny bit of musk has a strange capacity for enhancing a perfume, giving it a special lift. In slightly larger quantities the animal note was more obvious, and some perfumes called for this. It was used in many European perfumes, and only in certain perfumes would the amount of musk have been specifically detectable. In fact, the scent of musk was regarded with suspicion. The nineteenth-century perfumer Piesse wrote: 'It is a fashion of the present day for people to say that they "do not like musk" ... Those substances containing it always take the preference in ready sale - so long as the vendor takes care to assure his customer "that there is no musk in it".'[45]

Quite different from the perfumes of the nineteenth (and twentieth) century with their limited use of musk as an enhancer were the perfumes used by the medieval Near Easterners. These contained very large percentages of musk and would be extremely strong and probably unbearable to the modern nose.

Musk was sometimes used by itself; Arabic poetry speaks of crumbs (*fatīt*): that is, grains of musk in the bedding of the beloved.[46] Most perfumes using musk were, however, compounded.[47] These were of different categories: unguents, liquids, incense and scented powders. The most important unguent was *ghāliya*, which was classically prepared from musk and ambergris in ben oil to make a buttery paste. The liquids included scented waters (*naḍūḥāt*), which were what we would call colognes, and oils (*adhān*). None of the early preserved formulas

---

[44] Al-Thaʿālibī, *Laṭāʾif al-maʿārif* (Cairo, n.d.), pp. 238-9.

[45] George Piesse, *Piesse's Art of Perfumery* (London, ^{3}1891), pp. 266-7.

[46] Imruʾ al-Qays, *Muʿallaqa*, l. 37 in al-Tibrīzī, *Kitāb sharḥ al-qaṣāʾid al-ʿashr*, ed. Charles Lyall (Calcutta, 1894), p. 17.

[47] Compound perfumes are discussed in the first chapter of my dissertation, and in my forthcoming work on the *Mukhtaṣar fī ʾl-ṭīb* of Sahlān ibn Kaysān.

is for alcohol-based perfumes such as most modern perfumes are, and even the early fourteenth-century encyclopaedia of al-Nuwayrī makes no mention of the use of alcohol in perfumery in its extensive discussion of perfume making. Incense was made to be placed on hot coals and smouldered; self-combusting incense was well known in China by this time but its manufacture had not yet travelled west. The most famous of the compound incenses was *nadd*; many different forms of *nadd* existed but most included musk as a basic ingredient. Scented powders were used for sprinkling on clothing; there were also balls of aromatic material for rubbing.

Compound perfumes were prepared from pure aromatic ingredients or with a base of inexpensive ingredients. The former were the more expensive and highly regarded perfumes, while the latter were often prepared to defraud customers. But they were probably used by many people who could not afford the pure perfumes. The *Kitāb kīmiyā' al-ʿiṭr wa'l-taṣʿīdāt* of pseudo-al-Kindī says at the conclusion of one of its *ghāliya* formulas made with a base of ground pistachios:

> It is enhanced according to three types: a type with musk, ambergris, and ben oil with, for every two parts of the foundation, a part of musk and ambergris. The patrician of the country (*baṭāriqat al-balad*), treasurer, judge and his associates, and the postmasters are perfumed (*ghullifa*) with it. The second level of it has three parts of base and a part of musk, a part of good *sukk*, and half a part of ambergris, and it is prepared with ben oil. The officers and those similar to them are perfumed with it. The third level has five parts of the base and a part of musk, two parts of *sukk*, two parts of crushed aloeswood, and a fourth of a part of ambergris and it is prepared with ben oil like the first. The soldiers, merchants, and other men are perfumed with it.[48]

This clearly shows the importance of musk; the more musk and other high quality aromatics a perfume contained, the more expensive and high class it was. Any perfume could be enhanced; musk was the usual ingredient for this process, which was often denoted by the Arabic verb *fataqa*, which means to 'break open', and is also used for putting leaven into dough.[49]

Most of the surviving formulas are for the better types and include high proportions of musk, ambergris, aloeswood and other expensive ingredients. One of the earliest indications of the composition of a fine *ghāliya* comes from the *Tārikh al-rusul wa'l-mulūk* of al-Ṭabarī in an anecdote dating to the time of the caliph Hārūn al-Rashīd (reg. 786-809). In the context of the anecdote, these ingredients were supposed to represent the most excellent *ghāliya*:

---

[48] Al-Kindī [attr.], *Kitāb Kīmiyā' al-ʿIṭr wa-t-Taṣʿīdāt: Buch über die Chemie des Parfüms und die Destillationen*, ed. and trans. Karl Garbers (Leipzig, 1948), #47.

[49] See the discussion in King, 'The Musk Trade', pp. 58-9.

> As for its musk, it is from the navels of the well-aged (*ʿatīqa*) Tibetan animals (*kilāb*),[50] and as for its ambergris, it is from the ambergris of the Gulf of Aden, and as for its ben oil, it is from a certain al-Madanī, well known for the goodness of his work, and as for its compounding, it is by a man in Basra knowledgeable in its composition and skilled in compounding it.[51]

In his chapter on *ghāliya* and *nadd* al-Nuwayrī quoted many formulas from the lost book of al-Tamīmī, *Jayb al-ʿarūs*, but al-Nuwayrī limits his selection to 'those made for caliphs, kings, and important people (*akābir*)'.[52] The very first *ghāliya* formula he gives from al-Tamīmī's book was quoted by him after al-Yaʿqūbī. It would presumably yield a *ghāliya* like that presented to Hārūn al-Rashīd if mixed with a little ben oil for use:

> A type of *ghāliya* for the caliphs according to Aḥmad ibn Abī Yaʿqūb: a hundred *mithqāls* of excellent (*nādir*) Tibetan musk are taken and pounded after being cleansed from its membranes and hair. It is sieved after pounding through thick-weaved Chinese silk, and then the pounding and sieving are resumed, and this is repeated until it becomes like dust. Then a Meccan bowl (*tawr makkī*) or a Chinese butter-dish (*zibdiyya ṣīnī* [*sic*]) is taken, and what is available of good, rare ben oil in a sufficient quantity is added. Fifty *mithqāls* of fatty, blue Shiḥrī ambergris is cut up in it, and the dish with the ben oil and ambergris in it is set on a gentle coal fire without smoke or smell because they would spoil it. It is stirred with a gold or silver spoon until the ambergris melts. Then it is removed from the fire, and when it becomes tepid, musk is cast into it, and it is beaten well with the hand until it has become a single part. Then that is put up in a gold or silver vessel, but the head must be tightly covered so one may seal it, or it can be placed in a clean, glass pot (*barniyya*) with its head plugged with a stopper that is Chinese silk filled with cotton, so that its scent will not arise from it. He said, this is the best *ghāliya* of all.[53]

This recipe calls for the most expensive and desirable varieties of musk and ambergris, the Tibetan and Shiḥrī. Shiḥr referred to the coast of the Indian Ocean in Yemen, and this ambergris was considered the best by many writers, although Indian, South Asian, and African varieties of ambergris were also regarded as excellent. The ingredients for this most excellent *ghāliya* were properly sieved only with silk, a detail found in many other formulas by other writers, and

50 Lit. 'dogs'. The term probably does not literally mean that musk was believed to originate from dogs, but rather some smallish mammal. The beaver is often called *kalb al-māʾ* 'dog of the water'. This anecdote, if authentic, is earlier than writers who had a better idea of the origins of musk, as discussed in chapter 6 of my dissertation.

51 Al-Ṭabarī, *Taʾrīkh al-rusul waʾl-mulūk*, vol. 33, pp. 744-5.

52 Al-Nuwayrī, *Nihāyat al-arab*, vol. 12, p. 53.

53 Al-Nuwayrī, *Nihāyat al-arab*, vol. 12, pp. 53-4.

prepared in expensive vessels such as imported porcelain and gold and silver. The entire preparation of this perfume was thus a very expensive process, as befitted a perfume for the caliphs. This particular formula produced *ghāliya* which was said to have greatly amazed the caliph al-Maʾmūn (reg. 813-33).

Perhaps the earliest collection of perfume formulas, disregarding the *Kitāb kīmiyāʾ al-ʿiṭr waʾl-taṣʿīdāt* of pseudo-al-Kindī, which is difficult to date, is contained in the medical encyclopaedia called *Firdaws al-ḥikma* of ʿAlī ibn Sahl Rabban al-Ṭabarī, written in 850. This book gives formulas for scented powders, *ghāliya*, oils and other aromatic preparations.[54] His four different *ghāliya* formulas range from very high quality with pure ingredients, to one made from *sukk* with a small bit of musk added. *Sukk* was an aromatic preparation made mostly from *rāmik*, which was prepared from oak galls. It was black in colour and often used to extend musky perfumes.[55]

The scented powder (*dharīra*) formulas given by al-Ṭabarī also include musk in smaller quantities than the *ghāliyas*; in these powders the musk was used as an enhancer rather than the dominant note of the compound. Typically he does not specify the quantity of musk and ambergris to be added, but calls for what one has available. Here is an example for a scented powder based on sandalwood:

> Take two parts Indian aloeswood and two parts sandalwood; they are pulverized and sieved through silk. They are kneaded with rosewater and drops of cologne (*naḍūḥ*) are dripped upon it, and it is crushed also until it has become mixed. It is censed with fragrant incense and crushed also upon the perfumer's stone until it has dried, and them what is available of musk and ambergris is added to it.[56]

Al-Ṭabarī gives several oil formulas, most of which are based on floral and woody scents. These do not include musk; but one oil, specified as being useful for kings, did. It was based on wallflower and other floral scents.[57] When mixed, musk was added 'in a quantity such that its scent would become apparent'.[58]

---

54 Al-Ṭabarī, *Firdausu'l-Ḥikmat, or, Paradise of Wisdom*, ed. Muhammad Z. Siddiqi (Berlin, 1928). These formulas appear in the last section of the book, which is largely devoted to an exposition of Indian medicine. Towards the end (p. 611), he remarks: 'These chapters are light in medicine, but will be an increase in the usefulness of the book and its excellence in the science of medicine. For perfume [*ṭīb*] and medicine [*ṭibb*] are analogous, and the *lakhlakhahs*, waters, rose water, *maysūses* are attributed to the drugs [*al-adwiyya*], and they are also perfumes' and then gives these formulas. They are manifestly not Indian formulas.

55 *Sukk* is discussed in King, 'The Musk Trade', pp. 60-61.

56 Al-Ṭabarī, *Firdaus*, p. 611.

57 Al-Ṭabarī, *Firdaus*, p. 616. The wallflower (*khīrī*) has a strong scent of cloves with floral elements.

58 Al-Ṭabarī, *Firdaus*, p. 616.

Al-Ṭabarī's formulas do not specify what type of musk was to be used, nor does he apparently discuss the different kinds of musk available to him elsewhere in his book. In the formularies of the tenth century, of al-Tamīmī and Sahlān ibn Kaysān, a specific type of musk is sometimes mentioned, and if it is mentioned, it is always Tibetan. Sahlān ibn Kaysān, who preferred Chinese musk to Tibetan in his description of the varieties of musk, still called for Tibetan musk in his recipes when he bothered to specify a type. This indicates that Tibetan musk was standard, even if other varieties were sometimes preferred.

Sahlān's first *nadd* formula includes much information for the preparation of the ingredients for making perfumes. It starts with discussion of the preparation of musk, specified as Tibetan, by removing impurities, pounding, and sieving it:

> Ten *mithqāls* of Tibetan musk are taken and pounded into a fine powder, and then sieved through close textured silk. One must prevent burning (*iḥtirāq*) of the musk during the pounding: the sign of its burning is that when the one making it passes the pestle over the musk with force and heaviness, on lifting the pestle there are traces like polish (*ṣaql*) evident upon it; that is the sign of its burning when the musk is dry. When it is moist and these traces appear on it, they are not from its burning. If there are membranes (*akrāsh*) and remains (*luqaṭ*), they are removed before pounding, and what appears during the pounding should be removed. When one reaches the end of the pounding and it does not get through the bottom of the sieve, there are remains of membranes in it, and hair remains in it which got into it from the pod. The one making it must not leave any hair or remains in it because they spoil all of it and it will stink when it is used. If there are many remains (*luqaṭ*) and he cannot remove them, then he breaks the grains (*shiyāf*) and moistens all of the musk on the perfumer's stone and leaves it for an hour. Then he sieves it with a small sieve which is not thickly woven, and what is in it of membranes (*akrāsh*) rise to the top.[59]

Following this procedure, the musk was ready to use in the formula. This first *nadd* formula is made exclusively from musk and ambergris in a one to one ratio; the mixture was formed into wicks (*fatā'il*) and dried.

These uses of musk are all a result of its scent and its powers in perfumery. But musk was extensively used in medicine as well. Diet and environment were considered critical factors in health, and aromatics like musk fit into this system in several ways. They were valued both for their intrinsic powers when compounded in a medicine. More importantly, aromatics could help adjust the air to equalize the balance of elements present in it.[60] Musk had a purifying effect and kept food from spoiling[61] and was also thought to drive away illness.

---

59 Sahlān ibn Kaysān, *Mukhtaṣar fī 'l-ṭīb*, p. 198.

60 Cf. Ibn Sīnā, *Al-Qānūn fī 'l-ṭibb* (3 vols, Būlāq, 1877), vol. 1, p. 182.

61 Ibn Sīnā, *Al-Qānūn*, vol. 1, p. 360.

In the medieval world the boundaries between modern fields like medicine and hygiene did not exist; the physician was required to take an interest in the whole life of his patients, and thus all of the uses of musk as a perfume fell under the subjects with which a physician would be acquainted, even if he did not prepare perfumes himself. That job was often left to professional perfumers, who are attested from early times, although physicians are responsible for some of our most important works on aromatics and how to prepare aromatic compounds.

The properties of musk in medieval perfumery were based on the understanding of how musk fitted into humoral theory. Musk was invariably considered hot and dry, although the exact degrees varied depending on the authority. Among aromatic substances it was often considered the opposite of the cold and dry camphor. Thus musk was a heating substance, suitable for drawing out moisture and balancing out cold temperaments. These perfumes were valued for their effect of stimulation. Al-Ṭabarī writes of a sandalwood powder enhanced with musk: 'Use it in your sleep; ʿAbd al-Malik ibn Marwān used it at the time of sex. It is among the most beneficial of the *dharīras* for stimulation.'[62] This belief was manifested in the use of camphor to balance out musk in perfumes used by people with hot temperaments and in hot weather. Muḥammad al-Washshāʾ noted that elegant people 'only use camphor in times of real heat because of its coldness, or for a serious ailment'.[63] Camphor was not as highly regarded as musk; Sahlān ibn Kaysān commented that the common people thought camphor as necessary to a perfume as salt was to a pot, but that the elegant people did not follow this belief.[64] For the elegant man, a musk-based perfume was basic.

To what extent was the use of musk in Near Eastern perfumery influenced by its use in the lands further to the east? In the area of perfumes, the use of musk in Arabic perfume formulas is quite unlike its use in Indian formulas. Musk appears to have come into use in India during the Gupta period (320-*c*.510); at least, this is when it is first attested in the poetry of Kālidāsa.[65] The earliest aromatic formulas which include musk are contained in the *Bṛhatsaṃhitā* of Varāhamihira, dating to the early sixth century.[66] Varāhamihira's incense pastes are based on plant ingredients, especially gum guggulu, a resin from a species of myrrh found in India. The ideal Arabic incense paste for *nadd* was made with ambergris, musk, and sometimes aloeswood and other aromatics. Ambergris had a negligible role

---

62 Al-Ṭabarī, *Firdaus*, p. 612.

63 Muḥammad ibn Aḥmad al-Washshāʾ, *Kitāb al-muwashshā*, ed. Rudolph E. Brünnow (Leiden, 1886), p. 183.

64 Sahlān ibn Kaysān, *Mukhtaṣar fī 'l-ṭīb*, p. 201.

65 E.g. Kālidāsa, *Meghadūta*, ed. Moreshvar Ramchandra Kale (Delhi, 1991), verse 55. See chapter 2 of my dissertation for information on the history of musk in India.

66 Varāhamihira, *Bṛhatsaṃhitā*, ed. and trans. M. Ramakrishna Bhat (2 vols, Delhi, 1981-82), vol. 2, pp. 704-18.

in early medieval Indian perfumery, and the spread of its use in India has been linked to relations with the Arabs.[67] Musk was used in small quantities in Indian perfumery, and its role there was to enhance the compound in a way similar to the use of musk as an enhancer in nineteenth-century European perfumery. One of Varāhamihira's incense compounds was made from sixteen different substances, all derived from plants except for onycha. Before the mixing, each of the ingredients was separately censed with musk and camphor to enhance it; this is called *bodha* in Sanskrit, which literally means 'awakening' or 'arousing'. In this work and in other Sanskrit works on perfumery the role of musk is more limited than its role in the strongly musk-based Near Eastern perfumery. Indian perfumery of the early medieval period used musk for enhancing a perfume, for its final 'finish', but not as an integral part. Indian perfumery made the same distinction between the heating of musk and the cooling of camphor as Arabic perfumery.

This more limited role of musk is true also in a Tibetan incense formula originally from the Sanskrit published by Berthold Laufer in 1896.[68] In this formula, half an ounce of musk figures in its 52 ounces of ingredients (half of which was gum guggulu), a little less than one per cent! Yet that quantity would have been sufficient to enhance the incense in a perceptible way. In any case, it was an incense nothing like the *nadd* of the Near East which could contain as much as half of their substance or more of musk.

It is therefore unlikely that the canons of Near Eastern perfume manufacture were influenced by Indian traditions of perfumery, and so the *nadd* and *ghāliya* of the Arabs were genuinely Near Eastern inventions.

In conclusion, musk was the most important aromatic substance used in the early medieval Near East. Arabic literature contains much data on the different varieties of musk, giving information on the lands which exported it. There was also a fair understanding of the nature of the animal which produced it, even if this knowledge was surrounded with fanciful elements. Once musk came to be imported into the Near East it was adopted for use in perfumery in ways which were completely new. Arabic perfumery used musk in high percentages in compounds unlike those prepared in India, or China, for that matter. The almost ubiquitous use of musk in Arabic perfume formulas of all types testifies to its importance as an enhancer in compounds which were not primarily musk based; the use of musk as an enhancer is widely attested in Asia. The only type of musk which is specifically mentioned in the perfume formulas is Tibetan musk, and we can assume that it was the standard type of musk used in Arabic perfumery. Most of the perfumes used in the daily life of those outside of the aristocracy

---

[67] Parshuram Krishna Gode, 'History of Ambergris in India between about A.D. 700 and 1900', in id., *Studies in Indian Cultural History*, vol. 1 (Hoshiarpur, 1961), p. 9.

[68] Berthold Laufer, 'Indisches Recept zur Herstellung von Räucherwerk', *Verhandlungen der Berliner Gesellschaft für Anthropologie, Ethnologie und Urgeschichte*, 18 July 1896, pp. 394-8.

cannot have contained musk in these vast quantities because of the cost, but small amounts of musk made it into their perfumes. Those perfumes which were more affordable were designed to mimic the musk perfumes as closely as possible, but given the ingredients easily available, these imitations can only have fallen short of the real thing.

Chapter 7
The Sarvāstivādin Buddhist Scholastic Method in Medieval Islam and Tibet[1]

Christopher I. Beckwith

INTRODUCTION

The medieval scholastic method, which is known to the modern academic world almost exclusively in its Western European form,[2] is widely believed to have a three or four-part structure consisting of 'arguments, [and] counter-arguments, the main thesis, and criticism of the arguments for the challenged opinion'.[3] The consensus among Europeanists is that the full scholastic method is an organic, logical, spontaneous growth out of the European tradition – in particular, the works of Peter Abelard[4] and Anselm of Canterbury.[5] This view has been

---

1 This article is an abbreviated and revised version of part of a lecture ('Central Asian Buddhist Sources of Early Scholasticism in Medieval Tibet, Islam, and Western Europe') in the Numata Distinguished Guest Speaker Series given at the Oriental Institute of Oxford University, Faculty of Oriental Studies, in association with the Oxford Centre for Buddhist Studies, on 12 June 2008. I am grateful to the sponsors, and would like to thank my host, Robert Mayer, for his amiable hospitality. I am also grateful to Collett Cox for very kindly sending me a prepublication copy of her joint translation, with Hiromichi Takeda, of part of the *Abhidharmamahāvibhāṣaśāstra*. See Hiromichi Takeda and Collett Cox, 'Existence in the Three Time Periods **Abhidharma-mahāvibhāṣaśāstra* (T.1545 pp.393a9-396b23) English Translation', in *Festschrift Volume for Ronald Nakasone* (forthcoming). I am in addition deeply indebted to Pascale Hugon, Helmut Krasser, Anne MacDonald, Richard Nance and Karin Preisendanz for their very generous, informative help, which has saved me from numerous errors. Of course, I alone am responsible for any mistakes that remain.

2 The classic study is Martin Grabmann, *Die Geschichte der scholastischen Methode* (2 vols, Graz, 1957). I know of no specialized studies of the Arabic or Indo-Tibetan scholastic methods.

3 George Makdisi, *The Rise of Colleges: Institutions of Learning in Islam and the West* (Edinburgh, 1981), p. 249; the bracketed addition is mine.

4 Makdisi, *Rise of Colleges*, pp. 246-9; Grabmann (*Geschichte der scholastischen Methode*, vol. 2, pp. 219-22) considers the full scholastic method to have developed 'indirectly' from Abelard's *Sic et non* (plus the supposedly 'missing' solutions) and, especially, the newly translated *Logica nova* works of Aristotle.

5 Grabmann (*Geschichte der scholastischen Methode*, vol. 1, pp. 318 and 336) considers the supposed three-part method, which he sees in Anselm and other pre-thirteenth-

challenged by George Makdisi, who argues that the Latin scholastic method was borrowed from the Islamic world along with the college.[6] Unfortunately, he does not support his argument with citations from the Latin translations of Arabic texts, nor does he cite any Arabic examples.[7] Considering the great extent of both bodies of literature, it is reasonable to expect the scholastic method to be attested in them, so the lack of any citations is a serious problem for his theory. That problem has now been emended with the discovery that the scholastic method is indeed used in a very well-known text, Ibn Sīnā's *Metaphysics* (*al-Ilāhiyyāt*), which was translated into Latin in Spain in the late twelfth century.[8] At precisely the same point in time, in 1180, Jocius of London returned from Jerusalem and founded the first European college, the Collège des Dix-huit, in Paris.[9] Because the college was an unprecedented institution in Europe, it is thus certain that it was introduced from the Islamic Near East. Although the scholastic method and the college are not *known* to have been mutually connected from the outset in Europe, within medieval Islamic intellectual civilization they are very closely connected, as Makdisi has shown.[10] In order for the European scholastic method to be a European innovation, it would have to be unattested elsewhere until after its development in Europe. But the scholastic method had appeared in Tibetan texts in the late eighth century,[11] and in the Islamic world in the early eleventh century, both in versions close to the Latin Western European one. It is

century writers, to be the foundation of the 'high scholastic' method of thirteenth-century scholasticism.

6 Makdisi, *Rise of Colleges*.

7 Makdisi (*Rise of Colleges*, pp. 254-6) notes as an example Ibn ʿAqīl (d. 1119) and contends that the scholastic method was mainly used in law, though he does not quote or cite actual examples. Makdisi (*Rise of Colleges*, pp. 252-3) follows Ernst Kantorowicz ('The *Quaestiones Disputatae* of the Glossators', *Revue d'histoire du droit*, 16 [1938]: pp. 1-67), who argues that the earliest *quaestiones disputatae* were in law and specifies that this was a specifically medieval development with no (Classical) literary source ('The *Quaestiones Disputatae* of the Glossators', pp. 58-9).

8 Beckwith ('Central Asian Buddhist Sources of Early Scholasticism'); see, e.g., the following translations of Ibn Sīnā's *Metaphysics*: *Avicenna Latinus: Liber De philosophia prima sive Scientia divina, V-X.*, ed. Simone van Riet (Louvain, 1980), vol. 2, pp. 326-46; *La Métaphysique du Shifā'*, trans. Georges C. Anawati (2 vols, Paris, 1978-85), vol. 2, pp. 36-47; *The Metaphysics of The Healing*, trans. Michael E. Marmura (Provo, 2005), pp. 194, 220-34.

9 Henricus Denifle, *Chartularium Universitatis Parisiensis* (4 vols, Paris, 1899; repr. Brussels, 1964), vol. 1, p. 49; cf. Makdisi (*Rise of Colleges*, pp. 225-6). It antedates the University of Paris, as well as the other colleges with which it eventually merged to become the Sorbonne.

10 Makdisi, *Rise of Colleges* and *The Rise of Humanism in Classical Islam and the Christian West, with Special Reference to Scholasticism* (Edinburgh, 1990).

11 See below on this method and on the later (quite different) argument discussed in Christopher I. Beckwith, 'The Medieval Scholastic Method in Tibet and the West', in Lawrence Epstein and Richard Sherburne (eds), *Reflections on Tibetan Culture: Essays in Memory of Turrell V. Wylie* (Lewiston, NY, 1990), pp. 307-13.

thus impossible to accept any of the many theories that attempt to explain the sudden appearance of the scholastic method in medieval Western Europe as an internal development.[12] The same analysis must apply to Tibet and the Islamic world: from whom did the medieval Tibetans and Muslims get the scholastic method, and how?

THE STRUCTURE, ORIGIN AND TRANSMISSION OF THE SCHOLASTIC METHOD

The reason for Makdisi's failure to discover the scholastic method in the Arabic texts or their translations into Latin is perhaps his apparent belief that its essential, salient characteristic is a tripartite or quadripartite argument structure. Analysis of actual examples of the full Latin scholastic method as used by its earliest practitioners, Robert of Courçon, Alexander of Hales, Albert the Great, and others, shows that the number of parts is irrelevant.[13] The scholastic method argument also does not bear the slightest resemblance to the traditional 'discursive' treatise argument or the traditional dialogue argument.

Texts written as traditional treatises, such as the works of Aristotle, have virtually no overt or covert structure:[14]

Treatise Book and Argument Structure

Title of Book

> The author's view begins and proceeds to discuss the topic, in extenso, with occasional comments on other views. The length of the work is irrelevant; if it is very long, it is usually broken up into chapters and sections. This is the structure of Aristotle's works, most of the Muslim Aristotelians' works, and most medieval works in general. The point is to present information to the reader. The treatise has no particular internal or external structure other than that determined by the topics of interest to the author, who can present them in any order he pleases. Like this paragraph, it just goes on and on until the end.

Texts written in the traditional dialogue or question-and-answer format are also completely different from the scholastic method. The Socratic dialogue, like

---

12 Beckwith ('Central Asian Buddhist Sources of Early Scholasticism'). This principle applies to the college as well.

13 Grabmann (*Geschichte der scholastischen Methode*, vol. 2, p. 495) points out that the full scholastic method is first used by Robert of Courçon (or 'Curzon', etc.) in his *summa* (*c.*1202), citing an argument (*Le traité "De usura" de Robert de Courçon*, ed. and trans. Georges Lefèvre [Lille, 1902], pp. 3-7) in which the parts are, in his analysis: 'Fragestellung, Argumente, Gegenargumente (contra), Lösung (corpus articuli), Kritik der für die entgegengesetzte Meinung angenommenen Argumente'.

14 The basic structure of the treatise may be summarized as: T, AAAAAAAAA.. (T: topic, A: author's view).

other such continuous two-voice structures, is actually a covert treatise, because despite the presence of an overt second voice (or voices), the latter is rarely presented as a genuine alternative to the view of the authorial voice.[15]

A book written according to the scholastic method does not consist of continuous authorial viewpoint, either overtly as in an Aristotelian treatise or covertly as in a Socratic dialogue. A scholastic method book is broken up into very many discrete arguments (topics or *quaestiones disputatae* 'disputed questions') on specific points. It typically has a general, encyclopedic title such as *Summa ... X* 'summary of [everything on the subject of] X', or *Quaestiones Disputatae ... Y* ('Disputed Questions on [the subject of] Y'). After the usual short preface or prologue, the text begins with the first argument, the Topic of which (typically its title) is usually presented as a statement or 'question' about the interpretation of a quotation from scripture or of other literature relevant to a point of doctrine, or about a problem in one of the sciences (including metaphysics). It is followed by a string of subarguments pro and contra the Topic statement. In them many variant views by other writers, as well as hypothetical arguments that *could* be made, are presented. This string of subarguments is followed by a second string of subarguments about the subarguments in the first list.[16] The subarguments of the second list are presented in the same order as the first,[17] usually refuting them, but sometimes simply accepting them without comment, e.g., 'As for the argument Z, it is admitted'. The author's view may be presented at the beginning (and often is in Arabic works), between the objections and the replies to them (usual in the Latin method, in which the author's view is normally a brief statement), or at the end of the full argument.[18] The author then moves on to the next topic, which is treated in exactly the same way. He does this topic by topic (i.e., in one scholastic argument after another) throughout the entire text, which typically consists of many dozens or hundreds of such Topics, most of which are treated in full scholastic method arguments:

---

15 The overt structure of the two-voice argument is thus: T, A(B)A(B)A(B)A(B)A(B)A(B) A(B)A(B)A(B)A(B)..., but its covert (actual) structure is T, AAAAAAAAAA...

16 In modern studies the subarguments in the first list are usually called 'objections', and those in the second list 'rebuttals' or the like, but both lists of subarguments may include views with which the author agrees. The argument *within* a subargument can follow treatise, dialogue or scholastic method structure. In the latter case, there are thus scholastic method arguments within scholastic method arguments.

17 The subarguments are typically identified not by number but by brief summary statements of their main point, or mention of the author or textual source of the subargument, and should appear in the exact same order. Although occasionally an author (e.g., Alexander of Hales) has one or two arguments out of order in the second list, most repeat the order verbatim. Some authors (e.g., Fakhr al-Dīn al-Rāzī, Thomas Aquinas) number their subarguments and follow the order of the numbers fairly carefully.

18 Some authors, such as Vasubandhu, repeat their own view several times. See note 21.

SCHOLASTIC METHOD BOOK AND ARGUMENT STRUCTURE

Title of Book

1. First Scholastic Method Argument

I. Topic (Title / Question / Argument)[19]

II. List of Subarguments_1[20] pro and contra the Topic in part I

[1] Subargument_1 *Pro* or *Contra* the topic

[2] Subargument_1 *Pro* or *Contra* the topic

[3] Subargument_1 *Pro* or *Contra* the topic

[4] Subargument_1 *Pro* or *Contra* the topic

[5] Subargument_1 *Pro* or *Contra* the topic

III. Author's View[21]

IV. List of Subarguments_2 about the Subarguments_1 listed in Part II[22]

[1] Subargument_2 *Pro* or *Contra* the Subargument_1 in 1

[2] Subargument_2 *Pro* or *Contra* the Subargument_1 in 2

[3] Subargument_2 *Pro* or *Contra* the Subargument_1 in 3

[4] Subargument_2 *Pro* or *Contra* the Subargument_1 in 4

[5] Subargument_2 *Pro* or *Contra* the Subargument_1 in 5

2. Second Scholastic Method Argument

I. Topic

II. List of Subarguments_1 pro and contra the Topic in part I

[1] Subargument_1 *Pro* or *Contra* the topic

[2] Subargument_1 *Pro* or *Contra* the topic

[3] Subargument_1 *Pro* or *Contra* the topic

III. Author's view

---

[19] The topic of the argument is usually the same as the title or question, which can simply be a quotation from scripture or another author. In some scholastic method books the topics are listed in a summary introduction to each chapter and then are only referred to by number at the beginning of each full argument. Other variations also occur.

[20] These are statements for or against the topic, and are by named individuals or texts, or they are suggested by the author as possible objections that could be made. Part II can contain any number of subarguments. It sometimes contains only one subargument, in which case Part IV will have only one, or even none if the author agrees with it.

[21] The location of the authorial position is unimportant. The author's view, or the view of his school, can occur before the first list of subarguments, after it, or after the second list of subarguments, depending on the tradition or the individual author. In the Latin tradition the usual position of the author's view is in the middle, as shown in the schematic presentations here. In all traditions it can be repeated, typically in different words but sometimes almost verbatim. In Albert the Great's usage (e.g., Edward Grant, *A Source Book in Medieval Science* [Cambridge, 1974], pp. 681-2) it can be found both in the middle and at the end. Ibn Sīnā often states his view in the beginning and one or more times later on. Vasubandhu repeats his view in the middle and at the end in Example 1.

[22] The subarguments_2 corresponding to the view or views accepted by the author are often omitted (regularly in some authors).

IV. List of $Subarguments_2$ about the $Subarguments_1$ listed in part II
[1] $Subargument_2$ *Pro* or *Contra* the $Subargument_1$ in 1
[2] $Subargument_2$ *Pro* or *Contra* the $Subargument_1$ in 2
[3] $Subargument_2$ *Pro* or *Contra* the $Subargument_1$ in 3
3. Third and following Scholastic Method Arguments: same structure as 1 and 2 above

The salient feature of the scholastic method is not the number or organization of whatever parts scholars might divide it up into, but its *two lists of arguments* representing *many different views*, both real or hypothetical, on a problem, with a rigorous and exhaustive *recursive* type of analysis. This new, radically scientific approach must have been exciting for the young intellectuals who first encountered it in the Middle Ages.

The structure of the scholastic method argument is also strikingly distinctive. It could not possibly be an independent, simultaneous, purely internal development in more than one culture, let alone three completely different linguistic and religious cultures. Because it is now known how the method made its way into medieval Western Europe, and it is unlikely that either the Muslims or the Tibetans borrowed the method from one another,[23] it must be concluded that the scholars of the latter two cultures borrowed the scholastic method from still another source.

It has been known for several decades, from both historical scholarship and archaeology, that the medieval Islamic college, or *madrasa*, is an Islamicized form of the earlier Central Asian Buddhist college, or *vihāra*.[24] In fact, the Nawbahār or Nava *Vihāra* ('New College')[25] of Balkh,[26] one of the most important Buddhist *vihāras* in pre-Islamic Central Asia, evidently continued to function for a century or more after the Arab conquest, as did many other *vihāras*. There were hundreds

[23] The Arab Empire and the Tibetan Empire were in direct contact off and on for almost two centuries, during which each ruled over part of Buddhist Central Asia, but this contact ended upon the breakup of the two empires during the collapse of the early medieval world order in the early-mid-ninth century. See Christopher I. Beckwith, *The Tibetan Empire in Central Asia: A History of the Struggle for Great Power among Tibetans, Turks, Arabs, and Chinese during the Early Middle Ages*, revised edition (Princeton, 1993) and *Empires of the Silk Road: A History of Central Eurasia from the Bronze Age to the Present* (Princeton, 2009).

[24] V.V. Bartol'd (Barthold), Сочинения, II, 2 (Moscow, 1964), p. 30; Litvinskij, article 'Ajina Tepe' in *EIr* and the article on madrasa in *EI*².

[25] See Beckwith, *Empires of the Silk Road*, for emendations to the description of the Nawbahār in Christopher I. Beckwith, 'The Plan of the City of Peace: Central Asian Iranian Factors in Early 'Abbâsid Design', *Acta Orientalia Academiae Scientiarum Hungaricae*, 38 (1984): pp. 128-47.

[26] Balkh was the most important city of ancient and medieval Bactria, or Tokharistan, a thoroughly Buddhist country stretching from west of the city east into what is now Tajikistan.

of them in the territory of Khuttal (then part of Tokharistan, now part of Tajikistan) at the time Hui-ch'ao passed through in *c*.726 CE.[27]

The Nava Vihāra was visited in 628 or 630 by Hsüan-tsang, who stayed there for over a month and studied with the master Prajñākara. While there he acquired a copy of the text of the *Abhidharmamahāvibhāṣaśāstra*, the greatest of the Sarvāstivādin *summas*, which he brought back to China and translated. This is a Late Classical period work, an extended commentary on the *Jñānaprasthāna*, one of the canonical texts of the Vaibhāṣika subsect of Sarvāstivāda. A massive text, the *Abhidharmamahāvibhāṣa* is a purely scholastic work in which Sarvāstivādin sectarian views on points of doctrine are presented and opposing positions are disputed.[28] It contains what appears to be the earliest attested use of the full scholastic method.[29] The rhetorical organization of the text and the form of its arguments are similar to those found in other related texts, such as the *Abhidharmakośabhāṣya*, a later Sautrāntika work.[30] Since examples of the scholastic method apparently do not occur in other, verifiably earlier Buddhist or non-Buddhist Indian texts, it seems to have developed within the Sarvāstivādin school. The scholastic method is used in the *Abhidharmakośabhāṣya* passage analysed in Appendix 1. The text's quotation of a scholastic method argument from the *Abhidharmamahāvibhāṣa* is analysed in Appendix 2.

The first Muslim writer to use the scholastic method in Arabic works was the great Central Asian scientist and philosopher Ibn Sīnā (Avicenna, 980-1037), who was from Afshana, near Bukhara.[31] Ibn Sīnā was educated in Central Asia and accordingly must have learned the method there. However, no translation of a Buddhist scholastic text is known to have been made into Arabic before Ibn Sīnā's

---

27 Walter Fuchs, 'Hui-ch'ao's Pilgerreise durch Nordwest-Indien und Zentral-Asien um 726', *Sitzungsberichte der Preussischen Akademie der Wissenschaften (philosophisch-historisiche Klasse)*, 30 (1938): pp. 426-69, at p. 452; cf. Litvinskij, 'Ajina Tepe' in *EIr*. Of the hundreds of *vihāras* that once existed in the area of Khuttal (in what is now southern Tajikistan) archaeologists have excavated the remains of several, including the four-*īwān* plan *vihāra* of Adzhina Tepa (Boris A. Litvinskij and Tamara I. Zeimal', Аджина-Тепа [Moscow, 1971]), which was destroyed during the mid-eighth century wars in the region.

28 It is believed that the original text (now lost) was in Sanskrit.

29 Beckwith ('Central Asian Buddhist Sources of Early Scholasticism'). For an annotated translation of a section of the text see Takeda and Cox, 'Existence in the Three Time Periods'.

30 Cf. the Vaibhāṣika work written to refute it, the *Nyāyānusāra*. See Collett Cox, *Disputed Dharmas: Early Buddhist Theories on Existence. An Annotated Translation of the Section on Factors Dissociated from Thought from Saṅghabhadra's* Nyāyānusāra (Tokyo, 1995), pp. 189-97.

31 Of course, many later scholars use it too, including Fakhr al-Dīn al-Rāzī (1149/1150-1210) in his *Kitāb al-arbaʿīn fī uṣūl al-dīn* (ed. Sayyid Zayn al-ʿĀbidīn al-Mūsawī [Hyderabad, 1934]), wherein he carefully numbers the subarguments; see Beckwith ('Central Asian Buddhist Sources of Early Scholasticism').

time. To establish the means of transmission of the method in the absence of Arabic translations, it is necessary to use logic, deduction and historical analysis.

It has been normal for teachers to teach orally, and at least since Antiquity typically in schools. Some of the ideas of the most famous thinkers of all time, such as Aristotle, are known only, or mainly, through student notes; the idea that a literary source is a necessary prerequisite for someone to learn anything must therefore be dismissed.[32] The question, then, is not whether Ibn Sīnā could have learned the scholastic method from a teacher or some other oral source; the question must be whether there were teachers in Central Asian schools who knew the method and could transmit it to him.

The accepted, traditional view of the early history of the Islamic college or *madrasa* is that it developed in what used to be called 'Eastern Islam', usually meaning Islamic Central Asia.[33] During Ibn Sīnā's lifetime many *madrasas* appeared in the area of Khuttal – where previously there had been many *vihāras*[34] – and elsewhere in Central Asia. This is certainly evidence of the conversion of the population to Islam, and along with the people, conversion of their institutions' religious affiliation – but not their architectural forms, functions or legal statuses, which remained essentially unchanged. Except for their religious affiliation, Central Asian *vihāras* and *madrasas* were virtually identical. According to the principle cited above, this cannot be accidental; it must be due to the direct transmission of the *vihāra* tradition by live people. *Madrasas* spread rapidly throughout Central Asia, from which region they soon spread to the Islamic Near East. Makdisi's work illuminates the great importance of public oral disputation in the medieval *madrasas* and in the medieval European colleges and universities. The same can be said about the *vihāras*. As Makdisi shows for medieval Islam and medieval Latin Europe, oral teaching and disputation were closely connected to literary teaching and disputation, both of which were very energetically practiced in the *madrasas* and colleges.

---

32 In addition, the existence of something intelligent or useful in a text does not mean that its message is accepted by the people into whose language the text has been translated.

33 The 'internal' theory of Pedersen, Makdisi, et al. (article 'Madrasa' in *EI*²) that claims the *madrasa* originated in the mosque (which is a purely Arab Islamic architectural form and institution) is contradicted by actual archaeological-architectural and historical evidence that solidly supports the traditional view. On the sharp distinction between mosque-schools and *madrasas*, and on the earliest attested *madrasas*, which for long were found only in Central Asia, see the same work (article 'Madrasa' in *EI*²), which states that unlike the mosque-schools, the *madrasas* 'were especially arranged for study and the maintenance of students'. R. Hillenbrand notes the purely 'eastern Iranian' (i.e., Central Asian) architectural origins of the *madrasa*, discusses Barthold's theory that the *madrasa* was simply an Islamicized *vihāra*, and mentions the often argued but impossible theory of origin from 'the typical Khurāsānī house' (article 'Madrasa' in *EI*²).

34 Litvinsky, 'Ajina Tepe' in *EIr*.

The scholastic method was introduced to Tibet during the imperial period by the Indian Buddhist scholar Śāntarakṣita (*c.*725-88) and his pupil Kamalaśīla (*c.*740-95). In Kamalaśīla's *Madhyamakāloka*, typically a brief mention of the topic is followed by the two lists of arguments, which are usually followed by a brief conclusion.[35] A similar method is referred to or used in earlier Indian works such as the *Vigrahavyāvartanī*, a Mādhyamika work attributed to Nāgārjuna.[36] Not too surprisingly, Tibetan Buddhist literature also includes a full translation of the famous *Abhidharmakośabhāṣya*,[37] in which the Central Asian Buddhist type of scholastic method is used, as described above. Nevertheless, neither version of the true scholastic method argument is followed by later Tibetans. Instead, the argument type usually referred to as *dgag gzhag spang gsum* – 'the three (-part argument consisting of) objections (of others, and arguments against them), establishing (one's own view, and) refutation (of further objections to one's view)' – was introduced, apparently by the influential teacher Rngog Lotsāba Blo ldan shes rab (1059-1109), who had studied in Kashmir and may have learned it there.[38] This structurally quite different argument[39] was adopted by one of

---

[35] For examples of his argument form see the study and partial translation of the *Madhyamakāloka* by Ryusei Keira, *Mādhyamika and Epistemology: A Study of Kamalaśīla's Method for Proving the Voidness of all Dharmas* (Vienna, 2004). However, not all parts are given in the translation (the topic of the first argument, for example, is omitted by Keira), and there is no explicit mention of the two list categories (given by Keira as *pūrvapakṣa* and *uttarapakṣa*) in the part of the Tibetan text he quotes.

[36] Kamaleswar Bhattacharya, *The Dialectical Method of Nāgārjuna* (Delhi, 1978). It is certainly later than Nāgārjuna's traditional (but doubtful) dates. Cf. the following note.

[37] The *Abhidharmakośa* itself is usually said to be a highly abbreviated summary in verse (*kārikā*) form of the main doctrinal points of the *Abhidharmamahāvibhāṣaśāstra*, the ultimate summa of the Vaibhāṣika school. Vasubandhu, who is traditionally believed to be the author both of the *Abhidharmakośa* and the *Abhidharmakośabhāṣya*, is thought to have written the *Abhidharmakośa* first and then rejected its positions in the *Abhidharmakośabhāṣya*, either in accordance with a clandestine plan or after converting to the Yogācāra school. This tradition is, however, problematic. Charles Willemen, *The Essence of Scholasticism: Abhidharmahṛdaya, T1550,* revised edition (Delhi, 2006), p. 20, says, "The *Kośabhāṣya* ... is ultimately based on the Bactrian *Abhidharmahṛdaya*" (of Dharmaśreṣṭhin).

[38] He is also said to have written a summary of Kamalaśīla's *Madhyamakāloka*; see Keira (*Mādhyamika and Epistemology*, p. 17 n. 41).

[39] It is a tripartite argument, for which reason I previously argued (in Beckwith, 'Medieval Scholastic Method') that it is directly comparable to the Arabic and Latin scholastic methods. However, as shown in this article, the key feature of the scholastic method is the two recursive lists of arguments, not the number of parts. Moreover, the first and third parts of this later Tibetan argument do not consist of recursive lists (i.e., the arguments in the third part do not refer directly to the arguments in the first part), among other differences. It is not, therefore, a type of scholastic method in the strict sense. My earlier view must accordingly be rejected.

the most famous scholars in Tibetan history, Saskya Paṇḍita (1182-1251),[40] and became a mainstream tradition in Tibet.[41]

CONCLUSION

The literary scholastic method originated within the encyclopaedic scholastic commentary literature of the Sarvāstivādin school of Buddhism, which flourished mainly in the region of Central Asia (especially Gandhāra, Bactria and East Turkistan) and Northwestern India (especially Kashmir).[42] Despite the spread of Islam, Sarvāstivādin Buddhism apparently continued to be practised in parts of Central Asia for several centuries after the Arab conquest. The highly distinctive structure of the scholastic method and the lack of any attested antecedents in earlier Arabic literature ensures that it must have been borrowed. The means of borrowing was evidently oral, via formerly Buddhist teachers and students who had converted to Islam along with the rest of the population and continued teaching and studying in their *vihāras*, which also had been converted to Islam and renamed *madrasas*. The earliest Arabic writer to use the scholastic method is Ibn Sīnā, possibly the single most influential writer of the great age of Islamic civilization. He lived at the same time that the *madrasa* – the Islamicized *vihāra* – was spreading across his Central Asian homeland. About a century and a half later, an identical, parallel development occurred in Western Europe. The college – the Christianized *madrasa* – and the Latin scholastic method both appeared at exactly the same time, and in fact in the same city, Paris, both having been introduced from the Islamic world. The colleges and the university of Paris became the main centres of oral teaching and literary scholastic method disputation.

In sum, the scholastic method of the Central Asian Sarvāstivādin Buddhists was transmitted to Islam via the institution of the Buddhist college, the *vihāra*, which was converted apparently unchanged into the Islamic college, the *madrasa*.[43] The teaching and disputation that had been practised in the Buddhist

---

40 Saskya Paṇḍita was also politically influential. He proffered the submission of Tibet to the Mongols under Ögedei Khan in 1247 (Beckwith, *Empires of the Silk Road*, p. 191).

41 However, according to Georges B. Dreyfus ('What is Debate for? The Rationality of Tibetan Debates and the Role of Humor', *Argumentation*, 22 [2008]: pp. 43-58), and *pace* R.A. Stein (*Tibetan Civilization* [Stanford, 1972], pp. 160-63), it bears no relation to the oral form of debate used by Tibetan monks today, which actually has the typical Question : Answer (AB) type of dialogue structure widely found in ancient and medieval literatures (see above). For another early Indian literary example, see Michael Torsten Much, 'Uddyotakaras Kritik der *Apoha*-Lehre (Nyāyavārttika *ad* NS II 2,66), *Wiener Zeitschrift für die Kunde Südasiens*, 38 [1994]: pp. 351-66.

42 Charles Willemen, Bart Dessein and Collett Cox, *Sarvāstivāda Buddhist Scholasticism* (Leiden, 1998), pp. 138-254.

43 Cf. Litvinskij ('Ajina Tepe' in *EIr*).

vihāras continued to be practised there, but with the Islamicization of the *vihāra* as the *madrasa*, the topics focused on were Islamic rather than Buddhist.

APPENDIX 1

An argument from the *Abhidharmakośabhāṣya*[44]

[Topic / Argument / Question]

Whether constituents[45] exist in the three time periods;[46] do {the *kleśas*,[47] and past and future objects, really exist?}

[Subarguments$_1$]

[1] {The Vaibhāṣikas maintain that past and future constituents really exist ... [argument based on quoted scripture]}

[2] {The Blessed One implicitly teaches the same doctrine when he says ... [argument based on scripture]}

[3] {A consciousness can arise given an object, but not if the object is not present. ... [argument from reason]}

[4] {If the past does not exist, how can good and bad action ... [argument from reason]}

{Therefore, because of the proofs from scripture and reasoning quoted above, the Vaibhāṣikas affirm the existence of both the past and the future.}[48]

---

44 The text is from Pruden (Louis de La Vallée Poussin, *Abhidharmakośabhāṣyam*, trans. Leo Pruden [Berkeley, 1989], pp. 806-20), which is based on the Chinese translation. The sources of the text here are: Chinese, Taishō 1558, 20: 104a–106b; Tibetan, Derge 140 (*ku*), 476(238 v°).2 ff.

45 Text I have translated is unmarked; text quoted from Pruden's translation is in {curly brackets}; explanatory remarks, including structural elements, which are not overtly present in the Chinese text (the basis of Louis de la Vallée Poussin's translation, and thus Pruden's) are in [square brackets]; clarifications of my translation, or Pruden's of his, are in (parentheses). I have silently converted Pruden's '*dharma*(*s*)' to 'constituent(s)' throughout, corrected typographical errors, changed his brackets to parentheses or vice versa to accord with the system of this article, and omitted his section numbers and page references from my quotations of his translation.

46 The topic is given in English by Pruden (*Abhidharmakośabhāṣyam*, p. viii) as 'Discussion: Do the *Dharmas* Exist in the Three Time Periods?' In fact, the argument occurs as a digression within the discussion of the *anuśayas* 'latent defilements', in which the 'three time periods' are raised in the text (p. 804): 'We must examine to what object a person is bound by a past, present, or future *anuśaya*.' The term *anuśaya* is translated as 'latent defilement(s)' (p. 767), but is usually left untranslated.

47 The term *kleśa* is translated as 'defilement' by Pruden, but he usually leaves it untranslated.

48 The commentary here quotes the Sarvāstivādins' own arguments from the *Abhidharmamahāvibhāṣaśāstra* about this essential point of their school, though Vasubandhu's text is somewhat different from the one used by Hsüan Tsang and is thus evidently based on a different recension. See Appendix 2 for this section. For discussion

[The View of the Author according to the Sautrāntika School]
{If the past and the future exist as things ... [Two pages of argument.] Consequently, ...}

[Subarguments$_2$]

[1] {The argument [1]... is pure verbiage, for, ...}
[2] {With regard to the argument [2] that the Blessed One taught ... we would also say ...}
[3] {As for the argument [3] ... Consequently the reason that the Sarvāstivādins gave ... does not hold.}
[4] [As for argument [4],] the {Sarvāstivādins also deduce an argument from the result of action. But the Sautrāntikas do not admit that ...}

[The View of the Author according to the Sautrāntika School]
{Consequently,} *sarvāstivāda*, 'saying that everything exists', (the view) {of the Sarvāstivādins who affirm the real existence of the past and the future, is not good within Buddhism. It is not in this sense that one should understand *sarvāstivāda*. Good *sarvāstivāda* consists in affirming the existence of 'all' by understanding the word 'all' as scripture understands it.[49]}

APPENDIX 2

The Sarvāstivādins' Own Argument, based on the *Abhidharmamahāvibhāṣaśāstra*[50]

[Topic / Argument / Question: the Meaning of *sarvāstivāda*]
{The masters who call themselves Sarvāstivādins,} 'those who say everything exists,' {maintain that the past and the future exist. ... (How many ways are there of understanding the doctrine of the existence of all (*sarvāstivāda*)? Which is the best?)}

[Subarguments$_1$: the Arguments of the Sarvāstivādin Masters]

[1] [The view of the] Bhadanta Dharmatrāta ...
[2] [The view of the] Bhadanta Ghoṣaka ...
[3] [The view of the] Bhadanta Vasumitra ...
[4] [The view of the] Bhadanta Buddhadeva ...

[Subarguments$_2$: the Sarvāstivādins' replies to the Subargments$_1$]

---

of the many different recensions that once existed see Willemen, Dessein and Cox, *Sarvāstivāda Buddhist Scholasticism*, pp. 233ff.

[49] Although Vasubandhu, the author of the *Abhidharmakośabhāṣya*, belongs to the Sautrāntika 'Scriptural' School (a Sarvāstivādin subsect), and sometimes essentially argues that the Sarvāstivādin teachings are wrong on the basis of this or that Sūtra quotation, like the later Muslim theologian al-Ghazālī he often uses logic and dialectical argumentation skilfully – the book contains other examples of scholastic method arguments besides the one quoted here.

[50] *Abhidharmakośabhāṣyam*, trans. Pruden, pp. 807-10.

[1] Among them, the first (master, Dharmatrāta), {professing ... may be refuted ...}
[2] Again,[51] the second (master, Ghoṣaka)'s {time periods ... are confounded ...}
[4] Again, the fourth (master, Buddhadeva)'s {three time periods exist at the same time ...}

[Conclusion: the View of the Sarvāstivādins Summarized]

'The third is the best.'[52] {Consequently, the best system} (within the Sarvāstivādin school, according to the Sarvāstivādins themselves) {is that of Vasumitra ... according to which the time periods and the conditions are established through the operation of the activity of a constituent: when a constituent does not accomplish its operation, it is future; when it is accomplishing it, it is present; and when its operation has come to an end, it is past.}

---

[51] The respective equivalents of 'again' or 'furthermore' are used like this in the Arabic and Latin scholastic methods too. This appears to be a significant detail.

[52] This sentence, as well as the omission of a reply to the third subargument (with the position of which the Sarvāstivādin authors agreed), is copied verbatim by Vasubandhu from the *Abhidharmamahāvibhāṣaśāstra*.

Chapter 8
Notes on the Religions in the Mongol Empire

Peter Zieme

INTRODUCTION

The general situation of the religions during the time of the Mongol Empire is quite well known. The so-called *pax mongolica* could equally be named the *pax religiosa*. Beside Shamanism and Buddhism, Christianity and Islam were tolerated in general as well as Daoism and Confucianism among the Chinese.[1]

In this contribution, after some general comments on the different religions adopted by the Uyghurs from the eighth to fourteenth centuries, I will argue that Tibetan Buddhism in the thirteenth and fourteenth centuries had a strong influence in the Turfan region even though this was also the period of Islamization. The Uyghur kingdom became part of the Mongol Empire after the Uyghur king, the Idukkut, surrendered at the beginning of the thirteenth century. As a mark of respect a Mongol princess was given to him in marriage and he was regarded as the fifth son of Genghis Khan.

Once they had become part of the Mongol Empire, Uyghurs played an important role as mediators of cultural influence into Mongol society. The Tarim basin was occupied by the Tibetans in the latter half of the seventh century, then lost to the Chinese in 692. After 751 Tibetans again held parts of the province Gansu, but it is unclear to what extent Tibetan hegemony continued in the north of the Tarim Basin, while in the southern regions, between Khotan and Miran, Tibetans still had a strong position as well as in Dunhuang, at least until the beginning of the eleventh century. During these centuries Tibetan Buddhism had already exercised a direct influence on the area. It reached the Turfan oasis again at the time of Qubilai, if not earlier, when Tibetan priests were chosen as

[1] Paul Demiéville, 'La situation religieuse en Chine au temps de Marco Polo', in *Oriente Poliano* (Rome, 1957), pp. 193-236; Jean-Paul Roux, 'Les religions dans les sociétés turco-mongoles', *Revue de d'histoire des religions*, 201 (1984): pp. 393-420; S. Kitagawa, Triangular Structure of the Christians, the Muslims and the Mongols, in 中近東文化センター研究会報告 *Chukintō bunka sentā kenkyū kai hōkoku*, 10 (1989): pp. 112-21, 273-86; Jens Peter Laut, 'Vielfalt türkischer Religionen', *Spirita*, 10 (1996): pp. 24-36; Peter Zieme, 'Religions of the Turks in the Pre-Islamic Period', in David J. Roxburgh (ed.), *Turks: A Journey of a Thousand Years, 600-1600* (London, 2005), pp. 32-7.

advisors at the Mongol court. This time, however, the form this influence took was rather indirect. Some Uyghur kings or *ıdukkuts*, for example, had Tibetan names like Könčök or Kiräshiz. Uyghurs were not only, to put it in Barthold's words, teachers of the Mongols, but they became influential in many spheres of Mongol society: in the sciences, culture, as official translators and in military affairs. The role of Uyghurs in the Mongol Empire can hardly be exaggerated and has already been the subject of studies by many scholars such as Chen Yuan, Igor de Rachewiltz and Thomas Allsen.[2]

GENERAL STATEMENTS ON RELIGIONS IN UYGHUR TEXTS OF THE YUAN PERIOD

THE CASE OF A MAITREYA HYMN

One text has to be mentioned in this context which throws some light on the general situation of religions in the Mongol Empire: a hymn on the veneration of the future Buddha Maitreya.[3] Since the character of this text is religious and not historiographical, it has to be treated with the necessary caution. Yet, it clearly tells us which religious groups were known to the Buddhist author. In expounding on his expectation that all peoples 'will finally venerate Maitreya' the poet evokes the titles of representatives of all religions known to him in addition to Buddhism. He starts with the Christians by referring to the Lord Messiah and Maryam. The term *mad Maryam*, 'Mother Mary', is known from the Creed which is partly preserved in Uyghur, too.[4] In second place the Maitreya

---

2 Ch'ên Yüan, *Western and Central Asians in China under the Mongols: Their Transformation into Chinese* (Los Angeles, 1966); Igor de Rachewiltz, 'Turks in China under the Mongols: A Preliminary Investigation of Turco-Mongol Relations in the 13th and 14th Centuries', in Morris Rossabi (ed.), *China among Equals: The Middle Kingdom and its Neighbours, 10th-14th Centuries* (Berkeley, 1983), pp. 281-310; Thomas Allsen, 'The Yüan Dynasty and the Uighurs of Turfan in the 13th Century', in Rossabi (ed.), *China among Equals*, pp. 243-80.

3 Semih Tezcan, *Das uigurische Insadi-Sūtra* (Berlin, 1974), pp. 58-76; Peter Zieme, 'Zur Interpretation einer Passage des alttürkischen Maitreya-Lobpreises (BT III, 1014-1047)', in Nurettin Demir and Erika Taube (eds), *Turkologie heute - Tradition und Perspektive: Materialien der dritten Deutschen Turkologenkonferenz, Leipzig 4.-7. Oktober 1994* (Wiesbaden, 1998), pp. 317-24.

4 Sencer Divitçioğlu ('Nebulous Nestorians in the Turkish Realm (VIIIth Century)', *Central Asiatic Journal*, 50 [2006]: pp. 9-15) presents ideas that have to be rejected for the greater part. For example: on p. 12 he refers to Pelliot Tib. 1283 (for a transcript and full bibliography see http://otdo.aa.tufs.ac.jp) which is an itinerary of an embassy sent to some tribes in Central Asia in the eighth century. One of the names of the tribes is in Tibetan script *go-kog* (line 66). Although the Tibetan text had been studied many times, no one had offered a solution. Divitçioğlu is the first to give an etymology by dividing the word into *gok-og* and by concluding that *gok* is equal to *kök* 'sky' and *og* to *ög* 'mother' (< *kök-ana*). He translates the term as 'Celestial Mother': 'It is without doubt a place of

hymn mentions Muslims by evoking the prophet Muhammad. In third place we find Manichaeans represented by the bishop and the magister. In a further stanza the author mentions Muslims and finally soothsayers.

The inclusion of Manichaeans is more problematic than that of Christians and Muslims. In his book on Uyghur Manichaeism, Takao Moriyasu has brought together arguments for a rapid disappearance of the religion of Light after the first half of the eleventh century.[5] Since we have only scarce, if any, evidence for the existence of Manichaeans in the thirteenth century, the author probably mentioned them for the sake of completeness. Although this religion was no longer practised in the Yuan period, people were still aware of its presence in previous times. As a whole, this Maitreya hymn is an original composition using the topoi known from Maitreya veneration literature in Chinese.[6]

One can list further examples in which elements from various religions were combined. One of them is a Christian booklet written in Syriac and Uyghur scripts. This prayer book contains a colophon including a passage of merit transfer typical also for Buddhist manuscripts and prints.[7] It would be an exaggeration though to interpret this feature as a kind of syncretism, since

---

worship or a temple where a female cult is worshipped. Concerning the house of kök-öğ (PM [i.e. the Tibetan text]) the text notes wryly: ' "elle n'a de querelle avec personne"; this means that they are living peacefully with their neighbours, practising their Heavenly Mother cult as the Nestorian church prescribes'. My objections are: there is neither a *kök ana* in Turk mythology, nor a *kök ög*. Divitçioglu quotes from Bacot's translation, but replacing the word 'qui' by 'elle', he manipulates the text and conveys the impression that *go-kog* is a female entity. In the Tibetan text itself it is a designation of a tribe or a geographical name. The nearest equivalent that comes to my mind is the biblical name of Gog (and Magog). Divitçioğlu then refers to the Ossetians who preserve in their oral tradition a goddess called Mady Mayram, who may indeed be our Mother Mary, but not *kök ana*! The text has been discussed in Jacques Bacot, 'Reconnaissance en Haute Asie Septentrionale', *Journal Asiatique*, 244 (1956): pp. 137-53; Gérard Clauson, 'À propos du manuscript Pelliot Tibétain 1283', *Journal Asiatique*, 245 (1957): pp. 11-24; Louis Ligeti, 'À propos du Rapport sur les rois demeurant dans le nord', in Ariane Macdonald (ed.), *Études Tibétaines dédiées à la mémoire de Marcelle Lalou* (Paris, 1971), pp. 166-89. Recently, Federica Venturi ('An Old Tibetan Document on the Uighurs: A New Translation and Interpretation', *Journal of Asian History*, 42 [2008]: pp. 1-35) revisited the whole document without mentioning Divitçioğlu's article or offering a solution for *go-kog*, see esp. p. 29 n. 89, 'hitherto unidentified'.

5 Takao Moriyasu, *Die Geschichte des uigurischen Manichäismus an der Seidenstraße: Forschungen zu manichäischen Quellen und ihrem geschichtlichen Hintergrund* (Wiesbaden, 2004), p. 208.

6 Peter Zieme, 'Ein alttürkischer Maitreya-Hymnus und mögliche Parallelen', in Proceedings of the conference *Die Erforschung des Tocharischen und die alttürkische Maitrisimit, Tagung 3. - 4. April 2008* (to be published in 2010).

7 Peter Zieme, 'Notes on a Bilingual Prayer Book from Bulayık', in D. Winkler and Li Tang (eds), *Hidden Treasures and Intercultural Encounters. Studies on East Syriac Christianity in China and Central Asia* (Münster et al., 2009), pp. 167-80.

it concerns only the 'exterior' of the text. On the other hand, it probably does suggest that Christian Uyghurs lived like their Buddhist 'brethren'.

In the sphere of economy, we find among the several Uyghur documents from the Yuan period people who acted as sellers or buyers etc. with clear Christian names such as Tınha,[8] Ushanna,[9] Barshaba,[10] Kövärgiz (George),[11] Särgis,[12] Savma,[13] Nisdiriz,[14] Shilimun[15] and Matay (Matthew).[16] Muslim names such as Muḥammad or Qiyāṣuddīn also appear in the documents, but the quantity of Buddhist names clearly shows that in the economic field Buddhists still were in the majority.

The rather objective tone of the Maitreya hymn contrasts with at least two other attitudes.

ATTITUDES TOWARD ISLAM

A clearly hostile attitude to Islam is attested in an anonymous Buddhist text from the Turfan oasis. This short poem written in Uyghur quotes some fundamental theses of Islam, presenting them, albeit not *expressis verbis*, as ridiculous or

---

8 Dai Matsui, 'Taxation and Tax-collecting Systems in Uiguristan under Mongol Rule', in *Research on Political and Economic Systems under Mongol Rule* (Osaka, 2002), pp. 87-127, here text H (Ch/U 6321v) l. 3, according to the editor from Syriac *denḥā* 'epiphany'.

9 Matsui, 'Taxation and Tax-collecting Systems', text D (U 4845v). In ll. 2 and 5 the name *ushaq-a* (resp. *ushaq*) appears. Instead of this reading I propose *ushana* to be derived from Syriac *ūshānā* 'Hosanna' ('a man's name still much used', as Arthur John Maclean says. See his *A Dictionary of the Dialects of Vernacular Syriac, as Spoken by the Eastern Syrians of Kurdistan, Northwest Persia, and the Plains of Mosul* [Oxford, 1901], 7a).

10 Matsui, 'Taxation and Tax-collecting Systems', text D (U 4845v), l. 7 instead of *payispa* < Tibetan 'Phags-pa I read *barshaba* < Syriac Barshabā (Barsabas), cf. Maclean, *Dictionary of the Dialects of Vernacular Syriac*, 38a.

11 Matsui, 'Taxation and Tax-collecting Systems', text H (Ch/U 6321v), l. 5, according to the editor from Syriac *giwargīs* 'George'.

12 Matsui, 'Taxation and Tax-collecting Systems', text H (Ch/U 6321v), l. 7, according to the editor from Syriac *sergīs* 'Sergios'; cf. Maclean, *Dictionary of the Dialects of Vernacular Syriac*, p. 230b: 'the latter form [*sergīs* instead of *sergīyūs*] still much used as a man's name'.

13 Matsui, 'Taxation and Tax-collecting Systems', text H (Ch/U 6321v), l. 8, according to the editor from Syriac *ṣawmā* 'fasting', cf. Maclean, *Dictionary of the Dialects of Vernacular Syriac*, p. 263b: *ṣōmā* 'a fast'.

14 Matsui, 'Taxation and Tax-collecting Systems', text J (U 5623), l. 3, according to the editor from Syriac *nesṭūriōs* (Nestorius), cf. Maclean, *Dictionary of the Dialects of Vernacular Syriac*, p. 215b.

15 Matsui, 'Taxation and Tax-collecting Systems', text J (U 5623), l. 2, according to the editor from Syriac *Shlēmūn* (Salomon), cf. Maclean, *Dictionary of the Dialects of Vernacular Syriac*, p. 307a: 'a man's name still much used'.

16 U 5267, l. 2, cf. Simone-Christiane Raschmann, *Alttürkische Handschriften*, Teil 13 Dokumente Teil 1 (Stuttgart, 2007).

nonsensical (cf. e.g. line 4 of the cited stanza). This poem starts with the following verses:

> [ ]
> the many trees and the mountains,
> the many living beings (*janvar*), all these
> God has created – thus they (i.e. the Muslims = *musurmanlar*) say.[17]

A second attitude is presented, always in poetical form, by Uyghur Buddhists who were threatened by the approaching Muslims. It is somewhat astonishing that they uttered their reactions usually in very cautious words. The poems did not contain any formal declarations of war, but are rather vague. One poem in which such criticism can be seen was edited by Kōgi Kudara on the basis of photographs preserved in the Library of Tokyo University.[18] The last stanza can be paraphrased as follows:

> When the discipline of the Tathāgata Buddha deteriorates,
> when the *āryasaṃgha*, the noble community, disappears,
> there will be mourning by all living beings,
> even if they have something to live on in poverty.

The second example comes from a wooden tablet preserved in the Museum of Asian Art in Berlin.[19] Both sides bear a rather long poem in alliterative stanzas. The third stanza can be rendered as follows:

> When the monks who give *dharmadāna*, have faith,
> when they ... go to China,
> then your ... has become useful:
> will you lean on the *dashman*?

The word *dashman*, derived from the New Persian *dānishmand* ('wise'), indicates Muslim scholars.

---

17 Semih Tezcan and Peter Zieme, 'Antiislamische Polemik in einem alttürkischen buddhistischen Gedicht aus Turfan', *Altorientalische Forschungen*, 17 (1990): pp. 146-51.

18 Kōgi Kudara, 'Saiiki shogo dankan shū (19.20) chōsa chūkan hōkoku', in *Tōkyō daigaku shozō bukkyō kankei kichōsho ten – tenji shiryō mokuroku* [*Precious Buddhist Manuscripts in the Library of the University of Tōkyō – Catalogue of the Exposed Materials*] (Tokyo, 2001), pp. 20-24.

19 The wooden tablet, apparently a kind of votive table, bears the shelf mark MIK III 7830: its find mark, T II, indicates that it was obtained during the second Prussian expedition.

This poem ends with the fifteenth stanza:

When you are now negligent,
in this disappearing wild country,
you will contradict
the words of the Exalted.

There is more material which supports the impression offered by these poems. In a panegyric poem from Dunhuang[20] the qualities of the ruler of Xining, Sulaymān Wang (reg. 1339-43),[21] are praised as glorious and outstanding. Here is one example:

Never before there was an extraordinary holy king
who condemns drinking of much wine and beer as poison,
who drinks little to bring welfare to the people
and never neglects the useful things.[22]

This Sulaymān Wang, Wang of Xining,[23] was a Muslim, but at least in Xining this did not prevent Buddhists from composing a eulogy in his honour. This suggests that he was probably not perceived as offensive by Buddhists.

Linguistically one can observe that the influence of Islam and languages used in the Muslim world like New Persian and Arabic is very weak, especially in the lexicon, but some traces can be identified.[24] The most striking example is the juncture *sadaqa bushı* for 'alms' in an omen text.[25] The first is a loan word from the Arabic (via New Persian) *ṣadaqa*. A relatively large number of words of Arabic/New Persian origin can be found in a late manuscript (thirteenth or fourteenth century) of popular songs on Muslim virtues which show Muslim influence not only in the lexicon, but also in the contents. This shows that Islam had already begun to penetrate into the Turfan oasis. From Rashīd al-Dīn we

20 Preserved in the Beijing University Library under the shelf number 'Beida D 154'.

21 Abdurishid Yakup, 'Two Alliterative Uighur Poems from Dunhuang', *Linguistic Research*, 17-18 (Kyoto, 1999): p. 4.

22 Abdurishid Yakup, 'On the Interlinear Uyghur Poetry in the Newly Unearthed Nestorian Text', in Mehmet Ölmez and Simone-Christiane Raschmann (eds), *Splitter aus der Gegend von Turfan: Festschrift für Peter Zieme anläßlich seines 60. Geburtstages* (Istanbul, 2002), pp. 409-17.

23 Cf. Herbert Franke, 'A 14th Century Mongolian Letter Fragment', *Asia Major*, N.S., 11 (1965): pp. 120-27, at pp. 121-2.

24 Peter Zieme, 'Arabische und neupersische Wörter in den altuigurischen Texten von Turfan und Dunhuang', in Dieter Weber (ed.), *Languages of Iran: Past and Present, Iranian Studies in Memoriam David Neil MacKenzie* (Wiesbaden, 2005), pp. 285-95.

25 Peter Zieme, 'Türkische Zuckungsbücher', in Ingeborg Hauenschild et al. (eds), *Scripta Ottomanica et Res Altaicae: Festschrift Barbara Kellner-Heinkele* (Wiesbaden, 2002), pp. 379-95.

know, for example, that in Bešbalık north of the Tianshan Muslim people were already in high positions strong enough to take over the supremacy.[26]

There are also a few Mongol texts from Xaraxoto showing Muslim influence in the lexicon.[27] We also find among the Mongol texts from Turfan similar cases of Muslim names etc. A booklet of the thirteenth or fourteenth century from Turfan contains a mixture of Uyghur and Mongol texts. It includes the Mongol version of the Alexander romance, in which the Islamic influence is obvious in the name *Sulqarnay* = *Dhū 'l-Qarnayn* as Alexander's name. Volker Rybatzki, however, has seen Nestorian influence in this text: 'It is, however, interesting to note that several episodes of the "Cinggis qan romance", showing striking similarities with some of the themes of the apocalyptic works mentioned before, were reported by Carpini to have been told to him by Nestorian priests.'[28]

To summarize: while Islamic influence in the cultures of the Uyghurs can be seen only exceptionally until the time of Genghis Khan, it increased during the thirteenth and fourteenth centuries. During the Mongol period (Yuan Dynasty, 1260-1368) the Muslims thrived and established themselves as an important part of Chinese society. The records of the Yuan Dynasty include, for example, many biographies of distinguished Muslims who were employed by the Mongols.

The Islamization of the whole region from Kashghar to Dunhuang was a long process and cannot be treated here. I would, however, like to mention one point. In his article on the cult of the saints in Kashgharia, Hodong Kim has mentioned the manuscript *Tazkira-i Boghra Khān*, where it is said that 'he [i.e. Boghra Khān] went for the holy war toward the direction of Khitay and for one year, by the grace of God, he made (the inhabitants of) Turfan Muslim. However, since he became ill, he could not attack the Uighurs of Turfan and came back to Kashghar.'[29] While some scholars believe that this account should not be taken at face value, Kim has tried to find other sources which support it. First of all he mentions the *Dīvān lugāt-at-turk* where struggles between Muslims and the adjacent territories of the Uyghurs are mentioned, namely in Mıŋlaq. Kim refers to Karaev who concluded that these battles took place in the latter half of the tenth century. The region to which the Qarakhanid, who established in the tenth century the first Muslim-Turkic state between Kashghar and Balasaghun,

---

26 Peter Zieme, 'Ordo uluš, Solmı, and Bešbalık', *Acta Orientalia Academiae Scientiarum Hungaricae*, 62 (2009): pp. 255-66.

27 György Kara, 'Mediaeval Mongol Documents from Khara Khoto and East Turkestan in the St. Petersburg Branch of the Institute of Oriental Studies', *Manuscripta Orientalia*, 9/2 (2003): pp. 3-40.

28 Volker Rybatzki, 'Linguistic Particularities in the Middle Mongol Alexander Romance', in Desmond Durkin-Meisterernst (ed.), *Turfan Revisited: The First Century of Research into the Arts and Cultures of the Silk Road* (Berlin, 2004), pp. 294-6, p. 295a.

29 Kim Ho-dong, 'The Cult of Saints in Easter Turkestan. The Case of Alp Ata in Turfan', in *Proceedings of the 35th Permanent International Altaistic Conference* (Taipei, 1993), pp. 199-226, at p. 207.

came was Jungaria north of the Turfan oasis. Kim writes: 'Therefore, the story in TBK [i.e. *Tazkira-i Boghra Khan*] cannot be simply regarded as being fabricated or unreliable.'[30] Then he examines the person Alp Ata, who was the successor of Satok Bugra Han (apparently a person in Muslim hagiography) and concludes: 'Alp Ata as a historical figure was a Muslim warrior who led Qarakhanid raids against the Buddhist Uighurs of Turfan in the latter half of the tenth century, but was killed at a battle and buried at Astana.'[31] On the other hand, Omeljan Pritsak had earlier expressed his doubts, because 'Satok Bugra Han' never occurs as a historical person.[32] And Akira Haneda followed him.[33]

NESTORIANISM OR THE CHURCH OF THE EAST

In our context Christianity cannot be left unmentioned, since it reached China and Tibet via Central Asia. The topic has been explored in many publications and conferences, but some questions remain. New material has come to light through investigation into Zayton, that is, Quanzhou.[34] Xaraxoto's treasures have not yet been fully investigated.[35] And even in Turfan itself, the Museum of Turfan is carrying out new excavations into the Christian settlements nearby: namely, Bulayık and Kurutka. Thus, we can expect that some new details may be discovered during this ongoing research in Xinjiang and elsewhere. On the other hand, much has been well worked on and is well-known, among them the religious attitudes of the Mongol Khans, their relation to the Pope and to other Christian representatives who came to China or were sent to the Near East and the influence of the Christian wives of Mongol Emperors.

A work written in Acemi Turkish reports for 1494 that an embassy reached the city of Turfan where they found most of the inhabitants to be infidels worshipping the cross.[36] More than two hundred years earlier, European travellers and merchants had mentioned Christians in many ways. Included among these were Piano Carpini in 1245-47, Rubruk in 1254 and Marco Polo in

---

30 Kim, 'The Cult of Saints in Easter Turkestan', p. 207.

31 Kim, 'The Cult of Saints in Easter Turkestan', p. 209.

32 Omeljan Pritsak, 'Karahanidische Streitfragen 1-4', *Oriens*, 3 (1950): pp. 209-28, at p. 217.

33 Akira Haneda, 'Problems of the Turkicization, Problems of the Islamization', *Acta Asiatica. Bulletin of the Institute of Eastern Culture*, 34 (1978): pp. 1-21, at pp. 17-18.

34 Lance Eccles, Majella Franzmann and Samuel Lieu, 'Observations on Select Christian Inscriptions in the Syriac Script from Zayton', in Iain Gardner, Samuel Lieu and Ken Parry (eds), *From Palmyra to Zayton: Epigraphy and Iconography* (Turnhout, 2005), pp. 247-78.

35 Recently, new results were published in Yoshida Jun'ichi and Chimeddorji, *Study on the Mongolian Documents Found at Qaraqota* (Tokyo, 2008).

36 Ildikó Bellér-Hann, *A History of Cathay: A Translation and Linguistic Analysis of a Fifteenth-Century Turkic Manuscript* (Bloomington, 1995).

1271-95.[37] Marco Polo mentions for all the places he visited on his journey the religious affinity of their inhabitants: for example in Kashghar Muslims and Nestorian Christians, in Yarkand mostly Muslims and some Nestorian Christians, in Khotan, Peyn, Ciracian and Lop only Muslims, in Shazhou Buddhists, some Nestorian Christians and some Muslims.

Religious tolerance in the Mongol Empire was maintained by their rulers due to the imperial theory that power was given as a mandate by Heaven. Thus all other religions, whatever they are, are only means to maintain this power. Regarding the attitudes of Mongol rulers to the related problem of conversion, Timothy May concludes that one of the reasons against conversion was their belief that they were ordained 'by the heavens'; another reason was their tolerance.[38]

UYGHURS AND TIBET

As Herbert Franke, János Szerb and many others have explored in detail in their works, the relationship between Tibetan Buddhism and Mongol Buddhism became very strong when Qubilai ascended the throne and mutual interest grew. What is of interest here is whether or how far this development became obvious in Turfan. During the Yuan period, many Buddhist texts were translated from Tibetan into Uyghur. This was a consequence of the growing influence of 'Phags pa and other Tibetan priests under Qubilai's rule. While the known translations and their colophons have already been discussed in other publications, mention needs to be made of an interesting sheet from Xaraxoto (G 120 verso), recently edited by György Kara. The sheet contains in one corner a Uyghur colophon stating that a work called *Lam-bras* = Skt. *Mārgaphala* ('Way and Fruit') was translated from Tibetan into Uyghur by one or two persons (it is unclear whether the two names in the text refer to the same person) that bear Tibetan names, Bkra-shis and Rin chen.[39] Bearing a Tibetan name does not necessarily mean that the person is Tibetan – as mentioned before Uyghur kings, Idukkuts, also sometimes had Tibetan names.

Furthermore, it should be mentioned that new manuscripts were found in the Mogao Northern Grottoes, among which there are also some Buddhist works of Tibetan origin.[40] One manuscript, albeit badly preserved, contains biographies of Lamas similar to the Mahāsiddhas.[41]

---

[37] Peter Jackson, *The Mongols and the West: 1221-1410* (Harlow, 2005).

[38] Timothy May, 'Attitudes towards a Conversion among the Elite in the Mongol Empire, E-ASPAC', *The Electronic Journal of Asian Studies on the Pacific Coast* (2002-03).

[39] Kara, 'Mediaeval Mongol Documents', pp. 30-34.

[40] Abdurishid Yakup, 'Uighurica from the Northern Grottoes of Dunhuang', in *A Festschrift in Honour of Professor Masahiro Shōgaito's Retirement: Studies on Eurasian Languages* (Kyoto, 2006), pp. 1-41.

[41] Mogao B 77:24.

To render the geographical name Tibet, Uyghur texts always write 'twypwt' = *töpöt*, but in a Mongol text edited recently, the form *töpün* appears. This supports the theory of Louis Bazin and James Hamilton[42] about a relationship between *töpö(n)* and *töpöt*. In colophons to Buddhist works translated from Tibetan, the expression *töpöt tili* 'Tibetan language' is used. As already mentioned above, we have some remains of Tantric Buddhist scriptures that found their way to the Uyghurs either directly or sometimes more probably via the Mongol capital.

In the sphere of art or pictorial representation as well, we observe a growing influence from the Tibetan side starting in the thirteenth century, as mentioned above. Here, I would like to mention a Tibetan-influenced Buddhist grotto in Kurutka (near the city of Turfan) which has been described in detail by Albert Grünwedel. It should be restudied, but this may be difficult or impossible as the original place seems to have been totally destroyed.[43] Thus Grünwedel's book remains the most valuable source. The author identified grotto 9 as the most interesting one since it shows paintings of tantricists. The ceiling is decorated with *vajras*. Both side walls are painted in four strips. The strips are divided into blocks each 40 cm wide. Altogether there are 88 small fields. Small cartouches contain the names of the painted *bakhshis*, and Grünwedel was convinced that these are an illustration of the 84 Mahāsiddhas.[44] To give an example: the figure (Fig. 160; see Figure 8.1 here)[45] of the 49th Mahāsiddha is described as follows:

---

42 Louis Bazin and James Hamilton, 'L'origine du nom Tibet', in Ernst Steinkellner (ed.), *Tibetan History and Language: Studies Dedicated to Uray Géza on his Seventieth Birthday* (Vienna, 1991), pp. 9-28.

43 In a letter written in Turfan on 17 August 1906 (preserved in MAK, Berlin) Grünwedel reports about the cave of the 84 Siddhas he had described already in 1902: 'besuchte ich auch die Höhlen bei Turfan selbst: zwischen den Dörfern Qûrutqa, Bâghrâ und Bûlaryôq. Die dortige Höhlengruppe ist sehr merkwürdig: jung, uigurischer Lamaismus, die Höhle der 84 Siddha's hatte nicht gelitten. Ich liess die besten Bilder aussägen. Die Namen der Siddha's sind in uigurischer Schrift, aber tibetischer Sprache, auch sind überall Lama's abgebildet.'

44 Albert Grünwedel, *Bericht über archäologische Arbeiten in Idikutschahri und Umgebung im Winter 1902-1903* (Munich, 1905).

45 Grünwedel, *Bericht über archäologische Arbeiten*, p. 171 (to Fig. 160): 'Wenn ich den daneben in uigur. Schrift geschriebenen Namen 'Tšiluk-pa bakši' richtig gelesen habe, ist er mit dem Siddha Tsi-lu-ki der tibet. Liste identisch.' Grünwedel is thinking of Celukapa; cf. *Masters of Mahāmudrā: Songs and Histories of the Eighty-Four Buddhist Siddhas*, trans. and comm. Keith Dowman (New York, 1985), pp. 280-85. Unfortunately Grünwedel hesitated, as he writes (p. 170), to publish his readings of the Uyghur inscriptions. The new fragment B77:24 from the Northern Grottoes of Mogao contains a list of Mahāsiddhas, mentioning their names, attributes and deeds. The *mahāsiddha* *Čilukpa does not appear in this text. But the whole fragment, although difficult to read, is to be studied and edited to get a better knowledge of Uyghur Tantric Buddhism, cf. the information in Jinzhang Peng and Jianjun Wang, *Dunhuang Mogaoku beiqu shiku* [Northern Grottoes of Mogaoku, Dunbuang] (3 vols, Beijing, 2000-04), as well as in Yakup, 'Uighurica from the Northern Grottoes of Dunhuang', p. 4.

Number 49 is grey-brown. He stands on his right leg almost as if dancing. He holds up both arms. He points with the index fingers of both hands with palms upwards to his forehead. His left foot is completely turned upwards and the knee outwards; the sole also faces upwards and is supported in the elbow of the left arm.[46]

Figure 8.1 One of the 84 Mahāsiddhas, after Albert Grünwedel, *Bericht über archäologische Arbeiten in Idikutschahri und Umgebung im Winter 1902-1903* (Munich, 1905), p. 171, fig. 160.

As Grünwedel has already pointed out, the names and attributes of these Mahāsiddhas may be different from other Tibetan groups,[47] but for the study of Tibetan Buddhism beyond the Tibetan central areas these remains are of great value.

What an astonishing phenomenon. In one locality (Kurutka) we find Christian and Buddhist remains side by side and probably even at the same time, all shortly before the advent of Islam.

The aim of my essay is not to give a general survey of all the questions raised here, but rather to present some insights into historical documents, mainly of the Uyghurs, discovered or investigated recently. I hope these will be taken into consideration in future research.

46 Grünwedel, *Bericht über archäologische Arbeiten*, p. 169.

47 Grünwedel, *Bericht über archäologische Arbeiten*, p. 170.

Chapter 9
Tibetans, Mongols and the Fusion of Eurasian Cultures[1]

Paul D. Buell

BACKGROUND

The establishment of the Mongolian Empire (1206-59) inaugurated an unprecedented era of new cultural exchanges within Eurasia and considerably enhanced those already taking place. At one level, this meant the physical movement of people and cultural goods from one end of Asia to the other and beyond. This included far-distant places such as the African kingdom of Mali and its neighbours, featured in detail in the geography of Mongol China.[2] At another, the Mongol era (until 1368 in China) was particularly noteworthy for its many attempts to create culturally mixed institutions that offered something for everyone.[3] These generally offered the most for the Mongols themselves who were able to use such mixed institutions to avoid getting too close to any of the conquered peoples. Willing collaborators in all of this, sometimes playing a very active role, were representatives of a variety of peoples hailing from almost

---

[1] Sections of this article are based upon my unpublished master's thesis, 'Some Aspects of the Origin and Development of the Religious Institutions of the Early Yüan Period' (University of Washington, 1968). I would like to thank the National Endowment for the Humanities for an individual fellowship permitting my continued work on 'Muslim' (*huihui* 回回) medicine in China and supporting the present research. Thanks also to Dan Martin and Olaf Czaja for detailed assistance in resolving some of the technical issues of the article and for bibliographical suggestions, and also to Gene Anderson and my wife Ngan Le for their more generalized discussion and proofing, and to the late T.V. Wylie, with whom I read the primary Tibetan source material used in this study, and who first introduced me to the serious study of Tibetan history, including its Sakya period. Needless to say, any errors or misconceptions are strictly my own.

[2] On the rich geographical knowledge of the Mongol period see, as an introduction, Walter Fuchs, *The 'Mongol Atlas' of China by Chu Ssu-Pen, and the Kuang Yü Thu* (Peiping, 1946).

[3] How this worked out in terms of the political institutions of the central government where a Chinese outward structure often hid an underlying Mongolian reality is discussed in detail in my unpublished doctoral dissertation. See Paul D. Buell, 'Tribe, Qan and Ulus in Early Mongol China: Some Prolegomena to Yüan History' (doctoral dissertation, University of Washington, 1977).

anywhere the Mongols touched, even points as far removed as Syria and Nepal. Among them no groups were as important for the Mongols as the various Turkic peoples serving them, particularly the Uyghurs and other Turkic-speakers of China. One of these, Rabban Sauma (fl. late thirteenth century), travelled as far as Europe in Mongol service,[4] while others played important roles as administrators and cultural intermediaries throughout the Mongolian Empire and during the times of its successor states.[5] Also key Mongol collaborators, nearly as widespread as the Turks geographically but far fewer on the ground, were Tibetans.[6]

The Mongols encountered Tibetan missionaries almost as soon as they began to penetrate outside of Mongolia, and these same missionaries, who had come at first to convert and serve others, for example Tanguts and others living in the then Xixia 西夏 Kingdom, quickly moved on to a whole new field of religious conversion, the Mongols themselves, conquerors of Xixia. Their efforts proved most successful among the Mongols of East Asia, whom they successfully enlisted, in a process taking several centuries, to the cause of Lamaism, but they were by no means inactive among other groups of Mongols as well, prior to the definitive conversion to Islam among the Mongols of the West. Iranian sources, for example, frequently mention Tibetan *bakhshī*, a term also meaning shaman.[7] Tibetans were also advisers to Mongol princes and potentates, among them Prince Qubilai (1215-94) who made a point of collecting the brightest and best

[4] On this interesting personage see Morris Rossabi, *Voyager from Xanadu: Rabban Sauma and the First Journey from China to the West* (Tokyo, 1992).

[5] For one major figure see Paul D. Buell, 'Chinqai (1169-1252): Architect of Mongolian Empire', in Edward H. Kaplan and Donald W. Whisenhunt (eds), *Opuscula Altaica: Essays Presented in Honor of Henry Schwarz* (Bellingham, 1994), pp. 168-86. On the key Turkic Önggüd of Inner Mongolia, who, as I argue, may have been Chinqai's own people and who were not only aware of steppe politics but played active roles in it, see Paul D. Buell, 'The Role of the Sino-Mongolian Frontier Zone in the Rise of Cinggis-qan', in Henry G. Schwarz (ed.), *Studies on Mongolia: Proceedings of the First North American Conference on Mongolian Studies* (Bellingham, 1979), pp. 63-76. On early contacts between the Islamic world, including its Turks, and the early Mongols in general see Morris Rossabi, 'Muslims in the Yüan Dynasty', in John Langlois (ed.), *China under Mongol Rule* (Princeton, 1981), pp. 257-95, and Xiao Qiqing 蕭啟慶, *Xiyuren yu Yuanchu zhengzhi* 西域人與元初政治 (Taibei 台北, 1966).

[6] For the purposes of this article, 'Tibetans' refers to all Tibetan-speaking peoples, resident in Tibet and elsewhere and those assimilated to Tibetan culture, including such persons living in and about Tangut domains.

[7] There is no full study of this topic, perhaps because the groups and individuals involved are barely noticed in Tibetan and Western sources, in large part because of the fact that the mission failed among the western Mongols of the time, by contrast to those of Mongolia and China. See Leonard van der Kuijp, 'Bagsi and Bagsi-s in Tibetan Historical, Biographical and Lexicographical Texts', *Central Asiatic Journal*, 39/2 (1995): pp. 275-302, and Nikolaus Pallisen, *Die alte Religion des mongolischen Volkes während der Herrschaft der Tschingisiden* (Posieux, 1953), which has a great deal on Iran and Tibetans there in passing.

in his personal brain trust. It later stood him in good stead when he sought to become the supreme Khan of the Mongolian world in succession to this brother Möngke (reg. 1251-59) in the face of considerable opposition.[8] Tibetans even held government posts. In Mongol China they were most commonly (though not exclusively) special religious officers.[9]

Tibetans were important in the Mongol Empire and in its successor states for two reasons. One was their religion, a sophisticated Tantraism that appealed to many. It ultimately became the dominant religion in Mongolia. Here it closely allied itself with, but ultimately largely replaced, similar native Mongol shamanic traditions. Scarcely less important was the role of Tibetans as cultural intermediaries and messengers. This occurred, above all, in the area of specialized Buddhist knowledge. Artistic conventions were very important in China, for example, but the Tibet of the time was also a repository of Indian and non-Indian knowledge of every sort. This included medical lore.[10] Some was Indian,[11] to be sure, but also important among the Tibetans of the time were the Eurasian medical traditions known in China later as 'Muslim' medicine[12] –

---

8 Among those present in Qubilai's entourage at the time, in addition to several Tibetans as will be seen below, was the Syrian physician Isa or Jesü (Aixie 愛薛), the effective founder of Mongol China's 'Muslim' medicine institutions. See Tu-chien Weng, 'Ai-hsieh: A Study of his Life' (doctoral thesis, Harvard University, 1938). I am grateful to Igor de Rachewiltz for discussing his own research on Isa with me and for supplying me with a copy of Weng's dissertation.

9 On Tibet's Sakya period, which was roughly equivalent to China's Mongol Yuan Dynasty, see Luciano Petech, *Central Tibet and the Mongols: The Yüan — Sa-Skya Period in Tibetan History* (Rome, 1990), and on Tibetans in Mongol China from the perspective of Chinese sources see also Herbert Franke, 'Tibetans in Yūan China', in Langlois (ed.), *China under Mongol Rule*, pp. 296-328.

10 On Tibetan medicine see, as an introduction, Fernand Meyer, *Gso-ba rig-pa: Le système medical tibétain* (Paris, 1981). For an accessible overview of Tibetan medicine along with other related Asian systems, see Jan van Alphen and Anthony Aris (eds), *Oriental Medicine: An Illustrated Guide to the Asian Arts of Healing* (London, 1995). See also the article by Dan Martin in this volume.

11 Strictly speaking, Tibetan medicine is not purely Ayurvedic and freely mixes native, Indian, Chinese and Western traditions to produce its own unique practice as reflected in the recently most important Tibetan medical text, the *rGyud-bzhi*, the 'Four Treatises'. This text is claimed to be Indian, although the Indian original has ever been found and probably never existed. As an introduction to this key text see Yuri Parfionovitch, Gyurme Dorje and Fernand Meyer (eds), *Tibetan Medical Paintings: Illustrations to the Blue Beryl Treatise of Sangye Gyamtso (1653-1705)* (London, 1992). For a translation of the first two tantras, see Barry Clark (trans.), *The Quintessence Tantras of Tibetan Medicine* (Ithaca, 1995). On Indian medicine in India see, as an introduction, Dominik Wujastyk, *The Roots of Ayurveda* (London, 1998).

12 Tibetan medical histories discussed by Martin in this volume mention important medical works by doctors of a number of nationalities, not just Indian, but also Tazig, or Persian (*sTag-gZig* or *Ta-zig-gi Lugs*), Uyghur (*Hor-gyi Lugs*), Tangut (*Mi-nyag-gi Lugs*),

although, strictly speaking, this term is somewhat of a misnomer. The medicine involved was Greek and came via the Near East, long before the Arabs played a role in world history. It was actively propagated by non-Muslims as well as Muslims. By Mongol times the primary language of the medical texts involved was Arabic, the common language. Persian was also important, including in Mongol China where it was one of the working languages of administration. The emergence of this literature had followed an unprecedented effort to translate and adapt other people's medicines, usually from Greek to Syriac and thence to Arabic and Persian.[13]

For the Mongolian world of the thirteenth and fourteenth centuries this 'Muslim' medicine became the mainstream, both in the Mongol east and in the west, but particularly in China. There it briefly superseded Chinese medicine in importance, at least at the court level. Its sources were many, among them Arabic texts, some Persian, some apparently Turkic, some Syriac. I will suggest that Tibetans played an important role in interpreting, since their own medicine involved some of the same mixes as the cosmopolitan 'Muslim' medicine of Mongol China. This included a Greek and even a Turkic tradition from the Uyghurs, whose doctors were so important in Mongol China. Greek medicine and even Turkic tradition was the domain of a special Tibetan lineage, the Bi-ci, from a word in Persian for doctor, although the originator of the line was probably a Byzantine (see below and Dan Martin's article in this volume). Though not spelled out in our sources, Tibetans may have been partially responsible for creating the kind of cultural construct freely mixing traditions and amalgamating them that 'Muslim' medicine became in China. As with other institutions of the period, there was indeed in the final medical product a little something for everyone. Tibetans certainly played a similar role in creating the mixed religious institutions of the dynasty. Tibetans at the time, in any case, were good at synthesizing varied, disparate and even seemingly contradictory traditions.

Khotanese (*Li'i Lugs*) and Phrom, Romano-Byzantine (*Khrom-gyi Lugs*). This is a remarkable profusion of influences. Among westerners quoted by the Tibetans was Galen, according to the Greek and not the expected Arabic spelling of his name. See Christopher Beckwith, 'The Introduction of Greek Medicine into Tibet in the Seventh and Eighth Centuries', *Journal of the American Oriental Society*, 99 (1979): pp. 297-313. See also Ronit Yoeli-Tlalim, 'On Urine Analysis and Tibetan Medicine's Connections with the West', in Sienna Craig et al. (eds), *Studies of Medical Pluralism in Tibetan History and Society* (Halle, 2011), pp. 195-211. On another Greek doctor associated with Tibet, Basileos, see Martin in this volume.

13 For a survey of mainstream 'Islamic' medicine see Manfred Ullmann, *Islamic Medicine* (Edinburgh, 1978), and Peter E. Pormann and Emilie Savage-Smith, *Medieval Islamic Medicine* (Edinburgh, 2007). For its Greek background see, as a brief overview, 'Medicine', in Simon Hornblower and Antony Spawforth (eds), *The Oxford Classical Dictionary* (Oxford, ^{3}1996), pp. 945-9.

PRE-MONGOL TIBET AND ITS EXTERNAL INFLUENCE AND MISSIONARIES

The cultural influence exerted by Tibetans in the Mongol world was uniquely associated with the character of Tibet of the twelfth and thirteenth centuries, when they first came into contact with the Mongols in important ways. During that time, Tibet was involved in a great renaissance of its culture. Late Indian Buddhism flooded over it. Competing clans seized on aspects of Buddhist teaching to assert their own independence and carve out political and economic power.[14] Knowledge, particularly Buddhist knowledge, was the key. Increasingly significant were various focuses of purely secular knowledge, including medicine which became particularly important among the Sakya (Sa-skya), a school of Tibetan Buddhism, who ultimately took the lead in contacting the Mongols.[15] As Dan Martin has shown in his contribution to the present volume, this medicine was quite complex. It was not just Indian, despite the importance of an Indian base, but uniquely a Tibetan synthesis.

To expand political and cultural influence, in part to shore up positions at home, some Tibetan groups not only engaged in an internal colonization by founding subordinate monasteries but also sent missionaries abroad. A particular target was Buddhist Mi-nyag, a term referring to Tangut settlements situated in and about the kingdom of Xixia in northwest China.[16] Here Tibetans and Mongols first came into direct contact. Mongol relations with Xixia began around 1205 with raids and culminated in 1227 in the complete conquest of the Tangut state. It never again re-emerged as a political entity, though the Tanguts did survive as a cultural entity for some time after the conquest. They continued to use their complex written language based upon Chinese but not using characters directly recognizable as such to any Chinese.

According to dPa'-bo gTsug-lag 'Phreng-ba, a sixteenth-century Tibetan historian who is unusually well-informed about events in the Mongolian empire, the first Tibetan missionary to come into direct contact with the Mongols was gTsang-pa Dung-khur (gTsang-pa Dung-khur-ba dBang-phyug bKra-shis).[17] He was from the mTshal-pa monastic domain. This domain, with Sakya and 'Bri-khung, was one of the then three dominant temporal and religious authorities in a divided Tibet, each sect controlling its own mini-state. Sometime during the latter part of the reign of Genghis Khan (reg. 1206-27), probably in 1221 or 1222,[18] gTsang-pa Dung-khur went to Mongolia along with six of his disciples, where he was employed as a shepherd by the local Mongolian 'yurt dwellers', suggesting

---

14 See Ronald M. Davidson, *Tibetan Renaissance: Tantric Buddhism in the Rebirth of Tibetan Culture* (New York, 2005).

15 Davidson, *Tibetan Renaissance*, p. 380.

16 Davidson, *Tibetan Renaissance*, pp. 323-4, 333-4, 448-9.

17 I am indebted to Dan Martin for help with this and other names.

18 Petech, *Central Tibet and the Mongols*, p. 6, gives dates of 1209-10, or perhaps 1215, but I am not sure on what basis.

that he may have been a captive. He may have been taken in a Mongolian raid on the Tangut border zone where he was almost certainly resident prior to contact with the Mongols.

The lama was able to impress the locals through his apparent control over the weather after a hail-storm and flash-flood. Other sheep were lost, but his emerged unscathed. At the time, weather magic was a major focus of native Mongolian religious figures; the Tibetan no doubt took advantage of this useful tradition.[19] Later the mTshal-pa lama had to leave Mongolia, after being slandered by representatives of other religious groups (including Taoists). This must have been towards the end of the reign of Genghis Khan when the Mongols began favouring the Taoists of the north Chinese Quanzhen 全真 sect. The lama took up residence in Xixia, in Tangut domains, probably for a second time, and there he met Genghis Khan when Mongol armies conquered the area in 1227. The Tibetan lama impressed Genghis with his religious power and cured an illness of one of the Khan's ministers, pointing up a connection between medical treatment and religious influence that was to persist in Mongol and Tibetan contacts. As a result of the lama's influence with the Mongol ruling house, the mTshal-pa were able to increase their apparent influence within the former Tangut domains and help restore its endangered Buddhism. Later gTsang-pa Dung-khur established a connection with Ögödei (reg. 1229-43), and a prince of the rival line descended from Tolui-noyon, Qubilai.[20]

At this point, Mongol–Tibetan connections were focused on the periphery of the Tibetan cultural sphere,[21] primarily in the former Tangut domains, and in nearby areas of China, but this was to change as Mongolian expansion continued. At the time, Tibet had no central government and none of its various monastic states and tribal groups had any real supremacy over the other. Each competed against the other to the extent of its power, even waging war in one well-known case when 'Bri-khung was destroyed at the end of the thirteenth century. Its anarchy aside, Tibet was well off the main trade routes, comparatively remote and not strategically important. It was initially neglected by the Mongols. China offered much better pickings than the austere monastic communities and other political authorities of Tibet: not much plunder there and what there was, was scattered across a geographically enormous expanse.

TIBETAN–MONGOL RELATIONS EXPAND

What changed the situation, and brought Mongols and Tibetans into closer contact was Mongolian penetration of what are now the Sino-Tibetan

19 See Buell, 'Some Aspects of the Origin and Development', pp. 19-20.

20 dPa'-bo gTsug-lag 'Phreng-ba, *mKhas-pa'i dGa'-ston*, ed. Lokesh Chandra, Shata-piṭaka 9 (1-3) (3 vols, New Delhi, 1959-61), p. 792.

21 On what did and did not constitute Tibet at the time see the discussion in Franke, 'Tibetans in Yūan China'.

borderlands. This came about at first to outflank the Jin 金 Dynasty (1125-1234), the Mongols' main enemy in the north, and then to attack Southern Song (1125-1279), in part through an indirect movement into the mountains of west and southwest China. In this connection, there seem to have been a series of major raids on outlying Tibet by Mongolian armies during the years 1238 to 1240, all limited in geographical extent, but alarming the Tibetans.[22]

In 1244, a Mongol ultimatum to Tibet followed. According to Tibetan sources, this ultimatum was in the form of a summons to the abbot of Sakya, Kun-dga' rGyal-mtshan (1182-1251), also known as the Sakya Paṇḍita, probably the most learned and famous lama of his day. The one making the summons was prince Köten (1205-51), charged by his brother Ögödei with taking charge of Kokonor and surrounding areas, including Tibet. He is said to have written the following to the Tibetan prelate:

> This is our order. These are words to be transmitted to the fine and glorious Kun-dga' rGyal-mtshan, the Sakya Paṇḍita. In order to repay the kindness of my parents, I have need of a chaplain. Having made inquiry, you came into my mind as suitable. Since you, the honored lord, are desirable of increasing the happiness and advantage of dharma-beings, you must not be shrinking from the difficulties of the road. If you say that you are old or sick, then do you not remember how formerly the Buddha gave himself on behalf of living beings in innumerable lives? If you do not come, then I will appoint the great hosts of a powerful army, and if I do harm to many sentient beings, then will you not be afraid?[23]

Sakya Paṇḍita came, our sources go on, but took three years on the road.[24] He finally arrived in 1247, after a Mongol interregnum had ended and a new Khan, Güyük (reg. 1246-47), the son of Ögödei, had been elected. Once with the Mongol prince, Sakya Paṇḍita is said to have cured him of a serious disease, although the

22 See 'Gos lo-tsā-ba gZhon-nu-dpal, *The Blue Annals*, trans. George Roerich (2 vols, Calcutta, 1949), vol. 2, p. 577, Ngag-dbang Blo-bzang rGya-mtsho, *rDzogs-ldan gZhon-nu'i dGa'-ston*, xylograph, volume dza (19) of the author's complete works, 52b; *mKhas-pa'i dGa'-ston*, vol. 3, p. 792. See also Turrell Verl Wylie, 'The First Mongol Conquest of Tibet Reinterpreted', *Harvard Journal of Asiatic Studies*, 37 (1977): pp. 103-33.

23 'Jigs-med Rig-pa'i rDo-rje, *Geschichte des Buddhism in der Mongolei*, ed. and trans. Georg Huth (2 vols, Strassburg, 1892-97), I, pp. 81-2 (Tibetan), II, pp. 130-31 (German); my translation from the Tibetan. A slightly different Sakya version of the letter from another source is quoted in T.W.D. Shakabpa, *Tibet: A Political History* (New Haven, 1967), pp. 61-2. Quite likely this letter has been piously doctored, but the opening and closing passages appear genuine and are entirely in accord with the Mongolian practice of the time. See also Dieter Schuh, *Erlasse und Sendschreiben mongolischer Herrscher für tibetische Geistliche* (St. Augustin, 1977).

24 mTshal-pa Kun-dga' rDo-rje, *Deb-ther dMar-po* (Gangtok, 1961), p. 42.

nature of the disease is not stated and the whole episode may be pious legend.[25] To be sure, Sakya Paṇḍita was celebrated for his medical knowledge, but there is no evidence that he was actually a practising physician, although he may have had physicians in his entourage.[26] On the other hand, if we may credit the Persian historian Juwaynī (1226-83), Köten may have believed that any illness he had was due more to witchcraft than to any strictly physiological cause.[27] Köten was, in any case, happy with his relationship with the Tibetan prelate. Sakya Paṇḍita seems to have had the good sense to secure the submission of other Tibetan powers: for example, 'Bri-khung, while on his way to the prince's court.[28] As a result, according to the Tibetan sources, Köten made Sakya Paṇḍita effectively his viceroy in Tibet, accepting submission and a local representative as an alternative to having to mount raids and direct invasion, a pattern that was to persist with Tibet never directly occupied by the Mongols, although the paraphernalia of Mongol rule, even if administered by Tibetans, were still obvious.[29]

Thus began more than a century of interaction between the steppe conquerors and the Sakya, who eventually used their position with the Mongols to dominate Tibet. Though both Köten and Sakya Paṇḍita soon died, the former in 1251, the latter perhaps a year or so later, their basic relationship was continued by other Sakya prelates and other Mongols, most notably by Sakya Paṇḍita's nephew 'Phags-pa (1235-80) and by Prince Qubilai, to whom the Sakya, willing

---

[25] dPa'-bo gTsug-lag 'Phreng-ba, *mKhas-pa'i dGa'-ston*, vol. 3, pp. 760-61, says that Sakya Paṇḍita was specifically summoned to cure the illness of the Mongol prince. See also pp. 794-5, where a shamanic illness is suggested.

[26] I am indebted to Olaf Czaja for this suggestion. I hope to explore this aspect of the Tibetan mission to the Mongols in more detail in a future publication.

[27] ʿAlāʾ al-Dīn ʿAṭā-Malik Juwaynī, *The History of the World Conqueror*, trans. John Andrew Boyle (2 vols, Manchester, 1958), vol. 1, pp. 245 and 251. Juwaynī implies in the first of the two passages that Köten died while Güyük was still Khan (i.e., in 1248 or before) but later has him among those greeting the election of Möngke at the time of his coronation. See *The History of the World Conqueror*, vol. 2, p. 568.

[28] dPa'-bo gTsug-lag 'Phreng-ba, *mKhas-pa'i dGa'-ston*, vol. 3, pp. 761 and 794. 'Bri-khung was located directly north of what is now Lhasa, on the main trade route leading into central Asia. See also Giuseppe Tucci, *Tibetan Painted Scrolls* (3 vols, Rome, 1949), vol. 1, pp. 8-9 and 19; Alfonsa Ferrari, *Mk'yen-brtse's Guide to the Holy Places of Central Tibet*, ed. Luciano Petech and Hugh Richardson (Rome, 1958), pp. 111-12.

[29] See the letter attributed to Sakya Paṇḍita quoted by Tucci in *Tibetan Painted Scrolls*, vol. 1, p. 11. This organization included the structuring of Tibet into chiliarchies and myriarchies, in the best Mongol style. On the myriarchies see Turrell Verl Wylie, *The Geography of Tibet according to the 'Dzam-Gling-Rgyas-Bshad* (doctoral thesis, University of Washington, 1958), p. 147. Within the Mongol empire, Tibet was most similar to Korea where the king and his court literally constituted the government of the Mongol province of Korea. On Mongol governmental practices in general see Buell, 'Tribe, Qan and Ulus in Early Mongol China'.

or unwilling, transferred his allegiance.[30] At the time of his death, Sakya Paṇḍita assigned his religious authority to ’Phags-pa. His other nephew, Phyag-na (1239-67), also with him at the court of Prince Köten, received secular authority over the home monastery. This pattern of split authority was standard for the ruling ’Khon family. It provided for a blood succession while the religious chief of the monastery, in theory at least, remained celibate.

The subsequent history of ’Phags-pa’s relations with Qubilai has been described elsewhere.[31] Qubilai first made ’Phags-pa his princely chaplain. Later, when Qubilai became ruler of the Mongol successor qanate of China, ’Phags-pa became his official chief of religion. Also described elsewhere are the overall religious interactions of Tibetans with the Mongols and others during the entire period in question (the Sakya and mTshal-pa were by no means the only groups represented).[32] Of more interest, beyond the conversion of the ruling house to Tibetan Buddhism or the resulting dominance of the Sakya within the religious establishment of Mongol China, are the contributions of Tibetans to the remarkable cultural mix of the Mongol era in China. One key part of this were Mongol China’s religious institutions. Another, and the focus of what follows, was the Tibetan contribution to the medicine of the times. Although this was in theory ‘Islamic’, the actual base of practice was a good deal more complex. Mongol China’s ‘Islamic’ medicine was as much a culturally mixed institution as were its political institutions and imperial religious structure.

As I have shown in earlier research, the religious institutions of Mongol China were not purely Tibetan. They constituted a response to the need to propagate and institutionalize Buddhism, but also they met the specific requirements of the Mongols with their strongly shamanic traditions and established conceptions about what was the religious realm and the religious man. I argue, for example, that the Tibetan lama in many ways replaced and complemented the Mongolian shaman and that the whole idea of having a chief lama as a religious head for the whole had old Mongol roots. The idea of a chief shaman, or chief shamans, was

---

30 According to the *Deb-ther dMar-po* (p. 43), which suggests force:

> Later, when Prince Qubilai was dwelling at lu-pe’i-shan, he was pleased at meeting Prince Mong-gor of Kökenuur and the lama ’Phags-pa traveling together. After the prince had sent one circle of one hundred Mongolian riders to the Kökenuur people, he got the Sakya man.

Mong-gor was the son of Köten. The place is unidentified. The Chinese sources say nothing of the military escort. See Nianchang 念常, *Fozu lidai tongzai* 佛祖歷代通載, Taishō daizōkyō 大正大藏經, 49, 725c.

31 See, as an introduction, Franke, ‘Tibetans in Yūan China’, although this is written entirely from the Chinese side, and Buell, ‘Some Aspects of the Origin and Development’.

32 dPa’-bo gTsug-lag ’Phreng-ba notes eleven different groups present at Möngke’s court (*mKhas-pa’i dGa’-ston*, vol. 3, p. 794). Tibetans were present at princely courts as well by this time.

well established among the early Mongols, and Tibetan lamas even participated in shamanic rituals on occasion.[33]

But the religious institutions of Mongol China were not just a reflection of an accommodation between Tibetan and shamanic traditions. They were also part and parcel of a Chinese structure of a 'Chinese' dynasty, but one with little that was actually Chinese about it except for its overall form and nomenclature, and had a non-Chinese reality behind it. This was true for nearly all of the institutions of the central government. Governmental structures existed behind other governmental structures, usually in sets, one Mongolian, the other Chinese, with the Mongolian dominant.[34]

MEDICINE

Mongol-era medicine exhibited a similar pattern, although most of the institutions involved were informal. Mongol China's 'Islamic' medicine[35] was a free combination of Chinese and non-Chinese elements and systems. It was humoral in base. It was Persian and Arabic in much of its nomenclature, as well as in the majority of *materia medica* and *dietetica* called for. But texts freely mix theoretical systems and ideas. As might be expected in Chinese-language documents, there is evidence of a pervasive Sinification of key ideas and approaches to medicine and healing. For example, the term *qi* 氣 is often applied in a purely Chinese way and the body is, more often than not, seen in Chinese terms. The terminology of disease borrows Chinese ideas freely, even when translating those from another system, in its use of the Chinese term wind (*feng* 風) as a pathological agent, for example. Nonetheless, there is clearly more than one cosmopolitan tradition at work, not just Middle Eastern or Chinese, and in the case of the Middle Eastern sides of the texts, there is a strong likelihood of Syrian Christian transmission of many of the ideas involved. Certainly the one physician participating in the system whose work is best known to use, Isa, was a Nestorian and did come from Syria. In fact, the formal 'Islamic'

---

33 See the detailed discussion in Buell, 'Some Aspects of the Origin and Development', and its summary of native Mongolian religious institutions and officers.

34 See Buell, 'Tribe, Qan and Ulus in Early Mongol China'. For another, non-institutional example, see the mixed court foodways based on similar principles discussed in Paul D. Buell, Eugene N. Anderson and Charles Perry, *A Soup for the Qan: Chinese Dietary Medicine of the Mongol Era as Seen in Hu Szu-hui's Yin-shan Cheng-yao,* second revised and expanded edition (Leiden and Boston, 2010).

35 The formal 'Muslim' medical institutions of Mongol China principally included the Guanghui si 廣惠司, 'Administration of Broad Compassion', charged with 'preparing and presenting "Muslim" drugs and preparations to the emperor in order to treat members of the bodyguard and poor people in the capital' (*Yuanshi* 元史, 'History of the Yuan Dynasty', Zhonghua shuju 中華書局, 1976, 88, 2221). This was part of the Xuanhui yuan 宣徽院, 'Bureau for Imperial Household Provisions', the new Chinese agency providing a cover for the old imperial bodyguard. See Buell, Anderson and Perry, *Soup for the Qan*, 2nd ed., pp. 24-5.

medical institutions of Mongol China appear, in many ways, to have started out as his private family practice under official Mongol patronage.[36]

But what of possible Tibetan influence? Did Tibetans in any way help transmit 'Islamic' medicine, or their brand of it, to China? Also, what role did Tibetans play in the reintroduction of Indian, Ayurvedic traditions to China and to the Mongols? Ayurvedic medicine already had a long history in China, particularly during the period of disunity and Tang times. It was even taught in local medical schools.[37] It seems to have gained renewed importance in Mongol times. Tibetans were the most likely agents of its renewed spread since Tibetans were present in some numbers in Mongol China and contacts with the Indian world, not conquered by the Mongols and no longer predominantly Buddhist, were only of minor importance for East Asia in Mongol times. Thereby the process whereby a mixed Tibetan medicine became the dominant medicine in Mongolia began. The influence of Tibetan medicine, in fact, has persisted into the present. The Mongolian variants of Tibetan medicine are currently undergoing a revival, both in the Mongolian People's Republic and among the Buriyats of Russian Siberia.[38] Bonding between medical traditions producing the Mongolian medicine of the present day seems to have already begun in the thirteenth century if we may judge from the specific mix of medical traditions in the *Huihui yaofang* 回回藥方, 'Muslims Medicinal Recipes' (*HHYF*)[39] to be discussed below, Tibetans may have been active agents and influences in this development, then as they certainly were later. The *Huihui yaofang* is one of two main sources detailing the medical mix and establishment of Mongol China, the environment out of which the present situation has developed with much evolution. It is a manuscript, in its present form from the early Ming 明 (1368-1644) Dynasty, the surviving fragments (484 pages) of what once was a great encyclopaedia of perhaps 3,200 dense pages. The other is the imperial dietary manual of Mongol China, the *Yinshan zhengyao*

---

36 See the early life of Isa as described in Weng, *Ai-hsieh*. Note that Isa returned, as an ambassador to the Mongolian West under Qubilai and is likely to have been involved in the physical movement of medical materials from East to West and possibly West to East. In China, Isa was a major figure of great political influence under two reigns while enjoying a special position during his time in Iran as Qubilai's envoy.

37 See now Chen Ming 陳明, *Shufang yiyao, Chutu wenshu yu xiyu yixue* 殊方異藥, 出土文書與西域醫學 (Beijing, 2005), an excellent survey based upon Dunhuang 敦煌 materials.

38 On Buriyat medicine see Natalia Bolsokhoyeva, 'Tibetan Medical Schools of the Aga Area (Chita Region)', *Asian Medicine: Tradition and Modernity*, 3/2 (2007): pp. 334-46.

39 S.Y. Kong 江潤祥 et al., *Huihui yaofang* 回回藥方 (Hong Kong, 1996). On the *HHYF* see Paul D. Buell, 'How Did Persian and Other Western Medical Knowledge Move East, and Chinese West? A Look at the Role of Rashīd al-Dīn and Others', *Asian Medicine, Tradition and Modernity*, 3/2 (2007): pp. 279-95. See also Paul D. Buell, 'Medical Globalization in the Mongol Era', in Ts. Ishdorj (ed.), *Mongol Sudlalyn Ogulluud: Essays on Mongol Studies* (Ulaanbaatar, 2007), pp. 138-47 and Paul D. Buell, 'Food, Medicine and the Silk Road: The Mongol-Era Exchanges', *Silk Road*, 5/2 (2007): pp. 22-35.

飲膳正要, 'Proper and Essential Things for the Emperor's Food and Drink' (*YSZY*), presented to court in 1330 by Hu sihui 忽思惠, who may have been a Turk or a Turkicized Chinese.[40] The *HHYF*, as its name implies, is primarily a compendium of 'Muslim' medicine. The work is in a semi-colloquial but highly technical Chinese of a type found in other documents from Mongol China. It includes substantial Persian and some Arabic material: for example, titles, terms, names of medicinals, are given both in Chinese transcription and, to a lesser degree, in the original Arabic script often in phrases that are grammatically Persian, the working language of the Middle Eastern side of the text. The *HHYF* is replete with quotations from the great 'doctors' of the 'Muslim' tradition (including many Greeks) and there is a great deal in the theoretical underpinnings of the text as a whole that is typical of the mainstream Arabic medicine of the period. Nonetheless, it appears also to have at least some Ayurvedic elements. There is also what may be seen as subtle Tibetan influences on the theoretical discussions found at various places in the text. In particular, the humoral system of the *HHYF* is highly assimilated to Indian *tridosa* doctrine. Such Ayurvedic influence is best explained through Tibetan mediation since the age of direct Indian influence on China was long over by the time that the *HHYF* was written and Tibetan influence is certainly the source of such ideas in later Mongolian medicine apparently already emerging at the time. The second source, the imperial dietary, includes a number of elements specifically labelled as Tibetan, and at least one Tibetan was involved in its compilation as a supervising editor and apparently contributor. Tibetans were known otherwise as dietary physicians in Mongol China as well.

Also showing possible Tibetan influence, alongside 'Islamic', or better, 'Western', are the veterinary texts of the era. Here the influences may be somewhat older, dating back to the time when the major source of horses for Northern Song 宋 (960-1125) was Tibet. Nonetheless, the surviving texts, including the first available manifestations of the Bo Le 伯 樂 tradition (1384),[41] are strongly associated with the Mongol era and the period immediately following, the golden age of Chinese veterinary medicine. With veterinarian Dave Ramey and Arabist Timothy May, I have examined some of this literature in a separate study.[42]

---

40 See Buell, Anderson and Perry, *Soup for the Qan*.

41 The historical Bo Le lived in the seventh century BCE in the state of Qin, and although legend associates him with horse physiognomy and even hippiatrics, and he is the reputed author of a number of now lost treatises and diagrams, no actual works survive until almost two thousand years after his death, namely the *Bo Le zhenjing* 伯樂鍼經, 'Bo Le's Needling Classic', and the very short *Bo Le Hualuo tu ge jue* 伯樂畫烙圖歌訣, 'The Song Secrets of the Diagram of Bo Le's Branding'. Both of these works have strong Western parallels and probably reflect imported ideas, ultimately Western but possibly transmitted by Tibetans. See the discussion in Paul D. Buell, David Ramey and Timothy May, 'Greek and Chinese Horse Medicine: Déjà vu All Over Again', *Sudhoffs Archiv*, 94 (2010), 1 (June), 31-57.

42 See Buell, Ramey and May, 'Greek and Chinese Horse Medicine', and Paul D. Buell, Dave Ramey and Timothy May, 'Chinese Horse Medicine: Texts and Illustrations', in

HUIHUI YAOFANG (HHYF)

The 'Muslim' medicine of the *HHYF* includes a mix of hundreds of simples and recipes for various conditions. The text describes procedures for such things as setting broken bones, including cranial factures with surgical indications, treating wounds and cauterization. It also contains theoretical discussions, many of them oriented to dietary therapy. Nearly all the Arabic script entries explain the original names and terms appearing in Chinese transcription, often in grammatically Persian phrases. Sometimes a brief commentary is added. The majority of the simples and recipes and a good deal of the text go back to Greek medical tradition.[43] Greek forms are also at the root of many Arabic

---

Vivienne Lo (ed.), *Imagining Chinese Medicine* (forthcoming).

[43] For example, note the following, purporting to be a recipe from Galen himself. The majority of the ingredients were, in fact, well known to the Greeks. Note that the subtexts are in smaller characters in the original and include Arabic script entries, as well as special directions. Texts in brackets are additions of the translator:

> Another, an Ointment of Jālinūs [Galenos, i.e., Galen] ([subtext] *Maʿjūn-i Jālinūs* ['electuary of Galen'])
> It specially treats left paralysis, right numbness, hemiphlegia, and blood vessel [*jin* 筋] looseness disease symptoms on account of phlegm, and turbid body weakness. It clears all kinds of turbid substances associated with wind phlegm [preponderance of the humor phlegm caused by an attack of 'evil wind' coming from outside the body] from a turbid body. If the body is feeble, it can open obstruction. It also treats leaking urine. It also treats hemiphlegia brain illness [and] head pain:
> [Ingredients:]
> [Pe.] *Shaḥm-i ḥanẓal* [pulp of the wild gourd, *Cucumis colocynthis*] ([subtext] [Pe.] *shaḥm-i ḥanẓal* ['pulp of the wild *ḥanẓal*'])
> [Ar.] *Ghārīqūn* [*Agaricus officinalis*] ([subtext] *ghārīqūn*)
> [Ar.] *Ishqīl* [*Allium cepa*] ([subtext] This is 'mountain onion' [*Allium victorialis*, *A. fistulosum*, and various *Veratrum* spp.]. Roast)
> [Ar.] *Ushaq* [gum ammoniac] ([subtext] *ushaq*)
> [Ar.] *Saqamūniyā* [scammony, *Convolvulus scamonia*] ([subtext] this is the croton bean)
> 'Black' [Ar.] *harbaq* [black hellebore] ([subtext] [Pe.] *harbaq-i siyāh* ['Black hellebore'])
> [Ar.] *Fāriqūn* [St. John's wort, *Hypericum perforatum*] ([subtext] [Ar.] *fāriqūn*)
> [Ar.] *Basbāyij* [common polypody, *Polypodium vulgare*] ([subtext] *basbāyij*)
> [Ar.] *Āftimūn* [*Cuscuta epithymum*] ([subtext] [Ar.] *āftimūn*)
> Benzoin
> [Pr.] *Kamāduriyūs* [medicinal germander, *Teucrium chamaedrys*]
> [Ar.] *Farāsiyūn* [horehound, *Marrubium vulgare*] ([subtext] This is steppe leek.)
> Tree peony skin [rootbark of *Paeonia suffruticosa*] ([subtext] Each eight *qian* 錢 [tenth of a Chinese ounce])
> Myrrh
> [Ar.] *Ṣaghyin* [= *ṣaghbīn*, sagapenum, root of *Ferula* spp] ([subtext] [Ar.] *ṣaghyin*)
> 'Long' [Ar.] *Zarāwand* [*Aristolochia longa*] ([subtext] [Ar.] *zarāwand ṭawīl*)

forms, although these are not distinguished in the examples given. Others stem from the ancient Near East. Also present specifically are a number of simples and recipes labelled as Indian, although much Indian medicine had already been assimilated to Arabic by the time that the *HHYF* was written. One example is given below. Most of the medicinal called for, in any case, are still Indian:

> [Pe.] *jawārish-i Hindī* recipe ([Subtext] This is a pill medicine formed from decocting various medicinals with black sand sugar.)
>
> It can treat [Ar.] *qūlnaj* ([Subtext] this is intestinal wind internal knotting) symptoms and pain of each bone joint, foot *qi* 氣 [beriberi] and stomach main artery weakness.
>
> [Ingredients:]
>
> [Ar.] *Shīṭaraj Hindī* [Fumitory, *Fumaria officinalis*, also pepperwort or rose-colored wort, *Lepidium latifolium* or *Plumbago rosea* of India] ([Subtext] [Ar.] *shīṭaraj Hindī*)
>
> [Ar.] *Sādhaj Hindī* [Indian malabathrum, *Laurus malabathrum*] ([Subtext] This is loquat leaf.[44] Each four *qian*)
>
> Nutmeg
>
> [Ar.] *Nānakhwah* [bishop's weed, *Ammi copticum*] ([Subtext] *nānakhwah*)
>
> Black myrobalans ([Subtext] Three *liang* 兩 [Chinese ounce])
>
> Long pepper ([Subtext] Each five *qian*)
>
> Dried ginger ([Subtext] Five *liang*)
>
> Pepper
>
> [Ar.] *Nārmushki* ([Subtext] This is musk or *dangmenzi* 當門子 [musk]. Two *liang*)
>
> Cloves ([Subtext] Five *qian*)
>
> Nutmeg flowers ([Subtext] Four *qian*)
>
> Black pepper
>
> White pepper
>
> Long Pepper
>
> Cinnamon
>
> [Pe.] *Jawāshir* [*Opopanax chironium* resin] ([subtext] [Pe.] *jawāshir*)
>
> [Pe.] *Khazmiyān* [castoreum] ([subtext] This is castoreum)
>
> Chinese angelica [*Angelica sinensis*] ([subtext] Each four *qian*)
>
> Medicinal aloe
>
> [Ar.] *Zaʿfarān* [saffron] ([subtext] This is the pistil of foreign safflower [*Gardenia jasminoides*] flower. Two *qian* of each)
>
> Make a power of those ingredients that are dry. Use liquor to transform and open the sticky ones. Combine with refined honey. Each time take four *qian*. Use a soup decocted from [Ar.] *afithīmūn* [dodder, *Cuscuta epthymum*] ([subtext] *afithīmūn*) to down it.

[44] The editors of the *HHYF* repeatedly attempted, usually not correctly, to equate foreign medicinals with better known local herbs, as is the case here.

> [Pe.] *Fanīdh* [sugar candy or sweetmeat] sand sugar ([Subtext] This is the sand sugar of the *Fanīdh* land. Ten *liang*)
> Combine the above ingredients according to method. Each dose is two *qian*. Take along with fresh grape liquor.[45]

Note that this recipe calls for musk, the usual origin of which at the time was Tibet (see Anya King's article in this volume and also her doctoral dissertation[46]). Although not labelled as Indian, there are quite a number of specifically musk recipes that can be studied as a complex in the *HHYF*; in fact there are a conspicuous number of musk recipes. There are also other medicinals and complexes of medicinals that are specifically Indian. Note that, in a very un-Arabic way, but typically Indian, this recipe calls for washing it down with grape wine. There are other examples and grape wine is a typical component of the recipes themselves. Tibet, of course, did know but did not see much wine since the grape will not grow there and Tibetan texts may simply be repeating old lore regarding grape wine, although grape wine may have been a rare medicinal in Tibet in Mongol times, along with many other even more rare products now moving freely thanks to the Mongols.

Whence such content? In the case of the *HHYF* the source is uncertain and Persian medicine, before the Islamic conquest, was already influenced by Indian and common Arabic medicine had many Indian elements too. Nonetheless, the recipe in question seems later, is distinctively different in content from most purely Arabic recipes of the period and may very well have come to be included in the *HHYF* via Tibet, although this cannot be said conclusively pending further research. There is also the question of the specific choice of medicinal in the other recipes of the text and how this choice compares to other, presumably unassimilated, Arabic collections: for example, the slightly earlier collection of al-Samarqandī.[47] To this end detailed statistical analysis of all *HHYF* medicinals will be undertaken as part of the final publication of the author's complete translation. In any case, preliminary examination suggests that frequencies of occurrence for many medicinals, for example, the various myrobalans, are closer to the norm for recent Tibetan or Indian medicine than for Arabic *per se*. Myrobalan was certainly used in the Arabic world at the time, but the number of different varieties of myrobalan called for in the *HHYF* is conspicuously different.

---

45 *HHYF*, p. 347.

46 Anya King, unpublished dissertation, 'The Musk Trade and the Near East in the Early Medieval Period' (Indiana University, 2007). See also Anna Akasoy and Ronit Yoeli-Tlalim, 'Along the Musk Routes. Exchanges between Tibet and the Islamic World', *Asian Medicine: Tradition and Modernity*, 3/2 (2007): pp. 217-40.

47 See Martin Levey and Noury al-Khaledi, *The Medical Formulary of al-Samarqandī and the Relation of Early Arabic Simples to Those Found in the Indigenous Medicine of the Near East and India* (Philadelphia, 1967).

Also of possibly Tibetan origin or perhaps intermediation, although this type of recipe is certainly well known in the Arabic tradition, are a number of *HHYF* recipes associated with the designation *bāsilīqūn*, ultimately Greek, from a proper name, if it does not mean simply 'royal'. Be their Arabic connection what it may, these simples are closely paralleled in a Tibetan collection of 'Roman', that is, Byzantine medicine that is discussed by Dan Martin in this volume.[48] As a consequence, we do not have to postulate an Arabic origin for the *HHYF*'s *bāsilīqūn* simples. The tradition was known in Tibet and may have come directly from a Greek source, although a Syriac intermediary is possible as well. The following is an example, one of once several such recipes from the text, the others now lost and known only from table of contents listings. The olive oil does not seem very Tibetan but other oils could be substituted, the practice I am sure in China, where olive oil was as rare as in Tibet:

> A greater [Ar.] *bāsilīqūn* ointment recipe ([Subtext] [Pe.] *ma'jūn-i bāsilīqūn*)
> One can paste on where there is swelling and pain.
> [Ingredients:]
> [Ar.] *Lātyanaj* [pine resin] ([Subtext] *lātyanaj*)
> [Ar.] *Zift* [pitch, bitumen] ([Subtext] *zift*. Each five *liang*)
> [Ar.] *Bārzad* [galbanum, resin of *Ferula galbaniflua*] ([Subtext] *bārzad*. Four *qian*)
> Finely powder the ingredients together. Use [Ar.] *zayt* [olive] oil ([subtext] This is oil produced from the [Ar.] *zaytūn* tree [olive tree] of the Sham [Syrian] land. Eight *liang*) and together put onto the fire and cook. Stir to form an ointment and paste on.[49]

Also possibly from Tibetan intermediation are some of the very sophisticated broken bone treatments in the last sections of the text (*juan* 卷 34). Much of the material in this chapter, although not without strong parallels in more mainstream Arabic medicine, is unique in the entire Eurasian tradition in the degree of its specificity. There is nothing airy and theoretical about it; the traditions of bone setting and wound treatment in the chapter are immensely practical and applied and many of the proposed treatments are, with variations, still used today; those relating to skull fracture, for example. The terminology seems mixed at best. Interestingly, one Tibetan text, the *Bi-ci'i pu-ti kha-ser*, 'The Yellow-Covered Volume of the Bi-ci', does offer a set of extremely similar materials. The connection will be further investigated. The *Bi-ci'i pu-ti kha-ser*

---

48 The text in question, mentioned in the medical histories, is the *Tshad pa'i 'Bros 'ded*, expressing the Phrom or Romano-Byzantine system of medicine, composed by bTsan-pa-shing-la-ha or Tsan-pa-shi-la-ha, which Martin understands as connected with the Greek name Basil or, as I suspect, the namesake of the *bāsilīqūn* of the *HHYF*. bTsan or Tsan, according to Martin's interpretation would be a place name, an affiliation, in this case one located on the northern coast of Anatolia.

49 *HHYF*, p. 409.

purports to contain the secret teachings of the descendants of a Western, that is, Byzantine doctor who ended up in Tibet (see the detailed discussion of this text in the contribution by Dan Martin in this volume), although surviving editions are recent. The least that can be said is that the traditions of bone setting and surgical intervention of this part of the *HHYF* have strong Tibetan parallels. Probably a great deal else does too.

Finally, there is the strongest evidence of possible Tibetan influence of all: the way in which the *HHYF* interprets the humours that lie at the basis of both Islamic and Ayurvedic medicine. While in Islamic medicine, taking over in this respect from the Greeks, there are four humours, blood, phlegm, yellow bile and black bile, there are only three in Indian and Tibetan medicine, namely air (also wind), bile and phlegm. Significantly, the *HHYF* also seems to function not in terms of the four traditional Islamic humours, but within an assimilated system of three: *qi*, rarely used in the strict Chinese sense; yellow liquid, that is, presumably yellow bile; and phlegm. Blood is mentioned, but it does not seem to be a humour. Black bile is not mentioned at all. The text does note 'black blood' but black bile is never associated with blood in the Graeco-Islamic system.[50] In this aspect of its theory, the *HHYF* does, in any case, seem more Indian and Tibetan than Islamic. The existence of such a mixed system within the theoretical discussions of the text does suggest that much in them is assimilated and a cultural construct, i.e. a carefully determined synthesis of elements from various sources, like other aspects of the official posture of Mongol China.

YINSHAN ZHENGYAO (YSZY)

By contrast to the *HHYF*, in the case of the *YSZY*, the other important text, Tibetan influences are often directly labelled as such. For example, the following medicinal food calls for pomegranate under its Tibetan name, although the recipe is assimilated to Mongol court tastes. Brackets indicate additions or explanations by the translator:[51]

> [Tib.] **Se'u bru*[52] [Pomegranate] (This is the name of a West Indian Food)
> It treats deficiency chill of the primordial storehouse, chill pain of the abdomen, and aching pain along the spinal column.

---

50 The theoretical section of the *HHYF* is lost but humors are frequently referred to and sometimes defined in the discussions sections of the text which introduce the simples and recipes. This material will be analysed and cross-compared in detail in the forthcoming publication of my full translation.

51 That is to say, this is another variant on the Mongol banquet soup or *šülen*. See Buell, Anderson and Perry, *Soup for the Qan*.

52 This is reconstructed incorrectly in Buell, Anderson and Perry, *Soup for the Qan*, first edition (London, 2000). See now the discussion in the second edition, pp. 292-3.

> Mutton (two legs, the head, and a set of hooves), tsaoko cardamoms (four), cinnamon (three *liang*), sprouting ginger (half a *jin* 斤 [= 8 *liang*]), [Pe.] *kasni* [asafetida] (big as two chickpeas)
> Boil ingredients into a soup using one [Tu.] *telir* of water. Pour into a stone top cooking pot. Add a *jin* of pomegranate fruits, two *liang* of black pepper, and a little salt. The pomegranate fruits should be baked using one cup of vegetable oil and a lump of asafetida the size of a garden pea. Roast [i.e., cook dry ingredients] until a fine yellow in colour, slightly black. Remove debris and oil in the soup. Strain clean. Use the smoke produced from roasting *jiaxiang* 甲香 [*operculum* of *Turbo cornutus* and related Turbo species], Chinese spikenard [*Nardostachys chinensis*], *kasni*, and butter to fumigate a jar. Seal up and store [the *Se'u bru* Soup] as desired.[53]

In this dish, the major spice is a large, smoky cardamom, a primarily Southeast Asian spice, although certainly known in India. Also a key spice is *kasni* or asafetida, later called for by its Chinese name. Asafetida clearly marks Persian-Indian influence in the *YSZY*, as witnessed by the use of its Persian name. A *telir* is a metal basket for boiling. The word is apparently Turkic. The storage method is without doubt Indian. Dan Martin notes that pomegranate is used in much the same way in Tibetan medicine as in the recipe.[54]

Elsewhere, there is a Bal-po Curry, using the Tibetan name for Nepal. It is also somewhat assimilated to Mongol tastes but nonetheless provides one of the earliest known curry recipes, with Tibetan intermediation apparent. The same recipe, with New World chilies now added, survives in Kashmir today:

> [Tib.] Bal-po Soup (This is the name of a Western Indian food.)
> It supplements the centre, and brings down *qi*. It extends the diaphragm.
> [Ingredients:]
> Mutton (leg; bone and cut up), *tsaoko* cardamoms (five), chickpeas (half a *sheng* 升 [about 16 cubic inches]; pulverize and remove the skins), Chinese radish.
> Boil ingredients together to make a soup. Strain [broth. Cut up meat and Chinese radish and put aside]. Add to the soup [the] mutton cut up into [Tu.] *sashuq* [coin]-sized pieces, [the] cooked Chinese radish cut up into *sashuq*-sized pieces, 1 *qian* of *za'farān* [saffron], 2 *qian* of Turmeric, 2 *qian* of Black ['Iranian'] Pepper, half a *qian* of *kasni*, coriander leaves. Evenly adjust flavours with a little salt. Eat over cooked aromatic non-glutinous rice. Add a little vinegar.[55]

There are also other stray references to things Tibetan, including 'Tibetan' tea, also known from Chinese medicinal handbooks. And the origins of these delightful recipes, intended, as are nearly all in the *YSZY*, to be medicinal,

---

53 Buell, Anderson and Perry, *Soup for the Qan*, 2nd ed., pp. 292-3.
54 Personal communication to the author in an email of March, 2007.
55 Buell, Anderson and Perry, *Soup for the Qan*, 2nd ed., pp. 272-3.

were probably Tibetans active at court. More specifically, one of the primary editor-sponsors of the text, the Dynastic lord Jinjienudoerzhi 金界奴朵兒只, probably, Kun-rgya rDo-rje, may have been the source.[56]

If not Jinjienudoerzhi, a more distant origin might be in the teachings of the *nökör* (a Mongolian term referring to associates or personal representatives of some powerful personage, including officials as high as governors) of imperial preceptor 'Phags-pa. Also influential may have been associates of the *bla-ma* known in Persian sources as Damba, that is, Sga A-gnyan Dan-pa (1230-1303), a most important figure, judging from the many references to him in both Tibetan and Chinese sources. Such *nökör*, with a knowledge of medicine, are specifically mentioned by Rashīd al-Dīn as managing the meals and dietary balance of Temür Khan (reg. 1294-1307) and possibly of his father Qubilai before him, since 'Phags-pa was long dead by the time of Temür.[57]

Thus we have a definite Tibetan trail in the case of the *YSZY*, although most of our Tibetan agents seem to have remained anonymous. It was Tibetan religious figures, often appearing as stereotypes, who were of more interest to the writers of our sources. This was especially true when they confounded common morality as in connection with the supposed sexual escapades of the last Mongol emperor, a well-known story at the time. Cooks and dietary physicians were a great deal less colourful and it is significant that their existence is mentioned at all, although by a Persian historian, not a Chinese one.

TIBET, THE POSSIBLE LONG-DISTANCE CONNECTIONS

So Tibetans operating within Yuan China influenced food and apparently medicine. Tibetan and directly adjacent areas had active connections with the eastern Mongols. Tibetans intermediated between India and the Mongols in particular. In short, Tibetans participated in truly international exchanges. We

56 Buell, Anderson and Perry, *Soup for the Qan*, 2nd ed., p. 380. In the introduction to the *YSZY* this man is also called, with a Sinified name, Zhang jinjienu 張金界奴 (p. 194). There he is called 'Hall of Literature Chief Officer-in-charge, the Grandee-who-brings affairs to the attention of the Emperor and Who-is-relied-upon-to-govern, the Governor of Daidu 大都, Imperial Steward, Chief Administration Office of the Beneficent Administration Office [of the empress] for Controlling Craftsmen of Textiles, Dye Stuffs and Various Commodities'. The title suggests some assimilation, but there were many West and Central Asians who knew Chinese during the era and this was nearly 100 years after the first appearance of Tibetans among the Mongols, including 70 years since the establishment of Mongol China. I cannot explain the *nu* of the transcription. Dan Martin (email to the author of March, 2007), has suggested a number of alternative transcriptions, including gZhon-nu rDo-rje with the first syllable a clan name. This is very possible. With further research it should be possible to identify this individual.

57 See the discussion in Christopher I. Beckwith, 'Tibetan Science at the Court of the Great Khans', *Journal of the Tibet Society*, 7 (1987): pp. 5-11, at pp. 6-7.

know, for example, that large numbers of Tibetans were present in the Mongolian west, Iran in particular, where they have left ruins, and many passing references in largely antagonistic Islamic sources (see the contribution by Arezou Azad in this volume). There is even Tibetan on Ilkhanid coins. Tibetans seem to have gone to what became Chagatay domains and even the Golden Horde. Some connections do seem to have been maintained with home monasteries, including the Sakya rival 'Bri-khung.[58]

In view of the importance of the Iran–China connection for the introduction of 'Islamic' medicine there, most notably in the movement of books from West to East, and the interest of the Tibetans of the time in a common tradition of Eurasian medicine, it seems reasonable to conclude that Tibetans were involved in the knowledge trade at least as much as the Nestorians were. A key Nestorian figure was Isa, known to have been in close connection with 'Phags-pa as part of Qubilai's brain trust. Isa the translator, as he was known in Iran, began his career as a physician. He was in charge of the Muslim medical institutions of Mongol China. Most importantly, he travelled back to the West at the orders of Qubilai Khan towards the end of the latter's reign, along with imperial minister Bolad,[59] with a career both in China and in Iran, where he stayed. Isa returned bringing, we must assume, many of the Persian and Arabic books that served as a basis for the chapters, including those lost, of what became the *HHYF*.

The trail is unfortunately a great deal colder for the Tibetans. Did Tibetans bring back books too, for their own consumption? Did more than religion flow along the routes of these contacts? Were Tibetans truly conduits of West–East, East–West interchange and, if so, what was the content of the interchanges involved? We may never have a reliable answer, due to the nature of our sources and the eventual disappearance of Tibetan religion in Iran, and surrounding areas. Nonetheless, given what we know about the Mongol age, it is likely that more than religion was involved in the cultural goods carried by Tibetans. This was, after all, the era of Rashīd al-Dīn (1247-1317).[60] We will have more to say after analysis of the sources, above all the *HHYF*, now being analysed by my own team.

---

[58] *Blue Annals*, vol. 2, p. 580; dPa'-bo gTsug-lag 'Phreng-ba, *mKhas-pa'i dGa'-ston*, vol. 3, p. 800. On the Sakya and 'Bri-kung war, in which supporters from eastern and Central Asian Mongols participated on the respective sides, and the monastery and presumably many of its records were destroyed, see Buell, 'Some Aspects of the Origin and Development', pp. 120 and 121.

[59] See the excellent discussion in Thomas T. Allsen, *Culture and Conquest in Mongol Eurasia* (Cambridge, 2001), pp. 63-80.

[60] See Buell, 'How Did Persian and Other Western Medical Knowledge Move East, and Chinese West?'.

Chapter 10

Three Rock-Cut Cave Sites in Iran and their Ilkhanid Buddhist Aspects Reconsidered

Arezou Azad[1]

INTRODUCTION

It is well documented that Mongol rule in the thirteenth and fourteenth centuries fostered the direct exchange of ideas and practices between diverse cultures and religions. Three rock-cut sites in the regions of Marāgha and Sulṭāniyya in Iran have occupied archaeologists, some of whom suggested that the caves had served as Buddhist temples and/or monasteries imported by the Mongol dynasty of Ilkhans who ruled in Iran *c.*1258 to 1335. However, scholars do not tell us who would have patronized the establishments, and who constituted the clergy – Mongol or Persian, élite or commoners. This article will reconsider the sites, first through the broader geographic environment in which they are found, the possible references to them in Persian contemporary chronicles, and their exact locations today. Section II of this article outlines our methodological approach, and Section III our assessment of their functions and dating in light of the features observed and reconsidered. The last section provides conclusions and ideas for future study.

[1] I wish to thank the Barakat Trust, the British Institute of Persian Studies and Oxford University's Sub-Faculty of Near East and Middle Eastern Studies for their support. On the ground, the members of the research team, Reza Rohani, Mazdak Mirramezani and Reza Sadeghi, provided invaluable assistance; the Iranian Cultural Heritage Organisation on-site guidance; Warwick Ball preparatory advice; Birgül Açikyildiz, Teresa Bernheimer, Edmund Herzig, Dan Martin and Charles Ramble gave useful comments on various drafts of this article, or parts of it. Any errors contained herein are naturally the authors.

I. BACKGROUND

I) GEOGRAPHY AND URBAN ENVIRONMENT[2]

Before discussing the three rock-cut sites, let us locate ourselves within the broader physical and historical space. Two of the sites are found in Marāgha, and one lies in Sulṭāniyya. Both provided the chief seasonal residences for the nomadic Mongol courts on the Iranian plateau.[3] Both towns are located in Azerbaijan province to the northwest of the plateau, and benefit from extensive pasturelands and the water drainage from the mountain slopes.

However, as mediaeval 'urban agglomerations' – to borrow Jean Aubin's phrase – the two places differ significantly.[4] Marāgha has an ancient pre-Islamic history, and in the early Islamic days became Azerbaijan's capital in the time of the caliph Hārūn al-Rashīd (d. 169/785).[5] In the Mongol period five centuries later, Marāgha became the focus of scholarly exchanges between Iranian and Chinese astronomers, after the creation of an observatory commissioned by the Ilkhan Hülegü (reg. 654/1256-663/1265) and supervised by the famous scholar Nāṣir al-Dīn Ṭūsī (d. 672/1274).[6]

---

2 The political influence of Buddhists in the courts of the Ilkhans based on the mediaeval primary sources is discussed elsewhere in this volume in the article by Paul Buell and introduction by Ronit Yoeli-Tlalim.

3 Even the later Mongol courts, like that of the Ilkhan Öljeitü, were peripatetic. See Charles Melville, 'The Itineraries of Sultan Öljeitü, 1304-1316', *Iran*, 28 (1990): pp. 55-70; for the seasonal residences of the various Ilkhans see Bertold Spuler, *Die Mongolen in Iran* (Berlin, ²1955), pp. 130-31.

4 Jean Aubin, 'Elements pour l'Étude des Agglomérations Urbaines dans l'Iran Médiéval', in Albert Hourani and Samuel Stern (eds), *The Islamic City* (Oxford, 1970), pp. 49-75.

5 On this caliph's relations with the Barmakids of Balkh, and their links to Buddhism, see the article by Kevin van Bladel in this volume.

6 See Vladimir Minorsky, 'Marāgha', *EI*²; Hans Daiber and Jamil Rageb, 'Nāṣir al-Dīn Ṭūsī', *EI*². The observatory headed by Nāṣir al-Dīn Ṭūsī (d. 672/1274) is described in Rashīd al-Dīn (d. 718/1318), *Jāmiʿ al-tawārīkh*, ed. Muḥammad Rawshan and Muṣṭafā Mūsawī (4 vols, Tehran, 1373 H.Sh./1994), vol. 2, p. 1024. It was still active under the supervision of Naṣīr al-Dīn al-Ṭūsī (Nāṣir al-Dīn's son), in the time of Öljeitü Khan (reg. 704-17/1304-16). See John A. Boyle, *The Cambridge History of Iran*, vol. 5 (Cambridge, 1968), p. 398. It was in ruins when Qazwīnī wrote in 740/1340. See Qazwīnī, *The Geographical Part of the Nuzhat al-qulub*, ed. Guy Le Strange (Leiden, 1919), p. 135. Allsen describes visits by Chinese astronomers to the observatory, and cites Aydin Sayili as the best source on the Marāgha observatory. See Thomas Allsen, *Culture and Conquest in Mongol Eurasia* (Cambridge, 2001), pp. 161-75, esp. p. 163. For an image of its remains, see David Morgan, *The Mongols* (Oxford, ²2007), p. 153.

In this study we are interested in the terms *butkhāna* (i.e. a place of 'buddha' or idols) and *bakhshī* in the primary sources.[7] The term *butkhāna* usually refers to Buddhist places of worship. However, *bakhshī* can denote either a Buddhist cleric or a shaman, and I shall use it only when it appears in conjunction with the term *butkhāna* or another marker of Buddhism.

On Marāgha, Rashīd al-Dīn, the vizier writing for the Ilkhan Ghāzān (reg. 694/1295-703/1304), mentions in passing that Abāqā Khan (reg. 663/1265-680/1282) had visited a *butkhāna* there, which apparently 'delighted and excited the *bakhshīs*'. He also mentions that Abāqā's predecessor, Hülegü (reg. 654/1256-663/1265), had commissioned *butkhānas* in Khūy, immediately to the west of Marāgha.[8] The author does not specify what type of ritual the Ilkhans had performed there, the abbot who presided over the processions, or the identity or number of Buddhist monks serving in it. Neither does Rashīd al-Dīn provide any details concerning the locations of the *butkhānas*, or what they may have looked like, i.e. whether they were rock-cut, and what statues, paintings or decorations they may have housed.[9]

Sulṭāniyya is very different from Marāgha. A mediaeval city, it was planned and built by the Mongols on the fields they called 'Qonqor Olong', previously known by their Persian name, Sharūyāz. Jacob Lassner observes that a city that is based on a preconceived plan ('as though it were poured into a mould and cast', citing Jāḥiẓ on the round city of Baghdad built 145-9/762-6 by the caliph al-Manṣūr) did not develop 'from the inside-out, but rather from the outside-in'.

---

7 Rashīd al-Dīn (d. 718/1318), *Jāmiʿ al-tawārīkh*, vol. 2, p. 1114. On the use of *but*, to refer to 'idol' or 'buddha', see Harold Bailey, 'The Word "but" in Iranian', *Bulletin of the School of Oriental and African Studies*, 6 (1931): pp. 279-83; also Gerhard Doerfer, *Türkische und Mongolische Elemente im Neupersischen* (5 vols, Wiesbaden, 1963-75), §716, vol. 2, pp. 261-2. On Abāqā Khān's entrusting of prince Ghāzān's education and care to the *bakhshīs* Yāriq Khitāyi and Bāijū, see Rashīd al-Dīn, *Jāmiʿ al-tawārīkh*, vol. 2, pp. 1210-11. On the Persian use of *bakhshī* to refer to Buddhist teachers or healers, see Doerfer, *Türkische und Mongolische Elemente im Neupersischen*, § 724, vol. 2, pp. 271-7.

8 Hülegü's proclivities for the *bakhshīs*, and his links to his appanage in western Tibet and to a Buddhist master have been documented by two Tibetologists: David Snellgrove, 'The Notion of Divine Kingship in Tantric Buddhism', in *La Regalità Sacra – Contributi al Tema dell' VIII Congresso Internazionale di Storia delle Religioni* (Leiden, 1959), pp. 204-18; and Luciano Petech, *Central Tibet and the Mongols: The Yüan-Sa-skya Period of Tibetan History* (Rome, 1990). See also Elliot Sperling, 'Hülegü and Tibet', *Acta Orientalia Academiae Hungariae*, 44 (1990), pp. 145-57.

9 Rashīd al-Dīn tells us that Ghāzān Khān, prior to his conversion to Islam, also built several *butkhānas* in Khābūshān, near the town of Bayhaq in the eastern province of Khurāsān where he had served as governor. See Rashīd al-Dīn, *Jāmiʿ al-tawārīkh*, vol. 2, p. 1048. On Ghāzān Khān's conversion to Islam in the 690s/1290s, see Rashīd al-Dīn, *Jāmiʿ al-tawārīkh*, vol. 2, p. 1254; also Charles Melville, 'Pādshāh-i Islām: The Conversion of Sultan Maḥmūd Ghazan Khān', in id. (ed.), *History and Literature in Iran: Persian and Islamic Studies in Honour of P.W. Avery* (London, 1990), pp. 159-77.

The workers and artisans and other construction-related staff settled and formed the embryonic social fabric of the city and its quarters.[10]

While the contemporary narratives on Sulṭāniyya are more detailed than on Marāgha, we still lack details about the buildings that interest us.[11] According to Qāshānī, the panegyrist of the Ilkhan Öljeitü (d. 716/1316), the city developed in the way that Lassner describes for Baghdad six centuries earlier. In Qonqor Olong, a city, named Sulṭāniyya ('The Imperial'), was built by the order (*yārlīgh*) of Arghūn Khan (reg. 683/1284-690/1291), and completed under Öljeitü Khān (reg. 703/1304-716/1316).[12] The aim was to build a city as grand as Tabrīz (the former Mongol capital), with, *inter alia*, a citadel and a palace - decorated with mirrors, marble, blue tiles, pearls, rubies and turquoises - and other buildings cut into the mountain rock, a hospital and public recreational spaces. Sulṭāniyya was to provide the means for extensive trade, so that as much Chinese silk would be sold as there was grass. The élites would come and invest in the city that was developed by its chief architect, Khwāja Tāj al-Dīn ʿAlīshāh Tabrīzī.[13]

According to Rashīd al-Dīn, a place called 'Qonqor Olong' continued to co-exist with Sulṭāniyya, the city proper. He explains that Qonqor Olong was a place where Arghun and other Ilkhans, as well as a certain 'Kashmir Bakhshī', would go to perform religious services (*bandagī kardan*). The term *butkhāna* does not feature in this account, but Kashmīr lay within the cultural area of Tibet where Buddhism was practised widely, and it seems reasonable to expect that this was a Buddhist monk, and that the site was therefore a place of Buddhist worship.[14] Whether this is in fact the site that we visited remains an open question to which I shall return below.

---

10 Jacob Lassner, 'The Caliph's Personal Domain', in Hourani and Stern, *The Islamic City*, pp. 103-5.

11 Today only a few ruins remain above ground, notably the famous octagonal tomb of Öljeitü. Illustrations in sixteenth- and seventeenth-century manuscripts depict a large city with a multitude of buildings, gates and walls surrounding it, circumscribed by a landscape filled with beasts of the hunt. On the monuments, see Sheila Blair, 'Sulṭāniyya - 2. Monuments', *EI*², and plates of sixteenth- and seventeenth-century depictions in her article 'The Mongol Capital of Sultaniyya, "The Imperial"', *Iran*, 24 (1986): pp. 139-51.

12 Shabānkāraʿī (*c.*697/1298-759/1358), who wrote during the last decades of the Ilkhanid era from his central Iranian town of Shabānkāra, confirms this. He also mentions that a fortress was built in 'Shahrdīyāz' (orthographically similar to 'Sharūyāz') that was called Sunqur (perhaps a misreading of Qonqor/Qunqur). See Shabānkāraʿī, *Majmaʿ al-ansāb*, ed. Mīr Hāshim Muḥaddith (Tehran, 1363 H.Sh./1984), p. 288.

13 For the most detailed account, see Qāshānī, *Tārīkh-i Ūljāytū*, ed. Abū al-Qāsim ʿAbd Allāh ibn Muḥammad al-Qāshānī (Tehran, 1348 H.Sh./1969), pp. 45-9; also Vladimir Minorsky, 'Sulṭāniyya - 1. History', *EI*².

14 Rashīd al-Dīn (d. 718/1318), *Jāmiʿ al-tawārīkh*, vol. 2, pp. 1165, 1208, 1245, 1251. Kashmiri monks came into early contact with the Mongol rulers after the Mongols subdued Kashmir in the early 600s/1200s. Kashmiri Buddhist ecclesiastic orders had strong links with their co-religionists in Tibet after the second/eighth century, particularly

(II) THE SITES: HOW TO FIND THEM

1. The Raṣadkhāna caves (Marāgha)
Marāgha today is located 150 km southeast of Tabrīz, off the Tehran–Tabrīz highway. From the roundabout at Maydān-i Gaz in Marāgha there are signs leading to the Raṣadkhāna observatory up a hill at the north end of town. Currently, the Ministry of Information has closed most of the site to the public. The caves are on the slope to the left of the road, just twenty metres before the actual observatory on top. The observatory enjoys an impressive view of Lake Urmiya to the west – the legendary birthplace of the Prophet Zoroaster according to some – and the Sahānd mountains to the east.

2. The Mihrī Temple/Imāmzāda Maʿṣūm caves (near Marāgha)
Some 6 km southeast of Marāgha, the Mihrī Temple is reached after passing the small town of Oliyeh (probably derived from Arabic *awliyāʾ* for 'saint, holy person') at the village (Pe. *rūstā*) of Warjūwī, pronounced '*Var-övi*' in the local Azeri dialect.

3. The Dāsh Kasan/Qonqor Olong rock-cut site (Sulṭāniyya)
The site lies off the old Tākistān-Zanjān highway (which runs parallel to the new highway). Driving in the direction towards Zanjān, we took the left exit some 15 km before the turn-off for Sulṭāniyya at Ṣunbul Ābād. A tarmac road running southwest across a plateau ends at Viyar village after 9 km. From here, we took a sign-posted dirt road for 5 km to the plateau also known as 'Utāq-i Farhād'.

II. FIELD RESEARCH QUESTIONS AND METHOD

The research team had three broad questions to answer for each site. First, did the caves have architectural, epigraphic, art-historical or artefactual features that were indisputably Buddhist, and if so, did they belong to any specific form of Buddhism, such as Vajrayāna that was strong in Tibet at the time? Second, based on the features of the sites, what kind of Buddhist establishment did they house – a monastery, a shrine or both? Third, did the sites have characteristics that could be dated to the Ilkhanid period (*c*.1258-1335)?

The team visited each site for three to four days, cross-checked the new observations against the reports in the literature, notably the floor plans published for each site (see below). The team noted additions and made corrections, and took photographs of important features. Back in Oxford, the authors compared the structures with those of other Buddhist sites that have

---

after the persecution of Buddhist institutions by the last Yarlung emperor, Lang Darma (Tib. Glang Dar-ma), who was assassinated in 842. See Jean Naudou, *Les bouddhistes kasmīriens au moyen age* (Paris, 1968).

been studied, notably in Afghanistan, but also in India where the Buddhist rock-cut structures first appeared and often served as models.

Before discussing the findings of the research team, we should consider what Buddhist rock-cut sites tend to look like. This can serve as a reference point for our analysis, given that there are no known Buddhist rock-cut sites in modern-day Iran.[15]

In India, Buddhist rock-cut structures (built from around 50 BCE to 700 CE) reproduced in stone the forms and style of the old wooden constructions. These consisted of a temple (*caityagṛha*) and a monastery (*vihāra*).[16] The Buddhist temples have four main elements: first, a rectangular hall with an apse at one end and a hemispherical dome used as a funerary monument (*stūpa*) placed in its centre. The dome rests on a circular terrace (used as a processional path) that is reached by a set of stairs; second, a double row of pillars divides the hall into a central nave and two lateral aisles that converge at the back of the *stūpa*; third, a semi-circular vault hovers above the main nave and part of the side aisles; and fourth, a large horseshoe-shaped opening faces the *stūpa* and forms its entrance.

The monasteries have three features: first, a veranda excavated in the rock at the entrance to the cave with a roof supported by a row of sculpted pillars; second, a central flat-roofed hall which serves as the entrance-hall to numerous cells (often used as a refectory); and third, the cells surrounding the hall on three sides which are small and dark, and contain one or two stone beds (used as personal rooms).

Closer to Iran, the Buddhist caves of Afghanistan (dated to at least the first–third/seventh–ninth centuries), exhibit a similar division and use of space to that in India. The difference lies in the type of rock and, consequently, their state of preservation. The Indian caves, cut into hard stone, have retained many of their original structural, iconographic and stylistic elements, while the Afghan caves are cut into soft limestone and have lost many structural details. The Iranian caves are also cut into limestone, and suffer from the same preservation problem.[17]

---

15 Iran has many rock-cut sites, but only a few have been studied. The best known is probably the Karaftū site in northwest Iran which features a Greek inscription to Herakles. See Aurel Stein's *Old Routes of Western Īrān* (London, 1940), pp. 324-46; and Robert Ker Porter's earlier account in *Travels in Georgia, Persia, Armenia, Ancient Babylonia, &c. &c.* (London, 1821-22), vol. 2, p. 544. In the 1980s, Mary Vance drew up several bibliographies related to cave architecture in dozens of countries, but not Iran. See, for example, Mary Vance, *Cave Temples: A Bibliography* (Monticello, Illinois, 1987).

16 See Étienne Lamotte, *History of Indian Buddhism: From the Origins to the Saka Era* (Louvain-la-Neuve, 1988), pp. 311-13. For floor plans of Buddhist rock-cut temples and monasteries, such as in Ajanta, Bhima Shankar, Nasik and Kanheri, see Vidya Dehejia, *Early Buddhist Rock Temples: A Chronological Study* (London, 1972), pp. 72 and 94; also Sheila Weiner, *Ajanta: Its Place in Buddhist Art* (Berkeley, 1977), pp. 3 and 57-8.

17 For recent scholarly works on Afghan and Tajik Buddhist caves, see Giovanni Verardi and Elio Paparatti, *Buddhist Caves of Jāghūrī and Qarabāgh-e Ghaznī, Afghanistan*

III. FIELD RESEARCH FINDINGS

(I) FINDINGS: ARCHITECTURAL FEATURES OF THE CAVES VISITED

1. The Raṣadkhāna caves (Marāgha)

Previous studies Robert Ker Porter visited the caves in the second decade of the nineteenth century and recorded in his diaries the 'local tradition' that they were Zoroastrian. André Godard described them briefly in the 1930s, suggesting that the caves were connected to the observatory nearby. John Bowman and J.A. Thompson conducted archaeological investigations of the caves in the 1960s, and concluded that they were the remains of an Ilkhanid church mentioned in the contemporary chronicles. Vladimir Minorsky supported their conclusion. Bowman and Thompson's study served as a basis for Warwick Ball's visit in the 1970s. Ball's experience of Afghan caves led him to identify the Raṣadkhāna site as Buddhist, a suggestion that David Morgan endorsed as most plausible on the grounds that it was in Marāgha where the early Ilkhans, who had Buddhist proclivities, dwelt. No foreign team has since written about the site. The Iranian archaeologist Parvīz Varjāvand described them in the late 1980s, and emphasized their ancient Mithraic elements, bringing us back to where Porter started in the early nineteenth century: relying on folklore and projecting the date back into antiquity.[18]

(Rome, 2004), pp. 103-4; and Boris A. Litvinskii and Tamara I. Zejmal', *The Buddhist Monastery of Ajina Tepa, Tajikistan: History and Art of Buddhism in Central Asia* (Rome, 2004), figs 23 and 65-6. On Tibetan Buddhist cave sites in Luri, in the Mustang area of Nepal, see, *inter alia*, Peter Matthiessen, *East of Lo Monthang: In the Land of Mustang* (Boston, 1995), p. 55; Mary Slusser and Lila Bishop, 'Another Luri: A Newly Discovered Cave *chörten* in Mustang', *Orientations*, 30/2 (1999): pp. 18-27; and on sites in Dungkar (Tib. Dung-dkar); and in the far west of Tibet, see Helmut Neumann, 'The 11th Century Wall-Paintings of the Rediscovered Caves of Dun-kar in Western Tibet', in Maurizio Taddei and Giuseppe de Marco (eds), *South Asian Archaeology 1997: Proceedings of the 14th International Conference of the European Association of South Asian Archaeologists*, vol. 3 (Rome, 2000), pp. 1383-1402; Thomas J. Pritzker, 'A Preliminary Report on Early Cave Paintings of Western Tibet', *Orientations*, 27/6 (1996): pp. 26-47; and Kimiaki Tanaka, 'The Usefulness of Buddhist Iconography in Analysing Style in Tibetan', *Tibet Journal*, 21/2 (1996): pp. 6-9. For other Tibetan sites, see Huo Wei, 'Newly Discovered Early Buddhist Grottoes in Western Tibet', in Amy Heller and Giacomella Orofino (eds), *Discoveries in Western Tibet and the Western Himalayas* (Leiden, 2007), pp. 23-39.

18 Porter, *Travels in Georgia, Persia, Armenia*, pp. 459-60; André Godard, *Les Monuments de Marāgha* (Paris, 1934), p. 20; John Bowman and J.A. Thompson, 'The Monastery-Church of Bar Hebraeus at Maragheh in West Azerbaijan', *Abr-Nahrain*, 7 (1968): pp. 35-61; Minorsky, 'Marāgha', *EI*². We have accounts that the Jacobite Maphrian Bar Hebraeus (d. 1286) had a strong affinity for astronomy and visited Marāgha at a time when Hülegü – whose wife Doghuz Khatun was a devout Christian – was probably still alive. The Nestorian Patriarch

Observations The Raṣadkhāna caves have a ground level and an underground area (see the floor plan in Figure 10.1). At the ground level, a forecourt leads to what Ball calls an antechamber,[19] which has been cut into the western-oriented limestone hill face. Chiselled on the ceiling is a football-sized rock-cut relief of concentric circles, and dotting the walls are lamp niches cut at eye-level. Cut into the north wall is a set of four small niches that once held a small, rectangular wooden door. The antechamber leads through very distinctive upwards-pointed pentagonal openings[20] to two slightly elevated adjacent chambers in the east (no. 3) and south (no. 4) respectively. Each encloses a rectangular block of limestone some 1.2 metres high, standing on a plinth (the block is cut out of the mountain rock and fixed in), and with a chiselled concave roof (Plate 10.1). The southern chamber (no. 4) also has a stepped niche with a rounded back, looking much like an eroded *miḥrāb*.[21]

Two sets of corridors lead around and to lower chambers. From the north wall of the antechamber (no. 2) a corridor winds around the back of chamber 3, and leads through a small round opening only about 1 metre high. Beyond this is an underground passage ends in a room with blackened walls (marked 'a') situated just underneath chamber 3. A similar trajectory winds from the southeast corner of the 'antechamber' to a room underneath chamber 4 (marked 'b'), which has a stepped niche much like the one in chamber 4 above it. The walls of the underground corridors are dotted with lamp niches, as well as larger concave niches that must have held items.

North of the forecourt (no. 1) and along the face of the mountain, are numerous small chambers, with little semi-circular windows, large concave-shaped niches and small lamp niches. Much of the exterior of these caves has crumbled and

---

Mar Yaballaha III (d. 1317) was based in a monastery at Marāgha, where Ghāzān Khān visited him twice. Prior to that Arghun Khān (d. 690/1291) had visited Mar Yaballaha III in Marāgha at a church 'tent'. Ghāzān built a church in Marāgha in which the vessels of Arghun's tent-church were placed. Bar Hebraeus writes that Hülegü and his wife were 'two great lights'. See *The Chronography of Gregory Abû'l-Faraj*, trans. Ernest A. Wallis Budge (London, 1932), vol. 1, pp. xv-lxiii and 444. Yaballaha III (d. 1317) also wrote of the churches built by Hülegü and/or his wife in Baghdad and Ala Taq. See *The Monks of Kûblâi Khân, Emperor of China*, trans. Ernest A. Wallis Budge (London, 1928), pp. 74-5, 223. See also Warwick Ball, 'Two Aspects of Iranian Buddhism', *Bulletin of the Asia Institute of Pahlavi University*, 1 (1976): pp. 127-43, as well as 'Some Rock-Cut Monuments in Southern Iran', *Iran*, 24 (1986): pp. 95-115; Parvīz Varjāvand, *Kawīsh-i Raṣadkhāna-yi Marāgha* (Tehran, 1366 H.Sh./1987-88), pp. 279-83.

19 Ball, 'Two Aspects', p. 129, chambers marked nos 1 and 2 respectively.

20 The pentagonal openings are reminiscent of the shape of the Mongolian tents, or *yurts* that can be identified in Mongolian and Tibetan structures. See N. Tsultem, *Mongolian Architecture*, ed. D. Bayarsaikhan (Ulan-Bator, 1988), pls 11, 40, 58-61, 67; Snellgrove, 'The Notion of Divine Kingship', p. 47.

21 A *miḥrāb* is the prayer niche in the mosque, and is meant to indicate the direction of Mecca, or the *qibla*.

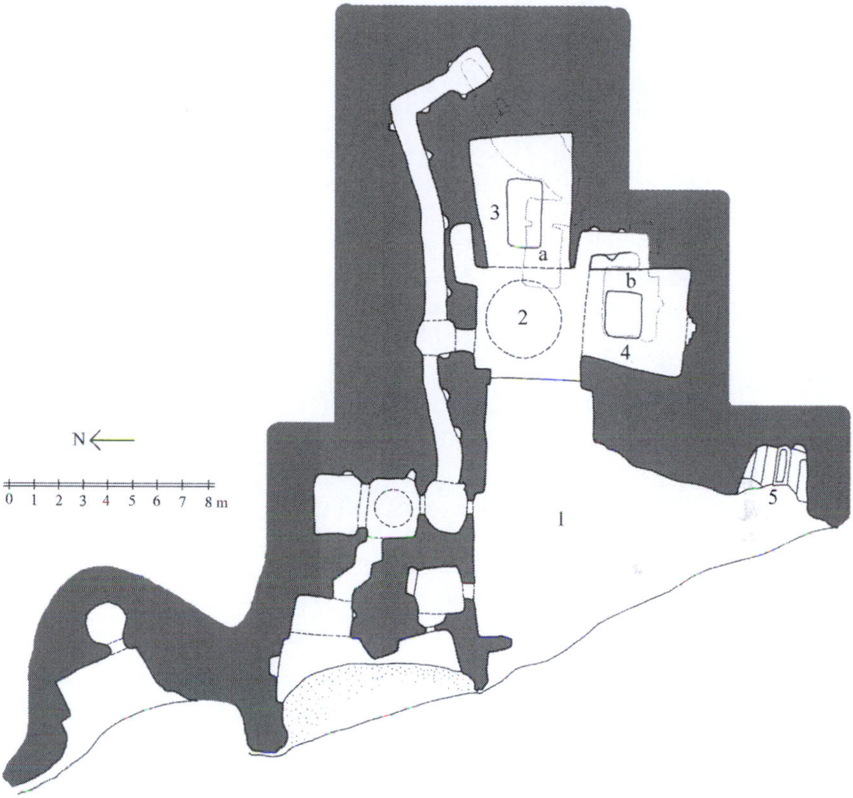

Figure 10.1 Floor plan of the Raṣadkhāna caves at Marāgha.

no original decorations or inscriptions remain. South of the forecourt along the face of the mountain is a shallow cave with three rock-cut tomb chambers (no. 5) that are now exposed and empty. Over a distance of some 50 metres further south are five semi-circular cave openings, but these are filled with earth and are inaccessible without excavation.[22] It seems that these are openings to more chambers or burial sites, as was already suggested by Bowman and Thompson.[23]

Function and dating The rectangular stone blocks in chambers a and b were identified as altars, and hence, the chambers as sanctuaries. To Ball they looked like the Buddhist circumambulatory pillar-caves of Afghanistan and Central

---

[22] These are not depicted in the floor plan (see Figure 10.1).

[23] Bowman and Thompson, 'The Monastery-Church of Bar Hebraeus', p. 56.

Asia,[24] and to Bowman and Thompson like the Jacobite style of dual sanctuaries.[25] I would also note a resemblance to the Sasanian fire altars of Balkh.[26] Ker Porter wrote: 'These secluded places [i.e. the caves] we are told, were not merely the habitations of Zoroaster himself and his Magi, but were used as temples.'[27] In the cave temples of the Mithraists (or *mithraea*), altars of such dimensions can also be found.[28] An ancient Mithraic use is likely given the similarities with Roman Mithraic temples, but it is the Ilkhanid period that is of greater interest to us.

The second set of observations revolves around the underground area and takes us into the Ilkhanid period. André Godard believed that the site was a mere extension of the Ilkhanid observatory and that the underground chamber served as a cold store.[29] The purpose of the underground spaces according to Bowman and Thompson was for storing precious items - manuscripts or relics.[30] Ball does not venture a guess about the purpose of the underground area. We can also not rule out the possibility that the underground passages served as escape routes. The soot along the underground walls may be the legacy of arson.[31] Caves lend themselves well to seekers of refuge, and the site may indeed have served persecuted Christians or Buddhists,[32] as it may have served the followers of Bābak, the famous rebel of several centuries earlier (201/816-17) described in the early Arabic sources.[33] However, we have no evidence to that effect, and can therefore not confirm that this area served any religious purpose.

---

24 Ball, 'Two Aspects', pp. 137-8.

25 Bowman and Thompson, 'The Monastery-Church of Bar Hebraeus', p. 43.

26 On the Balkh altars, see A.D.H. Bivar, 'Fire-Altars of the Sassanian Period in Balkh', *Journal of Warburg and Courtauld Institutes*, 17 (1954): pp. 182-3 and pls 25-6, pl. 25.

27 Porter, *Travels in Georgia, Persia, Armenia*, vol. 2, p. 496.

28 See Varjāvand, *Kawīsh-i Raṣadkhāna-yi Marāgha*, pp. 279-83. On the history and belief system of Mithraism which developed with the conquest of Persia by Alexander the Great in 331 BCE, see Franz Cumont, *Les Mystères de Mithra* (Brussels, 1913) and Taufiq Wahby, *The Remnants of Mithraism in Hatra and Iraqi Kurdistan and its Traces in Yazīdism* (London, 1962).

29 Godard, *Les Monuments de Marāgha*, p. 20.

30 Bowman and Thompson, 'The Monastery-Church of Bar Hebraeus', p. 53.

31 Fires may have been lit intentionally or may have been caused by natural disasters. The Marāgha area has been earthquake-prone for centuries, and earthquakes would have caused fires in places where oil lamps or candles were burning. The many notches in the walls of the *Raṣadkhāna* caves tell us that this was the case. See Charles Melville, 'Historical Monuments and Earthquakes in Tabriz', *Iran*, 19 (1981): pp. 159, 162-3 and 168. Fires may also, of course, have been used for cooking or heating the caves in this area that reaches freezing temperatures in the winter.

32 On the persecution of Christians during the Ilkhanate, Yaballaha III states that 'that accursed and damned man, Nawrūz [i.e. one of the Ilkhanid rebels in Khorasan], the hater of justice, the enemy of the truth and the lover of falsehood' destroyed a number of Christian churches. See Budge, *Monks of Kûblâi Khân*, p. 224.

33 For a recent description of the rebel, see Dominique Sourdel, 'Bābak', *EI*^{2}.

The third set of observations refers to the small chambers further north. Ball suggests that these are the cells of a monastery.[34] Due to the fact that much of the hill rock has crumbled away it is difficult to ascertain any structural constellation of cells that would match the template outlined by Lamotte. Bowman and Thompson propose that these were Christian monastic cells.[35]

Despite the literary evidence for Ilkhanid monastery-churches in Marāgha, it is difficult to identify the Raṣadkhāna caves to be one of them. Godard convincingly asks why the Ilkhans would not build a free-standing, richly decorated and imposing church, like the other Ilkhanid churches described in the contemporary chronicles.[36]

In the absence of any specifically Buddhist epigraphy, iconography or artefacts, it is difficult to confirm that the Raṣadkhāna site served as an Ilkhanid Buddhist monastery or temple. In fact, some Afghan caves were identified as Buddhist only on account of the Buddhist themes painted on their walls (see below), rather than their architecture. It is fair to assume that the Raṣadkhāna caves have served different troglodyte groups since prehistoric times, including Mithraists, and possibly Buddhists or Christians. Systematic archaeological reconnaissance and secured excavations of the caves and the surrounding area could help us to ascertain the Ilkhanid Buddhist use of the site.

2. Mihrī Temple/ Imāmzāda Maʿṣūm (near Marāgha)

Previous studies The first archaeologist to describe this site was Parvīz Varjāvand in the early 1970s. Warwick Ball provided a more accurate overview by factoring in the inscriptions and decorated stonework in the complex, as well as the adjacent cemetery, and a more detailed floor plan.[37] Recent Iranian excavations highlight further architectural features (see floor plan in Figure 10.2).

Observations In the outskirts of Marāgha lies the site of the Mihrī Temple, also known as the Imāmzāda Maʿṣūm. This site is far less known than the last, although it is just as mysterious, and therefore deserves more attention. The site has three accessible areas: a main space surrounded by four domed chambers (nos 2, 4, 5, 6, 7); a four-domed hall with a full-size pillar in its centre (no. 3); and a set of three long chambers some 100 metres away.

---

[34] Ball, 'Two Aspects', p. 131.

[35] Bowman and Thompson, 'The Monastery-Church of Bar Hebraeus', pp. 43-5.

[36] Godard, *Les Monuments de Marāgha*, p. 20; on Ilkhanid churches, see Minorsky, 'Marāgha, *EI*[2].

[37] Parvīz Varjāvand, 'The Imāmzādeh Maʿsūm Varjovi near Marāgheh', *East and West*, 25/3-4 (1975): pp. 435-8, at p. 436, figs 1 and 2; Warwick Ball, 'The Imāmzādeh Maʿsūm at Vardjovī. A Rock-Cut Īlkhānid Complex near Marāgheh', *Archäologische Mitteilungen aus Iran*, 12 (1979): pp. 329-40, at p. 331.

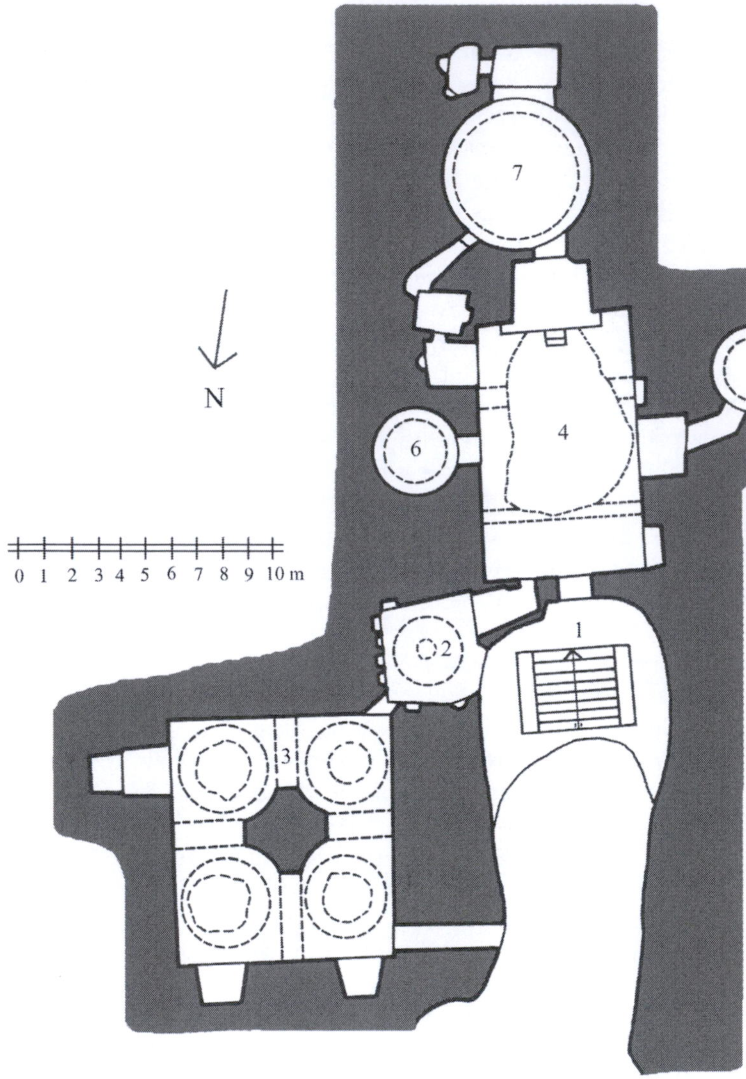

Figure 10.2 Floor plan of the Mihrī Temple/Imāmzāda Maʿṣūm, near Marāgha.

The main space: An elm tree and a stone stairway lead down to what Ball calls the antechamber (no. 1). A parallelogram-shaped opening with a rough semi-circular roof and a single step of masonry blocks crosses into the central chamber (no. 4). The original roof has collapsed, and is now replaced by a makeshift modern brick roof. Ball suggests that the roof was originally divided into three by two shallow semi-circular arches. He notes the four symmetrical notches along the opening, two on either side, indicating where a rectangular wooden door had been fitted. Recent Iranian excavations have revealed direct access from the central chamber (no. 4) to the largest of the domed chambers (no. 7) through two corridors; to another domed chamber not previously recorded (no. 6); and to the square room with a domed roof to the northeast (no. 2). Ball had already recorded the access from the middle of the west wall of chamber 4 through a semi-circular vaulted alcove with a tunnel leading to yet another domed chamber which is now free of rubble (no. 5). Flanking the vaulted alcove is a badly eroded east-facing *miḥrāb*, a square niche to its south and a band of Qurʾānic inscriptions.[38]

On the south side of the main chamber (no. 4) is a large square-roofed alcove. Ball observed the deliberate obliteration of frescoes here, but the author could not confirm that. The roof is blackened by what seems to be smoke, and next to it is a small wall opening that looks like an airshaft. The alcove leads to a little cavity that contains two niches. A second access to the largest domed room (no. 7) leads through an opening on the southern end of the east wall of chamber no. 4 via a passageway. The domed chamber no. 7 has a remarkably well-preserved ceiling faceted in the Ilkhanid stalactite style (Plate 10.3). Each facet is a square or triangle and only one facet has any decoration left on it. Not remarked on by Ball are tracings in *naskhī* script on the walls, which may indicate that the calligraphic artwork was left incomplete, and possibly brought to an abrupt halt. The second part: The pillared hall (no. 3) is accessed from the main chamber (no. 4) via a small roughly square chamber surmounted by a dome with practically no zone of transition or squinches (no. 2). It has a light shaft in its ceiling and contains a row of four roughly elliptical niches set at eye-level on its east wall and two elongated niches on the adjacent walls (Plate 10.4). The pillared hall itself was largely filled with the rubble of its collapsed ceiling when Ball visited, but has now been cleared out by the Iranian Cultural Heritage Organisation. It is a large square, divided into four smaller squares by semi-circular arches, each surmounted by a (now collapsed) dome, possibly pierced by a light shaft like in chamber no. 2. Ball guessed rightly that the hall had 'at least two alcoves'[39] – in fact, there are three; one cut in the east wall and two in the north wall. What Ball could not see is the abundance of niches cut into the chamber and pillar walls. The pillar's hexagonal stem (Plate 10.5) has 12 finely-carved niches grouped into four (Plate 10.6). The niches on the chamber walls are largely eroded, but two are well preserved. Also newly revealed are carved door notches on the western wall and low-lying rock-cut pegs. The opening in the western wall leading to the stairway antechamber (no. 1) seems to be recent and was probably not an original feature of the building.

The third part: Located just 100 metres to the east of the complex is a set of one transversal and two lateral chambers.[40] These were largely filled when Ball

38 See also photos in Ali Matin, *East Azerbaijan* (Tehran, 1384 H.Sh./2005-06), pp. 72-3.

39 Ball, 'The Imāmzādeh Maʿsūm at Vardjovī', p. 333.

40 The third part of the site is not indicated in the floor plan (Fig. 10.2).

visited,[41] but recent excavations reveal an array of large trough-like niches or basins with pegs carved in the rock (Plate 10.7). Some features include a little opening in the ground (now covered) and a large elevated rock-cut platform.

Function and dating Our research team found that the site remains an active Islamic shrine venerated by local pilgrims today. The largest domed chamber (no. 7) houses the shrine of Maʿṣūm, presumably the wife of a local dignitary who created the shrine for her. The smaller domed chamber (no. 5) is said to be the shrine of the dignitary himself.[42]

Here again, Ball suggests that this is one of the *butkhānas* configured as an Islamic building after the Ilkhan Ghāzān (reg. 694/1295-703/1304) converted to Islam. Ball contends that the oldest tombstone at the adjacent cemetery is dated to the eighth/fourteenth century: we were not able to identify that tombstone. He supports his Buddhist thesis with two main arguments: that the niches in chamber no. 2 leading to the pillar-cave (no. 3) may have contained rows of images such as those in the *stūpas* of Haḍḍa and Bāmiyān in Afghanistan; and that circumambulatory pillar-caves are found in Buddhist cave complexes in other places, such as at Basāwal and Fīlkhāna in Afghanistan, and at Qara Tepe and Turfan further east.[43] However, here again, Ball does not explain why these cave establishments would be built so much later than the Afghan or Central Asian ones. As with the nearby Raṣadkhāna site, Varjāvand suggests that it was Mithraic, seeing (unspecified) parallels with the Masjid-i sangī (the stone mosque) of Dārābjird and of Īj in Iran and with the *mithraeum* near Āzarshahr in the East Azerbaijan province of Iran.[44]

---

41 Ball, 'The Imāmzādeh Maʿsum at Vardjovī', p. 335.

42 Local residents told us that pilgrims used to make offerings at the shrine for fertility or good health, but stopped after the shrine was looted some years ago. It is still where the annual *taʿziya* procession is performed; the *taʿziya* is the Islamic passion play that re-enacts the suffering and death of Ḥusayn ibn ʿAlī ibn Abī Ṭālib (d. 61/680).

43 See Ball, 'The Imāmzādeh Maʿsum at Vardjovī', pp. 338-9. To take Ball's argument further, it can be surmised that if there had been a *stūpa* in this site it would have been in chamber 7. The domed chamber exhibits the greatest similarities with the Indian or Tibetan *caitya* that houses *stūpas*. On Tibetan *chörten* and monastery architecture, see Adrian Snodgrass, *The Symbolism of the Stupa* (Delhi, 1992); Niels Gutschow and David N. Gellner, *The Nepalese Caitya: 1500 Years of Buddhist Votive Architecture in the Kathmandu Valley* (Stuttgart, 1997).

44 Varjāvand, 'The Imāmzādeh Maʿsūm Varjovi near Marāgheh', pp. 437-8. The primary name of the site, Mihrī, may also be significant. Wahby in his study of Mithraic elements in the Yazīdī religion of the Kurds (citing Cumont, *Mystères de Mithra*), explains that 'Mithra' – the Indo-Aryan god of light, guardian of the truth and enemy of the lie and error – became the god of the sun and contracts, in the Iranian context, where his name was modified to 'Mihr' in the first century CE. Wahby also refers to numerous cave temple sites in Iraq. See his *Remnants of Mithraism*, pp. 3 and 12-14.

Neither Ball nor Varjāvand factor into their analyses the third part of the complex – the three long chambers. It is reasonable to presume that the elevated platform served as a kitchen space, and that the opening in the ground (now filled) led to underground cool stores. Furthermore, the trough-like niches and pegs are reminiscent of stables: the niches would have held fodder for horses or cattle tethered to rock-cut pegs. Such domestic uses may have served secular households as well as religious establishments.[45]

As with the Raṣadkhāna site, the Mihrī Temple lacks evidence that can allow us to take Ball's argument any further. The epigraphy, the stalactite style of the *miḥrābs* and the domed roof of the main shrine (chamber 7) point to an Ilkhanid Muslim use. It does not seem that was a new Ilkhanid construction as Ball suggests, but rather that the Ilkhans added their own signature to a structure that already existed.

3. Dāsh Kasan / Qonqor Olong

Previous studies Gianroberto Scarcia and a team of archaeologists from Venice visited the site when a significant portion was still under rubble (which has been cleared today). In a brief article in the mid-1970s he suggested that the figural representations on it were Buddhist. Wolfram Kleiss describes it briefly with photos and a rough plan in a 1997 article.[46]

Observations This site lies in Zanjān province near the late Ilkhanid capital of Sulṭāniyya. At the village of Viyar on a plateau the Mongols called Qonqor Olong, one comes across an imposing Ilkhanid horseshoe-shaped façade that faces north towards the Safīd Kūh mountains. The name of the village of Viyar might itself be an indication that a Buddhist building once stood here. The name Viyar/ Viar is common in Iran and Central Asia, and may be a cognate of *vihāra*.[47] The façade encloses a generous open space of some 30 x 70 metres (Plate 10.8), which

---

45 Not recorded, and probably unknown to Ball, is another long room, some twenty metres away from the 'third part' of the site, that features similar trough-like niches. It now serves as the underground chicken coop of a local resident's house some twenty metres away. Moreover, recent informal excavations have revealed an extensive site, now underground, only seven hundred metres southwest of Mihrī that spans a wide plain on a hill known as Pīr Hāshim. The Iranian Cultural Heritage and Tourism Organisation dug dozens of holes into the ground, two to three metres in diameter, that reveal an intricate system of stairs, wells and chambers. To the south of the plain, across a narrow river and along a low mountain range, another set of cave openings, niches,and built walls can be seen.

46 See Gianroberto Scarcia, 'The "Vihār" of Qonqor-olong – Preliminary Report', *East and West*, 25/3-4 (1975): pp. 99-104; and Wolfram Kleiss, 'Bauten und Siedlungsplätze in der Umgebung von Soltaniyeh', *Archäologische Mitteilungen aus Iran und Turan*, 29 (1997): pp. 341-91, pls 9 and 42.

47 The name 'Viyar' is reminiscent of Richard Bulliet's study of the place name 'Viar' and its cognate, *bahar*, which is common in north-east Iran. See his 'Naw Bahār and the

opens up to a stunning wide plain. Gianroberto Scarcia provided a floor plan of the external site, but described only a few structural details, probably because of the rubble fill.[48] The site is still peppered with fallen building blocks, but the Iranian Cultural Heritage Organisation has cleared the blocks to the periphery. This has laid bare much of the floors and the façade, which I shall now describe.[49]

The Qonqor Olong site, also known today as 'Dāsh Kasan', lies on an elevation rising on three shallow levels along the slope of the hill. Approaching the site at its first and lowest level, the open space, though largely dilapidated, gives the impression of having been a grand entrance. Ruins of staircase-like structures flank the entrance vertically to its east and west, and horizontal steps appear to have connected this level to the next. While the high walls of the façade at the first level have largely crumbled, the remains indicate a chiseled herring-bone pattern. On the eastern side of the enclosed space lies a rectangular sandpit-like structure framed by large rectangular rocks.

On the second level, the east and west walls feature cave openings, all of which are sealed. The light colouring of the damaged façade indicates that the rock fall was recent. This is not surprising given the soft consistency of the hill rock. The walls, albeit spoilt, are finely smoothed, geometrically refined and rich in decorative detail. They were partly obscured by rubble in Scarcia's time as can be seen from his photos and incomplete plan.[50] The recent clearing of the open space has brought to light the symmetrical juxtaposition of decorative relief on a vertical plane and of structure on a horizontal axis. Cut into the eastern and western walls is a pair of large relief carvings of a framed dragon (Plate 10.9). The dragon on the west wall was not visible when Scarcia visited. As with the minor cave openings, the dragons are directly opposite one another. Unfortunately, the structure above the dragons has largely broken off, but one can make out a wide niche, which may have housed a large statue.

At the third and most-elevated level, another sealed cave opening is now largely obscured from lower-level view due to the collapse of the weathered roof of the south-western part of the façade. An unconventional set of adjacent stalactite *miḥrābs* flank the central cave opening at the outer edges of the south wall and on either side of the eastern and western walls (Plate 10.10). The *miḥrābs* are facing north, east and west, when according to traditional practice they should be facing Mecca, which lies in a south-south-westerly direction. An intricate symmetry of carved pillars is found on the southern wall.

Survival of Iranian Buddhism', *Iran*, 14 (1976): pp. 140-45. A similar argument has been made for the etymology of the name Bukhara: see the article on the city in *EI*[2].

48 Scarcia, 'The "Vihār" of Qonqor-olong', p. 103.

49 No floor plan will be given here. The Iranian Cultural Heritage and Tourism Organisation has issued a report on its recent excavations written by Dr Mīr-Fattāḥ, but the research team was not able to locate it in time for this article.

50 Scarcia, 'The "Vihār" of Qonqor-olong', p. 103.

Another *miḥrāb* – only revealed recently – can be seen to the right of the dragon relief on the western wall. This *miḥrāb* differs in shape from the others in that it is long and narrow with some decorative deviations, such as reliefs of pillars and arches. While the eastern wall directly opposite has broken off, it is likely that the same *miḥrāb* format and symmetrical harmony was executed here.

Function and dating Scarcia suggests that the characteristic features of the complex – structural, stylistic and iconographic – are markers of Ilkhanid Buddhism, notably that of Arghun Khān who started the construction of Sulṭāniyya. That the building is Ilkhanid may be gleaned from contemporary literary references to Qonqor Olong discussed above. The confines of Sulṭāniyya extended beyond where the famous tomb of Oljeitü is found today, and may well have included this building.[51] The *miḥrāb* carvings may have been added when the Ilkhan Öljeitü embraced Islam.[52]

Scarcia does not suggest what the function of the building may have been, and it is indeed difficult to ascertain. Perhaps the Qonqor Olong site was a hunting lodge for the Ilkhan and his entourage, and it may also have contained a temple. Unlike Marāgha, this site has the aura of a regal entrance to a palatial building and boasts the grandeur of a powerful ruler. It does not include any convincing elements of Lamotte's profiling of a Buddhist monastery or temple, but then again, too little of it is visible today. Even the façade is too ruined, and without further excavations, we will not know whether it held any Buddhist objects of worship. However, as mentioned earlier, Rashīd al-Dīn and Qāshānī provide some evidence that there was a place of worship (*bandagī*) in Qonqor Olong attended by the Ilkhans and *bakhshīs*, and it is not impossible that this is the site to which they are referring.

The table below summarizes the elements that could possibly fall into Lamotte's description of Indian Buddhist rock-cut caves. The ticked boxes are a crude and approximate indication. We cannot say that these features were necessarily Buddhist, but they are shared with early Indian Buddhist cave temples and monasteries.

[51] The wall of Sulṭāniyya at the time of Arghun Khān reached 12,000 paces in circumference. His son and successor, Öljeitü, began to enlarge the town in 703/1305 (up to 30,000 paces in circumference). See Minorsky, 'Sulṭāniyya', *EI*², citing Qāshānī.

[52] Sufi *shaykhs*, in particular, seem to have found the favour of the Ilkhan Öljeitü. See Reuven Amitai-Preiss, 'Sufis and Shamans: Some Remarks on the Islamization of the Mongols in the Īlkhānate', *Journal of the Economic and Social History of the Orient*, 42 (1999): p. 35.

Table 10.1 Features of the Iranian cave sites that are shared with Indian Buddhist cave temples and monasteries

TEMPLE					MONASTERY		
Features/ Sites	*Rectangular hall, stairs (for stūpa)*	*Double row of pillars*	*Vaulted nave*	*Semi-circular opening (to stūpa)*	*Verandas*	*Flat-roofed central hall*	*Small cells*
Raṣadkhāna	√	--	√		?	?	√
Mihrī Temple	√	--	?		--	--	?
Qonqor Olong	--	--	--		--	--	--

(II) FINDINGS: EPIGRAPHY AND IMAGES AT THE ROCK-CUT SITES

Unfortunately, none of the sites displays any epigraphy that was written in the languages of Buddhism – Sanskrit, Pali, Tibetan, Chinese, Ghandari etc. In fact, the only epigraphy visible at all is a finely cut wall inscription at Mihrī (Plate 10.2) of a Qur'ānic text in the Arabic *naskhī* script. Ball transcribed the remnants of the inscription – more has been lost since – and identified excerpts from the 'Victory' *sūra* 48.[53] The inscription runs horizontally at eye-level along the walls of the various chambers of The Mihrī Temple.

The plaques that are incised on the façade of the Qonqor Olong site appear to have displayed some kind of writing as well. The Viyar village elder told the research team that in his youth the village children used to chip off carved writings from the façade. Apparently, the site was still used as a caravanserai and local festival hall with a fountain (perhaps the sandpit-like structure mentioned above) in his lifetime, until it was set alight by a local ruler.[54] No epigraphy is visible at the site today.

Similarly, while frescoes with Buddhist iconographic detail are a common feature in Buddhist art and adorn the Afghan and Central Asian cave sites,[55] none

53 Ball, 'The Imāmzādeh Maʿsūm at Vardjovī', pp. 332-3.

54 Interview with Ḥājjī ʿAbdul Ḥusayn, at Viyar, 24 September 2006. Writing in the early eighth/fourteenth century, the Persian chronicler Waṣṣāf, a protégé of the Ilkhanid vizier Rashīd al-Dīn, describes Sulṭāniyya's magnificent buildings and provides extensive details of an ornate fountain studded with jewels at Öljeitü's palace. Waṣṣāf, *Taḥrīr-i Tārīkh-i Waṣṣāf* (completed c.727/1326), ed. ʿAbd al-Muḥammad ʿĀyatī (Tehran, 1993), pp. 337-9.

55 See examples of Buddhist wall paintings of Afghanistan in André Godard, Joseph Hackin and Paul Pelliot, *Les Antiquités Bouddhiques de Bamiyan* (Paris, 1928), pls XVIII-XXVIII; Daniel Schlumberger, 'Le palais ghaznévide de Lashkari Bazar', *Syria*, 24 (1952):

is visible at the Iranian caves today. Ball observed remnants of red and yellow paint at Mihrī.[56] It cannot be excluded that frescoes adorned the walls at some point and that they were erased, but whether they were Buddhist may never be known.

At Qonqor Olong there are figural representations, notably a large pair of dragons finely carved in rock at an extremely high relief (more than 20 cm deep) flanking the two vertical walls of the horseshoe-shaped façade (Plate 10.9). Although the dragon is frequently found in pre-Islamic and Islamic artistic repertories – for example, in depictions of dragon-slaying events that feature in Persian epics – the wall carving of dragons of such a large size is unusual.[57] The dragons have serpent-like bodies, lashing tails and gaping mouths. They resemble Chinese dragons, and are almost identical to the dragons painted on the tiles of nearby Takht-i Sulaymān of the same period. This matches the commonly accepted notion that the prototype for the Islamic dragon is Chinese, possibly adopted by artists from China or Central Asia. The accurate identification of Sulṭāniyya on the Chinese map described by Bretschneider and dated to the mid-fourteenth century only strengthens the argument for interactions between Iran and the Far East. The dragons reflect an eastern style, but it would be speculative to cite them as strong evidence for the practice of Buddhism in Iran.[58] Other icons, such as images of the Buddha, bodhisattvas or the turning wheel (*cakra*) would be far more convincing clues for a Buddhist purpose of the rock-cut site.

Carvings of vegetal reliefs line the arches of the *miḥrāb* carvings, and also flank them. The *miḥrāb* carvings are superimposed by rock-cut plaques. At the

pp. 251-70, pls. XXXI and XXXII; examples of Qizil and Qumtura in *Painted Buddhas of Xinjiang* (London, 2002); Tibetan examples in Ian Alsop, 'The Wall Paintings of Mustang', in Pratapaditya Pal (ed.), *Nepal: Old Images, New Insights* (Mumbai, 2004), pp. 130-31.

[56] Ball, 'Two Aspects', p. 134.

[57] For dragon images in Islamic and pre-Islamic art in general, see Giovanni Curatola, *Draghi: La tradizione artistica orientale e i disegni del tesoro del Topkapï* (Venice, 1989), pp. 45-81, figs 20-78; on tiles, see Linda Komaroff and Stefano Carboni, *The Legacy of Genghis Khan: Courtly Art and Culture in Western Asia, 1256-1353* (New York, 2002), figs 59, 100, 102, 106, 275; and Rudolf Naumann, *Die Ruinen des Tachte Suleiman and Zendan-e Suleiman und Umgebung* (Berlin, 1977), figs 70, 81; in metalwork, see Daphne Lange Rosenzweig, 'Stalking the Persian Dragon: Chinese Prototypes for the Miniature Representations', *Kunst des Orients*, 12 (1978-79): pp. 150-76 (metalwork); and in carpets, see Taher Sabahi, 'The Eagle and the Serpent, the Phoenix and the Dragon', *Oriental Carpet and Textile Studies*, 5 (1999): pp. 137-44. Giovanni Curatola wrote an article on the Viyar dragons, which I was not able to read in time for this article: See his *Solṭāniya II* (Venice, 1979).

[58] In China, the dragon does not necessarily have a Buddhist meaning, as the Taoists and Confucians accepted it as a secular symbol of benevolence and power. See Curatola, *Draghi*, p. 17; and Rosenzweig, 'Stalking the Persian Dragon', pp. 150-51. Gerardus van der Leeuw explains the dragon found in such a multitude of religions through phenomenology in his *Religion in Essence and Manifestation* (London, 1938), pp. 66 and 76.

third level of the Qonqor Olong site, on the southern wall, directly above and precisely centred with the apexes of the *miḥrāb* arches, are two carvings of what appear to be 'tree of life' depictions: an image that is common to many religions.[59] As Scarcia already pointed out, the artistic style in Viyar seems to fall distinctly into the form found in Sasanian-type stucco reliefs such as those of Ṭāq-i Būstān (in Kirmānshāh, Iran) that reappear in mediaeval Islamic monuments.[60] Seen in this light, the image may have been associated with both Buddhist and neo-Sasanian stylistic repertoires of the Ilkhanid period.

The only other animate object of note is the carving of what Ball suggests[61] to be two entangled snakes surmounted by two diamond-like bosses on the wall of the central hall at The Mihrī Temple (Plate 10.11). The snake has been an iconographic symbol of various religions since prehistoric times, and therefore does not help us to identify the religion(s) practised in this cave.

We encountered no texts or movable artefacts, such as scrolls or statues, and not even ceramic sherds. Bowman and Thompson, who dug at the Raṣadkhāna site in Marāgha in the 1960s, recovered what appears to have been a lid fragment at one of the graves. One of its slabs had a small depression 'such as one finds in "Assyrian" cemeteries'.[62] Some 25 feet south of the tomb area along traces of another opening, the researchers excavated bits of human bone and two small pieces of 'mediaeval glazed Arab pottery' at what may have been another burial site.[63] The village elder of Viyar recalled that the Qonqor Olong site had been rich in artefacts, including coins and pottery, but that 'gold-diggers' had sold them off to international art dealers.[64] Future excavators may retrieve artefacts at the Marāgha and Zanjān sites, which have sealed entrances and may be connected to larger networks of chambers.

IV. CONCLUSION: A LEGACY LOST IN TRANSLATION?

This study has *not* provided convincing evidence that Buddhism imported in the Mongol period left a significant legacy in Iran. Although we know that some

59 See van der Leeuw, *Religion in Essence and Manifestation*, pp. 56-8, and Roger Cook, *The Tree of Life: Symbol of the Centre* (London, 1974).

60 Scarcia, 'The "Vihār" of Qonqor-olong', p. 104. Sasanian tree depictions come in a variety of floral and vegetal designs, such as strips of beads, chevrons, lotus buds, arch-shaped rosettes, demi-palmettes, leaf-scrolls and acorns. Examples on stucco from Varāmīn, Ctesiphon and Tāq-i Būstān can be seen in Roman Ghirshman, *Iran: Parthians and Sassanians* (London, 1962), p. 189; and Shinji Fukai and Kiyoharu Horiuchi, *Tāq-i Būstān* (Tokyo, 1969), pls IV-VIII, LVII-LIX. For later usage of this style, see Arthur Pope, *A Survey of Persian Art: From Prehistoric Times to the Present* (London, 1938), vol. 5, pp. 511-13.

61 Ball, 'The Imāmzādeh Maʿsūm at Vardjovī', p. 330.

62 Bowman and Thompson, 'The Monastery-Church of Bar Hebraeus', p. 49.

63 Bowman and Thompson, 'The Monastery-Church of Bar Hebraeus', p. 56.

64 Interview with Ḥajjī ʿAbd al-Ḥusayn in Viyar, 24 September 2006.

Mongol rulers did practise Buddhism, we are in the dark on whether Iranians converted to the religion or if there was already a Buddhist minority that would have provided the Ilkhanid import with an obvious home. We do not know who would have patronized the establishments, and who constituted the clergy – Mongol or Persian, élite or commoner.

There is much material for archaeologists and art-historians to explore, and the cross-cultural and multi-disciplinary aspects of the topic would require collaborations between Iranian and international researchers with expertise in Buddhist and Islamic architecture and texts. Work at the Sulṭāniyya site in Iran's Zanjān province holds the greatest promise for Ilkhanid Buddhism on account of its geographic location, and the frequency and detail of textual references. The Iranian Cultural Heritage Organisation has invested significant resources in debris removal and maintaining the integrity of the site. The story behind the monumental mélange of Sasanian, Islamic and eastern icons at the site deserves to be told, and its ideological and aesthetic significance understood.

Further studies of the Sulṭāniyya site should try to draw on the findings of the excavations being carried out since 2000 at the early Mongol capital of Qaraqorum (in modern-day Mongolia). Interesting parallels may also be contained in the Ilkhan Hülegü's burial site and castle discovered on the island of Shāhī, near Marāgha.

In Marāgha itself, further studies of the rock-hewn underground passages that probably connect the Raṣadkhāna site to the observatory would inevitably hold more solid clues. However, the current co-location of governmental information services at the observatory may prove to be an obstacle to further researches at this point. At the Mihrī Temple site, on the other hand, the distinctively Ilkhanid features and its connections to the underground city nearby hold promise for fruitful archaeological research.

Any further studies on the two Marāgha sites, which most probably have pre-Islamic antecedents, should include expertise in Roman Mithraic architecture, which has enjoyed significant scholarly attention. The Roman parallels could supplement the little-studied aspects of Mithraic architecture in Iran. There are plenty of pre-Islamic parallels of rock-cut architecture in Iran itself, and these should be catalogued and made available to a general scholarly readership. The Chihilkhāna site in Bushehr, for example, which was studied by Ball in the 1970s (and this field research team, as well as a Japanese team in 2008) appears to have served as a pre-Islamic Buddhist or Hindu refuge, possibly for Indian merchants. There are other sites that have received hardly any scholarly attention, notably the enigmatic 'Bunwū' (also spelled 'Bonwoo') site in southern Iran, which features shallow, geometrical fountains and epigraphy in Devanagari script painted in red on its walls and surrounding rock structures.

Ilkhanid Iran was a melting pot of religions and cultures; and the Buddhist influences on it have melted into its history and become indiscernible. This study has shown that the practice of 'Buddhism' in Iran cannot be studied without significant financial and material (and possibly, political) investment, and the risks of failure may prove prohibitive. The concept of religiosity is complex, and understanding it requires data, which in this case are sparse. But, we know that an exchange of ideas and techniques occurred, and that a plurality of people coexisted, and so we cannot reject the possibility of a Buddhist legacy.

Chapter 11
The Muslim Queens of the Himalayas: Princess Exchanges in Baltistan and Ladakh

Georgios T. Halkias

INTRODUCTION: MUSLIM QUEENS IN BUDDHIST KINGDOMS[1]

The practice of exchanging princesses (giving and/or receiving them as brides) was a prevalent feature of ancient diplomacy that was widely practised in Tibet[2] and in the states of the north-western Himalayas. Accounts of bride exchange[3] can be found in Ladakhi and Balti histories and in folksongs that commemorate the birth and accomplishments of Kings (*rgyal-po*) and Lords (*jo-bo*),[4] Queens (*rgyal-mo*) and Noble Ladies (*jo-jo*) and other important historical figures, such as ministers, priests and famous artists. In this article, we will look at folksongs concerning Ladakh's 'royal era' (*rgyal-dus*) that celebrate the extraordinary lives of Muslim princesses who were sent as brides to the court of Ladakh and became known as *Khatuns*, Muslim queens of Buddhist kingdoms.

---

[1] This article would not have been possible without the AHRC providing funding for two fieldwork trips in Ladakh in the summers of 2007 and 2008. Photographs taken during these journeys are available on http://warburg.sas.ac.uk/islamtibet/documents.html (see also Plate 11.1). Special thanks go to the following individuals for their advice, guidance and assistance: Ladakhi historian Tashi Rabgyas for meeting with me on several occasions at his son's home in Leh and guiding me through the vast oral and written sources on the history of Ladakh, and to Abdul Ghani Sheikh for availing his knowledge of Muslim traditions. I am also grateful to the editors and to Christopher Beckwith, Brandon Dotson and John Bray for their valuable comments.

[2] The union of matrimony and politics had already driven Tibet's foreign relations during the imperial period; see Brandon Dotson, 'The 'Nephew–Uncle' Relationship in the International Diplomacy of the Tibetan Empire (Seventh–Ninth Centuries)', in id. et al. (eds), *Contemporary Visions in Tibetan Studies* (Chicago, 2009).

[3] This early and most fundamental exchange between one group and another was first discussed in terms of alliance theory in kinship by Claude Lévi Strauss in *Les structures élémentaires de la parenté* (Paris, 1949) and n. 41 below.

[4] While *Yabgo* (a title from Turkestan) was the proper name of a ruling lineage or dynasty in Baltistan, 'the title of the ruler of Khapalu was the Tibetan word *Cho*' (Tib. *jo-bo*; lord, master): Richard Emerson, 'Charismatic Kingship: A Study of State-Formation and Authority in Baltistan', *Politics and Society*, 12 (1983): pp. 413-44, at p. 423.

Cultural historians and social anthropologists of Islam and of Tibet may wish to re-examine the neglected subject of Buddhist–Muslim marriage alliances; for by their frequency, such exchanges gave rise to intricate forms of interdependence between families and lineages that challenge stereotypes of cultural homogeneity and religious exclusivity and introduce important ways to evaluate the intricate history of Tibetan–Muslim relations in the Himalayas. Furthermore, the Muslim queens in Ladakh are important for reconstructing the Central Asian legacy of Muslim women as symbols of sovereignty.[5] It is well documented that after the Mongol invasion in Central Asia and Persia the thrones of Muslim states were 'occupied by an impressive number of women with the privileges of the *khutba* and coining of money': that is, the most important expressions of sovereignty in the Muslim world.[6] Not unlike the Mongol Khatuns, the Muslim queens of Ladakh, who bear the same title, are the outcome of the spread of Islamic civilization in Central Asia and its borderlands.

The Muslim queens of our folksongs witness to a rich cultural heritage, an old blend of Arab, Persian, Mongol, Indian and Tibetan elements. They inspired their own legacies for the people of Baltistan ('Little Tibet') and Ladakh ('Middle Tibet'), which shared epic and oral traditions as well as Tibetan Buddhism from the times of the Tibetan Empire (seventh–ninth centuries).[7] Ever since the conversion of the Baltis to Islam in the fourteenth–fifteenth centuries partly by Sayyid ʿAlī Hamadānī of Srinagar and mainly by his principal disciple, the *khalīfa* Sayyid Muḥammad Nūrbakhsh (1392-1464),[8] the Muslim princess-brides stood as promises of unity and peace and as means of alleviating conflict between the warring houses of Baltistan and the Buddhist kingdoms of Ladakh.

---

5 This study complements Fatima Mernissi's work on the history of Muslim women ascending the thrones of Muslim states from the thirteenth to the seventeenth centuries. Mernissi reports, for example, the marriage of Padishah Khatun to Abaqa Khan, Hulegu's son who was a Buddhist; see *The Forgotten Queens of Islam* (Minneapolis, 1993), p. 100.

6 Mernissi, *The Forgotten Queens*, p. 99. The Mongols had fewer reservations in regard to entrusting the governing of states to women than the Abbasid caliphs. The Mongol Khatuns appear to have held prominent positions and were honoured both at the court and in the mosque (ibid., pp. 99-107).

7 For the position of Ladakhi and Baltī in the Tibetan language family see Bettina Zeisler, 'On the Position of Ladakhi and Balti in the Tibetan Language Family', in John Bray (ed.), *Ladakhi Histories: Local and Regional Perspectives* (Leiden, 2005), pp. 41-64. For the Baltīs and Baltistan see M.A. Stein, *Ancient Geography of Kashmir* (Calcutta, 1899). For Persian references on medieval Ladakh and Baltistan, see Jigar Mohammed, 'Mughal Sources on Medieval Ladakh, Baltistan and Western Tibet', in *Recent Research on Ladakh 2007* (Leh, 2007), pp. 35-42.

8 A.S. Bazmee Ansari, 'Baltistān', *EI*^{2}. For the spread of Islam see Wolfgang Holzwarth, 'Islam in Baltistan: Problems of Research in the Formative Period', in Irmtraud Stellrecht (ed.), *The Past in the Present: Horizons of Remembering in the Pakistan Himalaya* (Cologne, 1997), pp. 1-40. For the development of the Nurbakhshi order, see n. 31 below and the contribution of Magnusson in this volume.

Unlike the Buddhist princess-brides received into Muslim harems (of which we hear little), the Khatuns of Ladakh were politically visible in court and, when caught in intrigues and public scandals, their notoriety preceded them. Yet, it is not surprising that Ladakh's seventeenth-century cultural renaissance coincided with the reigns of the two most famous Balti queens, Gyal Khatun and Kelsang Drolma. For in the realms of arts, architecture and religion they are celebrated as builders of mosques and patrons of Islamic culture as well as promoters of Buddhism and symbols of the Mahāyāna faith. Beyond their noted public contributions, the Khatuns of Ladakh participated in other intimate and important ways: as close kin with ties to Muslim sovereign houses, partners to Ladakhi kings and queen-mothers to their son-successors.

Future studies on the oral traditions of the north-western Himalayas will undoubtedly contribute to our greater understanding of the political, religious and cultural assumptions that governed matrimonial exchanges among the Muslim and Buddhist sovereigns,[9] the hierarchies and expectations of the bride-givers vis-à-vis the bride-receivers, and the possibilities for mobility for junior princesses in Muslim and Buddhist harems respectively.[10] Here we will focus on the folk traditions.

HIMALAYAN FOLK LITERATURE: KHATUN SONGS FROM THE ROYAL ERA

The rich and relatively unexplored traditions of folk literature in Ladakh and Baltistan are celebrated in festivals, songs and hymns, fables and proverbs, dances, music and drama.[11] Folk literature in the Indian Himalayas was greatly

---

[9] It appears that cultural assumptions governing royal marriages did not reflect those operating on a more general level in the marriages of commoners; see for example the status of the Argons (*'ar-gon*) or 'cultural hybrids', a term applied 'to all offspring of a Ladakhi mother converted to Islam and of a Muslim father, without regard to ethnic origin (Kashmir, Punjab, Yarkand, Baltistan, etc) as well as their descendants'; see Pascale Dollfus, 'The History of Muslims in Central Ladakh', *The Tibet Journal*, 20/3 (1995): pp. 35-58, at p. 42, and Gerhard Emmer, 'The Condition of the Argons in Leh', in *Recent Research on Ladakh 2007*, pp. 179-87. Inter-religious marriages have tended to be quite common in Ladakh, at least until recently.

[10] Polygamy was a custom for Baltī and Buddhist sovereigns alike. Commonly, the Muslim queens were junior wives to the Kings of Ladakh. They had to compete to secure the succession of their sons in the nobility in Leh or that of the minor Buddhist kingdoms of Zanskar, Nubra, Mulbekh, Purig and so forth. Adoption, common among Tibetan nobles, was not an option for royal succession. For kingship in Ladakh see Peter Schwieger, 'Power and Territory in the Kingdom of Ladakh', in Thierry Dodin and Heinz Räther (eds), *Recent Research on Ladakh 7* (Ulm, 1997), pp. 427-34.

[11] The folk traditions of Ladakh have, until now, received much less attention than they justly deserve, especially since they are under threat from modern societies. The present survey draws from the following collections and studies: Nawang Tsering

influenced by literary traditions from Tibet and monastic and lay forms of Tibetan Buddhism. Since the advent of Islam in the area there has been an arrival of Persian and Arabic literature. Among the Persian and Arabic stories introduced in some parts of Ladakh, the most influential are the famous Persian Epic *Shāhnāmeh* and *Ali Baba and the Forty Thieves*.[12]

The remarkably diverse collection of Ladakhi folk songs (*glu*) span over a period of more than a thousand years. They are often accompanied by instrumental music (*dbyangs*)[13] and have been classified on the basis of their purpose, social function or subject-matter.[14] For example, there are numerous heroic folksongs (*'gying-glu*) inspired by epic sagas like Gesar of Ling, Druguma and Api Cho;[15] songs sung by Dard immigrants to the region; religious songs of the Buddhist (*chos-glu*) and Muslim hymns (*hamd*, *qasida* or *manqabat*, *marsia*, and *bahre tawils*); songs of love (*grogs-glu*), teasing (*tshig-glu*) and songs sung in marriage (*bag-ston gyi glu*), dance (*shon-glu*), drinking (*chang-glu*) songs and others, covering a wide range of occasions, topics and moods.

Folksongs are the soul and body of Ladakhi folk literature. For generations poems celebrated kings as symbols of legitimate sovereignty and guardians of the common people. Hence, songs about Khatuns belong to the genre of heroic oral literature, the glorious and romanticized times of the *rgyal-dus*, the royal era. In a heroic Ladakhi song, the *Yaisha Castle* (*Yai-sha pho-brang*), among the blessings of heaven and earth, the presence of queens is a gift to all women:

Shakspo (*The Culture of Ladakh through Song and Dance* [Leh, 2008]; *Songs from the Himalaya: Ladakhi Folk Songs* [Leh, 1985]); Tashi Rabgyas (*Poems and Songs -'Jig rten kun tu dga' ba'i glu* [Leh, 2007]); Kacho Sikandar Khan Sikandar (*Ladakh in the Mirror of her Folklore: A Comprehensive Survey of the Folklore of Ladakh* [Kargil, 1997]); Abdul Gani Sheikh ('Folksongs and Dances of Ladakh', in *Recent Researches on the Himalaya* [Delhi, 1998], pp. 56-61); A.H. Francke ('Ladakhi Songs', *The Indian Antiquary*, 31 [1902]: pp. 87-106; *A History of Western Tibet* [London, 1907]; *Antiquities of Indian Tibet*, part II [Calcutta, 1926]; Historical Songs from Ladakh in the Leipzig Archives, see n. 42 below); and Banat Gul Afridi (*Baltistan in History* [Peshawar, 1988]).

12 For the influence of Arabic and Persian literature see Khan, *Ladakh in the Mirror*, p. 52. For Muslim and Tibetan elements in Ladakhi vocal and instrumental music, see Mark Trewin, 'A Cross-cultural Study of Instrumental Music in Ladakh', in Gudrun Meier and Lydia Icke-Schwalbe (eds), *Wissenschaftsgeschichte und gegenwärtige Forschungen in Nordwest-Indien* (Dresden, 1990), pp. 273-6, and Mark Trewin and Susan Stephens, *The Music Culture of Ladakh: City University Ladakh Expedition* (London, 1987).

13 See Eric Larson, 'Ladakhi Folk Songs and Instrumental Music', in Patrick Kaplanian (ed.), *Ladakh Himalaya Occidental Ethnologie, Écologie* (Pau, 2000), pp. 73-5.

14 For contemporary classifications and examples, see Khan, *Ladakh in the Mirror* and Tsering Shakspo, *The Culture of Ladakh*.

15 Api Cho was believed to have been one of old Baltistan's popular heroes living near Shigar. Khan (*Ladakh in the Mirror*, p. 48) explains that 'according to a tradition, Api Tso [Cho] was killed at the hands of Kesar.'

On the high horizon of Yaisha Castle
There exist ye twain bodies of Sun and Moon;
If ye twain bodies of sun and moon
Do so exist,
A blessing will it be
For us winged beings.
...
Inside (The) High Yaisha Castle
There livest thou The Father King;
If thou the Father King Dost so live,
A blessing will it be for (the union of) us
King and subjects.
Inside the high castle of Yaisha
There livest thou
The Mother Queen;
If thou the Mother Queen
Dost so live,
A blessing will it be for us
The fair sex.[16]

FOLKSONGS OF MUSLIM QUEENS FROM LADAKH AND BALTISTAN

I. MUSULU BEKIM, THE CHARM OF A THOUSAND QUEENS

The second half of the fifteenth century witnessed the rise of a new Ladakhi dynasty descending from King Tri Tsugde (*c.*1380-1410). His son Drag Bumde (*c.*1410-35)[17] succeeded his father on the throne and is remembered as a devout Buddhist ruler with strong ties in Central Tibet. Bumde sponsored many Buddhist temples, among them Spituk monastery,[18] the first establishment of the reformed school of Buddhism (Gelug) in Ladakh. He is famous for his royal edict abolishing what may have been a widely-held practice of animal sacrifice.

---

16 Translation by Khan, *Ladakh in the Mirror*, p. 202.

17 Unless otherwise indicated, dating follows Luciano Petech, *The Kingdom of Ladakh* (Rome, 1977) and *A Study on the Chronicles of Ladakh (Indian Tibet)* (Calcutta, 1939). Tashi Rabgyas provides different regnal dates for the Ladakhi kings in *History of Ladakh called the Mirror which Illuminates All* (*Mar yul la dwags kyi sngon rabs kun gsal me long*) (Leh, 2006).

18 An original eleventh-century temple on this site was said to have been erected by the King of Guge (Western Tibet), eventually becoming a monastery of the Kadampa school of Tibetan Buddhism: Geneviéve Tchekhoff and Yvan Comolli, *Buddhist Sanctuaries of Ladakh* (Bangkok, 1987), p. 77.

Not far from Mulbekh lies the village of Pashkum.[19] According to tradition, King Bumde had a castle built in Pashkum after his marriage to Ganga Rānī, a Kashmiri princess known by her Indian name. According to Sikandar Khan, in the folksong *The Great Pashkum,* the Muslim princess is known as the Queen Muslim Bekim (Tib. rGyal-mo Mu-su-lu Be-kim).[20] Besides her distinguished beauty and charm noted by the folk tradition, not much else is known of her life. It is likely that she was requested as a bride by King Drag Bumde to serve as an ambassador of goodwill, given the immanent threat of Muslim forces led by Rai Madari of Kashmir.[21] Her son with King Bumde received the Tibetan-Muslim name Drungpa 'Alī.[22]

The Great Pashkum

(Sikandar Khan, *Ladakh in the Mirror*, pp. 73-4)

Lo! The Royal Palace of Great Pashkum
Having been erected
Is touching the sky!
The Great Palace of Great Pashkum
Having been built is equaling the sky!
The Royal Palace of Great Pashkum
Is all aglow with the light of
Sun and Moon.
Not the light of Sun and moon it is
But the charming complexion of
'Queen Muslim Bekim', The Queen!
Not the glow of the full moon it is
But the charming appearance of

---

19 The village of Pashkum (Pashkyum) is located in the Suru valley in Purig.

20 Khan, *Ladakh in the Mirror*, p. 73. Be-kim is probably a title derived from *begum* (Indo-Persian *begam*); see Ansari, 'Baltistān'. Musulu Bekim must have been the junior wife, for a colophon mentions the King and the name of his Ladakhi wife, a Queen Jowo Kyab Pha (Petech, *The Kingdom of Ladakh*, p. 22).

21 The conquering of Baltistan by Rai Madari during the reign of Sikandar (1394-1416) may have heralded the Islamic conversion of Baltistan (Petech, *The Kingdom of Ladakh*, p. 22).

22 Francke, *A History of Western Tibet*, p. 81. For the tradition of granting half-Tibetan half-Muslim names to princes of Buddhist-Muslim descent, see n. 51. Nawang Tsering Shakspo reports on a different tradition of Muslim-Buddhist names in the village of Khuksho (120 km from Leh): 'According to village custom the eldest son of the family receives a Muslim name. Others would have "mixed" names such as Ali Tsering, Musa Namgyal, Sonam Bibi, Fatima Tsering and so on': 'The Significance of Khuksho in the Cultural History of Ladakh', in Henry Osmaston and Philip Denwood (eds), *Recent Research on Ladakh, 4 & 5* (London, 1995), pp. 181-7.

Queen Muslim Bekim!
Verily, Queen Muslim Bekim
Does excel
A hundred queens;
Verily, Queen Muslim Bekim does possess
The grace and charm of
A thousand queens.

II. GYAL KHATUN AND GYAL KELSANG, THE BALTI CHAIN OF QUEENS

ʿAlī Mīr and Jamyang Namgyal

The history of relations between the Ladakhi dynasties and the warrior-clans of Baltistan was marked by reciprocal territorial invasions and plundering followed by times of peace sustained between the Balti warrior clans[23] and the royal house of Leh. Earlier Ladakhi incursions into Baltistan met with little resistance up until the reign of the greatest figure in Balti history, ʿAlī shīr khān (1580-1624),[24] or ʿAlī Mīr of the *Ladakhi Royal Chronicles* (*La dwags rgyal rabs*).[25]

ʿAlī khān was a man talented in statesmanship and diplomacy.[26] It appears that he enticed the Ladakhi king, Jamyang Namgyal (*c.*1575-95), to lead an army to aid the sultan of Chigtan who was in conflict with the sultan of Kartse. This move proved disastrous for the people of Ladakh who were left behind defenceless. Outmanoeuvred and resourceless in enemy territory, King Jamyang had to surrender himself and his noble prisoners to the powerful sultan of Skardo. The Baltis seized the opportunity to invade Ladakh, plundering and ravaging Buddhist temples and religious treasures with memorable vengeance and iconoclastic fever.[27]

---

23 The local title of the Balti rulers was makpon/maqpon (Tib. *dmag-dpon*, lit. army leader); see Petech, *The Kingdom of Ladakh*, p. 33, n. 3. In old folksongs they are known as Cho (Jo-bo).

24 Dates provided by Afridi, *Baltistan in History*, p. 40.

25 The alleged founder of the lines of Baltī chiefs, ʿAlī shīr khān mentioned by Alexander Cunningham (*Ladák, Physical, Statistical, and Historical* [London, 1854]), Shridhar H.N. Kaul (*Ladakh through the Ages: Towards a New Identity* [Delhi, 1992]) and Afridi (*Baltistan in History*), can be no other than the ʿAlī Mīr who invaded Ladakh and kept captive the Ladakhi King Jamyang Namgyal and his army; see Petech, *A Study on the Chronicles*, pp. 134-6; Francke, *A History of Western Tibet*, pp. 92-6 and *Antiquities of Indian Tibet*, pp. 184-7. Rabgyas (*History of Ladakh*, p. 168) provides his full title, Ali Mir Sher Khān.

26 In 1591, he gave 'a daughter in marriage to prince Salim, the heir-apparent of the Moghul empire; and he appears again in the Moghul texts of 1603': Petech, *The Kingdom of Ladakh*, p. 33.

27 For an account of the damage on Ladakh's religious heritage see Janet Rizvi, *Ladakh: Crossroads of High Asia* (Delhi, 1996), p. 66.

Popular tradition, backed by the *Royal Chronicles,* recalls that while Jamyang Namgyal was in prison, ʿAlī Mīr's daughter was placed in his attendance. 'In due course, the princess and the king exchanged vows of marriage and she became pregnant. Her father having examined her and "seeing the damage that had been done, he gave his daughter to the king and allowed him to return to Ladakh together with his nobles."'[28] Whatever the circumstances may have been, ʿAlī Mīr released King Jamyang but not before giving his daughter, later known as Gyal Khatun, as his bride[29] with the stipulation that her son must inherit the Ladakhi throne. Following this mandate, Jamyang's two sons with his first wife, Queen Tsering, were *ipso facto* banned from royal succession and were sent off to Central Tibet.[30]

Muslim-Buddhist marriages

The royal marriage must have been an elaborate and expensive affair for both parties. The Rajas of Baltistan were known to give very lavish and generous dowries, which usually came in the shape of both movable and immovable property. Movable property included 'gold, silver, precious stone, jewellery, fine and costly clothing, swords, guns and 12 sets of house-hold utensils. As regards immovable property, village or villages are given in dowry.'[31] Tradition recalls that part of Gyal Khatun's movable dowry was 'a bevy of Muslim maids,

---

28 Petech, *The Kingdom of Ladakh*, p. 34.

29 Afridi (*Baltistan in History*, p. 43) argues that 'it was Sher Gazi, Raja of Saling, Khaplu, who gave his daughter Rgial Khatoon, in marriage to' Jamyang Namgyal. The Khaplu ruler had also achieved his release from the Raja of Ladakh who agreed that Gyal Khatun's children should be given preference in succession to those of the first queen; see Hashmatullah Khan, *History of Baltistan* (Islamabad, 1987), pp. 122-3, and Kaul, *Ladakh through the Ages*, p. 49. Afridi's contention is not supported by Ladakhi historical sources and the rock inscription at Mulbekh which addresses Gyal Khatun as Mir Khatun, the daughter of 'Alī Mīr Khān; see Prem Jinq Jina, *Tibetan Manuscripts and Inscriptions* (Delhi, 1998), pp. 91-2. There seems to be some mix up here, for Hashmatullah Khan (*History of Baltistan*, p. 123) reports that 'after her death, a portion of taxes continued to be paid to the Raja of Khaplu for a long time in the form of 2 maunds of phuli (Tr. note: probably rice) and 12 maunds of salt.' Sheikh Mohammad Jawad Zubdavi offers a compromise when he says that 'tradition has it that she was the sister of Salmulday, the Raja of Khapalu in Baltistan' and not the Raja's daughter ('History of Balti Settlements in the Indus Valley around Leh' [unpublished paper delivered at Kargil Conference, Kargil, Ladakh 2005]).

30 After their banishment we hear nothing of them (Petech, *A Study on the Chronicles*, p. 137).

31 Ibid., p. 200. Evidence of the princess' movable dowry can be seen today at the Stok Palace Museum which preserves the Queen's necklace or stomacher consisting of thirteen rows of silver beads.

a host of male servants and a band of Balti musicians' sent to Ladakh with the marriage party.[32]

There are no actual records of what wealth was exchanged between the two royal houses. King Jamyang may have had to pay bride-price to his Balti overlords. This would entail *khamital*, whereby the parents of the boy send presents to the parents of the girl.[33] After *khamital*, the parents of the boy ought to follow the custom of *rintho*, or *onarin*, a term signifying the payment of the price of milk that the girl was fed during the period of her suckling. The payment consists of 24 *tolas* of gold and 24 goats, after which the date of marriage is considered fixed.[34]

Apart from exchanging honours and marital gifts, both parties were expected to respect each other's faith. Foreign queens were allowed to retain their Muslim faith[35] and the Ladakhi kings reigned according to the country's Tibetan Buddhist customs. King Jamyang, even though initially forced to acknowledge Islam, continued his reign as a generous patron of Buddhism while the Ladakhi lamas, eager to neutralize what they may have perceived as an unmistakable Islamic infringement on the royal blood line, welcomed Gyal Khatun as an emanation of the Buddhist divinity of long life, the white Tārā. Even though the tribute to her in Buddhist folklore was flattering, she appears to have remained Muslim until her death, while private mosques were built for her and her servants in Leh and Shey.[36]

---

[32] Later, the Muslim musicians who settled in Leh had their status elevated to 'Kharmon' or 'royal musicians'. In 'A Brief History of Muslims in Ladakh', in *Recent Research on Ladakh, 4 & 5*, p. 190, Sheikh further reports that 'several hundred Balti Muslims are thought to have migrated from Baltistan and Purig to Shey and Chhushot during the reign of Jamyang Namgyal. Their descendants' number has now swelled to some 6,000. According to oral tradition, the King also granted land to Kashmiri Muslim traders to settle permanently in Leh. These traders were called "Kharchongpa" or "palace/royal traders".'

[33] 'Khamital' is a typical Balti term composed of 'kha' ('tongue') and 'mital' ('not to exceed') meaning that a seal has been fixed on the tongues of the parents of the girl (Afridi, *Baltistan in History*, p. 195).

[34] Ibid.

[35] Unlike Kashmir that was predominantly Sunni, Baltī princesses from the Magpon houses of Skardo were Shiite, or if they originated from the houses of Khaplu and Shigar, they may have been Nurbakhshi. The Nurbakhshis are a Sufi order that combines Shiite and Sunni elements, named after Sayyid Muhammad Nūrbakhsh (1392-1464). It is still adhered to in Ladakh and Baltistan; see Andreas Rieck, 'The Nurbakhshis of Baltistan: Crisis and Revival of a Five Centuries Old Community', *Die Welt des Islams*, N.S., 35 (1995): pp. 159-88, and Shahzad Bashir, *Messianic Hopes and Visions: The Nūrbakshīya between Medieval and Modern Islam* (Columbia, 2003).

[36] Later Muslim queens of Ladakh used to offer prayer in these mosques; see Sheikh, 'A Brief History', p. 190.

The fame of Gyal Khatun

The Balti princess, daughter of ʿAlī shīr khān, was destined to be the most renowned of all Muslim Khatuns in Ladakh. Praised in the oral traditions for her personal charisma and beauty, she is famous for giving birth to the 'Lion King' of Ladakh, Senge Namgyal (*c.*1616-23); see Plate 11.2. The name of the greatest conqueror king of Ladakh[37] is still heard on the lips of the people. A famous ballad from Ladakh narrates the birth of ʿAlī Mīr's grandson, Senge Namgyal in the arms of his mother Gyal Khatun, known as Zi-Zi:[38]

> Today the old king's name shall resound through the universe, for see the lovely babe his grandson, born today. See him in the arms of his mother, this child whose name shall be famous in all the world. See him in the arms of Zi-Zi the queen, this child whose name shall be famous in all the world.[39]

After the death of King Jamyang Namgyal, the Balti queen appears to have carried on the government in the interregnum on behalf of her elder son Senge Namgyal who was still a minor,[40] before retiring to the palace of Hondar in Nubra to spend her last days in religious activities.[41] Like most Ladakhi Khatuns her real name is not known. The name Gyal Khatun is a half-Tibetan (*rgyal*) half-Turkish (*khātūn*) title of sovereignty.[42] Given her high esteem among the Ladakhi people, she may be Si-li-ma in the Ladakhi folksong of praise to *Silima Khatun*.

---

37 Senge Namgyal's life and exploits are recounted in the *Royal Chronicles*. The Jesuit priest, Francisco de Azevedo, described him as 'a man of tall stature, of a brown colour, with something of the Javanese in his features and of stern appearance ... His hair hung down to his shoulders, either ear was adorned with turquoise and a large coral, whilst he wore a string of skull bones round his neck to remind himself of death'; see Petech, *A Study on the Chronicles*, p. 149.

38 Zi-zi was a title given to Muslim queens of Ladakh. Francke (*Antiquities of Indian Tibet*, p. 146) defines *zi-zi*, a duplication of *zi*, for lady in Urdu (or Persian).

39 Rizvi, *Ladakh*, pp. 170-71.

40 Petech, *The Kingdom of Ladakh*, p. 38.

41 According to Hashmatullah Khan (*History of Baltistan*, p. 123), in [Nubrah] 'with the purpose of gaining merit for the soul of her husband, she [Gyal Khatun] had two grand serais built, which exist to this day. She also built a sacred mosque near the palace and she is buried near this mosque'.

42 Just as *malika, sulṭāna, al-ḥurra* were titles used for women who ruled in the Arab world, the title of *khatun* is most often found in Asian Islam; see Mernissi, *The Forgotten Queens of Islam*, p. 21. A junior Queen Khatun (Tib. *btsan-mo ga-tun*), either a Turkic or 'A-zha princess, whose funeral is recorded in the *Old Tibetan Annals* for the year 708-709, appears to have tried to place her son, Lha Bal-po, on the Tibetan imperial throne; see Brandon Dotson, *Tibet's First History: An Annotated Translation of the Old Tibetan Annals* (Vienna, 2009), pp. 18-19, 105, and Christopher Beckwith, *The Tibetan Empire in Central Asia* (Princeton, 1993), pp. 68-70. The earliest reference to a Buddhist–Muslim princess exchange in the western Himalayas is that of an Arab lady Tagzig-ma (Tib. sTag-

The Song of Silima Khatun

My famous queen is like the rising sun,
The precious Silima Queen is brilliant like a vision of light.
My famous queen is like the shining full moon
To he lee [utterance to fill the rhythm].
My precious Silima Queen you are brilliant like a vision of light,
Even your royal line is god-like, brilliant like a vision of light.
Silima Khatun your royal line is the line of sugar-cane wood,
Precious Silima Queen your race may flourish like leaves.
Your name and qualities have become known all over the world [*ʿālam*, Arabic for world]
Oh precious Silima Khatun Queen, brilliant like a vision of light.[43]

Senge Namgyal's Balti queen

If ʿAlī shīr khān intended to install a Muslim queen-mother to the throne as an expedient to introduce Islam in Ladakh he must have been sorely disappointed. King Senge Namgyal's devotion to his Buddhist teacher Tagtsang Repa of the Drukpa School saw the zealous construction of many temples and monasteries and the granting of donations of landed estates to the Buddhist clergy.[44] This period marked by a Buddhist renaissance in Ladakh produced the fortress-palace of Leh, monasteries of the Drukpa school of Buddhism (He-mis, lCe-bde, sTag-sna), ornate temples (Basgo, Shel), and the crafting of the Tibetan Buddhist canon in gold and silver.

Senge Namgyal was not alone in his religious activities. Being half Balti on his mother's side he long entertained friendly relations with his Skardo kin and married probably a cousin, a Balti princess, the famous Muslim Queen Kelsang (sKal-bzang). Her name recurs in many Buddhist dedications jointly with the king, and like Gyal Khatun, she was held to be an incarnation of Tārā, 'a title that is never absent from the inscriptions'.[45] A small shrine to Buddha Maitreya near

gzigs-ma, lit. Arab lady), one of the four wives of King Kyide Nyima Gon, the founder of the first Ladakhi dynasty; see Petech, 'Western Tibet. Historical Introduction', in Deborah Klimburg-Salter (ed.), *Tabo: A Lamp for the Kingdom. Early Indo-Tibetan Buddhist Art in the Western Himalaya* (Milan, 1997), pp. 229-55, at p. 232.

43 My translation. The Tibetan text is preserved in the Leipzig Archives, Germany, see Michael Hahn, *August Hermann Francke und die Westhimalaya-Mission der Herrnhuter Brüdergemeine: eine Bibliographie mit Standortnachweisen der tibetischen Drucke* (Stuttgart, 1992), Historical Songs from Ladakh (95.1.24).

44 Petech, *A Study on the Chronicles*, p. 149.

45 Petech, *A Study on the Chronicles*, p. 138. Kelsang Drolma (sKal-bzang sgrol-ma) is a common Tibetan Buddhist name and one to have been easy for the Ladakhis to identify with. The identification of foreign queens with the Buddhist divinity Tārā is reminiscent of the Chinese and Nepalese brides to Tibet's emperor Srongtsen Gampo (*c.*605-50); see

the Serzang Temple in Basgo contains a 1642 inscription dedicated by Kelsang Tārā.[46] It would appear to have been constructed as an act of merit for King Senge Namgyal.[47]

The problem of Senge Namgyal's succession was not settled at once, and for some time the dowager queen Kelsang acted as a regent for her three sons.[48] With Delden Namgyal the elder son as the successor ruler of Ladakh, the kingdom was divided among the three brothers with Khatun Kelsang receiving Matro, Yigu and Purang as her personal estate. Queen Kelsang continued promoting the construction of Buddhist monuments, and upon her request, in February 1647, Tagtsang Repa laid the foundations of the main temple in the Shey palace.[49] A small temple in Shey with an image of Buddha Amitāyus is likely to have been a benefaction of our Balti princess.[50]

The old queen was active during her last years. In 1649 she sent to Central Tibet a mission on behalf of the court, and in 1650, against the advice of her revered teacher, she undertook a long journey, breathing her last in Zanskar. Her corpse was brought to Shey, were the funeral rites were performed.[51]

III. THE RETURN OF THE BUDDHIST PRINCESS FROM THE HAREM OF 'ALĪ SHĪR KHĀN

Receiving Muslim brides was a common practice among the Buddhist rulers of the northern Indian Himalayan kingdoms. There appears to have been a reciprocal practice whereby Buddhist princesses were given as brides to the Muslim sultans of Baltistan and Kashmir. During the reign of ʿAlī shīr khān (1580-1624), noble brides from Buddhist families were sought after and had a choice in rejecting marital offers. The following folksong contains an anonymous confession by a noble lady probably from one of the minor royal houses of Ladakh:

(Afridi, *Baltistan in History*, p. 183)

> For months and years, the sky has been clear (of clouds) but what a time has come that despite this no sunrays have appeared on the mountains.

Sarat Chandra Das, *Journey to Lhasa and Central Tibet* (Delhi, 1988), p. 165. Kelsang Drolma appears in two folkdances which may date to the times of the Baltī queen (Francke, 'Ladakhi Songs', p. 104; Shakspo, *The Culture of Ladakh*, pp. 55-7).

46 David Snellgrove and Tadeusz Skorupski, *The Cultural Heritage of Ladakh* (Warminister, 1977), p. 97.

47 Petech, *The Kingdom of Ladakh*, pp. 56-7, also mentions the construction of the main temple of Tsede (lCe-bde) consecrated by Lama Tagtsang Repa, finished in 1645-46.

48 Petech, *The Kingdom of Ladakh*.

49 Petech, *The Kingdom of Ladakh*, p. 58.

50 Snellgrove and Skorupski, *The Cultural Heritage of Ladakh*, p. 91.

51 Petech, *The Kingdom of Ladakh*, pp. 58-9. The sources remain silent concerning which kind of funeral rituals were performed.

> The sky has been cloudy for months and years but what a time has come that no dew appears on the ground.
> Maqpon Ali Sher Khan sends people to sue for my hand,
> No I shall not accede to his request, for, my dearest, I have taken an oath not to do so.
> The Kalon[52] of Ladakh requests me to marry him; no I cannot accept his offer, because my friend, I have made a promise to you (to marry you).
> The Malik[53] of Kashmir makes an offer marriage; but I cannot accept that offer since I have already chosen you as my spouse.

Our knowledge of Buddhist bride-giving to Muslim rulers derives primarily from Balti histories and folksongs. The *Royal Chronicles* remain silent on such exchanges. If the Ladakhi historians did not find them important, two cases included in Hashmatulla Khan's *History of Baltistan*[54] are sufficiently embarrassing to warrant their omission from the Ladakhi chronicles. Both incidents took place during the reign of the Ladakhi King Delden Namgyal (*c.*1640-75).

The first case involved a bride-request by King Delden. Troubled by the incursions and attacks of his relative Shīr Khān, he sent a messenger to the Rājā of Shigar with the following message:

> Forgive my past mistakes. Sher Khan troubles me greatly and I have never seen a more quarrelsome person before in my life. I feel a strong repulsion towards him and I am ashamed of being his relative. The weight of this shame has not lifted from my heart, though I have severely mauled his army. I wish your son to marry my daughter to double our unity through such a link. Then we can together punish this evil character.[55]

The Rājā of Shigar wrote back:

> No matter how one treats a piece of sandstone, it can never become a ruby, but friendship and unity is good for all times and can be strengthened without any further measures.

---

52 Kalon is the title referring to a minister of Ladakh.

53 Ar. 'king'; for its usage see Mernissi, *The Forgotten Queens*, pp. 12, 13, 72.

54 Maulvi Al Haj Hashmatullah Khan's text, first published in Urdu in 1968 (Lahore: Hassan Publishing), remains the most important published source on the history of Baltistan. He conducted his study while travelling extensively in Baltistan for both research and in the administrative capacity as *wazir-i-wazarat* (governor) of Ladakh and Baltistan for the Dogra government of Jammu-Kashmir. His work is based on records of the ruling families, oral traditions of the region and the *Shagharnama,* a Persian chronicle written in the court of Imam Quli Khan, ruler of the Balti state of Shigar in about 1700; see Emerson, 'Charismatic Kingship', p. 3.

55 Hashmatullah Khan (*History of Baltistan*, p. 62).

Hashmatullah Khan concludes that Delden Namgyal was deeply disappointed and, with the intention of giving aid to Hatīm Khān, he attacked Khapalu 'giving the Musulmans cause to worry'.[56]

A second incident is reported by Hashmatullah.[57] Shīr Khān was apparently delighted to hear that the Buddhists of Ladakh 'did not remain true to their faith and started making preparations for war'. Seizing upon this opportunity, he sent the following message to the king of Ladakh:

> I am your friend and well-wisher, and will be loyal to you as long as I live; my only condition is that you give your daughter in marriage for my son. If you accept this bond, our family is your liege and all of Tibet lies at your feet.

The message reached the king of Ladakh who conferred with his ministers and advisors and unanimously accepted his proposal. Shīr Khān was elated with the news and proceeded to make preparations for the marriage. He sent his son to Ladakh in order to consummate the marriage, and along with this, he sent a request for ten thousand soldiers so that he might destroy his enemies at Skardo and Shigar. This must have been Khān's plan all along but it came as a surprise to Delden Namgyal, for Hashmatullah concludes that 'the Raja of Ladakh hid his head when he received this request'.[58]

The Balti song (*sbal-glu*) *Hilal Bagh*, preserves another embarrassing incident. King Jamyang Namgyal (*c.*1575-95) is said to have given his daughter as bride to ʿAlī shīr khān (1580-1624) during his turbulent reign. Given the political standstill between Baltistan and Ladakh with King Jamyang held hostage to the Baltis, princesses may have been exchanged as part of a reciprocal agreement between the two rulers. However, since a matrimonial swap has not been recorded in the *Royal Chronicles*, it is possible that King Jamyang offered his daughter to ʿAlī khān as a way of negotiating his way out of prison.

As narrated in the *Hilal Bagh*, the Ladakhi bride, Queen Mandok by some counts,[59] was sent from Leh with a large marital procession of horses and men. Upon her arrival in Skardo she had a royal reception stepping on turquoise. If the

---

[56] Ibid. The folksong *The Treasure House Rshingo Rshing*, recalls another case of a marriage requested to settle a family dispute between the king of Ladakh and Tsering Malik of Chigtan, who bears a half-Tibetan name (Khan, *Ladakh in the Mirror of her Folklore*, p. 101).

[57] Ibid., p. 71.

[58] Ibid. Two other cases of Buddhist matrimonial exchange are reported. The first involves the daughter of the Ladakhi king given to the Rājā of Khapalu, Yabgo Behram (1494-1550) who bore him Yabgo Sikam, his successor (Hashmatullah Khan, *History of Baltistan*, p. 120). Another Ladakhi princess was sent as bride to the son of Sher Gazi, as reported by Afridi (*Baltistan in History*, p. 120).

[59] Kaul, *Ladakh through the Ages*, p. 49. Concerning the name of the Ladakhi princess, Gyal-mo (Tib. *rgyal-mo*; queen) Mandok, Afridi (*Baltistan in History*, p. 44) suggests that

folksong is accurate in recounting these events, it must have been disappointing for the Ladakhi king to receive his daughter back divorced from ʿAlī khān.[60] The folksong *Garden of Hilal* narrates the lonely departure of the Ladakhi princess from Baltistan and celebrates ʿAlī shīr khān, the Great:

Hilal Bagh

(Afridi, *Baltistan in History*, pp. 44-5)

Behold the red rose blossoming
In the Hilal Bagh (Hilal garden)[61] of the Broq Maqpon.
Oh, it was not the red rose; it was Maqpon Ali Sher Khan.
Behold the 'Halo' flower blossoming, in Broq Maqpon, Hilal Bagh.
Oh: it was not the 'Halo' flower, it was Anchan[62] Ali Sher Khan.
When the queen was brought (to Skardo)
She was accompanied by hundreds of men and horses
When the queen was brought, she was to tread on steps made of turquoise
(as a mark of honour) the steps leading to the palace had been adorned with turquoise.
When the Queen was sent back, there was not a single person or horse to go with her.
Despite these (indignities), O, Anchan Ali Sher Khan
I may lay down my life for your glory and happiness.

'Hashmatullah erroneously took' Jamyang Namgyal's daughter for the famous queen Mindoq Gyalmo.

60 Returning a bride may have been construed as an insult and even the cause for war; as in the case of Senge Namgyal conquering the King of Guge for refusing to receive his sister as a bride; see Petech, *A Study on the Chronicles*, p. 140.

61 The *hilal bagh* were the royal gardens below the Mindoq-khar Flower Palace (Afridi, *Baltistan in History*, p. 44). According to Hashmutallah Khan (*History of Baltisan*, p. 18), when 'Alī Shīr Khān left for Gilgit, the Ladakhi Queen wishing not to stay with the people of Skardo, had a separate palace constructed outside the fort. It was called after her name the Mindoq-khar.

62 *Anchan* is used as an epithet for 'Alī Khān meaning 'the great'.

IV. THE LONGING OF THE MUSLIM QUEEN OF ZANSKAR

It appears that Khri Mohammed Sultan of Kartse[63] had no male son to succeed him.[64] In a folksong dedicated to the people of Suru Karche, the Sultan's sister betrothed to the King of Zanskar[65] is haunted by the thought that the ancestral throne will perish after her brother's death. The anonymous Muslim queen of Zanskar prays for the birth of a successor son for the Sultan, anxious to leave her foreign husband and return to her native land of Suru Karche.

The People of Suru Karche

(Khan, *Ladakh in the Mirror*, pp. 118-20)

If the people of Suru Karche
If the people are truly lucky,
May my, the girl's, Brother
Be blessed with a noble son!
If the people of Suru Karche,
If really lucky the people are,
May King Thi Sultan, The King,
Be blessed with a Noble son!
O King of Zanskar I beg of thee,
Do send me, the princess, back
To her native land:
According to ye Buddhists a noble deed
Equal to erecting a Mani[66] will it be!
O King of Zanskar I pray thee!
Do send the princess back to Suru Karche;

---

63 The principality of Kartse or Karche (dKar-rtse) lies in the fertile valley of Suru. The relations between Kartse and Ladakh have not been without their share of strife. During the reign of king Delek Namgyal (*c.*1675-1705) it is reported that his commander-in-chief Sakya Gyatso lead expeditions in Purig taking prisoner to Ladakh the Khri (Thi) Sultan of Kartse (Petech, *A Study on the Chronicles*, p. 153).

64 Curiously, another folksong preserves a story of King Nyima Namgyal being adopted as a son and successor to the Sultan of Karche, Cho (King) Tri (Khri) Mohammed (Khan, *Ladakh in the Mirror*, p. 75).

65 Zanskar covers an area of 2,700 square miles. According to the *Chronicles of Zanskar*, the area was under Kashmir before it was seized by the Tibetans; Francke, *A History of Western Tibet*, p. 136. Since Nyima Gon's (*c.*tenth century) death, it was an independent kingdom conquered in the seventeenth century by Senge Namgyal who gave it as an apanage to his third son Demchok Namgyal. The latter founded a new Zanskar dynasty which lasted until the Dogra conquest in 1841 (Petech, *A Study on the Chronicles*, p. 155).

66 Referring to a *mani*-wall: a wall made of stone-blocks loosely stacked one over another and often inscribed with the six-syllable mantra of the bodhisattva of compassion.

According to us Muslims a noble deed
Equal to erecting a Mosque will it be.
O turquoise-blue pigeon on the wings!
Lucky do I think [O] pigeon thou art!
Fly on, fly on, to alight on the
Palace roof of this girl's brother.
O turquoise pigeon flying in the sky!
(How) lucky though art O turquoise pigeon!
Fly on, to alight on the façade of
King Thi Sultan's Palace!
O smoothly flowing river, hear!
Lucky thou art O river, do I feel!
Flow on, flow on, to touch the palace wall
Of my, this sister's, Brother!
O swiftly flowing river, hear!
Lucky thou art O river, do I feel.
Flow on to flow beneath the palace wall of Thi Sultan, the King!

V. GYALMO BI-BI, THE TRAGIC QUEEN OF LADAKH

In the history of Ladakhi Kings, Tsewang Namgyal (*c.*1753-82) stands out as one odd exception.[67] He earned his notoriety for an obsession for Central Asian horses (collecting as many as 500) and for surrounding himself by Muslim favourites and becoming estranged and indifferent to Buddhism. A man eccentric to the ways of the Buddhist court, he fell under the spell of Bi-bi from Kartse, and was eventually abandoned by the Zangla lady from Zanskar, his first queen.

With his new Muslim wife Queen Bi-bi or Bhe-mo Gyal, Tsewang Namgyal undertook to crush the Ladakhi nobles and officials opposed to their marriage by killing Kunkyob his minister and the village headman of Tingmosgang while chaining some aristocrats in the dungeons. To top that, he increased taxes and appointed as his new minister no other than Nasib Ali, Queen Bi-bi's brother. The tyrannical couple did not anticipate that the growing resentment of the people would turn into an angry and violent protest. From what followed, it appears that the local population blamed Queen Bi-bi entirely for the political ineptitude and flawed character of their king. While King Tsewang was not physically harmed but allowed to continue his reign until he had to abdicate,[68] Queen Bi-bi met a horrific end nailed to the door of the bazaar in Leh and publicly flogged to death by the Buddhist mob.

---

67 For a detailed description of the events, see Petech, *The Kingdom of Ladakh*, p. 116.

68 Tsewang Namgyal abdicated in 1782 but not before marrying another Muslim wife (Petech, *The Kingdom of Ladakh*, p. 135).

It is fitting for the folk traditions to preserve the *Da ltong biru ltong*,[69] a song of self-praise sung by Gyalmo Bi-bi. A narrative, inflated like Queen Bi-bi's reckless actions in the Ladakhi court, it reads with a certain irony, given the martyrdom that followed.

Da ltong biru-ltong

(Khan, *Ladakh in the Mirror*, pp. 179-80)

Climb the lofty peak of Da-ltong biru-ltong,
Ascend the Da-ltong biru-ltong Mount of Delight;
The Father land that gave birth
Is just under the nose!
The land of [S]higar[70] and Skardo[71]
Is close by!
The fatherland that gave birth
Has three kinds of castles;
Yea, the land of Shigar and Skardu
Possess three kinds of Castles!
One castle is the castle 'The Great Castle'
One castle are the parents who gave birth and
One castle am [I] the girl myself:
One castle am I, Rgyal Bi bi myself!
The like of me, the girl, is
Nowhere on the earth to be found;
The like of Rgyal Bi Bi is
Nowhere in the world to be found;
Thanks to the parents who gave
Rgyal Bi Bi birth;
Thanks to the Mirs and Akhons[72]
Who named Rgyal Bi Bi, Rgyal Bi Bi.

---

69 In the absence of a Tibetan transcription of the folksong we cannot be certain, but the title of the song could mean *mda' gtong bi ru gtong*, literally 'shoot the arrow, shoot it at Bi-bi'.

70 The little chiefship of Shigar had its own Gyalpo who has been subject to the kings of Baltistan (Cunningham, *Ladák*, p. 32).

71 Balti-yul is often called Skardo by the Tibetans (*skar-mdo* or *skar-ma-mdo*, lit. starry place) (Cunningham, *Ladák*, p. 34).

72 *Akhon* is a Central Asian expression designating scholars of Qur'anic law (*mollah*) (Dollfus, 'The History of Muslims', p. 55, n. 24). This reference to Bi-bi's noble descent is not altogether clear. Our historical Bi-bi Khatun has passed down in history as a low-caste (Bhegar) Muslim woman. Ruling out historical inaccuracy or altogether a Queen Bi-bi other than King Jamyang's wife, the folksong may have been popularized by

CONCLUSION: MUSLIM QUEENS UNTIL THE END OF THE DYNASTY

Songs celebrating the fame of khatuns were composed up until the end of Ladakh's dynastic era. At times, notoriety served as a reason for being noted in the official pages of history. The *Royal Chronicles* preserves the story of Queen Bi-bi the Martyr who served as a scapegoat for the political and economic ills of the times. There have been other khatuns who maintained positions of secular power by promoting their agendas and favouring their kin. Political ingenuity and manipulation are found in the story of Zi-zi Khatun, wife to King Nyima Namgyal (*c.*1694-1723).

Nyima Namgyal's first queen belonged to a noble family from Central Tibet but died soon after giving birth to his eldest son and successor Dekyong Namgyal. His second wife Zi-zi Khatun[73] from Purig, granddaughter of Hatim Khān and niece to Daulat Khān of Khaplu, appears to have forced her way into the Ladakhi court. A document from Wam-le, dating sometime after her giving birth to Tashi Namgyal and Princess Tashi Wangmo, reads like an appeal by Zi-zi Khatun to be granted authority at the Ladakhi court.

The Wam-le appeal

> Thus said Queen Zi-zi:
>
> On the occasion when a *prima facie* relationship was established at Kha-ha-phu-loo [Kha-pa-lu],[74] my paternal grandfather Ha-da-khan [Haidar-Khān] and my uncle Rdab-lad-khan [Daulat-Khān],[75] gave Zi-zi [as wife to the Ladakhi king], [with the stipulation] that should a boy be born, Steng-mkhar[76] will be given [to him]. However, since Zi-zi's 'power of speech' [kha dbang; authority]

Ladakhi Muslims intent on celebrating their Muslim queen as a symbol of power, glossing over her humble origins and humbling death.

73 Francke (*Antiquities of Indian Tibet*, p. 191) claims to have identified her Muslim burial-ground at Hundar in Nubra valley under the name 'A-yum-khri-rgyal-om. Her story as recounted can be found in Petech (*The Kingdom of Ladakh*, pp. 95-8).

74 Khapalu stretched 25 miles further down Shayok river according to Cunningham (*Ladák*, p. 28). The chiefs of Khapalu have been for generations under the supremacy of the Balti kings and 'their ancestors most probably had possession of the country for several centuries before the rise of the Balti dynasty, whose very title *Makpon*, or "General," betrays that they are the descendants of some military chief' (ibid.).

75 A Daolut Khan is listed in Cunningham's (*Ladák*, pp. 29-30) index of the Gyalpos of Khapalu (Khapolor). Cunningham's dating of the kings must be treated with caution.

76 I have not been able to identify this place or castle (Tib. *steng-mkhar*, lit. upper citadel or castle).

> was not established, we have ignored it. Henceforth, Zi-zi has the authority [maturity of speech] and it is necessary to hear her.[77]

Actively, she helped her son Prince Tashi Namgyal to take possession of Mulbek and make it his capital. While Nyima Namgyal was still alive, Muslim Zi-zi came in direct opposition with Dekyong Namgyal and his ministers over the issue of marrying her daughter, Tashi Wangmo, to the Muslim Rājā of Kishtwar.[78] The old royal couple succeeded in holding the wedding. Tashi missed the atmosphere of freedom in Leh and appealed to her kin. Zi-zi Khatun recalled her daughter back to Leh but the Rājā of Kishtwar would not let her return alone. The khatun, fearing that her son-in-law might eventually compete over the rule of Purig with her own son Tashi Namgyal, sent a trusted servant to join the party with secret instructions that the Rājā be killed on the way. The servant obeyed, pushing the young man off a bridge so that he drowned.

Tashi Wangmo did not remain a widow for long but soon married into the royal house of Khaplu. However, the truth about the murder leaked out, causing considerable damage to the reputation of the house of Leh. The Queen mother of Kishtwar entreated the Mughals to send a punitive expedition against the Ladakhis for the unjust loss of her son. The Ladakhis managed to stop the expedition by bribing the imperial court. The mother of the victim had no other recourse than to employ Indian Brahmans to curse the Ladakhi dynasty.[79] The action of Zi-zi was openly denounced by the people and cast an ineffaceable slur on her.

The negative publicity generated by Zi-zi Khatun did not prevent subsequent Ladakhi kings from taking Balti princesses as brides. On the contrary, marrying Muslim princesses appears to have been in vogue in the eighteenth–nineteenth centuries. For after Queen Bi-bi's tragic death by flogging, King Tsewang took another Muslim wife, a Bhe-kim of Purig who bore him his eldest son and throne successor Tseten Namgyal (*c.*1782-1802). This short-lived prince also acquired a woman known as Zi-zi Khatun from Pashkyum and when his brother Tsepal Namgyal succeeded him to the throne he married his Muslim widow. She bore him a son, Tsewang Rabten, the last scion of the Ladakhi dynasty. In 1835, Prince Tsewang Rabten took two wives, among them Zo-ra Khatun, the last Muslim Queen of Ladakh who gave birth to his son, Tenrung Yulgyal.[80] Tsewang Rabten Namgyal died in exile in 1839 in Bashahar after a personal clash with Dogra leader Zorawar Singh who had defeated the Ladakhi army in 1835.

---

77 My translation; the Tibetan text is found in Francke (*Antiquities of Indian Tibet*, p. 190).

78 According to Petech (*The Kingdom of Ladakh*, p. 98), the Kishtwar family converted to Islam in 1687.

79 'To these curses all the subsequent troubles in the family, early deaths etc., were attributed' (Petech, *The Kingdom of Ladakh*, p. 98).

80 Petech, *The Kingdom of Ladakh*, pp. 135-7.

The legacy of the Muslim queens ends with the last vestiges of Buddhist sovereignty in Ladakh. A love-song (*grogs-glu*) composed in the nineteenth century, the very end of the *rgyal-dus* era, is about the famous minister Nodrup Tenzin and the beautiful Salam Khatun of Skardo:[81]

Love Song

(Shakspo, *The Culture of Ladakh*, pp. 40-44)

> In a colourful silky garden, a lucky lotus flower blossomed,
> It was not a lucky lotus flower, but was the beautiful Salam Khatoon [Khatun].
> In the capital town of Skardu, a hundred and one streams flow.
> Though such streams flow, yet our beloved chief feels it [is] as muddy water.
> If our beloved feels the water as muddy, may Salam Khatoon become a mountain stream,
> If dNos-grub bstan-hdsin feels the water as muddy, may I become a mountain stream.
> On the sands of the sandy plain, the feet of dNos-grub bstan-hdsin are burning.
> On the sands of the sandy plain, the head of dNos-grub bstan-hdsin is burning.
> If the head of my chief is burning, may I become a parasol.
> If the head of dNos-grub bstan-hdsin is burning,
> may Salam Khatoon become a parasol.

The exchange of foreign princesses was a prevalent form of international diplomacy between Ladakh and the Muslim ruling houses of Purig, Chigtan, Shigar, Khaplu, Karche, Skardo and Kishtwar. Matrimonial exchanges were politically motivated and served as diplomatic means for the exercise of sovereign choices between states.[82] It would appear that marriage alliances were at the forefront of Ladakh's foreign policy, preoccupied with its Muslim neighbours and the encroaching presence of the Mughal Empire. By the mid-seventeenth

---

[81] The Leh minister is also known for composing *The King's Garden at Leh* (Francke, 'Ladakhi Songs', p. 89). He served as regent for some time after the deposition of Tsepal Namgyal by the Dogra overlords (Petech, *The Kingdom of Ladakh*, p. 142).

[82] Ladakh and Baltistan would appear to form an exception to Geoffrey Samuel's characterization of Tibetan-speaking communities in the Himalayas as 'stateless societies' ('Tibet as a Stateless Society and Some Islamic Parallels', *The Journal of Asian Studies*, 41/2 [1982]: pp. 215-29). Unlike other stateless societies, the kingdom of Ladakh did not abide by the Tibetan Buddhist model of shared power (religious and secular) and was clearly acting as a centralized state in the Himalayas in competition with another Tibetan-speaking people formerly organized into small agrarian states. Emerson ('Charismatic Kingship', p. 413) argues that Baltistan, even though composed of small sovereign political units '(ranging from about forty thousand to one hundred thousand people, as estimated back from the British census of India), they clearly met the defining features of a state'.

century, Ladakh was closer to speaking the language of diplomacy of the Muslim sultans in its western frontiers than that of its distant cousins, the central Tibetans in the east with their monastic celibates in joint positions of secular and spiritual power.[83]

To conclude, the anonymous Muslim queens of Ladakh, known mainly by their common Tibetan (*rgyal-mo*) and Persian titles of power (Zi-zi and Khatun), were daughters, wives, advisors and lovers to the kings and often mothers to their successors. They contributed to an extensive network of horizontal kinship relations forged through the blood-line.[84] In other capacities, they served as cultural and political ambassadors, peace-makers in times of trouble, secret agents and even dowager queens for their respective courts. Over the centuries, their legacy shaped the diplomatic relations between Buddhists and Muslims and enriched the religious and cultural landscape of the Indian north-western Himalayas.

Table 11.1 Muslim Queens in the Buddhist Court of Leh

Ladakhi kings	Regnal years	Muslim queens and their origins
Kyide Nyima Gon	10th century	Tagzig-ma (Arab)
Drag Bumde	c.1400-44	Be-kim (Kashmir)
Jamyang Namgyal	c.1595-1616	Gyal Khatun (Skardo)
Senge Namgyal	c.1616-23	Kelsang Khatun (Skardo)
Nyima Namgyal	c.1694-1723	Zi-zi Khatun (Purig)
Tsewang Namgyal	c.1753-82	Bi-bi Khatun (Karche) Bhe-kim (Purig)
Tseten Namgyal	c.1782-1802	Zi-zi Khatun (Purig)
Tsewang Rabten (prince)	d.1834	Zo-ra Khatun (unknown place)

83 During the Tibet-Ladakh-Mughal war of 1679-84, Ladakh allied with the Mughals to repel the Tibetan incursion by Gaden Tsewang. Previous attempts at international diplomacy prompted two Ladakhi embassies to be sent to Lhasa in 1664 and 1667. These missions failed at their task, mocked by the government in Lhasa; see Zahiruddin Ahmad, 'New Light on the Tibet-Ladakh-Mughal War of 1679-84', *East and West*, 18/3 (1968): pp. 340-61, at p. 342.

84 The offspring of Muslim queens and Ladakhi kings gave rise to important relations of kinship from the side of the mother's family.

Chapter 12
The Discovery of the Muslims of Tibet by the First Portuguese Missionaries[1]

Marc Gaborieau

This article is at the crossroads between two paths of research: on the one hand that of historians dealing with the first Portuguese missionaries in Tibet and Central Asia, to which I will return later, and on the other hand my own ethnological studies of Muslims in the Himalayas which I have conducted during the last forty-five years.

The presence of Muslims in Tibet has been well known in the West since the end of the eighteenth century when the first English explorers visited the region. The number of these Muslims was fairly small, but they existed. I have published some documents pertaining to their presence which I had found in Nepal in my book *Récit d'un voyageur musulman au Tibet*. What was not known is when these Muslims came to Tibet.

The Kashmiri Muslims, who constitute the oldest Muslim community in Central Tibet, trace their arrival to the region back to the Fifth Dalai Lama, the 'founder' of modern Tibet, who reigned from 1642 until 1682. An oral tradition recorded at the end of the nineteenth century from Kashmiri Muslims in Tibet tells the story of an Indian Sufi who came originally from the Indian city of Patna. After a competition in magic with the Dalai Lama he obtained the right for the Muslims to settle in Tibet. They were also granted a land on which to build a mosque and a cemetery. These oral traditions, however, are rarely cross-checked by external sources.

By chance, we have an early cross-check through the first Westerners who visited Tibet: Portuguese missionaries who reached there at the beginning of the seventeenth century. I will begin this article with an account of their first journeys. In the following two parts, based on their testimonies, I will address two questions. First, how do their reports relate to these oral traditions about the origin of the Muslims of Tibet? And, taking the earliest Portuguese documents

---

[1] This article was originally the transcript of an oral presentation in French at the international conference held in Paris (11-13 May 1998) on the occasion of the fifth centenary of the arrival of Vasco da Gama in India; it was published in *Vasco da Gama e a India* (Lisbon, 1999), vol. 1, pp. 41-4. For this English translation, I have corrected, updated and adapted the original text; but I have kept its oral style.

as a starting-point, what role did Muslims play in the formation of our image of Tibet in the West?

THE FIRST PORTUGUESE MISSIONARIES IN TIBET

Here is a brief account of the first journeys of Portuguese missionaries to Tibet. At the beginning of the seventeenth century, Tibet was under the authority of the Mongols, who had also contributed to installing the theocracy of the Dalai Lama - the title Dalai Lama is, not by chance, a Mongol expression. At that time, the country was relatively open to foreign merchants and travellers, notably to Muslims and Armenians. It was only with the establishment of Chinese sovereignty over Tibet in 1720 that the land was closed to any foreign influences other than those of the Chinese. The first Portuguese missions to Tibet at the beginning of the seventeenth century resulted from the presence of Jesuit missionaries at the Mughal court in north India. This mission had been founded in 1580 at the request of the emperor Akbar (reg. 1556-1605). The Catholic mission in India continued without interruption, albeit with ups and downs, until the conquest of Delhi by the British in 1803. It was particularly active during the reign of Akbar and his son Jahangir (reg. 1605-27). Using north India as their base, the Jesuits decided during the reign of these two Mughal emperors to set out in the direction of Central Asia and Tibet in order to spread Christianity there. These Portuguese missionaries in Central Asia and Tibet have been studied by several historians of whom I would like to mention here only the earliest and the latest. The first noteworthy study was a book by Cornelius Wessels with the title *Early Jesuit Travellers in Central Asia*, published in 1924 in The Hague. The most recent study was published by Hughes Didier under the title *Les Portugais au Tibet* in 1996 in Paris.

Let us then deal with these expeditions. A first expedition, led by Brother Bento de Goes from 1602 to 1607, crossed Central Asia following the tracks of the Silk Road. Departing from the north of India, he travelled as far as the Chinese border. Three further expeditions, between 1624 and 1635, had Tibet as their destination. For two of them, which were directed towards Western Tibet, the point of departure was Delhi, which was under the control of the Jesuit province of Goa. The first one to leave was led by Father António de Andrade in 1624-25 and limited to Tsaparang, the capital of the Tibetan kingdom of Guge. The second expedition was that of Father Francisco de Azevedo in 1631-32 who went to Tsaparang and then to Leh, the capital of Ladakh. The third expedition, however, was not directed towards Western, but Central Tibet. In terms of chronology, it took place between the two journeys just mentioned. Unlike the two others, this third expedition was no longer connected to the province of Goa, but to that of Cochin. Taking place in 1627-28, it was led by Father Estêvão Cacela and Father João Cabral. Having departed from Hooghly in the Bengal Delta, and passing Dhaka (now the capital of Bangladesh), Assam and Cooch Behar (in present-day

India), and then Bhutan, they reached the Central Tibetan province of Utsang where they established a short-lived mission. The travellers also visited the great cities of Gyantse and Shigatse in the vicinity of Lhasa, but they never entered Lhasa itself. They returned to Hooghly passing Kathmandu in Nepal and Patna in India, from where they went down the Ganges valley, which led them back to their original point of departure. It is mainly from the reports and the correspondence written in the course of these three missionary journeys that we extract our earliest Western accounts of the Muslims of Tibet.

Before dealing in more detail with the sources related to these missions, I would like to mention in passing that in the ensuing years, Tibet was explored sporadically by the Portuguese between 1635 and 1640. After that, they completely left this field. The Tibetan mission was only resumed much later and only briefly in 1715 by the Italian Jesuit Ippolito Desideri. He had to leave it when the Vatican decided to withdraw the mission in Tibet and Nepal from the Jesuits and entrust the Capuchins with it.

WHAT DID THESE MISSIONARIES SAY ABOUT THE PRESENCE OF MUSLIMS IN TIBET?

Turning now to the testimony of the first Portuguese missionaries, I would like to address the first question: what do they tell us about the presence of Muslims in Tibet?

The testimonies of these earliest missionaries are important historical documents: they are the first Western sources which confirm the presence of Muslims in Tibet. In 1624, for example, Father de Andrade mentioned Muslim Kashmiri merchants in Tsaparang in Western Tibet. Describing a meeting with the king of Tibet (i.e. the king of Tsaparang), he says:

> Furthermore, he [i.e. the king] ordered a letter to be written in Persian to use for the Muslims and had it signed and sealed with his coat of arms. The letter commanded all the Kashmiris of Agra and Lahore who traded with his lands to do what they were ordered, either by myself or by any other Father, and to transport our belongings by their own means to Tibet as if they were the baggage of the king himself.[2]

Three years later, in 1627, Father Cacela, who wrote from Bhutan, spoke of Kashmiri Muslims who came to Tsaparang and extended their business up to Gyantse and Lhasa in Central Tibet.

[2] Hughes Didier (ed. and trans.), *Les Portugais au Tibet: Les premières relations jésuites (1624-1635)* (Paris, 1996), p. 53.

> It [i.e. Tibet] also trades with Kashmir, taking the route via Tsaparang, as well as with the lands which are neighbours of this kingdom. Many strangers travel to Gyantse, the court of Demba Cemba (*sDe pa gTsaṅ pa*), the most powerful king of Potente [i.e. Tibet]. It is eight days away. Many people travel to Lhasa as well.[3]

The first Portuguese missionaries thus prove beyond any doubt that Muslims were well settled in Tibet at that time, that is, from the first quarter of the seventeenth century onwards: in other words even before the reign of the Fifth Dalai Lama to whom oral tradition attributes the introduction of Muslims in Tibet. They were present even in Lhasa, the religious and political capital which remains the heart of modern Tibet just as it has been in the past. This in itself is not astonishing. As Rolf Alfred Stein pointed out in his classical study about Tibetan civilization which appeared in 1962, Lhasa as well as the other great Tibetan cities were in those days cosmopolitan centres which welcomed numerous curious travellers and foreign merchants.

In this second part, I have emphasized the presence of Muslims in Central Tibet as evidenced by the documents connected with the mission of Cacela and Cabral. However, since these travellers did not spend much time in Central Tibet, we are hardly told any details about the Muslims except for the fact of their presence there. In order to learn more about their role, we have to turn to the missions directed towards Western Tibet.

WHAT ROLE DID MUSLIMS PLAY IN SHAPING THE WESTERN IMAGE OF TIBET?

In this third part I will mainly rely both on my own research and on the recent study by Hughes Didier. In order to answer the second question, that is, What role did Muslims play in shaping the Western image of Tibet?, I will first deal with the Muslims as intermediaries between the West and Tibet, while in the second section of this third part I will discuss how far they also constituted a barrier between the West and Tibet.

Muslims had always been indispensable intermediaries. It is well known that the earliest Western knowledge of Tibet – as, essentially, of the rest of the East before the seventeenth century – was obtained via Muslims. The name 'Tibet' itself, which is of Turkish origin, came to us through the Persian *Tibbat*.[4] The same can definitely be said about the Portuguese missionaries at the beginning of the seventeenth century, since Muslims served them as indispensable intermediaries. When reading the reports of Father de Andrade one notices just how significant Muslims were for missionaries who wanted to travel to Tibet. The missionaries had to use Persian for communication – Persian which they

---

3 Didier, *Les Portugais au Tibet*, p. 249.

4 See the contribution by Peter Zieme in this volume.

had learned due to the mission at the Mughal court and which more generally was the most important language of communication for large parts of the population of the East. It was also the official language of the Mughal Empire. The missionaries even dressed like Muslim merchants, a habit which continued until the nineteenth century. When at the beginning of the nineteenth century, the explorer William Moorcroft (1767-1825) went into Western Tibet, he was still disguised as a Muslim merchant.[5] Furthermore, with the help of the king of Tsaparang, the missionaries used the guilds of Muslim merchants in order to travel through India and Tibet.

Muslims also served as indispensable cultural intermediaries to shape the Western understanding of Buddhism. Until the nineteenth century Muslims had developed an image of Buddhism as a form of degenerate monotheism. For instance Father de Andrade had decided to travel to Tibet after he had heard at the Mughal court that this mysterious country was actually Christian. Once there, he reconsidered his views, but continued to believe, not unlike the Muslims, that, to put it in Didier's words, this Tibetan sect had features derived from Christianity. He saw Buddhism as a form of Christiano-pagan syncretism.[6] Introducing his travel report, Father de Andrade explains that 'we were in possession of numerous reports, diligently obtained from different sources, thanks to which we were certain that those kingdoms were inhabited by Christians, without taking into account that for the last twenty years rumours confirming this had reached the fathers'.[7]

If we keep to the facts considered up to now, for the missionaries, the Muslim was something like an *alter ego*: the Christians adopted the language, clothes and techniques of the Muslims; and even more, they saw Tibet with the eyes of Muslims.

But did this kind of interaction last? Here, I come to the second part of my second question: that is, whether the Muslims also constituted a barrier in the encounter between missionaries and Tibetans. Indeed, the Muslims at a certain point began to appear like an obstacle for the missionaries, who regarded the Buddhists as lost brothers, as lost Christians. One should not forget here the messianic vision in the West, most notably in Portugal until the seventeenth century, as well as the anti-Muslim aims of the missionaries. The missionaries still believed in the myth of Prester John and the lost Christians who were to be found somewhere beyond the Muslim world. Their aim was to forge an alliance with these lost Christians against the Muslims. This is what Father de Andrade aimed at when he sought an alliance with the Buddhist authorities of Tsaparang against the Muslims whom he had previously served. A series of misunderstandings followed, which I will not discuss in detail here, and which

---

5 See the contribution by John Bray in this volume.

6 See the introduction by Didier in *Les Portugais au Tibet*, p. 10, and pp. 88-90 for discussions concerning differences in belief.

7 Didier, *Les Portugais au Tibet*, p. 29. See also p. 49.

led at the same time to the downfall of Tsaparang, which fell under the control of Ladakh in 1630, and to the end of the Catholic mission in Tsaparang.

The first Portuguese missionaries in Tibet did not succeed in passing round the obstacle presented by the Muslims. This only happened with the Italian Jesuit Ippolito Desideri in 1715 he initiated a tradition of understanding Buddhism independent of the Muslim intermediary who had up to that time served as a filter. It is with him that modern Tibetology started to develop.

CONCLUSIONS

The Portuguese missionaries in Tibet who gave the earliest Western testimonies to the existence of Muslims there did not limit themselves to merely noting that presence; they also engaged with them in complex transactions which progressed from friendliness, through rivalry to hostility. There was in fact a curious game in which the Muslim was first seen as an *alter ego*, and later treated as an enemy. Muslims were first close to the Christians and translated for them, thus allowing them to approach the Tibetans and Asians in general. But these friendly transactions were progressively replaced by hostility, since the ultimate aim of the missionaries was to eliminate this link in order to find their lost brothers who lived beyond the Muslims, according to their understanding of the pagans of Asia. I have tried to analyse here the basic principles of this dialectic which was in many ways a failure.

I would like to conclude with a telling anecdote which gives evidence of this failure and at the same time presents the Muslim as the *alter ego* of the Christian. Ironically, to the Tibetans this similarity between Christians and Muslims was more obvious than the Portuguese missionaries would have imagined. When the mission in Tsaparang closed down in 1635, their few converts who had become strangers in the Buddhist society, were joined by the Tibetan authorities with the other foreign religious community, that of the Muslims. This shows how from the point of view of Asian religions – as is still the case for Hindus in Nepal and India – Muslims and Christians belong to the same category and are almost interchangeable.

BIBLIOGRAPHY AND FURTHER READING

Laurent Deshayes, *Histoire du Tibet* (Paris, 1997).

Hughes Didier, 'Interférences islamo-chrétiennes dans les représentations du bouddhisme', *Islamochristiana*, 16 (1990): pp. 115-38.

Hughes Didier (ed. and trans.), *Les Portugais au Tibet: Les premières relations jésuites (1624-1635)* (Paris, 1996).

Marc Gaborieau, *Récit d'un voyageur musulman au Tibet* (Paris, 1973).

Marc Gaborieau, 'Pouvoirs et autorités des soufis dans l'Himalaya', in Véronique Bouillier et Gérard Toffin (eds), *Prêtrise, pouvoirs et autorité en Himalaya* (Paris, 1989), pp. 215-38.
Marc Gaborieau (ed.), *Tibetan Muslims*, special issue of *The Tibet Journal*, 20/3 (1995).
Marc Gaborieau, Article 'Tubbat', §2 'Recent and contemporary history ethnology', in *EI*[2].
Sir Edward Maclagan, *The Jesuits and the Great Mogul* (London, 1932; repr. New York, 1972).
Avril Ann Powell, *Muslims and Missionaries in Pre-Mutiny India* (London, 1993).
Rolf Alfred Stein, *La civilisation tibétaine* (Paris, 1962).
Cornelius Wessels, *Early Jesuit Travellers in Central Asia: 1603-1721* (The Hague, 1924).
Thierry Zarcone (ed.), *Musulmans et soufis du Tibet* (Milan, 2005).

Chapter 13
So Close to Samarkand, Lhasa: Sufi Hagiographies, Founder Myths and Sacred Space in Himalayan Islam

Alexandre Papas

A few days' march from Samarkand lies the land of Tibet (…)

Benjamin of Tudela

INTRODUCTION: PROFANE NARRATIVES, SACRED SPACE

In his famous book *Das Heilige und das Profane: Vom Wesen des Religiösen* (1954),[1] Mircea Eliade gives to understand – though without any clear demonstration – that the conception of a sacred space is intimately linked to the creation of profane narratives. The religious experience of territory is saturated with signs, symbols, myths and legends which grant meanings to places. Hence the sacredness of such and such space is not only marked and named but also, necessarily, narrated. In Islam, the word *ḥaram* (sanctuary), also the term *ḥimā* (sacred land), which both come from pre-Islamic Arabia, designate the concept of sacred space. *Ḥaram* is derived from the Arabic root *ḥrm* denoting what is forbidden, not permitted or taboo; it also produces terms like *ḥurm* (refuge), *ḥarām* (unlawful, illicit), *iḥrām* (sanctification ritual during the *ḥajj*) and so forth. Whereas the Qurʾān contains about eighty occurrences of the root *ḥrm*, a famous *ḥadīth* makes a restrictive list of the Muslim sacred places, that is Mecca (Ar. *al-masjid al-ḥarām*), Jerusalem (*al-masjid al-aqṣā*) and Medina.[2] Yet, besides the Sacred Book and the Prophetic sayings, an exceptionally rich literature, hagiographical in particular, provides a much longer list including mosques, shrines and Sufi buildings.

From a Tibetan perspective, say Buddhist, Shamanic and Bon-po, the notion of *gnas* denotes, rather than the interdiction, the abode, the fact of abiding.

---

1 English translation: *The Sacred and the Profane: The Nature of Religion* (New York, 1961); French translation: *Le Sacré et le profane* (Paris, 1965).

2 For instance, see *Ṣaḥīḥ al-Bukhārī: The Translation of the Meanings of Ṣaḥīḥ al-Bukhārī*, ed. Muhammad Muhsin Khan (Medina, n.d.), vol. 2, p. 160, n. 288. Catherine Mayeur-Jaouen, 'Tombeaux, mosquées et zâwiya : la polarité des lieux saints musulmans', in André Vauchez (ed.), *Lieux sacrés, lieux de culte, sanctuaires* (Rome, 2000), pp. 133-47.

It generates various terms such as *gnas-skor* (pilgrimage), *gnas-chen* (powerful places), *gnas-yul* (sacred lands) and *sgrub-gnas* (places of realization).[3] Here too, a profusion of profane accounts – pilgrimage guides, legends, hagiographies – give content and intelligibility to consecrated places.

At the crossroads of Islamic Central Asia and the Himalayan regions, Xinjiang or Eastern Turkestan presents the edifying case of a sacred space fully nourished by mystical narratives (*tadhkira* and *manāqib*). Masami Hamada[4] has recently discussed the question of Muslim holy places and their power in the Tarim Basin during the modern and contemporary periods. Analysing the modes of discovering the tombs of saints, Hamada shows that, at the origin of a tomb discovery, stands a legendary tale where a saint appears in someone's dream, points out where his body is buried and enjoins him to build a shrine. These narratives are historically governed by political and religious motivations (gaining charisma, confessional rivalry, organization of the cult). Nevertheless, beyond politico-religious agendas, at the anthropological level, they define a sacred space in terms of holy men and saintly activities: saints accomplish miracles such as creating springs or moving mountains; they complete marvellous journeys that reach far-distant places or have heroic encounters; they turn a common place into a sacred one through their auspiciousness, their spiritual influence (Ar. *baraka*).

THE CASE OF THE HIMALAYAN MUSLIMS

Central Asian Muslim saints played an important role in bringing Islam and Sufism to Western China, Northern India and the mountainous ranges running between. As early as the sixteenth century, in his chronicle (ch. 83), the historian Mīrzā Muḥammad Ḥaydar Dughlāt relates that:

> In the spring of that year, the Khán [Sulṭān Saʿīd Khān, reg. 1514-33] resolved to conduct a holy war against Tibet. Previous to this, [his] Amirs had frequently invaded and plundered that country, but on account of their ignorance and folly, Islám had made no progress, and there were still numberless infidels in Tibet, besides those whom Amirs has subdued. The Khán had always been animated by a desire to carry on holy wars in the path of God, and especially so now that *he had just assumed the saintly ways of the Khwájas* [emphasis mine].

---

3 On these notions see Toni Huber (ed.), *Sacred Spaces and Powerful Places in Tibetan Culture: A Collection of Essays* (Dharamsala, 1999).

4 Masami Hamada, 'Le pouvoir des lieux saints dans le Turkestan oriental', *Annales. Histoire, Sciences Sociales*, 59/5-6 (2004): pp. 1019-40. The same author provides several Turkic primary sources containing a large number of saints' biographies related to holy sites: *Hagiographies du Turkestan oriental: Textes čaġatay édités, traduits en japonais et annotés avec une introduction analytique et historique* (Kyoto, 2006) (mostly in Japanese).

> He was always ready to devote himself to the cause of the faith, and felt that the holy war was one to the surest roads to salvation and union with God. Prompted by such pious feelings as these, at the end of the year 938 [1532] he set out to invade Tibet.[5]

This assertion is, actually, one of the first as well as one of the rare historical – not hagiographical – attestations to Central Asian missions oriented towards Tibet.[6] What is interesting in these lines is the allusion to the holy Khwājas and to the initiation of Sultan Saʿīd Khān: the same source states that the ruler of Kashgaria has been initiated to the Khwājagān-i Naqshbandiyya Sufi order by, successively, two Central Asian Shaykhs, first the Samarqandī Mawlānā Qāsim, then the Bukharan Khwāja Khāwand Maḥmūd.[7] Although the conquest attempt of Sultan Saʿīd did not succeed, the Khwāja's proselytizing ambition continued, as if the dream to convert Tibet to Sunni Islam would have been a religious duty, similar to the will to convert China. This corresponds to the Naqshbandiyya ideology which aims to convert non-Muslims to Sunni Islam; though late, the sixteenth and seventeenth centuries correspond also to the last period of the Islamization of Central Asia. This religious duty could possibly have been shared by Himalayan rulers: one knows the case of an anonymous Balti prince who, at the beginning of the seventeenth century, called *ʿulamāʾ* from Kashgar to teach the *sunna* in the region, to the detriment of Ismaili Shiism. During the seventeenth and eighteenth centuries there occurred a series of conversion waves initialised by Sufi Shaykhs themselves, coming from Central Asia (Kashgaria and further West). Quite well documented is the next period when, again, Samarqandī Shaykhs initiated Himalayan Muslims to Sufism.[8]

These remarks are only meant to provide some first reference points. It is not the place here to discuss this long and complex religious history in detail,

---

5 Ḥaydar Mīrzā, *A History of the Moghuls in India: Being the Tarikh-i-Rashidi of Mirza Muhammad Haidar, Dughlat*, ed. Ney Elias, trans. Edward Denison Ross (London, 1898; repr. New Delhi, 1986), p. 403. The text edited and translated by Wheeler McIntosh Thackston differs here, see *Mirza Haydar Dughlat's Tarikh-i Rashidi: A History of the Khans of Moghulistan* (Harvard, 1996), p. 76.

6 One would expect an earlier attestation, especially in the early medieval period (*c*.tenth–thirteenth centuries) given the fact that, after the conversion to Islam of the Karakhanid ruler Satuq Bughrā Khān (d. 955), his descendants and later missionaries led intensive Islamization activities against Buddhism in the Tarim Basin, at the gates of the Tibetan world. The present-day religious landscape of Southern Xinjiang presents a large number of mausoleums (accompanied by many legends) where these saints are buried, or supposed to be buried. See Rahilä Davut, *Uyghur mazarliri* [*The Mausoleums of the Uyghurs*] (Urumchi, 2001).

7 Ḥaydar Mīrzā, *History of the Moghuls in India*, pp. 213, 395, 398.

8 See my 'Note sur la Naqshbandiyya-Mujaddidiyya en Asie centrale chinoise (XVIIIe-XIXe siècles)', *Journal of the History of Sufism*, 5 (2007 = special issue on the Naqshbandiyya-Khâlidiyya Sufi order): pp. 319-28.

not least for the reason that such an account remains to be written. As we have seen and shall see repeatedly, a second reason is that any historicist endeavour faces a lack of sources or their legendary nature. In a sense, we shall continuously tread a delicate path between history and legend along collective memory and representations. Such is the limit, and at the same time the possible benefit, of the present study: if narratives are not records, if they only spin us stories, it is no less true that they inform us, better than anything else, about the beliefs, about the imagination, about faith and piety. All these are elements which might help us to understand Himalayan Islam based on its main features such as sacred spaces.

In the collective memory of both Central Asian Muslims and Muslim communities of Himalaya or greater Tibet (that is, Tibet properly but also Ladakh and the Chinese provinces of Qinghai and Gansu) there remains a common remembrance of the Central Asian saints' missions. More precisely, one notices a remarkable historico-geographical coincidence: the assertion of the Samarqandī origin of Tibetan Islam.[9] Through popular etymology, conversion narratives and founder myths related to several Muslim groups, such as Lusar,[10] Huang Fan (Yellow Tibetans),[11] Bonan, Salar or Dongxiang, even Hui, the city of Samarkand or its region appears as a land from where Muslim population groups are said to have migrated to Himalaya or from where Muslim proselyte groups or individuals are said to have came to Islamize Tibet. From the constellation of versions and variations emerges the general picture of a religious geography, linking Muslim isolated minorities to the Muslim world (Ar. *Dār al-Islām*) across Central Asia by the symbolic routes of etymology, hagiography and myth.

After having first examined some popular etymologies referring to Central Asia and Samarkand in particular, I wish to contrast Turkestani Sufi hagiographical texts with Himalayan legendary items. Then I shall focus on the Salar case: this is a Turkic Muslim ethnic group living in the former Amdo region, who represents an interesting case of religious and cultural contacts. I will make use of two main types of sources: (1) nineteenth–early twentieth century expedition reports by Western travellers or missionaries (British, German, Russian, French), such as Douglas Forsyth (1827-86), Josef Trippner (1899-1970), Nikolai Mikhailovich Przhevalskij (1839-88), Henri d'Ollone (1868-1945) and Fernand Grenard (1866-95), and (2) Central Asian hagiographies preserved in manuscripts written in Persian or Chaghatay Turkic during the eighteenth and nineteenth centuries.

---

[9] For ideas concerning the origin of the Tibetans in medieval Arabic literature see the contribution by Anna Akasoy on Tibet in Islamic geography and cartography in this volume.

[10] Lusars or Losars were Turkic people living in Kumbum (near Xining).

[11] They were Muslim Tibetans according to Louis M.J. Schram, 'The Monguors of the Kansu-Tibetan Frontier: Part III. Records of the Monguor Clans. History of the Monguors in Huangchung and the Chronicles of the Lu Family', *Transactions of the American Philosophical Society*, N.S., 51/3 (1961): pp. 1-117, at pp. 18, 26 *passim*.

THE QUESTION OF NAMES

Muslim historians such as Abū Jaʿfar Muḥammad al-Ṭabarī (ninth–tenth century) or Abū Saʿīd ʿAbd al-Ḥayy Gardīzī (eleventh century) attributed a Yemenite origin to the Tibetan kings.[12] It seems that this was a common belief among Muslim scholars throughout the medieval period. In a more precise way, the traveller and polygraph Yāqūt al-Ḥamawī (twelfth–thirteenth century) presumed that the Yemenite ruler called Tubbaʿ 'started from Yemen, crossed the Jayḥūn river and marched up to Samarkand. Finding the area inhabited, he founded a city there, rested for a few days and then proceeded towards China.' There he founded another city that he named Tibet. An anonymous ninth-century Arabian poet similarly wrote that 'these are the people who first gave Samarkand its name; Tibet also was founded by them'. Interestingly, these two quotations come from Abu Bakr Amiruddin Nadwi's book published in 1979, recently translated into English under the title *Tibet and Tibetan Muslims*.[13] Under the pen of the Tibetan Muslim author, this medieval legend becomes a philological etymology, that is to say historical evidence, about the origin of Tibet; moreover, it associates clearly the city of Samarkand and Tibet.

Another illustration of such unclear, though widespread, etymologies associating Himalayan Muslims with Central Asia is the range of ethnic names. As is well known, Dongxiang is a Mongol Muslim minority in China with a population of about 370,000 (1990 census), of which the majority lives in Gansu and Qinghai. Whereas their origin remains unclear (they are supposed to have came with Genghis Khan's garrisons from Iran and Afghanistan), they call themselves Santa or Sarta, that is in fact *Sart/Sārt*,[14] which refers in Turkic languages to the settled inhabitants of Central Asia, and particularly the Persian-speaking population, in the same sense as Tajik (see below). The case of Bonan (Ch. Baoan) is no less confusing since they are said to be descended from Muslim Mongol soldiers – mixed with the Central Asian population – stationed in Qinghai during the Yuan or Ming dynasties and to have settled in the Gansu province during the reign of the Qing Emperor Tongzhi (1861–75).[15] The Salars (Ch. Sala) are Turkic Muslims

---

12 Vasili Barthol'd, Clifford Edmund Bosworth and Marc Gaborieau, 'L'islam au Tibet', in Thierry Zarcone (ed.), *Musulmans et soufis du Tibet* (Milan, 2005), p. 2. The same article (p. 3) mentions the village of Samarqandāq which would be located, according to the famous Persian geography *Ḥudūd al-ʿālam*, in present-day Wakhan, between Tibet and Central Asia. See *Ḥudūd al-ʿālam: The Regions of the World. A Persian Geography*, trans. Vladimir Minorsky (London, 1937), p. 121 and commentary p. 309. See also the article by Akasoy in this volume.

13 Abu Bakr Amir-uddin Nadwi, *Islam and Tibetan Muslims* (Dharamsala, 2004), p. 6. See my book review in the *Tibet Journal* (forthcoming).

14 See the article 'Sārt' in *EI*[2].

15 Others consider that they converted to Islam early in the 1800s: James Stuart Olson, *An Ethnohistorical Dictionary of China* (London, 1998), pp. 30-32. Himalayan Muslim groups living across the border of Xinjiang, Gansu, Qinghai and Tibet, remain poorly

living also in Gansu and Qinghai; they number more than 104,000 people (2000 census). They used to mix with the Tibetan populations through intermarriage or by the conversion to Islam, as was the case with the Kargan(g) Tibetans who became Muslims under Salar influence.[16] Their language itself is 'a mixed language of Turkic origin with heavy Chinese and Tibetan adstrata'.[17] We know of the existence of manuscripts among the Salars composed in both Persian and Tibetan;[18] we even find Red Hat Muslims among the Salars mentioned which may be analogous to Red Hat Buddhists.[19] As for the etymology, according to d'Ollone's interviews, the Salars claim their origins from Samarkand,[20] and they connect their name to the Turkic Oghuz people living in the Samarkand area.[21] I will return later to this point and, more extensively, to the Salars.

The Hui are not Tibetan but Chinese Muslims, although several groups have been acculturated to non-Han communities.[22] The so-called Tibetan Hui (Ch. Zang Hui), for example, live in Lhasa and count about 6,000 souls.[23] Since the history of the Hui has already attracted a great deal of attention, I shall limit my remarks to two details:

Firstly, the Turkic name of the Hui - used in Central Asian sources (in Turki, that is, the Chaghatay Turkic language, and in Persian) and still used today in Kazakhstan and in Kirghizstan as an ethnic appellation - is Dungan or Tungan(i). This name has no clear etymology. The late Joseph F. Fletcher wrote that

---

known. Besides some ethnographical publications in Chinese, there are some examples of Himalayan Muslim groups visited by the Russian explorer Przhevalskij in the 1880s, see N.M. Przhevalskij, *Ot' Kjakhty na istoki Zheltoj Reki: Izsledovanie severnoj okrainy Tibeta i put' cherez' Lob'-Nor' po Bassejnu Tarima* [*From Kiakhta to the Source of the Yellow River. Explorations of the Northern Regions of Tibet and Trip along Lop Nor down the Tarim Basin*] (St. Petersburg, 1888), pp. 300-316, 362-3, 368-71, 374, etc.

16 William Woodville Rockhill, 'A Journey in Mongolia and Tibet', *The Geographical Journal*, 3/5 (1894): pp. 357-84, at p. 362; Josef Trippner, 'Die Salaren, ihre ersten Glaubensstreitigkeiten, und ihr Aufstand 1781', *Central Asiatic Journal*, 9/4 (1964): pp. 241-76, at p. 257.

17 Arienne Dwyer in Ma Wei, Ma Jianzhong and Kevin Stuart, *The Folklore of China's Islamic Salar Nationality* (Lewiston, NY, 2001), p. 1.

18 Henri Marie Gustave d'Ollone, 'Recherches sur les musulmans chinois. Mission d'Ollone', *Revue du Monde Musulman*, 9/12 (1909): pp. 522-98, at p. 583.

19 D'Ollone, 'Recherches sur les musulmans chinois', p. 540.

20 D'Ollone, 'Recherches sur les musulmans chinois', p. 539.

21 Beyond the name and etymology, they perceive themselves as brothers of the Oğuz Turks: see the interesting discussion between a Salar *müderris* and the Tatar traveller Abdurreşîd İbrâhîm (in Beijing) in Abdurreşîd İbrâhîm, *Âlem-i İslâm ve Japonya'da İslâmiyet'in Yayılması* [*The World of Islam and the Spread of Islamity in Japon*] (Istanbul, 1910-13; repr. 2003), vol. 2, pp. 157-61.

22 See the article by Diana Altner in this volume.

23 See notably Dru C. Gladney, *Muslim Chinese: Ethnic Nationalism in the People's Republic* (Cambridge, 1991), pp. 33-4.

> Marshall Broomhall, *Islam in China*, pp. xvi and 147, has given wide currency to an etymology derived from the Turkish *don-* / Chaghatay **tong-*, meaning 'to be converted.' But how early and where is the Chaghatay form attested? The use of the adjectival ī in the form 'Tunganī' would seem to indicate that 'Tungan' is no longer felt as a participial form from as early as the seventeenth century.[24]

More exactly, the Turkish verb *dönmek* (or the Uzbek form *dönmoq*) means 'to turn, to return', thus 'to turn towards Islam, to convert to' – in the same way that the Chinese word *hui* 回 has the meaning of 'to return, to go back to'. It is worth remarking, as a lead to follow up, that we find in the Ottoman dictionary of the Chaghatay language by Bukhārī an entry for the verb *dūnmāk*.[25] Composed at the end of the nineteenth century, this work is a late lexicon, yet it remains reliable as it is based on samples from classical Chaghatay literature. While this kind of attestation does not allow a scientific etymology, it testifies to the existence of an early Central Asian ethnic designation for the Hui.[26]

My second point: even though the Hui are generally believed to be descendants of the first Arab or Persian people who came to China by sea during the Tang dynasty, many of them claim that their ancestors come from Central Asia (Khwarezm and Samarkand in particular). There are historical bases to this 'genealogy': a Chinese record such as the *Liaoshi*, compiled in 1343-44, lists several tribes (Ch. *dashibu*), among them the Huihui, living in the region of Samarkand (Ch. Xunsigan).[27] More generally, it is well documented in Chinese and Persian sources that the Mongols who first conquered these Transoxanian areas recruited the local population (Huihui) not only as soldiers in the campaigns to conquer China but also as artisans, architects, literate men for the administrative services, etc.[28] The favourable policy of the Mongol emperors towards Muslims in China contributed to the unprecedented increase of the Muslim population and also to their significant social, economic and political role under the Yuan dynasty. The Muslim communities of Northwest and Central China were thus founded by Central Asian Muslims during the Mongol period and there is evidence that they were mainly Muslims from Samarkand and Khwarezm.[29] The relevant element for us is the exceptional status attributed to the great Central Asian oasis.

---

[24] Joseph F. Fletcher, 'The Naqshbandiyya in Northwest China', in *Studies on Chinese and Islamic Inner Asia* (London, 1995), article XI, p. 12, n. 4.

[25] See Şeyh Süleymân Efendî Buhârî, *Lugat-i Çagatâyi ve Turkî-yi Osmânî* [*Chaghatay and Ottoman Turkic Lexicon*] (Istanbul, 1298/1880-81), p. 173.

[26] As a comparable example, the name *Qalmāq*, which designates the Jungar Mongols in Persian and Turki sources, corresponds, in the popular etymology, to a Turkic verb meaning 'to stay, to remain'. The Jungars are thus defined as 'those who remained Infidels', contrary to the Dungans.

[27] Quoted by Michael Dillon, *China's Muslim Hui Community* (Richmond, 1999), p. 13.

[28] See the articles by Azad and Buell in this volume.

[29] Dillon, *China's Muslim Hui*, ch. 2 (pp. 11-26).

A last name that does not refer to Himalayan Muslims, but remains worth mentioning in a discussion about the relationship between Samarkand and Tibet, is the famous 'Ol-mo-lung-ring, part of or identical to Stag-gzig, the mythical region of origin of Bon-po. Against the former hypothesis on the identification of this toponym – especially the theory of the late Bronislav I. Kuznetsov – Dan Martin suggested that 'we may say that all the various sources we have brought forward point to a location for 'Ol-mo-lung-ring not precisely in Persia, but in the lands between northern Persia and the (changing) western borders of Tibet'.[30] Notwithstanding the necessarily imprecise geography of such a location, it refers apparently, once again, to the Persian-speaking part of Central Asia, that is, the land of the Tajiks according to Islamic sources,[31] including present-day Tajikistan and Southern Uzbekistan, more precisely the Bukhara and the Samarkand areas. Apart from the question of the origin of Bon-po, one can perceive the name Stag-gzig/Tajik as a memory, in Tibetan culture, of its Central Asian roots.

To sum up this section, I believe that all these names suggest, rather than a historical background, an anthropological reality. Through popular etymologies, Himalayan Muslims – some of them at least – express their religious affinity with Islamic Central Asia, manifesting a fascination or even devotion for the holy city of Samarkand which offers a real or an imagined homeland for the scattered communities.

SUFI HAGIOGRAPHIES AND MUSLIM HIMALAYAN LEGENDS

In addition to these various etymologies, one finds another way to connect Tibet and Central Asia: hagiographical traditions, more precisely, Sufi conversion narratives. It is often said, for instance, that Rinchana Bhoti, king of Ladakh in the fourteenth century, had been converted to Islam by a Turkestani Sufi belonging to the Suhrawardī order called Sharaf al-Dīn;[32] the king then had a mausoleum built for a certain Bulbul Shāh, a Persian, who had taught him the Qur'ān.[33] Another case is the two vicars (Ar. *khalīfa*) of the aforementioned Bukharan Naqshbandī Shaykh Khwāja Khāwand Maḥmūd who were sent to Little Tibet (Baltistan) in 1608.[34] More interesting for us are the Turkestani

[30] Dan Martin, "Ol-mo-lung-ring, the Original Holy Place', in Huber (ed.), *Sacred Spaces*, pp. 258-301, at p. 278.

[31] About the controversies on the etymology, see the article 'Tādjīk' in *EI*[2].

[32] Mohammad Ishaq Khan, *Kashmir's Transition to Islam: The Role of the Muslim Rishis (Fifteenth to Eighteenth Century)* (New Delhi, [3]2002), pp. 62-3.

[33] Charles-Eudes Bonin, 'La Conquête du Petit-Tibet', *Revue du Monde Musulman*, 11/6 (1910): pp. 207-31, at p. 210.

[34] David W. Damrel, 'Forgotten Grace: Khwâja Khâwand Mahmûd Naqshbandî in Central Asia and Mughal India' (PhD thesis, Duke University, 1991), pp. 93, 169.

Sufi hagiographies which describe the religious activities of the Naqshbandī Khwājas. These Sufis are all descendants of the great Samarqandī Shaykh Aḥmad Kāsānī Dahbīdī, also called Makhdūm-i Aʿẓam, that is, 'the great master' (1464-1542).[35] For instance, a text like the *Tadhkira-yi ʿazīzān* [*Collection of the Holy Men*],[36] written in Chaghatay Turkic by Muḥammad Ṣādiq Kāshgarī at the beginning of the nineteenth century, relates the travels of one of these descendants called Hidāyat Allāh (1626-94), also known under the honorific nickname (Ar. *takhalluṣ*) Āfāq Khwāja or Apaq Khoja.[37]

These two last names require an explanation since they are not commonly used in the Muslim world: the first one is actually the Arabic plural of the term *ufuq* which means 'horizon, heaven, universe'. It refers firstly to Qurʾān (41:53): 'We shall show them our signs in the horizons and in themselves, till it is clear to them that it is true. Suffices it not as to thy Lord, that He is witness over everything?'[38] Secondly, it refers to the Sufi hagiology according to which the saint rules over the world and human destinies; he is considered the axis (Ar. *quṭb*) of the world. Indeed, Āfāq Khwāja was extraordinarily popular throughout the Tarim Basin. The Turkic appellation *apaq*, or rather *appaq* in Modern Uyghur, means 1. 'pure white' and 2. 'beloved, lovable'. According to Uyghur historians, this name has been given to the Sufi leader by the Jungar Mongol Khan Galdan.[39] But this fact has been recently questioned.[40] Still, we also find Mongol names including Āfāq such as Abakh Khuja, Qun Abakh and Turlugh

---

35 On this figure see Bakhtjar Babadjanov, 'Makhdum-i A'zam', in *Islam na Territorii byvshej Rossiskoj imperii. Entsiklopedicheskij slovar' I* (Moscow, 2006), pp. 262-3.

36 There are several manuscripts of this text, one of the most complete is preserved in Tashkent: Muḥammad Ṣādiq Kāshgharī, *Tadhkira-yi ʿazīzān* (274 fols), Institut Vostokovedenija Akademii nauk Uzbekistana 45/I. A very partial translation in English has been realized by Robert B. Shaw, 'The History of the Khojas of Eastern Turkestan Summarised from the Tazkara-i-Khwâjagân of Muhammad Sâdiq Kâshgarî', edited with introduction and notes by N. Elias, published as Supplement to the *Journal of the Asiatic Society of Bengal*, 66/1 (1897). I use here the Uyghur edition: Qäshqäri Muhämmäd Sadiq, *Täzkiräyi äzizan*, ed. Nijat Mukhlis and Shämsidin Ämät (Kashgar, 1988).

37 I have dealt extensively with this figure in my *Soufisme et politique entre Chine, Tibet et Turkestan* (Paris, 2005).

38 *The Koran Interpreted*, trans. Arthur J. Arberry (London, 1955).

39 Haji Nur Haji and Chen Guoguang, *Shinjang islam tarikhi* [*History of Islam in Xinjiang*] (Urumchi, 1995), pp. 281-2.

40 Dolqun Abdurehim, '"Apaq Khoja" digän namning kelip chiqishi toghrisida qisqichä mulahizä' [Brief Reflection about the Appearance of the Name 'Apaq Khoja'], *Shinjang Ijtimayi Pänlär Tätqiqati*, 2 (2006): pp. 49-52. However, the name Āfāq can be found in few other cases in Central Asia (Khans and Begs essentially). See, for instance, the anonymous *Tārīkh-i Kāshgar*, facsimile edition by Oleg O. Akimushkin, *Tārīx-i Kāshgar: Anonimnaja tjurskaja khronika vladetelej Vostochnogo Turkestana po konets XVII veka* [*History of Kashgar: An Anonymous Turkic Chronicle of the Sovereigns of Eastern Turkestan until the End of the Seventeenth Century*] (St Petersburg, 2001).

Abakh.[41] All these examples show the widespread reputation of the saint among Turkic but also Mongol and Chinese Muslim populations. Last but not least, the names Āfāq (Ofoq in Uzbek) or Apaq are still very popular today in Xinjiang and the Central Asian republics. The shrine of the Shaykh, located near Kashgar, is still visited and venerated by Uyghurs and Hui pilgrims who come from Xinjiang or even farther afield, Gansu and Qinghai.[42]

Such use of names may find further motivations in the politico-religious context of seventeenth-century Inner Asia. Once again, I restrict myself to a few aspects. The seventeenth century is generally - and rightly - considered as the Golden Age of Tibet in the sense that important changes took place in the central region: intense cultural and religious activities; political strength inside and outside the frontiers of Tibet; reunification of the territory under the rule of the Fifth Dalai Lama and his successors.[43] This Mongol–Tibetan titulature of Dalai Lama, meaning 'oceanic master', appeared in 1562 when the Mongol Altan Khan gave the title of Dalai Lama to bSod-nams rgya-mtsho (1543-88), hence officializing a patronage relationship between the Mongol Khan and the Tibetan lama - *cho-yon (mchod-yon)* in Tibetan.[44] This politico-religious system reached its peak with the Qoshut Mongol Gushri Khan and the Fifth Dalai Lama, Ngag-dbang blo-bzang rgya-mtsho (1617-82), who founded a Lamaic theocracy in Tibet. It is not a matter of coincidence that we find such an analogous titulature in Kashgaria where Āfāq Khwāja founded an Islamic theocracy in 1680. Likewise, the Chinese supreme titulature *tianzi* - son of heaven - expressed the mystico-religious essence of power in late post-Mongol Inner Asia. No doubt this analogy is not only nominal.

Let us return to the *Tadhkira-yi ʿazīzān*. The text asserts that during the 1670s, the Naqshbandī Shaykh Āfāq Khwāja travelled - because of a forced exile - in Gansu and Qinghai but also, seemingly, in Tibet properly, and more precisely to Lhasa, called *Ju* or *Jo* in the text.[45] This term could originate from *Jo-khang*, the famous temple in Lhasa. We read that Āfāq Khwāja arrived at the idol temple (Pe. *butkhāna*) of Mullā Mānī, that is Śākyamuni. The Sufi master, aware of the magical powers of the Dalai Lama (Uy. *shäykh brahmanlar*), engaged in a miracle contest with him. The Tibetans and the Dalai Lama himself were so impressed

41 Nizamiddin Hüsäyn, '3. Qabahät äqidä. (yä'ni bir qätim Appaq Khoja toghrisida)' ['An Odious Belief (once again about Appaq Khoja)'], *Shinjang mädäniyati*, 2-3 (1989): pp. 113-54, at p. 127.

42 See my article 'Les tombeaux de saints musulmans au Xinjiang. Culte, réforme, histoire', *Archives de sciences sociales des religions*, 142 (2008): pp. 47-62.

43 Among others, see Françoise Pommaret (ed.), *Lhasa: Lieu du divin. La capitale du Dalaï-Lama au 17e siècle* (Geneva, 1997).

44 This institution existed long time before, in fact since the thirteenth century with Qubilai Khan and 'Phags-pa bla-ma blo-gros rgyal-mtshan. See the articles by Azad and Buell in this volume.

45 *Täzkiräyi äzizan*, pp. 48-50.

by his powers that they decided to help him return to his homeland. Thierry Zarcone has shown that this account is similar to a legend collected by Marc Gaborieau about the foundation of the first Muslim community in Lhasa.[46] An Indian Sufi named Khayr al-Dīn, endowed with supernatural powers, impressed the Fifth Dalai Lama who then provided a cult place in Lhasa to the Muslims. There are so many analogies with the case of Āfāq Khwāja that we can suppose that the legend of Khayr al-Dīn originates in the story of Āfāq Khwāja,[47] although the lack of other textual evidences prevents us from going further.

Be this as it may, the sequel of the anecdote is intriguing too. The *Tadhkira-yi ʿazīzān* explains that, after the 'victory' of Āfāq over the Dalai Lama, the former was given an official letter by the latter to deliver to the aforementioned Galdan Boshoqtu Khan (reg. 1670-97). This letter stipulated that:

> Ey Boshoqtu Khān, Āfāq is a great man, he is a perfect master in his religion, he is a khwāja of Kashgar and Yarkand. Ismāʿīl Khān seized his country, you have to give him soldiers. If you give him he will recapture it back, if you don't he won't succeed.[48]

The following events show that Āfāq Khwāja and his followers joined the Jungar contingents and conquered Kashgaria with their support.[49] However, some historians, like Vladimir Kuznetsov, think that Galdan was not enfeoffed to the Dalai Lama and that this letter only provided an excuse for the attack.[50] But, according to Mullā Mūsā Sāyrāmī's *Tārīkh-i Ḥāmidī* [*The Chronicle of Ḥāmid*], a nineteenth-century Turkic record, Āfāq came to an agreement with Galdan, and told him: 'if you give me soldiers, the Altishahr[51] is yours; I shall give it to

46 Marc Gaborieau, 'Pouvoirs et autorité des soufis dans l'Himalaya', in Zarcone (ed.), *Musulmans et soufis du Tibet*, pp. 27-31, and *Récit d'un voyageur musulman* (Paris, 1973), pp. 17, 115-17; Thierry Zarcone, 'Soufis d'Asie centrale au Tibet', in Zarcone (ed.), *Musulmans et soufis du Tibet*, pp. 62-8.

47 This kind of transmission of legends is not uncommon. In a comparable context, see John Brough, 'Legends of Khotan and Nepal', *Bulletin of the School of Oriental and African Studies*, 12/2 (1948): pp. 333-9.

48 Shaw, 'The History of the Khojas of Eastern Turkestan', pp. 36-7, n. 15. It seems that several sources mention this letter. See Jinshin Li, *Shinjang ötkän islam khanliqlirning qisqichä tarikhi* [*A Concise History of the Former Muslim Khanates in Xinjiang*] (Urumchi, 2003), p. 410.

49 Papas, *Soufisme et politique*, pp. 126-30.

50 Viacheslav S. Kuznetsov, 'K voprosu o vladychestve Djungarskogo khanstva nad Vostochnym Turkestanom' ['About the Domination of the Jungar Khanate in Eastern Turkestan'], *Materialy po istorii i filologii Central'noj Azii. Trudy Burjatskogo Instituta obshchestvennykh nauk*, 13 (1970): pp. 21-8. Many thanks to my colleague Sergei Abashin who brought this article to my attention.

51 Altishahr means 'the six cities': that is, Kashgar, Yarkand, Yangi Hisar, Khotan, Aqsu, and Ush Turfan.

you.'[52] Sāyrāmī explains that, underlying this offer was Āfāq Khwāja's will to take hold of the Khanate and depose Ismāʿīl Khān. From a larger perspective, and in spite of the difficult relations between Galdan and the Fifth Dalai Lama, one has to keep in mind that the *cho-yon* was not a formal institution where the Dalai Lama played 'merely' a symbolic role; in a time of high piety and strong religious feelings, his status was sacred and his influence decisive on Mongol Khans.

Whether historical or legendary, this episode refers to a *broader* tradition among the Muslims of both Himalaya and Central Asia. It is the tradition of the secret conversion to Islam of prominent Buddhist figures. Indeed, there is a version of Khayr al-Dīn's legend, mentioned by Marc Gaborieau, which claims that the Fifth Dalai Lama converted secretly to Islam.[53] Moreover, during the same period, namely, the seventeenth century, there was a belief that Galdan Boshoqtu Khan, who was a Lamaist, had converted to Islam under the influence of Kashgarian Turkic Muslims.[54] Likewise, in Kashgaria, a popular belief claimed that the Emperor of China himself had secretly adopted Islam, though he never dared to show it openly.[55] The Turkestani hagiographical tradition developed this topic too. For example, the *Hidāyatnāma* [*Book of Guidance*] of Mawlānā Mīr Khāl al-Dīn al-Yārkandī, written in Persian in 1730, describes at length the encounter between the aforementioned Āfāq Khwāja with the Emperor of China, Kangxi, at this time.[56] The story evokes the miraculous cure of the sick Emperor by the Sufi saint and ends, not with the Emperor's conversion, but with the official protection of Muslims by the Emperor.

Another example is the little-known anonymous *ʿIqd al-gūhar* [*String of Jewels*]; composed in Persian (the unique manuscript is preserved in the Bodleian Library),[57] the text explains in detail the proselyte activities of the father of Āfāq Khwāja, Yūsuf Khwāja (1590-1653).[58] This Naqshbandī Shaykh is said to have travelled to India and, on his way back to Kashgaria, stopped in the *diyār-i farang*. Meaning literally the 'country of Franks (i.e. Christians)', the locution

---

52 Mullā Mūsā Sāyrāmī, *Tarikhi hämidi*, ed. Änvär Baytur (Beijing, 1986), p. 130.

53 Gaborieau, *Récit d'un voyageur musulman*, p. 17.

54 According to the Chinese source *Qingzheng pingding shuomo fanglue*, in Peter C. Perdue, *China Marches West: The Qing Conquest of Central Eurasia* (Cambridge, 2005), p. 179. For a detailed discussion, see the article by Thierry Zarcone in this volume.

55 Charles Henri Auguste Schefer, *Notice sur les relations des peuples musulmans avec les chinois, depuis l'extension de l'islamisme jusqu'à la fin du XVe siècle* (Paris, 1895), p. 30.

56 Papas, *Soufisme et politique*, pp. 115-21.

57 Ms. Indian Institute, Persian 117 (57 fols).

58 Papas, *Soufisme et politique*, pp. 65-6. A recent article, dealing with Yūsuf Khwāja, has been published in Japanese by Minoru Sawada, 'Oasis wo shihai shita hitobito-17seiki yarkand no jirei' ['Those who Dominated the Oasis: The Case of Yarkand in the Seventeenth Century'], in Masatake Matsubara, Yuki Konagaya and Haiying Yang (eds), *Yûrashia sôgen kara no message-yûboku kenkyû no saizensen* [*The Message from the Eurasian Steppes: Recent Research in the Study of Nomadic People*] (Tokyo, 2005), pp. 290-315. I thank Ryoko Sekiguchi for having translated this reference.

corresponds in fact to the Himalayan area, and could also – this is a suggestion by Marc Gaborieau based on the phonological resonance – match with the city of Tsaparang in Western Tibet (Guge kingdom in the mid-seventeenth century). The inhabitants are what the text calls the *millat-i tarsāʾī*: that is, possibly, the people of the Buddhists. Here again, the expression means literally the 'people of Fearfuls (usually Christians)'. There – according to the *ʿIqd al-gūhar* – the Sufi saint visited the area of temples (Pe. *maḥal-i butkhāna*), stayed six months, accomplished numerous miracles and converted many infidels (*kāfir*). Finally, the high figure called *pādishāh-i farang* (lit. 'king of the Franks'), maybe a great lama, was defeated by the powers of the Muslim saint. The entire lexis seems to designate Christians, and could actually refer to the Jesuit mission of Guge founded by the Portuguese António de Andrade in 1625.[59] However, the Central Asian Islamic sources use often a more precise vocabulary to designate Christians. Moreover, in Persian the terms *tarsā* and *farang* do not exclusively designate Christians and Westerners but also Buddhists.[60] A final important argument is the fact that Yūsuf Khwāja had effectively led conversion missions to Northwest China, as appears clearly in the *Sayyid Āfāq Khwājam Tazkiralari*, a popular and widespread Turkic hagiography.[61] Today, the Salars (see below) consider Yūsuf Khwāja as one of their main religious heroes. To sum up, the passage in the *ʿIqd al-gūhar* probably describes an encounter between Sufi masters and Lamas, in which Samarqandī and Tibetan spiritual masters meet face to face.

We see how hagiographies and legends connect Central Asia and Tibet. Himalayan Muslim communities present traditions which follow a similar model: a holy Muslim man from Central Asia, a Samarqandī, makes a long journey to Tibet, encounters a great holy non-Muslim man, requests divine help, and in the end founds a Muslim community. In other words, the founder

---

59 Ippolito Desideri, *An Account of Tibet: The Travels of Ippolito Desideri 1712-1727*, ed. Filippo de Filippi with an introduction by Cornelius Wessels (London, 1937; repr. New Delhi, 1995), pp. 5-19. In his account, which takes place around the 1720s, Desideri rarely alludes to Muslims in Tibet, but includes the following interesting passage (pp. 177-8):

> They once had a place of burial near Lhasá, this was destroyed and they were ordered to make a new one farther away from the town. Although because they are foreigners they are not molested, they are called Mutekbà, or infidels, and are considered low, vile, and despicable people, not so much on account of their lies and incontinence, as because they kill animals with their own hands, a thing looked upon as infamous in these countries and only done by the Scembà or public executioner.

60 See ʿAlī Akbar Dihkhudā, *Lughatnāma*, Digital Version (Tehran, 2006). The Persian word *but* (idol) corresponds probably to *Buddha*: see Daniel Gimaret, 'Bouddha et les bouddhistes dans la tradition musulmane', *Journal Asiatique*, 257 (1969): pp. 273-316.

61 Quoted in Fletcher, 'The Naqshbandiyya in Northwest China', pp. 12-13. In Southern Xinjiang, recent handwritten copies of this text still circulate.

myths of Muslim communities in Himalaya coincide with the Sufi hagiographies and reveal a specific religious identity. From this perspective, one of the most interesting case is, I believe, that of the Salar, since it presents a founder myth which synthesizes almost all of these characteristics.

THE FOUNDER MYTH OF THE SALARS

The Salars attracted attention when they conducted violent uprisings against the Qings in the course of the eighteenth and nineteenth centuries. Ever since the publication of Jonathan N. Lipman's book, *Familiar Strangers*, we have a clear idea not only of the political events but of their actors: that is, the Salar Sufi groups.[62] It appears that all of them trace their spiritual chain of transmission (Ar. *silsila*) to Central Asian saints, most particularly Āfāq Khwāja (sometimes not directly but by the link of famous Chinese Shaykhs, such as Ma Laichi[63] and Ma Mingxin, both spiritual descendants of Āfāq Khwāja and Yūsuf Khwāja). What is remarkable here is again the historical background which pertains to the Eastern Turkestan Khwājas: that is, Sufi saints of Samarkand origin. The introduction of Naqshbandī Sufism among the Salars is indeed the work of the Khwājas, which can be dated back perhaps even to the late sixteenth century and the other envoy of Makhdūm-i Aʿẓam named Isḥāq Khwāja (d. 1599).[64] However, the history of Salar Sufism – Naqshbandī or other orders – is far from being entirely clear.

The origin of the Salars remains equally unclear despite the progress of historical research on this ethnic group. According to the Japanese scholar Toru Saguchi, 'it may be quite probable that some of the Turkmen-Salors have migrated from Central Asia to North-west China in the latter half of the fourteenth century under the Mongolian Empire ...'.[65] Their namesakes were the Turkmen Salars in the oasis of Sarakhs in Khwarezm. But another theory claims

---

62 Jonathan N. Lipman, *Familiar Strangers: A History of Muslims in Northwest China* (Seattle, 1997), pp. 138-61. Previously, Joseph Fletcher has done pioneering work on their history. Among the first ethnographic studies, we find mainly Russian scholars like Sergej E. Malov who visited the Salars in Gansu during autumn 1910, then Edham R. Tenishev who visited them in summer 1957. Later, in spring 1960, Zsuzsa Karkuk led interviews with Salar speakers in Beijing. These three authors published valuable linguistic and text materials.

63 This Shaykh is reputed to have converted Tibetans and Mongols to Islam: Lipman, *Familiar Strangers*, p. 67. Interestingly, Trippner mentions a theological debate between Ma Laichi and a rimpoche, at the end of which Tibetans converted to Islam: Joseph Trippner, 'Islamische Gruppen und Gräberkult in Nordwest-China', *Die Welt des Islams*, 7 (1961): pp. 142-71, at pp. 154-5.

64 Papas, *Soufisme et politique*, p. 108.

65 Tôru Saguchi, 'On the Origin of the Ch'in-Hai Salars', *Tarih Araştırmaları Dergisi*, 6/10-11 (1968): pp. 225-9, at p. 229. We find the name Salor or Salur in *EI*², see the article 'Salar'.

that they originated in the sixteenth century when they were driven to the Himalayas by the ruler of Qomul/Hami (in northern Xinjiang).[66] An alternative thesis asserts that they came to China as early as the Tang period and settled in Qinghai later.[67] Lastly, Dutreuil de Rhins argues that they simply came from the Turfan region in the sixteenth century, but they were converted to Islam by a companion of the Prophet, Saʿd ibn Abī Waqqāṣ,[68] who flew (*sic*) from Samarkand to Suzhou (at the border of Xinjiang and Gansu) in 628.[69] However most traditions associate the Salars with Samarkand: they may have come to the Yellow River in the thirteenth century or in the fourteenth century, on the occasion of the conquest of Turfan in 1368 by the Chaghatayid Khizr Khoja.

Whatever the exact history of the Salar people, more relevant for us is their collective memory and their founder myth for what they tell us about the Himalayan Muslim identity of this minority. Recorded by Ma Jianzhong and Kevin Stuart, the Salar founder myth tells the story of a people's migration from Samarkand to the Koko Nor region (Xunhua district). The legend is as follows:[70]

At a time, there were two brothers in Samarkand, Imām Qariman[71] and Imām Aḥmad, who were oppressed by the head of the place and could not live there any longer. Then leading their people (lit. clan brothers: Sa. *kumsin aghini*), and a white camel (Sa. *ah döye*), carrying a bowl of soil and a kettle of water from Samarkand, also carrying a Qur'ān, they left, looking for a good place (Sa. *yahxi otkhän or*) to live. They crossed the Tian Shan, passed Suzhou, and after having rested for a time, went forward again. As their camel was tired, hungry and thirsty, they stopped on the Fire Mountain (Sa. *otus dagh*; from Pe. *ātash*) at the village of Six Sons (Sa. Alitiuli). At midnight, Qariman woke up and realized that their camel was gone. Immediately he called his companions together, looking for the camel everywhere. Then, feeling thirsty, they went to look for water. They went and found their camel turned into stone, resting by a spring source

---

66 Charles-Eudes Bonin, 'Les Mahométans du Kansou et leur dernière révolte', *Revue du Monde Musulman*, 10/2 (1910): pp. 210-33, at p. 213.

67 Louis M.J. Schram, 'The Monguors of the Kansu-Tibetan Frontier. Their Origin, History, and Social Organization', *Transactions of the American Philosophical Society*, N.S., 44/1 (1954): pp. 1-164, at p. 23.

68 On this figure (that Dutreuil de Rhins erroneously considers as a parent of Muhammad), see the article in *EI*².

69 Jules Léon Dutreuil de Rhins, *Mission scientifique dans la Haute Asie 1890-1895* (3 vols, Paris, 1897-98), vol. 1, pp. 464-5.

70 I summarize Ma Wei, Ma Jianzhong and Stuart, *The Folklore of China's Islamic Salar Nationality*, pp. 7-10. I have modified slightly translations and transcriptions. I have also indicated some etymologies which show the large number of Persian terms.

71 The name Qariman/Kharamang probably comes from the widespread Turkic ethnonym *Karaman*. See the entry 'Kharamang' in Edham R. Tenishev, *Stroj salarskogo jazyka* [*The System of the Salar Language*] (Moscow, 1976), p. 461. An alternative assumption is that Qariman corresponds to the Persian name or title *qahramān*, meaning 'warrior, hero'.

while water ran out of its mouth. So Qariman and his followers (Sa. *kharimanglär*) removed the kettle, the soil and the Qur'ān from the camel's back. Thinking of the camel going through hardships to come here together with them, all wept. Then Qariman and his followers opened the Qur'ān, they prayed (Sa. *dovu etmix*; from Ar. *du'ā'*) asking for God's (Sa. *huda*; from Pe. *khudā*) blessings. Later, when they drank the spring water, it was sweet, they compared it with the water they brought [from Samarkand], and it was the same. Also they compared the soil, and they were the same as well. Thus believing that God [Allāh] had helped them find a good place (Sa. *yahxi yiur*), they settled there.

This story represents a fascinating, and still overlooked, overlapping of Tibetan and Muslim traditions. On the one hand, the myth finds a kind of distant echo in the Tibetan legends related to the Blue Lake (Koko Nor; Xöx nuur in Mongolian; mTsho sngon-po in Tibetan) in Amdo: one of the versions evokes two figures (a father and his son) looking for water, finding a big rock similar in appearance to a sheep, with water beneath.[72] On the other hand, we find a closer echo in the Islamic prophetic traditions related to the first mosque (Quba mosque), located nearby the Mabrak al-Nāqa hill ('kneeling place of the she-camel'), on the outskirts of Medina. Upon his arrival in Medina the Prophet Muhammad let loose his camel named Qaswā' to wander and choose where he would stay. Where the camel knelt, the Prophet himself settled. In al-Bukhārī's , we find the following report:

> Allah's Apostle [Muhammad] stayed with Banî 'Amr bin 'Awf for ten nights and established the mosque (mosque of Quba) which was founded on piety. Allah's Apostle prayed in it and then mounted his she-camel and proceeded on, accompanied by the people till his she-camel knelt down at (the place of) the Mosque of Allah's Apostle at Medina. Some Muslims used to pray there in those days, and that place was a yard for drying dates belonging to Suhayl and Sahl, the orphan boys who were under the guardianship of As'ad bin Zurâra. When his she-camel knelt down, Allah's Apostle said, 'This place, Allah willing, will be our abiding place.' Allah's Apostle then called the two boys and told them to suggest a price for that yard so that he might take it as a mosque. The two boys said, 'No, but we will give it as a gift, O Allah's Apostle!' Allah's Apostle then built a mosque there.[73]

---

[72] Katia Buffetrille, 'The Blue Lake in A-mdo and its Island', in Huber (ed.), *Sacred Spaces*, pp. 105-24, at p. 111.

[73] *Ṣaḥīḥ al-Bukhārī*, vol. 5, pp. 166-7, n. 245. Prophetic Traditions differ on certain details, see 'Masdjid' in *EI*². Though highly hypothetical, the tale could also refer to the story of Ṣāliḥ that appears in the Qur'ān (26:141-58 *passim*), in *ḥadīth* (e.g. Bukhārī, *Ṣaḥīḥ*, vol. 4, p. 360 [n. 562]), and in the biographies (*sīra*) and stories (*qiṣaṣ*) of the Prophet. The people of the Thamūd were unbelievers who did not listen to the prophet Ṣāliḥ enjoining them to convert to Islam. Ṣāliḥ left his people and went to a mountain where he found a fountain, performed a prayer, entered a cave and fell asleep for 40 years. God then woke

What is more pertinent for us is that we find in this myth several elements which correspond to the pattern we have identified: the city of Samarkand, the holy Muslim man, the long journey to Tibet and the foundation of a Muslim community there. Nothing seems to be lacking but the encounter with a Lamaist or, for that matter, any non-Muslim religious authority. In fact, this last element is present somewhere else. The Salar founding legend produced a type of play called *döye oyna*, that is the 'camel play' which still exists today in Qinghai, though it is now performed on stage and no longer on threshing grounds or family courtyards.[74] The play recounts the myth summarized above, but it adds one very interesting element: a third character who is a non-Muslim. He is a Mongol (or a Tibetan) and he is the interlocutor of the two Imams (Sa. *ahong*; from Persian *ākhūnd*), called 'Blind Man' since he represents the one ignorant of Islam. Although I have not found any evidence in the literature, I would not be surprised if some versions of this story recount the conversion of this Mongol man. At least – but this is very significant – other versions say that the Mongols happily sold or even gave the land to the Salar migrants.[75] Thus the Muslim community is given by the infidels a land to settle in.

To go further than Ma Jianzhong and Kevin Stuart, I would like to underline that this story is much more than a play or a folk legend; it is a myth that explains the foundation of a community in religious terms. The issue at stake is not only an identity or a minority discourse but the sacralization of its settlement. In fact, the narrative corresponds to a territorial reality, visible on the Himalayan ground itself: in the town called Jiezi (former Ketzekung) in Xunhua county, stands what is supposedly the field of the petrified camel where a large mosque and the (supposedly) fourteenth-century shrine of Ahmad and Qariman have been erected.[76] This is a major holy place for the pious Salars.

---

him up and sent him again to the Thamūd who demanded a sign of God's power. Ṣāliḥ brought a she-camel out of the rock so that the Thamūd could enjoy its abundant milk on the condition of the animal's exclusive access to their only source of water on alternate days. When the Thamūd finally killed the camel, God destroyed them and their city al-Ḥijr. Ṣāliḥ and a few faithful went to the land of Shām. Confronting both legends, the Salar myth may appear as a completely reserve version of Ṣāliḥ's story, in the course of the events as well as in the events themselves: the journey, the forbidden place (*ḥijr*), the camel coming out of the mountain, the source and the prayer. For a detailed analysis of Ṣāliḥ's story see Jaroslav Stetkevych, *Muḥammad and the Golden Bough: Reconstructing Arabian Myth* (Bloomington, 1996).

[74] Ma Jianzhong and Kevin Stuart, 'Stone Camels and Clear Springs: The Salar's Samarkand Origins', *Asian Folklore Studies*, 55/2 (1996): pp. 287-98.

[75] Li Yue Wei and Kevin Stuart, 'The Xunhua Sala', *Asian Folkore Studies*, 49/1 (1990): pp. 39-52, at p. 42.

[76] Abbot Low Moffat, 'The Salar Muhammadans', *The Geographical Journal*, 85/5 (1935): pp. 525-30. See Plates 13.1-3.

EPILOGUE: FOLLOWING THE TRACKS, SHAPING A SACRED SPACE

In each etymology, conversion narrative and legend that we have outlined here, Samarkand and the Himalayan regions, included Lhasa, were joined, even twinned, maybe doubled, symbolically by the meetings of saints, concretely by the crossing points in space. Such associations in space are typical of religious minorities and their representation of the world. Instead of being unique or exceptional, this pattern is a universal mode of shaping identity for religious minorities. But the question is not so much the form of representation as its *content*, and more precisely its religious signification: in other words, not how but *what* does the narrative tell us about the religious consciousness of Tibetan Muslim societies?

No doubt, for Muslims in general, the centre of the world is located at the Kaaba and Mecca, even for remote minorities like the Tibetan Muslims (as witnessed by the ubiquitous Kaaba posters stuck on the walls of Muslim houses or mosques).[77] Yet, in Himalayan Islam, Samarkand or its region appear as a subsidiary and symbolic holy centre, perhaps more familiar or more relevant to the Tibetan, Mongol and Turko-Mongol believers, due to the historical background of their Islamization. Apart from the Tibetan and the Indian legacies, the Central Asian heritage – both historical and legendary – represents a main feature of Himalayan Islam. I have tried elsewhere to shed some light on the history of Sufi masters and orders (the Naqshbandiyya mainly) which spread from Turkestan throughout Xinjiang, Gansu and Qinghai during the sixteenth, seventeenth and eighteenth centuries. In the present article, I have focused on the representation of a sacred space which integrates Samarkand as a holy city through the memory of itinerant Sufi holy men. My conclusion is that extraordinary journeys of this kind, which reduce space and bring communities closer, are a main concern for Inner Asian Muslims.[78] For, after all, these words, tales or myths, are spiritual travelogues, or rather pilgrimage narratives, the purpose of which is to integrate isolated communities into a larger religious territory, the *Dār al-Islām*.

Such oral and written accounts prove to be particularly effective in the Himalayan context where holy places and sacred spaces have an essential function, since piety is not only public but also mobile. What do these accounts

---

77 Central Asia abounds in traditions which claim that the Kaaba has been first settled by Allāh in Turkestan, then has been moved to Arabia. The Oxus (Amu Darya) river is believed to have flowed under the Kaaba. See, among others, Ármin Vámbéry, *Voyages d'un faux derviche dans l'Asie centrale de Téhéran a Khiva, Bokhara et Samarcand par le grand désert turkoman*, Nouvelle édition revue et corrigée d'après celle de 1873 revue par l'auteur (Paris, 1987), pp. 93, 98.

78 A tradition among the Khotan people claims that the famous Persian hero Rustam travelled from Kashgar to Lhasa: William H. Johnson, 'Report on his Journey to Ilchi, the Capital of Khotan, in Chinese Tartary', *Journal of the Royal Geographical Society of London*, 37 (1867): pp. 1-47, at p. 11.

mean for this Ladakhi lama 'who studied medical science as well as theology, [who] visited the main sacred places, crossed Nepal, Kashmir, parts of India, stayed for a long time in Turkestan and Mongolia where he was a horse dealer, [who] travelled as far as China and Eastern Tibet ...'?;[79] or for a man such as Ḥājjī Qurbān, 'a peasant by birth, who, as a knife-grinder, has traversed the whole of Asia, has been as far as Constantinople and Mecca, had visited upon occasions Tibet and Calcutta, and twice the Kirghish Steppe, to Orenburg and Taganrok'?[80] Brought and spread along the Inner Asian tracks, profane narratives travel with pilgrims and pious traders, who, in a sense, repeat their events and episodes; they relate their own travels and describe their spiritual experience. In the past world of the Himalayan caravans,[81] while travellers as well as locals were negotiating, discussing and praying, a communal space materialized between Islam and Tibet. Over and above this practical aspect, the representation of space, once experienced by the pilgrimages and their narrations, received a sacred dimension able to synthesize, even to go beyond, Islamic and Tibetan conceptions, that is – in short, as we have seen in the Introduction – the forbidden and the abode, towards, maybe, the transgressing and the crossing.

Thus, shaping a sacred space is not a simple imaginary creation or a poetic feeling; it is a system of beliefs where legend and history continuously overlap. At the extremities of legend and history, within the crossing and the transgressing, two facts deserve to be merely mentioned, without further comment. The first one is a folk tradition from the Turkani people (a bygone ethnic group in Northwestern China) relating that Islam had been brought to China by Alexander the Great (Iskandar in the Islamic tradition),[82] which means not from the Prophet and from the Hijaz but, long before, from the Greek ruler of Central Asia or the Oxus area. The second is a historical and somewhat symptomatic fact: in 1896, during the violent uprisings of Muslims in Gansu and the harsh repression in response by the Sino-Manchu forces, certain Muslims sought to take refuge in Samarkand,[83] as if the famous Central Asian oasis, rather than the canonical Islamic sanctuaries, appeared as a natural land of welcome.

---

[79] Dutreuil de Rhins, *Mission scientifique dans la Haute Asie 1890-1895*, vol. 1, pp. 363-4.

[80] Vámbéry, *Voyages d'un faux derviche dans l'Asie centrale*, p. 25.

[81] See Janet Rizvi, *Trans-Himalayan Caravans: Merchant Princes and Peasant Traders in Ladakh* (New Delhi, 2001).

[82] D'Ollone, 'Recherches sur les musulmans chinois', p. 547.

[83] Bonin, 'Les Mahométans du Kansou et leur dernière révolte', pp. 230-32. More prosaically, Bonin explains that the leader of these rebels, called Lieou-se-fou, had his father living in a Dungan (Hui) village in Semireche, near the Russo–Chinese border. Still, Samarkand is far from Semireche and, therefore, represents a mythical destination.

Chapter 14

Between Legend and History: About the 'Conversion' to Islam of Two Prominent Lamaists in the Seventeenth-Eighteenth Centuries

Thierry Zarcone

At the end of the seventeenth century, the Northern part of Eastern Turkestan and Qinghai were dominated by the Mongol Jungghars who recognized the spiritual jurisdiction of the Dalai Lama. The Jungghars (like the Torgut) belonged to the nomadic Oirat confederation which was also known as Qalmaq (Kalmuk), or Eleuth in Western sources. Meanwhile the Muslims of Kashgaria were politically divided. Although the Mongols were considered infidels and traditional enemies of Islam, Āfāq Khwāja (d. 1694), a member of the famous Sufi family of the Khwājas, both a spiritual and political dynasty, and a pretender to the throne of Kashgaria, went to Lhasa and requested the help of the Fifth Dalai Lama (d. 1682) and of the Jungghar Khan Ghaldan (d. 1697) against his Muslim rival. Thanks to the Jungghar army, Āfāq Khwāja recovered the throne of Kashgaria in 1680.[1]

This set of events is recorded in a surprising form in several Persian hagiographies of the Khwāja dynasty (written in the eighteenth century), in Eastern Turkish poetry and in oral tradition where legends and historical facts mingle. In these sources, the head of the Lamaist church and the Jungghar sovereign were either converted to Islam and Sufism or convinced of the supremacy of Islam after being defeated through magical competitions, and as a consequence they provided help to Āfāq Khwāja. In this article, my aim is to analyse how legends and history intertwine in these competing narratives and conversion stories.

[1] In one historical source of the nineteenth century, a major historian does not mention any coming of Āfāq Khwāja to Tibet or mediation by the Dalai Lama, but only the coming of Āfāq to Ili in order to meet Ghaldan and to ask his help against his enemies. See Mullā Mūsā Sāyrāmī, *Tarikhi hämidi*, ed. Änvär Baytur (Beijing, 1986), p. 130.

THE ALLEGED SUBMISSION AND/OR CONVERSION OF THE FIFTH DALAI LAMA (D. 1682)

In an article published in 1995 I have already discussed this encounter between the Naqshbandī Sufi Āfāq Khwāja and the leader of Tibet and I would like to mention here only the most salient aspects of this event.[2] My intention here is not to debate whether or not Āfāq Khwāja actually met the Dalai Lama in Lhasa, but to investigate under what circumstances, in the eyes of the Muslims, this event occurred.

According to the *Tadhkara-yi khwājagān* of Muhammad Sadiq Kashgārī, a hagiography preserved in an eighteenth- or nineteenth-century manuscript, having arrived in Lhasa in around 1671-75,[3] Āfāq Khwāja learned that the priest of the Tibetans (literally the *shaykh-brahman* of the infidels)[4] was performing miracles. Therefore, he also performed miracles and impressed the Buddhist population of the city. Following this event, the Khwāja asked for help against his Muslim enemies and obtained from the Lama a letter of recommendation for the ruler of the Mongol Jungghars, Ghaldan (called 'Qāmālqning tūrasī' = king of the Qalmaq, and 'Bushūrkhān').[5] In another version of this hagiography,[6] the Lama is clearly depicted as the Dalai Lama (*Dālāylāmālār*) and the encounter between the two men turned into a magical competition. Āfāq Khwāja defeated the Dalai Lama because his miracles (*kārāmāt*) were saintly miracles similar to prophetic miracles, unlike the magical performance of his opponent which was described as mere magic. The term used for magic by the hagiographer is *istidrāj* ('divine deception') which in the Sufi tradition refers to an extraordinary action performed by a person who neither believes nor performs good deeds.[7]

---

2 Several versions of this hagiography exist; I have used Ms 3357 (Eastern Turkish, copied in the nineteenth century), Institut de France, Paris. See Thierry Zarcone, 'Sufism from Central Asia among the Tibetans in the 16th-17th Centuries', *The Tibet Journal*, 20/3 (1995): pp. 96-114, at pp. 102-5; see also the more extensive version of this article, 'Soufis d'Asie centrale au Tibet aux XVIe et XVIIe siècles', in Thierry Zarcone (ed.), *Inde-Asie centrale: Routes du commerce et des idées* (Aix-en-Provence, 1996), pp. 325-44; repr. in Thierry Zarcone (ed.), *Musulmans et Soufis du Tibet* (Paris, 2005), pp. 53-76. See also the analysis of this event by Alexandre Papas, *Soufisme et Politique entre Chine, Tibet et Turkestan: Etudes sur les khwajas naqshbandis du Turkestan oriental* (Paris, 2005), pp. 90-102.

3 According to Papas, *Soufisme et Politique*, p. 92.

4 *Kāfirlarning brahman shayhlārī.*

5 Muḥammad Ṣādiq Yārkandī, *Tadhkira-i Khwājagān*, ms. Paris, Institut de France, no. 3357, fols 24^{r}-25^{r}.

6 Translated by Martin Hartmann, *Der Islamische Orient*, VI-X, Ein Heiligenstaat im Islam: Das Ende der Caghataiden und die Herrschaft der Choğas in Kašgarien (Berlin, 1905). The meeting with the Dalai Lama is mentioned on pp. 210-13.

7 For this concept see Florian Sobieroj, 'Divine Machinations: A Sufi Tract on the Gradual Deception (*istidrâj*) of Sinful People', *Journal of the History of Sufism*, 5 (2007): pp. 253-89.

We should bear in mind here that the Fifth Dalai Lama was a mystic more than a politician, and a practitioner of Tantric magic who authorized several books on occult and magic rituals.[8] Finally, after Āfāq Khwāja defeated him, the Tibetans were deceived by their lama and, recognizing the superiority of the Sufi, they submitted to him. We may speculate that the hagiographer intimates that the head of the Lamaist church and his subjects became Muslims, although this is not explicitly mentioned in the text.

In another legend of Indian origin, of which there are also several versions, analysed by Marc Gaborieau,[9] Khayr al-Dīn, a Sufi from Patna in India who performs miracles (*kārāmāt*), goes to Lhasa and enters a magical competition with the Fifth Dalai Lama, who is again only credited with producing *istidrāj*, as in the Āfāq Khwāja story. However, at the end of the competition, according to a later version of this legend, the leader of the Tibetans is supposed to have been secretly converted to Islam. It is quite certain that the historical background for this second story is the establishment of the first Muslim community in Lhasa when Kashmirī Muslims were authorized by the Fifth Dalai Lama to settle in this city and open a mosque.[10] Because of this parallel I first thought that either the story of Āfāq Khwāja was the origin for the legend of Khayr al-Dīn, or that Khayr al-Dīn's legend inspired the author of the hagiography on Āfāq Khwāja. However, it is in fact equally possible that there is no such direct connection between these two stories, but that they rather follow the same pattern of conversion stories (magical competition) which exists throughout the Islamic world.[11]

It should also be mentioned here that the Fifth Dalai Lama was the ruler of the whole Tibetan-Buddhist world from Lhasa to Mongolia, while the Qalmaq maintained the military supremacy. This also explains why Āfāq Khwāja should have preferred to visit the leader of the Tibetans in Lhasa before reaching the camp of the Jungghars in Ili to meet Ghaldan. In fact, in the seventeenth century Lhasa was one of the major places for any political decision-making regarding Central Asia.[12] Furthermore, the Fifth Dalai Lama was a man with a profound

---

[8] Zahiruddin Ahmad, *Sino-Tibetan Relations in the Seventeenth Century* (Rome, 1970), pp. 134-5; Samten Gyaltsen Karmay, *Secret Visions of the Fifth Dalai Lama: The Gold Manuscript in the Fournier Collection* (London, 1988), p. 19.

[9] Marc Gaborieau, 'Pouvoirs et autorité des soufis dans l'Himalaya', in Véronique Bouillier and Gérard Toffin (eds), *Prêtrise, pouvoirs et autorité en Himalaya* (Paris, 1989), pp. 215-38.

[10] About the status of this community, see Marc Gaborieau, *Récit d'un voyageur musulman au Tibet* (Paris, 1973), pp. 24-5; Papas, *Soufisme et Politique*, p. 98.

[11] See, for example, Simon Digby, 'Encounters with Jogîs in Indian Sūfī Hagiography', unpublished paper presented at the seminar on Aspects of Religion in South Asia, University of London, January 1970, and Raziuddin Aquil, 'Conversion in Chishtī Sufi Literature (13th-14th Centuries)', *Indian Historical Review*, 24/1-2 (1997-98): pp. 70-94.

[12] See Elliot Sperling, 'Tibétains, Mongols et Manchous', in Françoise Pommaret (ed.), *Lhasa, lieu du divin: La capitale des Dalaï-Lama au 17e siècle* (Paris, 1997), pp. 147-61, p. 155; English translation: *Lhasa in the Seventeenth Century* (Boston, 2002).

appreciation for other cultures. He invited Indian scholars to Tibet and renewed cultural relations with India, the Mongols and even the Manchus.[13]

Nevertheless, the story did not finish with Āfāq Khwāja's return to Central Asia and his meeting with the Qalmaq Ghaldan who, responding to the letter of the Dalai Lama, helped him to conquer Kashgharia in 1680. What I was unaware of in my earlier publication of 1995 is that the encounter between Āfāq Khwāja and the Jungghar ruler is also described in the form of a conversion story.[14]

THE ALLEGED CONVERSION OF GHALDAN TO ISLAM AND SUFISM

Before Ghaldan became the leader of the Mongols, he had taken monastic vows and studied for ten years in a Buddhist monastery in Tibet, since he had been recognized as the rebirth of a famous Tibetan lama who had died the year before. In Tibet, Ghaldan became the disciple of both the first Panchen Lama and the Fifth Dalai Lama. From Tibetan sources we know that Ghaldan met the Dalai Lama for the first time in 1656 when he began to study Buddhism in a monastery. In 1666, the Dalai Lama bestowed on him a 'benediction of longevity *Grub-rgyal* style together with a monk's robe and other many gifts, instructed him to make his supervision beneficial to Buddhist policies, and when he was about to leave, handed him a rosary of pearls'.[15] Ghaldan then left Tibet in order to become the leader of the Jungghars, a few years before Āfāq Khwāja reached Lhasa. In 1671, Ghaldan was granted the title of *Qungtajī* (*khongtaiji*) by the Fifth Dalai Lama (a political title usually given to the Jungghar Khan by the Dalai Lama), and in 1678 he was bestowed with the religious title of *boshūrkhān* (as it is transliterated into Turkish from the Tibetan: *bsTan-'dzin Bo-shog-thu Khang*), which made him the Khan of all the Oirat tribes and the leader of the Oirat Lamaists. In the Turkish sources Ghaldan is often mentioned equally under these two titles: *Qungtajī* and *boshūrkhān*.

---

[13] W.D. Tsepon Shakabpa, *Tibet: A Political History* (New Haven, 1967), pp. 114 and 123. According to a manuscript with the title *Borqum Avliya*, quoted by a Uyghur scholar (without any references), Āfāq Khwāja never fought against the Dalai Lama but was very respectful towards him; Ablät Masät and Rishat Ablät, 'Quntäyji vä Abakh Ghoja', *Ili Däryasi*, 4 (1996): pp. 77-9, at p. 78.

[14] This fact was also ignored by Masät and Ablät, 'Quntäyji vä Abakh Ghoja', pp. 77-9.

[15] From the *Za hor gyi bande ngag dbang blo bzang rgya mtsho'i 'di snang 'khrul pa'i rol rtsed rtogs brjod kyi tshul du bkod pa du kû la'i gos bzang* quoted in Junko Miyawaki, 'The Birth of the Oyirad Khanship', *Central Asian Journal*, 41/1 (1997): pp. 38-75, at pp. 66 and 69-71; ead., 'The Dzungars and the Torguts (Kalmuks), and the Peoples of Southern Siberia - Part One: History of the Dzungars: Introductory Survey', in *History of Civilizations of Central Asia*, vol. 5, *Development in Contrast: From the Sixteenth to the Mid-Nineteeth Century*, ed. Charyar Adle and Irfan Habib (Paris, 2003), pp. 147-8. See also Jean Baptiste du Halde, *Description géographique de l'empire de la Chine et de la Tartarie chinoise* (4 vols, Paris, 1735), vol. 4, p. 41; Ahmad, *Sino-Tibetan Relations in the Seventeenth Century*, p. 232.

Oral tradition preserves a new account of the relations between Āfāq Khwāja and Ghaldan, and an explanation of why the Jungghar sovereign agreed to provide Āfāq Khwāja with military help. This new story was collected in 1885 by a Tatar scholar, Qurbān ʿAlī Khālidī (d. 1913), in the Turfan district in Eastern Turkestan. Qurbān ʿAlī Khālidī published a substantial amount of written and oral material which includes myths and legends regarding the saints and shrines of the oasis. The name of Āfāq Khwāja was particularly venerated in the oasis of Turfan, where two shrines and a mosque commemorate the coming of the Sufi king to this part of Eastern Turkestan.[16]

One of the legends collected by Qurbān ʿAlī Khālidī concerns Ghaldan's conversion to Islam; whether fiction or historic fact, it has been kept alive in the memory of the inhabitants of the area since the end of the seventeenth century. In this story, however, the Fifth Dalai Lama is not involved in Ghaldan's decision. This oral tradition was written down by Qurbān ʿAlī Khālidī as follows:

> The famous Sufi Mashrab (*Dīvāna-yi Mashrab*) was a disciple of Āfāq Khwāja and a camel-rider (*sārbān/tuwaji*) in the service of the Khan Qungtajī [Ghaldan]. The Khan, having seen several miracles performed by Mashrab, asked him how he had reached such a degree [of holiness]. Mashrab answered that he was in the service of Āfāq Khwāja. Then Qungtajī adopted the faith of Islam (*īmāngha kīlib*) and offered Mashrab to marry his daughter. The Sufi told the Khan that his adoption of Islam was sufficient and that he was not obliged to give him his daughter. He expressed his particular wish that none of the cities [of the Qalmaq Empire] should be deprived of Islam and thrown into hell (*jahannam*), and that he was delighted to see, after years of service to the Khan, that – may God be praised – the Khan had adopted Islam. After having told this, Mashrab disappeared from human eyes (*ghāyib būlmushlār*). Afterwards Qungtajī [Ghaldan] became the disciple (*murīd mukhliṣ*) of Āfāq Khwāja. Thanks to the help of the Khan, Āfāq Khwāja conquered the city of Khotan and recovered his power over the kingdom [or: government] of the Six Cities. But, as a consequence, his kingdom was far from being independent, since he was linked to the Qalmaq Empire. Qungtajī made his subjects convert to Islam through their fear of him, but his intention was to have them adopt

16 The first shrine is a 'resting-place' (*qadamgāh*), actually a part of the funerary complex of the Tuyugh mausoleum or Ashāb al-Kahf; see Yasushi Shinmen, 'The History of the Mausoleum of the Ashâb al-Kahf in Turfan', *The Memoirs of the Toyo Bunko*, 61 (2003): pp. 83-104, at pp. 86-7 and 92; the second shrine is a mausoleum located in the village of Sayyid Khān; see Rahila Davut, *Uyghur Mazarliri* (Ürümchi, 2001), pp. 213-14; the third place is a mosque named after Āfāq Khwāja in the village of Qarakoja; see the picture of this mosque in Carl Gustaf Mannerheim, *Across Asia from West to East in 1906-1908* (Helsinki, 1940; repr. Oosterhout, 1969), p. 360.

this religion gradually. However, God did not find these impure Magi[17] [i.e. the Qalmaq population] worthy of entering paradise. After the death of Āfāq Khwāja and Qungtajī, they [gave up Islam and] returned to infidelity (*kufr*).

Dīwāna-yi Mashrab'ka Khwājam'ning murīdlarīdīn dūr Qungtajī'ning sārbānī ya'nī tuwajisī būlūb Khān ol zātindin nicha karāmātlar gūrūb bū darajayi qāydīn tābting dīb sūrghānda Hazrat Āfaq'ning khizmatidin tābtīm dīgānda Qungtajī īmāngha kīlib Dīwāna'ka qizīnī berkānda islāmgha gelkānning kifāya qizininggha hājat yūqtūr sizlārnī khusūsān ushbū kul chahra islāmdin bī-bahra qālmasūn jahanamda kūymasūn uchūn mūncha yillār khizmatinda būlūb idīm al-Hamdulillah islāma kelding murādima yettim dīb ghayib būlmushlār ba'de mazbūr Qungtajī Hazrat Khwājam'gha murīd mukhlis būlūb Khwājam āning i'ānatī birla Qotan shahrnī almaq Ālta Shahr hukūmatinī yina kolī Khwājam'gha tāqshūrmish binābarīn Khwājam'ning hukūmatī bilā-istiqlāl būlmay tūrūb bir tarafī Qālmāq khānlarīgha mulāzamat wa murāja'at birla būlmūsh dūr Qungtajī halqidin khawf bila imāninī ketim itīb līkīn niyatī Qālmāq tā'ifasinī tadrīj birla imān keltūrmāk maqsad wa mutalabī ikān Haq Ta'alī ol tā'ifa majūs najaslargha jannatī lāyiq kūrmāy Hazrat Āfāq'ning halqida Qungtajī tekhī dunyādin otūb tā'ifa majūs kufrīnde bar qarā[r]qāldīlar.[18]

This new story provides us with another explanation for why the Jungghar ruler should have helped Āfāq Khwāja to recover his power over the Six Cities kingdom. Oral history here claims that Ghaldan became a Muslim because he was fascinated by the miracles performed by a disciple of the Naqshbandī Sufi Āfāq. Actually, he converted not only to Islam, but to Sufism. Mashrab (d. 1711), who is presented as a disciple of Āfāq Khwāja and the man who introduced Ghaldan to his spiritual master, was one of the major figures of Sufi poetry and popular Sufism in Central Asia, and a famous name in Central Asian folklore. His poetry was edited in the form of a popular folk work in verse and prose and published under the titles of 'Diwan of Mashrab' (*Dīwāna-i Mashrab*) or 'Story of Mashrab' (*Qiṣṣa-yi Mashrab*).[19] His verses were sung in Sufi and profane circles

---

17 The word used for the Buddhist Qalmaq is *majūs*/magi, i.e. Zoroastrian, and in another source with the same legend we find the word *tarsā* (Christian) used to qualify the same people (*Kissa-i Mashrab*, ed. Mamatkul Juraev Sayfiddin Raf'iddin [Tashkent, 1992], p. 52, n. 19). This is, presumably, because of the lack of words to qualify the Buddhists.

18 I used here the manuscript version of Qurbān ʿAlī Khālidī's book, *Tārīkh-i jarīda-yi jadīda*, ms. India Office Library (now British Library), London, Turki no. 2, fols 21ᵛ-22ʳ. With the exception of a few minor changes, this paragraph is virtually the same in the printed version: Qurbān ʿAlī Valid-i Khālid Ḥājjī Ayaghūzī, *Tārīkh-i jarīda-yi jadīda* (Kazan, 1889), p. 22. There is also an edition of this manuscript in modern Uyghur: Qurban Ali Khalidi, *Kitab tarikh järidäi jädidi* (Urumchi, 1989), pp. 58-9.

19 See Mashrab, *Divana-i-Mashrab'*, trans. N.S. Lykoshin (in *Srednjaja Azija* [Tashkent], 7-12 [February] 1910; repr. Tashkent, 1992); *Kissa-i Mashrab*, pp. 3-4. A selection of his poetry was translated into German and French: *Machrab: Le vagabond flamboyant. Anecdotes*

and are even nowadays very popular.[20] The conversion story of Ghaldan is partly corroborated by Mashrab's poetry, and there is no doubt that the story collected in the Turfan oasis by Qurbān ʿAlī Khālidī is a shortened and late version of the *Qiṣṣa* of Mashrab. However, there is an important difference between the two stories - I will return to this later. For the story collected in the Turfan oasis in 1885 refers to the reconquest by Āfāq Khwāja in 1680 of the Six Cities kingdom with the help of Ghaldan's army, whereas the story in Mashrab's poetry points to the following decade (1687-97) when Ghaldan was engaged in a war with other Qalmaq tribes, and later with the Chinese Empire. In these years, unlike the first period, it was Ghaldan who needed the support of the Muslims and who may have made new political alliances with them.[21]

Nevertheless, the question of the conversion to Islam of Ghaldan can be discussed independently from the problem of the historical context of the event - studied below - to which these two stories refer.

From the *Qiṣṣa*, we learn that Mashrab fell in love with Qungtajī's daughter, and that, although depicted as a disciple of the Naqshbandī Āfāq Khwāja, he was presented as a follower of another Sufi order, the Qalandariyya.[22] Ghaldan's daughter told him that he must give up Islam and adopt Buddhism if he wanted to be loved. Mashrab did not accept this, but started working for his beloved as a herdsman looking after her camels. Actually, Mashrab's aim was not to be loved by Qungtajī's daughter, but to 'free her from hell', for she was a pagan Buddhist. While established in the mountains and looking after the camels of his beloved, Mashrab started ascetic exercises (*riyāḍāt*). Then, Qungtajī learned that a Qalandar dervish, a 'lover of God' who lived in his territory, had fallen in love with his daughter. He ordered this dervish to be brought to him. Qungtajī, who

---

et poèmes soufis, trans. Hamid Ismaïlov (Paris, 1993); Martin Hartmann, 'Mešreb, der weise Narr und fromme Ketzer. Ein Zentral-asiatisches Volksbuch', in *Der islamische Orient: Berichte und Forschungen, 1* (Berlin, 1902), pp. 147-93. There is another treatise attributed to Mashrab in which his mystical doctrine is clearly exposed, see Boborahim Mashrab, *Mabdai Nur*, ed. Hoji Ismatulloh Abdulloh (Tashkent, 1994).

20 See Sigrid Kleinmichel, *Halpa in Choresm (Ḫwārazm) und Ātin Āyi im Ferghanatal: Zur Geschichte des Lesens in Usbekistan* (2 vols, Berlin, 2000), vol. 2, pp. 267-8. A 'Biography of Shah Mashrab' (nineteenth century), was bought in 1929 in Kashghar by Gunnar Jarring (ms. Lund University Library, Jarring Prov. no. 272). Mashrab's poetry is also praised by Muslim Shamans; see Vladimir N. Basilov, 'Malika-Apa. Peripheral Forms of Shamanism? An Example from Middle Asia', in Denise Aigle, Bénédicte Brac de la Perrière and Jean-Pierre Chaumeil (eds), *La Politique des esprits: Chamanismes et Religions universalistes* (Nanterre, 2000), pp. 361-9, at p. 366.

21 See Peter C. Perdue, *China Marches West: The Qing Conquest of Central Eurasia* (Cambridge, 2005), pp. 148ff.

22 The passages in the *Kissa-i Mashrab* regarding Mashrab's relations with Qungtajī's daughter and on the conversion to Islam of the Qalmaq ruler are on pp. 46-60. The pages concerning this event in the Russian translation by Lykoshin (*Divana-i-Mashrab'*) are on pp. 76-93.

was threatened by several enemies, wanted to pay Mashrab with gold if he agreed to pray for him:, that is, to bring him victory with his prayers and his magic. This suggests that, in the eyes of the Qalmaq sovereign, Mashrab had access to holy and/or magical powers and belonged to a powerful religion. Qungtajī declared that Mashrab's God was right and his religion true. Mashrab, however, told Qungtajī that he had to convert to Islam if he wanted him to read prayers. Finally the Qalmaq ruler adopted Islam and pronounced the Muslim declaration of faith (*shahāda*), but under the strict condition that the Muslims should help him. Later Qungtajī became a disciple of Āfāq Khwāja and recognized him as his spiritual mentor (*pīr*).

Due to the important place the fighting of the Muslims against the pagan or Buddhist Mongols (Qalmaq, Qalmuq) received in the history and legends of Central Asian Muslims, their literature includes various cases of Tibetan priests or Buddhists who converted to Islam or Sufism. Several Central Asian epics focus in particular on the war against the Qalmaqs: the Kazakh *Qambar-batïr*, the Uzbek epic of *Alpamish*, the Kirghiz *Manas* etc. We are told by Karl Reichl, a specialist on Central Asian epics, that 'the choice of the Kalmuck khan as Qambar's rival [in the epic of *Qambar-batïr*] brings the epic poem into line with other heroic epics of the Turks of Central Asia, in which the Kalmucks are the Turks' enemies *par excellence*'.[23] Besides, as has been shown in detail by Papas, the Naqshbandī hagiographies have regarded the Qalmaq as the most dangerous among the infidels. Qalmaqs were considered by Āfāqī Sufis as one of their three major enemies, the two other being sleep and women.[24]

I would like to suggest that these epics and especially that of Alpamish may have, albeit indirectly, played the role of a model in the elaboration of the story of Ghaldan and Mashrab; for Alpamish's epic was well known to the Turkic peoples of Central Asia in general and of those of Chinese Turkestan in particular. In the Uzbek version of Alpamish's story, Alpamish converted the Qalmaq ruler Qarajan, who was a Lamaist Buddhist, to Islam with the help of saints and djinns who had lent him magical powers.[25] Moreover, in the Kirghiz version of the same epic, as in the *Qiṣṣa* of Mashrab, 'Qalandar' spirits help the hero.

The Qalandariyya Sufi order is generally described as a marginal and antinomian Sufi trend represented by unmarried and wandering Sufis and very different from the orthodox and rigorist Naqshbandiyya to which Mashrab also belonged.[26] However, in Central Asia, many Qalandars respected Naqshbandī

---

23 Karl Reichl, *Turkic Oral Epic Poetry* (New York, 1992), p. 148.

24 See Papas, *Soufisme et Politique*, pp. 100-101.

25 Reichl, *Turkic Oral Epic Poetry*, p. 166.

26 For a discussion of the Qalandariyya and Mashrab, see Lykoshin, *Divana-i-Mashrab'*, pp. 5-6. On the Qalandriyya in Central Asia, see A.L. Troitskaja, 'Iz proshlogo kalandarov i maddakhov v Uzbekistane', in *Domusulmanskie verovanija i obrjady ve Srednej Azii* (Moscow, 1975), pp. 191-223, and Gunnar Jarring, *Dervish and Qalandar: Texts from Kashghar* (Stockholm, 1987).

teachings: for example, the famous poet Muḥammad Ṣādiq Dhalīlī (born 1676 or 1680), a contemporary of the events analysed in this article.[27] The border between these two brotherhoods is thus not always easy to determine.[28] In the case of Mashrab, it is striking that both traditions, orthodox and heterodox, are followed, and that Mashrab, although a disciple of Āfāq Khwāja, appeared twice at least as a follower of the mysticism of Manṣūr Ḥallāj, a Sufi commonly regarded as one of the major 'heretics' in Islam. He quoted several times in his poetry the famous formula of Ḥallāj 'I am God (or the True, or: I am the Truth)' (*ana al-ḥaqq*). No wonder, therefore, that Mashrab was hanged (like Ḥallāj) by a Persian ruler. The resemblance of some Qalandarī practices to those of Tibetan Buddhist beggars (wandering monks?) may have intrigued the Qalmaq and Ghaldan – particularly their Sufi dance when connected with litanies (*dhikr*). The French explorer Fernand Grenard compared these practices at the beginning of twentieth century when he was in central Tibet coming from Xinjiang. He noticed that his Muslims servants had watched enthusiastically the dances of Tibetan beggars wearing masks and accompanied by drums and that they participated also by chanting their litanies.[29] The common origin may be here the shamanistic background of both Qalandariyya and Tibetan Buddhist beggars.

Moreover, as mentioned above, the term 'Qalandar' was used also for spirits, as in Alpamish's epic and in popular Islam in Central Asia. In the Kirghiz Alpamish epic, the hero is protected by seven Qalandars (*jitī qalandar*), coming from the unknown world (world of the spirit). The Qalmaq sovereign wonders if Alpamish is a saint or a wizard (*jādū kūy*). Although he enjoys the help of saints himself, the Qalmaq king is defeated by Alpamish because the seven Qalandars are too

---

27 His complete works were published in 1985, *Zälili Divānī* (Beijing, 1985). See also Abdushukur Turdī, 'Zälili ijadiyiti vä unung 'Säpärnamä' dastani' ['Zalili's Literary Composition and his Epic "Säpärnamä" (Travelogue)'], in *Uyghur Ädibiyati Tughrisida* (Urumchi, 1982), pp. 202-16, at pp. 202-5.

28 A manuscript on the Qalandariyya in the Biruni Library (Tashkent) gives us some clues for understanding this association, but it is well know that the great majority of the Naqshbandiyya regard the heterodox practices and doctrines of the Qalandars as alien. The same association existed also in the Ottoman Empire.

29 Jules Léon Dutreuil de Rhins, *Mission scientifique dans la Haute Asie 1890-1895* (3 vols, Paris, 1897-98), vol. 2, pp. 236-7:

> Chose curieuse! J'ai retrouvé au fond du Tibet la même danse dansée par des mendiants tibétains, avec les mêmes gestes, les mêmes jeux de physionomie et, sinon la même chanson, du moins le même air; seulement les mendiants tibétains se couvrent la figure d'un masque et s'accompagnent de tambourins. La ressemblance est telle qu'elle frappa nos domestiques musulmans non moins que nous et qu'ils se mirent à battre la mesure en criant : Ya Allah : inchâh Allah ! Il n'est pas probable que cette ressemblance soit fortuite.

powerful, and he finally converts to Islam.[30] The description of the Qalandars in this epic fits the drawing of a Qalandar of Eastern Turkestan as seen by Chinese eyes in the middle of the eighteenth century[31] and with photographs of these wandering dervishes at the end of the nineteenth and beginning of the twentieth century (see Plates 14.1 and 14.2). These Qalandars wear *janda* ('beggar's gabardine') with conical hats (*kulah*) on their heads. These are certainly also the kind of clothes Mashrab would have worn.[32]

In the Uzbek version of Alpamish, many other saints and Sufis are called upon by the hero to help him escape and fight the Qalmaqs: among these saints are the Naqshbandī Sufis Khwāja Ahrar (d. 1490), Ṣūfī Allāhyār (d. 1724) and Khwāja Isḥāq (d. 1598), the latter an ancestor of the Khwāja family.[33] In another popular hagiography widespread in Central Asia, the well-known Arab saint Ibrāhīm ibn Adham al-ʿIjlī al-Balkhī (d. 777 or 778) converts the daughter of a Qalmaq king and marries her. Qalandars are present at his wedding as witnesses and to ensure that the ceremony follows Islamic rules (this event does not appear in the earlier versions of the hagiography).[34]

The conversion story of Ghaldan/Qungtajī belongs thus to a genre well known in Central Asian hagiographical and even profane literature. Whereas the infidels here are Lamaist Buddhists, in other parts of Western Asia they are Christians or Zoroastrians.

BETWEEN LEGEND AND HISTORY

To sum up, the legends of the defeat and/or conversion of the Dalai Lama and of the conversion of Ghaldan constitute a fictional, imaginary background for two major historical events: namely, unusual alliances between Muslims and Buddhists, who had been confronting each other for centuries. These alliances *contre nature*, both of which occurred at the end of the seventeenth century, were

30 *Alpamys'-Batyr*, ed. A.A. Divaev (Tashkent, 1901), pp. 4, 14 and 17. English translation of this epic: Hasan Bulent Paksoy, *Alpamysh: Central Asian Identity under Russian Rule* (Hartford, 1989).

31 *Hui-jiang-zhi*, ed. Yong Gui, dated 29th year of Qian-long reign, 1764, University of Kyoto.

32 For further discussion of the clothes of the Qalandars, see Jarring, *Dervish and Qalandar*, pp. 25-6. It is striking that in Henry G. Schwarz's dictionary, *janda* is defined as a 'patched outer garment worn by Buddhist monk'. *An Uyghur-English Dictionary* (Washington, 1992).

33 *Alpomish*, ed. Hodi Zarif and Töra Mirzaev (Tashkent, 1993), pp. 103-5. See also Karl Reichl, 'Hero and Saint. Islamic Elements in Uighur Oral Epics', *Journal of the History of Sufism*, 3 (2001-2002): pp. 7-24, at pp. 18-20.

34 From the *Tārīkh-i Uwaysī*, trans. Julian Baldick in his *Imaginary Muslims: The Uwaysi Sufis of Central Asia* (London, 1993), pp. 185-6. On Ibrāhīm ibn Adham's popular hagiography in Central Asia, see Kleinmichel, *Halpa in Choresm*, vol. 2, pp. 256-8.

formed against the backdrop of the ongoing struggles for political power: first, in 1680, Muslims joined the Qalmaq in order to put an end to internecine quarrels in their own kingdom; secondly, between 1690 and 1697, the Qalmaqs needed the Muslims to be their allies to fight against other Mongols and to resist the Chinese Empire. From the *Qiṣṣa* of Mashrab, we learn, that after Ghaldan converted to Islam because of Mashrab, he met Āfāq Khwāja, became his disciple, and, as he had done with Mashrab, asked his help to defeat his enemies.[35]

So the question arises: why have Muslim hagiographers turned these alliances into conversion stories? I would like to suggest that they wanted to give Islam a glorious role and minimize the help provided to them by the Tibetan Buddhists. That is to say that, in their eyes, Muslims and only Muslims – here new converts, that is, Tibetan Buddhists – and not infidels gave military support to Āfāq to recover his throne, and only Muslims helped other Muslims (in the case of Ghaldan after 1690). Anything else would have been disgraceful in the eyes of the believers. The aim of any Muslim hagiography and legend is in fact twofold: first, to display historical facts in the form of a story, and, secondly, to present the miracles and the valour of the hero whose goal is the glorification of Islam through Sufism. In a sense, a holy war was launched against Tibet by Central Asia Muslims during the fifteenth and sixteenth centuries in order to Islamicize the roof of the world and all the Tibetan Buddhists of the region, and this holy war continued in the imagination of the hagiographers.

Regarding the historical veracity of these conversion legends, we must state that there are no proofs, no documentary evidence, that Āfāq Khwāja and the Dalai Lama did in fact meet in Lhasa or elsewhere in Tibet. However, they certainly had diplomatic exchanges, since Lhasa at this time was a major political centre in Central and Inner Asia. Hence, the decision by the Jungghars to help Āfāq Khwāja and to invade the Six Cities kingdom was perhaps taken in Tibet.[36] If we turn now to the second event, the sources tell us that Ghaldan invaded Northern Mongolia and directed a series of campaigns in the steppe between 1690 and 1697 before he was killed in a battle against the Chinese. Surprisingly, the Chinese Emperor Kangxi suspected him of looking for allies among the Muslims of the area and sending some of them into China as spies. Furthermore, to quote Peter Perdue, the emperor stressed that Ghaldan 'had claimed support from the princes of Kokonor, the Russians and "China's Muslims"'(*Zhongguo Huizi*[37]) in order to launch an attack on China and to set up a Muslim as its ruler'.[38] Even more, Kangxi believed that Ghaldan had become a Muslim. This is confirmed by a letter sent by the Emperor to Ghaldan, a copy of which was sent to the Sixth

---

35 *Kissa-i Mashrab*, p. 59.

36 For further discussion of the relationship between the Dalai Lama and the Mongolian Khans as 'protected' and 'protector', see Ahmad, *Sino-Tibetan Relations in the Seventeenth Century*, pp. 79 and 145ff.

37 Here *Huizi* does not distinguish Turkic and Chinese Muslims.

38 Perdure, *China Marches West*, pp. 179 and 191-2.

Dalai Lama in 1694, that states that the Jungghar sovereign has 'destroyed the law of Tsongkhaba', that is, the founder of the Gelugpa order of Tibetan Buddhism, and converted to the religion of the Muslims (*Hui-zi*).[39] Does the *Qiṣṣa* of Mashrab then reflect a historical fact corroborated by Kangxi's statement? Unfortunately this question will remain unanswered for lack of more detailed and reliable documents. In particular, we do not know whether Kangxi's assertion was based on serious proofs of the conversion of the Qalmaq king or only on a presumption he used later as a strategy against him.

To conclude, in the oral legend collected by Qurbān ʿAlī Khālidī in the Turfan oasis in 1885, we are told that after the death of Ghaldan and Āfāq Khwāja the Qalmaq population returned to their first faith: that is, Tibetan Buddhism. On the other hand, we are told by an Uyghur scholar in 1989 that the memory of Āfāq Khwāja as 'Abakh Khoja', 'Torlug Abakh' or 'Qun Abakh' is still honoured in contemporary Xinjiang by certain 'Mongols and Tangut'.[40] *Qun* is a high Mongol title. So, we may wonder to what extent these Mongols who venerate today the memory of Āfāq Khwāja could be descendants of the Qalmaqs linked to Ghaldan. We do know that the Qalmaq population was decimated after the fall of the Jungghar Empire because of smallpox[41] and that few of them stayed in the Ili area.[42] Later, Torgut Mongols (another tribe of the Oirat confederation) left the Volga region and established themselves in the Ili area in 1771,[43] still keeping their Lamaist faith. Further research in this area and in Qalmaq folklore and written traditions will help us to understand why and by whom exactly Qun Abakh is venerated, and whether these Mongols are Muslims, and also if their veneration of Āfāq Khwāja has any link with the event of the alleged conversion of Ghaldan to Islam and Sufism. This is a question I would like to investigate in the future.

---

39 The Chinese text is 'Huai Zong-Ka-Ba zhi fa, ni hui-zi zhi jiao'; in *Qinzheng Pingding Shuomo Fanglue* 親征平定朔漠方略, ed. Zhang Yushu, j. 15, 34/4 gengzi, p. 12. I would like to thank my colleague Hamada Masami (University of Kyoto) who has read and translated this text for me.

40 Nizamüddin Hüsäyin, '3. Qabahät 'Äqidä' (Yäni bir Qätim Appaq Khoja Toghrisida)', *Shinjang Mädäniyati* (Urumchi), 2/3 (1989): pp. 113-54, at p. 127, see Plate 14.3.

41 Miyawaki, 'The Dzungars and the Torguts (Kalmuks)', p. 150.

42 On the Mongol tribes of contemporary Xinjiang, see Marie-Lise Beffa and Marie-Dominique Even, 'Les Mongols (Oïrates) du Xinjiang', *La Lettre d'Asie centrale* (Paris), 3 (1995): pp. 14-16 and 4 (1995): pp. 14-16.

43 Miyawaki, 'The Dzungars and the Torguts (Kalmuks)', pp. 145 and 150-51.

Chapter 15
Ritual Theory across the Buddhist–Muslim Divide in Late Imperial China

Johan Elverskog

In the contemporary world the meeting of Buddhism and Islam is most often imagined as one of confrontation. Indeed, if anything is known about this 'clash of civilizations' it is that Muslims destroyed the last vestiges of Buddhism in its homeland of India.[1] And although this was not really the case historically,[2] the idea of Muslim persecution of Buddhism was recently vividly revived in the popular imagination when the Taliban destroyed the 'idolatrous' statues at Bamiyan. This wanton act of destruction seemed to readily confirm the narrative that Buddhist historiography has maintained for centuries, which claims the demise of Buddhism was solely the fault of Muslims rather than their own failure to secure imperial support or distinguish Buddhism from the amorphous category of Hinduism in an age of *tantra* and *bhakti*. Moreover, the negative view of Islam that permeates the Buddhist tradition also neatly coincides with contemporary notions about these two traditions. Namely, Islam is bad and violent, while Buddhism is good and peaceful, a view readily apotheosized in our media-saturated culture by the iconic images of the scowling and menacing Osama bin Laden on the one hand, and the jolly and benevolent Dalai Lama on the other. Of course, such views are nothing new.[3] As a range of scholars following in the footsteps of Edward Said have shown, the Western 'construction' of Buddhism and Islam in the eighteenth and nineteenth centuries followed two distinct paths: while Buddhism was held up as a rational, post-enlightenment

---

[1] This is the common view in both popular and academic literature, see, for example, Lawrence Sutin, *All is Change: The Two Thousand-Year Journey of Buddhism to the West* (New York, 2006), pp. 45-6; and Jonathan S. Walters, *Finding Buddhists in Global History* (Washington, 1998), pp. 45-6.

[2] See for example Richard M. Eaton, 'Temple Desecration and Indo-Muslim States', in id. (ed.), *Essays on Islam and Indian History* (New Delhi, 2000), pp. 94-132.

[3] Tomoko Masuzawa, *The Invention of World Religions* (Chicago, 2005), pp. 121-46, 179-80.

philosophy,[4] Islam was characterized as an inherently violent and irrational religion.[5]

Although these two discourses continue to have implications in the contemporary world it also behoves us to recall that such constructions of 'the other' within structures of power are not solely the preserve of the imperial West, as many postcolonial scholars would have us believe. Indeed, as briefly noted above, the 'Orientalist' view of Islam had been a fundamental theological and historiographical component of the Buddhist tradition for nearly a millennium. In fact the earliest extant Buddhist response to Islam as evidenced in the *Kālacakratantra* is largely negative. And over time, much as Hindu nationalists today blame much of India's woes on 500 years of Islamic rule, Buddhist historiography came to regard Muslims as the ones who single-handedly destroyed the Dharma in its homeland and elsewhere. Of course, as hinted above, there were certainly other factors involved in the demise of Buddhism in India. Moreover, counter to received wisdom, it is important to recognize that Buddhists actually worked with Muslims in order to attack Hindus in the misguided hope of reviving their previous glory days.[6] This was inevitably not to be; however, blaming the Muslims for the destruction of the famous Nalanda University in later historiography offered not only a scapegoat for their own failures, but also a powerful narrative of closure. It was also one that unfortunately continues to resonate today across the Buddhist world in places such as southern Thailand and Myanmar's Arakan province.

Yet what of Muslims, how did they see Buddhism?[7] On one level they shared the West's view of 'the East' as a land of riches. In the medieval period China in particular was seen or remembered in Muslim sources in favourable terms

---

[4] On the western construction of Buddhism see, for example, Phillip Almond, *The British Discovery of Buddhism* (Cambridge, 1988); Gregory Schopen, 'Archaeology and Protestant Suppositions in the Study of Indian Buddhism', *History of Religions*, 31 (1991): pp. 1-23; Bernard Faure, *The Rhetoric of Immediacy: A Cultural Critique of Chan/Zen Buddhism* (Princeton, 1991); Thomas A. Tweed, *The American Encounter with Buddhism 1844-1912: Victorian Culture and the Limits of Dissent* (Bloomington, 1992); Jonathan Silk, 'The Victorian Creation of Buddhism', *Journal of Indian Philosophy*, 22 (1994): pp. 171-96; Donald S. Lopez (ed.), *Curators of the Buddha: The Study of Buddhism under Colonialism* (Chicago, 1995); Stephen Prothero, *The White Buddhist: The Asian Odyssey of Henry Steel Olcott* (Bloomington, 1996); Donald S. Lopez, *Prisoners of Shangri-La: Tibetan Buddhism and the West* (Chicago, 1998); Donald S. Lopez (ed.), *A Modern Buddhist Bible: Essential Readings from East and West* (Boston, 2002).

[5] Although there is a great deal of literature on this topic, a fine overview of this discourse can be found in Emran Qureshi and Michael A. Sells (eds), *The New Crusades: Constructing the Muslim Enemy* (New York, 2003).

[6] *Tāranātha's History of Buddhism in India*, trans. Lama Chimpa and Alaka Chattopadhyaya (Delhi, 1990), p. 319.

[7] See Daniel Gimaret, 'Bouddha et les bouddhistes dans la tradition musulmane', *Journale Asiatique*, 257 (1969): pp. 273-316.

and even the Dharma was not a major concern.[8] This sentiment was even shared by the Arab armies that invaded Afghanistan and first came into contact with Buddhism. Much as they responded to non-Muslim religions elsewhere, Buddhism was allowed to continue unmolested.[9] Moreover, counter to notions of Muslim aniconism there actually developed a lively trade in Buddhist statues, and the word for Buddha, *but*, even became a synonym for beauty in Persian poetry.[10] Moreover, as van Bladel notes in his study of the Barmakids, during the early Arab state there was a lively tradition of translating Indic sources, such as the *Pañcatantra* (*Kalīla wa-Dimna)* and the *Kitāb Bilawhar wa-Yūdāsaf*, a compilation from various sources of the Buddha biography that became the prototype for the Christian legend of Barlaam and Josaphat.

Such ecumenicalism, however, was not always the case, as evidenced by the hatred and violence in other times and places. One need only travel to the Buddhist cave sites along the Silk Road and see the eyes gouged out of murals to witness earlier anti-Buddhist fervour, a sentiment well-captured in a folksong from Kāshgarī's twelfth-century Turkic dictionary:

> We came down on them like a flood,
> We went out among their cities,
> We tore down the idol-temples,
> We shat on the Buddha's head![11]

Thus, as is the case with all religious encounters, one can easily find the good, the bad and the ugly. However, we should recall that not all Muslims were bent on the Dharma's destruction. Indeed, as seen in Akasoy's article on Tibet in Arabic literature, the most common trope was one of laughter. Yet not all Arabs saw Tibet or Buddhism as a fantastic funhouse, some tried to make sense of it, or at least catalogue it as one of the components of the human experience.

One of the earliest was Jayhānī, whose description of Buddhism in his now lost *Kitāb al-masālik* provided material on Buddhist thought for both Maqdisī and Gardīzī in their brief descriptions of religion in India. More detailed descriptions of the Dharma, as well as the standard categorization of Indian religions, are found in al-Nadīm's *Fihrist* (987) and Shahrastānī's *Kitāb al-milal wa'l-niḥal* (1125), works only superseded by Rashīd al-Dīn, who had the good fortune to have at

---

8 Michal Biran, *The Empire of the Qara Khitai in Eurasian History: Between China and the Islamic World* (Cambridge, 2005), pp. 97-101, 209-10.

9 On early Muslim theory and practices regarding non-Muslims, see Patricia Crone, *God's Rule: Government and Islam* (New York, 2004), pp. 358-92; Derryl N. MacLean, *Religion and Society in Arab Sind* (Leiden, 1989).

10 A.S. Melikian-Chirvani, 'Buddhism in Islamic Times', *EIr*.

11 Maḥmūd el-Kāşgarī, *Compendium of the Turkic Languages (Diwan Lugat at-Turk)*, ed. and trans. Robert Dankoff and James Kelly (3 vols, Cambridge, 1982-85), vol. 1, p. 270.

hand the Kashmiri informant Kamalashri.[12] Some Muslims though went beyond simple description, such as the Chinese Muslim scholar Liu Zhi, who compared the Daoist concept of *wuwei* (non-action), the Buddhist concept of emptiness and the Chinese Islamic concept of *Zhenyi*, the True and One.[13]

Yet what of the Buddhists? Besides the *Kālacakratantra* and the standard narrative of Muslim destruction in Buddhist historiography what records do we have of their critical engagement with Islam? Unfortunately, the sources are sparse. While we know Buddhists certainly came into contact with Muslims in both the political and economic spheres (see King in this volume), how they actually responded to them - as witnessed at the conference where this paper was originally given - can often only be inferred from small fragments (Zieme's Uyghur poems), enticing possibilities (Buell's foodways) or various roundabout ways (Martin's medical texts). This is not to say there are no extant Buddhist voices on Islam. As Newman has shown in his study of the *Kālacakratantra*, there were some later Tibetan scholars who engaged with Islam.[14] Yet as with the scholars he notes, and others such as the Great Fifth Dalai Lama and Rölpé Dorjé, all consistently follow the same anti-Islamic paradigm stretching back to the *Kālacakratantra* itself. A valid question is therefore whether there are any other pre-modern Buddhist interpretations of Islam?

This article explores one such voice, that of the nineteenth-century Mongol nobleman and fiction-writer Injannashi (1837-92). He wrote at a time of Buddhist–Muslim civil war in Qing Inner Asia, but instead of following the conventional Buddhist anti-Muslim polemic, he used a form of ritual theory to argue that Muslims and their rituals were actually just like those of the Buddhists.

THE QUESTION OF *ḤALĀL* AND THE BUDDHIST–MUSLIM DIVIDE

The main ritual that separated Inner Asian Buddhists and Muslims was that of preparing *ḥalāl* meat. On one level the Buddhist argument against this practice could have been made on the grounds of vegetarianism; however, although the latter is much lauded in Tibetan Buddhist literature,[15] the reality is that Tibetans

---

12 Johan Elverskog, 'Islam and Buddhism', in Robert Buswell (ed.), *Encyclopedia of Buddhism* (New York, 2003), pp. 380-82; Karl Jahn, *Rashid al-Din's History of India: Collected Essays with Facsimiles and Indices* (The Hague, 1965) and Rashīd al-Dīn, *Die Indiengeschichte des Rašīd ad-Dīn*, trans. Karl Jahn (Vienna, 1980).

13 James D. Frankel, 'Liu Zhi's Journey through Ritual Law to Allah's Chinese Name: Conceptual Antecedents and Theological Obstacles to the Confucian-Islamic Harmonization of the Tianfang Dianli' (PhD thesis, Columbia University, 2005).

14 John Newman, 'Islam in the Kalacakra Tantra', *Journal of the International Association of Buddhist Studies*, 21/2 (1998).

15 See, for example, Shabkar, *The Life of Shabkar: The Autobiography of a Tibetan Yogin*, trans. Matthieu Ricard et al. (Albany, 1994), pp. 195, 327, 411, 541-2, 582, 585.

and Mongols all eat meat.[16] For the Mongols in particular, what was appalling about the preparation of *ḥalāl* meat was the slitting of an animal's throat in order to expel the blood. In the Mongol view this was absolutely monstrous and went against all norms of civilized society, the reason being that Mongols believe blood from slaughter should never touch the sacred mother earth and thus Mongols slaughter animals by cutting open the animal's belly and pinching the aorta, thereby ensuring that all the blood is retained within the carcass. This is clearly the antithesis of *ḥalāl* and it was this foodway that initially generated a major fault-line between the Mongols and the Islamic world.

On one level this differentiation of foodways may seem trivial, yet one need only look at the pork belt that is southern Europe, in order to understand that food and its rituals are a powerful means of drawing boundaries.[17] Indeed, the seriousness of this issue was readily confirmed during the course of this conference. Namely, the day after this paper was presented in November 2006, one of the London tabloids had a front-page article about a school that was planning on serving a 'halal chicken' for the school's Christmas party.[18] The response was inevitable: not serving a turkey prepared in the 'traditional' way was tantamount to the end of Britishness and the legitimation of 'Eurabia'.[19]

A similar uproar occurred in the thirteenth century when a group of Muslims refused to eat the meat offered at an imperial Mongol banquet hosted by Qubilai Khan. They, of course, wanted the meat to be *ḥalāl* instead of the blood-soaked Mongol affair. Much like the concerned British parents of today, Qubilai Khan was not pleased. He issued an edict in 1280 prohibiting *ḥalāl* practices and imposing the death sentence on violators.[20] This was no doubt extreme, yet it captures well the powerful tensions that existed between these communities. Moreover, as the Mongols became increasingly more Buddhist during the course of the Yuan dynasty (1272-1368) and absorbed through osmosis the ingrained anti-Muslim bent of the Dharma, these two tendencies acted synergistically.

---

16 For an exploration of how Tibetans deal with the karmic mandate to not kill and the reality of meat consumption, see Geoff Childs, *Tibetan Diary: From Birth to Death and Beyond in a Himalayan Valley of Nepal* (Berkeley, 2004), pp. 125-8.

17 Amongst the extensive scholarship on the importance of foodways in defining religious, cultural, and ethnic boundaries, one may mention, as particularly relevant, Claudine Fabre-Vassas, *The Singular Beast: Jews, Christians, and the Pig* (New York, 1997); Uradyn E. Bulag, *Nationalism and Hybridity in Mongolia* (Oxford, 1998), pp. 194-211; Maris Boyd Gillette, *Between Mecca and Beijing: Modernization and Consumption among Urban Chinese Muslims* (Stanford, 2000), pp. 114-66.

18 Paul Jeeves, 'Fury over Halal Christmas Dinner', *Daily Express*, 18 November 2006.

19 Paul Stokes, 'School U-Turns on Halal Christmas Menu', *Daily Telegraph*, 18 November 2006.

20 Morris Rossabi, *Khubilai Khan: His Life and Times* (Berkeley, 1988), p. 200. The actual edict is translated in Francis Woodman Cleaves, 'The Rescript of Qubilai Prohibiting the Slaughtering of Animals by Slitting the Throat', *Journal of Turkish Studies*, 16 (1992): pp. 67-89.

Indeed, as Newman has shown, the negative Buddhist description of Muslim foodways goes all the way back to the *Kālacakratantra*. It bemoans at some length Islamic foodways in relation to brahmanical norms:

> [The barbarians] kill camels, horses, and cattle, and briefly cook their flesh together with blood. They cook beef and amniotic fluid with butter and spice, rice mixed together with vegetables, and forest fruit, all at once on the fire. Men eat that, O king, and drink bird eggs, in the place of the demon [barbarians].[21]

This presentation was no doubt shaped by the historical context of the *Kālacakratantra*'s composition, one in which there was increasing conflict between not only Hindus and Buddhists, but also Muslims, who at this time were moving into northwest India in ever larger numbers. And it was no doubt because of this reality and the Buddhists' awareness of their waning influence that Islam came to occupy a central role in the eschatology of the *Kālacakratantra*, which was not only grossly negative and ultimately violent, but also one that was to shape Buddhist views of Islam for centuries.[22] For, as the Shambhala myth maintains, when Islam has taken over the world, the Buddhist saviour will ride forth and kill all the infidels.[23] It was no doubt such conceptualizations that held aloft the historical narrative that it was Muslims who destroyed the final vestiges and institutions of Buddhism in India. Yet, by pointing this out I do not want to minimize the complex and at times violent process of Islamization in Inner Asia which no doubt helped colour Buddhist views of Muslims as the antithesis of the civilized Dharma.[24] As the Fifth Dalai in fact made clear in his *History of Tibet*: before the introduction of Buddhism to the Mongols they were 'barbarians' like the Muslims.[25]

I relate this instance of Oriental Orientalism not to reaffirm the fact that Buddhists have long harboured animosity toward Islam, but also to note that, aside from the issue of *ḥalāl*, in the early Mongol world this anti-Islamic

---

21 Quoted in John Newman, 'Islam in the Kalacakra Tantra', *Journal of the International Association of Buddhist Studies*, 21/2 (1998): pp. 311-71, at p. 319.

22 See John Newman, 'Eschatology in the Wheel of Time Tantra', in Donald S. Lopez (ed.), *Buddhism in Practice* (Princeton, 1995), pp. 284-9.

23 On the myth of Shambhala see Edwin Bernbaum, *The Way to Shambhala: A Search for the Mythical Kingdom Beyond the Himalayas* (Garden City, NY, 1980); and Luboš Bělka, *Buddhistická Eschatologie: Šambhalský mýtus* (Brno, 2004).

24 On the Buddhist response to Islam, see, for example, Peter Zieme, 'Antiislamische Polemik in einem alttürkischen buddhistischen Gedicht aus Turfan', *Altorientalische Forschungen*, 17/1 (1990): pp. 146-51. On the larger dynamics of Islamization in Inner Asia see Devin DeWeese, *Islamization and Native Religion in the Golden Horde: Baba Tükles and Conversion to Islam in Historical and Epic Tradition* (University Park, 1994).

25 *A History of Tibet by the Fifth Dalai Lama of Tibet*, trans. Zahiruddin Ahmad (Bloomington, 1995), p. 193.

discourse was actually minimal.[26] In point of fact, Muslims were signatories to the Baljuna Covenant that brought Genghis Khan to power.[27] Moreover, their political and economic power was legendary during the Yuan dynasty, and subsequently infamous in the hands of later Chinese historians who blamed them, and interestingly Tibetan Buddhist lamas as well,[28] for all the dynasty's woes.[29] Though more to the point, the map of Islam would not be what it is today without the Mongol empire and its successor states that adopted Islam as the state religion. Yet, be that as it may, it is important to recognize that even with all this Mongol–Muslim interaction Mongol sources are quiet on the issue of Islam. Even after the Mongols' reconversion to Buddhism in the sixteenth century they never mention Islam. In fact, only in the nineteenth century do Mongol authors start writing about Islam.

THE SHAMBHALA MYTH IN THE NINETEENTH CENTURY

In the nineteenth century Mongol authors begin discussing not only Islam for the first time, but also situating Muslims in relation to the *Kālacakratantra*, especially its myth of Shambhala. In his 1848 *Crystal Mirror* (*Bolor Toli*) Jimbadorji, for example, points out that 'the Turkestanis, they are a people without the pure majestic Dharma'.[30] The 1835 *Pearl Rosary* (*Subud Erike*), on the other hand, records a prophecy based on the *Mañjuśrīmūlatantra* that asserts Genghis Khan was to be born at a time of many Muslims, whom he was to crush.[31] Moreover, this

---

26 In Sufi historiography the rise of Genghis Khan and the destruction of the Muslim world was seen as a positive development. Sufi leaders were even said to have helped Genghis Khan with his invasions. See Devin DeWeese, '"Stuck in the Throat of Chingiz Khan": Envisioning the Mongol Conquests in Some Sufi Accounts from the 14th to 17th Centuries', in Judith Pfeiffer and Sholeh A. Quinn (eds), *History and Historiography of Post-Mongol Central Asia and the Middle East: Studies in Honor of John E. Woods* (Wiesbaden, 2006), pp. 23-60.

27 Igor de Rachewiltz, *The Secret History of the Mongols: A Mongolian Epic Chronicle of the Thirteenth Century* (Leiden, 2006), pp. 657-8.

28 Herbert Franke, 'Tibetans in Yüan China', in John Langlois, Jr. (ed.), *China under Mongol Rule* (Princeton, 1981), pp. 296-328.

29 Hok-Lam Chan, 'The Demise of Yüan Rule in Mongolian and Chinese Legends', in Géza Bethlenfalvy et al. (eds), *Altaic Religious Beliefs and Practices: Proceedings of the 33rd Meeting of the Permanent International Altaistic Conference* (Budapest, 1992), pp. 65-82.

30 Jimbadorji, *Bolor Toli*, ed. Liu Jinsuo (Beijing, 1984), p. 366. Hereafter BT.

31 Johan Elverskog, *The Pearl Rosary: Mongol Historiography in Early Nineteenth-Century Ordos* (Bloomington, 2007), pp. 36-7. In the same way as Roerich has pointed out that Tibetans used this prophecy about Nepal from the *Mañjuśrīmūlatantra* to explain early Tibetan Buddhist history ('Gos lo-tsā-ba Gzhon-nu-dpal, *The Blue Annals*, trans. George Roerich [2 vols, Delhi, 1976], vol. 1, pp. x-xi), the same appears to have occurred in this case as well. However, the Mongol prophecy signals the birth of Genghis Khan; though,

prophecy is put into the mouth of the Panchen Lama, not only whose previous incarnation was the ruler of Shambhala who had organized the teachings of the *Kālacakratantra*, but also whose future incarnation will be Kalkin Raudra Cakrin, who will ride forth with his Buddhist army, annihilate the Muslim enemies and usher in a new age of pure Buddhism.[32] We can therefore see that in the nineteenth century the Mongols for the first time began drawing upon the vast reservoir of Buddhist anti-Muslim rhetoric and once again the key practice that confirmed Islamic perfidy was: 'According to those Muslims, they say that you cannot eat the meat of animals that die naturally. To kill an animal according to their own wrong view, one will be saved if, while cutting the neck with a knife, you recite the Lord's Dharani, Bismillah.'[33]

To explain this outburst of anti-Islamic polemic in late imperial China we need to recall the Muslim revival among the Hui that began in the mid-eighteenth century.[34] The Hui had long since transformed their religious practices and community into a localized Sino–Islamic one, and had for centuries worked within the shifting political winds emanating out of Beijing.[35] In the 1760s, however, there was a revival spearheaded by two Shaykhs, Ma Mingxin and Ma Laichi, who had returned from studying in Mecca and the Yemen and thus carried the legitimacy of having studied in the West. And although both had studied with Muḥammad ibn Zayn they developed differing views on the practice of *dhikr*, which was to have catastrophic results.[36]

---

unlike Bu-ston's *History of the Dharma* or the fifteenth-century *Blue Annals* which cite the prophecy *in toto* (Evgenij E. Obermiller, *History of Buddhism (Chos-'byung)* [2 vols, Leipzig, 1931-32], vol. 1, pp. 111-21), the *Pearl Rosary* uses only one passage: 'there will be different kinds of mlecchas (kla-klo)' (*The Blue Annals*, p. 45).

32 On the development of the connection between the Panchen Lamas and the Shambhala kings, see Damdinsüren, 'Ülger domgiin jargalant oron Shambal' ['Shambhala the Happy Land of Legends'], *Zentralasiatische Studien*, 11 (1977): pp. 351-87, at pp. 373-7, which is translated in Charles R. Bawden, 'The Wish-Prayer for Shambhala Again', *Monumenta Serica*, 36 (1984-85): pp. 453-509, at pp. 454-8.

33 *Sambala-yin oron-u teüke orosiba* [*History of the Land of Shambhala*], MS p. 19 (Zhongguo Menggu wen guji zongmu bianhui, *Catalogue of Ancient Mongolian Books and Documents of China* [Beijing, 1999], no. 4633). This passage and the condemnation of *ḥalāl* meat preparation – 'slit[ting] the throats of animals while saying the mantra of their demonic deity Visavimla, "Withered by Poison"; that is, *bismillah* – "in the name of Allah"' – derives from the *Kālacakratantra* (See Newman, 'Islam in the Kalacakra Tantra', p. 324).

34 The following interpretation is drawn from Johan Elverskog, *Our Great Qing: The Mongols, Buddhism, and the State in Late Imperial China* (Honolulu, 2006), pp. 139-46.

35 On the development of Sino–Islamic culture, see Zvi Ben-Dor Benite, *The Dao of Muhammad: A Cultural History of Muslims in Late Imperial China* (Cambridge, 2005).

36 The following historical summary is based on Jonathan N. Lipman, *Familiar Strangers: A History of Muslims in Northwest China* (Seattle, 1997), pp. 114-15; the articles collected in Joseph F. Fletcher, *Studies on Chinese and Islamic Inner Asia*, ed. Beatrice Manz (Aldershot, 1995); and Anthony Garnaut, 'Pen of the Jahriyya: A Commentary of *The History of the Soul* by Zheng Chengzhi', *Inner Asia*, 8 (2006): pp. 29-50.

Ma Laichi left Yemen first and upon returning to China he established a thriving Sufi community in the Hezhou and Xunhua districts of Gansu. When Ma Mingxin returned he initially joined this community and recognized the authority of Ma Laichi; however, as Ma Mingxin began to advocate the view that *dhikr* should be performed aloud (*jahrī*) in opposition to Ma Laichi's practice of silent (*khafī*) ritual prayer, two groups differentiated on the basis of this practice began to form. In the beginning the two groups were largely cordial, but tensions between them escalated, especially after the death of Ma Laichi, when issues of authority and control of resources was brought to the fore. To resolve these issues the two groups went to court and in their deliberations the Qing authorities sided with Ma Laichi's son since they deemed the Khafiyya ('Silentists') to be orthodox and Ma Mingxin's Jahriyya ('Aloudists') to be heterodox. Yet Ma Mingxin was not to be dissuaded and he continued with his teaching, which invariably resulted in further legal confrontations with the Khafiyya. In response, the Qing authorities eventually forbade Ma Mingxin to teach in Xunhua district, and seven years later in 1769 he was ordered to leave Hezhou and return to his home village.

Ma Mingxin moved instead to Guanchuan from where he travelled and acquired followers in Xinjiang, Ningxia and Shaanxi. But even though he no longer went to Xunhua he continued to have followers there, especially among the Turkic Salars, and tensions between the two groups there remained high, no doubt since the Qing continued to support the Khafiyya. Ultimately things came to a head in 1781 when one of Ma Mingxin's followers, nicknamed 'Su Forty-Three', led a group of Jahriyya in an attack on the Khafiyya that left over a hundred people dead, including the garrison commander of Lanzhou. At this turn of events Ma Mingxin was arrested as a rebel leader and brought to Lanzhou. 'Su Forty-Three' and his band followed and demanded his release. The Qing official at the prison rejected their pleas and instead had him executed.

This action resulted in a full-scale rebellion among Ma Mingxin's followers across northwest China. In response the Manchu court sent Grand Secretary Agui from Beijing to lead a battalion of troops to suppress the uprising. After arriving in the west they thus set about killing all the Jahriyya leaders and exiling the followers to the frontiers of the Qing Empire. Yet even after these heavy-handed tactics the Jahriyya rose up again three years later under the leadership of Ma Mingxin's disciple, Tian Wu. His revolt was also brutally suppressed by Qing forces and inevitably the tensions between the court and this particular Muslim group continued to fester through the generations, such as when the third leader of the Jahriyya, Ma Datian, was charged with sedition in 1818 and then died en route to his place of exile in Manchuria. This cycle of imperial suppression and Muslim response continued and reached its final apogee during the Hui rebellions of the mid-nineteenth century in both the north and the south.[37]

[37] On the Hui rebellions in the south, see David G. Atwill, *The Chinese Sultanate: Islam, Ethnicity, and the Panthay Rebellion in Southwest China, 1856-1873* (Stanford, 2006).

To make sense of this spiral of violence between local Muslim groups and the Qing state we need to recall Manchu religious policies. Prior to the 1760s, although Chinese officials had repeatedly petitioned the court to outlaw Islam entirely in the empire, the Manchu emperors had maintained that Islam fell within the bounds of civilization and that Muslims should receive the same treatment as all imperial subjects. However, as the Qing became involved on one side of this internal theological dispute, the imperial rhetoric did not necessarily accord with actions on the ground. This resulted in a spiral of communal and state violence, and the subsequent or tandem growth of the supposedly 'anti-Qing' Jahriyya. Moreover, on account of Qing bureaucratic malfeasance the local economies of these Muslim areas were devastated, and this further spurred the escalating sense of distrust and alienation. Tensions were further exacerbated when in violation of Qing universalist theory the court began implementing laws that discriminated against Muslims based solely on their religion.

The Board of Punishments passed the first of these laws in 1762 in the wake of the earliest lawsuits filed between the Khafiyya and Jahriyya. It mandated that all Muslim leaders had to report any inappropriate behaviour within their community to the authorities, and local officials had to report Muslim criminal acts to the state authorities. As might have been expected, court records began to fill with Muslim acts of criminality, and local officials inundated the court with reports of Muslim bandits and their intrinsic propensity for violence. In response, the Qing authorities became more suspicious and drafted further regulations concerning Muslims. Thus Muslims found in groups of three or more with any weapon were deemed immediately as criminals. In the 1770s, the Qing court even created a new criminal category, *dou'ou* 'brawling', that could be used as a pretence to arrest Muslims specifically. As an inevitable result, Muslims who might not initially have sided with the Jahriyya teachings joined them in protesting Qing policy, thus further reinforcing the court's fear of a growing Islamic anti-Qing movement.

As noted above, this mutual animosity culminated in 1781 when Ma Mingxin was executed. Yet it was further exacerbated by faulty intelligence. Namely, a Qing official sent to quell the violence between the Khafiyya and Jahriyya informed one group who he thought were Khafiyya that the Qing would exterminate all followers of the Jahriyya tradition. To his dismay, his audience turned out to be Jahriyya followers and they summarily executed him. With the death of another Qing official at the hands of the Jahriyya the Qing court responded with the 'pacification' campaign led by Grand Secretary Agui. And although it was successful at first it also bred animosity among the Jahriyya. This anger was further compounded by local leaders, who, in trying to impress the court, were overly zealous in killing perceived enemies of the state. As a result the Jahriyya continued to grow and thus Tian Wu was able to launch another revolt in 1784.

At this turn of events, the Qianlong emperor was baffled, and he wrote in a letter to one of his ministers:

> Why would Muslims from far and near join up and follow them like sheep? ... did news of Li Shiyao's investigations of Muslims leak out, so rebels could start rumors flying of [a government campaign to] 'exterminate Muslims' as an excuse to incite riots? I have thought of all these things, but none seems to be the true reason. In the end, why did they rebel? We must get to the bottom of this![38]

Whether they got to the bottom of it is unknown. What is clear is that the 1784 rebellion was suppressed, and as an interim solution the Qing instituted a virtual military occupation of northwest China. While it held the peace for the next half a century, when Qing forces had to move south in the 1850s to fight the growing Christian Taiping rebellion, internal and external violence erupted again in the northwest, culminating in the devastating Muslim rebellions of the 1860 and 1870s.

It was therefore within this course of events – the revival of Sufism and its internal theological disputes, the official categorization of Muslims as violent and anti-Qing, and the militarization of northwest China along the border of Mongol territory – that the appearance of the Shambhala myth in Mongol sources needs to be situated. Indeed, at such a time, when tensions were running high and military conflict was under way, it is perhaps understandable that Mongol Buddhists began to draw upon the apocalyptic visions of the *Kālacakratantra*'s Shambhala myth. And, as noted above, one of these Mongols was Jimbadorji, who included descriptions of the Muslim world in his *Crystal Mirror*:

> Outside their territories there is a stone surrounded with three hundred gates. Between each two gates there is, according to their reckoning, 360 miles, according to Chinese reckoning, 720 miles. The King's palace has 24 gates. The tower of the central palace is constructed of gold, and the palaces in the four directions are made of porcelain of four colours ... Every one or two years there is a disastrous wind in that country, and buildings and cities are destroyed. The people are of 12 tribes, with different languages. Gold and silver coins are scattered by the King over men who attain felicity. The people make the lips of their wells, and their water vessels, from gold and silver, and inlay them with all sorts of jewels ... To the south of the people of Küngker is a blue stone known as Mecca, the shrine of the heretics. It is about a eighty centimetres in size. It is fixed in the air, and, for four or five spans all around, nothing touches the ground. Its height is about that of the hand of a man on horseback.
>
> Near it is the temple of the heretics. It is a huge temple, its inner extent being about five or six bow shots. It has not a single pillar or beam, and it is called the great Rangjung temple. Quite some way from that temple is a shrine of the heretics, known as Mahasuri-yin Bilaya. It has a white stone with a hole in it

[38] Lipman, *Familiar Strangers*, pp. 114-15.

> like the human genitals, and it touches nothing either. The fact is that this, too, is fixed in the air by the force of magnetism.[39]

Although this text does have its fantastical elements and residual traces of the *Kālacakratantra*, it also reflects the growing awareness of world geography and international politics ushered in by the eighteenth-century works of Sumba Khenpo and Jikme Linkpa that provide first-hand descriptions not only of Mughal-Ottoman relations but also Mecca and Istanbul.[40] However, even with the growing cosmopolitanism of the mid-Qing period the Mongol view of Islam, especially during the Hui uprisings, still came to be shaped by the anti-Muslim views of the *Kālacakratantra*. As seen again in the work of Jimbadorji:

> As for what is called the land of Mecca, which is on the bank of the Sita river: Mecca is a word that means Muslim. Those La Loo[41] are all Muslims. Now, after the present period, the false beliefs of those Muslims will be disseminated more and more, and the majority of the people in this earthly continent will be Muslim. As for the beliefs of the Muslims: they do not eat the meat of the beasts which have died of themselves. They kill their beasts to the best of their ability according to their false belief, saying that if they cut the throats of the creatures with a razor after having pronounced the dharani of Bismillah their god, they will be delivered.[42]

Thus even with all the other historical realities of the eighteenth and nineteenth centuries the dividing line between the Buddhist and Muslim world continued to be the issue of *ḥalāl*. However, in the course of the Qing's 'war on terror' there was one dissenting view on the nature of Muslims and their foodways.

---

39 BT 367, translation based on Bawden, 'The Wish-Prayer for Shambhala Again', pp. 459-60.

40 See Michael Aris, 'India and the British according to a Tibetan Text of the Later Eighteenth Century', in Per Kvaerne (ed.), *Tibetan Studies: Proceedings of the 6th Seminar of the IATS, Fagernes 1992* (2 vols, Oslo, 1994), vol. 1, pp. 7-25; and Matthew Kapstein, 'Just Where on Jambudvipa are We? New Geographical Knowledge and Old Cosmological Schemes in 18th Century Tibet', in Sheldon Pollack (ed.), *Forms of Knowledge in Early Modern South Asia* (Durham, NC: Duke University Press, forthcoming).

41 The Mongolian 'La Loo' is a transcription of the Tibetan *kla-klo*, which is a translation of the Sanskrit *mleccha*, meaning 'barbarian' and more specifically in Tibet: the Muslims.

42 BT 368, translation based on Bawden, 'The Wish-Prayer for Shambhala Again', p. 465.

INJANNASHI AND THE QUESTION OF ISLAM

Injannashi came from a distinguished noble family that had fallen on hard times.[43] Their businesses, including a coalmine, had collapsed; and in seeking solace Injannashi turned to writing. As well as two novels, he wrote a massive fictionalized account of the life of Genghis Khan which, following the tradition of rewriting the *Hongloumeng* 紅樓夢, tells the tale of the Chinese gentry family of Bei Hou. All these works also include fascinating prefaces that lay out Injannashi's own ideas, including the question of Islam.

Injannashi's initial comments about Muslims are negative. However, his animosity does not arise from the standard repertoire of Buddhist anti-Muslim polemics. Rather, Injannashi is upset by the fact that Muslims are allowed to take the civil service examination while Mongols are not:

> But then, in this Great Qing Empire, regarding those Muslims who submitted to the empire later than the Mongols did, and who did not contribute to the founding of the dynasty as the Mongols did, care is being taken so as not to let the learned among them be neglected by selecting from among them, according to their schooling, persons to employ in ministerial positions. Why are Mongols alone singled out and excluded from this examination system? Therefore, I tried to reason to myself as follows: Is it because the Mongols are so uncouth and stupid that they will never be able to pass the examination, so that no examination system is necessary for them?[44]

To put this critique into context, we need to recall that the civil service exam was the engine of social status creation and maintenance in late imperial China, thus being excluded had grave consequences.[45] For Injannashi this was especially poignant since the central thrust of his work was precisely to advocate educational reform; or at least education for the nobility so that they could retain their status in the changing realities of late nineteenth-century China.[46] Yet, while he does use Muslims as a whipping post in regard to this particular issue, he also looks at Islam in another light, one that is completely at odds with the anti-Muslim tenor of the times.

---

43 For a bibliography of scholarship on Injannashi see Charles R. Bawden, 'A Chinese Source for an Episode in Injanasi's Novel *Nigen Dabqur Asar*', in Karenina Kollmar-Paulenz and Christian Peter (eds), *Tractata Tibetica et Mongolica: Festschrift für Klaus Sagaster zum 65. Geburtstag* (Wiesbaden, 2002), pp. 21-2.

44 John Gombojab Hangin, *Köke Sudur (The Blue Chronicle): A Study of the First Mongolian Historical Novel by Injannasi* (Wiesbaden, 1973), p. 63. Hereafter KS.

45 See Benjamin A. Elman, *A Cultural History of Civil Examinations in Late Imperial China* (Berkeley, 2000).

46 See Johan Elverskog, 'Injannashi, the Anti-Cervantes', in id. (ed.), *Biographies of Eminent Mongol Buddhists* (Sankt Augustin, 2008), pp. 75-98.

Injannashi does this by means of cross-cultural comparison, in particular through the study of ritual. To this end Injannashi begins by comparing various mourning rites, starting with a description from the *Wanbaozhuan*, a popular Chinese encyclopaedia, which records the following:

> There is a small nation by the name Jinwoguo in the environs of the ancient Man nation on an island of the Southern Sea. They make their living by hunting the beasts and birds of their mountains and plains, and sometimes this nation is also referred to as the Manluowu. At times, when the ships and boats of China by dint of wind arrive at their shores, the natives come in hordes and seize those on the ship, kill them and eat their flesh. They make utensils out of human skulls and marrow bones. They curse their parents day and night, hoping they will die sooner. When their parents die, they beat great drums and summon their neighbours to come to feast on the flesh of the dead.[47]

This description was no doubt disturbing for a Chinese reader since what could be worse than actually consuming one's parents?[48] For those steeped in the Confucian world of filial piety this was certainly beyond the pale, and the *Wanbaozhuan* readily confirms, 'they are a nation who knows not of humanity'.

Of course, representing 'the other' as monstrous is nothing new. Indeed, this portrayal of the Jinwoguo in the *Wanbaozhuan*, in particular its fascination with cannibalism, is in many ways no different from many early European accounts of South Sea cultures. Moreover, in much the same way as scholars now analyse the discourses shaping these Victorian anthropological representations in relation to empire, race and the like,[49] Injannashi wanted to elucidate why Chinese scholars presented the Jinwoguo in the way they did?

His rather simple and direct answer was that their prejudices arose out of ignorance and selfishness. He thus takes Chinese scholars to task for not only being unfamiliar with the underlying logic and rationale of this particular mourning rite, but also for operating from a stance of moral superiority. Thus, much as Orsi has questioned how most scholars view the Christian

---

47 KS 95.

48 On the discourses of eating and cannibalism in China see Gang Yue, *The Mouth that Begs: Hunger, Cannibalism, and the Politics of Eating in Modern China* (Durham, 1999). The purported cannibalism practised by South Seas people had a long history in the Chinese historical tradition. So much so in fact that it was not only repeated in the works of Marco Polo and Odoric of Pordenone, but plagiarized verbatim in the wildly popular forgery of John Maundeville (Linda L. Barnes, *Needles, Herbs, Gods, and Ghosts: China, Healing, and the West to 1848* [Cambridge, 2005], p. 31).

49 On the anthropological fascination with cannibalism see Peggy R. Sandave, *Divine Hunger: Cannibalism as a Cultural System* (Cambridge, 1988); Laurence R. Goldman (ed.), *The Anthropology of Cannibalism* (Westport, 1999); Francis Parker et al. (eds), *Cannibalism and the Colonial World* (Cambridge, 2004); Gananath Obeyesekere, *Cannibal Talk: The Man-Eating Myth and Human Sacrifice in the South Seas* (Berkeley, 2005).

snakehandlers of the American south,[50] Injannashi does the same with Chinese scholars:

> Some learned ones believe that only the Middle Kingdom is the kingdom of heaven, and that it alone possesses humanity. They believe this land alone receives the major benefits of sun and moon, and this land alone gives birth to intellects and wise ones, great minds and scholars. They not only explain all the rest to be strange, alien, perverse and evil, peculiar and queer, they even believe this to be true in their hearts.[51]

He then goes on to puncture this image of superiority by humorously pointing out the absurdity of Chinese scholars, who for 3,000 years claimed to be at the centre of civilization, and yet for all that time continued to miscalculate solar and lunar eclipses. A mistake that Injannashi points out with relish was only rectified with the arrival of the Belgian Jesuit Ferdinand Verbiest at the Kangxi emperor's court in the seventeenth century.

To drive his point home Injannashi continues his critique of misrepresenting 'the other' by discussing Mongol and Tibetan burial rites. He thus imagines how a Chinese person may misunderstand a Mongolian cremation as an act of vengeance against one's parents since lamas wave swords and spears over a burning corpse:

> Suppose those Chinese from the interior who inter their parents in gold and jade should witness a Mongol cremation, since they do not know the reason, they will likewise say the same thing as about the people of Jinwoguo. They will say that the Mongols, having cursed their parents to death, not only burn their dead, but call upon those red and yellow robed, queue-less,[52] bald and shaven people and make them wield sword and spear over the dead and pour oils over the dead to inflame the fire, whereby they take vengeance upon their dead parents. They certainly will not believe that actually it is a rite to offer the flesh of the dead for the Buddha to partake of it, thereby making them Buddhas.[53]

---

50 Robert Orsi, *Between Heaven and Earth: The Religious Worlds People Make and the Scholars who Study them* (Princeton, 2005), pp. 177-203 ('Snakes Alive: Religious Studies between Heaven and Earth').

51 KS 96.

52 On the importance of the queue in Qing society, see Phillip Kuhn, *Soulstealers: The Chinese Sorcery Scare of 1768* (Cambridge, 1990); and Weikun Cheng, 'Politics of the Queue: Agitation and Resistance in the Beginning and End of Qing China', in Alf Hiltebeitel and Barbara Miller (eds), *Hair: Its Power and Meaning in Asian Cultures* (Albany, 1998), pp. 123-42.

53 KS 98.

Injannashi thus returns to his central theme of needing to understand the rationale behind the ritual. One cannot simply look at the external practice, one must elucidate the internal logic.

To this end Injannashi turns to the Tibetan sky burial which, much like cannibalism, has been fetishized in both the East and West. Yet rather than exoticizing or condemning this practice he explains the reason behind this rite. He claims that in the Tibetan view vultures are sacred Dharma protectors and by consuming the flesh of a corpse the sins of the deceased are cleansed and thus the soul will find a good incarnation. Moreover, he makes the same assertion about the Jinwoguo and their funeral cannibalism:

> Even those people of Jinwoguo, because of their great population and lack of land and having no domesticated animals, have long since known the taste of human flesh. Therefore when a parent dies, they will call upon their tribes and members of their family to have a great feast, thereby obtaining the merit of making satiated the great hunger of many, and the soul of the dead will go to heaven. To sum it up, all of them possess a kind of mourning rite.[54]

In this way Injannashi not only explains the rationale behind the seemingly bizarre ritual of parental cannibalism, but also validates the humanity of the Jinwoguo. As he declares, 'even those who devour the flesh of their parents possess justice and goodness. Such being the case, can any teaching be without just principle?'[55]

This notion is indeed part of Injannashi's central argument: any teaching, or religion, must by definition be premised on goodness. His argument is clearly based on Confucian precedent, especially Mencius;[56] however, Injannashi takes the traditional Confucian view of inherent human goodness and the value of ritual for instilling and nurturing positive values in a new direction by putting it in a comparative context. It is thus not only Confucian mourning rites that are proper, but all mourning rites are valid since inherently they too are premised on human goodness. In Injannashi's view the reason for this is that a religion would not have followers if that were not the case:

> I think the founder of a religion cannot profit ... [if he] devises a new evil doctrine. What would he gain by it? I think each of these teachings has its good points and never intended to be evil. Only that we know not the fine details of these teachings and theories and true characters, and we believe them to be unacceptable and wrong. Naturally, the founder of a religion cannot say

54 KS 99.

55 KS 99.

56 For an excellent interpretation of Mencius, see Edward Slingerland, *Effortless Action: Wu-wei as Conceptual Metaphor and Spiritual Ideal in Early China* (Oxford, 2003), pp. 131-73.

> 'My religion is no good; my religion is wrong; the other teachings are right; you all follow them; leave my religion; don't follow my religion; do not study my religion.' Since it is being called a teaching, it is founded for the purpose of teaching people. It simply cannot be evil ...[57]

Thus as any contemporary introductory textbook on world religions will maintain: all religions have value, we simply need to understand them.[58]

Or as Injannashi writes: 'is it not simply that customs appear to differ in each place and their concept seems to be strange to each other, but the aims are all the same?'[59] Thus all religions and their rites, no matter how difficult to understand from an outsider's perspective, actually derive out of human goodness and should therefore be tolerated:

> Even the peculiarities of the Muslims, and the customs of the Jinwoguo have their righteousness and goodness ... Since all of them are for the good of men, how could there be wrong and malice? I have even talked to some of those learned among the European and Muslim devils, and found they too speak of the cultivation of virtues and self-control. Certainly they do not teach the harming of others with selfishness.[60]

Yet it is not only on the phenomenological level that Injannashi's work parallels the modern study of religion, he also premises his analysis on the ground of scepticism. As he explains on whether he was to include 'matters of gods and demons and strange magic and sorcery' in his work he proclaims that 'since I was born, [I have] never believed in such matters of which there is no proof nor matters which are not in congruence with logic and laws [of nature]'.[61] Yet even so, he decided to include them since people believed in them in the past; however, he hopes that 'future readers of this work will not think of me as they do of mendacious lamas'.[62]

Thus, having established his theoretical paradigm, Injannashi finally turns to the volatile issue of Muslim foodways. He writes:

> Even those Muslim butchers of sheep and cows, not able to bear simply killing sheep and cows for meat, perform some kind of ritual to direct the souls of the slaughtered animals to heaven, and offer prayers and bless their knives before they proceed to kill. They may not be able to dispatch the slaughtered souls

57 KS 97.

58 On the historical development of the comparative study of religion see, for example, Eric J. Sharpe, *Comparative Religion: A History* (London, ^{2}1986).

59 KS 99.

60 KS 99, 100.

61 KS 75-6.

62 KS 76.

> to heaven, but if you compare the present day Chinese and Mongols who simply butcher their animals without any kind of ritual, for meat and profit, those Muslims certainly have good hearts. Those not informed often simply follow the crowd by custom and defame the Muslims as having an animal origin, and say that they adhere to evil teaching and false doctrine. Alas, how unjust this is![63]

By means of his sceptical phenomenological approach Injannashi is thus able to challenge nearly a millennium of Buddhist polemics against Islam and argue that *ḥalāl* practices actually derive out of human goodness.

To confirm this point he concludes by comparing *ḥalāl* butchering practices with the Tibetan Buddhist practice of praying for rebirth in Buddha Amitābha's paradise.[64] Namely, even though both religious specialists 'are not sure whether they are able to commit the soul as they hope, they certainly do not believe that they are committing the soul to hell instead. The intentions are the same in both cases, except the difference that one [=animal] is killed and the other [=human] died naturally.'[65] Injannashi thus reaffirms his main thesis based on Confucian theories of humanity that all religions and rituals actually derive out of human goodness. 'They all seek the best according to their own custom. The outer aspects may differ but the thought behind them are the same'. In this way Injannashi is finally able to argue that the intentions of both Muslims and Buddhists are inherently the same thereby overcoming the problem of 'prejudice'.

CONCLUSION

A final question to ponder is invariably whether Injannashi's intellectual project actually resolves the problem of prejudice, or whether we should even take his moral argument seriously? Indeed, does Injannashi offer us any guidance in the current conflagrations related to a new Muslim revival, or how Europe should grapple with Muslim immigration? To some this suggestion may seem odd, and that itself reflects a lingering prejudice, yet it is no doubt a valid question, one that goes to the heart of much recent scholarship related to the issues of

---

63 KS 96-7.

64 On the worship of Amitābha in Tibet, see Matthew T. Kapstein, 'Pure Land Buddhism in Tibet?', in Richard Payne and Kenneth Tanaka (eds), *Approaching the Land of Bliss: Religious Praxis in the Cult of Amitābha* (Honolulu, 2004), pp. 16-41; Georgios Halkias, 'Pure-Lands and Other Visions in Seventeenth-Century Tibet: A Gnam-chos sādhana for the Pure-Land Sukhāvatī Revealed in 1658 by Gnam-chos Mi-'gyur-rdo-rje (1645-1667)', in Bryan J. Cuevas and Kurtis R. Schaeffer (eds), *Power, Politics and the Reinvention of Tradition: Tibet in the Seventeenth and Eighteenth Century* (Leiden, 2006), pp. 121-51.

65 KS 97.

representing the other as well as giving voice to 'the native'. Even so, whether or not Injannashi's argument can begin to address the problems and moral quandaries of the contemporary world is far beyond the scope of this article.

Another question that can be answered, however, is whether or not Injannashi's work had any impact in his own day. The answer is no. Up through the Republican period Tibetan and Mongol Buddhists continued to draw upon the deep reservoir of anti-Muslim sentiment, albeit within new theoretical frameworks such as the nation-state.[66] This, however, is not to diminish Injannashi's work. Rather it is to point out that the value of his work lies precisely in that he was willing to challenge conventional wisdom. Thus even though his comparison of mourning rites was nothing new, edicts of the Kangxi emperor in the seventeenth century had said much the same thing,[67] but that he did so at this particular moment in time is what makes it important. Others were not doing so and that gives Injannashi's work value beyond its interesting Confucian theorizing and his sceptical discourse analysis. While it is therefore important to situate Injannashi among the increasingly 'modern' and 'secular' intellectuals of the late Qing period,[68] it is also vital to recall that on the issue of Islam he was a lone voice, and much like Edward Said a century later, he challenged the very foundations of imperial Orientalism.

---

[66] Gray Tuttle, *Tibetan Buddhists in the Making of Modern China* (New York, 2005), pp. 143-4.

[67] According to Saghang Sechen's *Precious Summary* (*Erdeni-yin tobci*), when the Kangxi emperor was conducting the funeral rites for his father in 1662 'he handed down a decree which promulgated mourning to the peoples of whatsoever direction each according to his own customs'. See Saang Secen, *Erdeni-yin Tobci ("Precious Summary"): A Mongolian Chronicle of 1662*, vol. 1, ed. Minoru Go et al. (Canberra, 1990), 96r.

[68] For the history of the Mongol intelligentsia, see Christopher P. Atwood, *Young Mongols and Vigilantes in Inner Mongolia's Interregnum Decades, 1911-1931* (Leiden, 2002).

Chapter 16
Trader, Middleman or Spy? The Dilemmas of a Kashmiri Muslim in Early Nineteenth-Century Tibet

John Bray

In September 1814 William Moorcroft (1770-1825), the East India Company veterinary surgeon and explorer, reported a meeting with Khwajah Ahmed Ali, the Patna representative of a Kashmiri commercial house with agents and depots in Dhaka, Kathmandu, Lhasa and Xining as well as Kashmir itself.[1] The topics that they discussed were highly sensitive. The Company had recently declared war on the Gorkha rulers of Nepal, and Ahmed Ali was a potential source of vital information on the most viable military and transport routes between the Nepal border and Kathmandu. He seemed willing to share this information in the hope of future reward, but at the same time was afraid of reprisals from the Nepalis and even from his fellow Kashmiris.

As it turned out, Moorcroft's meeting was the first in a series of encounters between Ahmed Ali and British officials. Like a classic three-act play, the story falls into three distinct episodes, each of which has its own set of files in the British records. In Act One, between September and November 1814, Ahmed Ali offers his services as a source of wartime intelligence. In Act Two, which takes place between September 1815 and October 1816, Moorcroft proposes Ahmed Ali as a potential British commercial agent in Lhasa, but the arrangement ultimately falls through. The denouement in Act Three begins to unfold in March 1831 when Brian Houghton Hodgson (1800-1894), the Acting Resident in Kathmandu,

[1] Memorandum by Moorcroft, 15 September 1814. *Papers Respecting the Nepaul War*, Printed in conformity to the resolution of the Court of Proprietors of East India Stock of 3rd March 1824 (London), pp. 85-6. A manuscript version of the same record is to be found in the British Library Oriental and India Office Collection (OIOC), H/645, pp. 79-88. On Moorcroft see Garry Alder, *Beyond Bokhara: The Life of William Moorcroft* (London, 1985).

In this initial memorandum Moorcroft refers to his visitor as 'the Cashmeree', but subsequent archival records – clearly concerning the same person – refer to him by name and title. There are many variant spellings: I use 'Ahmed Ali' throughout, but reproduce the original spellings in the quotations. 'Khwajah' is a Persian/Urdu word literally meaning 'lord' or 'master', and widely used as a title by Kashmiri Muslims. It is also used as the family name of one of the most prominent Muslim families in Ladakh.

receives a desperate appeal from Ahmed Ali who has now been imprisoned in Lhasa on charges of being a British spy.

Ahmed Ali's story concerns the life and personal dilemmas of a particular individual. However, it also serves as an illustration of the wider role played by the Kashmiri merchants who travelled between northern India, Nepal, Tibet and western China between the seventeenth and early twentieth centuries. Trade and a number of specialist crafts provided their prime sources of livelihood. However, since they were one of the few communities with extensive family and commercial networks on both sides of the Himalaya, they also served as important sources of knowledge for all the parties with whom they dealt, and even as diplomatic go-betweens. In the best case, they became trusted intermediaries, honoured, respected and rewarded by all sides. In the worst case, they risked denunciation as untrustworthy outsiders, and even as spies.

The British records show that Ahmed Ali was always acutely conscious of the risks and opportunities that came with his middleman status, and was forever calculating how to use his position – and, above all, his sources of information – to best advantage. This article reviews his calculations as a means of shedding light on the history of the wider Kashmiri community in the region. Continuing with the theatrical metaphor, it sets the scene with a 'prologue' reviewing the earlier history of the Kashmiri merchants' international network, before embarking on a more detailed discussion of Ahmed Ali's personal three-act drama and its wider implications.

PROLOGUE: A COMMUNITY OF GO-BETWEENS

The Kashmiri Muslim merchant community had begun its expansion into Ladakh, Central Tibet, Turkestan (now Xinjiang) and as far as north-west China by the late sixteenth and early seventeenth centuries, if not earlier.[2] In all these regions, representatives of the leading merchant families established permanent bases and married local women, thus establishing kinship networks that extended across the entire region. However, despite these strong local connections, they retained their Muslim identity as well as their affiliation with the wider world of Islamic learning. The Persian language remained a critically important medium of communication linking a wide range of cities in or bordering on Central Asia including – in due course – the commercial thoroughfares of British India.

---

[2] In the same period merchants from Multan were extending similar networks across Afghanistan, Iran, Turan and even as far as European Russia. See Stephen Frederic Dale, *Indian Merchants and Eurasian Trade 1600-1750* (Cambridge, 1994). For a broader discussion of early modern South and South-East Asian trading networks see Denys Lombard and Jean Aubin (eds), *Asian Merchants and Businessmen in the Indian Ocean and the China Sea* (New Delhi, 2000). This includes an essay on Kashmiri Muslims by Marc Gaborieau.

According to oral tradition, the Kashmiri merchant presence in Ladakh dates back to the turn of the sixteenth and seventeenth century when King Jamyang Namgyal ('Jam-dbyangs rnam-rgyal – reg. *c.*1595-1616) offered land to a select group of traders known as *mkhar tshong pa* or 'palace traders', encouraging them to settle permanently in Leh.[3] The *mkhar tshong pa* enjoyed special privileges in the wool trade between Western Tibet via Ladakh to Kashmir. Many married local women: their mixed-race descendants are known as Argons, and are an important constituent of the local population in Leh to this day.[4] In addition to their commercial acumen, many Kashmiri settlers had other specialist skills. For example, the founder of the Zergar family in Ladakh was invited to Leh to strike coins.[5] Similarly, it is said that the Ladakhi kings invited the Khwajah family to assist with their Persian-language correspondence with the Mughal governors of Kashmir.[6]

The origins of the Kha-che or Kashmiri Muslim community in Lhasa appear to be similar. Prince Peter of Greece and Denmark writes that the first arrivals were almost certainly traders.[7] However, he also notes theories suggesting that the Fifth Dalai Lama applied to the Mughal Emperor for advisors, or that he caused Muslims to come to Lhasa in a 'purely representative capacity' so that he could show that people from the whole world attended his *levées*. The Kha-che traditions cited by Marc Gaborieau link the foundation stories of the Lhasa community with Khair-ud-Din, a Muslim saint who had come from Patna – Ahmed Ali's home town – in the mid-seventeenth century and, according to one version, secretly converted the Fifth Dalai Lama to Islam.[8]

A notable example of the way in which leading Kha-che families combined commercial and semi-diplomatic roles concerns the triennial *lo-phyag* mission from Leh to Lhasa, which was set up under the terms of the 1684 Treaty of

---

3 Abdul Ghani Sheikh, 'A Brief History of Muslims in Ladakh', in Henry Osmaston and Philip Denwood (eds), *Recent Research on Ladakh 4 & 5* (London, 1995), pp. 189-92, at p. 190.

4 For nineteenth- and early twentieth-century perspectives on the Argons' trading networks see in particular Janet Rizvi, *Trans-Himalayan Caravans: Merchant Princes and Peasant Traders in Ladakh* (New Delhi, 1999); Jacqueline Fewkes and Abdul Nasir Khan, 'Social Networks and Transnational Trade in Early 20th Century Ladakh', in John Bray (ed.), *Ladakhi Histories: Local and Regional Perspectives* (Leiden, 2005), pp. 321-34.

5 Sheikh, 'A Brief History', p. 190. See also Luciano Petech, *The Kingdom of Ladakh c. 950-1842 A.D.* (Rome, 1977), p. 117.

6 Sheikh, 'A Brief History', p. 190.

7 Prince Peter of Greece and Denmark, 'The Moslems of Central Tibet', *Journal of the Royal Central Asian Society*, 39 (1952): pp. 233-40, at p. 238.

8 Marc Gaborieau, *Récit d'un voyageur musulman au Tibet* (Paris, 1973), pp. 17-18; id., 'Pouvoirs et autorité des Soufis dans l'Himalaya', in Thierry Zarcone (ed.), *Musulmans et Soufis du Tibet* (Milan, 2005), pp. 27-33, and Gaborieau in this volume.

Temisgang (gTing-mo-sgang) between Ladakh and Tibet.[9] The mission combined trade with the offering of a prescribed set of ceremonial gifts to the Dalai Lama. The ceremonial head of the mission was always a Buddhist, but by the early twentieth century – and possibly much earlier – the Khwajah family had assumed responsibility for organizing and actually managing the mission. It was particularly well placed to do so because of its kinship networks in both Ladakh and Tibet and, for that matter, in Turkestan.

The Kashmiris' international connections and bilingual skills in Persian and Tibetan meant that they were well equipped to assist pioneer Western travellers in the region.[10] The Italian Capuchin missionaries, who first arrived in Lhasa in 1707, received welcome assistance initially from Armenian merchants and subsequently from their Kashmiri counterparts.[11] For example, in the 1720s a Kashmiri named Iusuf helped transmit funds from Rome on the last stage across the Himalayas to the Capuchins in Lhasa.[12] Similarly, when the two Jesuits Ippolito Desideri and Manoel Freyre travelled from Kashmir via Ladakh to Central Tibet in 1715-16, they took with them a Muslim Persian-speaking interpreter. While still in Ladakh, they met a Kashmiri coming from Rudok. In an apparent reference to the Capuchins in Lhasa, he told them that he had been to Central Tibet and that he had seen 'certain poor men wearing shaggy woollen capes and felt caps which hung down in the back, who were distributing many kinds of medicine to the people, and he knew for certain that they were Europeans'.[13]

In 1775 George Bogle (1747-81) visited the court of the Third Panchen Lama in Tashi Lhunpo as an emissary from the British Governor-general Warren Hastings. Hastings believed that the capture of the Kathmandu valley by Gorkha ruler Prithvi Narayan Shah had disrupted an important trade route between northern India and Tibet, and he hoped to establish or strengthen new commercial connections via Bhutan. Bogle found that the Kashmiris were well established in the region:

---

9 On the *lo-phyag* mission see in particular Roger Lloyd Kennion, 'The Lapchak', in id., *Sport and Life in the Further Himalaya* (Edinburgh, 1910), pp. 241-61; Abdul Wahid Radhu, *Caravane tibétaine* (Paris, 1981); John Bray, 'The Lapchak Mission from Leh to Lhasa in British Indian Foreign Policy', *Tibet Journal*, 15/4 (1990): pp. 75-96.

10 See Marc Gaborieau's article in this volume.

11 On the Armenian connection see Hugh Richardson, 'Armenians in India and Tibet', *Journal of the Tibet Society*, 1 (1981): pp. 63-7, repr. in *High Peaks: Pure Earth*, ed. Michael Aris (London, 1998), pp. 462-7. Armenian trading activities between northern India and Tibet paralleled those of the Kashmiris, but appear to have faded by the late eighteenth century.

12 Adelhelm Jann, 'Zur Kulturarbeit der katholischen Kirche in Innerasien', in Leo Helbling (ed.), *Studien aus dem Gebiete von Kirche and Kultur: Festschrift Gustav Schnürer* (Paderborn, 1930), pp. 128-207, at p. 147.

13 Michael J. Sweet, 'Desperately Seeking Capuchins: Manoel Freyre's Report on the Tibets and their Routes (Tibetorum ac eorum Relatio Viarum) and the Desideri Mission to Tibet', *Journal of the International Association of Tibetan Studies*, 2/2 (August 2006) [www.thdl.org?id=T2722]: pp. 1-33, at p. 17.

> The Kashmiris settled in Tibet are mostly the offspring of Tibetans, a sixth or eighth part only being natives of Kashmir. They have been long settled in this country and from the wealth which they acquire from their extensive commerce form a very respectable, though not very numerous body.[14]

Apparently the Kashmiris and the Gosains[15] enjoyed a comparative advantage in the Trans-Himalayan trade since Tibetan merchants felt unable to travel to India on account of the climate:

> They [the Tibetan merchants] said that being born in a cold country they were afraid of going into a hot one; that their people would die in Bengal; that they had heard from tradition that about eight hundred years ago the people of this country used to travel into Bengal, but that eight out of ten died before their return; that the Kashmiris and Gosains travelled into different countries, but that they could not.[16]

In addition to their trading activities, the Kashmiris also served in diplomatic roles. For example, in 1780 Bogle wrote that the Panchen Lama's court in Tashi Lhunpo included a *munshi* (secretary/interpreter), who was able to translate letters into Persian for onward transmission to the British.[17] Similarly, in 1789 the Regent in Tashi Lhunpo chose two Kashmiris, Mohammed Rajeb and Mohammed Wali, to carry letters to Calcutta for the Governor-general Lord Cornwallis.[18] The Kashmiris performed similar services for the British. For example in November 1792 Abdul Kadir Khan, who was serving as a British agent in Kathmandu, recommended that the British employ a Kashmiri named Sulaiman, who knew Chinese, Tibetan and Nepali, as a Tibetan translator.[19]

---

[14] George Bogle, 'Political and Ethnographical Notes on Tibet and Other Parts of Asia', in Alastair Lamb (ed.), *Bhutan and Tibet: The Travels of George Bogle and Alexander Hamilton. 1774-1777* (Hertingfordbury, 2002), p. 287.

[15] The Gosains were Indian religious devotees who combined pilgrimage with trade across northern India and the Himalayan region. Bogle himself received extensive assistance and guidance from a highly talented Gosain named Purangir. However, their influence in Tibet seems to have declined in the late eighteenth century, possibly because they were perceived to be too close to the British. On the wider regional background of the Gosains see Bernard S. Cohn, 'The Role of the Gosains in the Economy of Eighteenth and Nineteenth Century Upper India', *Indian Economic and Social History Review*, 1 (1963-64): pp. 175-82.

[16] Lamb, *Bhutan and Tibet*, p. 260.

[17] Bogle to Hastings, Rangpur, 30 September 1780. In Lamb, *Bhutan and Tibet*, p. 444.

[18] Lamb, *Bhutan and Tibet*, p. 470.

[19] Abdul Kadir Khan, 17 November 1792. Cited in Isrun Engelhardt, 'The Closing of the Gates: Tibetan-European Relations at the End of the Eighteenth Century', in Henk Blezer (ed.), *Tibet: Past and Present* (Leiden, 2002), p. 238, n. 33. Abdul Kadir Khan was a Shiite Muslim from Benares. On his background see Christopher Alan Bayly, *Empire and*

The context of the Tibetan exchanges with the British in 1789 and 1792 was a series of conflicts between Nepal and Tibet.[20] The eventual outcome of these conflicts was the consolidation of Manchu authority over Tibet, exercised through two Ambans (commissioners) in Lhasa, and this in turn meant that the country was barred to Europeans even more effectively than before. However, Kashmiri merchants continued to trade on both sides of the Himalaya, and therefore remained one of the prime sources of information on Tibet that was still available to the British in northern India.

An early nineteenth-century illustration of the Kashmiris' role as a source of British knowledge comes from Walter Hamilton's *East India Gazetteer* where the entry on Tibet draws heavily on details provided by 'Abdul Russool, a Cashmerian merchant of Lassa' who had evidently been in contact with Norman MacLeod, a British official based in Cooch Behar in around 1816. Abdul Russool is cited as a source of information on gold mines, imports and exports and taxes. Speaking of his own community, he reported:

> The natives of Cashmere established with their families at Lassa are computed at 150 persons, who carry on a considerable trade between that capital and their native country, from which they import shawls, numdee, a very thick woollen cloth, saffron and dried fruit. The exports to Cashmere are silver bullion, and tea, of which last article to the value of 1,50,000 rupees is annually exported from Lassa to Cashmere.[21]

One final contemporary illustration of the importance of Kashmir and the Persian language as an entry point for Western studies of Tibet comes from the career of the Hungarian linguist Alexander Csoma de Kőrös (1784-1842). Csoma was inspired to take up the study of Tibetan following a meeting with Moorcroft in Ladakh in 1822. In a letter written in 1825, Csoma reports that he owed his first lessons in the language to the conversation and instruction of an unnamed 'intelligent person' in Ladakh – almost certainly a Muslim of Kashmiri origin – 'who was well acquainted with the Tibetan and Persian languages'.[22] Those early lessons culminated in Csoma's groundbreaking *Essay Towards a Dictionary, Tibetan and English* (1834).[23]

Information: Intelligence Gathering and Social Communication in India, 1780-1870 (Cambridge, 1996), pp. 82-3. It was a reference in Bayly's work (p. 108) that first set me on the trail of Ahmed Ali, and I gratefully acknowledge this source of inspiration.

[20] For a more detailed discussion of these events see Alastair Lamb, *British India and Tibet, 1766-1910* (London, ²1986); id., *Bhutan and Tibet*; Englehardt, 'The Closing of the Gates'.

[21] Walter Hamilton, *The East India Gazetteer; Containing Particular Descriptions of ... Hindostan, and the Adjacent Countries ...* (London, ²1828), vol. 2, p. 643.

[22] Csoma to Captain Kennedy, 28 January 1824. Reproduced in Peter Marczell, *Alexander Csoma de Kőrös*, vol. 2 *British-Indian Source Documents* (Kolkata, 2007), p. 56.

[23] Alexander Csoma de Kőrös, *Essay towards a Dictionary: Tibetan and English*, Prepared with the Assistance of Sangs-rgyas phun-tshogs (Calcutta, 1834). There is now an extensive literature on Csoma, starting with Theodore Duka, *Life and Works of Alexander*

ACT ONE: AN OFFER OF INTELLIGENCE

At the outbreak of the war with Nepal in 1814, the East India Company found itself facing a shortage of intelligence in two critical respects:[24]

- The first was local and tactical. Few Westerners had travelled in Nepal and, as a matter of state security, the Gorkhas had prevented them from acquiring detailed information on the various alternative routes into the country, and their military defences.
- The second was regional and strategic. Since its military victory over Nepal in 1792, China regarded Nepal as – at least loosely – a subordinate state. Lord Hastings, the Governor-general, was uncertain of China's intentions and wished to ensure that the Emperor did not intervene on Nepal's behalf, or take reprisals against emerging British interests in Canton.

Against this background, the British struggled to muster whatever sources of intelligence they possessed, and Moorcroft proved an eager volunteer. Moorcroft's official role was to manage the Company's stud, an important responsibility in an era when armies were still heavily dependent on horsepower (and, in India, the odd elephant). However, in 1812 he had already undertaken a covert journey across Gorkha-ruled Kumaon and Garhwal into Western Tibet, thus demonstrating a characteristic taste for intrigue combined with an irrepressible enthusiasm for new discoveries.[25] Now he scoured his extensive list of personal contacts for possible intelligence sources. Potential candidates included Francis Neville, the son of a French father and a Newari mother who had been born in the Kathmandu valley; the Gosains ('faqueers'), whom he praises for their powers of observation; a Mishur horse-dealer; and – as discussed in

---

Csoma de Kőrös (London, 1885). See also József Térjek, *Alexander Csoma de Kőrös 1784-1842: A Short Biography* (Budapest, 1984).

[24] For the wider political background to the war see Lamb, *British India and Tibet*, pp. 26-42; Ludwig Stiller, *The Rise of the House of Gorkha* (Kathmandu, [2]1995), pp. 283-90. Contemporary accounts of the war include Henry Thoby Prinsep, *History of the Political and Military Transactions in India during the Administration of the Marquess of Hastings 1813-1823* (London, 1825); and the official publication *Papers Respecting the Nepaul War* (1824). John Pemble gives a detailed account of the military conduct of the war in *The Invasion of Nepal: John Company at War* (Oxford, 1971). Christopher A. Bayly offers a brilliant analysis of how the British in India managed – and failed to manage – their various sources of intelligence in his *Empire and Information*.

[25] Moorcroft gave his own account of the journey in 'A Journey to Lake Mánasaróvara in Ún-dés, a Province of Little Tibet', *Asiatick Researches*, 12 (1816): pp. 375-534. See also Alder, *Beyond Bokhara*, pp. 135-78.

the memorandum of 14 September – Ahmed Ali.[26] In introducing him, Moorcroft himself played the role of a middleman, speaking enthusiastically of Ahmed Ali's qualities, but at the same time distancing himself in case his information turned out to be unsatisfactory.

Moorcroft described Ahmed Ali's background in the opening paragraphs of the memorandum, which was addressed to John Adam, secretary to the government's Political and Secret Department. It seems that he belonged to a Kashmiri commercial house which had been established in Patna some two centuries previously, and had representatives in Kashmir, Nepal, Lhasa, Xining and Dhaka.[27] Its principal business in Patna was to collect otter skins through a network of agents in Dhaka and its neighbourhood, and to despatch these via Nepal to Tibet and China in return for gold.[28] Moorcroft had long been in contact with him because of his own interest in spreading the practice of vaccination in 'Hither China'.

Now Ahmed Ali had approached him bewailing his current misfortunes. The war would disrupt communications with Nepal and Tibet, thus preventing him from receiving money that he was owed, and causing financial embarrassment in India. A further problem, as he explained a week later, was that a 'great body of furs prepared for the China market remained on his hands', and he feared that they might be damaged by the delay caused by the conflict.[29] The war therefore presented him with a series of dilemmas. As Moorcroft puts it:

> This man balances between the two interests. He fears for his property in Nepaul; and he fears losing his connection there, should the British arms not be successful, and it were discovered that he had been in any respect active. Whether it would be worthwhile to secure such a man as this, by the promise of his property being respected, or by anything else, you are a better judge than myself.[30]

Already at the first meeting, Ahmed Ali had interesting intelligence to report. According to his agent in Tibet, the Raja of Nepal had sent a letter to the 'principal Chinese Tajun [Amban] residing at Lassa' a year previously, and asked him to forward a second letter to the Emperor of China requesting assistance in the likely event of war between Nepal and the British. Moorcroft duly passed on

---

26 Moorcroft to John Adam, Hajipur, 11 September and 14 September 1814, *Papers Respecting the Nepaul War*, pp. 82-6.

27 Moorcroft memorandum, 14 September 1814, *Papers Respecting the Nepaul War*, p. 85.

28 To the Silk Route and the Musk Route of contemporary historiography must now be added the Otter-skin Route.

29 Moorcroft to Adam, 23 September 1814, *Papers Respecting the Nepaul War*, pp. 86-8.

30 Memorandum by Moorcroft, 15 September 1814, *Papers Respecting the Nepaul War*, p. 85.

this information, but with the qualification that he had no means of ascertaining whether it were true or false, since 'the Cashmeereans are convenient agents in all kinds of chicane'.

At the second meeting a week later, Ahmed Ali made clear – apparently after some hesitation – that 'he wished for some remuneration for the loss he contemplated or, in fact to be paid, under some other name, for the information he might furnish'.[31] He now had two main items of intelligence to offer. The first was to give more details than the British then possessed on the roads from the Nepal border to Kathmandu, and he summarized this in an accompanying note. The second concerned the source of his information on the letter from Nepal to the Chinese Emperor. In response to Moorcroft's observation that it was unlikely that a foreigner residing in Lhasa for commercial purposes should be acquainted with important political events, Ahmed Ali replied that:

> ... the [commercial] house having been established for near two centuries at Lassa, its members were considered as domiciliated or naturalized, and were held in such high respect by the [Dalai] Lama, as always to be presented with tea by the hand of the Pontiff himself when they visited his durbar, to which they had free access.
>
> Being the channel of much beneficial commerce, and enjoying much consideration also with the Chinese Tajaas, the resident Cashmeerees have abundant opportunities of becoming acquainted with every circumstance which may importantly affect the interest of the neighbouring countries.[32]

Moorcroft nevertheless retained his suspicions of Ahmed Ali's honesty and reported that:

> I examined the countenance, gesture, voice, and general demeanour of the deponent, with great attention, during the whole of our conversation, but discovered nothing, save what was naturally deducible from a struggle between hope and fear.[33]

At a third meeting, Ahmed Ali produced the letter from Lhasa to which he had referred.[34] The letter and its contents were of 'such Sitburrooa Nepaul paper as is common both in Nepaul and Tibet' and, at least to outward appearances, Moorcroft judged it to be authentic. Ahmed Ali refused to allow Moorcroft's munshi to see any portion of it, but allowed Moorcroft himself to read the key

---

31 Moorcroft to Adam, 23 September 1814, *Papers Respecting the Nepaul War*, p. 87.

32 Ibid., p. 88.

33 Ibid., p. 87.

34 Moorcroft to Adam, 8 October 1814, *Papers Respecting the Nepaul War*, pp. 91-2.

extract concerning the Emperor of China, and to make a copy. Translated from the Persian, the extract read:

> Further it has been heard from the Great Tajim of Lassa, that the Rajah of Nepaul made three requests to the Emperor. 1st. That the mundermullee [currency] of Nepaul should pass current in Lhasa as formerly.[35] 2d. That the Emperor should permit a passage for the Rajah's troops to Asham. 3d. That the Emperor should assist him with men and treasure to wage war against the Feringees.
>
> The Emperor declared that he would assist the Rajah with men and treasure, to the extent which might be required: he also agreed to the passage of the Rajah's troops to Asham. The Emperor wrote in the most encouraging terms to the Rajah, but refused to admit of the circulation of the mundermulee.[36]

The official correspondence on Ahmed Ali continued into November 1814. On 3 November Moorcroft wrote that he had requested Mr H. Douglas, a British official based in Patna, to ascertain whether Ahmed Ali or his servants might be able to provide information on the roads leading from the Nepal border to Kathmandu.[37] Douglas evidently interviewed Ahmed Ali in public and, because he did not wish his connection with the British to be made known, he had replied in the negative. As Moorcroft wrote:

> It appeared that through fear of his Connection with me being made known to other Kashmeerean Merchants or to Nepalees Khojah Uhmed Ulee when interrogated in Court by Mr Douglas, as to having people in his service capable of acting as interpreters in Nipaul thought himself prudentially obliged to answer in the negative.[38]

---

35 There had been a longstanding dispute between Nepal and Tibet concerning the quality of silver in Nepali rupees circulating in Tibet. The Nepali coinage was started by King Mahendra Malla of Kathmandu (1560-74), and the main silver coin was therefore known as the *mahendramalli*. See Schuyler Camman, *Trade Through the Himalayas* (Westport, 1970 [1st ed. 1950]), pp. 108-11; Vijay Kumar Manandhar, *A Comprehensive History of Nepal-China Relations up to 1955 A.D.* (New Delhi, 2004), p. 72. In October 1815, the mint-master was asked to strike coins for Tibet. See Nicholas G. Rhodes, Karl Gabrisch and Carlo Valderetto, *The Coinage of Nepal from the Earliest Times until 1911* (London, 1989), p. 206.

36 *Papers Respecting the Nepaul War*, p. 92. Subsequent intelligence confirmed that the Raja of Nepal had written to the Emperor, a point that obviously was of crucial importance to the British. However, contrary to British fears, the Chinese sent neither money nor troops to support the Nepalis against the Company.

37 Moorcroft to Adam, Gamakhun, 8 November 1814. OIOC. H/646, pp. 623-6.

38 Moorcroft to Adam, Anah, 22 November 1814, OIOC. H/647. p. 107. Underlining in the original.

In subsequent negotiations, Ahmed Ali dwelt not only on the prospect of financial reward bestowed by the British government on persons who had been politically serviceable, but also 'the rank and credit they enjoyed in society'.[39] Ultimately, Moorcroft was persuaded that Ahmed Ali did have the 'power to shew the shortest and best road to Kathmandu' as well as 'the disposition so to do on the prospect of a proportionate remuneration'.

However, a further setback occurred after Ahmed Ali deputed one of his servants to provide the information the British were looking for. The servant was allowed to return home in order to prepare for the journey to the border and 'whilst there was prevailed upon to abandon his intentions to plead ignorance of the road and to pretend that his master had misunderstood him'.[40] In the end, Ahmed Ali himself chose to brave 'the resentment of his countrymen' to proceed to the camp of the military force led by Major-General Bennet Marley in the hope of discovering a hidden road leading into the Nepal hills.[41]

After weeks of prevarication, Ahmed Ali had clearly and openly committed himself to the British cause. In the event Marley's military campaign proved singularly ineffective, and on 10 February 1815 he went so far as to abandon his camp without telling anyone where he was going.[42] Against this background of official incompetence, it is doubtful whether Ahmed Ali's intelligence information yielded the British any real advantage. Nevertheless, he naturally felt that he deserved to be rewarded for the risks that he had taken.

ACT TWO: A COMMERCIAL PROPOSAL

In September 1815, before the Anglo-Nepal war had come to a final conclusion, Moorcroft again approached Adam with a new proposal on Ahmed Ali's behalf. This time the proposal was more overtly commercial. It was in the British interest to promote trade with Tibet, and Moorcroft therefore suggested the government might be interested in sponsoring Ahmed Ali in a trading venture with Lhasa. Once again, Moorcroft plays the role of an anxious but enthusiastic middleman. It is his letter that proposes the trading venture. By contrast Ahmed Ali's accompanying note is both more cautious and less specific. After outlining his past services, he proposes – at least ostensibly – to embark on a life of devoted contemplation:

> I therefore humbly hope that your Lordship [the Governor-general] in your gracious favour will be pleased to grant a provision for my support so that I

39 Ibid., p. 110.

40 Moorcroft to Adam, Hajipur, 20 December 1814. OIOC. H/651, pp. 37-8.

41 Ibid.

42 See Pemble, *Invasion of Nepal*, pp. 210-28.

> may remain occupied in prayer for your Lordship's prosperity and be ready to manifest my devotion to the British Government.[43]

Two themes dominate the subsequent correspondence. On the one hand, we again see Ahmed Ali anxiously weighing up the balance between commercial opportunity and all manner of personal and financial risks. As Moorcroft observed, he seemed to 'view difficulties through a magnifying glass'.[44] On their side, the British authorities were concerned about the political and diplomatic risks of working with a local intermediary whom they could not be certain of controlling.

In presenting Ahmed Ali's case, Moorcroft pointed out that there were special considerations:

> Uhmed Ulee has drawn upon himself the resentment of the other Kashmeereean merchants who traffic from Patna to Lassa by his having been active in the British cause, (although fruitlessly from circumstances not under his control) and I would willingly hope that on this account as well as from his former connections with Tibet he may be deemed worthy of the patronage of the British Government.[45]

Bearing in mind the political sensitivities, he suggested that the government's sponsorship should be covert. The government might offer financial support, but it would be better for the venture to 'wear the appearance of being conducted by Uhmud Ulee for his own use to avoid exciting jealousy'.

The Governor-general in Council took a favourable view of the proposal but, according to Adam's subsequent reply to Moorcroft, expressed reservations about using a local trader as an intermediary. The main risk was that he might exceed his authority:

> The principal objection to employing native agents of this description is the fear that they will exceed their powers, and that in pursuit of their own interest they will by assuming the character of authorized officers of Government commit its credit with the chiefs and people of the country in which they are employed and thus both involve the British Government in immediate embarrassment and ultimately defeat or delay the success of the plans which they were employed to promote.[46]

---

43 Translation of a petition from Ahmed Alli, 16 November 1816, OIOC. F/4/552/13385, p. 7.

44 Moorcroft to Adam, 22 September 1816, OIOC. F/4/552/13385, pp. 27-33.

45 William Moorcroft to John Adam, Calcutta, 19 September 1815, OIOC. F/4/552/13385, p. 5.

46 Adam to Moorcroft, Calcutta, 13 January 1816, OIOC. F/4/552/13385, pp. 9-10.

The Council therefore came up with a slightly modified proposal suggesting that the venture should be 'not merely ostensibly but really' on Ahmed Ali's account. The government would supply him with goods in the form of a loan to be repaid at the rate of six per cent per annum. Provided that appearances were maintained, the loan would not be strictly enforced.[47] If the plan failed, the government would not insist on repayment. However, if it were successful it would give favourable consideration to Ahmed Ali's 'claim to further employment and reward'.

Alongside his commercial activities, Ahmed Ali would also be encouraged to collect information both about Sikkim – which was then favoured as a potential new trade and communications route to Tibet – as well as Tibet itself:

> In like manner he should be desired to report largely on the commercial resources and relations of Lassa & the countries with which that city maintains a mercantile intercourse, and to procure and bring back with him specimens of the productions and manufactures of those countries also.[48]

As will be seen, this suggestion was to take on particular significance in Act Three of Ahmed Ali's story.

Finally, lest there should be any room for misunderstanding, Adam concluded his letter by insisting that Ahmed Ali should not see himself as an official representative of the Company in any sense at all:

> ... he is to be strictly cautioned not to assume the character of an agent of the British government and not to engage in any transaction of a political nature, and he should be distinctly informed that any deviation from this rule will subject him to the entire forfeiture of the favour and protection of the government.[49]

The correspondence between the Council and Ahmed Ali continued back and forth for over a year, with Moorcroft as the go-between. On 17 February 1816, following further consultations with Ahmed Ali, Moorcroft highlighted the risks involved in a new venture 'in a country wholly unconnected with British influence'. He therefore suggested first that Ahmed Ali's brother might be sent to Lhasa instead of himself.[50] Secondly, he commented that Ahmed Ali's funds had been depleted by his losses on the fur trade, and suggested that he might himself offer him a loan on the understanding that this would be backed by the government. The Council agreed to the suggestions of a loan as long as

47 Ibid., p. 11.

48 Ibid., p. 15.

49 Ibid., pp. 15-16.

50 Moorcroft to Adam, 17 February 1816, OIOC. F/4/552/13385, pp. 21-4.

it 'assumed the appearance of a private transaction' between Moorcroft and Ahmed Ali.[51]

On 22 September, Moorcroft came back with a further report.[52] Ahmed Ali offered a new explanation of why he could not go to Lhasa in person:

> It appeared that one of his ancestors many years back had established at Lassa through personal communication with the Lama and his minister a commercial House and that ever since the business of that house had been carried on by agents and relations to the principals who have not themselves visited the concern on account of the large presents which would be expected on such occasion as inferred from the cost attending the 1st establishment of the connection.[53]

Furthermore, in order to minimize the risk, he now asked for a monopoly on the trade in otter skins from Chittagong and Dhaka, which Moorcroft described as 'a most profitable article of trade with the inhabitants of the China Frontier'. He would be prepared to send British cloth to Lhasa, but only at the risk of the government, and he was hoping for a delay in starting the new venture. At the same time, perhaps hoping to emphasize his usefulness, he offered recently acquired intelligence concerning a meeting between Nepali officials and a Chinese general who had just arrived in Tibet.[54]

By this time the Council had had enough. On 5 October, Adam sent a letter to Moorcroft stating that, since Ahmed Ali was unwilling to travel to Lhasa in person, the Governor-general in Council had 'determined to relinquish the scheme of employing his agency'.[55] At the same time, responding to the somewhat defensive tone of Moorcroft's most recent letter, the Council expressed appreciation for:

> ... the active spirit of public zeal which has uniformly stimulated your endeavours to promote objects of national interest, whether immediately connected with your proper department [i.e. the Company stud] or embracing a wider range...[56]

Moorcroft's promotion of Ahmed Ali's services had not in the end proved successful but, from the government's perspective, he was not to be blamed.

---

51 Adam to Moorcroft, 2 March 1816, OIOC. F/4/552/13385, p. 24.

52 Moorcroft to Adam, 22 September 1816, OIOC. F/4/552/13385, pp. 27-33.

53 Ibid., p. 28.

54 On the Chinese general see Lamb, *Britain and Tibet*, p. 35; Pemble, *Invasion of Nepal*, pp. 342-3. To Hastings' relief, the Chinese accepted the British explanation that their quarrel was solely with the Gorkhas and that they had no designs on Tibet.

55 Adam to Moorcroft, 5 October 1816, OIOC. F/4/552/13385, p. 34.

56 Ibid.

Ahmed Ali approached the government once again in early 1817, having received invitations to Tibet from two commercial agents in Lhasa, but the Council refused to change its view. It now favoured a *laissez-faire* approach and had decided 'to leave to the operation of natural Causes that extension of the Commercial intercourse in question'.[57] It was therefore unnecessary to offer Ahmed Ali any financial support. The Council was happy to approve of Moorcroft's supplying Ahmed Ali with cloth and other British manufactures on his own account. However, he was to explain distinctly to the Kashmiri that: '... Government took no further interest in the concern and that he was in no wise to consider himself as employed by the Government as its agent in any capacity'.[58]

As far as the British authorities were concerned, this was the end of the matter. Events were to prove them wrong.

ACT THREE: AN ESPIONAGE CASE IN TIBET

Act Three begins with an urgent plea for assistance received in March 1831 by Brian Houghton Hodgson, the East India Company's Acting Resident in Nepal.[59] Ahmed Ali had been imprisoned in Lhasa on charges of espionage and, in his capacity as a 'dependent and servant of the British Government', he appealed for British assistance to secure his release. This time Ahmed Ali's affairs – far from being a private affair involving a few senior officials – sparked a diplomatic incident involving the governments of India, Nepal and China.

The immediate crisis passed relatively quickly. On 20 April 1831 Hodgson was able to report that Ahmed Ali had already been released, and was winding up his affairs in Lhasa before leaving the country.[60] On 2 June Ahmed Ali arrived in Kathmandu in person, and immediately claimed Hodgson's protection at the British Residency.[61] Hodgson was able to persuade him that he was now quite safe and could more conveniently stay in the city while preparing for his onward journey to India.

Hodgson and his colleagues in Calcutta now had the task of understanding Ahmed Ali's previous relationship with the British authorities, while avoiding

---

57 Note by George Swinton, Chief Secretary, 22 July 1831, Calcutta, OIOC F/4/1384/55154, pp. 55-9.

58 Ibid.

59 Urzee (petition) of Khaja Ahmed Alli, a well-wisher of the British Goverrnment from Lassa. Dated 21 August 1830, received 20 March 1831, OIOC. F/4/1384/55154, pp. 25-8. On Hodgson see in particular: William Wilson Hunter, *Life of Brian Houghton Hodgson, British Resident at the Court of Nepal* (London, 1896); David Waterhouse (ed.), *The Origins of Himalayan Studies: Brian Houghton Hodgson in Nepal and Darjeeling 1820-1858* (London, 2004).

60 Hodgson to H.T. Prinsep, Secretary to the Governor General, Kathmandu, 20 April 1831, OIOC. F/4/1384/55154, p. 31.

61 Hodgson to Prinsep, Kathmandu, 5 June 1831, OIOC. F/4/1384/55154, p. 39.

antagonizing their counterparts in Kathmandu, Lhasa and Peking. Their task was made more complicated by the fact that Moorcroft – the official who had known him best – had died in northern Afghanistan in 1825 on his way back from his epic journey to Bukhara.[62] John Adam, who had handled the correspondence with Ahmed Ali on behalf of the Governor-general, had died in the same year.

Hodgson evidently formed a certain regard for Ahmed Ali, describing him as:

> ... a man of great respectability, evidently, and of considerable intelligence and he doubtless possesses general information about Tibet which (especially the commercial part of it) would be cheaply purchased by the gift of a few hundred or even thousands of rupees.[63]

At the same time, he was frustrated by Ahmed Ali's negotiating style: the latter evidently regarded information as a precious resource, and released it only slowly, and with apparent reluctance.

AHMED ALI'S QUARREL WITH HIS FAMILY

It emerged that the immediate cause of Ahmed Ali's woes was a quarrel with his younger brothers Abdullah and Ashraf Ali. All three had been involved in the family business in Lhasa. However, Ahmed Ali had fallen out both with his siblings, and with his agent, one 'Fuzuloolah Fukro of the Kashmeerian tribe but born in Bootan'.[64] As Hodgson later observed, the quarrel was 'of long standing and involves a world of affairs, the discussion of which belongs properly to a court of Justice'.[65]

Ahmed Ali had in fact intended to bring a lawsuit against his brothers in Tibet. However, as a counter-move, they denounced him to the Lhasa authorities, claiming that he had been employed by the British authorities to construct a map of the country.[66] When he was arrested, three Persian-language manuscript volumes containing a compilation of information on Tibet were found in his possession, together with 'a document containing 16 paragraphs granted by

[62] On Moorcroft's journey to Bukhara see William Moorcroft and George Trebeck, *Travels in the Himalayan Provinces of Hindustan and the Panjab, in Ladakh and Kashmir, in Peshawar, Kabul, Kunduz and Bokhara*, ed. H.H. Wilson (2 vols, London, 1841). On the circumstances of his death, see Alder, *Beyond Bukhara*, pp. 344-60.

[63] Hodgson to Prinsep, Kathmandu, 15 June 1831, OIOC. F/4/1384/55154, p. 49.

[64] Urzee of Khaja Ahmed Alli, 21 August 1830, OIOC. F/4/1384/55154, pp. 25-8. In accordance with eighteenth- and early nineteenth-century usage 'Bootan' here almost certainly refers to Tibet.

[65] Hodgson to Prinsep, Kathmandu, 10 February 1832, OIOC. F/4/1384/55154, p. 111.

[66] Khajah Fukheeroolla to Secretary to the Governor General, 29 December 1830, OIOC. F/4/1384/55154, pp. 23-4.

government through the medium of the late Mr W. Moorcroft'. The discovery of these documents lent credence to the charges that Ahmed Ali was a British spy.

CHINESE INVESTIGATIONS AND ACCUSATIONS

Having arrested Ahmed Ali, the Chinese authorities commissioned a translation of all his papers from Persian into Chinese, an indication of the seriousness with which they viewed the espionage allegations. With perhaps a touch of exaggeration, Ahmed Ali later claimed that a group of Kashmiris residing in Lhasa were employed on this task day and night for two months.[67] As Hodgson observed, the fact that such translators were available is testimony to the cosmopolitan nature of Lhasa society at the time:

> With respect to the means possessed by the Chinese Viceroy [Amban] of interpreting Persian letters and documents and corresponding in that language, these means are regularly supplied to him, by the maintenance of a Persian translator attached to the office of the foreign Secretary at Lhassa. Bhotiah, Newaree, Parbattiah [Nepali], Cashmeeree, Moghal and Tartar translators are similarly attached to that Office.
>
> Out of the multitude of Mohamadans resorting continually to Lhassa from the plains of India, Cashmir, Ladâkh, and Bucharia, and some of whom are domiciled at Lhassa, there can be seldom a difficulty in selecting a suitable person for the post of Persian translator to the government, though of course the qualifications of the successive tenants of the office will be apt to vary.[68]

Having prepared the translation, the Ambans sought instructions from the Emperor's court in Peking. The Emperor's verdict was conveyed in a letter of complaint that the Ambans sent via Sikkim to the 'ruler of the city of Calcutta', alias the Governor-general.[69] The letter was written in Chinese and accompanied by a Persian translation. It began with a summary of the contents of Ahmed Ali's manuscripts:

> The different boundaries of this kingdom, the situation of the roads, mountains and rivers, the nature of the soil, the general outline and face of the country

---

[67] Translation of Ahmed Ali's Reply to the Questions put to him by the acting Resident at Kathmandoo, in obedience to instructions from Calcutta. n.d. OIOC. F/4/1384/55154, p. 102.

[68] Hodgson to Swinton, Kathmandu, 2 September 1831, OIOC F/4/1384/55154, p. 89.

[69] Translation of a letter from the Chinese Authorities on the frontier of Lepcha thro' the medium of a Persian translation which accompanied the original. Dated 25 July 1831, OIOC. F/4/1384/55154, pp. 64-8.

> and the distance and vicinities of the public routes are all marked and written down in these volumes. The stations of the troops of Kathay and China are all marked and written down in these volumes.[70]

The letter then summarized the law concerning foreign traders: they were expected to solicit permission from the border authorities and to return home once the period assigned to them had expired:

> Such is the Rule observed towards the merchants of Cashmeer, the Newar tribe and others who come to this country for purposes of trade. But for any other class to come like spies in order to find out the affairs and state of the kingdom under the garb of merchants is not within the law and statutes of the empire...[71]

Despite this offence, the Emperor had decided to spare Ahmed Ali's life and to inflict no further punishment other than expelling him from the country. The Ambans expected the Governor-general to receive this news with appropriate deference:

> You will reflect upon the Imperial generosity and kindness and, occupying yourself with the exercise of humility within the sphere of your zemindary [domain], remain in amity and concord with the neighbours on your frontier, by which you will give pleasure and satisfaction to the Celestial King [the Emperor] who has shown such mercy to poor strangers notwithstanding such preposterous proceedings.[72]

The first act of contemplation on the part of the Governor-general's colleagues was to consult official files in order to work out who exactly Ahmed Ali was, and whether he had really been acting upon government orders.

THE ORIGINAL DOCUMENTS

The main outlines of the story emerged bit by bit between June and September 1831. On 15 June, soon after their initial meeting, Hodgson explained to Ahmed Ali that he was 'deceived, no doubt, in fancying he ever had a commission from the government to furnish information relative to Tibet', but at the same time sought further clarification from Calcutta.[73] On 22 July George Swinton, the Chief Secretary to the Government, prepared a summary of the files concerning

---

70 Ibid.

71 Ibid.

72 Ibid.

73 Hodgson to Prinsep, Kathmandu, 15 June 1831, OIOC. F/4/1384/55154, p. 49.

Ahmed Ali's proposed mission to Lhasa in 1815-16.[74] From Calcutta's perspective, the position was clear: Ahmed Ali's proposals had failed, and the government therefore had no formal obligations towards him.

Ahmed Ali responded to the Governor-general's disclaimer 'with every appearance of extreme dejection'.[75] However on 25 July, shortly before leaving Kathmandu for India, he changed his tack, admitting that:

> ... he had never been authorised or directed by Government to collect information relative to Bhote [Tibet] and that he could not, consequently, ground any claim of right upon his doings and sufferings there. But he insisted that he could and did rest such a claim upon his secret services during the Nepal war, services never yet remunerated notwithstanding promises to that effect.[76]

Hodgson upbraided him for confusing matters by 'laying the stress in the wrong place' by alluding to Tibet instead of Nepal 'as the scene of those acts upon the merit of which he desired to be base his pretensions to favour or reward'.

Hodgson continued to correspond with Ahmed Ali after his departure for India and, over the following weeks, a coherent picture emerged of the papers confiscated by the Lhasa authorities, and of Ahmed Ali's relationship with British officialdom. In August Hodgson summarised his findings as follows:

- The three volumes confiscated by the Chinese authorities were Ahmed Ali's manuscript account of what he had seen and heard. No other book was found upon him.
- The Persian-language papers included a *sanad* (grant/decree) from the government, and this was most likely a rough draft of the agreement under which it had been proposed to send Ahmed Ali to Lhasa.
- He also had a copy of the peace treaty between the East India Company and Nepal, which he had obtained from the munshi of Major Bradshaw, one of the British negotiators.
- In addition, he had a 'scrap of paper containing queries relative to the people and country of Bhote'. This came from 'one Habeeb Oollah, a fellow merchant'. Ahmed Ali supposed that it came from Edward Gardner, the former British Resident in Kathmandu, although he had nothing to confirm this.[77]

---

[74] Note by the Secretary, Calcutta, 22 July 1831, OIOC. F/4/1384/55154, pp. 55-9.

[75] Hodgson to Prinsep, Kathmandu, 26 June 1831, OIOC. F/4/1384/55154, p. 71.

[76] Hodgson to Prinsep, Kathmandu, 26 July 1831, OIOC. F/4/1384/55154, p. 82. Underlining in the original.

[77] Hodgson to Swinton, Kathmandu, 2 September 1831, OIOC. F/4/1384/55154, p. 81.

Hodgson commented that both Gardner and he himself had used Kashmiri merchants as a source of information on Tibet and the routes to China. Ironically enough, it occurred to him some weeks later that the paper of queries from Nepal might be the same as one that he had himself – as a private individual – given to a Kashmiri merchant called Ahmedullah in 1826, and that it might have been passed on to Ahmed Ali at third or fourth hand.[78] He duly sent a copy of his list of questions to Ahmed Ali who promptly confirmed the questions were indeed the same as the ones that he had received, although Hodgson commented that he still had some doubts given that the Kashmiri was always seeking 'to give to his researches the semblance of acts done by something like official authority…'.[79]

The overall conclusion was that no British official had formally requested Ahmed Ali to collect information on Tibet, but that he had been given to believe that he might in due course be rewarded for doing so. This belief was plausible enough given that both Hodgson and other officials had in the past sought information from Kashmiris travelling from Tibet. In Hodgson's view, there was one other personal factor: 'the simple truth appears to be that Mr Moorcroft had fired him [Ahmed Ali] with a spark of his own ardent curiosity'.[80] Like his patron, Ahmed Ali had developed a personal enthusiasm for geographical discovery and information gathering.

As it happened, Hodgson himself subsequently published a report on the route from Nepal via Tibet to China, apparently based on information from another Kashmiri/Tibetan called Amir.[81] The report contained a shorter version of the kind of information that Ahmed Ali must himself have collected, including – for example – information about the 500 troops (musketeers and archers) stationed at the Nepal/Tibetan border town of Kutti, and the fact that the gates of Lhasa are 'cautiously guarded – especially that leading to China – to get through which costs the traveller a whole day of solicitation, and sundry rupees in presents'.[82] It is a matter for regret that Ahmed Ali was never able to share his own findings.

THE ROLE OF THE NEPAL GOVERNMENT

In the 1830s – as still today – Nepal's sensitive strategic location meant that it was keen to avoid provoking either China or India. Ahmed Ali's original letter had suggested that the British might ask Bhimsen Thapa, the most powerful minister

---

78 Hodgson to Swinton, Kathmandu, 4 October 1831, OIOC. F/4/1384/55154, pp. 101-2.

79 Ibid.

80 Ibid.

81 Brian Houghton Hodgson, 'Route from Kathmandu, in Nepal, to Tazedo, on the Chinese Frontier, with Some Occasional Allusions to the Manners and Customs of the Bhotiahs, by Amir, a Cashmiro-Bhotiah by Birth, and by Vocation an Interpreter to the Traders on the Route Described', *Asiatic Researches*, 17 (1832): pp. 513-34.

82 Ibid., pp. 516 and 531.

in the Nepal government, to help secure his release.[83] In the event, Bhimsen Thapa's intervention was not needed, and it is in any case unlikely that he would have responded to Ahmed Ali's appeal for fear of provoking the Chinese.

When the Chinese authorities expelled Ahmed Ali they requested the Nepalis to ensure that he proceeded on to British India without delay. At Hodgson's request the Nepal government wrote to Lhasa proposing that Ahmed Ali's departure should be delayed until later in the year when there was a reduced risk of succumbing to malaria in the Terai (the forested lowland area between the Nepal hills and the Indian border). However, they received an unfavourable answer. The Ambans pleaded 'the Emperor's Commands as an insuperable reason for Ahmed Ali's instant departure to the plains'.[84] Hodgson felt that he had no choice but to comply with the combined requests of the Chinese and the Nepal governments, but provided Ahmed Ali with 'elephants and doolies for his speedy and comfortable passage of the malarious tract'.[85]

The Nepal government's wish to avoid provoking the Chinese authorities in Lhasa was also reflected in their initial reluctance to forward a letter from Calcutta to Lhasa giving the British response to the Ambans' accusations that Ahmed Ali had been a spy, although they did eventually agree to do so.

THE BRITISH RESPONSE TO THE CHINESE

The message contained in the British reply was polite but forthright.[86] It began by stating that Ahmed Ali held no office and had never been employed to collect information. Somewhat disingenuously, it claimed that there was no need to do so since such information was readily available in books published in all parts of the world, and from the 'gazettes and official records of Pekin, which are translated into English, and from many other sources'. Merchants were free to come and go in British dominions, and no one prevented them from gathering information. The letter therefore asked rhetorically:

> Why should you punish Ahmed Ali or any other merchant for taking notes of roads and countries and writing what they see and hear? Such things have always been and always will be done, so long as trade is not carried on by the blind and the deaf and by people who cannot write.[87]

---

83 Urzee of Khaja Ahmed Alli, Lhasa, 21 August 1830, OIOC. F/4/1384/55154, p. 28.

84 Hodgson to Prinsep, Kathmandu, 16 July 1831, OIOC. F/4/1384/55154, p. 76.

85 Hodgson to Prinsep, Kathamandu, 26 July 1831, OIOC. F/4/1384/55154, p. 82.

86 Copy of letter to Lhasa authorities. Prinsep to Hodgson, 7 October 1831, OIOC. F/4/1384/55154, pp. 91-3.

87 Ibid.

Nevertheless the letter concluded by stating that the government was 'sensible of the consideration' which led the Chinese authorities to refrain from punishing him. With that – in the British view – the matter was closed.

THE QUESTION OF COMPENSATION

There was one more piece of unfinished business. Ahmed Ali was a respectable merchant who – however unwisely – had acted with the best of intentions. How – if at all – should he be rewarded? The official view was that his services in the Nepal war had been too far in the past for there to be any question of compensation now. At the same time, if the government rewarded him for his unsuccessful information-gathering in Tibet, it would lend credence to the notion that he had after all been a spy. However, there was one further possibility. Ahmed Ali had lost almost all of his property in Lhasa, but had managed to take with him three chests and one large leather bag containing samples of goods produced and sold in Tibet.[88] In the hope of winning some form of recompense, he now offered them for sale to the government.

On Swinton's instructions, Ahmed Ali's Tibetan goods were sent to Horace Hayman Wilson (1786-1880), the Secretary of the Asiatic Society, with a request that he should examine them and report 'whether any of them would be acceptable as curiosities to be deposited in the Museum of the Asiatic Society'.[89] Wilson consulted Csoma de Kőrös, who was then serving as the Asiatic Society's librarian. They reported that the principal goods were 'articles of dress worn in the countries beyond the Himalaya and specimens of woollen cloths and silks, the latter of Chinese manufacture'. There were also samples of tea and a few dried fruits. Wilson suggested that the perishables should be sold and that Society might select a few items for its museum.[90] The remainder should be sent back to London 'either for the Museum at India House, or as samples of the manufactures for which there is a demand in Tibet'.

The final question concerned the amount to be paid to Ahmed Ali. He had asked for Rs 5,000. Wilson and Csoma had valued the items at Rs 1618 and 8 annas. The government settled for Rs 2,500, apparently out of consideration for his 'respectable character and distressed circumstances'.[91] At least from the British perspective, honour had now been satisfied. Ahmed Ali's view is not recorded.

---

[88] W.R. Jennings, Collector of Customs Patna to Thomas Pakenham, Private Secretary to Lord William Bentinck, OIOC. F/4/1384/55154, p. 119.

[89] Swinton to Wilson, Calcutta, 13 August 1832, OIOC. F/4/1384/55154, p. 153.

[90] Wilson to Swinton, Calcutta, 13 August 1832, OIOC. F/4/1384/55154, pp. 229-34.

[91] Political, 25 March, No. 4 of 1834, OIOC. E/4/470. Reprinted in Marczell, *Alexander Csoma de Kőrös*, vol. 2, p. 395.

WIDER REPERCUSSIONS

As Moorcroft had made clear in 1814, Ahmed Ali risked the hostility of his fellow-Kashmiris when he openly sided with the British during the Anglo-Nepal war. In doing so he put their interests at risk, as well as his own, because of the possibility of reprisals against Kashmiris in Kathmandu. Similarly in the 1830s, by appearing to be too close to the British, he ruined his own position in Tibet, and other Kha-che Muslims in Lhasa must have feared that he would damage the reputation of the entire community.

In practice this does not seem to have happened, perhaps because there were Kashmiris on both sides of the affair: his own brothers had denounced him to the Chinese authorities, and other members of his community helped translate his Persian manuscripts for the Ambans. No doubt the incident placed the Chinese even more on their guard and, at the behest of the Manchus as much as the Tibetans themselves, the official bar on European travellers in Tibet remained in place until the Younghusband expedition of 1904. However, the Kha-che community as a whole continued to prosper.

It also continued to serve as a source of information both for the British and for the Chinese. To cite two illustrative examples, in 1846 Chinese officials in Lhasa reported back to Beijing that Muslim traders had passed on information about the 'Senpa' (Sikhs) on Tibet's western borders.[92] And in July 1877 Major Henderson, a British official in Kashmir, passed on information on Chinese and Tibetan government policy as reported by Gholam Shah, a Ladakhi Argon merchant who had left Lhasa three months previously.[93] When Khwajah Ghulam Muhammad (1857-1928), a Kashmiri based in Kathmandu, travelled to Lhasa in 1886, he found that the Kha-che Muslims were both prosperous and well-respected by the Tibetan host community.[94] Western travellers to Lhasa in the twentieth century painted a similar picture.[95]

EPILOGUE: AHMED ALI AND WILLIAM MOORCROFT'S 'AFTERLIFE'

As for Ahmed Ali himself, once his affairs had been settled to the Governor-general's satisfaction, he disappears from Western records. Or perhaps not quite.

---

[92] Schuyler Cammann, 'New Light on Huc and Gabet: their Expulsion from Lhasa in 1846', *The Far Eastern Quarterly*, 1/4 (Aug., 1942): pp. 355-6.

[93] Major P.D. Henderson to T.H. Thornton Esq., Secretary to Government of India Foreign Department, Kashmir, 30 July 1877, Ney Elias Papers. Royal Geographical Society, London.

[94] Gaborieau, *Récit d'un Musulman*.

[95] See for example: Austine Waddell, *Lhasa and its Mysteries*, p. 346; Charles Bell, *Tibet Past and Present* (Oxford, 1924), p. 243; F. Spencer Chapman, *Lhasa: The Holy City* (London, 1940), p. 96.

A decade and a half later, two European travellers in Tibet picked up what may have been a final echo of the sensation surrounding his arrest.

In 1846 two French priests, Régis Évariste Huc and Joseph Gabet travelled from north-east China to Lhasa. The leader of the Lhasa Kha-che community was deputed to look after them – yet another case of a member of the Lhasa Muslim community playing a sensitive role as an intermediary between the Tibetans and Western travellers. Huc reports that the Tibetans were welcoming, but that pressure from the Chinese authorities – as represented in Tibet by the two Ambans – meant that they were forced to leave Lhasa after only a few weeks. However, before doing so, they collected some surprising news concerning the fate of Ahmed Ali's old patron, William Moorcroft.[96]

Far from dying in northern Afghanistan, Moorcroft had – according to Huc's sources – travelled on to Lhasa in disguise as a Kashmiri Muslim, arriving some time in 1826. He spoke Persian so fluently that he was able to fool his Kashmiri 'compatriots' into taking him as one of their own. From his Lhasa base he purchased some herds of goats and yaks, which were entrusted to shepherds in the surrounding mountains. On the pretext of inspecting his livestock, 'Moorcroft' frequently travelled through the Tibetan countryside, and took advantage of the opportunity to make drawings and maps. Finally, after a dozen years in the Tibetan capital, he set out for Ladakh but was attacked and killed by robbers in the western Tibetan province of Ngari. It was only when the robbers inspected his baggage and found the maps that 'Moorcroft's' true identity came to light.

Huc had never heard of Moorcroft before his stay in Lhasa, and he reports that the story was corroborated by several sources, including 'Moorcroft's' former Lhasa servant Nisan who had himself been taken in by the disguise. Nisan had been given a letter of recommendation, apparently written in Roman characters and to be used in case he ever travelled to Calcutta. However, Nisan had destroyed it after the discovery of his master's maps and drawings.

Over the years Huc's account has prompted wide speculation. Moorcroft's journey to Tibet in 1812 points to his taste for disguise and intrigue. So might his 'after-life' in Lhasa just possibly be true?

Perhaps disappointingly, in a careful review of the evidence, Robert Fazy argues that the story is implausible because – among other reasons – it is hard to believe that Moorcroft could have mustered the necessary language skills to persuade the local Muslim community that he was one of their own.[97] In a more recent assessment, Philip Denwood makes a similar point, and suggests that the murdered man could have been a Kashmiri who had been commissioned by Moorcroft to gather information. The discovery of letters or papers bearing

---

96 Régis-Évariste Huc, *Souvenirs d'un voyage dans la Tartarie et le Thibet* (Peking, 1924 [1st ed. 1850]), vol. 2, pp. 318-22.

97 Robert Fazy, 'Le cas Moorcroft, un problème de l'exploration tibétaine', *T'oung Pao*, 35 (1940): pp. 155-84.

his name might have led the Tibetans to assume that the victim was Moorcroft himself.[98]

If Denwood's theory is correct, then Ahmed Ali is certainly a potential candidate. The Tibetans clearly associated Ahmed Ali with Moorcroft, and the discovery of hidden maps and documents is a key element of both stories. Ahmed Ali's story does not match that of Huc's spy in all respects, because of course he lived to return safely to British India. Nevertheless, it seems plausible to suggest that Huc had picked up a garbled version of the Ahmed Ali affair 15 years earlier.

The Calcutta authorities had always been concerned with matters of representation: how far could they trust Ahmed Ali to identify with – and speak for – British interests? Ultimately, it seems that the Kashmiri trader came to represent his old spymaster to a degree and in a fashion that no one ever expected.

98 Philip Denwood, 'William Moorcroft – an Assessment', in Osmaston and Denwood (eds), *Recent Research on Ladakh 4&5*, pp. 39-53, at p. 53.

Chapter 17
Do All the Muslims of Tibet Belong to the Hui Nationality?

Diana Altner

The Chinese state currently classifies all Muslims living in Tibetan areas as belonging to the Muslim minority of the 'Hui'. Tibetans distinguish different Muslim groups according to the origin of their ancestors. In the present article, the origin and development of the Chinese term 'Hui' will be discussed as well as the equivalent terms in the Tibetan language and the Tibetan terms used for the individual Muslim groups living in the Tibetan areas.

THE ETHNIC GROUP HUI (*HUIZU* 回族)

The Hui or Huihui, who live in China, represent an independent ethnic group which numbered 9,816,805 people in 2000 according to the official census. The older name for the Hui, 'Chinese Muslims', reflects the significance of religion for the ethnic identity of the Hui. The distinct identity of the Hui is often denied by Han Chinese who argue that the Hui are actually Han who do not eat pork and practise Islam. The cultural differences according to the Han Chinese are very limited.[1]

The Hui are, however, recognized by the Chinese government as a separate nationality. This official acknowledgment of the Hui as an ethnic group suggests that their identity is indeed more than a religious one. Compared to the other national minorities who profess to Islam – the Uyghur (*Weiwu'erzu* 维吾尔族), Khazak (*Hasake zu* 哈萨克族), Uzbeks (*Wuzibieke zu* 乌孜别克族), Kirgis (*Ke'erkezi zu* 柯尔克孜族), Tatar (*Tata'er zu* 塔塔尔族), Dongxiang (*Dongxiang zu* 东乡族), Bonan (*Bao'an zu* 保安族), Tajik (*Tajike zu* 塔吉克族) and Salar (*Sala zu* 撒拉族), the Hui are numerically the largest group.

Rather than living exclusively in any particular part of China, the Hui are scattered throughout the whole country. While they can be found in all provinces and cities in China, their settlements are concentrated in areas around mosques. These settlements are most numerous in the Ningxia Hui Autonomous Region (*Ningxia Huizu zizhiqu* 宁夏回族自治区) (17.7%), Gansu province (*Gansu sheng*

---

1 Thomas Hoppe, *Die ethnischen Gruppen Xinjiangs: Kulturunterschiede und interethnische Beziehungen* (Hamburg, 1995), pp. 350-51.

甘肃省) (12.7%), Henan province (*Henan sheng* 河南省) (10.1%), Qinghai province (*Qinghai sheng* 青海省) (7.4%) and the Xinjiang Autonomous Region (*Xinjiang zizhiqu* 新疆自治区) (7.9%).[2]

GENERAL CHARACTERISTICS OF THE HUI

The Hui are distinct within their surroundings because of their religion and the lifestyle it requires: they follow Islamic traditions in dietary habits, funeral services, marriage ceremonies and holiday celebrations. Most of them specialize in certain professions such as being traders, farmers, butchers, tanners, or practising other crafts.

On the other hand, the fact that the Hui generally speak Chinese contributes to their assimilation. In most parts of China they use the local Chinese dialects and the languages of other nationalities. At the same time they use a large number of Arabic and Persian words and Arabic script in decoration and for religious purposes.[3] In their daily life, the Hui wear Chinese dress or the dress of other nationalities and use Chinese names in public. Because of their various social contexts, Hui communities differ considerably among each other.[4] Hui who abandon the religious community still remain Hui. 'These days Hui atheists and agnostics abound, and their "Huiness" consists not in what they believe but in their ancestry and in some of the customs that characterize their daily lives and commonly accompany their families' births, weddings, and deaths.'[5]

DIFFERENCES BETWEEN THE HUI AND THE OTHER MUSLIM MINORITIES OF CHINA

While the Uyghur, Kazak, Kirgis, Salar, Uzbeks and Tatar can be regarded as Turkish peoples, the Dongxiang and Bonan belong to the Mongolian peoples and the Tajik are an Iranian people, the Hui cannot be classified as any of these larger ethnic and cultural groups. While the other Muslim minorities speak their own language with a Turkish, Mongolian or Iranian origin, the Hui are more deeply assimilated: they do not have their own language. There are words that are only used among Hui but they cannot be regarded as belonging to a 'Hui language'.

The Hui claim that they originated in the 'Islamic world': Central Asia, Persia and Arabia. Persians, Arabs, Turkic-speakers and other peoples belong to the

---

[2] Ingo Nentwig, 'Hui/Dunganen, Huihui, Huizu', in *Bertelsmann Lexikon: Die Völker der Erde. Kulturen und Nationalitäten von A-Z* (Gütersloh, 1992), p. 152.

[3] Michael Dillon, *China's Muslim Hui Community: Migration, Settlement and Sects* (Richmond, 1999), pp. 5-6.

[4] Hoppe, *Die ethnischen Gruppen Xinjiangs*, p. 352.

[5] Ibid., p. 359.

ancestors of the Hui. These groups arrived in China via different routes and spread gradually over the whole of China. Compared to the Hui, the other Muslim minorities of China are concentrated in fewer provinces: 99.7% of the Uyghur, 99.5% of the Kazak, 98.75% of the Kirgis, 99.9% of the Tajik, 99.6% of the Uzbeks and 98.9% of the Tatar are settled in the Xinjiang Autonomous Region; 83% of the Dongxiang and 90.6% of the Bonan live in the Gansu province; 87.8% of the Salar live in the Qinghai province.[6] The wide distribution of the Hui throughout China can be seen as one reason for the pressure of assimilation. They adapt to Chinese society to a much higher degree than the other Muslim minorities, but without losing specific characteristics.

By underlining cultural characteristics, the Hui emphasize the uniqueness of their way of life which distinguishes them from the ethnic groups settling around them. Compared to the Chinese or the Tibetans, they emphasize their religious lifestyle. Compared to other Muslim minorities also practising Islam, they try to distinguish themselves by other characteristics. In Xinjiang, for instance, the Hui emphasize their origin from the inner Chinese provinces by decorating their mosques not with Arabic calligraphy but with Chinese characters.[7]

The other Muslim minorities regard the Hui as fellow Muslims but ethnically they rank them among the Han Chinese.

ORIGINS OF THE ETHNIC GROUP HUI

Arab merchants came to China via two routes: overland along the Silk Road and through Southeast Asia by sea. Within one century after Muhammad's death, Muslims came to China via the Silk Road from the northwest.[8] These people were mainly interested in establishing economic relations with the Chinese. They did not travel to China for missionary reasons; religion was simply a part of their culture. Since these early Muslim visitors to China were exclusively traders and merchants, Islam mainly spread out along the trading routes and Islamic communities became established in the important trading towns.[9] Unlike the Muslims who came to China by sea, the Muslims who came to China via land spread out more in western China.[10]

Muslim merchants came to China by sea also from the seventh century onwards. When sea traffic to China increased greatly in the eighth century, Arab and Persian traders came to southern Chinese harbours and soon settled in the

[6] Statistics for the census of 1990 presented by Ingo Nentwig in the seminar *The Hui and Islam in China*, summer term 2001, Leipzig University.

[7] Hoppe, *Die ethnischen Gruppen Xinjiangs*, p. 352.

[8] Morris Rossabi, 'Muslims in the Yüan Dynasty', in John Langlois (ed.), *China under Mongol Rule* (Princeton, 1981), p. 257.

[9] Werner Eichhorn, *Die Religionen Chinas* (Stuttgart, 1973), p. 261.

[10] Dillon, *China's Muslim Hui Community*, p. 1.

towns close to harbours such as Guangzhou 广州, Quanzhou 泉州, Hangzhou 杭州 and Yangzhou 扬州. The arrival of Muslims via the coastal areas was important because it took place in a geographically very limited area. The coastal towns offered members of foreign cultures the opportunity to develop structures for a vibrant cultural life and thus to maintain their religious customs as well. These circumstances facilitated the establishment of a foreign religion in China.[11] In the thirteenth century these costal areas were the home of more than 100,000 foreigners.[12]

The first political contacts between Chinese and Arabs by land can be traced back to the Tang Dynasty (618-907).[13] The dynasty's expansive foreign policy left traces in the cultural and religious landscape. As a result of the opening to the outside world, a number of important foreign embassies visited the Chinese emperors. In 638, Yazdegerd III of Persia, the last Sasanian ruler, stayed at the Chinese court, and in 651 an embassy of the third Islamic Caliph, ʿUthmān ibn ʿAffān, visited the Tang emperor.[14] A new phase began in 749, with the revolution of the Abbasids, referred to as 'black-robed Arabs' in Chinese historical records. Under al-Manṣūr (reg. 754-75), the first alliance between China and the Abbasids was built.[15] Between 756 and 762 the Chinese emperor Suzong and his son, the later emperor Daizong, were supported by foreign soldiers from Persia to suppress the An Lushan rebellion. Muslim sources mention 4,000 soldiers settled in North China, many of whom stayed and married Chinese women.[16]

The Song Dynasty (960-1259) also supported trade with foreigners; especially trade by sea became more and more important. The main reason for this development was the changed borderline of the Song Dynasty – compared to the former Tang Dynasty. Important areas in Northern and Northwestern China that belonged to the traditional routes of the caravans were not ruled by the Chinese emperors any longer.

Chinese historical records include many reports about Islam in Islamic countries, but only a few descriptions of the practice of the Islam in Chinese society. In one report about foreigners living in Guangzhou in the year 1192, some descriptions of their everyday life and religious practice can be found:

---

11 Imke Mees, *Die Hui - Eine moslemische Minderheit in China: Assimiliationsprozesse und politische Rolle vor 1949* (Munich, 1984), p. 15-16.

12 Hoppe, *Die ethnischen Gruppen Xinjiangs*, p. 355.

13 Marshall Broomhall, *Islam in China, a Neglected Problem* (London, 1910), p. 11. More recent studies on Islam in China include Raphael Israeli, *Islam in China: Religion, Ethnicity, Culture, and Politics* (Lanham, 2002); Donald Daniel Leslie, Yang Daye and Ahmed Youssef, *Islam in Traditional China: A Bibliographical Guide* (Sankt Augustin, 2006).

14 Dieter Kuhn, *Status und Ritus: Das China der Aristokraten von den Anfängen bis zum 10. Jahrhundert nach Christus* (Heidelberg, 1991), p. 553.

15 Broomhall, *Islam in China*, pp. 25-6.

16 Donald Daniel Leslie, *The Integration of Religious Minorities in China: The Case of the Chinese Muslims* (Canberra, 1998), p. 12.

> In the foreign quarter in Guangzhou reside all the people from behind the sea ... The sea barbarians [*hailiao*] are by nature superstitious (honour devils) and love cleanliness. Every day they prostrate themselves and pray for blessing. They have a hall there where they worship, just like the Buddhists in China, except that they do not set up images ... When they meet in the morning to eat, they do not use chopsticks or spoon ... All the diners put their right (a mistake for left) hand under the cushion and do not use it for eating, saying it is only for use in the privy. All use the left (a mistake for right) hand to pick up the food, and when the meal is over, they wash with water.[17]

The situation for Muslims had hardly changed since the Tang with the exception that they were clearly settlers, had mosques in most of the big cities and even special Muslim cemeteries. Donald Daniel Leslie prefers the term 'Muslim settlers in China' for Muslims living in China during that time rather than 'Chinese Muslims'.[18]

The Muslims started to integrate into Chinese society in the Song period, but their number remained small. That situation started to change when China was ruled by the Yuan (1279-1368) and a large number of Persians, Arabs and Turks were employed as soldiers and civil servants. In addition to that, the number of merchants increased. The 'Chinese Muslims' – the Hui – are the descendants of these immigrants, who mixed with the Chinese who later converted to Islam.[19] A large group of immigrants to China were Muslims who were sent by Genghis Khan from 1219 onwards as soldiers and civil servants to the East. After the military conflicts ended, many of these Muslims decided to stay in these eastern areas and became farmers.[20]

Other kinds of contacts between the Islamic world and China were established in the fields of medicine. As Beckwith has noted, 'Persian or Arab doctors could be found not only in Ch'ang-an, the T'ang capital, but in nearly every port of China.'[21]

Another source for the enlargement of the Hui communities was the conversion of individual people from other ethnic groups such as the Han Chinese, Mongols and Tibetans.[22]

---

17 Leslie, *Integration of Religious Minorities*, p. 18.

18 Ibid., pp. 17-20.

19 Ingo Nentwig, 'Religion im heutigen China', in Claudius Müller (ed.), *Wege der Götter und Menschen: Religionen im traditionellen China* (Berlin, 1989), p. 67.

20 Hoppe, *Die ethnischen Gruppen Xinjiangs*, p. 356.

21 Christopher Beckwith, 'The Introduction of Greek Medicine into Tibet in the Seventh and Eighth Centuries', *Journal of the American Oriental Society*, 99 (1979): pp. 297-313, at p. 297. See also the contribution by Paul Buell in this volume for further references.

22 Hoppe, *Die ethnischen Gruppen Xinjiangs*, p. 356.

THE ORIGIN OF THE TERM 'HUI'

There was no special term for Muslims in Chinese history until the twelfth century. In Tang history, where Muslims are mentioned for the first time, they were called *Tashi* 大食.[23] 'Tashi' was the common name for Arabs during the Sui und Tang dynasties. It is not clear whether 'Tashi' is derived from the Arabic word for 'trader' (*tājir*) or what Broomhall has referred to as 'a Persian corruption of an ancient Aramean word, *Ta'i* for Nomad'[24] (presumably from the root ṭ^ᵓ = to wander). Stein argues that the word 'Tashi' goes back to the Iranian people of the Tajik who are called Stag gzigs in Tibetan.[25]

The Mongols also did not give the Muslims a special name, but regarded them generally as foreigners:

> By identifying Muslims and several other non-Chinese groups as a separate class, the *Se-mu jen* [*Semuren*] 色目人, it isolated them from the *Han-jen* [*Hanren*] 汉人 (Northern Chinese, Jurchens and Khitans) and the *Nan-jen* [*Nanren*] 南人 (Southern Chinese). The Court also lumped all Muslims, be they natives of Central Asia, the Middle East, or China itself, into one group, ... The Court ... did not distinguish between the Muslims and other foreigners ...[26]

The term *Huihui* 回回 appears for the first time in the twelfth century,[27] when it is applied generally to all Muslim people. Clear distinctions between the Hui and other Muslim groups were not established until the time of the People's Republic of China.[28]

The historians of the Ming period used the term 'Huihui' as the name for all Muslims living in China.[29] Since the middle of the Ming Dynasty, 'Huihui' was used, by extension, for all Muslims outside of China and Islam was called 'Huihui religion' (*Huihui jiao* 回回教).[30] During the Qing Dynasty, the term 'Huihui' was generally shortened to 'Hui'.[31]

While a definite satisfactory explanation for the terms 'Huihui' and 'Hui' has not yet been achieved, there are currently several competing theories: According to Professor Giles' dictionary, the term *hui* in daily use means 'to come

---

23 Emil Bretschneider, *Mediaeval Researches from Eastern Asiatic Sources: Fragments towards the Knowledge of the Geography and History of Central and Western Asia from the 13th to 17th Century*, 2 vols (London, 1888), I, p. 267.

24 Broomhall, *Islam in China*, p. 13.

25 Rolf Stein, *Die Kultur Tibets* (Berlin, 1989), p. 57.

26 Rossabi, 'Muslims in the Yüan Dynasty', p. 259.

27 Broomhall, *Islam in China*, p. 13.

28 Hoppe, *Die ethnischen Gruppen Xinjiangs*, p. 357.

29 Bretschneider, *Mediaeval Researches*, I, p. 274.

30 Jianping Wang, *Concord and Conflict: The Hui Communities of Yunnan Society in a Historical Perspective* (Lund, 1996), p. 19.

31 Wang, *Concord and Conflict*, p. 19.

or go back to the starting point; to return'. There is a theory that the doubling of the term *hui* imitates the Arabic with the meaning of 'to return and to submit'.[32] Dabry de Thiersant defends the idea that the term *hui* means the return and complete submission to God.[33] Broomhall suggested a similar theory: 'it is quite possible that the dominant thought of submission and return to God may have given rise to the name of the Double Return, especially if the invariable custom of turning towards Mecca in prayer and even returning thence in pilgrimage be considered'.[34] Emil Bretschneider supports the idea that the term occurs first in the *Liao shi* and that later in the *Yuan shi*, the term 'Huihui' for Muslims is met with only in a few instances. They are generally referred to there as 'Hui-ho' or 'Hui-hu'.[35] Julia Ching suggested that 'Muslims became known in Chinese as Hui-hui (literally: return) – we are not sure why. Perhaps the name had to do with their custom of turning to face Mecca when they prayed; or perhaps it sounded like "Uighur", since Uighurs had converted to Islam.'[36] Tafel also refers to a connection between the term *huihui* and the Uyghur.[37]

During the time of the Chinese Republic, all Muslims living in China were included under the term 'Hui'. After the foundation of the People's Republic of China, the ethnic groups who professed Islam were divided into Uyghur, Kazak, Uzbeks, Tajik, Bonan, Dongxiang, Tatar, Salar and Hui.[38]

The religion of the Muslims is called *Huihui jiao* 回回教, *Qing zhen jiao* 清真教 ('the pure and true religion') but also *Xiao jiao* 小教 ('the small sect' in contrast to Confucianism) by the Chinese.[39]

HUI IN THE TIBETAN AREAS

Muslims living in Tibetan settlement areas speak Tibetan or Chinese in daily life and adopt Tibetan or Chinese clothing and lifestyle. While the Chinese government regards all Muslims living in Tibet as Hui, the Tibetans distinguish between them according to their places of origin.

32 Broomhall, *Islam in China*, p. 167.

33 Claude Philibert Dabry de Thiersant, *Le Mahométisme en Chine et dans le Turkestan Oriental* (Paris, 1878), p. 2.

34 Broomhall, *Islam in China*, p. 168.

35 Bretschneider, *Mediaeval Researches*, I, p. 267.

36 Julia Ching, *Chinese Religions* (London, 1993), p. 180.

37 Albert Tafel, *Meine Tibetreise* (Stuttgart, 1914), p. 116.

38 Wang, *Concord and Conflict*, p. 19.

39 Broomhall, *Islam in China*, p. 167.

TIBETAN TERMS FOR HUI

The general Tibetan term for Muslims is 'Kha che'. This term refers to the name of the land where the ancestors of some of the Muslims living in Tibet came from: Kha che yul, that is, Kashmir.[40]

According to the Tibetan–Chinese dictionary (*Bod rgya tshig mdzod chen mo/Zang Han da cidian* 藏汉大词典) 'Kha che' is translated as 'Huizu' for the Hui nationality but also as *Keshimi'er* 克什米尔 for Kashmiri.[41] According to the Chinese–Tibetan dictionary (*Han Zang duizhao cidian* 汉藏对照词典/*rGya bod shan sbyar tshig mdzod*), however, the Chinese term 'Huizu' is translated into Tibetan as 'Hu'i rigs' (Hui-nationality), but not as 'Kha che'.[42] The term 'Kha che' is translated as Muslims but also as Kashmiris.[43]

CHINESE TRANSCRIPTIONS FOR THE TERM KHA CHE

There are different Chinese transcriptions for the Tibetan term 'Kha che': *Keshe* 克什, *Kaji* 卡基 and *Kajia* 喀迦.

Fang Jianchang 房建昌 mentions in his article 'Xizang Musilin de laiyuan jiqi shenghuo' 西藏穆斯林的来源及其生活 ('Origin and Life of the Muslims in Tibet') Chinese terms for Muslims used as transcriptions for Tibetan terms in addition to the term Hui. According to that article, Muslims are generally called *Keshe* 克什. Muslims with origins in China are called *Jia* 加 *keshi* (*jia* means Han); Muslims with origins in Ladakh are called *Ladakeshe* 拉达克什.[44] *Keshe* seems to be a Chinese transcription for Kha che which I have not been able to find in any dictionary. In his other article on historical activities of Muslims in Tibet, 'Lishi shang Musilin zai Xizang de Huodong' 历史上穆斯林在西藏的活动 ('Historical Activities of the Muslims in Tibet'), Fang Jianchang transcribes Kha che as *Kaji* 卡基.[45]

Another transcription for Kha che is used by Song Xiaoji 宋晓嵇 in his article 'Lasa de qingzhensi' 拉萨的清真寺 ('The Mosques of Lhasa'): *Kajia* 喀迦, according to the old Chinese name for Kashmir *Jiashimiluo* 迦湿弥罗. He translated that term into Chinese as Hui.[46]

---

40 Prince Peter of Greece and Denmark, 'The Moslems of Central Tibet', *Journal of the Royal Central Asiatic Society*, 39 (1952): pp. 233-40, at p. 234.

41 Zhang Yisun, *Bod rgya tshig mdzod chen mo/Zang Han da cidian* (Beijing, 1998), p. 192.

42 *Han Zang duizhao cidian/rGya bod shan sbyar tshig mdzod* (Beijing, 1991), p. 450.

43 Melvin Goldstein, *The New Tibetan-English Dictionary of Modern Tibetan* (Berkeley, 2001), p. 93.

44 Fang Jianchang, 'Xizang Musilin de laiyuan jiqi shenghuo', *Ningxia Shihui Kexue*, 3 (1986): pp. 66-8, at p. 68.

45 Fang Jianchang, 'Lishi shang Musilin zai Xizang de Huodong', *Sixiang Zhanxian*, 4 (1987): pp. 81-3, at p. 83.

46 Song Xiaoji, 'Lasa de qingzhensi', *Xueyu Wenhua*, 1/9 (1991): pp. 38-9, at p. 38.

Wu Congzhong 吴从众 mentions in his work *Xizang jingnei de Menbazu, Luobazu he Huizu* 西藏境内的门巴族 珞巴族和回族 ('The Menba, Lhoba and Hui within the Borders of Tibet') that Hui nationality 回族 is translated by the Tibetans as *Jiakaji* 甲卡基. *Jia* means Han (Chinese) and *kaji* is the phonetic translation for Kashmir.[47]

Originally the term 'Kha che' was the name for people coming from Kashmir. During the centuries the term developed into a general term for Muslims. For the Chinese term *jia* two different characters are used: 加 and 甲. A phonetic parallel to the Tibetan word *rgya*, which refers to China, is clearly to be seen.

KHA CHE IN LHASA

While the Muslims in Tibet generally are called Kha che, in Lhasa they were traditionally divided into three main groups: the Lhasa kha che, the Gharīb and the Wa bak gling.

At the end of the nineteenth century, most of the Kha che who came to Tibet as traders lived in the centre of Lhasa. The so-called Lhasa kha che are not a homogeneous group but can be divided into three subgroups.[48]

The majority of the Lhasa kha che belonged to the group of the Zā'īdah.[49] As descendants of the first immigrant traders from Kashmir they formed the heart of the community. They often use Muslim names such as Sayyid, Shayk, Kwajah, Baba etc.[50] A recent article in Tibetan on Lhasa Muslims refers to them both as Lhasa kha che and as Bar skor kyi kha che. The latter refers to the area where most of the Kha che still carry out their business: the Bar skor.[51]

In addition to the Zā'īdah, two other groups of Lhasa kha che existed: the La dwags kha che or La dwags pa,[52] whose ancestors came from Ladakh, and the Siring pa or Singhpa kha che, whose ancestors came from India.[53] The members of the last group are said to be the descendants of the soldiers who came to Lhasa during the Dogra wars. Originally they were Hindus, who later converted to Islam under the influence of the Kha che in Lhasa. The Siring pa or Singhpa Kha che were also called 'Dogra Muslims'.[54]

---

47 Wu Congzhong, *Xizang jingnei de Menbazu, Luobazu he Huizu* [*The Menba, Luoba and Hui within the Borders of Tibet*] (Beijing, 1989), p. 65.

48 Marc Gaborieau, *Récit d'un voyageur musulman au Tibet* (Paris, 1973), p. 22.

49 Persian: 'born' (in Tibet), according to Gaborieau, *Récit d'un voyageur musulman*, p. 34, n. 65.

50 Gaborieau, *Récit d'un voyageur musulman*, p. 22.

51 Tshe rdor, 'Lha sa'i kha che', *Bod kyi rtsom rig sgyu rtsal* [*Tibetan Art and Literature*], 4 (1992): pp. 112-28, at p. 112.

52 Prince Peter of Greece and Denmark, 'The Moslems of Central Tibet', p. 234.

53 Gaborieau, *Récit d'un voyageur musulman*, p. 22.

54 Abdul Ghani Sheikh, 'Tibetan Muslims', *Tibet Journal*, 16 (1991): pp. 86-9, at p. 87.

The ancestors of the Lhasa kha che came exclusively from India, three-quarters of them from Kashmir.[55] Corneille Jest writes that in Tibet the Kha che were considered Indian citizens, thus having the status of foreigners.[56]

In contrast to the Kashmiris, another group, consisting of 10 to 12 families, were called the Gharīb.[57] The Arabic word *gharīb* (lit. 'stranger') contrasts with the words *amīr* or *sharīf* which are used for persons with a high political or social status. In the context of Lhasa, the Gharīb are the poor in contrast to the rich traders from Kashmir on whom they depended.[58] The Gharīb probably belonged to fringe and banished groups or convicted people.[59] While they lived as beggars, they also acted as service personnel for the local police and in prisons.[60] Nowadays the Gharīb are no longer present in Lhasa since they emigrated to India during the years 1961 and 1962.[61]

Wa bak gling (Chinese: *Hebalin* 河坝林) is the name for Muslims who come from China, who were also called Hao pa gling, and also Ho pa gling,[62] Kha che or Huihui/Hui.[63] The name Ho pa gling refers to the neighbourhood where this group of Muslims lives.[64] The Tibetanised form *wa bak* is derived from the Chinese word *heba. Heba* means 'dam' or 'wall', *gling* means 'garden'. On the northern shore of the Lhasa river (Lhasa skyid chu) close to the mosque, a wall was built because of the danger of flooding. Since that time the settlement quarter and the Muslims themselves have been called 'Wa bak gling'.[65] The Tibetans call the Muslims who came from China also Rgya[66] kha che.[67]

---

55 Prince Peter of Greece and Denmark, 'The Moslems of Central Tibet', p. 234.

56 Corneille Jest, '*Kha che* and *Gya-Kha che*: Muslim Communities in Lhasa (1990)', *Tibet Journal*, 20/3 (1995): pp. 8-20, at p. 9.

57 Gaborieau, *Récit d'un voyageur musulman*, pp. 26-7.

58 Ibid., p. 27.

59 Roland Barraux, *Geschichte der Dalai Lamas: Göttliches Mitleid und irdische Politik* (Düsseldorf, 1995), p. 57.

60 This kind of double function as beggars and policemen can also be found in a group known as the *rāgībah* or, in its Tibetanised form, the *ra gya pa*. This group of Tibetans were responsible for removing corpses from Lhasa and cutting them into pieces for the sky burial. The *ra gya pa* belonged to the lowest level of the traditional Tibetan society (together with butchers and beggars), but they were very powerful and did not beg like beggars. See Gaborieau, *Récit d'un voyageur musulman*, p. 27.

61 Gaborieau, *Récit d'un voyageur musulman*, p. 29.

62 *Ho pa gling* is the term commonly found in Western literature.

63 Prince Peter of Greece and Denmark, 'The Moslems of Central Tibet', p. 234.

64 Gaborieau, *Récit d'un voyageur musulman*, p. 27.

65 Tshe rdor, 'Lha sa'i kha che', p. 112.

66 rgya – short for: rgya nag, i.e. China.

67 Prince Peter of Greece and Denmark, 'The Moslems of Central Tibet', p. 236.

The origin of the Wa bak gling is not clear. It is assumed that they came from Chinese areas where Islam had already been established.[68] According to this theory, their ancestors came from the Chinese provinces Gansu, Shanxi, Qinghai, Sichuan and Yunnan. At the beginning of the eighteenth century, during the reign of the Qing emperor Kangxi (reg. 1661-1722 under the Chinese name Shengzu) Chinese Muslims began settling in Lhasa. Some of them were the descendants of soldiers of the Chinese army who fought against the Gurkhas.[69] Nowadays the Wa bak gling form the majority of the Muslims in Lhasa.

MUSLIM QUARTERS IN LHASA[70]

In contrast to the rest of China where the Hui are widely scattered, in the Tibetan Autonomous Region the Hui are concentrated in single locations. The largest Muslim communities and most mosques and Muslim cemeteries can be found in Lhasa.

For centuries Lhasa was the religious, political and economic centre of the Tibetan world, where people from all Tibetan areas came for various reasons. Lhasa offered perfect conditions for local and foreign traders. Mosques and Muslim communities in Lhasa are historically attested since the reign of the Fifth Dalai Lama. Ladakhi Muslims were already well known in Western Tibet, and after that Dalai Lama had brought Ladakh within his sphere of religious influence, a small community of these Muslims began to grow in Lhasa. Most of them were traders, but there were also some butchers.[71]

The Muslim community in Lhasa is divided into two groups distinguished by the two areas in which they live: Kha che gling ga and Wa bak gling ga. Kha che gling ga is situated 3 km to the west of the Potala. There are residential buildings, two mosques and a cemetery. Kha che gling ga became a settlement area for Muslims in the eighteenth century.[72] The ancestors of the Muslims who live in that area were mainly traders and came from Kashmir, northern India and Nepal: Kha che gling ga is the home of the Lhasa kha che. (See Plate 17.1 which shows the new entrance to Kha che gling ga.) The Chinese name of this area is *Huizu yuanlin* 回族园林 ('garden of the Hui').

---

68 Ibid., p. 240.

69 People from Nepal; Tibetan: Gor kha. Gurkha invasion 1788-1792. See Jest, '*Kha che* and *Gya-Kha che*', p. 11.

70 During the years 2003 and 2004 I had the chance to do some fieldwork on Tibetan Muslims in Lhasa. This research was a by-product of my fieldwork for my PhD thesis on Tibetan fishermen.

71 David Snellgrove and Hugh Richardson, *A Cultural History of Tibet* (Boston, 1995), p. 203.

72 *Xizang Lishi Wenhua Cidian* [*Dictionary of the History and Culture of Tibet*] (Hangzhou, 1998), p. 40.

Wa bak gling ga is situated in the centre of Lhasa around the main mosque *Hebalin qingzhen si* 河坝林清真寺 and is inhabited by Muslims whose ancestors came from China or who came from China themselves: the Hui or Wa bak gling. There are many Muslim restaurants and butcher shops along the streets (Plate 17.2). The Wa bak gling used to supply meat to the court of the Dalai Lama.[73]

Next to the main mosque[74] (Plate 17.3) there are two other little mosques in Wa ba gling ga. The area also has its own cemetery. Nowadays Wa bak gling ga is the home of the main Muslim community with a large number of Muslims who came to Lhasa from different parts of China.

THE CASE OF THE 'TIBETAN HUI'

The special term for so-called 'Tibetan Hui', *zang Hui* 藏回, raises the question: Who belongs to this group?

In the Hualong Hui Autonomous County (*Hualong Huizu zizhixian* 花龙回族自治县) in the eastern part of the Qinghai province there is a region called Kaligang. According to the Chinese sources, *Hualong huizu zizhixiang gaikuang* 花龙回族自治县概况 (*Survey of the Hualong Hui Autonomous County*) and the *Hualong huizu zizhixian huizu shehui lishi diaocha* 花龙回族自治县回族社会历史调查 (*Investigation of the Society and History of the Hui in the Hualong Hui Autonomous County*), there are Hui, Han, Tibetans, Salar, Tu and Dongxiang living in Hualong. Since the second half of the twentieth century, the Hui are numerically the largest group, followed by Han Chinese and Tibetans. The balance between Hui and Tibetans has shifted more and more in favour of the Hui:

During the census of 1919, 1,681 Tibetan households with 6,026 (36.5%) Tibetans, 1,429 households with 5,631 (34.1%) Hui, 1,011 households with 4,349 (26.3%) Han and 137 households with 503 Salar were registered.[75] The census of 1982 registered the number of Hui at 86,735 (49.35%), the number of Han Chinese at 42,346 (24.09%), the number of Tibetans at 38,313 (21.8%) and the number of Salar at 7,943 (4.52%).[76] In 1990, more than 100,000 Hui had settled in Hualong.[77]

---

73 Abdul Wahid Radhu, *Islam in Tibet: Tibetan Caravans* (Louisville, 1997), p. 160.

74 Also: *Lhasa Da Qingzhen Si* (Fang Jianchang, 'Xizang Huizu yu qingzhensi yanjiu de ruogan wenti' ['Some Questions Concerning the Research on Hui and their Mosques in Tibet'], *Huizu Yanjiu*, 2 [1992]: pp. 27-30, at p. 28); Tibetan: *rGyal lha khang*; also: *Bara Masjid*, 'big mosque' (Jose Cabezón, 'Islam in the Tibetan Cultural Sphere', in Abdul Wahid Radhu, *Islam in Tibet*, p. 15).

75 *Hualong Huizu Zizhixian gaikuang* [*Survey of the Huizu Autonomous County*] (Xining, 1984), p. 17.

76 Ibid., p. 19.

77 Qiu Shusen, *Zhongguo Huizu da cidian* [*Great Dictionary of the Hui Nationalitiy in China*] (Nanjing, 1992), p. 118.

The so-called *Kaligang Hui* 卡力岗回 still settle in the Kaligang region in the communities *Dehelong* 德恒陇 and *Ashilong* 阿石陇; more than 8,000 Hui have settled in that area. Most of them speak Tibetan and follow Tibetan customs and traditions. Their houses are built in Tibetan style. Their ancestors were Tibetans who converted to Islam.[78] The Kaligang Hui are divided into *Jia-Hui* 加回 (also *Han-Hui* 汉回) who moved into that area from elsewhere and *O-Hui* 哦回 (also *Zang-Hui* 藏回) – the so-called 'Tibetan Hui' – who work as farmers.[79]

THE STORY OF MA LAICHI 马来尺 (1681-1766)[80]

Most Kaligang Hui claim that the visit of Ma Laichi was the beginning of the conversion of their ancestors to Islam.[81] Ma Laichi descended from a rich family in Gansu. In 1728 he went on pilgrimage to Mecca, but also visited Baghdad, Damascus, Cairo and other central places.[82] In around 1750 he arrived in the Kaligang region. According to the legend, Ma Laichi lived in the house of Tibetans. It is said that the landlord subjected him to an examination. He wanted to know whether Ma Laichi was a wise man and offered him boiled eggs to eat. Ma Laichi had to decide which eggs were good or bad. He ate the good ones and returned the bad ones, and in that way, convinced the landlord that he really was a wise man.[83]

Afterwards Ma Laichi converted some Tibetans to Islam.[84] It is said that he used special teaching methods and strategies.[85] After his death, Ma Laichi was buried in his home town.[86] Since that time the Tibetans of the Kaligang region have converted step by step to Islam.[87]

CONCLUSIONS

It is confusing that, in the People's Republic of China, different Muslim groups with different origins are classified under the ethnonym Hui, such as, for

---

[78] 'Hualong Huizu zizhixian gaikuang Huizu lishi diaocha', in *Qinghai Sheng Huizu Salazu Hasakezu shehui lishi diaocha* [*A Survey of the Society and History of of Qinghai's Hui, Salar and Kazakh peoples*] (Xining, 1995), p. 28.

[79] Qiu, *Zhongguo Huizu da cidian*, p. 24.

[80] Ibid., p. 943. See the article by Johan Elverskog in this volume.

[81] Li Gengyan and Xu Likui, 'Yisilanjiao zai Kaligang' ['Islam in Kaligang'], in *Yisilanjiao zai zhonguo* (Yinchuan, 1982), p. 421.

[82] Qiu, *Zhongguo Huizu da cidian*, p. 943.

[83] Li and Xu, 'Yisilanjiao zai Kaligang', p. 421.

[84] Qiu, *Zhongguo Huizu da cidian*, p. 943.

[85] Li and Xu, 'Yisilanjiao zai Kaligang', p. 421.

[86] Qiu, *Zhongguo Huizu da cidian*, p. 943.

[87] *Hualong Huizu Zizhixian gaikuang*, p. 194.

instance, Muslims who have completely adopted the lifestyle of Tibetans and other nationalities. This classification goes hand in hand with a popular tendency to regard the Hui as ethnically homogeneous. Such an interpretation cannot be historically sustained because the Hui derive from disparate origins.

I have presented here different groups of Muslims living in Tibetan areas who belong nowadays officially to the so-called Hui nationality in China: the Lhasa kha che, the Wa bak gling and the Zang Hui (Tibetan Hui). The origins of these groups are completely different: the ancestors of the Lhasa kha che come from Ladakh, Kashmir and India, the Wa bak gling are descended from Muslims coming from China (the 'real' Hui?) and the ancestors of the Zang Hui were Tibetans who converted to Islam. These different origins of the individual Muslim groups show that the Hui definitely cannot be regarded as a 'racial entity'. It seems that all Muslims who do not belong to one of the other Muslim minorities in China are also subsumed under the ethnonym 'Hui'.

The Tibetan terms for Muslims and the Chinese translations and transcriptions are confusing. An interesting field for future research that I would like to engage in is how all these groups of Muslims in Tibet identify themselves. I doubt, for instance, that the Lhasa kha che in the Kha che gling ga area regard themselves as Hui.

Chapter 18
Greater Ladakh and the Mobilization of Tradition in the Contemporary Baltistan Movement

Jan Magnusson

FROM LADAKH WAZARAT TO GREATER LADAKH

The Balti are a group of people living in the western Himalayas. They are ethnically related to Tibetans and speak a Tibetan dialect, but are predominantly Muslims. Post-colonial geopolitical conflicts between India and Pakistan separated the Balti in two groups, one living in the areas of Baltistan and Ghanche in Pakistan, and another living in the areas of Kargil and Ladakh in India. Before Partition in 1947 the Balti and their homeland were part of an administrative domain called Ladakh Wazarat within the Dogra-ruled princely state of Jammu and Kashmir established after the Anglo–Sikh wars in the mid-nineteenth century.[1] It extended southeast across the valleys along the Indus and Shyok rivers from where the Karakoram Highway now cuts north towards Gilgit, over the present districts of Baltistan and Ghanche in Pakistan, Kargil (including Zanskar) and Ladakh (including Nubra) in India. Today Kargil as well as Ladakh have been given 'hill tribe' status[2] within India while Baltistan is a federally administered

---

1 The Dogra made Baltistan a so-called *kardari* (sub-division) and in 1899 it became part of the Frontier District. Ladakh Wazarat was established in 1901 and incorporated Skardu (Baltistan), Kargil and Leh. See Ahmad Hasan Dani, *History of Northern Areas of Pakistan* (Lahore, 2001), p. 314.

2 After Partition Ladakh and Kargil were part of the state of Jammu and Kashmir but became separate districts in 1979. The term 'hill tribe' refers to the provision of the so-called Sixth Schedule in the Indian constitution that allows for self-government rights to minority groups through the establishment of autonomous district councils (ADC). The councils have less power than states but more power than local governments. When India's constitution was promulgated in 1950 the ADC framework was intended as a strategy to incorporate the populations of northeastern India in the Indian nation state. The same strategy has been used by the Indian state to manage demands for self-governance from a number of populations along the Indian–Himalayan borderlands. Demands for autonomy from Jammu and Kashmir and regional identity movements led to the creation of Ladakh Autonomous Hill Council in 1995 and Kargil Autonomous Hill Council in 2003. See David Stuligross, 'Autonomous Councils in Northeast India: Theory

area within the state of Pakistan.[3] The Balti in Nubra are living in the part of the Shyok Valley that was annexed by India in the 1971 war with Pakistan. The people of Baltistan and Kargil are Muslims, mainly Shiite, Nūrbakhshī (a Shiite–Sufi sect inspired by messianic ideas) or Sunni groups. The Kargil district also includes the Tibetan Buddhist community in Zanskar. People in Ladakh and Nubra are mainly Tibetan Buddhists while the Muslim minority belongs to the same groups as in Baltistan and Kargil.

Greater Ladakh, a concept to which I will return in detail shortly, is a contemporary political vision with Balti activists as the driving force that has emerged in the western Himalayas in the past decades. The imagined geographical boundaries of Greater Ladakh are drawn differently by different local groups. The most wide-ranging border extends from Chitral in northwestern Pakistan across Gilgit and Baltistan, into India over Kargil, Zanskar, Nubra and Ladakh, to Chang Tang, Lahaul and Spiti in the east. Sometimes Kashmir and Azad Kashmir are included too.

The most common boundary replicates Ladakh Wazarat much as it was before Partition. On the yellow T-shirts with a map of Greater Ladakh printed on the front and worn by some young activists in Kargil today, the western boundary of Greater Ladakh is drawn approximately at the peak Haramosh (7,409 m) that is located roughly where the Indus bends south and the road to Skardu[4] from the Karakoram Highway in Pakistan begins. The northern border is the border with China/Tibet. The southern border is drawn around Zanskar, Lahaul and Spiti while the eastern border runs around Nubra and Chang Tang.

Greater Ladakh claims to include both Muslim and Buddhist areas but so far it has not found much of a foothold in the latter. An important reason for the lack of positive response is probably the communal conflicts in Ladakh, especially the social boycott against Muslims from 1989 to 1992 and its continuing aftermath. This alienation seems to have been present in Buddhist–Muslim relations since Partition when many Muslims wanted the entire Ladakh Wazarat to accede

and Practice', *Alternatives: Social Transformation and Humane Governance*, 24/4 (1999): pp. 497-526; Selma K. Sonntag, *National Minority Rights in the Himalayas*, Heidelberg Papers in South Asian and Comparative Politics, Working paper no. 21 (Heidelberg: South Asia Institute, 2004).

[3] Baltistan/Ghanche is governed directly by the Federal Minister for Kashmiri Affairs, Northern Areas, States and Frontier Region. Baltistan/Ghanche hold 6/3 out of 24 seats in The Northern Areas Legislative Council instituted in 1994 as a part of the so-called Northern Areas Rule of Business. The council elects a Deputy Chief Executive, an office that holds the status of a federal minister. But the council can only exercise nominal power as all of its decisions must be approved by the Federal Minister before they can be enacted (IUCN Pakistan Programme, *NACS Support Project: Northern Areas Strategy for Sustainable Development. Background Paper on Governance*, final draft, October 2002).

[4] Skardu is the main town of Baltistan.

to Pakistan.[5] My Buddhist informants in Ladakh are generally sceptical about Greater Ladakh and seem inclined to link the idea with a threat of Balti and Muslim dominance over the region. But there are also other legacies involved. In Ladakh, at least around Leh,[6] Balti have been considered by Buddhists as well as Sunnis to be at the bottom of the social hierarchy. Historically they have generally been looked down on for their different dialect and for their Shiite faith. Balti immigrants looking for work have been hired only to do the most menial jobs.[7] As we shall see in the discussion of the revival of language and script below, some of the current Balti activities also react against Budddhist cultural politics in Ladakh.[8]

THE DYNAMICS OF A SOCIAL MOVEMENT

As a student of exile-Tibetan culture and society in India, the Balti cultural revival caught my attention in the mid-1990s. As a sociologist I have approached it as a social movement. This makes my focus different from an anthropological study that would probably have a much more ethnographic character or a political science study that would probably deal more with the political debate and competition, or the security aspect. The field I am interested in is the dynamics of social and cultural change as expressed in activities of so-called Social Movement Organizations (SMO), activists and intellectuals, and the cultural politics and products that accompany this process.

The Baltistan Movement, as I will call the revival, initially emerged in Baltistan and soon spread to Kargil and Nubra. Whereas the inclusion of the annexed Balti villages in Nubra may seem natural, the inclusion of Kargil as a stronghold for the movement may, at least at first glance, seem odd as the population in Kargil is officially based on a Purig majority, the so-called Purki (about 70%), whereas the

---

5 See Kim Gutschow, 'The Politics of Being Buddhist in Zangskar: Partition and Today', *India Review*, 5/3-4 (2006): pp. 470-98. Van Beek argues that the conflict between Muslims and Buddhists in Ladakh must be understood as a consequence of the colonial ordering of the people in the region as *communities* based on religious affiliation. See Martijn van Beek, 'Beyond Identity Fetishism: "Communal" Conflict in Ladakh and the Limits of Autonomy', *Cultural Anthropology*, 15/4 (2001): pp. 525-69. Grist suggests that the suspension of democratic politics in Jammu and Kashmir between 1990 and 1996 encouraged the religious division. See Nicola Grist, *Local Politics in the Suru Valley of Northern India* (PhD thesis, Goldsmiths, University of London, 1998), pp. 190-93.

6 Leh is the main town of Ladakh.

7 Pascale Dolfuss, 'The History of Muslims in Central Ladakh', *Tibet Journal*, 20/3 (1995): pp. 35-58, at p. 45.

8 The communal conflict is an important context in the socio-political dynamics of the area today. But since the topic of this text is the mobilization of tradition in the Baltistan Movement it will have to be dealt with another time. For a detailed description and analysis, see van Beek, 'Beyond Identity Fetishism'.

Baltis are a minority. But in reality many people in the area look at themselves as so-called Argons, an ethnic mix that is not officially recognized by the Indian state as a tribe. When the name first came in use it referred to children with a Ladakhi mother who had converted to Islam, and with a Muslim father, and did not specify any particular ethnic affiliation. This is not necessarily the case any more. The Argon families often had trans-Himalayan bonds and because of this their community came to be rather influential. They were primarily business people living in the towns and did not represent a threat to the Balti farmers.[9] Since Argons/Purkis aspire to the same cultural ideas and traditions as the Balti they are integral in the movement. In oral accounts of local history it is often stated that Baltistan is the intellectual and religious model for Kargil.

The Baltistan Movement started to emerge in Balti student circles in the 1980s but it has not yet developed into a full-scale popular movement. The leading activists are groups of college-educated men and some local literary scholars and historians. I have chosen to concentrate my attention on three specific Social Movement Organizations (SMO) and their creative mobilization of tradition and cultural politics: the Baltistan Culture Foundation (BCF), founded in 1998 and based in Skardu, the Kargil Social and Cultural Organization (KASCO), founded in 1995 and based in Kargil,[10] and the Society for Knowledge and Responsibilities of Culture, Health, Education and Nature (Skarchen),[11] founded in 1997 and based in the Nubra Valley/Leh. The respondents are predominantly intellectuals and activists who are active in these three organizations and/or in Balti cultural politics. All three organizations can be described as local NGOs funded mostly through small government grants and donor grants. So far, both Skarchen and KASCO have obtained a large proportion of their resources by serving as so-called PIAs (Project Implementation Agencies) in the large-scale Watershed Development Project in India.[12] In 2002, the BCF was taken over by the Aga Khan Cultural Support Program[13] that is now using it as an implementation agency for its cultural support programme in Baltistan, a development I have dealt

---

9 Dolfuss, 'The History of Muslims in Central Ladakh', p. 42.

10 The Kargil district and its main town share the same name.

11 The word 'Skarchen' means 'morning star' and is considered to be an auspicious symbol by the people of the Nubra Valley. It is also the name of a location in the Nubra Valley.

12 Land and water resource management for sustainable development of natural resources and communal empowerment. It was introduced in Ladakh in 1996 (www.dolr.nic.in/fguidelines.htm, last accessed 2 August 2008).

13 The Aga Khan Cultural Support Program is an organization within the Aga Khan Development Network, a large NGO led by the Imam of the Ismailis, Sir Sultan Mahomed Shah Aga Khan (www.akdn.org).

with elsewhere.[14] Data for the study was primarily collected during fieldwork in Baltistan, Kargil, Ladakh and Nubra between 2004 and 2006.[15]

THE EMERGENCE OF THE BALTISTAN MOVEMENT

The Baltistan Movement emerged in the western Himalayas as a challenge to the prevailing social orders and the geopolitics of the Pakistani and Indian nation states. But why did it emerge at this particular point in time? In order to answer this question I would like to discuss two kinds of causes: present socio-political conditions, and long-term historical and cultural traditions.

One possible socio-political condition behind the emergence of the movement is the post-colonial cultural hegemony of modern Pakistan and India in the region.[16] From such a perspective, the movement can be interpreted as a counter-reaction to the changes brought about by the integration into the nation states, especially regarding the Kashmir issue and the disadvantages caused by the undetermined territorial status of the Northern Areas in Pakistan after Partition. Other socio-political conditions include a lack of development opportunities, the migration (of men) in order to work and study outside the region, the significance of ethnic identity in the present world as well as globalization in terms of increased mobility, access to information and markets leading to new demands and a new awareness of the world.

Possible long-term historical and cultural traditions include the region's relatively independent geographical location in a transit zone between Tibet, South Asia and Central Asia and the cultural interaction it invites. Long-lasting Balti traditions include vernacular Tibetan and pre-Partition memories but, most of all, a historical context that during long periods has been different from that of South Asia.

One can say that the emergence of the Baltistan Movement and later the vision of Greater Ladakh were shaped by enduring western Himalayan traditions and induced by the post-Partition conditions in the region. The movement is a context in which history and cultural traditions are reinvented to fit the vision

---

14 Jan Magnusson, 'The Baltistan Movement: Tibetan History and Identity in the Northern Areas of Pakistan', in P. Christiaan Klieger (ed.), *Tibetan Borderlands: Proceedings of the Tenth Seminar of the International Association for Tibetan Studies, Oxford, 2003* (Leiden, 2006), pp. 191-207.

15 I would like to thank Mohammad Hassan, Gulzar Hussain Munshi, Aijas Hussain Munshi, Sonam Joldan and Dawa Tsering and his family for their friendship, support, and hospitality, and Tenzin for his safe driving and patience.

16 Cf. Sökefeld's work on the Northern Areas of Pakistan where he talks about independence as the transition from one mode of domination and subalternity to another. Martin Sökefeld, 'From Colonialism to Postcolonial Colonialism: Changing Modes of Domination in the Northern Areas of Pakistan', *Journal of Asian Studies*, 64/4 (2005): pp. 939-73, at pp. 940 and 963.

arising from present needs for social and cultural mobilization. Historical and cultural elements which distinguish Greater Ladakh from neighbouring and contending regions, from Pakistan and India, and lend it a specific identity in the world are selected and formatted for this purpose. For instance, even though it often reaches back to the days of the Tibetan Empire to gain historical authenticity, the vision tends to bring out a specific Balti history rather than a common western Himalayan history. That could explain why, for instance, intellectuals belonging to the movement often emphasize Tibetan and not Muslim elements of Baltistan's history in order to distinguish the Balti people from their fellow Muslims of Pakistan, Kashmir and, as we shall see, maybe also Ladakh.

MOBILIZATION OF TRADITION

In their book about music and social movements, the sociologists Ron Eyerman and Andrew Jamison investigate how traditions are mobilized by social movements.[17] The *mobilization of tradition*, according to the authors, includes a selective reworking of cultural materials (poetry, music, performance) and leads to a renewed collective identity, creating political consciousness among people on an emotional rather than intellectual level.

Traditions[18] do not have to be old to serve this purpose. Nor do they have to be historically accurate. For our present aim, tradition may be best understood as a tool for legitimizing cultural practice and identity.[19] In his influential work *The Invention of Tradition*, Hobsbawm refers to tradition as a set of practices meant to establish continuity with a suitable past.[20] At the heart of his argument is the assertion that traditions are selected and used as a response to a present situation. It is a creative use, in Eyerman and Jamison's vocabulary, of selected cultural and historic elements picked out of the past and mixed with various novel and contemporary elements.

In the case of Greater Ladakh and the Baltistan movement I would like to suggest that tradition is mobilized as a strategy in the reassertion of a cultural, political and regional identity that is different from that of the two dominant

---

17 R. Eyerman and A. Jamison, *Music and Social Movements: Mobilizing Tradition in the Twentieth Century* (Cambridge, 1998).

18 In this context the term 'tradition' does not mean 'anti-modern', 'conservative' or 'reactionary', nor does it mean a 'custom' that is less articulated and more easily altered, and not a 'habit' which is an individualized form of behaviour.

19 Frank J. Korom, *Hosay Trinidad: Muharram Performances in an Indo-Caribbean Diaspora* (Philadelphia, 2003), p. 211.

20 Eric Hobsbawm, 'Introduction: Inventing Traditions', in Eric Hobsbawm and Terence Ranger (eds), *The Invention of Tradition* (Cambridge, 1983).

nation states, and transcends the border between them.[21] Elements of tradition and history become 'weapons of the weak', as Scott has put it,[22] in a political project to navigate away from an unfortunate situation and find a road to a new awareness of cultural identity. For instance, as I will discuss below, the reworking of traditional poetry by mixing it with pop music in Kargil has made it more accessible to people and has provided an emotive popular context for a collective vision of Greater Ladakh.

In the following sections I will look at the Baltistan Movement's mobilization of tradition first by discussing the historic narratives of Greater Ladakh and then by focusing on two particular examples: 1. The attempts to reintroduce Tibetan script in Baltistan and Kargil, and 2. The production of so called pop *ghazals* in Kargil.

HISTORICAL VISION OF GREATER LADAKH

Historical narratives within the Baltistan movement are based on a reworking of elements from a conventional western Himalayan historic context to support the visions of Greater Ladakh. The purpose seems clear enough: to distinguish and demarcate Greater Ladakh as an independent geographical and cultural entity in the world today.

Talking about their history, my informants from Baltistan, Kargil and Nubra often conjure up Golden Ages when the region was either under Tibetan influence or an independent kingdom. In a promotional leaflet in English directed at outsiders and foreign donor agencies, Skarchen presents the following vision of Balti history and language. Similar visions are propagated by most intellectuals affiliated with the movement in Skardu and Kargil:

> Indian historian have name [Baltistan] Little Tibet, as the majority of population being ethnically and linguistically of Tibetan origin and the area is geographically located on the Tibetan plateau and for centuries remained a part of the Tibetan Empire. The local people themselves referred and for centuries remained a part of the Tibetan Empire. The local people themselves referred to their homeland as 'BALTIYUL' (Land of Baltis). The population of Baltistan is a heterogeneous mixture of ethnic groups and Tibetan is the principal ethnic group in this area. The language spoken by the entire

[21] Korom, *Hosay Trinidad*, p. 208.

[22] James C. Scott, *Weapons of the Weak: Everyday Forms of Peasant Resistance* (New Haven, 1985). In this study of a Malaysian village, Scot explores everyday forms of resistance that are not framed as open organized political activity. It is a kind of resistance that avoids direct symbolic confrontation in the 'struggle over the appropriation of symbols, how the past and present should be labelled, a struggle to identify causes and assess blame, a contentious effort to give partisan meaning to local history' (p. xvii).

> population is called BALTI, which is an archaic dialect of Tibetan language. Presently Balti has been heavily influenced by Burushaski, Turkish and Urdu and affected by Muslim literature in Persian. With the result it has deviated from the original Tibetan language.[23]

When I discussed with a Skarchen informant why the organization has chosen to focus on pre-Islamic Tibetan history he pulled out a pack of well-thumbed photocopies from an unidentified book. It proved to be a chronological list of rulers in Baltistan from 1190 to 1915. He pointed to the Tibetan names which appeared in the list before the first Muslim ruler, Ibrāhīm Shāh in the thirteenth century, who is said to be the founder of the Maqpon dynasty that ruled Baltistan for 24 generations. He went on to describe the Tibetans as the authentic lineage of Balti kings, and the Muslim kings as representatives of a foreign political force. He blamed the recent erosion of Balti culture on modernization forces in general but more importantly he claimed that Islam was the prime reason for the oppression of authentic expressions of Balti culture even up until today, an issue I will return to below.

The views about Balti history and culture circulating among intellectuals and activists of the movement are far from clear-cut, and they are increasingly re-formatted to fit the changing political visions of Greater Ladakh. For instance, in a paper written by the Balti activist Ismail Khan and circulated in Pakistan and India the author speaks of a 'highjacked history' where an independent historical Greater Ladakh was appropriated and subsumed under the history of Jammu and Kashmir. In reality, the author argues, for 900 years starting from the middle of the tenth century Greater Ladakh had been an independent kingdom ruled by dynasties descending from the kings of 'old Tibet'. Some activists in Kargil, however, flatly deny that Greater Ladakh was ever under Tibetan influence. They hold that the original inhabitants of the region were Dards but that a massive migration of Tibetans 'more than a thousand years ago overwhelmed the culture of the Dards and moped up their racial characters'.[24] In the same text the region is described as a battleground between Tibet and China in the seventh century. In the eighth century, the author(s) argue(s), the Arabs 'jumped in' and conquered Kashgar in order to gain control over Central Asia and introduce Islam. However, by that time a ruler from Kashmir called Laltadita had conquered Ladakh which became a buffer state between Tibet and China. The result was that the original Greater Ladakh was split, the text concludes.

The Nubra activists do not make any historical claims. They stress the point that they are *ethnic* Tibetans:[25] that is, that they are of a Tibetan *race* (genetically Tibetan) and direct descendants of Tibetan nomads who migrated south to find

---

23 Skarchen, undated flyer in English, faithfully reproduced.

24 Undated flyer in English called *Greater Ladakh* produced by KASCO.

25 The same view is held by some intellectuals in Baltistan, for example Abbas Kazmi and Syed Muhammad, 'The Balti Language', in P.N. Pushp and K. Warikoo (eds),

pastures for their livestock a long time ago. As evidence of their origin they bring up their customs in food and clothing and their 'system of living' which they claim to be genuinely Tibetan. However, this claim is discarded by most Balti activists elsewhere.

In academic studies of the regional history it is often stated that the Tibetans occupied the region while attempting to gain control over Turkistan (Xinjiang) during the seventh and eighth centuries, and that Tibetan *u-chen (dbu can)* scripts as well as Buddhist doctrine were introduced during this time. As eminent historians of the Western Tibetan Empire[26] have established, there are not that many sources to draw on.

The Pakistani historian Ahmad Hasan Dani distinguishes two periods of Buddhism in the history of Baltistan: the period between the first and second centuries CE when Buddhism was introduced either from Kashmir or Gilgit, and the time of the Tibetan conquest of Baltistan in the eighth century.[27] According to Dani, the Tibetan interest in Baltistan was a result of the consolidation of dynastic rule in Tibet.[28] At the end of the ninth century, Dani continues, a new state power started to develop and Baltistan remained independent until the time of the Mughals. This account supports the way history is promoted in the Baltistan Movement.

However, according to Dolfuss, external influence in the area began as early as the fourteenth century when Muslims conquered Kashmir.[29] This was followed by sporadic frontier raids as well as attempts to gain permanent control.[30] At the beginning of the fifteenth century Ladakh was temporarily occupied by Sultan Zayn al-ʿĀbidīn and in 1483 Baltistan was invaded by Sayyid Hasa.[31] Dolfuss emphasizes opportunities for trade rather than religious zeal as a primary cause of change, and mentions, for instance, how Mīrzā Ḥaydar Dughlāt seized both Baltistan and Ladakh in 1548 in order to ensure access to trade routes to Central Asia, not in order to convert people to the Islamic faith. According to Dolfuss, it was in fact trade and the resulting influx of Muslim trading communities and

Jammu, Kashmir and Ladakh: Linguistic Predicament (New Delhi, 2005). KASCO seems to be ambiguous on the issue.

26 Christopher I. Beckwith, *The Tibetan Empire in Central Asia: A History of the Struggle for Great Power among Tibetans, Turks, Arabs, and Chinese during the Early Middle Ages* (Princeton, 1987); Helmut Hoffman, 'Early and Medieval Tibet', in Denis Sinor (ed.), *The Cambridge History of Early Inner Asia* (Cambridge, 1990), pp. 371-99.

27 Dani, *History of Northern Areas of Pakistan*, p. 213.

28 Ibid., p. 214.

29 Dolfuss, 'The History of Muslims in Central Ladakh'.

30 Wolfgang Holzwarth, 'Change in Pre-Colonial Times: An Evaluation of Sources on the Karakorum and Eastern Hindukush Regions (from 1500 to 1800)', in Irmtraud Stellrecht (ed.), *Karakorum - Hindukush - Himalaya: Dynamics of Change*, Part 2 (Cologne, 1998), pp. 297-336, at p. 302.

31 Dolfuss, 'The History of Muslims in Central Ladakh'.

their religious authorities in the area that led to the spread of Islam.[32] Holzwarth also points out that Baltistan served as a refuge for exiled Nūrbakhshī leaders from Kashmir.[33] One of the most notable of these leaders was Mīr Dāniyāl who, according to Rieck, used his time there to win converts to his sect.[34]

Independent or not, at the time of the rule of the Mughals the region was in economic recession as a result of rerouted trade caravans, and in 1679 the king of Ladakh had to approach the Mughals for protection against a Mongolo–Tibetan military expansion.[35]

Many historians have particularly paid attention to Islamization in the area and expressed various views as to when it took place. Francke has argued local rulers tended to ignore their Tibetan origin and fabricated new pedigrees including as many Muslim names as possible.[36] He concludes that since the oldest of the recorded pedigrees he could find starts with Sultan Sikandar in the late fourteenth century, it is likely that Islam was introduced at that time. Dani, however, argues that Buddhism was practised until 'the advent of Amir-i-Kabir Sayyid Ali Hamadani himself'[37] who is locally known to have won a debate against a Buddhist monk, leading to the construction of the famous Kashmiri-style Chakchan mosque in Khaplu. From the evidence of Ḥashmatullāh's *Tārīkh-i Jammu*, another Pakistani historian argues that Hamadānī never visited Baltistan.[38] It was really his nephew and disciple Muḥammad Nūrbakhsh who converted the people in Baltistan from Buddhism, he suggests. In fact, several modern studies suggest that not even Nūrbakhsh reached Baltistan.[39] Sufis, on the other hand, tend to hold that it was an Iraqi preacher called Mīr Shams al-Dīn ʿIrāqī (a.k.a. Shaykh Shams al-Dīn Muḥammad al-Iṣfahānī) who, after being expelled from Kashmir, came to Baltistan and converted people to Shiism in the late fifteenth century.[40] Quoting *Tārīkh-i Firishta*, Holzwarth mentions a certain ʿAlī Rāy as the first Muslim ruler of Baltistan (1570-78).[41]

---

32 Compare this with Stellrecht's view of conflicts in the Himalayas as generally being over *road control* and how the *transit potential* is at the core of the relationship with the lowland powers. Irmtraud Stellrecht, 'Economic and Political Relationships between Northern Pakistan and Central as well as South Asia in the Nineteenth and Twentieth Century', in Stellrecht (ed.), *Karakorum*, pp. 3-20.

33 Holzwarth, 'Change in Pre-Colonial Times'.

34 Andreas Rieck, 'The Nurbakhshis of Baltistan: Crisis and Revival of a Five Centuries Old Community', *Die Welt des Islams*, 35/2 (1995): pp. 159-88, at p. 161.

35 Dolfuss, 'The History of Muslims in Central Ladakh'.

36 August Hermann Francke, *A History of Western Tibet, One of the Unknown Empires* (London, 1907), p. 90.

37 Dani, *History of Northern Areas of Pakistan*, p. 232, most likely referring to the Persian Sufi ʿAlī ibn Shihāb al-Dīn Hamadānī (1314-84).

38 Banat Gul Afridi, *Baltistan in History* (Peshawar, 1988), p. 26.

39 Rieck, 'The Nurbakhshis of Baltistan', p. 161.

40 Rieck, 'The Nurbakhshis of Baltistan'.

41 Holzwarth, 'Change in Pre-Colonial Times', p. 302.

Grist, on the other hand, rejects the image of Islam 'sweeping in' and a mass-conversion of the people in the region.[42] Institutional religion could not be found here until the seventeenth century, she argues, and goes on to state that both Islam and Buddhism should be perceived as integral parts of the Himalayan world and that the structural change from one religion to the other is perhaps not as dramatic as it might seem. This view is supported by Srinivas's emphasis on the historical integration rather than division between Muslim and Buddhist communities in Ladakh.[43] Rieck cautions us not to overrate the presence of religious authorities and suggests that Islam may only have been a 'thin layer over a plethora of pre-Islamic beliefs and superstitions until the late nineteenth century'.[44]

As Eaton has noted, historians do not always distinguish between conversion to the Islamic faith and the rule of Muslims, since people often submitted to the military arm of the Muslim state and not to the Islamic faith.[45] The issue is further complicated by the fact that people may display the official religious faith of their ruler in order to receive favours and protection.[46]

One should bear in mind that the conversion to Islam in this region was taking place on the periphery of the Muslim sphere of influence. Baltistan and Ladakh were far away from the centres of Muslim power. What is more, they were far away from the centres of Buddhist and Hindu power too. As Grist suggests, people in this region were hardly fully integrated into any mass-religious system.[47]

To this one might add that the polarization of religious communities parallels Hobsbawn's 'invention of tradition' with 'tradition' as a product of the colonial era which facilitates a historical narrative based on a struggle between the communities. In practice, religions, especially their local practice on geographical margins, are much less closed, self-contained or mutually exclusive than such a narrative may presume.

The results of my fieldwork support both Grist's view and Eaton's thesis: the blurred line between Islam and Buddhism seems to be innate in the revival of

42 Nicola Grist, 'Muslims in Western Ladakh', *Tibet Journal*, 20/3 (1995): pp. 59-70.

43 Smriti Srinivas, 'Conjunction, Parallelism and Cross-Cutting Ties among the Muslims of Ladakh', *Tibet Journal*, 20/3 (1995): pp. 71-95.

44 Rieck, 'The Nurbakhshis of Baltistan', p. 165. The observations are similar to those of the British anthropologist Charles Ramble, who found that for the Tepa people in present-day Mustang, Buddhism as a system is used more as a 'raw material, divisible stuff which they have broken up and employed in the construction or elaboration of a local tradition'. See Charles Ramble, 'How Buddhist are Buddhist Communities? The Construction of Tradition in Two Lamaist Villages', *Journal of the Anthropological Society of Oxford*, 21/2 (1990): pp. 185-97, at p. 194.

45 The 'religion of the sword thesis' as Eaton puts it. See Richard Eaton, *The Rise of Islam and the Bengal Frontier 1204-1760* (Berkeley, 1993), p. 113.

46 The 'religion of patronage thesis' according to Eaton, *Rise of Islam and the Bengal Frontier*, p. 116.

47 Grist, 'Muslims in Western Ladakh'.

Balti cultural expressions, and Islamic and Buddhist symbols are freely mixed in cultural products of Balti activists. At times the display of religious faith even seems to be used as a strategy to secure various political ends and patronage and to negotiate contemporary Balti culture with Islam.

Something that caught my attention in Skarchen's discourse of Balti culture as 'disappearing' and 'diminishing' so that 'necessary steps' have to be taken in order to preserve it, was the argument that Islam has been suppressing Balti culture. The 'domination of Islam' has 'muffled' Balti culture as one informant put it.

The separation of religion and culture into two separate spheres struck me as a rather pragmatic attitude. It is significant that the informants often described Muslims in the third person plural, and the practice of Islam as something to be upheld or put aside depending on the practical circumstances of the situation. This observation seems to find support in Rieck's theory of Islam as a 'thin layer' and Grist's conclusion regarding the rather late institutionalization of religion in this part of the Himalayas.

The Nubra Balti informants' views about Islam were also different from those of my informants in Baltistan and Kargil who seemed to be able place their religious belief at the heart of their cultural identity. They did not, as did the Nubra Balti, describe Islam to be in opposition to their cultural traditions. On the contrary, Balti religious teachers and their books were seen by the Balti and Kargili informants as an advanced and prestigious form of Islamic practice and scholarship, and as a central part of contemporary Balti culture. On the other hand, their views probably suggest that Grist's observation concerning a structural similarity and Eaton's above-mentioned conclusions regarding Islam in Indian history can be applied to the Nubra Balti.

In comparison to the Nubra Baltis, the activists in Baltistan and Kargil have been careful to negotiate every project with local religious leaders to obtain their approval and convince them of the necessity to revitalize and preserve local history and traditions. Their common interest is the recognition of the region and its people by the central government in order to attract development resources to the area. This 'unholy alliance' rests fully on the separation of culture and religion principle and also confirms Grist's theory.

Here, the activists in Kargil have an advantage over their friends across the border. In the Baltistan Movement intellectuals and activists do not generally occupy any influential positions in society and are thus at the mercy of those who are. In Kargil many of their fellow activists are leading citizens in government offices and school boards. This may in fact partly explain why contemporary Balti cultural life is more active in Kargil than in Skardu.

From the mid-nineteenth century until Partition, Baltistan, Kargil and Ladakh were ruled by the Dogra, a Kashmiri dynasty. It was backed by the British who sought to protect the northwest frontier from Russian influence. The business-oriented Dogra revamped the regional economy and constructed a large new bazaar in Leh.[48] But by the time India was preparing itself for independence the number of large caravans passing through the region had started to decrease and the region once again found itself in economic recession.

During the days of the Ladakh Wazarat public administration, economic relationships (trade and property) and family bonds reached across the region. At Partition, despite the fact that the large majority of people in the region were Muslim, the Hindu ruler decided to incorporate Jammu and Kashmir in the Indian state. But strong Muslim forces in the Northern Areas (then called the Gilgit Agency) wanted to be part of the new Islamic State of Pakistan and a rebellion broke out. Pakistan's new government was supportive of the rebels' claim. As a result Kashmir was split into two parts and Baltistan came under the control of Pakistan.[49] Neither Ladakh nor Kargil took an active part in this turmoil. Contacts were subsequently reduced to a minimum with Kargil and Ladakh on the Indian side of the border (or Line of Control [LOC] as it is most often referred to) and Baltistan on the Pakistani side.

In his work on the history of Kashmir, Mridu Rai has pointed out the lack of legitimacy for the Hindu Dogra among Jammu and Kashmir's Muslim citizens, and how it gave rise to the Kashmiriyat, a specific Kashmiri cultural identity, and its pan-Islamism.[50] This lack of legitimacy probably explains part of the rebels' incentives. When they joined the Islamic state of Pakistan, Muslims in the Gilgit Agency relied on the Pakistani government to provide them with full citizenship as well as the material and cultural rights they felt deprived of under the Dogra. However, because of the disputed status of the territory and the Kashmir conflict, their expectations were not fulfilled, and the vision of a Greater Ladakh has partly emerged as a response to this.

The aim of my analysis of the Baltistan Movement's use of history and academic literature on this history was to highlight the different historical narratives rather than to harmonize them and arrive at one version. The main reason is, of course, that no such a master narrative can exist. Historical narratives are always contested and mobilized to support different communities' claims of identity and rights.[51]

In post-colonial South Asia the enterprise of writing history has been closely related to the crafting of a top-down nation-building master narrative. Contending narratives of communities like the people of Baltistan, Kargil and Ladakh, on the margins of nation-states and far away from mainstream events, were often 'wrenched' from them, as the Indian historian Shahid Amin argues in his study of the infamous Chaudi Chaura incident in 1922 when

---

48 Dolfuss, 'The History of Muslims in Central Ladakh', p. 41.

49 Alistair Lamb, *Kashmir: A Disputed Legacy 1846-1990* (Karachi, 1991).

50 Mridu Rai, *Hindu Rulers, Muslim Subjects: Islam, Rights, and the History of Kashmir* (London, 2004).

51 This has been put forward by the 'history from below', 'subaltern studies' and 'minority history' paradigms.

villagers attacked and burned down a local police station in Uttar Pradesh in what they believed to be an act of Gandhian civil disobedience.[52] Contending narratives are appropriated into the logic of the master narrative, omitting the communities' own agency, logic and beliefs. The narrative of Greater Ladakh is, from this perspective, 'what seeps through the gaps, fissures, interstices'[53] of the Indian and Pakistani master narratives as competing narratives of neglected communities reasserting their identity and demands for social justice.[54]

My own argument in this context is that the vision of Greater Ladakh finds its meaning primarily against the backdrop of present day geopolitical boundaries and socio-economic conditions. Before Partition Baltistan, Kargil and Ladakh were geographically and politically remote areas on the transit zones between the British, Russian and Chinese empires and formally held together as parts of a princely Indian state. After Partition, they were divided and pulled into the dynamics of the Kashmir conflict, and this condition has continued to determine the development of the region.[55] In my view, the emergence of the Baltistan Movement and the visions of Greater Ladakh should be understood as a counter-reaction to this situation.

As for the interest in supporting this vision with Tibetan historic elements, it should be taken into account that the region was and continues to be in the borderlands of Tibet and has been constantly subjected to Tibetan cultural influence, especially when the Tibetan Empire was at its peak. At the same time it is interesting to note that, in general, the affinity and loyalty to Tibet among the people living in the Himalayan borderlands seems to be waning as a result of the economic and political advantages of belonging to a comparatively well-developed state like India. This is the case even in a religious context where, for instance, many of the leading centres of learning of Tibetan Buddhism are now placed outside Tibet.[56] But, however dominant this trend might be, it is not evident in the Baltistan Movement's vision. Here, a return to Tibetan cultural elements is key to the claim for independence from post-colonial India and Pakistan. However, this seeming contradiction might be a result of the way academic research is structured. As Aggarwal has pointed out, research on the Himalayas has tended to follow the geopolitics of the modern nation states. This is also obvious in area studies where South Asian and East Asian studies or, one may add, Central Asian studies, South Asian studies and Tibetan studies

---

52 Shahid Amin, *Chaudi Chaura 1922-1992: Metaphor, Memory* (Berkeley, 1995).

53 Gyan Prakash, 'Subaltern Studies as Post-Colonial Criticism', *The American Historical Review*, 99/5 (1994): pp. 1475-90, at p. 1482.

54 Dipesh Chakrabarty, 'Minority Histories, Subaltern Pasts', *Postcolonial Studies*, 1/1 (1998): pp. 15-29.

55 Cf. Meredith Weiss, *The Jammu and Kashmir Conflict*, Yale Working Paper CAR/CS05, The MacMillan Centre, 2002. http://128.36.236.77/workpaper (last accessed 3 August 2008).

56 Klieger (ed.), *Tibetan Borderlands*.

are insufficiently connected.[57] Transnational perspectives situating Baltistan, Kargil and Ladakh in a wider Himalayan context with Tibet have thus largely been missing.[58]

THE BATTLE OVER TIBETAN SCRIPT

Under the rule of the Mughals the common language spoken in the empire was called Hindustani. Its name was later changed to Urdu. It is written in a Perso-Arabic script called *nastaʿlīq*. Urdu was also used as the language of administration in British India. At the time of Partition language had come to be associated with religious communities (Muslims/Hindus), and Urdu/*nastaʿlīq* was claimed as a Muslim language as well as the national language of Pakistan while the Hindu language and national language of India was to be Hindi (written in *devanagiri* script). In some northern Indian states like Jammu and Kashmir, Urdu/*nastaʿlīq* was later instituted as the official state language/script. As Anderson has shown, national languages, especially in printed form, have been crucial in the creation of the modern nation state, and in many cases communities living in the margins of nation states or across their borders were, often forcibly, pulled into the national community by the structure of the educational system, requirements for employment and so on.[59]

The dominant vernacular language of Baltistan, Kargil and Ladakh was, and continues to be, a western Tibetan dialect. Unlike the dialects of central Tibet, many words reflect older pronunciation. That is, they are pronounced more or less as they are spelled, and the dialect is perhaps closer to the one spoken in Kham, a region located in the eastern part of Tibet. Even though it is difficult, if not impossible, to adapt *nastaʿlīq* to the Tibetan phonetics, the *u-chen* (*dbu-can*) Tibetan script was replaced by *nastaʿlīq* already under the Mughals. Urdu/*nastaʿlīq* was upheld after Independence as the official state language on both sides of the LOC. Up until today the medium of instruction in schools in Baltistan and Kargil continue to be Urdu/*nastaʿlīq* (and English), and it is also used in courts, offices, media and so on. Urdu is the administrative language in Ladakh although Tibetan is taught in schools.

The reintroduction of *u-chen* is an activity that has engaged and inspired intellectuals and activists in the Baltistan movement. The fight for the right to use an indigenous language and the resistance against the dominance of the

57 Ravina Aggarwal, *Beyond Lines of Control: Performance and Politics on the Disputed Borders of Ladakh, India* (Durham, 2004).

58 For more on this debate see Geoffrey Samuel, 'Tibet and the Southeast Asian Highlands', in Per Kværne (ed.), *Tibetan Studies: Proceedings of the Seminar of the International Association for Tibetan Studies, Fagernes 1992* (Oslo, 1994), pp. 679-710.

59 Benedict Anderson, *Imagined Communities: Reflections on the Origin and Spread of Nationalism* (London, 1991).

language of the hegemonic state has been common among communities that feel marginalized in post-colonial nation states. But for the Baltistan Movement's intellectuals the issue has an additional twist as it has evolved into a conflict with Buddhist groups in Ladakh that claim that the vernacular Tibetan spoken in Baltistan, Kargil and Ladakh, *bodhic*, and *u-chen*should be used exclusively by Buddhists. In fact, the terms *bodhic* and *ladakhi* are used interchangeably in the debate over language. In the following section I will use only *bodhic*.

But before I move into a more detailed description of this interesting conflict I would like to present two examples of the counter-hegemonic strategies of the Baltistan Movement related to the introduction of Tibetan language and script in elementary education. An attempt to do this was made by the BCF in Baltistan starting in 1999. A similar project has been initiated by KASCO in Kargil.

With funding from the UK-based Tibet Foundation which maintains close ties with the Tibetan community in exile, the BCF launched a twofold strategy: the erection of store signs in *u-chen* in local bazaars, and the production of Tibetan textbooks for elementary schools. The purpose was not only to revive the use of *u-chen* script but also to increase people's awareness of their 'unique Balti heritage'. About 100 store-boards were put up (see Plate 18.1). But the 1000 textbooks that were printed never reached an elementary school. One of the most important reasons for the failure of the project was most likely the publication of a competing textbook written by a person propagating the use of *nastaʿlīq* for Balti in response to the BCF's initiative. In the public debate *u-chen* was branded as 'unislamic' by its opponents and local (public) support for the project quickly faded away. However, the store-boards have not yet been taken down.[60] What is interesting is that although the majority of people passing them cannot read *u-chen*, the script has assumed a symbolic value as an expression and reconfirmation of Balti identity.

KASCO's strategy has been somewhat shrewder. Instead of approaching already existing elementary schools the organization has set up its own private English medium school, the Munshi Habib-Ullah Mission School,[61] funded primarily by fees paid by the parents. Their plan is to begin with a pre-nursery, nursery and so-called LKG (lower kindergarten) school and then expand while letting the school slowly build a solid local reputation. Language teaching will then be introduced softly, voluntarily and in dialogue with the parents. The founders of the school are careful to avoid using the label *bodhic* for the script and opt for the more neutral *Tibetan*, alternatively *ngati skad* ('our language'), instead.

The reintroduction of *u-chen* has several religious connotations. In Baltistan some groups perceive the use of the script as a challenge to Islam. At first glance this is perhaps less surprising than the resistance from some Buddhist

60 Magnusson, 'The Baltistan Movement'.

61 Mission school in this case has nothing to do with Christianity but signifies the social involvement of the founders.

intellectuals in Ladakh towards recognition of *u-chen* as the script of Muslim Tibetan-speaking groups in Kargil and Nubra. But the history of the battle over language and script in Ladakh and Kargil reaches back at least to the nineteenth century and the Moravian missionary A.H. Francke's attempts to introduce a combination of colloquial and classical *bodhic*.[62] Even before that, the rise of the Dogra dynasty had ended the patronage of *bodhic* and the script was replaced by *nasta'līq*. At the same time English was finding its way into the school syllabuses.

After Partition Urdu became the officially recognized language of Jammu and Kashmir (to which Ladakh then belonged). Although *bodhic* was not recognized it was still taught in schools, and became symbolic for Ladakhi nationalism. In 1952 the prominent Ladakhi political leader Kusho Bakula, then a member of the Jammu and Kashmir Assembly, distributed flyers in the assembly making a case for the official recognition of *u-chen* as a script for *bodhic*, linking it exclusively with Buddhism and Buddhist culture. The trend intensified during the cultural revival in Ladakh in the 1970s when language took on a symbolic significance, guarding cultural boundaries.[63]

Needless to say, the language issue has been politicized. For instance, in a case similar to the BCF's schoolbook project in Baltistan, the Ladakhi leader Tshetan Phuntsog's suggestion to simplify the spelling system by eliminating the letter *a-chen* was denounced as being anti-Buddhist since this letter is used in the sacred mantra *Om Mani Padme Hum*.[64] Aggarwal distinguishes three positions in the political debate over *bodhic* in Ladakh:[65]

1. Buddhist Ladakh is threatened by modern life. To protect it, knowledge of classical Buddhist texts is necessary and the religious context of the language should be preserved. This view is held by a group of Buddhist scholars working at the Central Institute for Buddhist Studies near Leh.
2. *Bodhic* should be standardized and secularized but fused with Tibetan phrases and grammar so as to keep its compatibility with the Buddhist canon and with other Himalayan languages such as Tibetan, Bhutanese and Sikkinese. This view is held by a group at the Jammu and Kashmir Academy of Art, Culture, and Languages in Leh.
3. *Bodhic* should be able to represent Ladakh's contemporary social realities. It should lose its religious context and be simplified so that it can be used to discuss modern, secular topics of public life. This view is held by a group of socially involved intellectuals who frequently take part in the public debate.

---

62 Ravina Aggarwal, 'Introduction', in Abdul Ghani Sheikh, *Forsaking Paradise: Stories from Ladakh* (New Delhi, 2001), pp. 7-37.

63 Ibid., pp. 12-13.

64 Ibid., p. 14. Tshetan Phuntsog held that the letter *a-chung* is more efficient for everyday use.

65 Ibid., pp. 13-16.

With the emergence of the Baltistan Movement the language issue has become more prominent and activists and intellectuals of the movement tend to support the third position. Over the years several seminars and meetings have been held to bridge the differences and reach a solution.[66] More recently local NGOs have made various petitions both to the central and the state government to recognize the language in the constitution as *bhoti*, thus losing the religious component of *bodhic* and the political component of *ladakhi*.

But the battle between these groups is still far from over. My informants among intellectuals and activists in Kargil dub this issue as perhaps the most important of them all, rhetorically begging the proponents of *bodhic*/Buddhism to 'release the script' to Tibetan-speaking Muslims. For them the access to language and script is intimately linked to their active production of Balti cultural products such as music, poetry and novels. The script is also a helpful tool when drawing the cultural boundary of Greater Ladakh. In their view, *u-chen* should be perceived as the script of Greater Ladakh without any religious implications.

POP *GHAZALS*

In the following section I intend to focus more on the Baltistan Movement's reinvention of Balti culture taking place in Kargil. Looking more specifically at the cultural construction of Greater Ladakh a single activity seems to dominate recent public discourse, namely the production, promotion and recording of so-called pop *ghazals*. Related to traditional Arabic poetry as well as contemporary Indian pop music it is perhaps the most significant Balti cultural activity that has taken place in Kargil in the 2000s.

Even though the production of Balti pop *ghazals* is a new development in this region, the pop *ghazal* is one of the most well-established genres in contemporary South Asian pop music. As I will discuss in more detail below, this development has been facilitated by the small-scale cassette production industry that has been established all over South Asia since the 1970s.

The musicologist Peter Manuel distinguishes pop *ghazals* as one of two general approaches to modern *ghazal* singing, the other being the light-classical *ghazal* song.[67] The former is fixed and pre-composed and frequently backed by a modern band consisting of a mix of Western and Indian instruments while the latter is characterized by improvisation and elaboration of the text.

The *ghazal* is primarily a poetic form and a literary genre in Arabic verse going back to the seventh century. In the thirteenth century it had become the

---

66 After the Kargil war in 1999 the commanding Indian General Arjun Ray even intervened to moderate between the contending groups, but without success.

67 Peter Manuel, 'A Historical Survey of the Urdu Ghazal-Song in India', *Asian Music*, 20/1 (1988-89): pp. 93-113.

dominant poetic form in Persian literature. As Persian was the literary language of the Muslim parts of South and Central Asia the *ghazal* spread and was adapted into Urdu, Pushto and Turkish. By the end of the eighteenth century the Urdu *ghazal* came to dominate the Indian scene. As Manuel points out, 'While retaining the stock imagery, metaphors, and formal elements of the Persian *ghazal*, the Urdu *ghazal* developed its own character and has flourished until this day, enjoyed and cultivated by Hindus as well as Muslims, and by lower-class and even illiterate aficionados as well as aristocrats.'[68]

A *ghazal* is structured as rhymed couplets that do not need to be thematically related. Each couplet can be self-sufficient and the format thus requires skilful linguistic condensation by means of a conventional symbolic and metaphorical vocabulary. The challenge for the poet is to fashion finely-created, ingenious couplets, while usually restricting himself only to the relatively fixed and stereotypical imagery, but also to the themes conventionally explored in the *ghazal*. These latter include mysticism, philosophy, ridicule of Islamic orthodoxy, celebration of madness and inebration, and, above all, unrequited love.[69]

Although it is the *ghazal* songs that are popular in South Asia today, the *ghazal* was intended to be read or chanted (*tarannum*) at a poetry recital (*mushāʿira*). Twentieth- and twenty-first-century South Asian *ghazal* songs have a simple structural form but also allow for a little improvisation. The improvisation 'lends a degree of suspense in anticipation of the return of the pre-composed melody such that the completion of the couplet with the end-rhyme may be a dramatic, even climactic moment, eliciting cries of approbation from listeners'.[70]

When records became mass-produced in India at the beginning of the twentieth century, *ghazals* dominated a large part of the market. By the mid-twentieth century cinema had emerged as the predominant medium for popular music in South Asia, creating a new platform for the modern *ghazal*. The format was even more simplified and fixed and resembled a regular *geet*, a catchy tune that the listener could easily pick up and hum.[71]

In the 1970s, however, the dominance of the film industry was challenged by the emergence of a so-called cassette-culture where small-scale independent producers were recording and marketing pop versions of regional folk music for local audiences. In the late 1980s Indians were buying 2.5 million cassette players annually and cassettes constituted 95% of the recorded music market. In 1991 alone, around 217 million cassettes were circulated in India.[72] The advent of this 'cassette culture' led to a revival of regional folk music. The technology was comparatively cheap and producers could aim for specialized regional markets

---

68 ibid., p. 94.

69 Ibid., p. 95.

70 Ibid., p. 99.

71 Ibid.,, p. 106.

72 Peter Manuel, *Cassette Culture: Popular Music and Technology in North India* (Chicago, 1993), pp. 62-3.

and still make a profit. Manuel comments that a profit could be made on as little as 100 cassettes although big hits, like the Punjabi–Pushto folksong *Tutuk Tutuk Tutiyan* sold an unimaginable 500,000 copies in 1989.[73] The emergence of the cassette culture also elevated the modern *ghazal* to new levels of popularity and eventually *ghazals* started to appear in regional languages like Punjabi, Marathi, Bengali, Pushto, Hindi and, more recently, Tibetan.

Cassettes provided a new vehicle for the cultural expression of marginalized communities and their socio-political mobilization.[74] As already mentioned at the beginning of this article, popular music, social identity and mobilization, and social movements go hand in hand. Music has the power to express or transmit ideologies, opinions and values to ordinary people and those who do not take an interest in politics.[75] The cassette culture, Manuel suggests in his study of popular music and technology in north India, contributes 'to the ability of diverse Indian communities to affirm, in language, style, and text content, their own social identities on the mass media in an unprecedented manner'.[76]

The production of cassettes is carried out locally and is not controlled by the central state or by big commercial production companies. Nor does a person have to be literate to get the message. Cassettes are also inexpensive to produce and affordable not only for rich consumers and thus easily available for extensive duplication and dissemination.[77] This is very clear in the case of the pop *ghazals* produced in Kargil. For instance, it would be more or less impossible to market these cassettes by conventional means in Pakistan today. But by using transnational networks between Kargil and Baltistan including common meeting places such as Shiite pilgrim sites in the Middle East and religious schools in Iran, the cassettes have been brought to Baltistan where they are duplicated and redistributed.

At the creative musical centre of the Balti *ghazal* is the dynamic Riyaz Munshi, a young Kargili composer who has written the music for virtually all of the songs that have been recorded so far. Riyaz is also the director of the Munshi Habib-Ullah Mission School mentioned above. He has very consciously added what he calls a musical modern touch to the *ghazals* and edited the original poems to fit the modern pop song format. His purpose has been both to attract the interest of young people and to make the product commercially viable. His *ghazals* have a conventional Hindi film/pop sound with driving drumbeats

---

73 Ibid., p. 73.

74 Cassettes were also used to spread Ayatollah Khomeini's speeches during the Iranian revolution, to circulate separatist songs in Kashmir, and to spread the speeches of Hindu nationalists in India, to mention some examples.

75 Compare with Dick Hebdige's studies of Caribbean music. Dick Hebdige, *Cut 'n' Mix: Culture, Identity and Caribbean Music* (London, 1987).

76 Manuel, *Cassette Culture*, p. 194.

77 Ibid., p. 99.

and so-called *laggi* sections between the verses.[78] The cassettes are recorded by an Indian producer in a commercial sound studio in New Delhi, and feature Indian session musicians. Most of the vocals are performed by three singers one of whom, Meena, is a professional Indian session singer. She does not speak Tibetan and just imitates the words phonetically. Another singer is Feyaz who was described to me as 'a guy with a British, serious look'. The most popular of the trio is Khadim the Pang, a mechanical engineer from Kargil nick-named after his booming voice and 'tough dude' image.

The combination of a cultural awareness program with business has been a big success with 10 albums and a VCD (Video Compact Disc), *Hai-Lay Hrgamo* ('Hey Joy'), released in the last three years by Skarchen Production and Balti Universal Music Zone, and circulated widely both in India and Pakistan. The album *Zoom* (2005) became a hit, selling around 5,000 copies. The title is a pun on the vernacular word *zooms*, meaning 'companion', and the English word *zoom* ('making a success'). With a wholesale price of Rs 40 and a production cost of around Rs 70,000 per cassette the producers made enough money to finance new albums. Other albums have titles like *Rgazoom* ('Admiring the Beauty', 2004), *Niyamtsar* (a name for a friend you grow up with and then marry, 2003), *Strogi Totee* ('Pigeon of Life', 2006), *Sning Tam* ('Talk of the Heart', 2005) and *Chakbu* ('Bunch of Flowers', 2005). The success of *Zoom* is specifically attributed to the hit song *Sham Sham*, 'Your name *Sham* [a common Urdu female name] is like light'. It differs from the other songs through its mix of Urdu and Balti lyrics.

As has been the fashion among modern *ghazal* vocalists in general, the producers have mixed old *ghazals* with new *ghazals* written by established Balti poets like Ustad Sadiq Ali Sadiq from Kargil, and *ghazals* written by up and coming poets like Bashir Wafa on the same cassette, serving the double purpose of reintroducing old material and providing a public platform for contemporary poetry. The album, *Tsarang Hasni's Special* (2006), contains some new *ghazals* written by Hassan Hasni, a Balti poet from Pakistan who linked up with Riyaz Munshi and KASCO during his visit to Kargil in 2005.

The cassettes have made a tremendous impact on the general awareness of Balti culture compared to the situation as it was before they were first released. Many of these songs are now widely known and sung by people in Kargil, Nubra and Baltistan. The VCD mobilizes and reworks elements of Balti traditions to paint a utopian image of Greater Ladakh. Although the Bollywood influence is strong, the videos are very clearly made with an intention to expose the viewer to Balti clothes, customs, dancing, poetry and values. The videos in the VCD are shot and cut in the Bollywood musical number style and are a mix between the symbolic visual language of modern Hindi movies and reconstructed traditional Balti symbols.

The producer of the VCD told me that the title (*Hey Joy*) signifies happiness in order to 'create a positive market image'. On a deeper level, however, the

---

78 The *laggi* consists of fast tempo music or just drums.

theme of the VCD can also be seen as a kind of dream of a happy Balti land that provides a leitmotif for the videos. For instance, in common with most of the other songs on the VCD, the song *Rjait Pa Mait Yang* ('I Can't Forget', lyrics: Sadiq Ali Sadiq, music: Riyaz Munshi) is an idealized version of Balti lovers played out by two actors dressed in more or less traditional Balti garments, moving in a scenic Himalayan landscape. In this particular song a cool modern man also walks through a village showing off his good looks in a parallel plot. The context implies that he is a Balti who has left his homeland to become 'modern' and now returns to lament his loss of 'tradition'. The singer, The Pang, stands by a jeep that seems to be parked in the vicinity. At the end of the song he is shown together with a group of happy, young Buddhist monks.

To another song, *Na Thong Mi Resi* ('Whenever I See You', Wahid Baltistani/ Riyaz Munshi), a group of men and women is shown dancing in traditional clothes. Even if the dance initially appears to be traditional it is new and choreographed entirely by Hussain Sagar, a young man in his twenties and a student in economics. About half way through the video the men suddenly change to modern, Western-style clothes and red baseball caps, and start doing Bollywood dance moves. The mix of selected traditional Balti cultural elements with contemporary elements selected from Indian popular culture is consciously intended by the producer to catch the attention and interest of an audience that might not show so much enthusiasm for regular folklore (although pop *ghazals* could perhaps be called folklore too), classical music or spoken poetry. In this way, the production of pop *ghazal* cassettes takes advantage of the benefits of the genre in Indian/South Asian popular culture in general, and the audiences' familiarity with it. It thus works well as a tool in the creation of cultural awareness. The VCD adds another dimension to this process by providing an opportunity to add visual cultural material to Greater Ladakh as a historical and cultural concept making it a more accessible backdrop to Greater Ladakh as a political idea.

DECOUPLE AND RECONNECT

Mobilization of tradition is clearly a strategy deployed by the three social movement organizations in the cultural politics of Greater Ladakh under investigation here. I have dealt with three empirical examples: the construction of a common regional historical narrative, the struggle for Tibetan language and script, and the construction of a common regional culture. The concept of Greater Ladakh decouples Baltistan, Kargil and Ladakh from the master narrative of the nation-state and reconnects them with a western Himalayan historical narrative and Tibet. In this narrative the six decades of being part of the nation-states of India and Pakistan are depicted as a historical parenthesis.

However, in an ironic twist, the rift between Muslims and Buddhists, with its legacy from the colonial era, and the recent conflicts between Muslims and Buddhists in Ladakh in their struggle for 'hill tribe' status, have made the regional Buddhist communities reluctant to join in. The fight for recognition as an independent political and ethnic group within the respective nation-states has made the Balti Muslims and the Ladakhi Buddhists point to their present differences rather than a common past.

Index of Proper Names

This index includes personal names (other than modern authors), and some places, races, languages and key terms. Books are listed under their authors, but under their titles if the authors are unknown. Regnal dates are given whenever possible. All dates are CE unless otherwise mentioned. A small number of significant terms have also been included. Tibetan names appear either in their Wylie transliteration, or in their simplified form, usually cross-referenced. Arabic names are usually given in the form in which they are found in the *Encyclopedia of Islam*, 2nd edition, with a modification of their orthography; 'al-' is ignored in alphabetical order. When a reference occurs in a footnote, an 'n' follows the page number.